Glory To God

PRIEST:

Glory to God in the highest.

PEOPLE:

And on earth peace to men of good will.
We praise you. We bless you. We worship you. We glorify you.
We give you thanks for your great glory.
Lord God, heavenly King, God the Father almighty.
Lord Jesus Christ, the only-begotten Son.
Lord God, Lamb of God, Son of the Father.
You, who take away the sins of the world,
    have mercy on us.
You, who take away the sins of the world,
    receive our prayer.
You, who sit at the right hand of the Father,
    have mercy on us.
For you alone are holy.
You alone are Lord.
You alone, O Jesus Christ, are most high,
With the Holy Spirit, in the glory of God the Father. Amen.

THE BOOK OF CATHOLIC WORSHIP

THE BOOK
OF
CATHOLIC
WORSHIP

THE LITURGICAL CONFERENCE
WASHINGTON, D.C.

The Liturgical Conference
2900 Newton Street, N.E.
Washington, D.C. 20018

This book is also distributed by:

Berliner & McGinnis, Inc., Nevada City, California
Gregorian Institute of America, Toledo, Ohio
Helicon Press, Inc., Baltimore, Maryland
McLaughlin & Reilly Co., Boston, Massachusetts
Palm Publishers, Montreal, P.Q., Canada
World Library of Sacred Music, Inc., Cincinnati, Ohio

Nihil Obstat: Carroll E. Satterfield
Censor Librorum

Imprimatur: Lawrence Cardinal Shehan, D.D.
Archbishop of Baltimore
January 12, 1966

Acknowledgements

GRATEFUL acknowledgement is made for the following translations and prayers:

The Grail, England, for the translation of Psalm 41 on page 595.

Oxford University Press for the prayer on page 781.

The Chair of Unity Apostolate for material in the Christian Unity Service.

The hymnal has been drawn from many sources; it contains selections from a number of Protestant and Catholic collections, as well as several hymns and many antiphons not published before. We wish to acknowledge the help and cooperation of the following:

The Commission on the Liturgy and Hymnal, Lutheran Church of America, for No. 15, 91, and the words of No. 99.

The Shawnee Press for No. 34.

J. Fischer and Brothers for music of No. 44.

Oxford University Press for music of No. 37, 51, 98 and the words of No. 37, 47, 60, 62, 85 and 98.

Rev. F. Bland Tucker for words of No. 51.

Msgr. Martin Hellriegel for words of No. 87.

Mr. Ernest Merrill for words of No. 57.

The Grail, England, for No. 112, 113, 118, 125 and 130.

Rev. Eugene Lindusky for No. 86.

Conception Abbey Press for No. 13, 64 and music of 140, 150 and 160.

The World Library of Sacred Music for No. 29 and 32.

The Liturgical Press for music of No. 25, 79 (second tune) and words of No. 1, 3, 25, 43 and 79.

The American Tract Society for No. 19.

Rev. Cyril Reilly for No. 92 and 161.

Rev. Joseph Roff for music of No. 24, 97, 139, 143, 144, 154 and 159; and for assistance in the arrangement of several other hymns.

McLaughlin & Reilly Company for music of No. 1, 21, 30, 35, 39, 79 (first tune), 137, 138, 141, 142, 147, 157, 158 and the words of No. 30, 35, 39, 41 and 94.

Rev. Joseph Nolan for words of refrain of No. 17.

Gregorian Institute of America for music of No. 43, 59, 63, 84 and the words of No. 14, 59 and 84.

The Syrian Antiochian Orthodox Archdiocese of N.Y. for No. 90.

Special acknowledgement and thanks are given to the following for their particularly generous and significant contributions:

Robert F. Twynham for music of No. 16, 42, 49, 56, 75, 102-111, 114-117, 119-124, 126-129, and 131-135.

The Church Pension Fund of the Protestant Episcopal Church in the U.S.A. for No. 2, 4, 5, 6, 7, 8, 9, 11, 12, 18, 20, 22, 23, 26, 27, 28, 31, 33, 36, 38, 40, 45, 46, 48, 50, 52, 53, 54, 55, 58, 65, 66, 68, 69, 70, 71, 72, 73, 74, 76, 77, 78, 80, 81, 82, 83, 89, 93, 95, 96, 100, 101; also the music of No. 14, 41, 47, 57, 60, 61, 67, 85, 94 and the words of No. 44.

Editorial Board of
The Book of Catholic Worship

Sister Mary Clare Mylett, S.N.D., Head of the Department of Music, Trinity College, Washington, D.C.

Joseph Nolan, Pastor of St. Patrick's Church, Galena, Kansas; Member of Diocesan Liturgical Commission.

C. Alexander Peloquin, Composer and Conductor; Director of Peloquin Chorale, Providence, Rhode Island.

H. A. Reinhold, Author of *The Dynamics of the Liturgy*, *The American Parish and the Roman Liturgy*, *Bringing the Mass to the People*.

Joseph Roff, Assistant Pastor, Sacred Hearts and St. Stephen Church, Brooklyn, N.Y.

Gerard S. Sloyan, Head of the Department of Religious Education at the Catholic University of America; Past President of the Liturgical Conference.

Virginia Sloyan, Staff member of the Liturgical Conference.

Robert Twynham, Composer and Conductor; Director of Music at the Cathedral of Mary Our Queen, Baltimore, Maryland.

Eugene A. Walsh, S.S., Professor of Education and Music at St. Mary's Seminary, Baltimore, Maryland.

Warren Werwage, Member of the Liturgical Commission for the Diocese of Cleveland.

Geoffrey Wood, S.A., Rector and Professor of Scripture, Atonement Seminary, Washington, D.C.

Table of Contents

THE HYMNAL

Sundays of the Year

When the date of a Sunday does not appear in the list below, the usual Sunday Mass is replaced by the Mass of a feast day.

1966	1967	1968	1969	1970	SUNDAY	PAGE
Jan 2			Jan 5	Jan 4	Holy Name of Jesus	24
Jan 9	Jan 8	Jan 7	Jan 12	Jan 11	Holy Family	29
Jan 16	Jan 15	Jan 14	Jan 19	Jan 18	Second Sunday after Epiphany	32
Jan 23		Jan 21	Jan 26		Third Sunday after Epiphany	33
Jan 30 ·		Jan 28			Fourth Sunday after Epiphany	33
		Feb 4			Fifth Sunday after Epiphany	33
Feb 6	Jan 22	Feb 11		Jan 25	Septuagesima Sunday	37
Feb 13	Jan 29	Feb 18	Feb 9	Feb 1	Sexagesima Sunday	38
Feb 20	Feb 5	Feb 25	Feb 16	Feb 8	Quinquagesima Sunday	40
Feb 27	Feb 12	Mar 3	Feb 23	Feb 15	First Sunday in Lent	45
Mar 6	Feb 19	Mar 10	Mar 2	Feb 22	Second Sunday in Lent	53
Mar 13	Feb 26	Mar 17	Mar 9	Mar 1	Third Sunday in Lent	60
Mar 20	Mar 5	Mar 24	Mar 16	Mar 8	Fourth Sunday in Lent	67
Mar 27	Mar 12	Mar 31	Mar 23	Mar 15	First Sunday in Passiontime	74
Apr 3	Mar 19	Apr 7	Mar 30	Mar 22	Second Sunday in Passiontime	80
Apr 10	Mar 26	Apr 14	Apr 6	Mar 29	Easter Sunday	108
Apr 17	Apr 2	Apr 21	Apr 13	Apr 5	First Sunday after Easter	116
Apr 24	Apr 9	Apr 28	Apr 20	Apr 12	Second Sunday after Easter	118
	Apr 16	May 5	Apr 27	Apr 19	Third Sunday after Easter	119
May 8	Apr 23	May 12	May 4	Apr 26	Fourth Sunday after Easter	120
May 15	Apr 30	May 19	May 11	May 3	Fifth Sunday after Easter	121
May 22	May 7	May 26	May 18	May 10	Sunday after the Ascension	126
May 29	May 14	June 2	May 25	May 17	Pentecost Sunday	130
June 5	May 21	June 9	June 1	May 24	Trinity Sunday	137
June 12	May 28	June 16	June 8	May 31	Second Sunday after Pentecost	142
June 19	June 4	June 23	June 15	June 7	Third Sunday after Pentecost	145
June 26	June 11	June 30	June 22	June 14	Fourth Sunday after Pentecost	146
July 3	June 18	July 7		June 21	Fifth Sunday after Pentecost	147
July 10	June 25	July 14	July 6	June 28	Sixth Sunday after Pentecost	149
July 17	July 2	July 21	July 13	July 5	Seventh Sunday after Pentecost	150
July 24	July 9	July 28	July 20	July 12	Eighth Sunday after Pentecost	151
July 31	July 16	Aug 4	July 27	July 19	Ninth Sunday after Pentecost	153
Aug 7	July 23	Aug 11	Aug 3	July 26	Tenth Sunday after Pentecost	154
Aug 14	July 30	Aug 18	Aug 10	Aug 2	Eleventh Sunday after Pentecost	156
Aug 21		Aug 25	Aug 17	Aug 9	Twelfth Sunday after Pentecost	157
Aug 28	Aug 13	Sept 1	Aug 24	Aug 16	Thirteenth Sunday after Pentecost	158
Sept 4	Aug 20	Sept 8	Aug 31	Aug 23	Fourteenth Sunday after Pentecost	160
Sept 11	Aug 27	Sept 15	Sept 7	Aug 30	Fifteenth Sunday after Pentecost	161
Sept 18	Sept 3	Sept 22		Sept 6	Sixteenth Sunday after Pentecost	162
Sept 25	Sept 10		Sept 21	Sept 13	Seventeenth Sunday after Pentecost	164
Oct 2	Sept 17	Oct 6	Sept 28	Sept 20	Eighteenth Sunday after Pentecost	168
Oct 9	Sept 24	Oct 13	Oct 5	Sept 27	Nineteenth Sunday after Pentecost	169
Oct 16	Oct 1	Oct 20	Oct 12	Oct 4	Twentieth Sunday after Pentecost	171
Oct 23	Oct 8		Oct 19	Oct 11	Twenty-first Sunday after Pentecost	172
Oct 30	Oct 29	Oct 27	Oct 26	Oct 25	Christ the King	283
	Oct 15	Nov 3		Oct 18	Twenty-second Sunday after Pentecost	174
Nov 6	Oct 22	Nov 10	Nov 2		Twenty-third Sunday after Pentecost	175
Nov 13		Nov 17			Twenty-fourth Sunday after Pentecost	175
	Nov 5		Nov 16	Nov 8	Twenty-fifth Sunday after Pentecost	175
	Nov 12			Nov 15	Twenty-sixth Sunday after Pentecost	175
	Nov 19				Twenty-seventh Sunday after Pentecost	175
Nov 20	Nov 26	Nov 24	Nov 23	Nov 22	Last Sunday after Pentecost	175
Nov 27	Dec 3	Dec 1	Nov 30	Nov 29	First Sunday in Advent	3
Dec 4	Dec 10		Dec 7	Dec 6	Second Sunday in Advent	4
Dec 11	Dec 17	Dec 15	Dec 14	Dec 13	Third Sunday in Advent	5
Dec 18		Dec 22	Dec 21	Dec 20	Fourth Sunday in Advent	10
	Dec 31	Dec 29	Dec 28	Dec 27	Sunday after Christmas	18

THE BOOK OF CATHOLIC WORSHIP

Introduction

FOR SOME TIME now it has been apparent that the celebration of the new liturgy requires an entirely new kind of liturgical book for the people. The restoration of the people's part in the Eucharist and the other sacraments has placed demands upon the congregation which their missals are not adequate to meet. The hand missal, essentially a translation of the altar missal with a commentary, remains an indispensable tool for private preparation and meditation, but it is not designed for use at the liturgical service of today, with its prayers and readings in English, its congregational singing and group recitation of prayers and psalms.

A pew book is needed, a book that can be picked up by whoever comes to church or chapel, whatever the occasion. Such a book should contain all, but only, the people's parts, not only of the Mass but of the sacraments and other public services. It should contain a large and carefully selected hymnal, and the entire Psalter arranged for group recitation. Above all, it should be flexible, providing for the many legitimate variations which may occur in the celebration of a particular rite.

THE BOOK OF CATHOLIC WORSHIP is such a book. It is designed to give the people all the materials they need to take part fully, actively and meaningfully in the services of their parish or community. Whether they come to Sunday Mass, to the celebration of a sacrament, to a bible service or to the stations of the cross, the people will find in this book everything they need to take their part.

THE BOOK OF CATHOLIC WORSHIP is not for the priest to use during the service. When the priest is proclaiming God's Word or praying aloud in the name of the entire community, the people should be listening to him, and thus such readings and prayers are not contained in this book, unless they might not be available elsewhere. The priest will use his missal or ritual, and by the inflection of his voice as he concludes a priestly prayer will invite the people's AMEN. The reader will have his lectionary. But the people will find in this book their part in any dialogue with the priest, as well as any prayers or recited verses they say by themselves or together with the priest.

The structure of each service is clearly indicated to help the people take an intelligent part in it, and everything the people may sing or say is contained in this book. But THE BOOK OF CATHOLIC WORSHIP is a tool, and is not designed to be followed page by page. The people open their books when they have need of them, and close them again to follow something for which they do not require text or music. During Mass, for example, few people will require a book for the Lord Have Mercy or for simple responses, even though these texts are included as a convenience on the inside front and back covers.

This book is by no means a substitute for the directions of a commentator, cantor, or other leader. He will direct the people as to what they are going to recite and what they are going to sing, and often the numbers of the hymns will be displayed on a sign. He will tell the people which of the many possible ways of taking part in a service they will use on a given day. But in THE BOOK OF CATHOLIC WORSHIP, the commentator will find the texts and hymns in which he will lead the people.

It is clearly understood that even though recent changes in the Mass and sacraments have been promulgated and the use of English encouraged, our entire liturgy rests upon our rich and continuous tradition of prayer and worship. No change has ever or will ever offend against our sacred heritage, preserved for us in the Church by the Holy Spirit. It is this heritage that remains the fundamental source and guiding principle of our prayer and worship.

How to Use this Book

THIS ENTIRE BOOK is designed so that its major parts can be found easily and quickly. The easily identifiable Hymnal will serve as a divider: before it come the Masses of the temporal and sanctoral cycles, common and votive Masses, and the Eucharistic Prayer; after the Hymnal come the Psalter, the sacraments, parish prayers and services. Within the temporal and sanctoral cycle Masses, those at which the entire congregation is likely to be present receive a larger typographical treatment.

AT MASS ON SUNDAYS AND FEAST DAYS

Before the Mass Begins

It is always well to read over the introduction, commentary and texts of the Mass of the day in your own missal at home the night before. The commentator will announce the Mass of the day and its page number, or you can find it for yourself by consulting the calendar on page xii. The entire Order of Worship with commentary and explanation is given on page 383. The Latin text of the dialogue and Ordinary chants may be found on pages 796 to 800.

Entrance Song

According to the directions of the commentator you may sing or recite the Entrance Song from the Mass of the day, and perhaps additional psalm verses from the Psalter. (The psalm you are looking for is easily found in the Psalter, since they are numbered consecutively from 1–150. The commentator will tell you the verses.) Or the commentator may recite the verses while you repeat the antiphon. Or he may direct you to the Hymnal (note that hymn numbers are always used rather than page numbers).

Lord Have Mercy

Again, this may be sung or recited at the direction of the commentator. Should you need your book for this, the text is printed on the inside front cover. Musical settings may be found near the end of the Hymnal.

Glory to God

If this is to be sung, the commentator will direct you to one of the musical settings near the end of the Hymnal, and the priest will sing the first few words. If the text is to be recited, you may wish to find it on the inside front cover.

Prayer

At any time the priest greets you with "The Lord be with you," you reply, "AND WITH YOUR SPIRIT." When he invites you to silent prayer with "Let us pray," you add your personal petitions to the general prayer. Then you follow the prayer as the priest says it, and respond "AMEN" at its conclusion.

First Reading

Sit and listen to the reading.

Songs of Meditation and Response

The commentator may direct you to sing or recite these texts from the Mass of the day. Or you may listen while they are sung or recited. Or you may sing one of the responses from the Hymnal.

Gospel and Homily

Stand for the Gospel, then sit for the Homily.

Creed

If this is to be sung, the commentator will direct you to the musical setting near the end of the Hymnal, and the priest will sing the first few words. If it is to be recited, you may wish to find the text on the inside back cover of the book.

Prayer of the Faithful

The commentator will direct you to sing or say your response, which is commonly, "LORD, HAVE MERCY," or "LORD, HEAR OUR PRAYER."

Song at the Preparation of the Gifts

The commentator will direct you to sing or say the text from the Mass of the day, perhaps with additional psalm verses from the Psalter. Or the commentator may recite the psalm verses while you repeat the antiphon. Or he may direct you to the Hymnal.

Prayer over the Gifts

Listen to the prayer of the priest and respond "AMEN." At this point in the Mass of the day you will find the page number on which the Eucharistic Prayer begins for the particular feast.

THE EUCHARISTIC PRAYER

This is the central prayer of the Mass, which has comparatively few variations apart from its introductory passage (preface), which is sung or said by the priest, and to which the people listen. It is, of course, not necessary to follow the prayer word by word, but is sufficient to be aware of its principal sentiments so that the response at the great "Amen," after the "Through Him and with Him and in Him," may be a genuine one.

If the hymn, Holy, Holy, Holy, is to be sung, the commentator may direct you to the musical setting near the end of the Hymnal. If you are to recite the Holy, Holy, Holy, you may wish to find the text of the prayer at the end of the first part (preface) of the Eucharistic Prayer.

The Eucharistic Banquet

This follows immediately after the Eucharistic Prayer. Again, it is not necessary to follow along word by word, and only the principal elements are printed here.

If you are to sing the Lord's Prayer and the Lamb of God, the commentator will direct you to the Hymnal. The texts of these two prayers and of the Lord, I Am Not Worthy may be found within the Eucharistic Banquet section.

Communion Song

The commentator may direct you to sing or recite this text from the Mass of the day before the distribution of communion. Once again, additional psalm verses may be used from the Psalter. Or the commentator may recite the psalm verses while you repeat the antiphon. Or the commentator may direct you to the Hymnal for a communion hymn.

Prayer after Communion

After the distribution of communion, respond to the greeting, "The Lord be with you," of the priest. After the priest's invitation, "Let us pray," add your petitions to those of the congregation, and respond, "AMEN," at the conclusion of the prayer.

Dismissal Rite

Respond to the greeting of the priest. Answer the priest when he sings or

says "The Mass is ended. Go in peace," by singing or saying, "THANKS
BE TO GOD." Kneel for the priest's blessing and respond, "AMEN."
The commentator will direct you to the Hymnal for a closing hymn.

THE STRUCTURE OF THE MASS

*The chart below indicates the principal parts of the Mass and where they can
be found in the book. Of course, it is not necessary to refer to the parts you know
from memory when taking part in the Mass.*

Entrance Rite

Entrance Song . . . . Mass of the day
Lord Have Mercy . . . . . Inside Front Cover (or Hymnal)
Glory to God . . . . . . Inside Front Cover (or Hymnal)
Prayer . . . . Listen to priest

THE LITURGY OF THE WORD

First Reading . . . . Listen to lector
Songs of Meditation and Response . . . . Mass of the day
Gospel . . . . Listen to priest or deacon
Homily . . . . Listen to priest
Creed . . . . Inside Back Cover (or Hymnal)
Prayer of the Faithful . . . . Respond to leader

THE LITURGY OF THE EUCHARIST

Song at the Preparation of the Gifts . . . . Mass of the day
Prayer over the Gifts . . . . Listen to priest
EUCHARISTIC PRAYER . . . Find page number in Mass of the day
Eucharistic Banquet . . . . . . Follows Eucharistic Prayer
Communion Song . . . . Mass of the day
Prayer after Communion . . . . Listen to priest

Dismissal Rite
Order of Worship

AT MASS ON WEEKDAYS

To find the Mass of the day: Find today's date in the Masses of the Sanctoral
Cycle. If no Mass is given, the Mass is of the preceding Sunday, except

from December 24 to January 13, during Lent, Easter Week, from Ascension to Pentecost, and during Pentecost week, when the proper weekday Mass will be found in the temporal cycle.

If a marriage Mass is to be celebrated, turn to Marriage (page 750); if a Mass of the Dead is to be celebrated, turn to the Liturgy of the Dead (page 767); Votive Masses may be found on pages 344 to 381.

To follow the Mass of the day: The structure of the Mass is as given above, except that some parts of the Mass may be omitted, such as the Glory to God, the Creed, the Homily and the Prayer of the Faithful, and others, which are well known from the Sunday Mass. Simply follow the leadership of the priest and the directions of the commentator.

The Eucharistic Prayer will always begin on page 405, except when seasonal prefaces are used (during Christmas, Epiphany, Lent, Passiontime, Easter, Ascension, and Pentecost Week), or when a particular preface is indicated in the Mass of the day.

AT THE SACRAMENTS
AND OTHER PARISH CELEBRATIONS

Find the service which is to be celebrated in the Table of Contents (pages ix to xi) or in the General Index (pages 805–807). The commentator will direct you to various hymns and psalms, and suggestions are made within the services themselves.

The priest or leader will have his own ritual or other book with all of his prayers and readings. This book contains only what you need to take your part.

FOR PRIVATE PRAYER

The Psalter is the single most authentic source of Christian prayer. You will find a helpful index of psalms and canticles for various occasions and themes on page 804. Consult the General Index on page 805 for other prayers.

HOW TO USE THE HYMNAL

An alphabetical listing of hymns and antiphons by first lines can be found on page 553. Helpful indices of hymns for various seasons and for various occasions can be found on page 803.

To find a particular hymn, remember that hymns and antiphons are always referred to by number (not by page number). The hymns and antiphons are numbered consecutively.

HOW TO USE THE PSALTER

The psalms are numbered consecutively from 1–150, and are always referred to by number (not by page number). The canticles follow the psalms.

Helpful indices for private use of the psalms are found on page 804.

For the recitation of the Divine Office, or of any part of it, you will need to know the numbers of the psalms and canticles which are to be sung or recited, so that you can find them in the Psalter.

MASSES
OF THE
TEMPORAL
CYCLE

ADVENT

THE ADVENT MASSES speak to us of the coming of the Lord. Christ came to us in history; he comes to us today, especially within his Church; he will come in glory at the end of time. Recalling the events of Christ's coming in history is more than mere pious recollection. It is a here and now meeting with Christ as he comes again in the Word, proclaimed to his people. Remembering the first coming of the Lord helps our faith that he is always and everywhere present to us. It is an immediate preparation for the feast of Christmas, when we will celebrate his coming in the flesh.

Most of all, the Advent season is a time of preparation for the final coming of the Lord in glory. Long ago, God promised through his prophets that he would come to save the world, and he kept his promise. Christ has promised us that he will come again to judge the world, and we believe that he will keep his word with us. The Advent Masses give us the grace to realize what Christ's growing presence in the world is now, and what we must make it become.

The first Sunday of Advent continues the idea of the concluding Sundays after Pentecost. It speaks to us of the judgment of the Lord: "There will be signs in the heavens." The following Sundays tell us how to prepare for the completion of the present age. Preparing for Christmas means intensifying our preparation for the last judgment. We listen to the words of John the Baptist and of the prophet Isaiah, who tell us to reform our lives so as to prepare the way of the Lord.

None of us knows when the Lord will come in glory, or when our own death will bring us before his face. As we prepare for his coming in grace at Christmas, we are also preparing for that great day on which we will clearly see his face.

First Sunday in Advent

Entrance Song

To you I lift up my soul; in you, O my God, I trust;
let me not be put to shame; let not my enemies exult over me.
No one who waits for you shall be put to shame.

> Your ways, O Lord, make known to me;
> teach me your paths. TURN TO PSALM 24

Glory be to the Father.

Lord Have Mercy   *Prayer*

THE LITURGY OF THE WORD

First Reading
ROMANS 13:11–14

Songs of Meditation and Response

No one who waits for you shall be put to shame.
Your ways, O Lord, make known to me;
teach me your paths. PSALM 24

> *When this Mass is repeated during the week,*
> *the following verses are not recited.*

Alleluia, alleluia.
Show us, O Lord, your kindness,
and grant us your salvation. Alleluia. PSALM 84

Gospel
LUKE 21:25–33

Homily   *Creed*   *Prayer of the Faithful*

THE LITURGY OF THE EUCHARIST

Song at the Preparation of the Gifts

To you I lift up my soul; in you, O my God, I trust;
let me not be put to shame; let not my enemies exult over me.
No one who waits for you shall be put to shame. TURN TO PSALM 24

Prayer over the Gifts

EUCHARISTIC PRAYER

TURN TO PAGE 406

Communion Song

The Lord will give his benefits:
and our land shall yield its increase. TURN TO PSALM 84

Prayer after Communion

Second Sunday in Advent

Entrance Song

People of Sion, behold the Lord shall come to save the nations;
and the Lord shall make the glory of his voice to be heard,
in the joy of your heart. ISAIAH 30:30

O shepherd of Israel, hearken,
O guide of the flock of Joseph! TURN TO PSALM 79
Glory be to the Father.

Lord Have Mercy   Prayer

THE LITURGY OF THE WORD

First Reading

ROMANS 15:4–13

Songs of Meditation and Response

From Sion, perfect in beauty, God shines forth.
Gather his faithful ones before him,
those who have made a covenant with him by sacrifice. PSALM 49

When this Mass is repeated during the week,
the following verses are not recited.

Alleluia, alleluia.
I rejoiced because they said to me:
"We will go up to the house of the Lord." Alleluia. PSALM 121

Gospel

MATTHEW 11:2–10

Homily   Creed   Prayer of the Faithful

THE LITURGY OF THE EUCHARIST

Song at the Preparation of the Gifts

Will you not, O God, give us life;
and shall not your people rejoice in you?
Show us, O Lord, your kindness,
and grant us your salvation. TURN TO PSALM 84

Prayer over the Gifts

EUCHARISTIC PRAYER

TURN TO PAGE 406

Communion Song

Up Jerusalem! stand upon the heights;
and behold the joy that comes to you from your God.

BARUCH 5:5, 4:36 TURN TO PSALM 147

Prayer after Communion

Third Sunday in Advent

Entrance Song

Rejoice in the Lord always: again I say, rejoice.
Let your moderation be known to all men: for the Lord is near.
Have no anxiety, but in everything, by prayer
let your petitions be made known to God. PHILIPPIANS 4:4–6

You have favored, O Lord, your land;
you have restored the well-being of Jacob. TURN TO PSALM 84

Glory be to the Father.

Lord Have Mercy   Prayer

First Reading

PHILIPPIANS 4:4–7

Songs of Meditation and Response

From your throne, O Lord, upon the cherubim,
rouse your power, and come.
O shepherd of Israel, hearken,
O guide of the flock of Joseph!   PSALM 79

> *When this Mass is repeated during the week,*
> *the following verses are not recited.*

Alleluia, alleluia.
Rouse, O Lord, your power,
and come to save us. Alleluia.   PSALM 79

Gospel

JOHN 1:19–28

Homily   Creed   Prayer of the Faithful

THE LITURGY OF THE EUCHARIST

Song at the Preparation of the Gifts

You have favored, O Lord, your land;
you have restored the well-being of Jacob.
You have forgiven the guilt of your people.

TURN TO PSALM 84

Prayer over the Gifts

EUCHARISTIC PRAYER
TURN TO PAGE 406

Communion Song

Say to those who are frightened: Be strong, fear not!
Here is our God, he comes to save us.

ISAIAH 35:4 TURN TO PSALM 49

Prayer after Communion

6

Entrance Song

Drop down dew, you heavens, from above,
and let the clouds rain the Just:
let the earth be opened and bud forth a savior.   ISAIAH 45:8

> The heavens declare the glory of God,
> and the firmament proclaims his handiwork.

Glory be to the Father.   TURN TO PSALM 18

First Reading
ISAIAH 2:2–5

Song of Meditation

Lift up, O gates, your lintels;
reach up, you ancient portals,
that the king of glory may come in!
Who can ascend the mountain of the Lord?
or who may stand in his holy place?
He whose hands are sinless, whose heart is clean.

PSALM 23

Second Reading
ISAIAH 7:10–15

Song of Meditation

The Lord is near to all who call upon him,
to all who call upon him in truth.
May my mouth speak the praise of the Lord,
and may all flesh bless his holy name.   PSALM 144

Gospel
LUKE 1:26–38

Song at the Preparation of the Gifts

Be strong, fear no longer!
For, behold, our God will bring judgment.
He himself will come to save us.

ISAIAH 35:4 TURN TO PSALM 18

Communion Song

Behold, the virgin shall be with child and bear a son,
and shall name him Emmanuel.

ISAIAH 7:14   TURN TO PSALM 84

Ember Friday in Advent

Entrance Song

You, O Lord, are near, and all your ways are truth.
Of old I know from your decrees that you are forever.

Happy are they whose way is blameless,
who walk in the law of the Lord.   TURN TO PSALM 118

Glory be to the Father.

First Reading
ISAIAH 11:1–5

Song of Meditation

Show us, O Lord, your kindness,
and grant us your salvation.
You have favored, O Lord, your land;
you have restored the well-being of Jacob.   PSALM 84

Gospel
LUKE 1:39–47

Song at the Preparation of the Gifts

Will you not, O God, give us life;
and shall not your people rejoice in you?
Show us, O Lord, your kindness,
and grant us your salvation.   TURN TO PSALM 84

Communion Song

Behold, the Lord shall come,
and all his holy ones with him:
and there shall be in that day a great light.

ZECHARIAH 14:5–6   TURN TO PSALM 79

Ember Saturday in Advent

Entrance Song

Come, O Lord, from your throne upon the cherubim;
if your face shine upon us, then we shall be safe.

O shepherd of Israel, hearken,
O guide of the flock of Joseph!   TURN TO PSALM 79
Glory be to the Father.

First Reading

ISAIAH 19:20–22

Song of Meditation

At one end of the heavens he comes forth,
and his course is to their other end.
The heavens declare the glory of God,
and the firmament proclaims his handiwork.   PSALM 18

Second Reading

2 THESSALONIANS 2:1–8

Song of Meditation

O shepherd of Israel, hearken,
O guide of the flock of Joseph!
From your throne upon the cherubim, shine forth
before Ephraim, Benjamin and Manasse.
Rouse your power, O Lord,
and come to save us.   PSALM 79

Gospel

LUKE 3:1–6

Song at the Preparation of the Gifts

Rejoice heartily, O daughter of Sion,
shout for joy, O daughter of Jerusalem!
See, your king shall come to you,
a just savior is he.   ZECHARIAH 9:9   TURN TO PSALM 79

9

Communion Song

He has rejoiced as a giant to run the way:
at one end of the heavens he comes forth,
and his course is to their other end.   TURN TO PSALM 18

Fourth Sunday in Advent

Entrance Song

Drop down dew, you heavens, from above,
and let the clouds rain the Just:
let the earth be opened and bud forth a savior.   ISAIAH 45:8

The heavens declare the glory of God,
and the firmament proclaims his handiwork.

Glory be to the Father.   TURN TO PSALM 18

Lord Have Mercy   *Prayer*

THE LITURGY OF THE WORD

First Reading
I CORINTHIANS 4:1-5

Songs of Meditation and Response

The Lord is near to all who call upon him,
to all who call upon him in truth.
May my mouth speak the praise of the Lord,
and may all flesh bless his holy name.   PSALM 144

*When this Mass is repeated during the week,
the following verses are not recited.*

Alleluia, alleluia.
Come, O Lord, and delay not;
forgive the sins of your people Israel. Alleluia.

Gospel
LUKE 3:1-6

Homily   Creed   Prayer of the Faithful

Song at the Preparation of the Gifts

Hail, Mary, full of grace, the Lord is with you,
blessed are you among women,
and blessed is the fruit of your womb.

LUKE 1:28   TURN TO PSALM 44

Prayer over the Gifts

EUCHARISTIC PRAYER

TURN TO PAGE 406

Communion Song

Behold, a virgin shall be with child and bear a son,
and shall name him Emmanuel.

ISAIAH 7:14   TURN TO PSALM 84

Prayer after Communion

CHRISTMAS

DURING ADVENT the Masses stressed the coming of the Lord. In the Christmas season they emphasize his presence. Beginning with the three Masses of Christmas Day, we rejoice that our Savior has appeared to us.

As we remember the great day of Christ's birth, we celebrate with joy and thanksgiving the great exchange: the Son of God became man so that men might become sons of God. Jesus took on human life of Mary so as to give us a share in his divine life. Our Lord has come to us so that we may have faith in his final coming in glory; he has shown himself to us so that we can believe that some day we will see the Father whom he has revealed.

The midnight Mass of Christmas recalls Christ's humble birth in Bethlehem. We remember and are glad because he is still present in the gifts of bread and wine, and in all who offer gifts.

The second Mass on Christmas day, originally celebrated at sunrise, reminds us that Jesus is the light of the world. His life and his teaching still enlighten men of good will to live the Christian life.

The third Mass, originally celebrated when the sun was highest in the heavens, reveals Jesus as the Lord of splendor and majesty. Though born of Mary, he is the Eternal Word! He is divine: "The Word was made flesh and came to dwell among us." He dwells with us now. He is Emmanuel, "God with us."

The other Masses of this season keep alive the Christmas spirit. The feasts of Stephen and John, the Sunday after Christmas, New Year's Day—all announce the Christmas message: Jesus lives among us, even till the consummation of the world.

The Vigil of Christmas

Entrance Song

This day you shall know that the Lord will come, and save us:
and in the morning you shall see his glory. <small>EXODUS 16:6–7</small>

> The Lord's are the earth and its fullness;
> the world and those who dwell in it. <small>TURN TO PSALM 23</small>

Glory be to the Father.

Lord Have Mercy   Prayer

THE LITURGY OF THE WORD

First Reading
ROMANS 1:1–6

Songs of Meditation and Response

This day you shall know that the Lord will come and save us:
and in the morning you shall see his glory. <small>EXODUS 16:6–7</small>

O shepherd of Israel, hearken,
O guide of the flock of Joseph!
From your throne upon the cherubim, shine forth
before Ephraim, Benjamin and Manasse. <small>PSALM 79</small>

> *The following verse is recited if the Vigil is on Sunday.*

Alleluia, alleluia.
Tomorrow shall the wickedness of the earth be abolished:
and the savior of the world shall reign over us. Alleluia.

Gospel
MATTHEW 1:18–21

Homily   Prayer of the Faithful

THE LITURGY OF THE EUCHARIST

Song at the Preparation of the Gifts

Lift up, O gates, your lintels;
reach up, you ancient portals,
that the king of glory may come in. <small>TURN TO PSALM 23</small>

Prayer over the Gifts

EUCHARISTIC PRAYER

TURN TO PAGE 405

Communion Song

The glory of the Lord shall be revealed,
and all mankind shall see the salvation of our God.

ISAIAH 40:5   TURN TO PSALM 79

Prayer after Communion

Christmas Midnight Mass

Entrance Song

The Lord said to me, "You are my son;
this day I have begotten you."
> Why do the nations rage
> and the people utter folly?   TURN TO PSALM 2
> Glory be to the Father.

Lord Have Mercy   Glory to God   Prayer

THE LITURGY OF THE WORD

First Reading
TITUS 2:11–15

Songs of Meditation and Response

Yours is princely power in the day of your birth,
in holy splendor; before the daystar, I have begotten you.
The Lord said to my Lord, "Sit at my right hand,
till I make your enemies your footstool."   PSALM 109
Alleluia, alleluia.
The Lord said to me, "You are my son;
this day I have begotten you." Alleluia.   PSALM 2

14

Gospel

LUKE 2:1–14

Homily   Creed   Prayer of the Faithful

THE LITURGY OF THE EUCHARIST

Song at the Preparation of the Gifts

Let the heavens be glad and the earth rejoice
before the Lord, for he comes.   TURN TO PSALM 95

Prayer over the Gifts

EUCHARISTIC PRAYER

TURN TO PAGE 391

Communion Song

In holy splendor,
before the daystar I have begotten you.
TURN TO PSALM 109

Prayer after Communion

Christmas Mass at Dawn

Entrance Song

A light shall shine upon us this day:
for the Lord is born to us:
and he shall be called wonderful, God, prince of peace,
Father of the world to come:
of whose reign there shall be no end.   ISAIAH 9:2, 6

The Lord is king, in splendor robed;
robed is the Lord and girt about with strength.
Glory be to the Father.   TURN TO PSALM 92

Lord Have Mercy   Glory to God   Prayer

THE LITURGY OF THE WORD

First Reading

TITUS 3:4–7

Songs of Meditation and Response

Blessed is he who comes in the name of the Lord;
the Lord is God, and he has given us light.
By the Lord has this been done;
it is wonderful in our eyes.   PSALM 117
Alleluia, alleluia.
The Lord is king, in splendor robed;
robed is the Lord and girt about with strength. Alleluia.

PSALM 92

Gospel

LUKE 2:15–20

Homily   Creed   Prayer of the Faithful

THE LITURGY OF THE EUCHARIST

Song at the Preparation of the Gifts

God has made the world firm,
not to be moved.
Your throne, O God, stands firm from of old;
from everlasting you are.   TURN TO PSALM 92

Prayer over the Gifts

EUCHARISTIC PRAYER
TURN TO PAGE 391

Communion Song

Rejoice heartily, O daughter Sion,
shout for joy, O daughter Jerusalem!
See, your king shall come,
a just savior of the world is he.

ZECHARIAH 9:9   TURN TO PSALM 109

Prayer after Communion

Christmas Mass in Daytime

Entrance Song

A child is born to us, a son is given to us;
upon his shoulder dominion rests;
and his name shall be called the angel of great counsel.

ISAIAH 9:6

Sing to the Lord a new song,
for he has done wondrous deeds. TURN TO PSALM 97
Glory be to the Father.

Lord Have Mercy   *Glory to God*   *Prayer*

THE LITURGY OF THE WORD

First Reading

HEBREWS 1:1–12

Songs of Meditation and Response

All the ends of the earth have seen
the salvation by our God.
Sing joyfully to God, all you lands.
The Lord has made his salvation known:
in the sight of the nations he has revealed his justice.

PSALM 97

Alleluia, alleluia.
A sanctified day has shone upon us;
come, you nations, and adore the Lord:
for this day a great light has descended upon the earth.
Alleluia.

Gospel

JOHN 1:1–14

Homily   *Creed*   *Prayer of the Faithful*

THE LITURGY OF THE EUCHARIST

Song at the Preparation of the Gifts

Yours are the heavens, and yours is the earth;
the world and its fullness you have founded.
Justice and judgment are the foundation of your throne.

TURN TO PSALM 88

Prayer over the Gifts

EUCHARISTIC PRAYER

TURN TO PAGE 391

Communion Song

All the ends of the earth have seen
the salvation by our God.

TURN TO PSALM 97

Prayer after Communion

Sunday after Christmas

Entrance Song

When a profound stillness compassed everything
and the night in its swift course was half spent,
your all-powerful word, O Lord,
bounded from heaven's royal throne.

WISDOM OF SOLOMON 18:14–15

The Lord is king, in splendor robed;
robed is the Lord and girt about with strength.

Glory be to the Father.

TURN TO PSALM 92

Lord Have Mercy   Glory to God   Prayer

THE LITURGY OF THE WORD

First Reading

GALATIANS 4:1–7

Songs of Meditation and Response

Fairer in beauty are you than the sons of men;
grace is poured out upon your lips.

My heart overflows with a goodly theme;
as I sing my ode to the king,
my tongue is nimble as the pen of a skillful scribe.

Alleluia, alleluia. PSALM 44
The Lord is king, in splendor robed;
robed is the Lord and girt about with strength. Alleluia.

PSALM 92

Gospel

LUKE 2:33–40

Homily Creed Prayer of the Faithful

THE LITURGY OF THE EUCHARIST

Song at the Preparation of the Gifts

God has made the world firm,
not to be moved.
Your throne, O God, stands firm from of old;
from everlasting you are. TURN TO PSALM 92

Prayer over the Gifts

EUCHARISTIC PRAYER

TURN TO PAGE 391

Communion Song

Take the child and his mother, and go into the land of Israel,
for those who sought the child's life are dead.

MATTHEW 2:20 TURN TO PSALM 92

Prayer after Communion

December 26 : Stephen : Martyr

Entrance Song

Princes met and talked against me,
and the wicked persecuted me wrongfully;
help me, O Lord my God,
for your servant meditates on your statutes.

Happy are they whose way is blameless,
who walk in the law of the Lord.   TURN TO PSALM 118

Glory be to the Father.

First Reading
ACTS OF THE APOSTLES 6:8–10, 7:54–59

Songs of Meditation and Response
Princes met and talked against me,
and the wicked persecuted me wrongfully.
Help me, O Lord my God:
rescue me because of your kindness.   PSALMS 118, 6

Alleluia, alleluia.
I see the heavens opened,
and Jesus standing on the right hand of the power of God.
Alleluia.   ACTS OF THE APOSTLES 7:56

Gospel
MATTHEW 23:34–39

Song at the Preparation of the Gifts
The apostles chose Stephen to be a levite,
a man full of faith and of the Holy Spirit:
whom the Jews stoned,
praying and saying,
"Lord Jesus, receive my spirit." Alleluia.

ACTS OF THE APOSTLES 6:5, 7:59   TURN TO PSALM 20

Communion Song
I see the heavens opened,
and Jesus standing on the right hand of the power of God:
Lord Jesus, receive my spirit,
and do not lay this sin against them.

ACTS OF THE APOSTLES 7:56, 59, 60   TURN TO PSALM 78

December 27 : John : Apostle

Entrance Song
In the midst of the assembly the Lord opened his mouth;
and filled him with the spirit of wisdom and understanding;
he clothed him with a robe of glory.   SIRACH 15:5

It is good to give thanks to the Lord,
to sing praise to your name, Most High.

Glory be to the Father. TURN TO PSALM 91

First Reading
SIRACH 15:1–6

Songs of Meditation and Response

This saying therefore went abroad among the brethren,
that that disciple was not to die.
But Jesus had not said, "He is not to die."
But rather, "So I wish him to remain until I come.
Follow me." JOHN 21:23, 22

Alleluia, alleluia.
This is that disciple who bears witness concerning these things:
and we know that his witness is true. Alleluia. JOHN 21:24

Gospel
JOHN 21:19–24

Song at the Preparation of the Gifts

The just man shall flourish like the palm tree,
like a cedar of Lebanon shall he grow. TURN TO PSALM 91

Communion Song

A saying went abroad among the brethren,
that that disciple was not to die.
But Jesus had not said, "He is not to die";
but rather, "So I wish him to remain until I come."

JOHN 21:23 TURN TO PSALM 111

December 28 : The Holy Innocents : Martyrs

Entrance Song

Out of the mouths of babes and of sucklings, O God,
you have fashioned praise because of your foes.

O Lord, our Lord,
how glorious is your name over all the earth!

Glory be to the Father. TURN TO PSALM 8

First Reading

REVELATION 14:1–5

Songs of Meditation and Response

We were rescued like a bird
from the fowlers' snare.
Broken was the snare,
and we were freed.
Our help is in the name of the Lord,
who made heaven and earth.   PSALM 123

Alleluia, alleluia.
Praise the Lord, you children,
praise the name of the Lord. Alleluia.   PSALM 112

Gospel

LUKE 2:13–18

Song at the Preparation of the Gifts

We were rescued like a bird
from the fowlers' snare.
Broken was the snare
and we were freed.   TURN TO PSALM 123

Communion Song

A voice was heard in Rama,
weeping and loud lamentation;
Rachel weeping for her children,
and she would not be comforted,
because they are no more.

MATTHEW 2:13–18   TURN TO PSALM 112

December 29 : Thomas à Becket
Bishop and Martyr

*Today's Mass is the daytime Mass of Christmas,
with a commemoration of Thomas.*

December 30

Today's Mass is the daytime Mass of Christmas.

*Today's Mass is the daytime Mass of Christmas,
with a commemoration of Sylvester.*

New Year's Day

Entrance Song

A child is born to us, a son is given to us;
upon his shoulder dominion rests;
and his name shall be called the angel of great counsel.

ISAIAH 9:6

Sing to the Lord a new song,
for he has done wondrous deeds.

TURN TO PSALM 97

Glory be to the Father.

Lord Have Mercy   Glory to God   Prayer

THE LITURGY OF THE WORD

First Reading

TITUS 2:11–15

Songs of Meditation and Response

All the ends of the earth have seen
the salvation by our God.
Sing joyfully to God, all you lands.
The Lord has made his salvation known:
in the sight of the nations he has revealed his justice.

PSALM 97

Alleluia, alleluia.
God, who in diverse ways spoke in times past
to the fathers by the prophets;
last of all, in these days, has spoken to us by his son.
Alleluia.

HEBREWS 1:1–2

Gospel

LUKE 2:21

23

Homily   Creed   Prayer of the Faithful

THE LITURGY OF THE EUCHARIST

Song at the Preparation of the Gifts

Yours are the heavens, and yours is the earth;
the world and its fullness you have founded.
Justice and judgment are the foundation of your throne.

TURN TO PSALM 88

Prayer over the Gifts

EUCHARISTIC PRAYER
TURN TO PAGE 391

Communion Song

All the ends of the earth have seen
the salvation by our God.   TURN TO PSALM 97

Prayer after Communion

The Holy Name of Jesus

The Sunday between New Year's and Epiphany or
January 2

Entrance Song

At the name of Jesus every knee should bend
of those in heaven, on earth, and under the earth,
and every tongue should confess
that the Lord Jesus Christ is in the glory of God the Father.

O Lord, our Lord,   PHILIPPIANS 2:10–11

how glorious is your name over all the earth!
Glory be to the Father.   TURN TO PSALM 8

Lord Have Mercy   Glory to God   Prayer

THE LITURGY OF THE WORD

First Reading

ACTS OF THE APOSTLES 4:8–12

Songs of Meditation and Response

Save us, O Lord, our God,
and gather us from among the nations,
that we may give thanks to your holy name
and glory in praising you.   PSALM 105
You, O Lord, are our Father and our redeemer,
from everlasting is your name.   ISAIAH 63:16

Alleluia, alleluia.
May my mouth speak the praise of the Lord,
and may all flesh bless his holy name. Alleluia.

PSALM 144

Gospel

LUKE 2:21

Homily   Creed   Prayer of the Faithful

THE LITURGY OF THE EUCHARIST

Song at the Preparation of the Gifts

I will give thanks to you, O Lord my God, with all my heart,
and I will glorify your name forever.
For you, O Lord, are good and forgiving,
abounding in kindness to all who call upon you. Alleluia.

TURN TO PSALM 85

Prayer over the Gifts

EUCHARISTIC PRAYER
TURN TO PAGE 391

Communion Song

All the nations you have made shall come
and worship you, O Lord,

and glorify your name.
For you are great and do wondrous deeds;
you alone are God. Alleluia. TURN TO PSALM 85

Prayer after Communion

January 2–4

The Mass is that of New Year's Day.

January 5 : Telesphorus : Pope and Martyr

*Today's Mass is that of New Year's Day,
with a commemoration of Telesphorus.*

EPIPHANY

EPIPHANY is the climax of the Advent-Christmas season. During Advent we stressed the coming of the Lord, and at Christmas time we rejoiced in his presence. Epiphany means showing forth, or manifestation. Now, during the time of Epiphany, we concentrate on Christ's manifestation of himself as a universal king, as the heavenly bridegroom, as savior and as judge.

In the Gospel of the feast we hear of the Magi, who recognized the infant as the universal king. The humble child of Christmas is the mighty king, whom all mankind are called to adore.

In the Church's tradition, the marriage feast of Cana is also remembered during this time. Cana was a twofold epiphany. Jesus worked his first public sign, changing water into wine. And he revealed himself at the marriage feast as the heavenly bridegroom who will love his bride, the Church, even to his death on the cross.

The baptism of Jesus in the Jordan was another epiphany. The voice from heaven and the thunder in the sky show him to be the savior. He saves us by the waters of baptism, whereby the Father becomes well-pleased with us.

During this whole time we learn to look toward the future. As we recall the manifestations of Christ in history, we look forward to his final epiphany when he will come to judge the world. The Masses of the season afford us the grace to prepare for that judgment.

Most of all, we seek during this time to recognize Christ as he shows himself to us today. Our lives are themselves epiphanies, Christ showing himself through us to all who have the eyes of faith to see. In every Mass we meet him—universal king, heavenly bridegroom, savior and judge—in the signs of bread and wine, in our families, our friends, in the people we work with. We ask the grace to recognize him.

The Lord's Epiphany

Entrance Song

Behold, the Lord the ruler is come;
and the kingdom is in his hand,
and power, and dominion.   1 CHRONICLES 29:12   MALACHI 3:1

O God, with your judgment endow the king,
and with your justice, the king's son.   TURN TO PSALM 71

Glory be to the Father.

Lord Have Mercy   Glory to God   Prayer

THE LITURGY OF THE WORD

First Reading

ISAIAH 60:1–6

Songs of Meditation and Response

All from Saba shall come,
bringing gold and frankincense,
and proclaiming the praises of the Lord.
Rise up in splendor, O Jerusalem,
for the glory of the Lord shines upon you.

Alleluia, alleluia.   ISAIAH 60:6, 1
We have seen his star in the East:
and have come with gifts to worship the Lord. Alleluia.

MATTHEW 2:2

Gospel

MATTHEW 2:1–12

Homily   Creed   Prayer of the Faithful

THE LITURGY OF THE EUCHARIST

Song at the Preparation of the Gifts

The kings of Tharsis and the isles shall offer gifts;
the kings of Arabia and Saba shall bring tribute.

28

All kings shall pay him homage,
all nations shall serve him. TURN TO PSALM 71

Prayer over the Gifts

EUCHARISTIC PRAYER
TURN TO PAGE 392

Communion Song

We have seen his star in the East
and have come with gifts to worship the Lord.

MATTHEW 2:2 TURN TO PSALM 71

Prayer after Communion

Weekdays between Epiphany and the Feast of the Holy Family

On these days the Mass of the Epiphany is celebrated.

January 11 : Hyginus : Pope

*Unless the Feast of the Holy Family comes on this day,
a commemoration of Hyginus is made.*

The Holy Family
First Sunday after Epiphany

Entrance Song

The father of the just will exult with glee;
let your father and mother have joy;
let her who bore you exult. PROVERBS 23:24–25

How lovely is your dwelling place,
O Lord of hosts!
My soul yearns and pines
for the courts of the Lord. TURN TO PSALM 83
Glory be to the Father.

Lord Have Mercy   Glory to God   Prayer

First Reading
COLOSSIANS 3:12–17

Songs of Meditation and Response

One thing I ask of the Lord; this I seek:
to dwell in the house of the Lord all the days of my life.

PSALM 26

Happy they who dwell in your house, O Lord!
continually they praise you.   PSALM 83

Alleluia, alleluia.
Truly you are a hidden God,
the God of Israel, the savior. Alleluia.   ISAIAH 45:15

Gospel
LUKE 2:42–52

Homily   Creed   Prayer of the Faithful

THE LITURGY OF THE EUCHARIST

Song at the Preparation of the Gifts

The parents of Jesus took him up to Jerusalem,
to present him to the Lord.   LUKE 2:22 TURN TO PSALM 83

Prayer over the Gifts

EUCHARISTIC PRAYER
TURN TO PAGE 392

Communion Song

Jesus went down with them, and came to Nazareth
and was subject to them.   LUKE 2:51 TURN TO PSALM 127

Prayer after Communion

Entrance Song

Upon a high throne I saw a man sitting,
whom a multitude of angels adore, singing in unison:
"Behold him, the name of whose empire is forever."

Sing joyfully to God, all you lands;
serve the Lord with gladness. TURN TO PSALM 99

Glory be to the Father.

First Reading

ROMANS 12:1–5

Songs of Meditation and Response

Blessed be the Lord, the God of Israel,
who alone does wondrous deeds.
The mountains shall yield peace for the people,
and the hills justice. PSALM 71

Alleluia, alleluia.
Sing joyfully to God, all you lands;
serve the Lord with gladness. Alleluia. PSALM 99

Gospel

LUKE 2:42–52

Song at the Preparation of the Gifts

Sing joyfully to God, all you lands;
serve the Lord with gladness;
come before him with joyful song.
Know that the Lord is God. TURN TO PSALM 99

Communion Song

"Son, why have you done so to us?
In sorrow your father and I have been seeking you."
"How is it that you sought me?
Did you not know that I must be about my father's business?"

LUKE 2:48–49   TURN TO PSALM 97

January 13 : The Baptism of Jesus

The Gospel is John 1:29–34.
For the rest of today's Mass turn to page 28.

Second Sunday after the Epiphany

Entrance Song

Let all on earth worship you, O God, and sing praise to you,
sing praise to your name, Most High.

> Shout joyfully to God, all you on earth,
> sing praise to the glory of his name;
> proclaim his glorious praise. TURN TO PSALM 65
> Glory be to the Father.

Lord Have Mercy   Glory to God   Prayer

THE LITURGY OF THE WORD

First Reading
ROMANS 12:6–16

Songs of Meditation and Response

> The Lord sent forth his word to heal them
> and to snatch them from destruction.
> Let them give thanks to the Lord for his kindness '
> and his wondrous deeds to the children of men.
> PSALM 106

> Alleluia, alleluia.
> Praise the Lord, all you his angels,
> praise him, all you his hosts. Alleluia. PSALM 148

Gospel
JOHN 2:1–11

Homily   Creed   Prayer of the Faithful

Song at the Preparation of the Gifts

Shout joyfully to God, all you on earth,
sing praise to the glory of his name.
Hear now, all you who fear God, while I declare
what the Lord has done for me.   TURN TO PSALM 65

Prayer over the Gifts

EUCHARISTIC PRAYER
TURN TO PAGE 406

Communion Song

The Lord said, "Fill the jars with water
and take to the chief steward."
When the chief steward had tasted the water
after it had become wine,
he said to the bridegroom,
"You have kept the good wine until now."
This first miracle Jesus worked in the presence of his disciples.

JOHN 2:7–11   TURN TO PSALM 65

Prayer after Communion

Sundays of Epiphany Season

*The number of Sundays after the Epiphany may vary from three to six,
depending on the date of Septuagesima.*

Entrance Song

Adore God, all you his angels:
Sion hears and is glad, and the cities of Juda rejoice.

The Lord is king; let the earth rejoice;
let the many isles be glad.   TURN TO PSALM 96
Glory be to the Father.

Lord Have Mercy   Glory to God   Prayer

First Reading

THIRD SUNDAY: ROMANS 12:16–21
FOURTH SUNDAY: ROMANS 13:8–10
FIFTH SUNDAY: COLOSSIANS 3:12–17
SIXTH SUNDAY: I THESSALONIANS 1:2–10

Songs of Meditation and Response

The nations shall revere your name, O Lord,
and all the kings of the earth your glory.
For the Lord has rebuilt Sion,
and he shall appear in his glory.   PSALM 101

Alleluia, alleluia.
The Lord is king; let the earth rejoice;
let the many isles be glad. Alleluia.   PSALM 96

Gospel

THIRD SUNDAY: MATTHEW 8:1–13
FOURTH SUNDAY: MATTHEW 8:23–27
FIFTH SUNDAY: MATTHEW 13:24–30
SIXTH SUNDAY: MATTHEW 13:31–35

Homily   Creed   Prayer of the Faithful

THE LITURGY OF THE EUCHARIST

Song at the Preparation of the Gifts

The right hand of the Lord has struck with power:
the right hand of the Lord has exalted me;
I shall not die, but live,
and declare the works of the Lord.   TURN TO PSALM 117

Prayer over the Gifts

EUCHARISTIC PRAYER
TURN TO PAGE 406

Communion Song

All marvelled at the words that came
from the mouth of God. LUKE 4:22 TURN TO PSALM 96

Prayer after Communion

LENT

ON SEPTUAGESIMA SUNDAY the Church begins to direct our minds toward the holy season of Lent. Lent, in turn, will be a preparation for Holy Week and the central feast of Christianity, Easter.

The Masses of this season unfold the great Christian mysteries, the things God does to fulfill his redemptive plan for us. God sent his Son, who became man, suffered, died and was raised up from the dead. These are the saving actions necessary to accomplish God's loving redemptive plan. By these actions of Jesus, we are saved from sin and given God's own life. Taken together, these saving actions are the mystery of Christianity.

God continues to act today in the Church. He still acts upon us and among us in the sacraments, especially in the Eucharist. The sacraments are mysteries because they signify and make present the saving actions of Christ. In the Eucharist we celebrate the core of the Christian mysteries, the great saving action of Christ, his dying and rising.

From Septuagesima to Pentecost, we focus on the solemn observance of the central action of history, our redemption. The Masses of Septuagesima and Lent speak to us of our new life in Christ. They remind us that in baptism we die to selfishness so as to rise with the Lord Jesus. They emphasize the fulfillment of this new life which we achieve each time we unite with our fellow Christians in the Eucharist of the risen Lord. In this sacrament, Christ's resurrection becomes our resurrection: "He who eats my flesh . . . I will raise him up on the last day."

The daily Lenten Masses also stress baptism within the celebration of the Eucharist. They urge us to change our lives by dying to narrowness and selfishness so as to come alive in the freedom and love of Christ. As we prepare for the great feast of Easter, they remind us to live as the risen people of God, "seeking the things that are above."

Septuagesima Sunday

Entrance Song

The terrors of death surged round about me,
the cords of the nether world enmeshed me.
In my distress I called upon the Lord;
from his holy temple he heard my voice.

I love you, O Lord, my strength,
O Lord, my rock, my fortress, my deliverer.
Glory be to the Father. TURN TO PSALM 17

Lord Have Mercy   Prayer

THE LITURGY OF THE WORD

First Reading

I CORINTHIANS 9:24–27, 10:1–5

Songs of Meditation and Response

A stronghold in times of distress;
they trust in you who cherish you;
for you forsake not those who seek you, O Lord.
For the needy shall not always be forgotten;
nor shall the hope of the afflicted forever perish;
rise, O Lord, let not man prevail. PSALM 9

*When this Mass is repeated during the week,
the following verses are not recited.*

Out of the depths I cry to you, O Lord;
Lord, hear my voice!
Let your ears be attentive
to the prayer of your servant.
If you, O Lord, mark iniquities,
Lord, who can stand it?
But with you is forgiveness,
and by reason of your law
I have waited for you, O Lord. PSALM 129

Gospel

MATTHEW 20:1–16

Homily   Creed   Prayer of the Faithful

THE LITURGY OF THE EUCHARIST

Song at the Preparation of the Gifts

It is good to give thanks to the Lord,
and to sing praise to your name, Most High.

TURN TO PSALM 91

Prayer over the Gifts

EUCHARISTIC PRAYER
TURN TO PAGE 406

Communion Song

Let your face shine upon your servant;
save me in your kindness.
O Lord, let me not be put to shame,
for I call upon you.   TURN TO PSALM 30

Prayer after Communion

Sexagesima Sunday

Entrance Song

Awake! Why are you asleep, O Lord?
Arise! Cast us not off forever!
Why do you hide your face, forgetting our oppression?
Our bodies are pressed to the earth.
Arise, O Lord, help us, and deliver us.

> O God, our ears have heard,
> our fathers have declared to us.   TURN TO PSALM 43
> Glory be to the Father.

Lord Have Mercy   Prayer

First Reading

2 CORINTHIANS 11:19–33, 12:1–9

Songs of Meditation and Response

Let the nations know that God is your name;
you alone are the Most High over all the earth.
O my God, make them like leaves in a whirlwind,
like chaff before the wind.   PSALM 82

*When this Mass is repeated during the week,
the following verses are not recited.*

You have rocked the country, O Lord, and split it open.
Repair the cracks in it, for it is tottering.
That they may flee out of bowshot;
that your loved ones may escape.   PSALM 59

Gospel

LUKE 8:4–15

Homily · Creed   Prayer of the Faithful

THE LITURGY OF THE EUCHARIST

Song at the Preparation of the Gifts

Make my steps steadfast in your paths,
that my feet may not falter.
Incline your ear to me; hear my word.
Show your wondrous kindness, O Lord,
savior of those who trust in you.   TURN TO PSALM 16

Prayer over the Gifts

EUCHARISTIC PRAYER
TURN TO PAGE 406

Communion Song

I will go in to the altar of God,
the God of my gladness and joy.   TURN TO PSALM 42

Prayer after Communion

Quinquagesima Sunday

Entrance Song

Be my rock of refuge, O God, a stronghold to give me safety.
You are my rock and my fortress;
for your name's sake you will lead and guide me.

In you, O Lord, I take refuge;
let me never be put to shame.
In your justice rescue me and deliver me. TURN TO PSALM 30

Glory be to the Father.

Lord Have Mercy   Prayer

THE LITURGY OF THE WORD

First Reading

I CORINTHIANS 13:1–13

Songs of Meditation and Response

You are the God who alone works wonders;
among the peoples you have made known your power.
With your strong arm you delivered your people,
the sons of Israel and Joseph. PSALM 76

> *When this Mass is repeated during the week,
> the following verses are not recited.*

Sing joyfully to God, all you lands;
serve the Lord with gladness.
Come before him with joyful song;
know that the Lord is God.
He made us, his we are;
his people, the flock he tends. PSALM 99

Gospel

LUKE 18:31–43

Homily   Creed   Prayer of the Faithful

Song at the Preparation of the Gifts

Blessed are you, O Lord;
teach me your statutes.
With my lips I declare
all the ordinances of your mouth. TURN TO PSALM 118

Prayer over the Gifts

EUCHARISTIC PRAYER
TURN TO PAGE 406

Communion Song

They ate and were wholly surfeited;
the Lord had brought them what they craved:
they were not defrauded of that which they craved.
TURN TO PSALM 77

Prayer after Communion

Ash Wednesday

THE BLESSING OF THE ASHES

Entrance Song

Hear us. O Lord, for bounteous is your kindness;
in your great mercy turn toward us, O Lord.

Save me, O God,
for the waters threaten my life. PSALM 68
Glory be to the Father.

The Prayer of Blessing

THE DISTRIBUTION OF THE ASHES

When distributing the ashes, the priest says:

Remember, man, that you are dust, and unto dust you shall return.

GENESIS 3:19

1. Let us change our garments for ashes and sackcloth:
   let us fast and lament before the Lord:
   for plenteous in mercy is our God to forgive our sins.

   JOEL 2:13

   Between the porch and the altar,
   let the priests, the ministers of the Lord, weep, and say,
   "Spare, O Lord, your people;
   and close not the mouths of those who sing to you, O Lord."

   JOEL 2:17   ESTHER 13:17

2. Let us amend for the better
   in those things in which we have sinned through ignorance,
   lest suddenly overtaken by the day of death,
   we seek time for repentance and are not able to find it.

   Attend, O Lord, and have mercy;
   for we have sinned against you.

   ESTHER 13, JOEL 2

   Help us, O God, our savior;
   and because of the glory of your name, O Lord, deliver us.

   PSALM 78

   Attend, O Lord, and have mercy
   for we have sinned against you.

   Glory be to the Father.

   Attend, O Lord, and have mercy
   for we have sinned against you.

The Prayer of Conclusion

THE MASS

Entrance Song

You have mercy on all, O Lord,
and hate none of the things which you have made,
overlooking the sins of men for the sake of repentance,
and sparing them: because you are the Lord our God.

WISDOM OF SOLOMON 11:24, 25, 27

Have pity on me, O God; have pity on me,
for in you I take refuge. TURN TO PSALM 56

Glory be to the Father.

First Reading

JOEL 2:12–19

Song of Meditation

Have pity on me, O God, have pity on me,
for in you I take refuge.
He has sent from heaven and saved me;
he has made those a reproach who trample upon me.

PSALM 56

Response

O Lord, deal with us not according to our sins,
nor requite us according to our crimes.　　PSALM 102

O Lord, remember not against us the iniquities of the past;
may your compassion quickly come to us,
for we are brought very low.
Help us, O God, our savior,
because of the glory of your name, O Lord;
deliver us and pardon our sins for your name's sake. PSALM 78

Gospel

MATTHEW 6:16–21

Song at the Preparation of the Gifts

I will extol you, O Lord, for you drew me clear
and did not let my enemies rejoice over me.
O Lord, I cried out to you and you healed me.

TURN TO PSALM 29

Communion Song

He who shall meditate day and night on the law of the Lord
shall yield his fruit in due season.　　TURN TO PSALM 1

Thursday after Ash Wednesday

Entrance Song

When I called upon the Lord, he heard my voice
and freed me from those who war against me;
and he humbled them,
who is before all ages and remains forever.
Cast your care upon the Lord,
and he will support you.

Hearken, O God, to my prayer;
turn not away from my pleading;
give heed to me, and answer me. TURN TO PSALM 54
Glory be to the Father.

First Reading
ISAIAH 38:1–6

Song of Meditation

Cast your care upon the Lord,
and he will support you.
When I called upon the Lord,
he heard my voice and freed me from those
who war against me. PSALM 54

Gospel
MATTHEW 8:5–13

Song at the Preparation of the Gifts

To you, O Lord, I lift up my soul:
in you, O my God, I trust;
let me not be put to shame,
let not my enemies exult over me.
No one who waits on you shall be put to shame.
TURN TO PSALM 24

Communion Song

You shall be pleased with due sacrifices,
burnt offerings and holocausts on your altar, O Lord.
TURN TO PSALM 50

Friday after Ash Wednesday

Entrance Song

The Lord has heard, and has had pity on me;
the Lord became my helper.

I will extol you, O Lord, for you drew me clear
and did not let my enemies rejoice over me.

Glory be to the Father. TURN TO PSALM 29

44

First Reading

ISAIAH 58:1–9

Song of Meditation

One thing I ask the Lord;
this I seek:
to dwell in the house of the Lord.
That I may gaze on the loveliness of the Lord
and be protected by his holy temple.   PSALM 26

Response as on Ash Wednesday.

Gospel

MATTHEW 5:43–48, 6:1–4

Song at the Preparation of the Gifts

O Lord, for the sake of your promise give me life,
that I may know your decrees.   TURN TO PSALM 118

Communion Song

Serve the Lord with fear, and rejoice before him with trembling;
embrace discipline, lest you perish from the just way.

TURN TO PSALM 2

Saturday after Ash Wednesday

The First Reading is Isaiah 58:9–14 and the Gospel is Mark 6:47–56.
For the rest of today's Mass turn to page 44.

First Sunday in Lent

Entrance Song

He shall call upon me, and I will answer him;
I will deliver him and glorify him;
with length of days I will gratify him.

You who dwell in the shelter of the Most High,
shall abide in the shadow of the Almighty.

Glory be to the Father.   TURN TO PSALM 90

Lord Have Mercy   Prayer

First Reading

2 CORINTHIANS 6:1–10

Songs of Meditation and Response

To his angels God has given command about you,
that they guard you in all your ways.
Upon their hands they shall bear you up,
lest you dash your foot against a stone.

You who dwell in the shelter of the Most High,
shall abide in the shadow of the Almighty.
Say to the Lord, "My refuge and my fortress,
my God, in whom I trust."
For he will rescue you from the snare of the fowler,
from the destroying pestilence.
With his pinions he will cover you,
and under his wings you shall take refuge.
His faithfulness is a buckler and a shield;
you shall not fear the terror of the night.
Nor the arrow that flies by day;
nor the pestilence that roams in darkness;
nor the devastating plague at noon.
Though a thousand fall at your side,
ten thousand at your right side,
near you it shall not come.
For to his angels he has given command about you,
that they may guard you in all your ways.
Upon their hands they shall bear you up,
lest you dash your foot against a stone.
You shall tread upon the asp and the viper;
you shall trample down the lion and the dragon.
Because he clings to me, I will deliver him;
I will set him on high because he acknowledges my name.
He shall call upon me, and I will answer him;
I will be with him in distress.

I will deliver him and glorify him;
with length of days I will gratify him
and will show him my salvation.
PSALM 90

Gospel

MATTHEW 4:1–11

Homily   Creed   Prayer of the Faithful

THE LITURGY OF THE EUCHARIST

Song at the Preparation of the Gifts

With his pinions the Lord will cover you,
and under his wings you shall take refuge;
his faithfulness is a buckler and a shield. TURN TO PSALM 90

Prayer over the Gifts

EUCHARISTIC PRAYER

TURN TO PAGE 393

Communion Song

With his pinions the Lord will cover you,
and under his wings you shall take refuge;
his faithfulness is a buckler and a shield. TURN TO PSALM 90

Prayer after Communion

Monday in the First Week in Lent

Entrance Song

As the eyes of servants are on the hands of their masters,
so are our eyes on the Lord, our God,
till he have pity on us.
Have pity on us, O Lord, have pity on us.

To you I lift up my eyes,
who are enthroned in heaven. TURN TO PSALM 122

Glory be to the Father.

First Reading

EZEKIEL 34:11-16

Song of Meditation

Behold, O God, our protector,
and look upon your servants.
O Lord God of hosts,
hear the prayers of your servants.   PSALM 83

Response

O Lord, deal not with us according to our sins,
nor requite us according to our crimes.   PSALM 102

O Lord, remember not against us the iniquities of the past;
may your compassion quickly come to us,
for we are brought very low.
Help us, O God, our savior,
because of the glory of your name, O Lord;
deliver us and pardon our sins for your name's sake.

PSALM 78

Gospel

MATTHEW 25:31-46

Song at the Preparation of the Gifts

I will lift up my eyes,
that I may consider your wonders, O Lord;
teach me your statutes;
give me discernment that I may learn your commands.
TURN TO PSALM 118

Communion Song

Amen I say to you:
What you did for one of these, the least of my brethren,
you did for me:
come, blessed of my Father,
take possession of the kingdom
prepared for you from the foundation of the world.
TURN TO PSALM 3
MATTHEW 25:40, 34

48

Tuesday in the First Week in Lent

Entrance Song

Lord, you have been our refuge
through all generations;
from everlasting to everlasting you are.

Before the mountains were begotten
and the earth and the world were brought forth,
from everlasting to everlasting, you are God.

Glory be to the Father. TURN TO PSALM 89

First Reading
ISAIAH 55:6–11

Song of Meditation

Let my prayer come like incense before you, O Lord.
The lifting up of my hands, like the evening sacrifice.

PSALM 140

Gospel
MATTHEW 21:10–17

Song at the Preparation of the Gifts

My trust is in you, O Lord;
I say, "You are my God."
In your hands is my destiny. TURN TO PSALM 30

Communion Song

When I call, answer me, O my just God,
you who relieve me when I am in distress;
have pity on me, O Lord, and hear my prayer!

TURN TO PSALM 4

Ember Wednesday in Lent

Entrance Song

Remember that your compassion, O Lord,
and your kindness are from of old;
let not our enemies exult over us;
deliver us, O God of Israel, from all our tribulations.

49

To you I lift up my soul, O Lord;
in you, O my God, I trust;
let me not be put to shame. TURN TO PSALM 24
Glory be to the Father.

First Reading
EXODUS 24:12–18

Song of Meditation
Relieve the troubles of my heart,
and bring me out of distress, O Lord.
Put an end to my affliction and my suffering,
and take away all my sins. PSALM 24

Second Reading
I KINGS 19:3–8

Song of Meditation
Bring me out of distress, O Lord;
put an end to my affliction and my suffering,
and take away all my sins.
To you, I lift up my soul, O Lord.
In you, O my God, I trust;
let me not be put to shame,
let not my enemies exult over me.
No one who waits for you shall be put to shame;
those shall be put to shame who heedlessly break faith.

PSALM 24

Gospel
MATTHEW 12:38–50

Song at the Preparation of the Gifts
I will delight in your commands,
which I love exceedingly.
And I will lift up my hands to your commands which I love.

TURN TO PSALM 118

Communion Song
Attend to my sighing,
heed my call for help,
my king and my God!
To you, I pray, O Lord. TURN TO PSALM 5

Entrance Song

Splendor and majesty go before him;
praise and grandeur are in his sanctuary.

> Sing to the Lord a new song;
> sing to the Lord, all you lands. TURN TO PSALM 95

> Glory be to the Father.

First Reading

EZEKIEL 18:1–9

Song of Meditation

Keep me, O Lord, as the apple of your eye;
hide me in the shadow of your wings.
From you let my judgment come;
your eyes behold what is right. PSALM 16

Gospel

MATTHEW 15:21–28

Song at the Preparation of the Gifts

The angel of the Lord encamps
around those who fear him, and delivers them.
Taste and see how good the Lord is. TURN TO PSALM 33

Communion Song

The bread that I will give
is my flesh for the life of the world.

JOHN 6:52 TURN TO PSALM 33

Ember Friday in Lent

Entrance Song

Bring me out of distress, O Lord;
put an end to my affliction and my suffering,
and take away all my sins.

To you, O Lord, I lift up my soul.
In you, O my God, I trust;
let me not be put to shame.TURN TO PSALM 24

Glory be to the Father.

First Reading
EZEKIEL 18:20–28

Song of Meditation

Save your servant, O my God, who trusts in you.
Hearken, O Lord, to my prayer.PSALM 85

The Response is recited as on Monday.

Gospel
JOHN 5:1–15

Song at the Preparation of the Gifts

Bless the Lord, O my soul,
and forget not all his benefits;
and your youth shall be renewed like the eagle's.

TURN TO PSALM 102

Communion Song

All my enemies shall be put to shame in utter terror;
they shall fall back in sudden shame.TURN TO PSALM 6

Ember Saturday in Lent

Entrance Song

Let my prayer come before you;
incline your ear to my call for help, O Lord.

O Lord, the God of my salvation, by day I cry out,
at night I clamor in your presence.TURN TO PSALM 87

Glory be to the Father.

First Reading
DEUTERONOMY 26:12–19

Song of Meditation

Pardon our sins, O Lord;
why should the nations say, "Where is their God?"
Help us, O God, our savior;
because of the glory of your name, O Lord, deliver us.

PSALM 78

Second Reading

I THESSALONIANS 5:14–23

Song of Meditation

Praise the Lord, all you nations;
glorify him, all you peoples!
For steadfast is his kindness toward us,
and the fidelity of the Lord endures forever.   PSALM 116

Gospel

MATTHEW 17:1–9

Song at the Preparation of the Gifts

O Lord, the God of my salvation, by day I cry out,
at night I clamor in your presence.
Let my prayer come before you, O Lord.
TURN TO PSALM 87

Communion Song

O Lord my God, in you I take refuge;
save me from all my pursuers and rescue me.
TURN TO PSALM 7

Second Sunday in Lent

Entrance Song

Remember that your compassion, O Lord,
and your kindness are from of old;
let not our enemies exult over us;
deliver us, O God of Israel, from all our tribulations.

To you I lift up my soul, O Lord;
in you, O my God, I trust;
let me not be put to shame.
Glory be to the Father.

TURN TO PSALM 24

Lord Have Mercy   Prayer

THE LITURGY OF THE WORD

First Reading

I THESSALONIANS 4:1–7

Songs of Meditation and Response

Relieve the troubles of my heart
and bring me out of my distress, O Lord.
Put an end to my affliction and my suffering,
and take away all my sins.

PSALM 24

Give thanks to the Lord, for he is good,
for his kindness endures forever.
Who can tell the mighty deeds of the Lord,
or proclaim all his praises?
Happy are they who observe what is right,
who do always what is just.
Remember us, O Lord, as you favor your people;
visit us with your saving help.

PSALM 105

Gospel

MATTHEW 17:1–9

Homily   Creed   Prayer of the Faithful

THE LITURGY OF THE EUCHARIST

Song at the Preparation of the Gifts

I will delight in your commands, which I love exceedingly;
and I will lift up my hands to your commands, which I love.

TURN TO PSALM 118

Prayer over the Gifts

Communion Song

Attend to my sighing;
heed my call for help,
my king and my God!
To you I pray, O Lord.

TURN TO PSALM 5

Prayer after Communion

Monday in the Second Week in Lent

Entrance Song

Redeem me, O Lord, and have pity on me;
my foot stands on level ground;
in the assemblies I will bless the Lord.

> Do me justice, O Lord! for I have walked in integrity,
> and in the Lord I trust without wavering.

> Glory be to the Father.

TURN TO PSALM 25

First Reading
DANIEL 9:15–19

Song of Meditation

You are my help and my deliverer;
O Lord, hold not back!
Let my enemies be put to shame and confounded,
who seek my life.

PSALM 69

Response

O Lord, deal not with us according to our sins,
nor requite us according to our crimes.

PSALM 102

O Lord, remember not against us the iniquities of the past;
may your compassion quickly come to us,
for we are brought very low.
Help us, O God, our savior,
because of the glory of your name, O Lord;
deliver us and pardon our sins for your name's sake.

PSALM 78

Gospel

JOHN 8:21–29

Song at the Preparation of the Gifts

I bless the Lord, who counsels me;
I set the Lord ever before me;
with him at my right hand, I shall not be moved.

TURN TO PSALM 15

Communion Song

O Lord, our Lord,
how glorious is your name over all the earth!

TURN TO PSALM 8

Tuesday in the Second Week in Lent

Entrance Song

To you my heart speaks;
you my glance seeks;
your presence, O Lord, I seek.
Hide not your face from me.

The Lord is my light and my salvation;
whom should I fear?

TURN TO PSALM 26

Glory be to the Father.

First Reading

1 KINGS 17:8–16

Song of Meditation

Cast your care upon the Lord, and he will support you.
When I called upon the Lord, he heard my voice
and freed me from those who war against me.   PSALM 54

Gospel

MATTHEW 23:1–12

Song at the Preparation of the Gifts

Have mercy on me, O Lord, in the greatness of your compassion;
O Lord, wipe out my offense.

TURN TO PSALM 50

Communion Song

I will declare all your wondrous deeds;
I will be glad and exult in you;
I will sing praise to your name, Most High.

TURN TO PSALM 9

Wednesday in the Second Week in Lent

Entrance Song

Forsake me not, O Lord; my God, be not far from me!
Hasten to help me, O Lord, my salvation!

O Lord, in your anger punish me not,
in your wrath chastise me not. TURN TO PSALM 37

Glory be to the Father.

First Reading

ESTHER 13:8–11, 15–17

Song of Meditation

Save your people, O Lord,
and bless your inheritance.
To you, O Lord, I call;
O my God, be not deaf to me,
lest I become one of those going down into the pit.

PSALM 27

The Response is recited as on Monday.

Gospel

MATTHEW 20:17–28

Song at the Preparation of the Gifts

To you I lift up my soul, O Lord.
In you, O my God, I trust;
let me not be put to shame,
let not my enemies exult over me.
No one who waits for you shall be put to shame.

TURN TO PSALM 24

Communion Song

The Lord is just, he loves just deeds;
the upright shall see his face. TURN TO PSALM 10

Thursday in the Second Week in Lent

Entrance Song

Deign, O God, to rescue me;
O Lord, make haste to help me;
let my enemies be put to shame and confounded who seek my life.

Let them be turned back in disgrace
who desire my ruin.   TURN TO PSALM 69

Glory be to the Father.

First Reading

JEREMIAH 17:5–10

Song of Meditation

Pardon our sins, O Lord;
why should the nations say, "Where is their God?"
Help us, O God, our savior;
because of the glory of your name, O Lord, deliver us.

PSALM 78

Gospel

LUKE 16:19–31

Song at the Preparation of the Gifts

Moses prayed in the sight of the Lord his God, and said,
"Why, O Lord, are you angry with your people?
Let the anger of your soul be appeased;
remember Abraham, Isaac and Jacob,
to whom you swore that you would give the land
flowing with milk and honey."
So the Lord relented in the punishment
he had threatened to inflict on his people.

EXODUS 32:11, 8, 13, 14   TURN TO PSALM 69

Communion Song

"He who eats my flesh, and drinks my blood,
abides in me, and I in him," says the Lord.

JOHN 6:57   TURN TO PSALM 33

Friday in the Second Week in Lent

Entrance Song

But I in justice shall behold your face;
I shall be content when your glory shall appear.

Hear, O Lord, a just suit;
attend to my outcry. TURN TO PSALM 16

Glory be to the Father.

First Reading
GENESIS 37:6–22

Song of Meditation

In my distress I called to the Lord,
and he answered me.
O Lord, deliver me from lying lip,
from treacherous tongue. PSALM 119

The Response is recited as on Monday.

Gospel
MATTHEW 21:33–46

Song at the Preparation of the Gifts

Deign, O Lord, to rescue me;
let all be put to shame and confusion
who seek to snatch away my life.
Deign, O Lord, to rescue me. TURN TO PSALM 39

Communion Song

You, O Lord, will keep us
and preserve us always from this generation.
TURN TO PSALM 11

Saturday in the Second Week in Lent

Entrance Song

The law of the Lord is perfect, refreshing the soul;
the decree of the Lord is trustworthy,
giving wisdom to the simple.

The heavens declare the glory of God,
and the firmament proclaims his handiwork.
Glory be to the Father. TURN TO PSALM 18

First Reading
GENESIS 27:6–39

Song of Meditation

It is good to give thanks to the Lord,
to sing praise to your name, Most High.
To proclaim your kindness at dawn
and your faithfulness throughout the night. PSALM 91

Gospel
LUKE 15:11–32

Song at the Preparation of the Gifts

Give light to my eyes that I may not sleep in death
lest my enemy say, "I have overcome him."
TURN TO PSALM 12

Communion Song

You ought to rejoice, my son,
for your brother was dead, and has come to life;
he was lost, and is found. LUKE 15:32 TURN TO PSALM 12

Third Sunday in Lent

Entrance Song

My eyes are ever toward the Lord,
for he will free my feet from the snare.
Look toward me, and have pity on me,
for I am alone and afflicted.

To you I lift up my soul, O Lord.
In you, O my God, I trust;
let me not be put to shame. TURN TO PSALM 24
Glory be to the Father.

Lord Have Mercy   Prayer

First Reading
EPHESIANS 5:1–9

Songs of Meditation and Response

Rise, O Lord, let not man prevail;
let the nations be judged in your presence.
Because my enemies are turned back,
overthrown and destroyed before you.   PSALM 9

To you I lift up my eyes,
who are enthroned in heaven.
Behold, as the eyes of servants
are on the hands of their masters.
As the eyes of a maid
are on the hands of her mistress,
so are our eyes on the Lord our God,
till he have pity on us.
Have pity on us, O Lord, have pity on us. PSALM 122

Gospel
LUKE 11:14–28

Homily   Creed   Prayer of the Faithful

THE LITURGY OF THE EUCHARIST

Song at the Preparation of the Gifts

The precepts of the Lord are right, rejoicing the heart,
and his ordinances are sweeter than syrup or honey from the comb;
therefore your servant is careful of them.   TURN TO PSALM 18

Prayer over the Gifts

EUCHARISTIC PRAYER
TURN TO PAGE 393
Communion Song

The sparrow finds a home,
and the swallow a nest

61

in which she puts her young:
your altars, O Lord of hosts,
my king and my God!
Happy they who dwell in your house!
continually they praise you.

TURN TO PSALM 83

Prayer after Communion

Monday in the Third Week in Lent
Entrance Song

In God, in whose promise I glory,
in the Lord whose word I praise,
in God I trust without fear;
what can flesh do against me?

> Have pity on me, O God, for men trample upon me;
> all the day they press their attack against me.

> Glory be to the Father.

TURN TO PSALM 55

First Reading
2 KINGS 5:1–15

Song of Meditation

O God, my wanderings you have counted;
my tears are recorded in your sight.
Have pity on me, O Lord, for men trample upon me;
all the day they press their attack against me. PSALM 55

Response

O Lord, deal not with us according to our sins,
nor requite us according to our crimes. PSALM 102

O Lord, remember not against us the iniquities of the past;
may your compassion quickly come to us,
for we are brought very low.
Help us, O God, our savior,
because of the glory of your name, O Lord;
deliver us and pardon our sins for your name's sake.

PSALM 78

Gospel

LUKE 4:23-30

Song at the Preparation of the Gifts

Hearken, O God, to my prayer;
turn not away from my pleading;
give heed to me, and answer me.   TURN TO PSALM 54

Communion Song

Oh, that out of Sion would come the salvation of Israel!
When the Lord restores the well-being of his people,
then shall Jacob exult and Israel be glad.   TURN TO PSALM 13

Tuesday in the Third Week in Lent

Entrance Song

I call upon you, for you will answer me, O God;
incline your ear to me; hear my word.
Keep me, O Lord, as the apple of your eye;
hide me in the shadow of your wings.

Hear, O Lord, a just suit;
attend to my outcry.   TURN TO PSALM 16

Glory be to the Father.

First Reading

2 KINGS 4:1-7

Song of Meditation

Cleanse me from my unknown faults, O Lord!
From wanton sin especially, restrain your servant.
Let it not rule over me.
Then shall I be blameless and innocent of serious sin.

PSALM 18

Gospel

MATTHEW 18:15-22

Song at the Preparation of the Gifts

The right hand of the Lord has struck with power:
the right hand of the Lord has exalted me;
I shall not die, but live,
and declare the works of the Lord. TURN TO PSALM 117

Communion Song

Lord, who shall sojourn in your tent?
Who shall dwell on your holy mountain?
He who walks blamelessly and does justice.
TURN TO PSALM 14

Wednesday in the Third Week in Lent

Entrance Song

My trust is in the Lord.
I will rejoice and be glad of your kindness,
when you have seen my affliction.

>In you, O Lord, I take refuge;
>let me never be put to shame.
>In your justice rescue me and deliver me. TURN TO PSALM 30
>Glory be to the Father.

First Reading
EXODUS 20:12–24

Song of Meditation

Have pity on me, O Lord, for I am languishing;
heal me, O Lord.
For my body is in terror;
my soul, too, is utterly terrified. PSALM 6

>*The Response is recited as on Monday.*

Gospel
MATTHEW 15:1–20

Song at the Preparation of the Gifts

O Lord, deal kindly with me for your name's sake; TURN TO PSALM 108
because your kindness is generous.

Communion Song

You will show me the path to life,
you will fill me with fullness of joys in your presence, O Lord.

TURN TO PSALM 15

Thursday in the Third Week in Lent

Entrance Song

"I am the salvation of the people," says the Lord.
"From whatever tribulation they shall cry to me,
I will hear them;
and I will be their Lord forever."

Hearken, my people, to my teaching;
incline your ears to the words of my mouth.

Glory be to the Father. TURN TO PSALM 77

First Reading
JEREMIAH 7:1–7

Song of Meditation

The eyes of all look hopefully to you, O Lord,
and you give them their food in due season.
You open your hand
and satisfy the desire of every living thing. PSALM 144

Gospel
LUKE 4:38–44

Song at the Preparation of the Gifts

Though I walk amid distress, you preserve me, O Lord;
against the anger of my enemies you raise your hand;
your right hand saves me. TURN TO PSALM 137

Communion Song

You have commanded that your precepts be diligently kept.
Oh, that I might be firm in the ways of keeping your statutes!

TURN TO PSALM 118

Friday in the Third Week in Lent

Entrance Song

Grant me, O Lord, a proof of your favor,
that my enemies may see, to their confusion,
that you, O Lord, have helped me and comforted me. .

> Incline your ear, O Lord; answer me,
> for I am afflicted and poor.　　　TURN TO PSALM 85
> Glory be to the Father.

First Reading

EXODUS 17:2, NUMBERS 20:1–3, 6–13

Song of Meditation

In God my heart trusts, and I find help;
then my heart exults, and with my song I give him thanks.
To you, O Lord, I call;
O my God, be not deaf to me,
do not abandon me.　　　PSALM 27

The Response is recited as on Monday.

Gospel

JOHN 4:5–42

Song at the Preparation of the Gifts

Heed my call for help, my king, and my God!
To you I pray, O Lord.　　　TURN TO PSALM 5

Communion Song

"He who drinks of the water that I will give him," says the Lord,
"shall find in himself a fountain of water,
springing up unto life everlasting."

JOHN 4:13, 14　TURN TO PSALM 16

Saturday in the Third Week in Lent

Entrance Song

Hearken to my words, O Lord, attend to my sighing.
Heed my call for help, my king and my God!

To you I pray, O Lord;
at dawn you hear my voice. TURN TO PSALM 5
Glory be to the Father.

First Reading
DANIEL 13:1–9, 15–17, 19–30, 33–62

Song of Meditation

Even though I walk in the dark valley,
I fear no evil; for you are at my side, O Lord.
With your rod and your staff
that give me courage. PSALM 22

Gospel
JOHN 8:1–11

Song at the Preparation of the Gifts

Steady my footsteps according to your promise,
and let no iniquity rule over me, O Lord.

TURN TO PSALM 118

Communion Song

Has no one condemned you, woman?
No one, Lord.
Neither will I condemn you; now sin no more.

JOHN 8:10–11 TURN TO PSALM 17

Fourth Sunday in Lent

Entrance Song

Rejoice, O Jerusalem,
and come together, all you who love her:
rejoice with joy, you who have been in sorrow:
that you may exult,
and be filled from the breasts of your consolation.

ISAIAH 66: 10, 11

I rejoiced because they said to me,
"We will go up to the house of the Lord."

Glory be to the Father. TURN TO PSALM 121

Lord Have Mercy   Prayer

First Reading

GALATIANS 4:22–31

Songs of Meditation and Response

I rejoiced because they said to me,
"We will go up to the house of the Lord."
May peace be within your walls,
prosperity in your buildings.   PSALM 121

They who trust in the Lord are like Mount Sion,
which is immovable; which forever stands.
Mountains are round about Jerusalem;
so the Lord is round about his people,
both now and forever.   PSALM 124

Gospel

JOHN 6:1–15

Homily   Creed   Prayer of the Faithful

THE LITURGY OF THE EUCHARIST

Song at the Preparation of the Gifts

Praise the Lord, for he is good;
sing praise to his name, for he is sweet;
all that he wills he does
in heaven and on earth.   TURN TO PSALM 134

Prayer over the Gifts

EUCHARISTIC PRAYER
TURN TO PAGE 393

Communion Song

Jerusalem, built as a city,
with compact unity:
to it the tribes go up,

the tribes of the Lord,
to give thanks to your name, O Lord. TURN TO PSALM 121

Prayer after Communion

Monday in the Fourth Week in Lent

Entrance Song

O God, by your name save me, and by your might deliver me.
O God, hear my prayer;
hearken to the words of my mouth.

For haughty men have risen up against me,
and fierce men seek my life. TURN TO PSALM 53
Glory be to the Father.

First Reading
I KINGS 3:16–28

Song of Meditation

Be my rock of refuge, O God,
a stronghold to give me safety.
In you, O God, I take refuge;
O Lord, let me never be put to shame. PSALM 30

Response

O Lord, deal not with us according to our sins,
nor requite us according to our crimes. PSALM 102
O Lord, remember not against us the iniquities of the past;
may your compassion quickly come to us,
for we are brought very low.
Help us, O God, our savior,
because of the glory of your name, O Lord;
deliver us and pardon our sins for your name's sake. PSALM 78

Gospel
JOHN 2:13–25

Song at the Preparation of the Gifts

Sing joyfully to God, all you lands;
serve the Lord with gladness;

come before him with joyful song:
know that the Lord is God. TURN TO PSALM 99

Communion Song

Cleanse me from my unknown faults, O Lord!
From wanton sin especially, restrain your servant.
TURN TO PSALM 18

Tuesday in the Fourth Week in Lent

Entrance Song

Hearken, O God, to my prayer;
turn not away from my pleading;
give heed to me, and answer me.

    I rock with grief, and am troubled
    at the voice of the enemy and the clamor of the wicked.
TURN TO PSALM 54

    Glory be to the Father.

First Reading
EXODUS 32:7–14

Song of Meditation

Arise, O Lord, help us!
Redeem us for your name's sake.
O God, our ears have heard,
our fathers have declared to us
the deeds you did in their days, in days of old. PSALM 43

Gospel
JOHN 7:14–31

Song at the Preparation of the Gifts

I have waited, waited for the Lord,
and he stooped toward me and heard my cry.
And he put a new song into my mouth, a hymn to our God.
TURN TO PSALM 39

Communion Song

May we shout for joy at your victory
and raise the standards in the name of the Lord our God.
TURN TO PSALM 19

Wednesday in the Fourth Week in Lent

Entrance Song

When I prove my holiness through you,
I will gather you from all the foreign lands;
and I will sprinkle clean water upon you
to cleanse you from all your impurities;
and I will give you a new spirit. EZEKIEL 36:23–26

I will bless the Lord at all times;
his praise shall be ever in my mouth. TURN TO PSALM 33
Glory be to the Father.

First Reading
EZEKIEL 36:23–28

Song of Meditation

Come, children, hear me;
I will teach you the fear of the Lord.
Look to him that you may be radiant with joy,
and your faces may not blush with shame. PSALM 33

Second Reading
ISAIAH 1:16–19

Song of Meditation

Happy the nation whose God is the Lord,
the people whom he has chosen for his own inheritance.
By the word of the Lord the heavens were made;
by the breath of his mouth all their host. PSALM 32

The Response is recited as on Monday.

Gospel
JOHN 9:1–38

Song at the Preparation of the Gifts

Bless the Lord our God, you peoples,
loudly sound his praise;
he has given life to my soul,

71

and has not let my feet slip.
Blessed be God,
who refused me not my prayer or his kindness.

TURN TO PSALM 65

Communion Song

"The Lord made clay of spittle, and anointed my eyes:
and I went, and I washed, and I saw,
and I have believed in God." JOHN 9:11 TURN TO PSALM 20

Thursday in the Fourth Week in Lent

Entrance Song

Rejoice, O hearts that seek the Lord!
Look to the Lord, and be strengthened;
seek his face evermore.

Give thanks to the Lord, invoke his name;
make known among the nations his deeds.

Glory be to the Father. TURN TO PSALM 104

First Reading
2 KINGS 4:25–38

Song of Meditation

Look, O Lord, to your covenant;
be not forever unmindful of the lives of your afflicted ones.
Arise, O Lord; defend your cause;
remember the reproaches of your servants. PSALM 73

Gospel
LUKE 7:11–16

Song at the Preparation of the Gifts

O Lord, make haste to help me.
Let all those be put to shame
who desire the ruin of your servants. TURN TO PSALM 69

Communion Song

O Lord, I will tell of your singular justice.
O God, you have taught me from my youth;
and now that I am old and gray,
O God, forsake me not. TURN TO PSALM 70

Friday in the Fourth Week in Lent

Entrance Song

Let the thought of my heart find favor before you, O Lord,
my rock and my redeemer.

> The heavens declare the glory of God,
> and the firmament proclaims his handiwork.
> Glory be to the Father.

TURN TO PSALM 18

First Reading

I KINGS 17:17–24

Song of Meditation

> It is better to take refuge in the Lord
> rather than to trust in man.
> It is better to take refuge in the Lord
> rather than to trust in princes.

PSALM 117

> *The Response is recited as on Monday.*

Gospel

JOHN 11:1–45

Song at the Preparation of the Gifts

Lowly people you save, O Lord,
but haughty eyes you bring low;
for who is God except you, O Lord?

TURN TO PSALM 17

Communion Song

The Lord, seeing the sisters of Lazarus weeping at the tomb,
wept before the Jews, and cried out:
"Lazarus, come forth";
and he who had been dead four days came forth,
bound hands and feet.

JOHN 11:33, 35, 43, 44, 39 TURN TO PSALM 30

Saturday in the Fourth Week in Lent

Entrance Song

"All you who thirst, come to the waters," says the Lord;
"and you who have no money, come and drink with joy."

ISAIAH 55:1

Hearken, my people, to my teaching;
incline your ears to the words of my mouth.

Glory be to the Father. TURN TO PSALM 77

First Reading

ISAIAH 49:8–15

Song of Meditation

On you, O Lord, the unfortunate man depends;
of the fatherless you are the helper.
Why, O Lord, do you stand aloof?
Why hide in times of distress?
While the wicked man is proud, the afflicted is set on fire.

PSALM 9

Gospel

JOHN 8:12–20

Song at the Preparation of the Gifts

The Lord is become my rock, my fortress, my deliverer;
and in him will I put my trust. TURN TO PSALM 17

Communion Song

The Lord is my shepherd; I shall not want.
In verdant pastures he gives me repose;
beside restful waters he leads me. TURN TO PSALM 22

First Sunday in Passiontime

Entrance Song

Do me justice, O God,
and fight my fight against a faithless people;
from the deceitful and impious man rescue me.
For you are my God and my strength.

Send forth your light and your fidelity;
they shall lead me on
and bring me to your holy mountain,
to your dwelling-place. TURN TO PSALM 42

Lord Have Mercy   Prayer

First Reading

HEBREWS 9:11–15

Songs of Meditation and Response

Rescue me from my enemies, O Lord;
teach me to do your will.   PSALM 142

O Lord, my deliverer from the angry nations,
truly above my adversaries you exalt me
and from the violent man you have rescued me. PSALM 17

Much have they oppressed me from my youth.
Let Israel say:
Much have they oppressed me from my youth.
Yet they have not prevailed against me;
upon my back the plowers plowed.
Long did they make their furrows.
But the just Lord has severed
the cords of the wicked.   PSALM 128

Gospel

JOHN 8:46–59

Homily   Creed   Prayer of the Faithful

Song at the Preparation of the Gifts

I praise you, O Lord, with all my heart;
be good to your servant, that I may live
and keep your words.
O Lord, give me life according to your word.

TURN TO PSALM 118

Prayer over the Gifts

EUCHARISTIC PRAYER

TURN TO PAGE 394

Communion Song

"This is my body, which shall be given up for you:
 this is the cup of the new covenant in my blood," says the Lord,
"do this as often as you receive it, in remembrance of me."

I CORINTHIANS 11:24–25   TURN TO PSALM 41

Prayer after Communion

Monday in the First Week in Passiontime

Entrance Song

Have pity on me, O Lord, for men trample upon me;
all the day they press their attack against me.

My adversaries trample upon me all the day;
yes, many fight against me.   TURN TO PSALM 55

First Reading
JONAH 3:1–10

Song of Meditation

O God, hear my prayer;
hearken to the words of my mouth.
O God, by your name save me,
and by your might deliver me.   PSALM 53

Response

O Lord, deal not with us according to our sins,
nor requite us according to our crimes.   PSALM 102

O Lord, remember not against us the iniquities of the past;
may your compassion quickly come to us,
for we are brought very low.
Help us, O God, our savior,
because of the glory of your name, O Lord;
deliver us and pardon our sins for your name's sake.   PSALM 78

Gospel
JOHN 7:32–39

Song at the Preparation of the Gifts

Return, O Lord, save my life;
rescue me because of your kindness. TURN TO PSALM 6

Communion Song

The Lord of hosts,
he is the king of glory. TURN TO PSALM 23

Tuesday in the First Week in Passiontime

Entrance Song

Wait for the Lord with courage;
be stouthearted, and wait for the Lord.

The Lord is my light and my salvation;
whom should I fear? TURN TO PSALM 26

First Reading

DANIEL 14:29–42

Song of Meditation

Fight my fight, O Lord;
from the deceitful and impious man rescue me.
Send forth your light and your fidelity;
they shall lead me on and bring me to your holy mountain.

PSALM 42

Gospel

JOHN 7:1–13

Song at the Preparation of the Gifts

They trust in you who cherish your name, O Lord,
for you forsake not those who seek you.
Sing praise to the Lord enthroned in Sion,
for he has not forgotten the cry of the afflicted.

TURN TO PSALM 9

Communion Song

Redeem me, O God of Israel,
from all my distress. TURN TO PSALM 24

Wednesday in the First Week in Passiontime

Entrance Song

My deliverer from the angry nations;
truly above my adversaries you exalt me
and from the violent man you have rescued me, O Lord.

I love you, O Lord, my strength,
O Lord, my rock, my fortress, my deliverer.

TURN TO PSALM 17

First Reading

LEVITICUS 19:1–2, 11–19, 25

Song of Meditation

I will extol you, O Lord, for you drew me clear
and did not let my enemies rejoice over me.
O Lord, my God, I cried out to you and you healed me.
O Lord, you brought me up from the nether world;
you preserved me from among those going down into the pit.

PSALM 29

The Response is recited as on Monday.

Gospel

JOHN 10:22–38

Song at the Preparation of the Gifts

Rescue me from my enemies, O my God;
from my adversaries defend me, O Lord.

TURN TO PSALM 58

Communion Song

I wash my hands in innocence,
and I go around your altar, O Lord,
giving voice to my thanks,
and recounting all your wondrous deeds.

TURN TO PSALM 25

Thursday in the First Week in Passiontime

Entrance Song

All that you have done to us, O Lord,
you have done in true judgment:

because we have sinned against you,
and have not obeyed your commandments:
but give glory to your name,
and deal with us according to the multitude of your mercy.

DANIEL 3:31

Happy are they whose way is blameless,
who walk in the law of the Lord.   TURN TO PSALM 118

First Reading

DANIEL 3:25, 34–45

Song of Meditation

Bring gifts and enter his courts;
worship the Lord in his holy court.   PSALM 95
The Lord strips the forests,
and in his temple all say, "Glory!"   PSALM 28

Gospel

LUKE 7:36–50

Song at the Preparation of the Gifts

By the streams of Babylon
we sat and wept when we remembered Sion.

TURN TO PSALM 136

Communion Song

Remember your word to your servant, O Lord,
since you have given me hope.
This is my comfort in my affliction.   TURN TO PSALM 118

Friday and Saturday in the First Week in Passiontime

Entrance Song

Have pity on me, O Lord, for I am in distress;
rescue me from the clutches of my enemies and my persecutors.
O Lord, let me not be put to shame,
for I call upon you.

In you, O Lord, I take refuge;
let me never be put to shame.
In your justice rescue me.   TURN TO PSALM 30

First Reading

FRIDAY: JEREMIAH 17:13–18
SATURDAY: JEREMIAH 18:18–23

Song of Meditation

My enemies spoke peaceably to me:
and in anger they afflicted me.
You, O Lord, have seen;
be not silent; be not far from me!   PSALM 34

The Response is recited as on Monday.

Gospel

FRIDAY: JOHN 11:47–54
SATURDAY: JOHN 12:10–36

Song at the Preparation of the Gifts

Blessed are you, O Lord; teach me your statutes.
Let not the proud oppress me;
so shall I have an answer for those who reproach me.

TURN TO PSALM 118

Communion Song

Give me not up, O Lord, to the wishes of my foes;
for false witnesses have risen up against me,
and such as breathe out violence.   TURN TO PSALM 26

Palm Sunday

Second Sunday in Passiontime

THE PROCESSION

Entrance Song

If this song is to be sung, turn to No. 151 in the hymnal.

Hosanna to the Son of David!
Blessed is he who comes in the name of the Lord.
O king of Israel: hosanna in the highest.   MATTHEW 21:9

Prayer

1. The children of the Hebrews, bearing olive branches,
    went to meet the Lord, crying aloud and saying,
   "Hosanna in the highest."

   The Lord's are the earth and its fullness;
       the world and those who dwell in it.
   For he founded it upon the seas
       and established it upon the rivers.
   Lift up, O gates, your lintels;
       reach up, you ancient portals,
       that the king of glory may come in!
   "Who is this king of glory?"
       "The Lord, strong and mighty,
       the Lord, mighty in battle."
   Lift up, O gates, your lintels;
       reach up, you ancient portals,
       that the king of glory may come in!
   "Who is this king of glory?"
       "The Lord of hosts; he is the king of glory."
       Glory be to the Father.

2. The Hebrew children spread their garments in the way,
    and shouted, saying,
   "Hosanna to the Son of David:
       blessed is he who comes in the name of the Lord."

TURN TO PSALM 46

Gospel

MATTHEW 21:1–9

The Procession

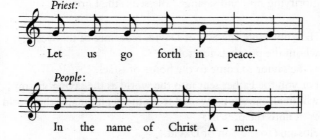

Priest: Let us go forth in peace.

People: In the name of Christ A - men.

During the procession any of the following may be sung or recited.

1. With flowers and palms the multitude run to meet the redeemer,
   and they give becoming honors to the triumphant victor:
   the nations utter the praises of the Son of God,
   and their voices thunder through the clouds
   in praise of Christ: "Hosanna."

2. With the angels and the children,
   let us be found faithful,
   acclaiming him who triumphs over death:
   "Hosanna in the highest."

3. The great crowd gathered for the feast day
   acclaimed the Lord:
   "Blessed is he who comes in the name of the Lord:
   Hosanna in the highest."

4. The whole company of those descending began to rejoice
   and to praise God with a loud voice
   for all the miracles they had seen, saying,
   "Blessed is he who comes as king, in the name of the Lord!
   Peace on earth, and glory in the highest." TURN TO PSALM 147

5. All join together in praising your name, and saying:
   "Blessed is he who comes in the name of the Lord:
   Hosanna in the highest."

6. Like splendid palm branches we are strewn in the Lord's path:
   let us all go to meet him with hymns and canticles,
   glorifying him and saying: "Blessed is the Lord."

7. Hail, our king, the Son of David, redeemer of the world,
   whom the prophets foretold
   as the savior to come to the house of Israel.
   For you the Father sent into the world as the saving victim
   whom all the saints awaited from the beginning of the world
   even unto the present:
   "Hosanna to the Son of David.

Blessed is he who comes in the name of the Lord.
Hosanna in the highest."

Hymn No. 7 is sung during the procession. Other hymns may also be sung.
As the priest enters the church all sing or recite:

8. When the Lord entered the holy city,
   the children of the Hebrews, foretelling the resurrection of life,
   carrying palm branches, cried out,
   "Hosanna in the highest."
   When the populace had heard that Jesus was coming to Jerusalem,
   they went out to meet him, carrying palm branches:
   "Hosanna in the highest," they cried.

Prayer of Conclusion

THE MASS

Entrance Song

O Lord, be not far from me;
O my help, hasten to aid me.
Save me from the lion's mouth;
from the horns of the wild bulls, my wretched life.

My God, my God, look upon me, why have you forsaken me?
Far from my salvation are the words of my sins.

TURN TO PSALM 21

Lord Have Mercy   Prayer

THE LITURGY OF THE WORD

First Reading
PHILIPPIANS 2:5–11

Songs of Meditation and Response

You have hold of my right hand;
with your counsel you guide me;
in the end you will receive me in glory.
How good God is to Israel,
to those who are clean of heart!

83

But, as for me, I almost lost my balance;
my feet all but slipped,
because I was envious of sinners
when I saw them prosper though they were wicked.   PSALM 72

My God, my God, look upon me: why have you forsaken me?
Far from my salvation, are the words of my sins.
O my God, I cry out by day and you answer not;
by night, and there is no relief.
But you are enthroned in the holy place,
O glory of Israel!
In you our fathers trusted;
they trusted and you delivered them.
To you they cried, and they escaped;
in you they trusted, and they were not put to shame.
But I am a worm, not a man;
the scorn of men, despised by the people.
All who see me, scoff at me;
they mock me with parted lips, they wag their heads.
"He relied on the Lord; let him deliver him,
let him rescue him, if he loves him."
But they look on and gloat over me;
they divide my garments among them,
and for my vesture they cast lots.
Save me from the lion's mouth;
from the horns of the wild bulls, my wretched life.
You who fear the Lord, praise him:
all you descendants of Jacob, give glory to him.
There shall be declared to the Lord a generation to come:
and the heavens shall show forth his justice.
To a people that shall be born,
which the Lord has made.   PSALM 21

Gospel

MATTHEW 26:36–75, 27:1–60

Homily   Creed   Prayer of the Faithful

Song at the Preparation of the Gifts

Insult has broken my heart, and I am weak;
I looked for sympathy, but there was none;
for comforters, and I found none.
Rather they put gall in my food
and in my thirst they gave me vinegar to drink.

TURN TO PSALM 68

Prayer over the Gifts

EUCHARISTIC PRAYER
TURN TO PAGE 394

Communion Song

Father, if this cup cannot pass away, unless I drink it,
your will be done.   MATTHEW 26:42   TURN TO PSALM 114

Prayer after Communion

Monday in Holy Week

Entrance Song

Judge, O Lord, those who wrong me;
war against those who make war upon me.
Take up the shield and buckler, and rise up in my defense,
O Lord, the strength of my salvation.
  Brandish the lance,
  and block the way in the face of my pursuers;
  say to my soul, "I am your salvation."   TURN TO PSALM 34

First Reading
ISAIAH 50:5–10

Song of Meditation

Awake, O Lord, and be vigilant in my defense,
my God and my Lord.
Brandish the lance,
and block the way in the face of my pursuers.   PSALM 34

Response

O Lord, deal not with us according to our sins,
nor requite us according to our crimes.　　PSALM 102
O Lord, remember not against us the iniquities of the past;
may your compassion quickly come to us,
for we are brought very low.
Help us, O God, our savior,
because of the glory of your name, O Lord;
deliver us and pardon our sins for your name's sake.

PSALM 78

Gospel

JOHN 12:1–9

Song at the Preparation of the Gifts

Rescue me from my enemies, O Lord,
for in you I hope.
Teach me to do your will,
for you are my God.　　TURN TO PSALM 142

Communion Song

Let all be put to shame and confounded
who are glad at my misfortune.
Let those be clothed with shame and disgrace
who glory over me.　　TURN TO PSALM 34

Tuesday in Holy Week

Entrance Song

But it behooves us to glory in the cross
of our Lord Jesus Christ:
in whom is our salvation, life, and resurrection;
by whom we are saved and delivered.　　GALATIANS 6:14

May God have pity on us and bless us;
may he let his face shine upon us;
and may he have pity on us.　　TURN TO PSALM 66

First Reading

JEREMIAH 11:18–20

86

Song of Meditation

But I, when they were ill, put on sackcloth.
I afflicted myself with fasting,
and poured forth my prayers within my bosom.
Judge, O Lord, those who wrong me;
war against those who make war upon me.
Take up the shield and buckler,
and rise up in my defense.   PSALM 34

Gospel
MARK 14:32–72, 15:1–46

Song at the Preparation of the Gifts

Save me, O Lord, from the hands of the wicked;
preserve me from violent men.

Communion Song

They who sit at the gate gossip about me;
and the drunkards make me the butt of their songs.
But I pray to you, O Lord;
for the time of your favor, O God,
in your great kindness answer me.

Entrance Song

At the name of Jesus every knee should bend,
of those in heaven, on earth and under the earth,
for the Lord became obedient unto death,
even to death on a cross.
Therefore our Lord Jesus Christ
is in the glory of God the Father.   PHILIPPIANS 2:10, 8, 11

O Lord, hear my prayer,
and let my cry come to you.

First Reading
ISAIAH 62:11, 63:1–7

Song of Meditation

Hide not your face from your servant;
in my distress, make haste to answer me.

87

Save me, O God,
for the waters threaten my life;
I am sunk in the abysmal swamp
where there is no foothold.   PSALM 68

Second Reading
ISAIAH 53:1–12

Song of Meditation

O Lord, hear my prayer,
and let my cry come to you.
Hide not your face from me;
in the day of my distress, incline your ear to me.
In the day when I call, answer me speedily.
For my days vanish like smoke,
and my bones burn like fire.
Withered and dried up like grass is my heart;
I forget to eat my bread.
You will arise, O Lord, and have mercy on Sion,
for it is time to pity her.   PSALM 101

Gospel
LUKE 22:39–71, 23:1–53

Song at the Preparation of the Gifts

O Lord, hear my prayer,
and let my cry come to you.
Hide not your face from me.   TURN TO PSALM 101

Communion Song

I mingle my drink with tears,
for you lifted me up only to throw me down,
and I wither like grass;
but you, O Lord, endure forever.
You will arise and have mercy on Sion,
for it is time to pity her.   TURN TO PSALM 101

Holy Thursday : Chrism Mass in Cathedrals

Entrance Song

You shall make the oil of anointing
and say to the sons of Israel:

As sacred anointing oil this shall belong to me
throughout your generations. EXODUS 30:25, 31

The favors of the Lord I will sing forever;
through all generations I shall proclaim your faithfulness.

TURN TO PSALM 88

First Reading
ISAIAH 61:1–4, 6, 8–9

Song of Meditation

In God my heart trusts, and I find help;
then my heart exults, and with my song I praise him.
The Lord is the strength of his people,
the saving refuge of his anointed. PSALM 27

Gospel
LUKE 4:16–22

Song at the Preparation of the Gifts

O Redeemer, receive the song
of those who sing your praise.

A tree made fruitful by the fostering light of the sun
brought forth this oil that it might be blessed.
Humbly we bring it to the Savior of the world.

In your kindness, O King of the eternal homeland,
consecrate this oil of olives as a sign of life,
a safeguard against the demon.

May both men and women be made new
by being anointed by the Chrism,
and may the wound to their glorious dignity be healed.

Our minds being cleansed at the sacred font,
let our sins be put to flight;
may holy gifts be lavished on those
whose foreheads are anointed.

You who were born from the heart of the Father,
and did fill the womb of the Virgin,
grant light, put an end to death
for those who share in the Chrism.

May this day be a festival for us
for ever and ever:
may it be made holy with worthy praise,
and may it not grow old with time.

EUCHARISTIC PRAYER

TURN TO PAGE 395

Communion Song

You love justice and hate wickedness:
therefore God, your God, has anointed you.

Holy Thursday of the Lord's Supper

Entrance Song

But it behooves us to glory in the cross
of our Lord Jesus Christ:
in whom is our salvation, life, and resurrection:
by whom we are saved and delivered.   GALATIANS 6:14

May God have pity on us and bless us;
may he let his face shine upon us;
and may he have pity on us.   TURN TO PSALM 66

Lord Have Mercy   Glory to God   Prayer

THE LITURGY OF THE WORD

First Reading

I CORINTHIANS 11:20–32

Song of Meditation

Christ became obedient for us unto death,
even to death on a cross.
Therefore, God also has exalted him
and has given him the name that is above every name.

PHILIPPIANS 2:8–9

Gospel

JOHN 13:1–15

Homily

*During the Washing of the Feet some or all of the following verses and refrains
may be recited or sung (No. 153). The following hymns are also appropriate:
32, 50, 112, 117.*

1. "A new commandment I give you,
   that you love one another, as I have loved you," says the Lord.
                                                    JOHN 13:34

      Happy are they whose way is blameless,
      who walk in the law of the Lord.   PSALM 118

2. After the Lord had risen from supper
   he poured water into a basin,
   and began to wash the feet of his disciples:
   to whom he gave this example.   JOHN 13:4, 5, 15

      Great is the Lord and wholly to be praised
      in the city of our God, his holy mountain.   PSALM 47

3. The Lord Jesus, after he had supped with his disciples,
   washed their feet, and said to them:
   "Do you know what I your Lord and master have done to you?
   I have given you an example, that so you also should do."
                                                    JOHN 13:12, 13, 15

      You have favored, O Lord, your land;
      you have restored the well being of Jacob.   PSALM 84

4. "Lord, do you wash my feet?"
   Jesus answered and said to him,
   "If I do not wash your feet, you shall have no part with me."
   He came to Simon Peter, and Peter said to him:
   "Lord, do you wash my feet?"
   Jesus answered and said to him,
   "If I do not wash your feet, you shall have no part with me.
   What I do, you know not now;
   but you shall know hereafter."   JOHN 13:6–8

5. "If I, your Lord and master, have washed your feet,
   how much more ought you to wash one another's feet?"
                                                    JOHN 13:14

      Hear this, all you peoples;
      hearken, all you, who dwell in the world.   PSALM 48

6. "By this shall all men know that you are my disciples,
   if you have love for one another,"
   Jesus said to his disciples.   JOHN 13:35

91

7. Let these three, faith, hope and charity, abide in you;
   but the greatest of these is charity.
   And now there remain faith, hope and charity, these three;
   but the greatest of these is charity.   I CORINTHIANS 13:13

The following hymn (No. 97) should always be recited or sung.

8. Where charity and love are, there is God.
   The love of Christ has gathered us together.
   Let us rejoice in him and be glad.
   Let us fear and love the living God.
   And let us love one another with a sincere heart.

   Where charity and love are, there is God.
   When, therefore, we are assembled together,
   let us take heed, that we be not divided in mind.
   Let malicious quarrels and contentions cease.
   And let Christ dwell among us.

   Where charity and love are, there is God.
   Let us also with the blessed see
   your face in glory, O Christ our God.
   There to possess immeasurable and happy joy
   for infinite ages of ages. Amen.

Concluding Prayer

Priest: Our Father . . . and lead us not into temptation.
People: BUT DELIVER US FROM EVIL.
Priest: You have given us your commandments, Lord.
People: TO BE KEPT FAITHFULLY.
Priest: You washed your disciples' feet.
People: DO NOT TURN AWAY FROM YOUR HANDIWORK.
Priest: Lord, listen to my prayer.
People: AND LET MY CRY COME TO YOU.

Prayer of the Faithful

THE LITURGY OF THE EUCHARIST

Song at the Preparation of the Gifts

The right hand of the Lord has struck with power:
the right hand of the Lord has exalted me;

I shall not die but live,
and declare the works of the Lord. TURN TO PSALM 117

Prayer over the Gifts

EUCHARISTIC PRAYER
TURN TO PAGE 394

Communion Song

The Lord Jesus, after he had supped with his disciples,
washed their feet, and said to them,
"Do you know what I, your Lord and Master, have done to you?
I have given you an example, that so you also should do."

JOHN 13:12–15 TURN TO PSALM 22

Prayer after Communion

After the prayer:
Priest: Let us bless the Lord.
People: THANKS BE TO GOD.

*Hymn No. 79 is sung while the Blessed Sacrament is taken from the altar to
a place where it is kept for communion on Good Friday. Afterwards the altar
cloths and furnishings are removed, and the following is recited:*

They divided my garments among them,
and for my vesture they cast lots. TURN TO PSALM 21

Good Friday

Of the Lord's Suffering and Death

Prayer

THE LITURGY OF THE WORD

First Reading

HOSEA 6:1–6

Song of Meditation

O Lord, I have heard your hearing and was afraid;
I have considered your works and trembled.
In the midst of two animals you shall be made known;

when the years shall draw near.
You shall be known;
when the time shall come, you shall be manifested.
When my soul shall be in trouble,
you will remember mercy, even in your wrath.
God will come from Lebanon,
and the Holy One from the shady and thickly covered mountain.
His majesty covered the heavens;
and the earth is full of his praise.   HABAKKUK 3:2–3

Second Reading
EXODUS 12:1–11

Song of Meditation

Deliver me, O Lord, from evil men;
preserve me from violent men.
From those who devise evil in their hearts,
and stir up wars every day.
They make their tongues sharp as those of serpents;
the venom of asps is under their lips.
Save me, O Lord, from the hands of the wicked;
preserve me from violent men.
Who plan to trip up my feet—
the proud who have hidden a trap for me.
They have spread cords for a net;
by the wayside they have laid snares for me.
I say to the Lord, you are my God;
hearken, O Lord, to my voice of supplication.
O Lord, my Lord, my strength and my salvation;
you are my helmet in the day of battle!
Give me not up from my desire to the wicked:
they have plotted against me.
Do not forsake me lest at any time they should triumph.
Those who surround me lift up their heads;
may the mischief which they threaten overwhelm them.
Surely the just shall give thanks to your name;
the upright shall dwell in your presence.   PSALM 139

Gospel

JOHN 18, 19

The Prayer of the Faithful

VENERATION OF THE HOLY CROSS

Priest:

Be-hold the wood of the Cross, on which was hung the sal - va - tion of the world.

People:

Come, let us a - dore.

Reproaches

The following are sung (No. 154) or recited during the veneration of the cross, or appropriate hymns may be sung (No. 95).

1. My people, what have I done unto you?
or in what have I offended you? Answer me.
Because I led you out of the land of Egypt,
you have prepared a cross for your savior.

Holy God. Holy God.
Holy, mighty One. Holy, mighty One.
Holy immortal One, have mercy on us.
Holy immortal One, have mercy on us.

Because I led you out through the desert forty years,
and fed you with manna, and brought you into a very good land,
you have prepared a cross for your savior.

Holy God. Holy God.
Holy, mighty One. Holy, mighty One.
Holy immortal One, have mercy on us.
Holy immortal One, have mercy on us.

What more should I have done, and did it not?
Behold, I have planted you as my fairest vine,
and you have become very bitter to me,
for you have quenched my thirst with vinegar,
and with a lance you have pierced your savior's side.

Holy God. Holy God.
Holy, mighty One. Holy, mighty One.
Holy immortal One, have mercy on us.
Holy immortal One, have mercy on us.

2. My people, what have I done to you,
    or in what have I offended you? Answer me.
            For you I scourged Egypt and its firstborn,
            and you have given me over to be scourged.

            I led you out of Egypt, overwhelming Pharao in the Red Sea,
            and you have delivered me to the chief priest.

            I opened the sea before you,
            and you have opened my side with a lance.

            I went before you in a pillar of cloud,
            and you have haled me to the judgment hall of Pilate.

            I fed you with manna through the desert
            and you have smitten me with buffets and with lashes.

            I gave you the water of salvation to drink from the rock,
            and you have given me gall and vinegar to drink.

            For you I smote the kings of the Chanaanites,
            and you have smitten my head with a reed.

            I gave you a royal sceptre,
            and you have given my head a crown of thorns.

            With great power I lifted you up,
            and you have hung me upon the gibbet of the cross.

3. We adore your cross, O Lord;
    we praise and glorify your holy resurrection.
    For behold, by reason of that wood,
    joy has come into all the world.
            May God have pity on us and bless us.
            May he let his face shine upon us, and have pity on us.

PSALM 66

96

The following hymn may also be sung (No. 21) or recited. The first verse may also be used as a refrain, repeating alternately the first four lines and the last two lines after the other verses.

4. Faithful cross, O tree all beauteous!
   Tree all peerless and divine.
   Not a grove on earth can show us
   Such a flower and leaf as thine.

   Sweet the nails, and sweet the wood,
   Laden with so sweet a load!

   Sing, my tongue, the Savior's glory;
   Tell his triumph far and wide;
   Tell aloud the famous story

   Of his body crucified.
   How upon the cross a victim,
   Vanquishing in death, he died.

   Eating of the tree forbidden,
   Man had sunk in Satan's snare,
   When our pitying Creator
   Did this second tree prepare;
   Destined, many ages later,
   That first evil to repair.

   Such the order God appointed
   When for sin he would atone;
   To the serpent thus opposing
   Schemes yet deeper than his own;
   Thence the remedy procuring,
   Whence the fatal wound had come.
   So when now at length the fullness
   Of the sacred time drew nigh,
   Then the Son, the world's Creator,
   Left his Father's throne on high;
   From a virgin's womb appearing,
   Clothed in our mortality.

   All within a lowly manger,
   Lo, a tender babe he lies!
   See his gentle Virgin Mother
   Lull to sleep his infant cries!
   While the limbs of God incarnate
   Round with swathing bands she ties.

97

Thus did Christ to perfect manhood
In our mortal flesh attain:
Then of his free choice he goeth
To a death of bitter pain;
And as a lamb, upon the altar
Of the Cross, for us is slain.

Lo, with gall his thirst he quenches!
See the thorns upon his brow!
Nails his tender flesh are rending!
See his side is opened now!
When, to cleanse the whole creation,
Streams of blood and water flow.

Lofty tree, bend down thy branches,
To embrace thy sacred load;
Oh, relax the native tension
Of that all too rigid wood;
Gently, gently bear the members
Of thy dying King and God.

Tree, which solely wast found worthy
the world's great victim to sustain
Harbor from the raging tempest!
Arc, that saved the world again.
Tree, with sacred blood anointed
Of the lamb for sinners slain.

Blessing, honor everlasting,
To the immortal Deity;
To the Father, Son, and Spirit,
Equal praises ever be;
Glory through the earth and heaven
To Trinity in Unity.
Amen.

THE COMMUNION LITURGY

Songs at the Procession to the Altar

As the Blessed Sacrament is brought to the altar, the following songs may be sung or recited. If the first song is to be sung, turn to No. 155 in the hymnal.

1. We adore you, O Christ, and we bless you,
   because by your holy cross you have redeemed the world.

2. By a tree we were made slaves,
and by the holy cross we are set free:
the fruit of the tree seduced us,
the Son of God has redeemed us.

3. Savior of the world, save us:
you who by your cross and blood have redeemed us,
help us, we implore you, our God.

The Lord's Prayer

*All together sing or recite the Our Father. Then the priest receives Communion,
and the people confess their sins.*

I confess to almighty God,
to blessed Mary ever Virgin,
to blessed Michael the Archangel,
to blessed John the Baptist,
to the holy apostles Peter and Paul,
to all the saints, and to you, father,
that I have sinned exceedingly in thought, word, and deed;
through my fault, through my fault,
through my most grievous fault.
Therefore I beseech blessed Mary ever Virgin,
blessed Michael the Archangel,
blessed John the Baptist,
the holy apostles Peter and Paul,
all the saints, and you, father,
to pray to the Lord our God for me.

Priest: May almighty God have mercy on you, forgive you your
sins, and bring you to life everlasting.
People: AMEN.
Priest: May the almighty and merciful Lord grant you pardon,
absolution, and remission of your sins.
People: AMEN.

Communion Song

TURN TO PSALM 21

Prayers after Communion

EASTER

Easter is the supreme Christian feast on which we celebrate the central mystery of our faith. Christ, in whom we believe, has triumphed over sin and death. He is risen, and our faith is not in vain.

What Christ accomplished on the first Easter is made real for us again in the sacraments. We are united in the life of the Risen Christ.

The Vigil Service of the Lord's resurrection places before us in a dramatic and stirring way what happens to the Christian by means of the continual saving action of the risen Christ in baptism and the Eucharist. Baptism is very real to us again as the new water is blessed, converts are baptised, and we renew the promises of our own baptism. We sing the joyful alleluias because we are risen with Christ to share his Easter meal. In every Mass, but especially during the Easter time, we are at table again with the Risen Christ and, like the disciples at Emmaus, we recognize him in the breaking of the bread, and our hearts burn within us as we hear his voice.

The Sundays immediately after Easter continue the Resurrection theme, recalling Christ's victory over sin and death. By our faith in his resurrection, we will overcome sin. By our faith in his resurrection, we also will triumph over death. Our physical death will be our journey in the risen Christ to our Father's house.

The Masses for this time bring us a special grace to make our faith in the resurrection more vital. We receive the grace to live a joyful Christian life, remembering that the sufferings of this world are not worthy to be compared with the glory that is to come because of the resurrection.

Easter is "the" Christian feast. All other feasts of the year are an unfolding of this central Christian mystery. All other feast days must be seen in the light of the dying and rising.

The Easter Vigil

Of the Lord's Resurrection

THE BAPTISM LITURGY

THE BLESSING OF THE FIRE AND THE EASTER CANDLE

Prayers

THE PROCESSION

Priest:

Light of Christ.

People:

Thanks be to God.

During the procession, the people's candles are lighted from the Easter candle. When the Easter candle has been given the place of honor in the church the deacon or priest calls the whole creation to be happy for the former darkness has been shattered by the great event of this night, the resurrection of Christ. He asks to be good enough to praise and explain Easter.

After the first summons to rejoice in this night the singer greets the people and invites them to join in his song.

> *Deacon:* The Lord be with you.
> *People:* AND WITH YOUR SPIRIT.
> *Deacon:* Lift up your hearts.
> *People:* THEY ARE LIFTED TO THE LORD.
> *Deacon:* Let us give thanks to the Lord our God.
> *People:* IT IS FITTING AND RIGHT TO DO SO.

The singer now praises this night by telling its history: how all things prepared for the resurrection, the wedding of man and God. He concludes with prayers for church and civil authorities, for all people, for peace and justice.

First Reading

GENESIS 1:1–2:2

Prayer

Second Reading

EXODUS 14:24–31, 15:1

Song of Response

I will sing to the Lord, for he is gloriously triumphant;
horse and chariot he has cast into the sea.
My strength and my courage is the Lord,
and he has been my savior.
He is my God, I praise him;
the God of my father, I extol him.
The Lord crushes hostile attacks,
Lord is his name!   EXODUS 15:1–3

Prayer

Third Reading

ISAIAH 4:2–6

Song of Response

My friend had a vineyard on a fertile hillside;
he spaded it, cleared it of stones, and planted the choicest vines;
within it he built a watchtower, and hewed out a wine press.
For the vineyard of the Lord of hosts is the house of Israel.

ISAIAH 5:1–2

Prayer

Fourth Reading

DEUTERONOMY 31:22–30

Song of Response

Give ear, O heavens, while I speak;
let the earth hearken to the words of my mouth.
May my instruction soak in like the rain,

and my discourse permeate like the dew,
Like a downpour upon the grass,
like a shower upon the crops.
For I sing the Lord's renown.
Oh, proclaim the greatness of our God!
The Rock—how faultless are his deeds,
how right his ways!
A faithful God, without deceit,
how just and upright is the Lord!   DEUTERONOMY 32:1–4

Prayer

THE LITANY (FIRST PART)

Lord, have mercy. CHRIST, HAVE MERCY.
Lord, have mercy. Christ, hear us. CHRIST, GRACIOUSLY HEAR US.
God, the Father of heaven, HAVE MERCY ON US.
God the Son, Redeemer of the world, HAVE MERCY ON US.
God the Holy Spirit, HAVE MERCY ON US.
Holy Trinity, one God, HAVE MERCY ON US.
Holy Mary, PRAY FOR US.
Holy Mother of God, PRAY FOR US.
Holy Virgin of virgins, PRAY FOR US.
Saint Michael, PRAY FOR US.
Saint Gabriel, PRAY FOR US.
Saint Raphael, PRAY FOR US.
All you holy angels and archangels, PRAY FOR US.
All you holy ranks of blessed spirits, PRAY FOR US.
Saint John the Baptist, PRAY FOR US.
Saint Joseph, PRAY FOR US.
All you holy patriarchs and prophets, PRAY FOR US.
Saint Peter, PRAY FOR US.
Saint Paul, PRAY FOR US.
Saint Andrew, PRAY FOR US.
Saint John, PRAY FOR US.
All you holy apostles and evangelists, PRAY FOR US.
All you holy disciples of the Lord, PRAY FOR US.

Saint Stephen, PRAY FOR US.
Saint Lawrence, PRAY FOR US.
Saint Vincent, PRAY FOR US.
All you holy martyrs, PRAY FOR US.
Saint Sylvester, PRAY FOR US.
Saint Gregory, PRAY FOR·US.
Saint Augustine, PRAY FOR US.
All you holy bishops and confessors, PRAY FOR US.
All you holy doctors, PRAY FOR US.
Saint Antony, PRAY FOR US.
Saint Benedict, PRAY FOR US.
Saint Dominic, PRAY FOR US.
Saint Francis, PRAY FOR US.
All you holy priests and clerics, PRAY FOR US.
All you holy monks and hermits, PRAY FOR US.
Saint Mary Magdalen, PRAY FOR US.
Saint Agnes, PRAY FOR US.
Saint Cecilia, PRAY FOR US.
Saint Agatha, PRAY FOR US.
Saint Anastasia, PRAY FOR US.
All you holy virgins and widows, PRAY FOR US.
All you holy men and women, saints of God, INTERCEDE FOR US.

THE BLESSING OF WATER FOR BAPTISM

Prayer

Preface of Blessing

Priest: The Lord be with you.
People: AND WITH YOUR SPIRIT.
Priest: Lift up your hearts.
People: THEY ARE LIFTED TO THE LORD.
Priest: Let us give thanks to the Lord our God.
People: THAT IS RIGHT AND JUST.

The water is made holy during this song of thanksgiving. In it the priest recalls the way God has used water to teach men, to help them, to heal them and finally to be a sign of man's sharing in Christ's resurrection. Plunged into the water of Baptism man dies and rises from the water living in Jesus. The waters of Baptism are the womb of our mother, the Church. During this blessing then the Easter candle, the sign of the risen Lord, is plunged deep into these waters of motherhood to make them rich with new life. The Spirit of Christ, the Holy Spirit, thus makes the waters alive and powerful, the sign of man's new life. Finally the holy oils, signs of the Spirit and of strength, are mixed with the water.

THE BAPTISM

TURN TO PAGE 713 OR PAGE 727

After the Baptism, or after the blessing of the water, the newly blessed water is taken to the baptistry.

Song at the Procession to the Font

As a hind longs for the running waters,
so my soul longs for you, O God.
Athirst is my soul for God, the living God.
When shall I go and behold the face of God?
My tears are my food day and night,
as they say to me day after day, "Where is your God?"

PSALM 41

Prayer

RENEWING THE PROMISES OF BAPTISM

Priest: Do you renounce Satan?
People: WE DO RENOUNCE HIM.
Priest: And all his works?
People: WE DO RENOUNCE THEM.
Priest: And all his allurements?
People: WE DO RENOUNCE THEM.
Priest: Do you believe in God, the Father almighty, creator of heaven and earth?
People: WE DO BELIEVE.
Priest: Do you believe in Jesus Christ, his only Son, our Lord, who was born into this world and who suffered?
People: WE DO BELIEVE.

105

Priest: Do you believe also in the Holy Spirit, the holy Catholic Church, the communion of saints, the forgiveness of sins, the resurrection of the body and life everlasting?

People: WE DO BELIEVE.

Priest: Now let us pray to God together, as our Lord Jesus Christ has taught us to pray:

People: OUR FATHER . . .

THE LITANY (SECOND PART)

Be merciful, SPARE US, LORD.
Be merciful, HEAR US, LORD.
From every evil, DELIVER US, LORD.
From every sin, DELIVER US, LORD.
From everlasting death, DELIVER US, LORD.
Through the mystery of your holy Incarnation, DELIVER US, LORD.
Through your coming, DELIVER US, LORD.
Through your birth, DELIVER US, LORD.
Through your baptism and holy fasting, DELIVER US, LORD.
Through your cross and passion, DELIVER US, LORD.
Through your death and burial, DELIVER US, LORD.
Through your holy resurrection, DELIVER US, LORD.
Through your wonderful ascension, DELIVER US, LORD.
Through the coming of the Holy Spirit, the Consoler,
DELIVER US, LORD
In the day of judgment, DELIVER US, LORD.

Sinners that we are, WE ASK YOU TO HEAR US.
That you would pardon us, THIS WE ASK YOU, HEAR OUR PRAYER.
That you would govern and preserve your holy Church,
THIS WE ASK YOU, HEAR OUR PRAYER.
That you would preserve the Apostolic Pope and all ranks
  in the Church in holy religion,
THIS WE ASK YOU, HEAR OUR PRAYER.
That you would humble the enemies of holy Church,
THIS WE ASK YOU, HEAR OUR PRAYER.
That you would give peace and true union of hearts to
  Christian kings and rulers,

THIS WE ASK YOU, HEAR OUR PRAYER.
That you would strengthen and keep us in your holy service,
THIS WE ASK YOU, HEAR OUR PRAYER.
That you would repay with everlasting goods all who have
    done good to us,
THIS WE ASK YOU, HEAR OUR PRAYER.
That you would give and preserve the fruits of the earth,
THIS WE ASK YOU, HEAR OUR PRAYER.
That you would grant eternal rest to all the faithful departed,
THIS WE ASK YOU, HEAR OUR PRAYER.
That you would listen to us, THIS WE ASK YOU, HEAR OUR PRAYER.

Lamb of God, who take away the sins of the world,
SPARE US, LORD.
Lamb of God, who take away the sins of the world,
HEAR US, LORD.
Lamb of God, who take away the sins of the world,
HAVE MERCY ON US.
Christ, hear us. CHRIST, GRACIOUSLY HEAR US.

Lord Have Mercy   Glory to God   Prayer

THE LITURGY OF THE WORD

First Reading
COLOSSIANS 3:1–4

Songs of Meditation and Response

Give thanks to the Lord, for he is good,
for his mercy endures forever.   PSALM 117

Praise the Lord, all you nations;
glorify him, all you peoples!
For steadfast is his kindness toward us,
and the fidelity of the Lord endures forever.   PSALM 116

Gospel
MATTHEW 28:1–7

Homily   Prayer of the Faithful

THE LITURGY OF THE EUCHARIST

Prayer over the Gifts

EUCHARISTIC PRAYER

TURN TO PAGE 396

LAUDS—THE SONGS OF PRAISE

Alleluia, alleluia, alleluia.   TURN TO PSALM 150

And very early in the morning
after the Sabbath, they came to the sepulchre
at sunrise, alleluia. TURN TO THE SONG OF ZACHARY, PAGE 709

Prayer

DISMISSAL

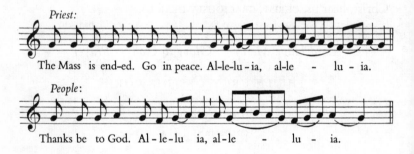

Priest:
The Mass is end-ed. Go in peace. Al-le-lu-ia,   alle - lu - ia.

People:
Thanks be to God. Al - le-lu   ia, al-le   - lu - ia.

Easter Mass During the Day

Entrance Song

I arose, and am still with you, alleluia;
you rest your hand upon me, alleluia;
your knowledge is too wonderful,
alleluia, alleluia.

O Lord, you have probed me and you know me;
you know when I sit and when I stand. TURN TO PSALM 138
Glory be to the Father.

Lord Have Mercy   Glory to God   Prayer

THE LITURGY OF THE WORD

First Reading
I CORINTHIANS 5:7-8

Songs of Meditation and Response

This is the day the Lord has made;
let us be glad and rejoice in it.
Give thanks to the Lord, for he is good,
for his mercy endures forever. PSALM 117
Alleluia, alleluia.
Christ, our passover, has been sacrificed. I CORINTHIANS 5:7
Christians, to the Paschal victim
  Offer your thankful praises!
A lamb the sheep redeemeth: Christ, who only is sinless,
  Reconcileth sinners to the Father.
Death and life have contended in that combat stupendous:
  The Prince of life, who died, reigns immortal.
Speak, Mary, declaring
  What thou sawest, wayfaring.
"The tomb of Christ, who is living,
  The glory of Jesus' resurrection;
Bright angels attesting,
  The shroud and napkin resting.
Yea, Christ my hope is arisen:
  To Galilee he goes before you."
Christ indeed from death is risen, our new life obtaining.
Have mercy, victor King, ever reigning! Amen. Alleluia.

Gospel
MARK 16:1-7

Homily   Creed   Prayer of the Faithful

Song at the Preparation of the Gifts

The earth feared and was silent
when God arose for judgment. Alleluia.

TURN TO PSALM 75

Prayer over the Gifts

EUCHARISTIC PRAYER
TURN TO PAGE 396

Communion Song

Christ, our passover, has been sacrificed, alleluia:
therefore let us keep festival
with the unleavened bread of sincerity and truth,
alleluia, alleluia, alleluia.

I CORINTHIANS 5:7–8 TURN TO PSALM 117

Prayer after Communion

Easter Monday

Entrance Song

The Lord has brought you into a land
flowing with milk and honey, alleluia:
thus the law of the Lord will ever be on your lips,
alleluia, alleluia.   EXODUS 13:5, 9

Give thanks to the Lord, invoke his name;
make known among the nations his deeds.

Glory be to the Father.   TURN TO PSALM 104

First Reading
ACTS OF THE APOSTLES 10:37–43

Songs of Meditation and Response

This is the day the Lord has made;
let us be glad and rejoice in it.
Let the house of Israel say that he is good,
that his mercy endures forever.   PSALM 117

Alleluia, alleluia.
An angel of the Lord came down from heaven,
and drawing near, rolled back the stone, and sat upon it.

MATTHEW 28:2

*The Response "Christians to the Paschal Victim" is recited
as in the Mass during the day on Easter.*

Gospel
LUKE 24:13–35

Song at the Preparation of the Gifts
An angel of the Lord came down from heaven,
and said to the women,
"He whom you seek is risen as he said." Alleluia.

MATTHEW 28:2, 5, 6   TURN TO PSALM 104

Communion Song
The Lord has risen,
and has appeared to Peter. Alleluia.

LUKE 24:34   TURN TO PSALM 113

Easter Tuesday

Entrance Song
He gave them the water of learning to drink, alleluia;
it shall be made strong in them,
and shall not be moved, alleluia,
and it shall exalt them forever,
alleluia, alleluia.

SIRACH 15:3, 4

Give thanks to the Lord, invoke his name;
make known among the nations his deeds.

Glory be to the Father.

TURN TO PSALM 104

First Reading
ACTS OF THE APOSTLES 13:16, 26–33

Songs of Meditation and Response
This is the day the Lord has made;
let us be glad and rejoice in it.

PSALM 117

Thus let the redeemed of the Lord say,
those whom he has redeemed from the hand of the foe
and gathered from the lands.

PSALM 106

Alleluia, alleluia.
The Lord is risen from the sepulchre,
who for us hung upon a tree.

The Response "Christians to the Paschal Victim" is recited
as in the Mass during the day on Easter.

Gospel
LUKE 24:36–47

Song at the Preparation of the Gifts

The Lord thundered from heaven,
and the Most High gave forth his voice:
and the fountains of waters appeared, alleluia.

TURN TO PSALM 17

Communion Song

If you have risen with Christ,
seek the things that are above,
where Christ is seated at the right hand of God, alleluia;
mind the things that are above, alleluia.

COLOSSIANS 3:1, 2 TURN TO PSALM 135

Easter Wednesday

Entrance Song

Come, blessed of my Father, receive the kingdom, alleluia,
which was prepared for you from the foundation of the world,
alleluia, alleluia, alleluia. MATTHEW 25:34

Sing to the Lord a new song;
sing to the Lord, all you lands. TURN TO PSALM 95

Glory be to the Father.

First Reading
ACTS OF THE APOSTLES 3:13–15, 17–19

Songs of Meditation and Response

This is the day the Lord has made;
let us be glad and rejoice in it.
The right hand of the Lord has struck with power:
the right hand of the Lord has exalted me. PSALM 117

Alleluia, alleluia.
The Lord is risen indeed,
and has appeared to Peter.   LUKE 24:34

*The Response "Christians to the Paschal Victim" is recited
as in the Mass during the day on Easter.*

Gospel
JOHN 21:1–14

Song at the Preparation of the Gifts

The Lord opened the doors of heaven;
he rained manna upon them for food
and gave them heavenly bread.
The bread of angels was eaten by men, alleluia.

TURN TO PSALM 77

Communion Song

Christ having risen from the dead,
dies now no more, alleluia;
death shall no longer have dominion over him,
alleluia, alleluia.   ROMANS 6:9   TURN TO PSALM 95

Easter Thursday

Entrance Song

They praised in unison your conquering hand, O Lord, alleluia,
because wisdom opened the mouths of the dumb,
and gave ready speech to infants,
alleluia, alleluia.   WISDOM OF SOLOMON 10:20, 21

Sing to the Lord a new song,
for he has done wondrous deeds.   TURN TO PSALM 97

Glory be to the Father.

First Reading
ACTS OF THE APOSTLES 8:26–40

Songs of Meditation and Response

This is the day the Lord has made;
let us be glad and rejoice in it.
The stone which the builders rejected

has become the cornerstone.
By the Lord has this been done;
it is wonderful in our eyes. PSALM 117

Alleluia, alleluia.
Christ is risen, who created all things,
and who had compassion upon the human race.

*The Response "Christians to the Paschal Victim" is recited
as in the Mass during the day on Easter.*

Gospel
JOHN 20:11–18

Song at the Preparation of the Gifts

"In the day of your solemnity," says the Lord,
"I will bring you into a land flowing with milk and honey."
Alleluia. EXODUS 13:5   TURN TO PSALM 106

Communion Song

O purchased people, proclaim the perfections of him, alleluia,
who has called you out of darkness
into his marvelous light, alleluia.

I PETER 2:9   TURN TO PSALM 97

Easter Friday

Entrance Song

The Lord led them on in hope, alleluia,
while he covered their enemies with the sea,
alleluia, alleluia, alleluia.

Hearken, my people, to my teaching:
incline your ears to the words of my mouth.

Glory be to the Father. TURN TO PSALM 77

First Reading
I PETER 3:18–22

Songs of Meditation and Response

This is the day the Lord has made;
let us be glad and rejoice in it.

Blessed is he who comes in the name of the Lord;
the Lord is God, and he has given us light.   PSALM 117

Alleluia, alleluia.
Say among the nations:
the Lord has reigned from a tree.   PSALM 95

*The Response "Christians to the Paschal Victim" is recited
as in the Mass during the day on Easter.*

Gospel
MATTHEW 28:16–20

Song at the Preparation of the Gifts

This day shall be a memorial feast for you, alleluia;
and you shall celebrate it as a solemn feast to the Lord
from generation to generation: an everlasting legal day,
alleluia, alleluia, alleluia.

EXODUS 12:14   TURN TO PSALM 99

Communion Song

All power in heaven and on earth
has been given to me, alleluia.
Go and make disciples of all nations,
baptizing them in the name of the Father,
and of the Son,
and of the Holy Spirit,
alleluia, alleluia.   MATTHEW 28:18, 19   TURN TO PSALM 117

Easter Saturday

Entrance Song

The Lord led forth his people with joy, alleluia;
with shouts of joy, his chosen ones,
alleluia, alleluia.

Give thanks to the Lord, invoke his name;
make known among the nations his deeds.

Glory be to the Father.   TURN TO PSALM 104

First Reading
I PETER 2:1–10

Songs of Meditation and Response

Alleluia, alleluia.
This is the day the Lord has made;
let us be glad and rejoice in it. Alleluia. PSALM 117

Praise, you servants of the Lord,
praise the name of the Lord. PSALM 112

*The Response "Christians to the Paschal Victim" is recited
as in the Mass during the day on Easter.*

Gospel

JOHN 20:1–9

Song at the Preparation of the Gifts

Blessed is he who comes in the name of the Lord;
we bless you from the house of the Lord.
The Lord is God, and he has given us light,
alleluia, alleluia. TURN TO PSALM 117

Communion Song

All you who have been baptized into Christ,
have put on Christ, alleluia.

GALATIANS 3:27 TURN TO PSALM 96

First Sunday after Easter

Entrance Song

Crave as newborn babes, alleluia:
pure spiritual milk:
alleluia, alleluia, alleluia. I PETER 2:2

Sing joyfully to God our strength;
acclaim the God of Jacob. TURN TO PSALM 80
Glory be to the Father.

Lord Have Mercy   Glory to God   Prayer

First Reading
I JOHN 5:4–10

Songs of Meditation and Response

Alleluia, alleluia.
"On the day of my resurrection," says the Lord,
"I will go before you into Galilee." Alleluia.

MATTHEW 28:7

After eight days, the doors being closed,
Jesus stood in the midst of his disciples,
and said, "Peace be to you!" Alleluia.   JOHN 20:26

Gospel
JOHN 20:19–31

Homily   Creed   Prayer of the Faithful

THE LITURGY OF THE EUCHARIST

Song at the Preparation of the Gifts

An angel of the Lord came down from heaven,
and said to the women,
"He whom you seek has risen even as he said." Alleluia.

MATTHEW 28:2, 5, 6   TURN TO PSALM 80

Prayer over the Gifts

EUCHARISTIC PRAYER
TURN TO PAGE 396

Communion Song

Put in your hand, and know the place of the nails, alleluia;
and be not unbelieving, but believing,
alleluia, alleluia.   JOHN 20:27   TURN TO PSALM 117

Prayer after Communion

Second Sunday after Easter

Entrance Song

Of the kindness of the Lord the earth is full, alleluia;
by the word of the Lord the heavens were made,
alleluia, alleluia.

Exult, you just, in the Lord;
praise from the upright is fitting. TURN TO PSALM 32
Glory be to the Father.

Lord Have Mercy   *Glory to God*   *Prayer*

THE LITURGY OF THE WORD

First Reading

I PETER 2:21–25

Songs of Meditation and Response

Alleluia, alleluia.
The disciples recognized the Lord Jesus
in the breaking of the bread. Alleluia.   LUKE 24:35

I am the good shepherd:
and I know my sheep, and mine know me. Alleluia.

JOHN 10:14

Gospel

JOHN 10:11–16

Homily   *Creed*   *Prayer of the Faithful*

THE LITURGY OF THE EUCHARIST

Song at the Preparation of the Gifts

O God, my God, to you do I watch at break of day,
and in your name I will lift up my hands, alleluia.

TURN TO PSALM 62

Prayer over the Gifts

EUCHARISTIC PRAYER

TURN TO PAGE 396

Communion Song

I am the good shepherd, alleluia:
and I know my sheep, and mine know me,
alleluia, alleluia.   JOHN 10:14   TURN TO PSALM 22

Prayer after Communion

Third Sunday after Easter

Entrance Song

Shout joyfully to God, all you on earth, alleluia;
sing praise to the glory of his name, alleluia;
proclaim his glorious praise,
alleluia, alleluia, alleluia.

Say to God, "How tremendous are your deeds, O Lord!
For your great strength your enemies fawn upon you."
Glory be to the Father.   TURN TO PSALM 65

Lord Have Mercy   Glory to God   Prayer

THE LITURGY OF THE WORD

First Reading
I PETER 2:11–19

Songs of Meditation and Response

Alleluia, alleluia.
The Lord has sent deliverance to his people. Alleluia. PSALM 110
It behooved Christ to suffer and to rise again from the dead,
and so to enter into his glory. Alleluia.   LUKE 24:46

Gospel
JOHN 16:16–22

Homily   Creed   Prayer of the Faithful

119

Song at the Preparation of the Gifts

Praise the Lord, O my soul;
I will praise the Lord all my life;
I will sing praise to my God while I live. Alleluia.

TURN TO PSALM 145

Prayer over the Gifts

EUCHARISTIC PRAYER
TURN TO PAGE 396

Communion Song

A little while, and you shall not see me, alleluia:
and again a little while, and you shall see me:
because I go to the Father.
Alleluia, alleluia. JOHN 16:16 TURN TO PSALM 65

Prayer after Communion

Fourth Sunday after Easter

Entrance Song

Sing to the Lord a new song, alleluia;
for the Lord has done wondrous deeds, alleluia;
in the sight of the nations he has revealed his justice:
alleluia, alleluia, alleluia.

His right hand has won victory for him,
his holy arm. TURN TO PSALM 97
Glory be to the Father.

Lord Have Mercy   Glory to God   Prayer

THE LITURGY OF THE WORD

First Reading

JAMES 1:17–21

Songs of Meditation and Response

Alleluia, alleluia.
The right hand of the Lord has struck with power;
the right hand of the Lord has exalted me. Alleluia. PSALM 117

Christ, having risen from the dead, dies now no more;
death shall no longer have dominion over him. Alleluia.

ROMANS 6:9

Gospel
JOHN 16:5-14

Homily   Creed   Prayer of the Faithful

THE LITURGY OF THE EUCHARIST

Song at the Preparation of the Gifts

Shout joyfully to God, all you on earth,
sing praise to the glory of his name;
hear now, all you who fear God, while I declare
what the Lord has done for me. Alleluia.

TURN TO PSALM 65

Prayer over the Gifts

EUCHARISTIC PRAYER
TURN TO PAGE 396

Communion Song

When the Paraclete has come, the Spirit of truth,
he will convict the world of sin,
and of justice, and of judgment,
alleluia, alleluia.   JOHN 16:8   TURN TO PSALM 97

Prayer after Communion

Fifth Sunday after Easter

Entrance Song

Declare the word of joy, and let it be heard, alleluia:
declare it even to the ends of the earth;

the Lord has delivered his people:
alleluia, alleluia. ISAIAH 48:20

> Shout joyfully to God, all you on earth,
> sing praise to the glory of his name;
> proclaim his glorious praise. TURN TO PSALM 65
> Glory be to the Father.

Lord Have Mercy   Glory to God   Prayer

THE LITURGY OF THE WORD

First Reading
JAMES 1:22–27

Songs of Meditation and Response

Alleluia, alleluia.
Christ is risen, and has shone upon us,
whom he redeemed with his blood. Alleluia.
I came forth from the Father, and have come into the world.
Again I leave the world, and go to the Father. Alleluia.

JOHN 16:28

Gospel
JOHN 16:23–30

Homily   Creed   Prayer of the Faithful

THE LITURGY OF THE EUCHARIST

Song at the Preparation of the Gifts

Bless the Lord our God, you peoples,
loudly sound his praise;
he has given life to my soul,
and has not let my feet slip.
Blessed be the Lord, who refused me not
my prayer, or his kindness. Alleluia. TURN TO PSALM 65

Prayer over the Gifts

EUCHARISTIC PRAYER

TURN TO PAGE 396

Communion Song

Sing to the Lord, alleluia;
sing to the Lord; bless his name;
announce his salvation day after day,
alleluia, alleluia.   TURN TO PSALM 95

Prayer after Communion

Rogation Days

*The days between the Fifth Sunday after Easter and the Ascension may be kept
as a time of special petition. If this is done the following Mass is celebrated after
the Litany of the Saints. These days may be celebrated at another time if this
seems more appropriate. The alleluias in parentheses are recited during Eastertime.* *For the Litany, turn to page 782.*

Entrance Song

From his holy temple he heard my voice, alleluia;
and my cry to him reached his ears.
(Alleluia, alleluia.)

> I love you, O Lord, my strength,
> O Lord, my rock, my fortress, my deliverer.

> Glory be to the Father.   TURN TO PSALM 17

First Reading
JAMES 5:16–20

Songs of Meditation and Response

Alleluia, alleluia.
Pardon our sins, O Lord;
why should the nations say,
"Where is their God?" Alleluia.   PSALM 78

I will rejoice and be glad of your kindness,
when you have seen my affliction
and watched over me in my distress. Alleluia.   PSALM 30

*If these days are celebrated outside of Eastertime
the following is recited instead:*

123

You saved us, O Lord, from our foes,
and those who hated us you put to shame.
In God we gloried day by day;
your name we praised always.   PSALM 43

Alleluia, alleluia.
Pardon our sins, O Lord;
why should the nations say,
"Where is their God?" Alleluia.   PSALM 78

Gospel
LUKE 11:5–13

Song at the Preparation of the Gifts

I will speak my thanks earnestly to the Lord,
and in the midst of the throng I will praise him,
for he stood at the right hand of the poor man,
to save me from those who would condemn me. Alleluia.

TURN TO PSALM 108

Communion Song

Ask, and you shall receive;
seek, and you shall find;
knock and it shall be opened to you.
For everyone who asks receives;
and he who seeks finds;
and to him who knocks, it shall be opened. (Alleluia.)

LUKE 11:9–10 TURN TO PSALM 30

Vigil of the Lord's Ascension

The First Reading is Ephesians 4:7–13, and the Gospel is John 17:1–11.
For the rest of today's Mass, turn to page 121.

The Lord's Ascension

Entrance Song

Men of Galilee,
why do you stand looking up to heaven? Alleluia.
He shall come in the same way

as you have seen him going up to heaven:
alleluia, alleluia, alleluia. ACTS OF THE APOSTLES 1:11

All you peoples, clap your hands,
shout to God with cries of gladness. TURN TO PSALM 46
Glory be to the Father.

Lord Have Mercy   Glory to God   Prayer

THE LITURGY OF THE WORD

First Reading

ACTS OF THE APOSTLES 1:1–11

Songs of Meditation and Response

Alleluia, alleluia.
God mounts his throne amid shouts of joy;
the Lord, amid trumpet blasts. Alleluia. PSALM 46

The Lord advances from Sinai to the sanctuary;
ascending on high, he has led captivity captive. Alleluia.
PSALM 67

Gospel

MARK 16:14–20

Homily   Creed   Prayer of the Faithful

THE LITURGY OF THE EUCHARIST

Song at the Preparation of the Gifts

God mounts his throne amid shouts of joy;
the Lord, amid trumpet blasts. Alleluia. TURN TO PSALM 46

Prayer over the Gifts

EUCHARISTIC PRAYER
TURN TO PAGE 397

Communion Song

Chant praise to the Lord,
who rises on the heights of the heavens to the east. Alleluia.
TURN TO PSALM 67

Prayer after Communion

Sunday after the Ascension

Entrance Song

Hear, O Lord, the sound of my call, alleluia;
to you my heart speaks; your glance I seek;
your presence, O Lord, I seek.
Hide not your face from me,
alleluia, alleluia.

> The Lord is my light and my salvation;
> whom should I fear? TURN TO PSALM 26
> Glory be to the Father.

Lord Have Mercy   Glory to God   Prayer

THE LITURGY OF THE WORD

First Reading
I PETER 4:7–11

Songs of Meditation and Response

Alleluia, alleluia.
The Lord reigns over all the nations,
God sits upon his holy throne. Alleluia. PSALM 46
I will not leave you orphans;
I go away and I come to you,
and your heart shall rejoice. Alleluia. JOHN 14:18

Gospel
JOHN 15:26–27, 16:1–4

Homily   Creed   Prayer of the Faithful

THE LITURGY OF THE EUCHARIST

Song at the Preparation of the Gifts

God mounts his throne amid shouts of joy;
the Lord, amid trumpet blasts. Alleluia. TURN TO PSALM 46

Prayer over the Gifts

126

Communion Song

Father, while I was with them,
I kept them whom you have given me, alleluia;
but now I am coming to you:
I do not pray that you take them out of the world,
but that you keep them from evil,
alleluia, alleluia. JOHN 17:12–13, 15 TURN TO PSALM 46

Prayer after Communion

THE PENTECOST SEASON

DURING PENTECOST we concentrate on the effects of our victory with Christ on Easter. The Pentecost Masses show us how Christ's victory is ours, and how our redemption is to transform the whole of human living. This is why the major portion of the Church's year is composed of the Sundays after Pentecost.

The Holy Spirit brings to the Church and to each individual the power of Christ's resurrection. The Father sent Jesus to redeem us. His mission is accomplished as Jesus in turn sends his Holy Spirit with a mission to make us temples of the living God, to work within us so as to remake us sons of God.

The Masses after Pentecost bring us special graces to live more Christ-centered lives. The texts deal with practical Christian living and the Christian ideal. We are reminded of our high calling: "No man can serve two masters"; "If you live according to the flesh you will die."

This is a time for us to realize that the same Jesus who taught the love of the Father, who healed the sick and the lame, who drove out the demons and raised the dead is still present with his power in the Eucharist. During this Pentecost season we come to him with our failure to love, our crippling selfishness, our possessive pride, and killing indifference, calling on his Eucharistic power. We are filled with joy because he continually saves us.

The Vigil of Pentecost

Entrance Song

When I prove my holiness through you,
I will gather you from all the foreign lands;
and I will sprinkle clean water upon you
to cleanse you from all your impurities;
and I will give you a new spirit,
alleluia, alleluia.   EZEKIEL 36:23–26

> I will bless the Lord at all times;
> his praise shall be ever in my mouth.   TURN TO PSALM 33
> Glory be to the Father.

First Reading
ACTS OF THE APOSTLES 19:1–8

Songs of Meditation and Response

Alleluia. Give thanks to the Lord, for he is good,
for his kindness endures forever.   PSALM 106

Praise the Lord, all you nations;
glorify him, all you peoples!
For steadfast is his kindness toward us,
and the fidelity of the Lord endures forever.   PSALM 116

Gospel
JOHN 14:15–21

Song at the Preparation of the Gifts

Send forth your spirit, and they shall be created,
and you shall renew the face of the earth.
May the glory of the Lord endure forever, alleluia.

TURN TO PSALM 103

EUCHARISTIC PRAYER
TURN TO PAGE 398

Communion Song

On the last day of the feast, Jesus said:
"He who believes in me,
from within him there shall flow rivers of living water."
He said this, however, of the Spirit,
whom they who believed in him were to receive,
alleluia, alleluia.   JOHN 7:37–39 TURN TO PSALM 67

Pentecost

Entrance Song

The spirit of the Lord fills the world, alleluia,
is all-embracing, and knows man's utterance,
alleluia, alleluia, alleluia. WISDOM OF SOLOMON 1:7

God arises; his enemies are scattered,
and those who hate him flee before him.

Glory be to the Father. TURN TO PSALM 67

Lord Have Mercy   Glory to God   Prayer

THE LITURGY OF THE WORD

First Reading

ACTS OF THE APOSTLES 2:1–11

Songs of Meditation and Response

Alleluia, alleluia.
Send forth your spirit, and they shall be created;
and you shall renew the face of the earth. PSALM 103
Alleluia.

Come, Holy Spirit, fill the hearts of your faithful:
and kindle in them the fire of your love.

Come, thou Holy Spirit, come!
And from thy celestial home
 Shed a ray of light divine!
Come, thou Father of the poor!
Come, thou source of all our store!
 Come, within our bosoms shine!

Thou, of comforters the best;
Thou, the soul's most welcome guest;
 Sweet refreshment here below;
In our labor, rest most sweet;
Grateful coolness in the heat;
 Solace in the midst of woe.

O most blessed Light divine,
Shine within these hearts of thine,
   And our inmost being fill!
Where thou art not, man hath naught,
Nothing good in deed or thought,
   Nothing free from taint of ill.

Heal our wounds, our strength renew;
On our dryness pour thy dew;
   Wash the stains of guilt away:
Bend the stubborn heart and will;
Melt the frozen, warm the chill;
   Guide the steps that go astray.

On the faithful, who adore
And confess thee, evermore
   In thy sev'nfold gift descend;
Give them virtue's sure reward;
Give them thy salvation, Lord;
   Give them joys that never end.
   Amen. Alleluia.

Gospel

JOHN 14:23–31

Homily   Creed   Prayer of the Faithful

THE LITURGY OF THE EUCHARIST

Song at the Preparation of the Gifts

Confirm, O God, what you have wrought in us;
from your temple, which is in Jerusalem,
kings shall offer gifts to you, alleluia.   TURN TO PSALM 67

Prayer over the Gifts

EUCHARISTIC PRAYER
TURN TO PAGE 398

Communion Song

Suddenly there came a sound from heaven,
as of a violent wind blowing,

where they were sitting, alleluia:
and they were all filled with the Holy Spirit,
speaking of the wonderful works of God,
alleluia, alleluia.

ACTS OF THE APOSTLES 2:2, 4   TURN TO PSALM 103

Prayer after Communion

Pentecost Monday

Entrance Song

He fed them with the best of wheat, alleluia:
and filled them with honey from the rock,
alleluia, alleluia.

Sing joyfully to God our strength;
acclaim the God of Jacob. TURN TO PSALM 80

Glory be to the Father.

First Reading
ACTS OF THE APOSTLES 10:34, 42–48

Songs of Meditation and Response

Alleluia, alleluia.
The apostles spoke in foreign tongues
the wonderful works of God. Alleluia.

ACTS OF THE APOSTLES 2:4

Come, Holy Spirit, fill the hearts of your faithful;
and kindle in them the fire of your love.

The Response "Come, thou Holy Spirit, come!"
is recited as on Pentecost.

Gospel
JOHN 3:16–21

Song at the Preparation of the Gifts

The Lord thundered from heaven,
the Most High gave forth his voice;
and the fountains of waters appeared, alleluia.

TURN TO PSALM 17

Communion Song

The Holy Spirit will teach you, alleluia:
whatever I have said to you,
alleluia, alleluia. JOHN 14:26 TURN TO PSALM 103

Pentecost Tuesday

Entrance Song

Receive the joy of your glory, alleluia:
giving thanks to God, alleluia,
who has called you to the heavenly kingdom,
alleluia, alleluia, alleluia. 4 ESDRAS 2:36, 37

Hearken, my people, to my teaching;
incline your ears to the words of my mouth.

Glory be to the Father. TURN TO PSALM 77

First Reading
ACTS OF THE APOSTLES 8:14–17

Songs of Meditation and Response

Alleluia, alleluia.
The Holy Spirit will teach you
whatever I have said to you. Alleluia. JOHN 14:26

Come, Holy Spirit, fill the hearts of your faithful;
and kindle in them the fire of your love.

The Response "Come, thou Holy Spirit, come!"
is recited as on Pentecost.

Gospel
JOHN 10:1–10

Song at the Preparation of the Gifts

The Lord opened the doors of heaven;
he rained manna upon them for food
and gave them heavenly bread.
The bread of the angels was eaten by men, alleluia.

TURN TO PSALM 77

Communion Song

The Spirit who proceeds from the Father, alleluia:
he will glorify me,
alleluia, alleluia.   JOHN 15:26, 16:14   TURN TO PSALM 47

Ember Wednesday

Entrance Song

O God, when you went forth at the head of your people,
making a passage for them,
dwelling in their midst, alleluia;
the earth quaked; it rained from heaven,
alleluia, alleluia.

> God arises; his enemies are scattered,
> and those who hate him flee before him.
>
> Glory be to the Father.   TURN TO PSALM 67

First Reading
ACTS OF THE APOSTLES 2:14–21

Song of Meditation

Alleluia. By the word of the Lord the heavens were made;
by the breath of his mouth all their host.   PSALM 32

Second Reading
ACTS OF THE APOSTLES 5:12–16

Song of Meditation

Alleluia, alleluia.
Come, Holy Spirit, fill the hearts of your faithful;
and kindle in them the fire of your love.

The Response "Come, thou Holy Spirit, come!"
is recited as on Pentecost.

Gospel
JOHN 6:44–52

Song at the Preparation of the Gifts

I will delight in your commands,
which I love exceedingly.
And I will lift up my hands to your commands,
which I love, alleluia.   TURN TO PSALM 118

Communion Song

Peace I leave with you, alleluia;
my peace I give to you, alleluia, alleluia.

JOHN 14:27   TURN TO PSALM 32

Pentecost Thursday

The First Reading is Acts of the Apostles 8:5–8 and the Gospel is Luke 9:1–6.
For the rest of today's Mass turn to page 130.

Ember Friday

Entrance Song

Let my mouth be filled with your praise, alleluia:
that I may sing, alleluia.
My lips shall shout for joy as I sing your praises,
alleluia, alleluia.

In you, O Lord, I take refuge;
let me never be put to shame.
In your justice rescue me, and deliver me.

Glory be to the Father.   TURN TO PSALM 70

First Reading
JOEL 2:23–24, 26–27

Songs of Meditation and Response

Alleluia, alleluia.
O how good and sweet
is your spirit, O Lord, within us! Alleluia.

WISDOM OF SOLOMON 12:1

Come, Holy Spirit, fill the hearts of your faithful;
and kindle in them the fire of your love.

The Response "Come, thou Holy Spirit, come!"
is recited as on Pentecost.

Gospel

LUKE 5:17–26

Song at the Preparation of the Gifts

Praise the Lord, O my soul;
I will praise the Lord all my life;
I will sing praise to my God while I live, alleluia.

TURN TO PSALM 145

Communion Song

I will not leave you orphans;
I will come to you again, alleluia:
and your hearts shall rejoice, alleluia.

JOHN 14:18   TURN TO PSALM 70

Ember Saturday

Entrance Song

The charity of God is poured forth in our hearts, alleluia:
by his Spirit dwelling in us,
alleluia, alleluia.

ROMANS 5:5

Bless the Lord, O my soul;
and all my being, bless his holy name.

Glory be to the Father.

TURN TO PSALM 102

First Reading
JOEL 2:28–32

Song of Meditation

Alleluia. It is the Spirit that gives life;
but the flesh profits nothing.

JOHN 6:64

Second Reading
ROMANS 5:1–5

Songs of Meditation and Response

Alleluia, alleluia.
Come, Holy Spirit, fill the hearts of your faithful;
and kindle in them the fire of your love.

The Response "Come, thou Holy Spirit, come!"
is recited as on Pentecost.

Gospel

LUKE 4:38-44

Song at the Preparation of the Gifts

O Lord, the God of my salvation, by day I cry out,
at night I clamor in your presence.
Let my prayer come before you, O Lord, alleluia.

TURN TO PSALM 87

Communion Song

The Spirit breathes where he will, and you hear his voice,
alleluia, alleluia;
but do not know whence he comes or where he goes,
alleluia, alleluia, alleluia. JOHN 3:8 TURN TO PSALM 103

Trinity Sunday

Entrance Song

Blessed be the Holy Trinity and undivided Unity:
we will give glory to him,
because he has shown his mercy to us. TOBIT 12:6

O Lord, our Lord,
how glorious is your name over all the earth! PSALM 8
Glory be to the Father.

Lord Have Mercy   Glory to God   Prayer

THE LITURGY OF THE WORD

First Reading

ROMANS 11:33-36

Songs of Meditation and Response

Blessed are you, O Lord,
who look into the depths from your throne upon the cherubim.
Blessed are you, O Lord, in the firmament of heaven,
and praiseworthy forever. DANIEL 3:55, 56
Alleluia, alleluia.

Blessed are you, O Lord, the God of our fathers,
and praiseworthy forever. Alleluia.   DANIEL 3:52

Gospel
MATTHEW 28:18–20

Homily   Creed   Prayer of the Faithful

THE LITURGY OF THE EUCHARIST

Song at the Preparation of the Gifts

Blessed be God the Father,
and the only-begotten Son of God,
and also the Holy Spirit:
because he has shown his mercy to us.

TOBIT 12:6   TURN TO PSALM 148

Prayer over the Gifts

EUCHARISTIC PRAYER
TURN TO PAGE 406

Communion Song

We bless the God of heaven,
and before all living we will praise him;
because he has shown his mercy to us.

TOBIT 12:6   TURN TO PSALM 150

Prayer after Communion

Weekdays between the First and Second Sundays after Pentecost

Entrance Song

O Lord, I trusted in your kindness.
Let my heart rejoice in your salvation;
let me sing of the Lord,
"He has been good to me."

How long, O Lord, will you utterly forget me?
How long will you hide your face from me?
Glory be to the Father. TURN TO PSALM 12

First Reading

I JOHN 4:8–21

Songs of Meditation and Response

I said, "O Lord, have pity on me;
heal my soul, for I have sinned against you."
Happy is he who has regard for the lowly and the poor;
in the day of misfortune the Lord will deliver him.
Alleluia, alleluia. PSALM 40

Hearken to my words, O Lord,
attend to my sighing. Alleluia. PSALM 5

Gospel

LUKE 6:36–42

Song at the Preparation of the Gifts

Heed my call for help,
my king and my God!
To you I pray, O Lord. TURN TO PSALM 5

Communion Song

I will declare all your wondrous deeds;
I will be glad and exult in you;
I will sing praise to your name, Most High.

TURN TO PSALM 9

Corpus Christi
Thursday after Trinity Sunday

Entrance Song

He fed them with the best of wheat, alleluia;
and filled them with honey from the rock,
alleluia, alleluia, alleluia.

Sing joyfully to God our strength;
acclaim the God of Jacob. TURN TO PSALM 80

Glory be to the Father.

Songs of Meditation and Response

The eyes of all look hopefully to you, O Lord;
and you give them their food in due season.
You open your hand;
and satisfy the desire of every living thing.   PSALM 144

Alleluia, alleluia.
My flesh is food indeed, and my blood is drink indeed.
He who eats my flesh, and drinks my blood,
abides in me and I in him.   JOHN 6:56–57

Laud, O Sion, thy salvation,
Laud with hymns of exultation,
    Christ, thy king and shepherd true:
Bring him all the praise thou knowest,
He is more than thou bestowest,
    Never canst thou reach his due.

Special theme for glad thanksgiving
Is the quick'ning and the living
    Bread today before thee set:
From his hands of old partaken,
As we know, by faith unshaken,
    Where the twelve at supper met.

Full and clear ring out thy chanting,
Joy nor sweetest grace be wanting,
    From thy heart let praises burst:
For today the feast is holden,
When the institution olden
    Of that supper was rehearsed.

Here the new law's new oblation,
By the new king's revelation,
    Ends the form of ancient rite:
Now the new the old effaceth,
Truth away the shadow chaseth,
    Light dispels the gloom of night.

What he did at supper seated,
Christ ordained to be repeated,

His memorial ne'er to cease:
And his rule for guidance taking,
Bread and wine we hallow, making
   Thus our sacrifice of peace.

This the truth each Christian learneth,
Bread into his flesh he turneth,
   To his precious blood the wine:
Sight hath fail'd, nor thought conceiveth,
But a dauntless faith believeth,
   Resting on a pow'r divine.

Here beneath these signs are hidden
Priceless things to sense forbidden;
   Signs, not things are all we see:
Blood is poured and flesh is broken,
Yet in either wondrous token
   Christ entire we know to be.

Whoso of this food partaketh,
Rendeth not the Lord nor breaketh;
   Christ is whole to all that taste:
Thousands are, as one, receivers,
One, as thousands of believers,
   Eats of him who cannot waste.

Bad and good the feast are sharing,
Of what divers dooms preparing,
   Endless death, or endless life.
Life to these, to those damnation,
See how like participation
   Is with unlike issues rife.

When the sacrament is broken,
Doubt not, but believe 'tis spoken,
   That each sever'd outward token doth the very
      whole contain.
Naught the precious gift divideth,
Breaking but the sign betideth
   Jesus still the same abideth, still unbroken doth
      remain.

Lo! the angels' food is given
To the pilgrim who hath striven;
   See the children's bread from heaven, which on

dogs may not be spent.
Truth the ancient types fulfilling,
Isaac bound, a victim willing,
  Paschal lamb, its life blood spilling, manna to the
  fathers sent.
Very bread, good shepherd, tend us,
Jesus, of thy love befriend us,
Thou refresh us, thou defend us,
Thine eternal goodness send us
  In the land of life to see.
Thou who all things canst and knowest,
Who on earth such food bestowest,
Grant us with thy saints, though lowest,
Where the heav'nly feast thou showest,
  Fellow heirs and guests to be. Amen.
Alleluia.

Gospel

JOHN 6:56–59

Song at the Preparation of the Gifts

The priests of the Lord offer incense and loaves to God,
and therefore they shall be sacred to their God
and shall not profane his name. Alleluia.

LEVITICUS 21:6   TURN TO PSALM 145

Communion Song

As often as you shall eat of this bread and drink the cup,
you proclaim the death of the Lord, until he comes.
Therefore whoever eats this bread
or drinks the cup of the Lord unworthily,
will be guilty of the body and blood of the Lord, alleluia.

I CORINTHIANS 11:26–27   TURN TO PSALM 33

Second Sunday after Pentecost

Entrance Song

The Lord came to my support.
He set me free in the open,
and rescued me, because he loves me.

I love you, O Lord, my strength,
O Lord, my rock, my fortress, my deliverer.
Glory be to the Father. TURN TO PSALM 17

Lord Have Mercy   Glory to God   Prayer

THE LITURGY OF THE WORD

First Reading

I JOHN 3:13–18

Songs of Meditation and Response

In my distress I called to the Lord,
and he answered me.
O Lord, deliver me from lying lip,
from treacherous tongue. PSALM 119
Alleluia, alleluia.
O Lord my God, in you I take refuge;
save me from all my pursuers and rescue me. Alleluia.

PSALM 7

Gospel

LUKE 14:16–24

Homily   Creed   Prayer of the Faithful

THE LITURGY OF THE EUCHARIST

Song at the Preparation of the Gifts

Return, O Lord, save my life;
rescue me because of your kindness. TURN TO PSALM 6

Prayer over the Gifts

EUCHARISTIC PRAYER
TURN TO PAGE 406

Communion Song

I will sing of the Lord, "He has been good to me";
and I will sing to the name of the Lord the Most High.

TURN TO PSALM 12

Prayer after Communion

143

Sacred Heart of Jesus
Friday following Second Sunday after Pentecost

Entrance Song

The thoughts of his heart are to all generations:
to deliver them from death
and preserve them in spite of famine.
> Exult, you just, in the Lord;
> praise from the upright is fitting. TURN TO PSALM 32
Glory be to the Father.

First Reading
EPHESIANS 3:8–12, 14–19

Songs of Meditation and Response

Good and upright is the Lord;
thus he shows sinners the way.
He guides the humble to justice;
he teaches the humble his way. PSALM 24

Alleluia, alleluia.
Take my yoke upon you, and learn from me,
for I am meek, and humble of heart:
and you will find rest for your souls. Alleluia.
MATTHEW 11:29

Gospel
JOHN 19:31–37

Song at the Preparation of the Gifts

My heart expected reproach and misery;
I looked for sympathy, but there was none;
and for comforters, and I found none. TURN TO PSALM 68

EUCHARISTIC PRAYER
TURN TO PAGE 399

Communion Song

One of the soldiers opened his side with a lance,
and immediately there came out blood and water.

JOHN 19:34 TURN TO PSALM 32

Third Sunday after Pentecost

Entrance Song

Look toward me, and have pity on me, O Lord,
for I am alone and afflicted.
Put an end to my affliction and my suffering,
and take away all my sins, O my God.

> To you, I lift up my soul, O Lord.
> In you, O my God, I trust;
> let me not be put to shame.　　TURN TO PSALM 24
> Glory be to the Father.

Lord Have Mercy　　Glory to God　　Prayer

THE LITURGY OF THE WORD

First Reading
I PETER 5:6–11

Songs of Meditation and Response

Cast your care upon the Lord,
and he will support you.
When I called upon the Lord,
he heard my voice
and freed me from those who war against me.　PSALM 54
Alleluia, alleluia.
A just judge is God, strong and patient;
is he angry every day? Alleluia.　　　　PSALM 7

Gospel
LUKE 15:1–10

Homily　　Creed　　Prayer of the Faithful

THE LITURGY OF THE EUCHARIST

Song at the Preparation of the Gifts

They trust in you who cherish your name, O Lord,
for you forsake not those who seek you.

Sing praise to the Lord enthroned in Sion,
for he has not forgotten the cry of the afflicted.

TURN TO PSALM 9

Prayer over the Gifts

EUCHARISTIC PRAYER

TURN TO PAGE 406

Communion Song

I say to you: there is joy among the angels of God
over one sinner who repents.   LUKE 15:10   TURN TO PSALM 24

Prayer after Communion

Fourth Sunday after Pentecost

Entrance Song

The Lord is my light and my salvation;
whom should I fear?
The Lord is my life's refuge;
of whom should I be afraid?
My enemies that trouble me, themselves stumble and fall.

Though an army encamp against me,
my heart will not fear.   TURN TO PSALM 26
Glory be to the Father.

Lord Have Mercy   Glory to God   Prayer

THE LITURGY OF THE WORD

First Reading

ROMANS 8:18–23

Songs of Meditation and Response

Pardon our sins, O Lord;
why should the nations say,
"Where is their God?"
Help us, O God our savior;
because of the glory of your name, O Lord, deliver us.

PSALM 78

Alleluia, alleluia.
O God, seated on your throne, judging justly:
be a stronghold for the oppressed
in times of distress. Alleluia.   PSALM 9

Gospel

LUKE 5:1–11

Homily   Creed   Prayer of the Faithful

THE LITURGY OF THE EUCHARIST

Song at the Preparation of the Gifts

Give light to my eyes that I may never sleep in death,
lest my enemy say, "I have overcome him."

TURN TO PSALM 12

Prayer over the Gifts

EUCHARISTIC PRAYER
TURN TO PAGE 406

Communion Song

O Lord, my rock, my fortress, my deliverer:
my God, my rock of refuge!   TURN TO PSALM 17

Prayer after Communion

Fifth Sunday after Pentecost

Entrance Song

Hear, O Lord, the sound of my call;
be my helper: forsake me not:
despise me not, O God my savior.

    The Lord is my light and my salvation;
    whom should I fear?   TURN TO PSALM 26
    Glory be to the Father.

Lord Have Mercy   Glory to God   Prayer

First Reading

I PETER 3:8–15

Songs of Meditation and Response

Behold, O God, our protector, and look on your servants.
O Lord God of hosts, hear the prayers of your servants.

Alleluia, alleluia. PSALM 83
O Lord, in your strength the king is glad;
in your victory how greatly he rejoices! Alleluia. PSALM 20

Gospel

MATTHEW 5:20–24

Homily   Creed   Prayer of the Faithful

THE LITURGY OF THE EUCHARIST

Song at the Preparation of the Gifts

I bless the Lord who counsels me;
I set God ever before me;
with him at my right hand I shall not be disturbed.

TURN TO PSALM 15

Prayer over the Gifts

EUCHARISTIC PRAYER
TURN TO PAGE 406

Communion Song

One thing I ask of the Lord;
this I seek:
to dwell in the house of the Lord
all the days of my life. TURN TO PSALM 26

Prayer after Communion

Sixth Sunday after Pentecost

Entrance Song

The Lord is the strength of his people,
the saving refuge of his anointed.
Save your people, O Lord, and bless your inheritance;
and rule them forever!

> To you, O Lord, I call;
> O my God, be not deaf to me,
> lest, if you heed me not,
> I become one of those going down into the pit.

TURN TO PSALM 27

> Glory be to the Father.

Lord Have Mercy   Glory to God   Prayer

THE LITURGY OF THE WORD

First Reading

ROMANS 6:3–11

Songs of Meditation and Response

Return, O Lord! How long?
Have pity on your servants!
O Lord, you have been our refuge
through all generations.   PSALM 89
Alleluia, alleluia.
In you, O Lord, I take refuge;
let me never be put to shame.
In your justice rescue me and release me,
incline your ear to me,
make haste to deliver me! Alleluia.   PSALM 30

Gospel

MARK 8:1–9

Homily   Creed   Prayer of the Faithful

Song at the Preparation of the Gifts

Make my steps steadfast in your paths,
that my feet may not falter.
Incline your ear to me;
Show your wondrous kindness, O Lord,
O savior of those who trust in you. TURN TO PSALM 16

Prayer over the Gifts

EUCHARISTIC PRAYER
TURN TO PAGE 406

Communion Song

I will go round and offer in his tent
sacrifices with shouts of gladness;
I will sing and chant praise to the Lord. TURN TO PSALM 26

Prayer after Communion

Seventh Sunday after Pentecost

Entrance Song

All you peoples, clap your hands,
shout to God with cries of gladness.

For the Lord, the Most High, the awesome,
is the great king over all the earth. TURN TO PSALM 46
Glory be to the Father.

Lord Have Mercy   *Glory to God*   *Prayer*

THE LITURGY OF THE WORD

First Reading
ROMANS 6:19–23

Songs of Meditation and Response

Come, children, hear me;
I will teach you the fear of the Lord.
Look to him that you may be radiant with joy,
and your faces may not blush with shame.   PSALM 33
Alleluia, alleluia.
All you peoples, clap your hands,
shout to God with cries of gladness. Alleluia.   PSALM 46

Gospel

MATTHEW 7:15–21

THE LITURGY OF THE EUCHARIST

Song at the Preparation of the Gifts

As though it were holocausts of rams and bullocks,
or thousands of fat lambs,
so let our sacrifice be in your presence today,
that it may please you;
for those who trust in you
cannot be put to shame, O Lord.

DANIEL 3:40 TURN TO PSALM 49

Prayer over the Gifts

EUCHARISTIC PRAYER
TURN TO PAGE 406

Communion Song

Incline your ear to me,
make haste to deliver me.   TURN TO PSALM 30

Prayer after Communion

Eighth Sunday after Pentecost

Entrance Song

O God, we ponder your kindness within your temple.
As your name, O God, so also your praise

reaches to the ends of the earth.
Of justice your right hand is full.

> Great is the Lord and wholly to be praised
> in the city of our God, his holy mountain.
> Glory be to the Father. TURN TO PSALM 47

Lord Have Mercy   Glory to God   Prayer

THE LITURGY OF THE WORD

First Reading
ROMANS 8:12–17

Songs of Meditation and Response

Be my rock of refuge, O God,
a stronghold to give me safety. PSALM 30
In you, O God, I take refuge;
O Lord, let me never be put to shame. PSALM 70
Alleluia, alleluia.
Great is the Lord and wholly to be praised
in the city of our God, his holy mountain. Alleluia.

PSALM 47

Gospel
LUKE 16:1–9

Homily   Creed   Prayer of the Faithful

THE LITURGY OF THE EUCHARIST

Song at the Preparation of the Gifts

Lowly people you save, O Lord,
but haughty eyes you bring low;
for who is God except you, O Lord? TURN TO PSALM 17

Prayer over the Gifts

EUCHARISTIC PRAYER
TURN TO PAGE 406

Communion Song

Taste and see how good the Lord is;
happy the man who takes refuge in him.

TURN TO PSALM 33

Prayer after Communion

Ninth Sunday after Pentecost

Entrance Song

Behold, God is my helper, the Lord sustains my life.
Turn back the evil upon my foes;
in your faithfulness destroy them, O Lord, my protector.

O God, by your name save me,
and by your might deliver me.   TURN TO PSALM 53
Glory be to the Father.

Lord Have Mercy   Glory to God   Prayer

THE LITURGY OF THE WORD

First Reading
I CORINTHIANS 10:6–13

Songs of Meditation and Response

O Lord, our Lord,
how glorious is your name over all the earth!
You have elevated your majesty above the heavens.
Alleluia, alleluia.   PSALM 8
Rescue me from my enemies, O my God;
from my adversaries defend me. Alleluia.   PSALM 58

Gospel
LUKE 19:41–47

Homily   Creed   Prayer of the Faithful

153

Song at the Preparation of the Gifts

The precepts of the Lord are right,
rejoicing the heart,
and his ordinances sweeter than syrup
or honey from the comb;
therefore your servant is careful of them.

TURN TO PSALM 18

Prayer over the Gifts

EUCHARISTIC PRAYER
TURN TO PAGE 406

Communion Song

"He who eats my flesh, and drinks my blood,
abides in me, and I in him," says the Lord.

JOHN 6:57 TURN TO PSALM 33

Prayer after Communion

Tenth Sunday after Pentecost

Entrance Song

When I called upon the Lord, he heard my voice
and freed me from those who war against me;
and he humbled them,
he who is before all ages, and remains forever:
cast your care upon the Lord, and he will support you.

Hearken, O God, to my prayer;
turn not away from my pleading;
give heed to me, and answer me. TURN TO PSALM 54
Glory be to the Father.

Lord Have Mercy   Glory to God   Prayer

THE LITURGY OF THE WORD

First Reading

I CORINTHIANS 12:2–11

Songs of Meditation and Response

Keep me, O Lord, as the apple of your eye;
hide me in the shadow of your wings.
From you let judgment come;
your eyes behold what is right.   PSALM 16
Alleluia, alleluia.
To you we owe our hymn of praise, O God, in Sion;
to you must vows be fulfilled in Jerusalem. Alleluia.

PSALM 64

Gospel

LUKE 18:9–14

Homily   Creed   Prayer of the Faithful

THE LITURGY OF THE EUCHARIST

Song at the Preparation of the Gifts

To you I lift up my soul, O Lord.
In you, O my God, I trust; let me not be put to shame,
let not my enemies exult over me.
No one who waits for you shall be put to shame.

TURN TO PSALM 24

Prayer over the Gifts

EUCHARISTIC PRAYER
TURN TO PAGE 406

Communion Song

You shall be pleased with due sacrifices,
burnt offerings and holocausts on your altar, O Lord.

TURN TO PSALM 50

Prayer after Communion

155

Eleventh Sunday after Pentecost

Entrance Song

God is in his holy dwelling,
God who makes men of one mind to dwell in a house;
he shall give power and strength to his people.

God arises; his enemies are scattered,
and those who hate him flee before him.

Glory be to the Father.   TURN TO PSALM 67

Lord Have Mercy   Glory to God   Prayer

THE LITURGY OF THE WORD

First Reading
I CORINTHIANS 15:1–10

Songs of Meditation and Response

In God my heart trusts, and I find help;
then my heart exults, and with my song I give him thanks.
To you, O Lord, I call;
O my God, be not deaf to me; depart not from me.   PSALM 27
Alleluia, alleluia.
Sing joyfully to God our strength;
acclaim the God of Jacob.
Take up a pleasant psalm with the harp. Alleluia.   PSALM 80

Gospel
MARK 7:31–37

Homily   Creed   Prayer of the Faithful

THE LITURGY OF THE EUCHARIST

Song at the Preparation of the Gifts

I will extol you, O Lord, for you drew me clear
and did not let my enemies rejoice over me;
O Lord, I cried out to you and you healed me.

TURN TO PSALM 29

156

Prayer over the Gifts

EUCHARISTIC PRAYER

TURN TO PAGE 406

Communion Song

Honor the Lord with your wealth,
with first fruits of all your produce.
Then will your barns be filled with grain,
with new wine your vats will overflow.

PROVERBS 3:9–10 TURN TO PSALM 67

Prayer after Communion

Twelfth Sunday after Pentecost

Entrance Song

Deign, O God, to rescue me; O Lord, make haste to help me.
Let them be put to shame and confounded who seek my life.

Let them be turned back in disgrace,
who desire my ruin. TURN TO PSALM 69
Glory be to the Father.

Lord Have Mercy   Glory to God   Prayer

THE LITURGY OF THE WORD

First Reading

2 CORINTHIANS 3:4–9

Songs of Meditation and Response

I will bless the Lord at all times;
his praise shall be ever in my mouth.
Let my soul glory in the Lord; the lowly will hear and be glad.
Alleluia, alleluia. PSALM 33
O Lord, the God of my salvation, by day I cry out,
at night I clamor in your presence. Alleluia. PSALM 87

Gospel

LUKE 10:23-37

Homily   Creed   Prayer of the Faithful

THE LITURGY OF THE EUCHARIST

Song at the Preparation of the Gifts

Moses prayed in the sight of the Lord his God and said,
"Why, O Lord, is your indignation enkindled against your people?
Let the anger of your mind cease;
remember Abraham, Isaac, and Jacob,
to whom you swore to give a land flowing with milk and honey."
And the Lord was appeased from doing the evil
which he had spoken of doing against his people.

EXODUS 32:11, 13, 14   TURN TO PSALM 105

Prayer over the Gifts

EUCHARISTIC PRAYER
TURN TO PAGE 406

Communion Song

The earth is replete with the fruit of your works, O Lord;
you produce bread from the earth,
and wine to gladden men's hearts,
so that their faces gleam with oil,
and bread fortifies the hearts of men.   TURN TO PSALM 103

Prayer after Communion

Thirteenth Sunday after Pentecost

Entrance Song

Look to your covenant, O Lord,
forsake not forever the lives of your afflicted ones.
Arise, O Lord; defend your cause;
be not unmindful of the voices of those who ask you.

Why, O God, have you cast us off forever?
Why does your anger smolder against the sheep of your pasture?
Glory be to the Father. TURN TO PSALM 73

Lord Have Mercy   Glory to God   Prayer

THE LITURGY OF THE WORD

First Reading

GALATIANS 3:16–22

Songs of Meditation and Response

Look to your covenant, O Lord,
be not unmindful of the lives of your afflicted ones.
Arise, O Lord; defend your cause;
remember the reproach of your servants. PSALM 73
Alleluia, alleluia.
O Lord, you have been our refuge
through all generations. Alleluia. PSALM 89

Gospel

LUKE 17:11–19

Homily   Creed   Prayer of the Faithful

THE LITURGY OF THE EUCHARIST

Song at the Preparation of the Gifts

My trust is in you, O Lord;
I say, "You are my God."
In your hands is my destiny. TURN TO PSALM 30

Prayer over the Gifts

EUCHARISTIC PRAYER
TURN TO PAGE 406

Communion Song

You have given us, O Lord, bread from heaven,
endowed with all delights and the sweetness of every taste.
WISDOM OF SOLOMON 16:20 TURN TO PSALM 77

Prayer after Communion

Fourteenth Sunday after Pentecost

Entrance Song

Behold, O God, our protector,
and look upon the face of your anointed.
Better is one day in your courts than a thousand elsewhere.

How lovely is your dwelling place,
O Lord of hosts!
My soul yearns and pines
for the courts of the Lord. TURN TO PSALM 83
Glory be to the Father.

Lord Have Mercy   Glory to God   Prayer

THE LITURGY OF THE WORD

First Reading

GALATIANS 5:16–24

Songs of Meditation and Response

It is better to take refuge in the Lord
than to trust in men.
It is better to take refuge in the Lord
than to trust in princes. PSALM 117
Alleluia, alleluia.
Come, let us sing joyfully to the Lord;
let us acclaim the God of our salvation. Alleluia.

PSALM 94

Gospel

MATTHEW 6:24–33

Homily   Creed   Prayer of the Faithful

THE LITURGY OF THE EUCHARIST

Song at the Preparation of the Gifts

The angel of the Lord encamps
around those who fear him, and delivers them.
Taste and see how good the Lord is. TURN TO PSALM 33

Prayer over the Gifts

EUCHARISTIC PRAYER
TURN TO PAGE 406

Communion Song

"Seek first the kingdom of God;
and all things shall be given you besides," says the Lord.

MATTHEW 6:33   TURN TO PSALM 22

Prayer after Communion

Fifteenth Sunday after Pentecost

Entrance Song

Incline your ear, O Lord; answer me;
save your servant, O my God, who trusts in you.
Have pity on me, O Lord, for to you I call all the day.

Gladden the soul of your servant,
for to you, O Lord, I lift up my soul. TURN TO PSALM 85
Glory be to the Father.

Lord Have Mercy   Glory to God   Prayer

THE LITURGY OF THE WORD

First Reading

GALATIANS 5:25–26, 6:1–10

Songs of Meditation and Response

It is good to give thanks to the Lord,
to sing to your name, Most High.
To proclaim your kindness at dawn
and your faithfulness throughout the night.   PSALM 91

Alleluia, alleluia.
For the Lord is a great God,
and a great king over all the earth. Alleluia.   PSALM 94

Gospel

LUKE 7:11–16

Homily   Creed   Prayer of the Faithful

THE LITURGY OF THE EUCHARIST

Song at the Preparation of the Gifts

I have waited, waited for the Lord,
and he stooped toward me, and heard my cry.
And he put a new song into my mouth,
a hymn to our God.   TURN TO PSALM 39

Prayer over the Gifts

EUCHARISTIC PRAYER
TURN TO PAGE 406

Communion Song

The bread that I will give
is my flesh for the life of the world.
JOHN 6:52   TURN TO PSALM 41

Prayer after Communion

Sixteenth Sunday after Pentecost

Entrance Song

Have pity on me, O Lord, for to you I call all the day;
for you, O Lord, are good and forgiving,
abounding in kindness to all who call upon you.

Incline your ear, O Lord; answer me,
for I am afflicted and poor.   TURN TO PSALM 85
Glory be to the Father.

Lord Have Mercy   Glory to God   Prayer

First Reading

EPHESIANS 3:13-21

Songs of Meditation and Response

The nations shall revere your name, O Lord,
and all the kings of the earth your glory.
For the Lord has rebuilt Sion,
and he shall appear in his glory.   PSALM 101
Alleluia, alleluia.
Sing to the Lord a new song,
for the Lord has done wondrous deeds. Alleluia.

PSALM 97

Gospel

LUKE 14:1-11

Homily   Creed   Prayer of the Faithful

Song at the Preparation of the Gifts

Deign, O Lord, to rescue me;
let all be put to shame and confusion
who seek to snatch away my life.
Deign, O Lord, to rescue me.   TURN TO PSALM 39

Prayer over the Gifts

EUCHARISTIC PRAYER
TURN TO PAGE 406

Communion Song

O Lord, I will tell of your singular justice;
O God, you have taught me from my youth;
and now that I am old and gray, O God, forsake me not.
TURN TO PSALM 83

Prayer after Communion

Seventeenth Sunday after Pentecost

Entrance Song

You are just, O Lord, and your ordinance is right.
Deal with your servant according to your kindness.

> Happy are they whose way is blameless,
> who walk in the law of the Lord.   TURN TO PSALM 118
> Glory be to the Father.

Lord Have Mercy   Glory to God   Prayer

THE LITURGY OF THE WORD

First Reading
EPHESIANS 4:1–6

Songs of Meditation and Response

Happy the nation whose God is the Lord,
the people the Lord has chosen for his own inheritance.
By the word of the Lord the heavens were made;
by the breath of his mouth all their host.   PSALM 32
Alleluia, alleluia.
O Lord, hear my prayer,
and let my cry come to you. Alleluia.   PSALM 101

Gospel
MATTHEW 22:34–46

Homily   Creed   Prayer of the Faithful

THE LITURGY OF THE EUCHARIST

Song at the Preparation of the Gifts

I, Daniel, prayed to my God, saying,
"Hear, O Lord, the prayers of your servant;
show your face upon your sanctuary,
and favorably look down upon this people,
upon whom your name is invoked, O God."

DANIEL 9:17–19   TURN TO PSALM 118

Prayer over the Gifts

EUCHARISTIC PRAYER

TURN TO PAGE 406

Communion Song

Make vows to the Lord, your God, and fulfill them;
let all round about him bring gifts to the terrible Lord
who checks the pride of princes,
who is terrible to the kings of the earth.

TURN TO PSALM 75

Prayer after Communion

Ember Wednesday in September

Entrance Song

Sing joyfully to God our strength;
acclaim the God of Jacob.
Take up a pleasant psalm with the harp;
blow the trumpet in the beginning of the month;
for it is a statute in Israel,
an ordinance of the God of Jacob.

He made it a decree for Joseph,
when he came forth from the land of Egypt:
he heard an unfamiliar speech. TURN TO PSALM 80

Glory be to the Father.

First Reading

AMOS 9:13-15

Song of Meditation

Who is like the Lord, our God, who is enthroned on high
and looks upon the heavens and the earth below?
He raises up the lowly from the dust:
from the dunghill he lifts up the poor. PSALM 112

Second Reading

NEHEMIAH 8:1-10

165

Song of Meditation

Happy the nation whose God is the Lord,
the people the Lord has chosen for his own inheritance.
By the word of the Lord the heavens were made;
by the breath of his mouth all their host.   PSALM 32

Gospel
MARK 9:16–28

Song at the Preparation of the Gifts

I will delight in your commands,
which I love exceedingly.
And I will lift up my hands to your commands,
which I love.   TURN TO PSALM 118

Communion Song

Eat fat meats, and drink sweet wine,
and send portions to those who have not prepared for themselves:
because it is the holy day of the Lord,
be not sad, for the joy of the Lord is our strength.

NEHEMIAH 8:10   TURN TO PSALM 80

Ember Friday in September

Entrance Song

Rejoice, O hearts that seek the Lord!
Look to the Lord, and be strengthened;
seek his face evermore.

> Give thanks to the Lord, invoke his name;
> make known among the nations his deeds.

Glory be to the Father.   TURN TO PSALM 104

First Reading
HOSEA 14:2–10

Song of Meditation

Return, O Lord! How long?
Have pity on your servants.
O Lord, you have been our refuge through all generations.
PSALM 89

Gospel

LUKE 7:36–50

Song at the Preparation of the Gifts

Bless the Lord, O my soul,
and forget not all his benefits;
and your youth shall be renewed like the eagle's.

TURN TO PSALM 102

Communion Song

Take away from me reproach and contempt,
for I observe your decrees, O Lord.
Your decrees are my delight. TURN TO PSALM 118

Ember Saturday in September

Entrance Song

Come, let us bow down in worship to God;
let us kneel before the Lord.
Let us weep before him who made us;
for he is the Lord our God.

Come, let us sing joyfully to the Lord;
let us acclaim God our savior. TURN TO PSALM 94

Glory be to the Father.

First Reading

LEVITICUS 23:26–32

Song of Meditation

Pardon our sins, O Lord;
why should the nations say, "Where is their God?"
Help us, O God our savior;
because of the glory of your name, O Lord, deliver us.

PSALM 78

Second Reading

HEBREWS 9:2–12

Song of Meditation

Praise the Lord, all you nations;
glorify him, all you peoples!

For steadfast is his kindness toward us,
and the fidelity of the Lord endures forever.   PSALM 116

Gospel
LUKE 13:6–17

Song at the Preparation of the Gifts

O Lord, the God of my salvation, by day I cry out,
at night I clamor in your presence.
Let my prayer come before you, O Lord.

TURN TO PSALM 87

Communion Song

In the seventh month you shall keep this feast,
as I made the Israelites dwell in booths,
when I led them out of the land of Egypt.
I, the Lord, am your God.

LEVITICUS 23:41, 43   TURN TO PSALM 94

Eighteenth Sunday after Pentecost

Entrance Song

Give peace, O Lord, to those who have hoped in you,
and let your prophets be proved true.
Hear the prayers of your servant, and of your people Israel.

I rejoiced because they said to me,   SIRACH 36:18
"We will go up to the house of the Lord."

Glory be to the Father.   TURN TO PSALM 121

Lord Have Mercy   Glory to God   Prayer

THE LITURGY OF THE WORD

First Reading
I CORINTHIANS 1:4–8

Songs of Meditation and Response

I rejoiced because they said to me,
"We will go up to the house of the Lord."

May peace be within your walls,
prosperity in your buildings.
PSALM 121
Alleluia, alleluia.
The nations shall revere your name, O Lord,
and all the kings of the earth your glory. Alleluia.
PSALM 101

Gospel
MATTHEW 9:1–8

Homily   Creed   Prayer of the Faithful

THE LITURGY OF THE EUCHARIST

Song at the Preparation of the Gifts

Moses consecrated an altar to the Lord,
offering upon it holocausts, and sacrificing victims:
he made an evening sacrifice to the Lord God
for an odor of sweetness, in the sight of the Israelites.
EXODUS 24:4, 5   TURN TO PSALM 64

Prayer over the Gifts

EUCHARISTIC PRAYER
TURN TO PAGE 406

Communion Song

Bring gifts and enter his courts;
worship the Lord in his holy court.
TURN TO PSALM 95

Prayer after Communion

Nineteenth Sunday after Pentecost

Entrance Song

"I am the salvation of the people," says the Lord;
"in whatever tribulation they shall cry to me, I will hear them;
and I will be their Lord forever."

Hearken, my people, to my teaching;
incline your ears to the words of my mouth.
Glory be to the Father. TURN TO PSALM 77

Lord Have Mercy   Glory to God   Prayer

THE LITURGY OF THE WORD

First Reading
EPHESIANS 4:23–28

Songs of Meditation and Response

Let my prayer come like incense before you, O Lord.
The lifting up of my hands, like the evening sacrifice.

Alleluia, alleluia. PSALM 140
Give thanks to the Lord, invoke his name;
make known among the nations his deeds. Alleluia.

PSALM 104

Gospel
MATTHEW 22:1–14

Homily   Creed   Prayer of the Faithful

THE LITURGY OF THE EUCHARIST

Song at the Preparation of the Gifts

Though I walk amid distress, you preserve me, O Lord;
against the anger of my enemies you raise your hand;
your right hand saves me. TURN TO PSALM 137

Prayer over the Gifts

EUCHARISTIC PRAYER
TURN TO PAGE 406

Communion Song

You have commanded that your precepts
be diligently kept.

Oh, that I might be firm in the ways
of keeping your statutes! TURN TO PSALM 118

Prayer after Communion

Twentieth Sunday after Pentecost

Entrance Song

All that you have done to us, O Lord,
you have done in true judgment,
because we have sinned against you,
and we have not obeyed your commandments;
but give glory to your name,
and deal with us according to the multitude of your mercy.

DANIEL 3:31, 29, 35

Happy are they whose way is blameless,
who walk in the law of the Lord. TURN TO PSALM 118

Glory be to the Father.

Lord Have Mercy   Glory to God   Prayer

THE LITURGY OF THE WORD

First Reading

EPHESIANS 5:15–21

Songs of Meditation and Response

The eyes of all look hopefully to you, O Lord,
and you give them their food in due season.
You open your hand
and satisfy the desire of every living thing. PSALM 144

Alleluia, alleluia.
My heart is steadfast, O God, my heart is steadfast;
I will sing and chant praise to you, my glory. Alleluia.

PSALM 107

Gospel

JOHN 4:46–53

Homily   Creed   Prayer of the Faithful

THE LITURGY OF THE EUCHARIST

Song at the Preparation of the Gifts

By the streams of Babylon
we sat and wept
when we remembered you, O Sion.   TURN TO PSALM 136

Prayer over the Gifts

EUCHARISTIC PRAYER
TURN TO PAGE 406

Communion Song

Remember your word to your servant, O Lord,
since you have given me hope.
This is my comfort in my affliction.   TURN TO PSALM 118

Prayer after Communion

Twenty-First Sunday after Pentecost

Entrance Song

In your will are all things, O Lord,
and there is none that can resist your will;
for you have made all things,
heaven and earth, and all things
that are under the cope of heaven.
You are Lord of all.   ESTHER 13:9, 10–11

Happy are they whose way is blameless,
who walk in the law of the Lord.   TURN TO PSALM 118
Glory be to the Father.

Lord Have Mercy   Glory to God   Prayer

First Reading

EPHESIANS 6:10–17

Songs of Meditation and Response

O Lord, you have been our refuge
through all generations.
Before the mountains were begotten
and the earth and the world were brought forth,
from everlasting to everlasting you are God.   PSALM 89
Alleluia, alleluia.
When Israel came forth from Egypt,
the house of Jacob from a people of alien tongue. Alleluia.

PSALM 113

Gospel

MATTHEW 18:23–35

Homily   Creed   Prayer of the Faithful

Song at the Preparation of the Gifts

There was a man in the land of Hus, whose name was Job,
simple, and upright, and fearing God,
whom Satan besought that he might tempt:
and power was given him from the Lord
over his possessions and his flesh;
and he destroyed all his substance and his children,
and wounded his flesh also with a grievous ulcer.

JOB 1   TURN TO PSALM 118

Prayer over the Gifts

EUCHARISTIC PRAYER
TURN TO PAGE 406

Communion Song

My soul pines for your salvation;
I hope in your word.

When will you do judgment on my persecutors?
The wicked persecuted me wrongfully;
help me, O Lord my God! TURN TO PSALM 118

Prayer after Communion

Twenty-Second Sunday after Pentecost

Entrance Song

If you, O Lord, mark iniquities, Lord, who can stand?
But with you is forgiveness, O God of Israel.

Out of the depths I cry to you, O Lord;
Lord, hear my voice! TURN TO PSALM 129

Glory be to the Father.

Lord Have Mercy   Glory to God   Prayer

THE LITURGY OF THE WORD

First Reading

PHILIPPIANS 1:6–11

Songs of Meditation and Response

Behold how good it is, and how pleasant
where brethren dwell as one!
It is as when the precious ointment upon the head
runs down over the beard, the beard of Aaron. PSALM 132

Alleluia, alleluia.
Those who fear the Lord trust in the Lord;
he is their help and their shield. Alleluia. PSALM 113

Gospel

MATTHEW 22:15–21

Homily   Creed   Prayer of the Faithful

Song at the Preparation of the Gifts

Remember me, O Lord, you who rule above all power:
and give a well-ordered speech in my mouth,
that my words may be pleasing in the sight of the prince.

ESTHER 14:12, 13   TURN TO PSALM 129

Prayer over the Gifts

EUCHARISTIC PRAYER

TURN TO PAGE 406

Communion Song

I call upon you, for you will answer me, O God;
incline your ear to me; hear my word.   TURN TO PSALM 16

Prayer after Communion

The Last Sundays after Pentecost

Each year has from 23 to 28 Sundays between Pentecost and Advent. The Sundays after the twenty-second all have the same songs, but their readings and prayers vary. The chants for these Sundays, together with the readings for the twenty-third Sunday after Pentecost and the Sunday before Advent, are given here. The readings for the Sundays between are the same as those given for the last four Sundays after the Epiphany, p. 34. If the twenty-third Sunday after Pentecost is also the last before Advent, the readings of the latter are used.

Entrance Song

The Lord says: "I think thoughts of peace, and not of affliction.
You shall call upon me, and I will hear you;
and I will bring back your captivity from all places."

JEREMIAH 29:11, 12, 14

You have favored, O Lord, your land;
you have restored the well-being of Jacob.   TURN TO PSALM 84

Glory be to the Father.

Lord Have Mercy   *Glory to God*   *Prayer*

First Reading

TWENTY-THIRD SUNDAY AFTER PENTECOST: PHILIPPIANS 3:17–4:3

LAST SUNDAY AFTER PENTECOST: COLOSSIANS 1:9–14

Songs of Meditation and Response

You saved us, O Lord, from our foes,
and those who hated us you put to shame.
In God we gloried day by day;
your name we praised always.   PSALM 49

Alleluia, alleluia.
Out of the depths I cry to you, O Lord;
Lord, hear my prayer! Alleluia.   PSALM 129

Gospel

TWENTY-THIRD SUNDAY AFTER PENTECOST: MATTHEW 9:18–26

LAST SUNDAY AFTER PENTECOST: MATTHEW 24:15–35

Homily   Creed   Prayer of the Faithful

THE LITURGY OF THE EUCHARIST

Song at the Preparation of the Gifts

Out of the depths I cry to you, O Lord;
Lord, hear my prayer!
Out of the depths I cry to you, O Lord.

TURN TO PSALM 129

Prayer over the Gifts

EUCHARISTIC PRAYER

TURN TO PAGE 406

Communion Song

Amen I say to you, all things whatever you ask for in prayer,
believe that you shall receive, and it shall be done to you.

MARK 11:24   TURN TO PSALM 84

Prayer after Communion

176

MASSES
OF THE
SANCTORAL
CYCLE

CHRIST IN HIS SAINTS

Christ is the center of Christian worship. The Mass is his offering to the Father, in which all men share as members of his Church.

The holiness of the saints is none other than the holiness of Christ. They are witnesses to the saving power of the redemption in a human life. We look to the saints as models because they lived out the life of Christ. We look to the saints for encouragement because they were men and women like us, transformed in the love of Christ. From all walks of life and from all classes of people have come realistic disciples of the Lord. They are the good trees that bear the good fruit. Their source of holiness is the tree of Calvary.

The Church has always had a special regard for the men and women who were closest to Jesus in the mystery of Redemption. The many feasts of Our Lady and the Apostles bear witness to this fact. Their free cooperation with grace made it possible for the Lord to carry out his plan of Redemption. These feast days are reminders of the marvel of God's love. That love is fully present in every Holy Mass; it is meant to be fully present in every human life.

From the earliest times the Church has also given us the example of the virgins, the martyrs, and other holy men and women as reminders of the Christian call to holiness of life. At Mass we beg their intercession and the grace to live the Gospel through Christ Our Lord. The grace that makes saints is present for us in each Holy Mass, wherein the communion of saints is made present in the sacred meal which Christians share.

Feasts from January 1 to January 13 are to be found among the Masses following Christmas in the Temporal Cycle, beginning on page 23.

January 14 : Hilary : Bishop and Doctor of the Church

For today's Mass turn to page 323.

January 15 : Paul : Hermit

Entrance Song

The just man shall flourish like the palm tree,
like a cedar of Lebanon shall he grow:
planted in the house of the Lord,
in the courts of the house of our God.

It is good to give thanks to the Lord,
to sing praise to your name, Most High.
Glory be to the Father. TURN TO PSALM 91

First Reading
PHILIPPIANS 3:7–12

Songs of Meditation and Response

The just man shall flourish like the palm tree,
like a cedar of Lebanon shall he grow in the house of the Lord.
To proclaim your kindness at dawn
and your faithfulness throughout the night. PSALM 91

Alleluia, alleluia.
The just man shall blossom like the lily,
and flourish forever before the Lord. Alleluia. HOSEA 14:6

Gospel
MATTHEW 11:25–30

Song at the Preparation of the Gifts

O Lord, in your strength the just man is glad;
in your victory how greatly he rejoices!
You have granted him his heart's desire. TURN TO PSALM 20

The just man is glad in the Lord and takes refuge in him;
all the upright of heart shall be praised.　　TURN TO PSALM 63

January 16 : Marcellus : Pope and Martyr

For today's Mass turn to page 310.

January 17 : Anthony : Abbot

The Gospel is Luke 12:35–40; for the rest of today's Mass turn to page 327.

January 18 : Prisca : Virgin and Martyr

The Mass is of the preceding Sunday with a commemoration of Prisca.

January 19 : Marius and His Family : Martyrs

The Mass is of the preceding Sunday with a commemoration of the Martyrs.

January 20 : Fabian and Sebastian : Martyrs

Entrance Song

Let the prisoners' sighing come before you, O Lord;
repay our neighbors sevenfold into their bosoms;
avenge the blood of your saints which has been shed.

O God, the nations have come into your inheritance;
they have defiled your holy temple,
they have made Jerusalem as a place to keep fruit.

Glory be to the Father.　　TURN TO PSALM 78

First Reading

HEBREWS 11:33–39

Songs of Meditation and Response

God is glorious in his saints,
wonderful in majesty, a worker of wonders.
Your right hand, O Lord, is magnificent in power;
your right hand has shattered the enemy.　　EXODUS 15:11, 6

Alleluia, alleluia.
Let your faithful ones bless you, O Lord.
Let them discourse of the glory of your kingdom. Alleluia.

PSALM 144

Gospel

LUKE 6:17–23

Song at the Preparation of the Gifts

Be glad in the Lord, and rejoice, you just;
exult, all you upright of heart.   TURN TO PSALM 31

Communion Song

A multitude of sick,
and those who were troubled with unclean spirits,
came to him;
for power went forth from him and healed all.

LUKE 6:18–19   TURN TO PSALM 144

January 21 : Agnes : Virgin and Martyr

Entrance Song

Sinners wait to destroy me,
but I pay heed to your decrees, O Lord.
I see that all fulfillment has its limits;
broad indeed is your command.

Happy are they whose way is blameless,
who walk in the law of the Lord.   TURN TO PSALM 118

Glory be to the Father.

First Reading

SIRACH 51:1–8, 12

Songs of Meditation and Response

Grace is poured out upon your lips;
thus God has blessed you forever.
Because of truth, and meekness, and justice;
and may your right hand show you wondrous deeds.

Alleluia, alleluia.   PSALM 44

The five wise virgins took oil in their vessels with the lamps;
and at midnight a cry arose,
"Behold the bridegroom is coming,
go forth to meet Christ our Lord." Alleluia.   MATTHEW 25:4, 6

Gospel
MATTHEW 25:1–13

Song at the Preparation of the Gifts

Behind her the virgins of her train are brought to the king.
Her neighbors are brought to you with gladness and joy;
they enter the palace of the Lord, the king.   TURN TO PSALM 44

Communion Song

The five wise virgins took oil in their vessels with the lamps;
and at midnight a cry arose,
"Behold the bridegroom is coming,
go forth to meet Christ our Lord."
MATTHEW 25:4, 6   TURN TO PSALM 44

January 22 : Vincent and Anastasius : Martyrs

For today's Mass turn to page 315.

January 23 : Raymond of Penafort : Confessor

For today's Mass turn to page 325.

January 24 : Timothy : Bishop and Martyr

The First Reading is 1 Timothy 6:11–16; for the rest of today's Mass turn to page 311.

January 25 : The Conversion of Paul the Apostle

Entrance Song

I know whom I have believed,
and I am certain that he is able to guard the trust
committed to me against that day,
being a just judge.   2 TIMOTHY 1:12

O Lord, you have probed me and you know me;
you know when I sit and when I stand. TURN TO PSALM 138
Glory be to the Father.

First Reading
ACTS OF THE APOSTLES 9:1–22

Songs of Meditation and Response

He who worked in Peter for the apostleship,
worked also in me among the Gentiles,
and they recognized the grace of God that was given to me.

GALATIANS 2:8–9

The grace of God in me has not been fruitless;
but his grace always remains in me. I CORINTHIANS 15:10

Before Septuagesima add:

Alleluia, alleluia.
The great saint Paul, a vessel of election,
is indeed worthy to be glorified,
for he was made worthy to sit upon the twelfth throne. Alleluia.

After Septuagesima add:

O holy Apostle Paul, you are a vessel of election
and indeed worthy to be glorified.
You are the preacher of truth
and teacher of the Gentiles in faith and truth.
Through you all nations have known the grace of God.
Intercede for us with God who chose you.

Gospel
MATTHEW 19:27–29

Song at the Preparation of the Gifts

To me, your friends, O God,
are made exceedingly honorable;
their principality is exceedingly strengthened.

TURN TO PSALM 138

EUCHARISTIC PRAYER

TURN TO PAGE 403

183

Communion Song

Amen, I say to you,
that you who have left all things, and followed me,
shall receive a hundredfold,
and shall possess life everlasting.

MATTHEW 19:28–29 TURN TO PSALM 18

January 26 : Polycarp : Bishop and Martyr

The First Reading is 1 John 3:10–16, and the Gospel is Matthew 10:26–32;
for the rest of today's Mass turn to page 312.

January 27 : John Chrysostom : Bishop and Doctor of the Church

The Songs of Meditation and Response are given below;
for the rest of today's Mass turn to page 323.

Songs of Meditation and Response

Behold, a great priest, who in his days pleased God.
There was not found the like to him,
who kept the law of the Most High.   SIRACH 44:16, 20

Before Septuagesima add:

Alleluia, alleluia.
Blessed is the man who endures temptation;
for when he has been tried,
he will receive the crown of life. Alleluia.   JAMES 1:12

After Septuagesima add:

Happy the man who fears the Lord,
who greatly delights in his commands.
His posterity shall be mighty upon the earth;
the upright generation shall be blessed.
Wealth and riches shall be in his house;
his generosity shall endure forever.   PSALM 111

January 28 : Peter Nolasco : Confessor

For today's Mass turn to page 326.

January 29 : Francis de Sales : Bishop and Doctor of the Church

For today's Mass turn to page 323.

January 30 : Martina : Virgin and Martyr

For today's Mass turn to page 329.

January 31 : John Bosco : Confessor

Entrance Song

God gave him wisdom and understanding exceeding much,
and largeness of heart as the sand that is on the seashore.

Praise, you servants of the Lord, I KINGS 4:29
praise the name of the Lord. TURN TO PSALM 112
Glory be to the Father.

First Reading

PHILIPPIANS 4:4–9

Songs of Meditation and Response

Trust in the Lord and do good,
that you may dwell in the land and be fed with its riches.
Take delight in the Lord,
and he will grant you your heart's requests.
Commit to the Lord your way;
trust in him, and he will act. PSALM 36

Before Septuagesima add:

Alleluia, alleluia.
The afflicted and the poor shall praise your name. Alleluia. PSALM 73

After Septuagesima add:

You are my refuge, O Lord,
a tower of strength against the enemy.
Oh, that I might lodge in your tent forever,
take refuge in the shelter of your wings!
You indeed, O God, have accepted my vows;
you granted me the heritage of those who fear your name. PSALM 60

Gospel

MATTHEW 18:1–5

Song at the Preparation of the Gifts

Come, children, hear me;
I will teach you the fear of the Lord. TURN TO PSALM 33

Communion Song

Hoping against hope he believed,
so that he became father of many nations,
according to what was said to him.

ROMANS 4:18 TURN TO PSALM 112

February 1 : Ignatius of Antioch
Bishop and Martyr

Entrance Song

But as for me,
God forbid that I should glory
save in the cross of our Lord Jesus Christ,
through whom the world is crucified to me,
and I to the world. GALATIANS 6:14

Remember, O Lord, David
and all his meekness. TURN TO PSALM 131

Glory be to the Father.

First Reading

ROMANS 8:35–39

Songs of Meditation and Response

Behold, a great priest who in his days pleased God.
There was not found the like to him,
who kept the law of the Most High. SIRACH 44:16, 20

Before Septuagesima add:

Alleluia, alleluia.
With Christ I am nailed to the cross.
It is now no longer I that live,
but Christ lives in me. Alleluia. GALATIANS 2:19–20

After Septuagesima add:

You have granted him his heart's desire;
you refused not the wish of his lips.
For you welcomed him with goodly blessings.
You placed on his head a crown of precious stones. PSALM 20

Gospel

JOHN 12:24–26

Song at the Preparation of the Gifts

O Lord, you crowned him with glory and honor
and you have given him rule over the works of your hands.

TURN TO PSALM 8

Communion Song

I am the wheat of Christ;
may I be ground by the teeth of beasts,
that I may be found pure bread. TURN TO PSALM 22

February 2 : The Purification of Mary

THE BLESSING OF CANDLES

Before the principal Mass on this feast candles are blessed and a procession takes place.

Priest: The Lord be with you.
People: AND WITH YOUR SPIRIT.

The priest prays that God will make the candles holy and useful and will listen to the prayers of those who burn them; that the Christian people may burn with love of God and so be presented to him; that the light of the Holy Spirit will end the darkness of sin and enable us to know and love Christ.

During the distribution of the candles the following may be sung or recited. The refrain, "A light of revelation, etc.," is repeated after each verse.

A light of revelation to the gentiles,
and a glory for your people Israel.

Now you dismiss your servant, O Lord,
according to your word, in peace.

Because my eyes have seen your salvation.

187

Which you have prepared
before the face of all people.

A light of revelation to the gentiles,
and a glory for your people Israel.

Glory be to the Father.

Priest: The Lord be with you.
People: AND WITH YOUR SPIRIT.

The priest prays that we may have the insight to understand the mystery being celebrated.

Priest: Let us go forth in peace.
People: IN THE NAME OF CHRIST. AMEN.

During the procession the following may be sung or recited.

1. Adorn your bridal chamber, Sion,
   and welcome Christ the King;
   embrace Mary, who is the gate of heaven,
   for she carries the glorious King of the new light.
   She remains a virgin,
   bearing in her hands the Son begotten before the daystar.
   Holding him in his arms, Simeon proclaimed to the peoples,
   "He is the Lord of life and death
   and the Savior of the World."

2. It had been revealed to Simeon by the Holy Spirit
   that he should not see death
   before he had seen the Christ of the Lord.
   And when they brought the child into the temple,
   he received him into his arms and blessed God, saying:
   "Now you dismiss your servant, O Lord, in peace."
   When his parents brought in the child Jesus,
   to do for him according to the custom of the Law,
   he received him into his arms.

3. They offered for him to the Lord
   a pair of turtledoves or two young pigeons,
   as it is written in the law of the Lord.
   After the days of Mary's purification were fulfilled,
   according to the law of Moses,

they took Jesus up to Jerusalem to present him to the Lord.
As it is written in the law of the Lord.
Glory be to the Father and to the Son
and to the Holy Spirit.
As it was in the beginning, is now and ever shall be,
world without end. Amen.
As it is written in the law of the Lord.

Entrance Song

O God, we ponder your kindness within your temple.
As your name, O God, so also your praise
reaches to the ends of the earth.
Of justice your right hand is full.

> Great is the Lord, and wholly to be praised
> in the city of our God, his holy mountain.

> Glory be to the Father. TURN TO PSALM 47

Lord Have Mercy　Glory to God　Prayer

THE LITURGY OF THE WORD

First Reading

MALACHI 3:1–4

Songs of Meditation and Response

O God, we ponder your kindness
within your temple.
As your name, O God, so also your praise
reaches to the ends of the earth.
As we have heard, so have we seen,
in the city of our God, in his holy mountain.　PSALM 47

Before Septuagesima add:
Alleluia, alleluia.
The old man carried the Child:
but the Child governed the old man. Alleluia.

After Septuagesima add:
Now you dismiss your servant, O Lord,
according to your word, in peace.

Because my eyes have seen your salvation.
Which you have prepared before the face of all peoples.
A light of revelation to the Gentiles,
and a glory for your people Israel.   LUKE 2:29–32

Gospel
LUKE 2:22–32

Homily   Creed   Prayer of the Faithful

THE LITURGY OF THE EUCHARIST

Song at the Preparation of the Gifts

Grace is poured out upon your lips;
thus God has blessed you forever and ever.

TURN TO PSALM 44

Prayer over the Gifts

EUCHARISTIC PRAYER
TURN TO PAGE 391

Communion Song

It was revealed to Simeon by the Holy Spirit
that he should not see death
before he had seen the Christ of the Lord.

LUKE 2:26   TURN TO PSALM 47

Prayer after Communion

February 3 : Blaise : Bishop and Martyr
The Mass is of the preceding Sunday with a commemoration of Blaise.

February 4 : Andrew Corsini : Bishop
For today's Mass turn to page 320.

February 5 : Agatha : Virgin and Martyr

Entrance Song

Let us all rejoice in the Lord,
celebrating the feast in honor of blessed Agatha,

Virgin and Martyr,
for whose passion the angels rejoice
and praise the Son of God.

> My heart overflows with a goodly theme;
> as I sing my ode to the king. TURN TO PSALM 44

> Glory be to the Father.

First Reading
I CORINTHIANS 1:26–31

Songs of Meditation and Response

God will help her with his countenance;
God is in her midst, she shall not be disturbed.
There is a stream whose runlets gladden the city of God;
the Most High has sanctified his dwelling. PSALM 45

Before Septuagesima add:

Alleluia, alleluia.
I will speak of your decrees before kings
without being ashamed. Alleluia. PSALM 118

After Septuagesima add:

Those that sow in tears
shall reap rejoicing.
Going, they went and wept,
casting their seeds.
But coming, they shall come with joyfulness
carrying their sheaves. PSALM 125

Gospel
MATTHEW 19:3–12

Song at the Preparation of the Gifts

Behind her the virgins of her train are brought to the king.
Her neighbors are brought to you. TURN TO PSALM 44

Communion Song

I invoke him, the living God,
who deigned to cure me of every wound,
and to restore my breast to my body. TURN TO PSALM 118

February 6 : Titus : Bishop

The Gospel is Luke 10:1–9; for the rest of today's Mass turn to page 320.

February 7 : Romuald : Abbot

For today's Mass turn to page 327.

February 8 : John of Matha : Confessor

For today's Mass turn to page 325.
During Lent, the Lenten weekday Mass is celebrated instead.

February 9 : Cyril of Alexandria : Bishop and Doctor of the Church

For today's Mass turn to page 323.
During Lent, the Lenten weekday Mass is celebrated instead,
with a commemoration of Cyril.

February 10 : Scholastica : Virgin

For today's Mass turn to page 332. During Lent, the Lenten weekday Mass
is celebrated instead, with a commemoration of Scholastica.

February 11 : Our Lady of Lourdes

During Lent, the Lenten weekday Mass is celebrated instead, with a commem-
oration of Our Lady of Lourdes.

Entrance Song

I saw the holy city, new Jerusalem,
coming down out of heaven from God,
made ready as a bride adorned for her husband.

REVELATION 21:2

My heart overflows with a goodly theme;
as I sing my ode to the king.   TURN TO PSALM 44

Glory be to the Father.

First Reading

REVELATION 11:19; 12:1, 10

Songs of Meditation and Response

The flowers appear in our land,
the time of pruning has come,
the song of the dove is heard in our land.
Arise, my beloved, my beautiful one, and come!
O my dove, in the clefts of the rock,
in the secret recesses of the cliff.

SONG OF SOLOMON 2:12, 10, 14

Before Septuagesima add:

Alleluia, alleluia.
Show me your face, let me hear your voice,
for your voice is sweet and your face is beautiful. Alleluia.

After Septuagesima add:

You are the glory of Jerusalem,
you are the joy of Israel,
you are the honor of our people. JUDITH 15:10

You are all beautiful, O Mary,
and there is in you no stain of original sin.
Happy are you, O holy Virgin Mary,
and most worthy of all praise,
for with your virgin foot you have crushed the serpent's head.

SONG OF SOLOMON 4:7

Gospel

LUKE 1:26–31

Song at the Preparation of the Gifts

Hail, full of grace, the Lord is with you.
Blessed are you among women.

LUKE 1:28 TURN TO PSALM 44

EUCHARISTIC PRAYER

TURN TO PAGE 401

Communion Song

You have visited the land and watered it;
greatly have you enriched it. TURN TO PSALM 64

February 12 : Founders of the Servite Order
Confessors

During Lent, the Lenten weekday Mass is celebrated instead, with a commemoration of the Confessors.

Entrance Song

The just sang, O Lord, your holy name
and praised in unison your conquering hand—
because wisdom opened the mouths of the dumb,
and gave ready speech to infants.

O Lord, our Lord,   WISDOM OF SOLOMON 10:20–21
how glorious is your name over all the earth!

Glory be to the Father.   TURN TO PSALM 8

First Reading
SIRACH 44:1–15

Songs of Meditation and Response

My elect shall not toil in vain,
nor beget children for sudden destruction;
for a race blessed by the Lord are they and their offspring.

Their bodies are buried in peace,   ISAIAH 65:23
and their name lives on and on.   SIRACH 44:14

Before Septuagesima add:
Alleluia, alleluia.
At gatherings their wisdom is retold,
and the assembly sings their praises. Alleluia.   SIRACH 44:15

After Septuagesima add:
Those that sow in tears
shall reap rejoicing.
Going, they went and wept,
casting their seeds.
But coming, they shall come with joyfulness,
carrying their sheaves.   PSALM 125

Gospel
MATTHEW 19:27–29

Song at the Preparation of the Gifts

I will bring them to my holy mountain,
and make them joyful in my house of prayer;
their holocausts and sacrifices will be acceptable on my altar.

ISAIAH 56:7 TURN TO PSALM 125

Communion Song

I have chosen you from the world
that you should go and bear fruit,
and that your fruit should remain.

JOHN 15:16 TURN TO PSALM 91

February 14 : Valentine : Martyr

*The Mass is of the preceding Sunday, with a commemoration of Valentine.
During Lent, the Lenten weekday Mass is celebrated instead, with a commemoration of Valentine.*

February 15 : Faustinus and Jovita : Martyrs

*The Mass is of the preceding Sunday, with a commemoration of the Martyrs.
During Lent, the Lenten weekday Mass is celebrated instead, with a commemoration of the Martyrs.*

February 18 : Simeon : Bishop and Martyr

*The Mass is of the preceding Sunday, with a commemoration of Simeon. During
Lent, the Lenten weekday Mass is celebrated instead, with a commemoration
of Simeon.*

February 22 : Peter's Chair

Entrance Song

The Lord made a covenant of friendship with him,
and made him a prince;
that he should possess the dignity of priesthood forever.

Remember, O Lord, David
and all his meekness.

SIRACH 45:30

TURN TO PSALM 131

Glory be to the Father.

195

First Reading

I PETER I:I–7

Songs of Meditation and Response

Let them extol him in the assembly of the people
and praise him in the council of the elders.
Let them give thanks to the Lord for his kindness
and his wondrous deeds to the children of men.   PSALM 106

You are Peter,
and upon this rock I will build my Church.
And the gates of hell shall not prevail against it.
And I will give you the keys of the kingdom of heaven.
And whatever you shall bind on earth
shall be bound in heaven.
And whatever you shall loose on earth
shall be loosed in heaven.   MATTHEW 16:18–19

Gospel

MATTHEW 16:13–19

Song at the Preparation of the Gifts

You are Peter,
and upon this rock I will build my Church,
and the gates of hell shall not prevail against it.
And I will give you the keys of the kingdom of heaven.
MATTHEW 16:18–19 TURN TO PSALM 131

EUCHARISTIC PRAYER
TURN TO PAGE 403

Communion Song

You are Peter,
and upon this rock I will build my Church.
MATTHEW 16:18 TURN TO PSALM 18

February 23 : Peter Damian : Bishop and Doctor of the Church

Today's Mass turn to page 323. During Lent, the Lenten weekday Mass is
celebrated instead, with a commemoration of Peter Damian.

February 24 : Matthias : Apostle

(February 25 in Leap Year)

Entrance Song

To me, your friends, O God,
are made exceedingly honorable;
their principality is exceedingly strengthened.

> O Lord, you have probed me and you know me;
> you know when I sit and when I stand.

> Glory be to the Father. TURN TO PSALM 138

First Reading

ACTS OF THE APOSTLES 1:15–26

Songs of Meditation and Response

Your friends, O God, are made exceedingly honorable;
their principality is exceedingly strengthened.
Were I to recount them,
they would outnumber the sands. PSALM 138

You have granted him his heart's desire;
you refused not the wish of his lips.
For you welcomed him with goodly blessings.
You placed on his head a crown of precious stones. PSALM 20

Gospel

MATTHEW 11:25–30

Song at the Preparation of the Gifts

You shall make them princes through all the land;
they shall remember your name, O Lord,
through all generations. TURN TO PSALM 44

EUCHARISTIC PRAYER

TURN TO PAGE 403

Communion Song

You who have followed me shall sit on thrones
judging the twelve tribes of Israel.

MATTHEW 19:28 TURN TO PSALM 18

197

February 27 : Gabriel : Confessor

(February 28 in Leap Year)

During Lent, the Lenten weekday Mass is celebrated, with a commemoration of Gabriel.

Entrance Song

The eye of God looks favorably upon him;
he raises him free of the vile dust, and lifts up his head
to the amazement of the many who glorify God.

SIRACH 11:13

How good is God to Israel,
to those who are clean of heart! TURN TO PSALM 72

Glory be to the Father.

First Reading

I JOHN 2:14–17

Songs of Meditation and Response

How great is the goodness, O Lord,
which you have in store for those who fear you.
And which, toward those who take refuge in you,
you show in the sight of men. PSALM 30

Happy the man whose strength you are!
his heart is set upon the pilgrimage
in the vale of tears, in the place he has set.
I had rather lie at the threshold of the house of my God
than dwell in the tents of the wicked.
He withholds no good thing
from those who walk in sincerity,
O Lord of hosts,
happy the man who trusts in you. PSALM 83

Gospel

MARK 10:13–21

Song at the Preparation of the Gifts

O Lord, I am your servant, the son of your handmaid;
you have loosed my bonds.
To you will I offer sacrifice of thanksgiving.

TURN TO PSALM 115

Communion Song

Behold, I stand at the door and knock.
If any man listens to my voice and opens the door to me,
I will come in to him and will sup with him,
and he with me. REVELATION 3:20 TURN TO PSALM 83

March 4 : Casimir : Confessor

For today's Mass turn to page 325. During Lent, the Lenten weekday Mass is celebrated, with a commemoration of Casimir.

March 6 : Perpetua and Felicitas : Martyrs

For today's Mass turn to page 335. During Lent, the Lenten weekday Mass is celebrated, with a commemoration of the Martyrs.

March 7 : Thomas Aquinas : Doctor of the Church

The Lenten weekday Mass is celebrated, with a commemoration of Thomas. If the Mass of St. Thomas is celebrated, the First Reading is Wisdom of Solomon 7:7–14, and the rest of the Mass is on page 323.

March 8 : John of God : Confessor

The Lenten weekday Mass is celebrated, with a commemoration of John.

March 9 : Frances of Rome : Holy Woman

The Lenten Mass is celebrated, with a commemoration of Frances.

March 10 : The Forty Martyrs

The Lenten weekday Mass is celebrated, with a commemoration of the Martyrs.

March 12 : Gregory the Great : Pope and Doctor of the Church

The Lenten weekday Mass is celebrated, with a commemoration of Gregory.

March 17 : Patrick : Bishop

The Lenten weekday Mass is celebrated, with a commemoration of Patrick.

March 18 : Cyril of Jerusalem : Bishop and Doctor of the Church

The Lenten weekday Mass is celebrated, with a commemoration of Cyril.

March 19 : Joseph : Husband of Our Lady

The alleluias in parentheses are recited during Eastertime.

Entrance Song

The just man shall flourish like the palm tree,
like a cedar of Lebanon shall he grow:
planted in the house of the Lord,
in the courts of the house of our God.
(Alleluia, alleluia.)

> It is good to give thanks to the Lord,
> to sing praise to your name, Most High.
>
> Glory be to the Father. TURN TO PSALM 91

First Reading

SIRACH 45:1–6

Songs of Meditation and Response

Before Easter:

O Lord, you welcomed him with goodly blessings,
you placed on his head a crown of precious stones.
He asked life of you;
you gave him length of days forever and ever. PSALM 20

Happy the man who fears the Lord,
who greatly delights in his commands.
His posterity shall be mighty upon the earth;
the upright generation shall be blessed.
Wealth and riches shall be in his house;
his generosity shall endure forever. PSALM 111

200

Alleluia, alleluia.
The Lord loved him, and adorned him;
he clothed him with a robe of glory. Alleluia.   SIRACH 45:9

The just man shall blossom as the lily;
and shall flourish forever before the Lord. Alleluia.   HOSEA 14:6

Gospel
MATTHEW 1:18–21

Song at the Preparation of the Gifts

My faithfulness and my kindness shall be with him,
and through my name shall his horn be exalted. (Alleluia.)

TURN TO PSALM 88

EUCHARISTIC PRAYER
TURN TO PAGE 402

Communion Song

Do not be afraid, Joseph, son of David,
to take to you Mary your wife,
for that which is begotten in her is of the Holy Spirit. (Alleluia.)

MATTHEW 1:20   TURN TO PSALM 126

March 21 : Benedict : Abbot

The Lenten weekday Mass is celebrated, with a commemoration of Benedict.

March 24 : Gabriel : Archangel

The Lenten weekday Mass is celebrated, with a commemoration of Gabriel.

March 25 : The Annunciation

The alleluias in parentheses are recited during Eastertime.

Entrance Song

All the rich among the people seek your favor.
Behind her the virgins of her train are brought to the king.
Her neighbors are brought to you with gladness and joy.
(Alleluia, alleluia.)

My heart overflows with a goodly theme;
as I sing my ode to the king. TURN TO PSALM 44

Glory be to the Father.

First Reading
ISAIAH 7:10–15

Songs of Meditation and Response

Before Easter:

Grace is poured out upon your lips;
thus God has blessed you forever.
Because of truth, and meekness, and justice;
may your right hand show you wondrous deeds.

Hear, O daughter, and see; turn your ear;
for the king shall desire your beauty.
All the rich among the people seek your favor;
the daughters of kings come to meet you.
Behind her the virgins of her train are brought to the king;
her neighbors are brought to you.
They are brought with gladness and joy;
they enter the palace of the king. PSALM 44

After Easter:

Alleluia, alleluia.
Hail, Mary, full of grace, the Lord is with you;
blessed are you among women. LUKE 1:28

The rod of Jesse has blossomed:
a Virgin has brought forth God and man:
God has given peace,
reconciling in himself the lowest with the highest. Alleluia.

Gospel
LUKE 1:26–38

Song at the Preparation of the Gifts

Hail, Mary, full of grace, the Lord is with you.
Blessed are you among women
and blessed is the fruit of your womb. (Alleluia.)

LUKE 1:28, 42 TURN TO PSALM 84

Communion Song

Behold, a virgin shall be with child, and bear a son,
and shall name him Emmanuel. (Alleluia.)

ISAIAH 7:14   TURN TO PSALM 24

March 27 : John Damascene : Doctor of the Church

The Lenten weekday Mass is celebrated, with a commemoration of John. In Easter week, the Mass of the weekday is celebrated.

March 28 : John Capistran : Confessor

The Lenten weekday Mass is celebrated, with a commemoration of John. In Easter week, the Mass of the weekday is celebrated.

April 2 : Francis of Paula : Confessor

The Lenten weekday Mass is celebrated, with a commemoration of Francis. In Easter week, the Mass of the weekday is celebrated.

April 4 : Isidore : Bishop and Doctor of the Church

For today's Mass turn to page 323. During Lent, the Lenten weekday Mass is celebrated, with a commemoration of Isidore. In Easter week, the Mass of the weekday is celebrated.

April 5 : Vincent Ferrer : Confessor

For today's Mass turn to page 325. During Lent, the Lenten weekday Mass is celebrated, with a commemoration of Vincent. In Easter week, the Mass of the weekday is celebrated.

April 11 : Leo I : Pope and Doctor of the Church

For today's Mass turn to page 310. During Lent, the Lenten weekday Mass is celebrated, with a commemoration of Leo. In Easter week, the Mass of the weekday is celebrated.

April 13.: Hermenegild : Martyr

The Gospel is Luke 14:26–33; for the rest of today's Mass turn to page 313. During Lent, the Lenten weekday Mass is celebrated, with a commemoration of Hermenegild. In Easter week, the Mass of the weekday is celebrated.

April 14 : Justin : Martyr

During Lent, the Lenten weekday Mass is celebrated, with a commemoration of Justin. In Easter week, the Mass of the weekday is celebrated. After the First Sunday after Easter the Mass below is celebrated:

Entrance Song

The wicked have told me fables, but not as your law.
I will speak of your decrees before kings
without being ashamed.
Alleluia, alleluia.

Happy are they whose way is blameless,
who walk in the law of the Lord.   TURN TO PSALM 118
Glory be to the Father.

First Reading

I CORINTHIANS 1:18–25, 30

Songs of Meditation and Response

Alleluia, alleluia.
The wisdom of this world is foolishness with God.
For it is written, "The Lord knows the thoughts of the wise,
that they are empty." Alleluia.   I CORINTHIANS 3:19–20

Nay more, I count everything loss,
because of the excelling knowledge of Jesus Christ, my Lord.
Alleluia.   PHILIPPIANS 3:8

Gospel

LUKE 12:2–8

Song at the Preparation of the Gifts

For I determined not to know anything among you,
except Jesus Christ and him crucified. Alleluia.

I CORINTHIANS 2:2   TURN TO PSALM 138

Communion Song

There is laid up for me a crown of justice,
which the Lord, the just Judge,
will give to me in that day. Alleluia.

2 TIMOTHY 4:8   TURN TO PSALM 118

April 17 : Anicetus : Pope and Martyr

During Easter week the Mass of the weekday is celebrated. After the First Sunday after Easter, the Mass is of the preceding Sunday, with a commemoration of Anicetus.

April 21 : Anselm : Bishop and Doctor of the Church

For today's Mass turn to page 323. During Easter week, the Mass of the weekday is celebrated.

April 22 : Soter and Caius : Popes and Martyrs

For today's Mass turn to page 310. During Easter week, the Mass of the weekday is celebrated.

April 23 : George : Martyr

The Mass of the preceding Sunday is celebrated, with a commemoration of George. During Easter week the Mass of the weekday is celebrated.

April 24 : Fidelis of Sigmaringen : Martyr

For today's Mass turn to page 319. During Easter week, the Mass of the weekday is celebrated.

April 25 : Rogation Day

If the Litany of Rogation is to be recited, turn to page 123. If there is no litany, the Mass is that of St. Mark, below.

April 25 : Mark : Evangelist

The First Reading is Ezekiel 1:10–14 and the Gospel is Luke 10:1–9; the Eucharistic Prayer is on page 403; for the rest of today's Mass turn to page 319. During Easter week, the Mass of the weekday is celebrated.

April 26 : Cletus and Marcellinus : Popes and Martyrs

For today's Mass turn to page 310. During Easter week, the weekday Mass is celebrated.

April 27 : Peter Canisius : Doctor of the Church

For today's Mass turn to page 323. During Easter week, the weekday Mass is celebrated.

April 28 : Paul of the Cross : Confessor

During Easter week, the weekday Mass is celebrated. After the First Sunday after Easter, the Mass below is celebrated.

Entrance Song

With Christ I am nailed to the cross.
It is now no longer I that live, but Christ lives in me.
I live in the faith of the Son of God,
who loved me and gave himself up for me.
Alleluia, alleluia. GALATIANS 2:19–20

Happy is he who has regard for the lowly and the poor;
in the day of misfortune the Lord will deliver him.

Glory be to the Father. TURN TO PSALM 40

First Reading

I CORINTHIANS 1:17–25

Songs of Meditation and Response

Alleluia, alleluia.
Christ died for all, in order that they who are alive
may live no longer for themselves,
but for him who died for them and rose again. Alleluia.

2 CORINTHIANS 5:15

If we are sons, we are heirs also:
heirs indeed of God and joint heirs with Christ,
provided, however, we suffer with him,
that we may also be glorified with him. Alleluia. ROMANS 8:17

Gospel

LUKE 10:1–9

Walk in love, as Christ also loved us,
and delivered himself up for us,
an offering and a sacrifice to God,
in fragrant odor. Alleluia.   EPHESIANS 5:2   TURN TO PSALM 21

Communion Song

Rejoice in as far as you are partakers
of the sufferings of Christ,
that you may also rejoice with exultation
in the revelation of his glory. Alleluia.

I PETER 4:13   TURN TO PSALM 21

April 29 : Peter of Verona : Martyr

*The First Reading is 2 Timothy 2:8–10; 3:10–12; for the rest of today's
Mass turn to page 319.*

April 30 : Catherine of Siena : Virgin

For today's Mass turn to page 332.

May 1 : Saint Joseph : the Worker

Entrance Song

Wisdom gave the holy ones the recompense of their labors,
and conducted them by a wondrous road,
and became a shelter for them by day
and a starry flame by night.
Alleluia, alleluia.   WISDOM OF SOLOMON 10:17

Unless the Lord build the house,
they labor in vain who build it.   TURN TO PSALM 126
Glory be to the Father.

Lord Have Mercy   Glory to God   Prayer

THE LITURGY OF THE WORD

First Reading

COLOSSIANS 3:14–15, 17, 23–24

Songs of Meditation and Response

Alleluia, alleluia.

In whatever trouble they shall call upon me, I will hear them,
and I will always be their protector. Alleluia.

Obtain for us grace to lead an innocent life, O Joseph;
and may it ever be secure under your protection. Alleluia.

Gospel

MATTHEW 13:54–58

Homily   Creed   Prayer of the Faithful

THE LITURGY OF THE EUCHARIST

Song at the Preparation of the Gifts

May the gracious care of the Lord our God be ours;
prosper the work of our hands for us!
Prosper the work of our hands! Alleluia. TURN TO PSALM 89

Prayer over the Gifts

EUCHARISTIC PRAYER

TURN TO PAGE 402

Communion Song

Where did he get this wisdom and these miracles?
Is not this the carpenter's son?
Is not his mother called Mary?
Alleluia.   MATTHEW 13:54–55 TURN TO PSALM 126

Prayer after Communion

May 2 : Athanasius : Bishop and Doctor of the Church

Entrance Song

In the midst of the assembly he opened his mouth;
and the Lord filled him

with the spirit of wisdom and understanding;
he clothed him with a robe of glory.
Alleluia, alleluia. SIRACH 15:5

It is good to give thanks to the Lord,
to sing praise to your name, Most High.
Glory be to the Father. TURN TO PSALM 91

First Reading
2 CORINTHIANS 4:5-14

Songs of Meditation and Response

Alleluia, alleluia.
You are a priest forever,
according to the order of Melchisedec. Alleluia. PSALM 109

Blessed is the man who endures temptation;
for when he has been tried,
he will receive the crown of life. Alleluia. JAMES 1:12

Gospel
MATTHEW 10:23-28

Song at the Preparation of the Gifts

I have found David, my servant;
with my holy oil I have anointed him,
that my hand may be always with him,
and that my arm may make him strong. Alleluia.
TURN TO PSALM 88

Communion Song

"What I tell you in darkness,
speak it in the light," says the Lord;
"and what you hear whispered,
preach it on the house-tops." Alleluia.
MATTHEW 10:27 TURN TO PSALM 131

May 3 : Alexander, Eventius, Theodulus and Juvenal : Martyrs

The Mass is of the preceding Sunday, with a commemoration of the Martyrs.

May 4 : Monica : Holy Woman

The First Reading is 1 Timothy 5:3–10; the Gospel is Luke 7:11–16; for the rest of today's Mass turn to page 336.

May 5 : Pius V : Pope

For today's Mass turn to page 310.

May 7 : Stanislaus : Bishop and Martyr

For today's Mass turn to page 319.

May 9 : Gregory Nazianzen : Bishop and Doctor of the Church

The First Reading is Sirach 39:6–14; for the rest of today's Mass turn to page 323.

May 10 : Antoninus : Bishop

For today's Mass turn to page 320.

May 11 : Philip and James : Apostles

Entrance Song

In the time of their tribulation they cried to you, O Lord,
and you heard them from heaven,
alleluia, alleluia.   NEHEMIAH 9:27

Exult, you just, in the Lord;
praise from the upright is fitting.   TURN TO PSALM 32
Glory be to the Father.

First Reading

WISDOM OF SOLOMON 5:1–5

Songs of Meditation and Response

Alleluia, alleluia.
The heavens proclaim your wonders, O Lord,
and your faithfulness, in the assembly of the holy ones. Alleluia.

PSALM 88

Have I been so long a time with you,
and you have not known me?
Philip, he who sees me, sees also my Father. Alleluia.

JOHN 14:9

Gospel
JOHN 14:1–13

Song at the Preparation of the Gifts

The heavens proclaim your wonders, O Lord,
and your faithfulness, in the assembly of the holy ones,
alleluia, alleluia.　　　TURN TO PSALM 88

EUCHARISTIC PRAYER
TURN TO PAGE 403

Communion Song

Have I been so long a time with you, and you have not known me?
Philip, he who sees me sees also my Father. Alleluia.
Do you not believe that I am in the Father and the Father in me?
Alleluia, alleluia.　　　JOHN 14:9–10　TURN TO PSALM 18

May 12 : Nereus, Achilleus, Domitilla and Pancras : Martyrs

Entrance Song

But see, the eyes of the Lord are upon those who fear him,
upon those who hope in his kindness, alleluia;
to deliver them from death;
for he is our help and our shield, alleluia.

Exult, you just, in the Lord;
praise from the upright is fitting.　　　TURN TO PSALM 32

Glory be to the Father.

First Reading
WISDOM OF SOLOMON 5:1–5

Songs of Meditation and Response

Alleluia, alleluia.
This is the true brotherhood,

which overcame the wickedness of the world;
it followed Christ,
attaining the glorious kingdom of heaven. Alleluia.

The white-robed army of Martyrs praises you, O Lord.
Alleluia.

Gospel
JOHN 4:46–53

Song at the Preparation of the Gifts

The heavens proclaim your wonders, O Lord,
and your faithfulness, in the assembly of the holy ones,
alleluia, alleluia. TURN TO PSALM 88

Communion Song

Exult, you just, in the Lord, alleluia;
praise from the upright is fitting, alleluia. TURN TO PSALM 32

May 13 : Robert Bellarmine : Bishop and Doctor of the Church

Entrance Song

In the midst of the assembly he opened his mouth;
and the Lord filled him
with the spirit of wisdom and understanding;
he clothed him with a robe of glory. SIRACH 15:5
Alleluia, alleluia.

It is good to give thanks to the Lord,
to sing praise to your name, Most High.

Glory be to the Father. TURN TO PSALM 91

First Reading
WISDOM OF SOLOMON 7:7–14

Songs of Meditation and Response

Alleluia, alleluia.
The wise shall shine brightly
like the splendor of the firmament. Alleluia.

Those who led the many to justice,
shall be like the stars forever. Alleluia. DANIEL 12:3

Gospel

MATTHEW 5:13–19

Song at the Preparation of the Gifts

But for me, to be near God is my good;
to make the Lord God my refuge.
I shall declare all your works
in the gates of the daughter of Sion. Alleluia.

TURN TO PSALM 72

Communion Song

You are the light of the world.
Even so, let your light shine before men,
in order that they may see your good works
and give glory to your Father in heaven. Alleluia.

MATTHEW 5:14, 16   TURN TO PSALM 91

May 14 : Boniface : Martyr

The Mass is of the preceding Sunday, with a commemoration of Boniface.

May 15 : John Baptist de la Salle : Confessor

The Gospel is Matthew 18:1–5; for the rest of today's Mass turn to page 325.

May 16 : Ubald : Bishop

For today's Mass turn to page 320.

May 17 : Paschal Baylon : Confessor

For today's Mass turn to page 325.

May 18 : Venantius : Martyr

For today's Mass turn to page 319.

May 19 : Peter Celestine : Pope

For today's Mass turn to page 310.

May 20 : Bernadine of Siena : Confessor

The Gospel is Matthew 19:27–29; for the rest of today's Mass turn to page 325.

May 25 : Gregory VII : Pope

For today's Mass turn to page 310.

May 26 : Philip Neri : Confessor

The alleluias in parentheses are recited only before Pentecost.

Entrance Song

The charity of God is poured forth in our hearts,
by his spirit dwelling within us.
(Alleluia, alleluia.) ROMANS 5:5

> Bless the Lord, O my soul;
> and, all my being, bless his holy name.
>
> Glory be to the Father. TURN TO PSALM 102

First Reading
WISDOM OF SOLOMON 7:7–14

Songs of Meditation and Response
Before Pentecost:

Alleluia, alleluia.
From on high he sent fire into my very frame
and instructed me. Alleluia. LAMENTATIONS 1:13

Hot grew my heart within me;
in my thoughts, a fire blazed forth. Alleluia. PSALM 38

After Trinity Sunday:

Come, children, hear me;
I will teach you the fear of the Lord.
Look to him that you may be radiant with joy,
and your faces may not blush with shame. PSALM 33

Alleluia, alleluia.
From on high he sent a fire into my very frame,
and instructed me. Alleluia. LAMENTATIONS 1:13

Gospel
LUKE 12:35–40

Song at the Preparation of the Gifts

I will run the way of your commands
when you give me a docile heart. (Alleluia.) TURN TO PSALM 118

Communion Song

My heart and my flesh
cry out for the living God. (Alleluia.) TURN TO PSALM 83

May 27 : Bede : Doctor of the Church

For today's Mass turn to page 323.

May 28 : Augustine of Canterbury : Bishop

The First Reading is 1 Thessalonians 2:2–9; the Gospel is Luke 10:1–9; for the rest of today's Mass turn to page 322.

May 29 : Mary Magdalen of Pazzi : Virgin

For today's Mass turn to page 332.

May 30 : Felix : Pope and Martyr

The Mass is of the preceding Sunday, with a commemoration of Felix.

May 31 : Mary Our Queen

The alleluias in parentheses are recited only before Pentecost.

Entrance Song

Let us all rejoice in the Lord, celebrating a feast
in honor of the Queenship of the Blessed Virgin Mary,
on whose solemnity the angels rejoice
and give praise to the Son of God.
(Alleluia, alleluia.)

My heart overflows with a goodly theme;
as I sing my ode to the king.   TURN TO PSALM 44
Glory be to the Father.

First Reading
SIRACH 24:5, 7, 9–11, 30–31

Songs of Meditation and Response

Before Pentecost:

Alleluia, alleluia.
Blessed are you, O Virgin Mary,
who stood beneath the cross of the Lord. Alleluia.

Now with him you reign forever. Alleluia.

After Trinity Sunday:

He has on his garment and on his thigh a name written:
"King of kings and Lord of lords."   REVELATION 19:16
The Queen takes her place at his right hand in gold of Ophir.

Alleluia, alleluia.   PSALM 44

Hail, Queen of mercy, protect us from the enemy,
and receive us at the hour of death. Alleluia.

Gospel

LUKE 1:26–33

Song at the Preparation of the Gifts

Sprung from a royal line, Mary shines with glory.
We devoutly plead to be helped by her prayers
in mind and in heart. (Alleluia.)   TURN TO PSALM 96

EUCHARISTIC PRAYER

TURN TO PAGE 401

Communion Song

Most worthy Queen of the world, Mary ever Virgin,
you bore Christ the Lord, the Savior of all men.
Intercede for our peace and salvation. (Alleluia.)

TURN TO PSALM 98

June 1 : Angela Merici : Virgin

For today's Mass turn to page 332.

June 2 : Marcellinus, Peter and Erasmus : Martyrs

The Mass is of the preceding Sunday, with a commemoration of the Martyrs.

June 4 : Francis Caracciolo : Confessor

The alleluias in parentheses are recited only before Pentecost.

Entrance Song

My heart has become like wax melting away within my bosom,
because zeal for your house consumes me.
(Alleluia, alleluia.) PSALM 21

> How good God is to Israel,
> to those who are clean of heart! TURN TO PSALM 72
>
> Glory be to the Father.

First Reading
WISDOM OF SOLOMON 4:8–14

Songs of Meditation and Response
After Trinity Sunday:

As the hind longs for the running waters,
so my soul longs for you, O God.
Athirst is my soul for the strong living God. PSALM 41

Alleluia, alleluia.
My flesh and my heart waste away;
God is the God of my heart and my portion forever. Alleluia.

PSALM 72

Before Pentecost:

Alleluia, alleluia.
Happy the man you choose
and bring to dwell in your courts. Alleluia. PSALM 64

Lavishly he gives to the poor;
his generosity shall endure forever. Alleluia. PSALM 111

Gospel
LUKE 12:35–40

Song at the Preparation of the Gifts

The just man shall flourish like the palm tree,
like a cedar of Lebanon shall he grow. (Alleluia.)

TURN TO PSALM 91

Communion Song

How great is the goodness, O Lord,
which you have in store for those who fear you. (Alleluia.)

TURN TO PSALM 30

June 5 : Boniface : Bishop and Martyr

The alleluias in parentheses are recited only before Pentecost.

Entrance Song

I will rejoice in Jerusalem and exult in my people.
No longer shall the sound of weeping be heard there,
or the sound of crying.
My elect shall not toil in vain,
nor beget children for sudden destruction;
for a race blessed by the Lord are they and their offspring.
(Alleluia, alleluia.) ISAIAH 65:19, 23

> O God, our ears have heard,
> our fathers have declared to us,
> the deeds you did in their days. TURN TO PSALM 43
>
> Glory be to the Father.

First Reading
SIRACH 44:1–15

Songs of Meditation and Response
After Trinity Sunday:

In as far as you are partakers of the sufferings of Christ, rejoice
that you may also rejoice with exultation
in the revelation of his glory.
If you are upbraided for the name of Christ,
blessed will you be,
because the honor, the glory and the power of God,
and his Spirit rest upon you. I PETER 4:13–14

Alleluia, alleluia.
I will spread prosperity over him like a river,
and glory like an overflowing torrent. Alleluia. ISAIAH 66:12

Before Pentecost:

Alleluia, alleluia.
Rejoice with Jerusalem and be glad because of her,
all you who love the Lord. Alleluia.

You shall see and your heart shall rejoice;
and the Lord's power shall be known to his servants. Alleluia.

ISAIAH 66:10, 14

Gospel
MATTHEW 5:1–12

Song at the Preparation of the Gifts

I bless the Lord who counsels me;
I set God ever before me;
with him at my right hand I shall not be disturbed. (Alleluia.)

TURN TO PSALM 15

Communion Song

He who overcomes,
I will permit him to sit with me upon my throne;
as I also have overcome
and have sat with my Father on his throne. (Alleluia.)

REVELATION 3:21 TURN TO PSALM 125˙

June 6 : Norbert : Bishop
For today's Mass turn to page 320.

June 9 : Primus and Felicianus : Martyrs
The Mass is of the preceding Sunday, with a commemoration of the Martyrs.

June 10 : Margaret : Holy Woman
For today's Mass turn to page 336.

June 11 : Barnabas : Apostle

Entrance Song

To me, your friends, O God,
are made exceedingly honorable;
their principality is exceedingly strengthened.

O Lord, you have probed me and you know me;
you know when I sit and when I stand.
Glory be to the Father.   TURN TO PSALM 138

First Reading
ACTS OF THE APOSTLES 11:21–26; 13:1–3

Songs of Meditation and Response

Through all the earth their voice resounds,
and to the ends of the world, their message.
The heavens declare the glory of God,
and the firmament proclaims his handiwork.   PSALM 18

Alleluia, alleluia.
I have chosen you out of the world,
that you should go and bear fruit,
and that your fruit should remain. Alleluia.   JOHN 15:16

Gospel
MATTHEW 10:16–22

Song at the Preparation of the Gifts

You shall make them princes through all the land;
they shall remember your name, O Lord,
through all generations.   TURN TO PSALM 44

EUCHARISTIC PRAYER
TURN TO PAGE 403

Communion Song

You who have followed me shall sit on thrones
judging the twelve tribes of Israel.
MATTHEW 19:28   TURN TO PSALM 18

June 12 : John of St. Facundus : Confessor
For today's Mass turn to page 325.

June 13 : Anthony of Padua : Doctor of the Church
For today's Mass turn to page 323.

June 14 : Basil the Great : Bishop and Doctor of the Church

Entrance Song

In the midst of the assembly he opened his mouth;
and the Lord filled him
with the spirit of wisdom and understanding;
he clothed him with a robe of glory. SIRACH 15:5

It is good to give thanks to the Lord,
to sing praise to your name, Most High.

Glory be to the Father. TURN TO PSALM 91

First Reading
2 TIMOTHY 4:1-8

Songs of Meditation and Response

The mouth of the just man tells of wisdom
and his tongue utters what is right.
The law of his God is in his heart,
and his steps do not falter. PSALM 36

Alleluia, alleluia.
I have found David, my servant;
with my holy oil I have anointed him. Alleluia. PSALM 88

Gospel
LUKE 14:26-35

Song at the Preparation of the Gifts

My faithfulness and my kindness shall be with him,
and through my name shall his horn be exalted. TURN TO PSALM 88

Communion Song

The faithful and prudent servant
whom the master will set over his household
to give them their ration of grain in due time. LUKE 12:42   TURN TO PSALM 36

June 15 : Vitus, Modest and Crescentia : Martyrs

The Mass is of the preceding Sunday, with a commemoration of the Martyrs.

June 17 : Gregory Barbadici : Bishop

For today's Mass turn to page 320.

June 18 : Ephraem : Doctor of the Church

For today's Mass turn to page 323.

June 19 : Juliana of Falconieri : Virgin

For today's Mass turn to page 332.

June 20 : Silverius : Pope

The Mass is of the preceding Sunday, with a commemoration of the Pope.

June 21 : Aloysius Gonzaga : Confessor

Entrance Song

You have made him little less than the angels,
and crowned him with glory and honor.   PSALM 8

Praise the Lord, all you his angels,
praise him, all you his hosts.   TURN TO PSALM 148

Glory be to the Father.

First Reading
SIRACH 31:8–11

Songs of Meditation and Response

O Lord, you are my trust from my youth;
I have been strengthened by you from birth;
from my mother's womb you are my protector.   PSALM 70

But because of my innocence you sustain me
and you establish me in your sight forever.   PSALM 40

Alleluia, alleluia.
Happy the man you choose and take to yourself.
He shall dwell in your courts. Alleluia.   PSALM 64

Gospel
MATTHEW 22:29–40

222

Song at the Preparation of the Gifts

Who can ascend the mountain of the Lord?
or who may stand in his holy place?
He whose hands are sinless, whose heart is clean.

TURN TO PSALM 23

Communion Song

He gave them the bread of heaven;
man ate the bread of angels. TURN TO PSALM 77

June 22 : Paulinus : Bishop

Entrance Song

May your priests, O Lord, be clothed with justice;
let your faithful ones shout merrily for joy.
For the sake of David your servant,
reject not the plea of your anointed.

Remember, O Lord, David
and all his meekness. TURN TO PSALM 131

Glory be to the Father.

First Reading
2 CORINTHIANS 8:9–15

Songs of Meditation and Response

Behold a great priest, who in his days pleased God.
There was not found the like to him,
who kept the law of the Most High. SIRACH 44:16, 20

Alleluia, alleluia.
You are a priest forever,
according to the order of Melchisedec. Alleluia.

PSALM 109

Gospel
LUKE 12:32–34

Song at the Preparation of the Gifts

I have found David, my servant;
with my holy oil I have anointed him,
that my hand may be always with him,
and that my arm may make him strong.

TURN TO PSALM 88

223

The faithful and prudent servant
whom the master will set over his household
to give them their ration of grain in due time.

LUKE 12:42   TURN TO PSALM 109

June 23 : Vigil of John the Baptist

Entrance Song

Do not be afraid, Zachary,
your petition has been heard,
and your wife Elizabeth shall bear you a son,
and you shall call his name John;
and he shall be great before the Lord,
and shall be filled with the Holy Spirit
even from his mother's womb;
and many will rejoice at his birth.   LUKE 1:13-15

O Lord, in your strength the king is glad;
in your salvation how greatly he rejoices!

Glory be to the Father.   TURN TO PSALM 20

First Reading
JEREMIAH 1:4-10

Song of Meditation

There was a man, one sent from God,
whose name was John.
This man came to bear witness concerning the light,
to prepare for the Lord a perfect people.   JOHN 1:6-7

Gospel
LUKE 1:5-17

Song at the Preparation of the Gifts

You crowned him with glory and honor.
You have given him rule over the works of your hands, O Lord.

TURN TO PSALM 8

Communion Song

Great is his glory in your salvation;
majesty and splendor you conferred upon him, O Lord.

TURN TO PSALM 20

June 24 : Birthday of John the Baptist

Entrance Song

From my mother's womb the Lord called me by my name,
and made my mouth a sharp-edged sword;
he concealed me in the shadow of his hand,
and made me a chosen arrow. ISAIAH 49:1, 2

> It is good to give thanks to the Lord,
> to sing praise to your name, Most High.
> Glory be to the Father. TURN TO PSALM 91

Lord Have Mercy   Glory to God   Prayer

THE LITURGY OF THE WORD

First Reading
ISAIAH 49:1–3, 6–7

Songs of Meditation and Response

Before I formed you in the womb, I knew you,
and before you were born, I dedicated you.
The Lord extended his hand,
and touched my mouth, and said to me. JEREMIAH 1:5, 9
Alleluia, alleluia.
You, child, shall be called the prophet of the Most High;
you shall go before the Lord to prepare his ways. Alleluia.

LUKE 1:76

Gospel
LUKE 1:57–68

Homily   Creed   Prayer of the Faithful

THE LITURGY OF THE EUCHARIST

Song at the Preparation of the Gifts

The just man shall flourish like the palm tree;
like a cedar of Lebanon shall he grow. TURN TO PSALM 91

Prayer over the Gifts

Communion Song

You, child, shall be called the prophet of the Most High;
for you shall go before the face of the Lord to prepare his ways.

LUKE 1:76 TURN TO PSALM 95

Prayer after Communion

June 25 : William : Abbot

For today's Mass turn to page 327.

June 26 : John and Paul : Martyrs

Entrance Song

Many are the troubles of the just;
but out of them all the Lord delivers them;
the Lord watches over all their bones;
not one of them shall be broken.

> I will bless the Lord at all times;
> his praise shall be ever in my mouth.   TURN TO PSALM 33
>
> Glory be to the Father.

First Reading

SIRACH 44:10–15

Songs of Meditation and Response

Behold, how good it is and how pleasant,
where brethren dwell as one!
It is as when the precious ointment upon the head
runs down over the beard, the beard of Aaron.   PSALM 132

Alleluia, alleluia.
This is the true brotherhood,
which overcame the wickedness of the world;
it followed Christ, attaining the glorious kingdom of heaven.
Alleluia.

Gospel

LUKE 12:1–8

Song at the Preparation of the Gifts

All who love your name shall glory in you,
for you, O Lord, bless the just man;
O Lord, you surround us with the shield of your good will.

TURN TO PSALM 5

Communion Song

For if before men they were punished, God tried them;
as gold in the furnace he proved them,
and as sacrificial offerings he took them to himself.

WISDOM OF SOLOMON 3:4–6 TURN TO PSALM 125

June 28 : Vigil of Peter and Paul

Entrance Song

The Lord said to Peter,
"When you were young you girded yourself
and walked where you would.
But when you are old you will stretch forth your hands,
and another will gird you,
and lead you where you would not."
Now this he said to signify by what manner of death
he should glorify God.   JOHN 21:18–19

The heavens declare the glory of God,
and the firmament proclaims his handiwork.

Glory be to the Father.   TURN TO PSALM 18

First Reading

ACTS OF THE APOSTLES 3:1–10

Song of Meditation

Through all the earth their voice resounds,
and to the ends of the world, their message.
The heavens declare the glory of God,
and the firmament proclaims his handiwork.   PSALM 18

Gospel

JOHN 21:15–19

Song at the Preparation of the Gifts

To me, your friends, O God,
are made exceedingly honorable;
their principality is exceedingly strengthened.

TURN TO PSALM 138

Communion Song

Simon, son of John, do you love me more than these do?
Lord, you know all things;
you know, Lord, that I love you.

JOHN 21:15, 17   TURN TO PSALM 88

June 29 : The Holy Apostles, Peter and Paul

Entrance Song

Now I know for certain that the Lord has sent his angel
and rescued me from the power of Herod
and from all that the Jewish people were expecting.

ACTS OF THE APOSTLES 12:11

O Lord, you have probed me and you know me;
you know when I sit and when I stand.

Glory be to the Father.

TURN TO PSALM 138

Lord Have Mercy   Glory to God   Prayer

THE LITURGY OF THE WORD

First Reading

ACTS OF THE APOSTLES 12:1–11

Songs of Meditation and Response

You shall make them princes through all the land;
they shall remember your name, O Lord.
The place of your fathers your sons shall have;
they shall remember your name, O Lord.
The place of your fathers your sons shall have;
therefore shall nations praise you.

PSALM 44

Alleluia, alleluia.
You are Peter,
and upon this rock I will build my Church. Alleluia.

MATTHEW 16:18

Gospel

MATTHEW 16:13-19

Homily   Creed   Prayer of the Faithful

THE LITURGY OF THE EUCHARIST

Song at the Preparation of the Gifts

You shall make them princes through all the land;
they shall remember your name, O Lord, through all generations.

TURN TO PSALM 44

Prayer over the Gifts

EUCHARISTIC PRAYER
TURN TO PAGE 403

Communion Song

You are Peter,
and upon this rock I will build my Church.

MATTHEW 16:18   TURN TO PSALM 18

Prayer after Communion

June 30 : Paul : Apostle

Entrance Song

I know whom I have believed,
and I am certain that he is able to guard the trust
committed to me against that day;
being a just judge.   2 TIMOTHY 1:12

O Lord, you have probed me and you know me;
you know when I sit and when I stand.

Glory be to the Father.   TURN TO PSALM 138

First Reading

GALATIANS 1:11-20

He who worked in Peter for the apostleship,
worked also in me among the Gentiles,
and they recognized the grace of God, that was given to me.

GALATIANS 2:8–9

The grace of God in me has not been fruitless;
but his grace always remains in me.   I CORINTHIANS 15:10

Alleluia, alleluia.
Holy Apostle Paul,
preacher of truth and teacher of the Gentiles,
intercede for us. Alleluia.

Gospel

MATTHEW 10:16–22

Song at the Preparation of the Gifts

To me, your friends, O God,
are made exceedingly honorable;
their principality is exceedingly strengthened.

TURN TO PSALM 138

EUCHARISTIC PRAYER

TURN TO PAGE 403

Communion Song

Amen I say to you
that you who have left all things and followed me,
shall receive a hundredfold,
and shall possess life everlasting.

MATTHEW 19:28–29   TURN TO PSALM 114

July 1 : Precious Blood

Entrance Song

You have redeemed us, O Lord, with your blood,
out of every tribe and tongue and people and nation,
and have made us for our God a kingdom. REVELATION 5:9–10

The favors of the Lord I will sing forever;
through all generations
my mouth shall proclaim your faithfulness.
Glory be to the Father. TURN TO PSALM 88

Lord Have Mercy   Glory to God   Prayer

THE LITURGY OF THE WORD

First Reading
HEBREWS 9:11–15

Songs of Meditation and Response

This is he who came in water and in blood, Jesus Christ;
not in the water only, but in the water and in the blood.
There are three that bear witness in heaven:
the Father, the Word, and the Holy Spirit;
and these three are one.
And there are three that bear witness on earth:
the Spirit, the water, and the blood;
and these three are one.   I JOHN 5:6, 7–8
Alleluia, alleluia.
If we receive the testimony of men,
the testimony of God is greater. Alleluia.   I JOHN 5:9

Gospel
JOHN 19:30–35

Homily   Creed   Prayer of the Faithful

THE LITURGY OF THE EUCHARIST

Song at the Preparation of the Gifts

The cup of blessing that we bless,
is it not the sharing of the blood of Christ?
And the bread that we break,
is it not the partaking of the body of the Lord?
        I CORINTHIANS 10:16   TURN TO PSALM 21

Prayer over the Gifts

EUCHARISTIC PRAYER

TURN TO PAGE 394

Communion Song

Christ was offered once to take away the sins of many;
the second time he will appear with no part in sin
to those who wait for him unto salvation.

HEBREWS 9:28   TURN TO PSALM 21

Prayer after Communion

July 2 : The Visitation

Entrance Song

Hail, holy Mother, who gave birth to the King
who rules heaven and earth forever and ever.

My heart overflows with a goodly theme;
as I sing my ode to the king.   TURN TO PSALM 44

Glory be to the Father.

First Reading

SONG OF SOLOMON 2:8–14

Songs of Meditation and Response

Blessed and venerable are you, O Virgin Mary,
for without stain to your virginity,
you became the Mother of the Savior.
O Virgin, Mother of God,
he whom the whole world cannot contain,
being made man, shut himself up within your womb.

Alleluia, alleluia.
Happy are you, O holy Virgin Mary,
and most worthy of all praise;
for out of you has risen the sun of justice,
Christ our God. Alleluia.

Gospel

LUKE 1:39–47

Song at the Preparation of the Gifts

Blessed are you, O Virgin Mary,
who bore the Creator of all things;
you brought forth him who made you,
and you remain forever a virgin. TURN TO PSALM 131

EUCHARISTIC PRAYER
TURN TO PAGE 401

Communion Song

Blessed is the womb of the Virgin Mary,
which bore the Son of the eternal Father.

TURN TO PSALM 33

July 3 : Irenaeus : Bishop and Martyr

Entrance Song

The law of truth was in his mouth,
and iniquity was not found on his lips.
He walked with me in peace, and in equity,
and turned many away from evil. MALACHI 2:6
Hearken, my people, to my law;
incline your ears to the words of my mouth.
Glory be to the Father. TURN TO PSALM 77

First Reading

2 TIMOTHY 3:14–17; 4:1–5

Songs of Meditation and Response

Because of my relatives and friends
I will say, "Peace be within you!" PSALM 121

Keep innocence, and behold equity;
for there is a future for the man of peace. PSALM 36

Alleluia, alleluia.
Stand in the multitude of the prudent priests
and from your heart join yourself to their wisdom
that you may hear every discourse of God. Alleluia.

SIRACH 6:35

Gospel

MATTHEW 10:28–33

Song at the Preparation of the Gifts

I send my teachings forth to all shining like the dawn,
and I will make them known afar off.

SIRACH 24:44   TURN TO PSALM 124

Communion Song

See that I have not labored for myself only,
but for all who seek the truth.

SIRACH 24:47   TURN TO PSALM 121

July 5 : Anthony Maria Zaccaria : Confessor

Entrance Song

My speech and my preaching
were not in the persuasive words of human wisdom,
but in the demonstration of the Spirit and of the power.

I CORINTHIANS 2:4

I will give thanks to you, O Lord, with all my heart
in the company and assembly of the just.

TURN TO PSALM 110

Glory be to the Father.

First Reading

I TIMOTHY 4:8–16

Songs of Meditation and Response

God is my witness how I long for you all
in the heart of Christ Jesus.
And this I pray, that your charity may more and more abound
in knowledge and all discernment.
That you may approve the better things,
that you may be upright
and without offense unto the day of Christ.

Alleluia, alleluia.
Filled with the fruit of justice,
through Jesus Christ, to the glory and praise of God. Alleluia.

PHILIPPIANS I:8–11

Gospel

MARK 10:15-21

Song at the Preparation of the Gifts

In the presence of the angels I will sing your praise;
I will worship at your holy temple
and give thanks to your name. TURN TO PSALM 137

Communion Song

Brethren, be imitators of me,
and mark those who walk after the pattern you have in us.

PHILIPPIANS 3:17 TURN TO PSALM 137

July 7 : Cyril and Methodius : Bishops

Entrance Song

May your priests, O Lord, be clothed with justice;
let your faithful ones shout merrily for joy.
For the sake of David, your servant,
reject not the plea of your anointed.

Remember, O Lord, David
and all his meekness. TURN TO PSALM 131

Glory be to the Father.

First Reading

HEBREWS 7:23-27

Songs of Meditation and Response

Her priests I will clothe with salvation,
and her faithful ones shall shout merrily for joy.
In her will I make a horn to sprout forth for David;
I will place a lamp for my anointed. PSALM 131

Alleluia, alleluia.
The Lord has sworn, and he will not repent:
"You are a priest forever,
according to the order of Melchisedec." Alleluia. PSALM 109

Gospel

LUKE 10:1-9

235

Song at the Preparation of the Gifts

God is wonderful in his saints;
the God of Israel gives power and strength to his people.
Blessed be God! TURN TO PSALM 67

Communion Song

"What I tell you in darkness,
 speak it in the light," says the Lord,
"and what you hear whispered,
 preach it on the housetops."

MATTHEW 10:27 TURN TO PSALM 91

July 8 : Elizabeth : Holy Woman

For today's Mass turn to page 336.

July 10 : Seven Holy Brothers, Rufina and Secunda : Martyrs

Entrance Song

Praise the Lord, you children,
praise the name of the Lord.
He established in her home the barren wife
as the joyful mother of children.

Blessed be the name of the Lord
both now and forever. TURN TO PSALM 112
Glory be to the Father.

First Reading

PROVERBS 31:10–31

Songs of Meditation and Response

We were rescued like a bird
from the fowlers' snare.
Broken was the snare,
and we were freed.
Our help is in the name of the Lord,
who made heaven and earth. PSALM 123

Alleluia, alleluia.
This is the true brotherhood,
which overcame the wickedness of the world;
it followed Christ,
attaining the glorious kingdom of heaven. Alleluia.

Gospel
MATTHEW 12:46–50

Song at the Preparation of the Gifts

We were rescued like a bird
from the fowlers' snare;
broken was the snare,
and we were freed. TURN TO PSALM 123

Communion Song

"Whoever does the will of my Father in heaven,
he is my brother and sister and mother," says the Lord.
MATTHEW 12:50   TURN TO PSALM 32

July 11 : Pius I : Pope and Martyr
The Mass is of the preceding Sunday, with a commemoration of Pius.

July 12 : John Gualbert : Abbot
The Gospel is Matthew 5:43–48; for the rest of today's Mass turn to page 327.

July 14 : Bonaventure
Bishop and Doctor of the Church
The second part of the Songs of Meditation and Response, and the Song at the Preparation of the Gifts, are given below; for the rest of today's Mass turn to page 323.

Song of Response

Alleluia, alleluia.
The Lord has sworn, and he will not repent:
"You are a priest forever,
according to the order of Melchisedec." Alleluia.
PSALM 109

Song at the Preparation of the Gifts

My faithfulness and my kindness shall be with him,
and through my name shall his horn be exalted.

TURN TO PSALM 88

July 15 : Henry : Confessor

For today's Mass turn to page 325.

July 16 : Our Lady of Mount Carmel

The Mass is of the preceding Sunday, with a commemoration of Our Lady.

July 17 : Alexis : Confessor

The Mass is of the preceding Sunday, with a commemoration of Alexis.

July 18 : Camillus de Lellis : Confessor

Entrance Song

Greater love than this no one has,
that one lay down his life for his friends. JOHN 15:13

Happy is he who has regard for the lowly and the poor;
in the day of misfortune the Lord will deliver him.

Glory be to the Father. TURN TO PSALM 40

First Reading
I JOHN 3:13–18

Songs of Meditation and Response

The mouth of the just man tells of wisdom,
and his tongue utters what is right.
The law of his God is in his heart,
and his steps do not falter. PSALM 36

Alleluia, alleluia.
Happy the man who fears the Lord,
who greatly delights in his commands. Alleluia.

PSALM III

Gospel
JOHN 15:12–16

Song at the Preparation of the Gifts

O Lord, in your strength the just man is glad;
in your victory how greatly he rejoices!
You have granted him his heart's desire.

TURN TO PSALM 20

Communion Song

I was sick and you visited me.
Amen, amen, I say to you,
as long as you did it for one of these,
the least of my brethren,
you did it for me. MATTHEW 25:36, 40 TURN TO PSALM 40

July 19 : Vincent de Paul : Confessor

The Gospel is Luke 10:1–9; for the rest of today's Mass turn to page 326.

July 20 : Jerome Emilian : Confessor

Entrance Song

My gall is poured out on the ground
because of the downfall of the daughter of my people,
as child and infant faint away in the open spaces of town.

Praise the Lord, you servants, LAMENTATIONS 2:11
praise the name of the Lord. TURN TO PSALM 112
Glory be to the Father.

First Reading
ISAIAH 58:7–11

Songs of Meditation and Response

Let your water sources be dispersed abroad,
and in the streets divide your waters. PROVERBS 5:16
Well for the man who is gracious and lends,
who conducts his affairs with justice;
he shall never be moved. PSALM 111
Alleluia, alleluia.
Lavishly he gives to the poor;
his generosity shall endure forever. Alleluia. PSALM 111

Gospel

MATTHEW 19:13-21

Song at the Preparation of the Gifts

When you prayed with tears, and buried the dead,
and left your dinner,
and hid the dead by day in your house,
and buried them by night,
I offered your prayer to the Lord.

TOBIAS 12:12   TURN TO PSALM 68

Communion Song

Religion pure and undefiled before God the Father, is this:
to give aid to orphans and widows in their tribulation,
and to keep oneself unspotted from this world.

JAMES 1:27   TURN TO PSALM 33

July 21 : Lawrence of Brindisi
Doctor of the Church

For today's Mass turn to page 323.

July 22 : Mary Magdalene : Penitent

Entrance Song

Sinners wait to destroy me,
but I pay heed to your decrees, O Lord.
I see that all fulfillment has its limits;
broad indeed is your command.

Happy are they whose way is blameless,
who walk in the law of the Lord.   TURN TO PSALM 118
Glory be to the Father.

First Reading

SONG OF SOLOMON 3:2-5, 8:6-7

Songs of Meditation and Response

You love justice and hate iniquity.
Therefore God, your God, has anointed you
with the oil of gladness.

240

Alleluia, alleluia.
Grace is poured out upon your lips;
thus God has blessed you forever. Alleluia. PSALM 44

Gospel
LUKE 7:36–50

Song at the Preparation of the Gifts

The daughters of kings come in your honor;
the queen takes her place at your right hand
in gold and colored clothing. TURN TO PSALM 44

Communion Song

I have fulfilled just ordinances, O Lord;
let not the proud oppress me.
For in all your precepts I go forward;
every false way I hate. TURN TO PSALM 118

July 23 : Apollinaris : Bishop and Martyr

Entrance Song

Priests of the Lord, bless the Lord;
holy men of humble heart, praise God.

Bless the Lord, all you works of the Lord,
praise and exalt him above all forever.

DANIEL 3:84, 87 TURN TO PSALM 148

Glory be to the Father.

First Reading
I PETER 5:1–11

Songs of Meditation and Response

I have found David, my servant;
with my holy oil I have anointed him,
that my hand may be always with him,
and that my arm may make him strong.
No enemy shall have an advantage over him,
nor shall the son of iniquity have power to hurt him.

PSALM 88

Alleluia, alleluia.
The Lord has sworn, and he will not repent:
"You are a priest forever,
  according to the order of Melchisedec." Alleluia.

PSALM 109

Gospel
LUKE 22:24–30

Song at the Preparation of the Gifts

My faithfulness and my kindness shall be with him,
and through my name shall his horn be exalted.

TURN TO PSALM 88

Communion Song

"Master, you delivered to me five talents;
  behold I have gained other five over and above."
"Well done, good and faithful servant;
  because you have been faithful over a few things,
  I will set you over many; enter into the joy of your master."

MATTHEW 25:20–21   TURN TO PSALM 91

July 24 : Christina : Virgin and Martyr
The Mass is of the preceding Sunday, with a commemoration of the Martyr.

July 25 : James : Apostle

Entrance Song

To me, your friends, O God,
are made exceedingly honorable;
  their principality is exceedingly strengthened.

  O Lord, you have probed me and you know me;
  you know when I sit and when I stand.

  Glory be to the Father.   TURN TO PSALM 138

First Reading
I CORINTHIANS 4:9–15

You shall make them princes through all the land;
they shall remember your name, O Lord.
The place of your fathers your sons shall have;
therefore shall nations praise you.   PSALM 44

Alleluia, alleluia.
I have chosen you out of the world,
that you should go and bear fruit,
and that your fruit should remain. Alleluia.   JOHN 15:16

Gospel
MATTHEW 20:20–23

Song at the Preparation of the Gifts

Through all the earth their voice resounds,
and to the ends of the world, their message.

TURN TO PSALM 18

EUCHARISTIC PRAYER
TURN TO PAGE 403

Communion Song

You who have followed me shall sit on thrones,
judging the twelve tribes of Israel.

MATTHEW 19:28   TURN TO PSALM 78

July 26 : Anne : Grandmother of the Lord

Entrance Song

Let us all rejoice in the Lord,
celebrating a feast in honor of blessed Anne,
on whose solemnity the angels rejoice
and give praise to the Son of God.

> My heart overflows with a goodly theme,
> as I sing my ode to the king.   TURN TO PSALM 44

> Glory be to the Father.

First Reading
PROVERBS 31:10–31

Songs of Meditation and Response

You love justice and hate wickedness.
Therefore God, your God, has anointed you
with the oil of gladness.

Alleluia, alleluia.
Grace is poured out upon your lips;
thus God has blessed you forever. Alleluia.   PSALM 44

Gospel
MATTHEW 13:44–52

Song at the Preparation of the Gifts

The daughters of kings come in your honor;
the queen takes her place at your right hand
in gold and colored clothing.   TURN TO PSALM 44

Communion Song

Grace is poured out upon your lips;
thus God has blessed you forever and ever.
TURN TO PSALM 44

July 27 : Pantaleon : Martyr

The Mass is of the preceding Sunday, with a commemoration of the Martyr

July 28 : Nazarius, Celsus, Victor and Innocent : Martyrs

The First Reading is Wisdom of Solomon 10:17–20; for the rest of today's Mass turn to page 315.

July 29 : Martha : Virgin

The Gospel is Luke 10:38–42; for the rest of today's Mass turn to page 332.

July 30 : Abdon and Sennen : Martyrs

The Mass is of the preceding Sunday, with a commemoration of the Martyrs.

July 31 : Ignatius of Loyola : Confessor

Entrance Song

At the name of Jesus every knee should bend
of those in heaven, on earth and under the earth,
and every tongue should confess
that the Lord Jesus Christ is in the glory of God the Father.

PHILIPPIANS 2:10-11

All who love your name shall glory in you,
for you bless the just man.   TURN TO PSALM 5

Glory be to the Father.

First Reading

2 TIMOTHY 2:8-10; 3:10-12

Songs of Meditation and Response

The just man shall flourish like the palm tree;
like a cedar of Lebanon shall he grow in the house of the Lord.
To proclaim your kindness at dawn
and your faithfulness throughout the night.   PSALM 91

Alleluia, alleluia.
Blessed is the man who endures temptation;
for when he has been tried,
he will receive the crown of life. Alleluia.   JAMES 1:12

Gospel

LUKE 10:1-9

Song at the Preparation of the Gifts

My faithfulness and my kindness shall be with him,
and through my name shall his horn be exalted.

TURN TO PSALM 88

Communion Song

I have come to cast fire upon the earth,
and what will I but that it be kindled?

LUKE 12:49   TURN TO PSALM 111

August 1 : The Maccabees : Martyrs

The Mass is of the preceding Sunday, with a commemoration of the Martyrs.

August 2 : Alphonsus de Liguori : Bishop
and Doctor of the Church

Entrance Song

The Spirit of the Lord is upon me,
because he has anointed me;
to bring good news to the poor he has sent me,
to heal the contrite of heart. LUKE 4:18

Hearken, my people, to my teaching;
incline your ears to the words of my mouth.

Glory be to the Father. TURN TO PSALM 77

First Reading

2 TIMOTHY 2:1–7

Songs of Meditation and Response

I remember your ordinances of old, O Lord,
and I am comforted.
Indignation seizes me
because of the wicked who forsake your law. PSALM 118

Your justice I kept not hid within my heart;
your faithfulness and your salvation I have spoken of.

PSALM 39

Alleluia, alleluia.
He was directed by God to the repentance of the nation,
and he took away the abominations of wickedness,
he turned to God with his whole heart,
and though times were evil, he practiced virtue. Alleluia.

SIRACH 49:3–4

Gospel

LUKE 10:1–9

Song at the Preparation of the Gifts

Honor the Lord with your wealth,
and give him the first fruits of all your produce.
Do not withhold him from doing good who is able;
if you are able, do good yourself also.

PROVERBS 3:9, 27 TURN TO PSALM 132

246

Communion Song

A great priest, who in his time renovated the house,
and in his days reinforced the temple,
as a bright fire,
and frankincense burning in the fire.

SIRACH 50:1, 9   TURN TO PSALM 18

August 4 : Dominic : Confessor

Entrance Song

The mouth of the just man tells of wisdom,
and his tongue utters what is right.
The law of his God is in his heart.

Be not vexed over evildoers,
nor jealous of those who do wrong. TURN TO PSALM 36
Glory be to the Father.

First Reading

2 TIMOTHY 4:1–8

Songs of Meditation and Response

The just man shall flourish like the palm tree,
like a cedar of Lebanon shall he grow in the house of the Lord.
To proclaim your kindness at dawn
and your faithfulness throughout the night.   PSALM 91
Alleluia, alleluia.
The just shall blossom like the lily
and flourish forever before the Lord. Alleluia.   HOSEA 14:6

Gospel

LUKE 12:35–40

Song at the Preparation of the Gifts

My faithfulness and my kindness shall be with him,
and through my name shall his horn be exalted.

TURN TO PSALM 88

Communion Song

The faithful and prudent servant
whom the master will set over his household
to give them their ration of grain in due time.

LUKE 12:42   TURN TO PSALM 132

247

August 5 : Dedication of the Church of St. Mary Major

For today's Mass turn to page 339.

August 6 : The Transfiguration

Entrance Song

Your lightning illumined the world;
the earth quivered and quaked.   PSALM 76

> How lovely is your dwelling place,
> O Lord of hosts!
> My soul yearns and pines
> for the courts of the Lord.   TURN TO PSALM 83
> Glory be to the Father.

Lord Have Mercy   Glory to God   Prayer

THE LITURGY OF THE WORD

First Reading
2 PETER 1:16–19

Songs of Meditation and Response

Fairer in beauty are you than the sons of men;
grace is poured out upon your lips.
My heart overflows with a goodly theme;
as I sing my ode to the king.   PSALM 44
Alleluia, alleluia.
He is the refulgence of eternal light,
the spotless mirror, and the image of his goodness. Alleluia.

WISDOM OF SOLOMON 7:26

Gospel
MATTHEW 17:1–9

Homily   Creed   Prayer of the Faithful

Song at the Preparation of the Gifts

Glory and wealth are in his house;
his generosity shall endure forever. Alleluia.

TURN TO PSALM 111

Prayer over the Gifts

EUCHARISTIC PRAYER
TURN TO PAGE 405

Communion Song

Tell the vision you have seen to no one,
till the Son of Man has risen from the dead.

MATTHEW 17:9 TURN TO PSALM 83

Prayer after Communion

August 7 : Cajetan : Confessor

The Gospel is Matthew 6:24–33; for the rest of today's Mass turn to page 325.

August 8 : John Mary Vianney : Confessor

For today's Mass turn to page 325.

August 9 : Vigil of Lawrence

Entrance Song

Lavishly he gives to the poor;
his generosity shall endure forever;
his horn shall be exalted in glory.

Happy the man who fears the Lord,
who greatly delights in his commands.

TURN TO PSALM 111

Glory be to the Father.

First Reading
SIRACH 51:1–8, 12

Song of Meditation

Lavishly he gives to the poor;
his generosity shall endure forever.
His posterity shall be mighty upon the earth;
the upright generation shall be blessed.   PSALM 111

Gospel
MATTHEW 6:24–27

Song at the Preparation of the Gifts

My prayer is pure,
and therefore I ask
that a place may be given to my voice in heaven;
for there is my judge,
and he who knows my conscience is on high.
Let my prayer ascend to the Lord.

JOB 16:20   TURN TO PSALM 85

Communion Song

He who wishes to come after me,
let him deny himself,
and take up his cross, and follow me.

MATTHEW 16:24   TURN TO PSALM 33

August 10 : Lawrence : Martyr

Entrance Song

Splendor and majesty go before him;
praise and grandeur are in his sanctuary.

Sing to the Lord a new song;
sing to the Lord, all you lands.   TURN TO PSALM 95
Glory be to the Father.

First Reading
2 CORINTHIANS 9:6–10

Songs of Meditation and Response

Though you test my heart, O Lord,
searching it in the night.
Though you try me with fire,
you shall find no malice in me.   PSALM 16

Alleluia, alleluia.
The Levite Lawrence performed a good work.
By the sign of the Cross, he gave sight to the blind. Alleluia.

Gospel
JOHN 12:24–26

Song at the Preparation of the Gifts

Splendor and majesty go before him;
praise and grandeur are in his sanctuary.

TURN TO PSALM 95

Communion Song

If anyone serve me, let him follow me;
and where I am there also shall my servant be.

JOHN 12:26 TURN TO PSALM 114

August 11 : Tibertius and Susanna : Martyrs

The Mass is of the preceding Sunday, with a commemoration of the Martyrs.

August 12 : Clare : Virgin

For today's Mass turn to page 332.

August 13 : Hippolytus and Cassian : Martyrs

The Mass is of the preceding Sunday, with a commemoration of the Martyrs.

August 14 : Vigil of the Assumption

The Song of Meditation is given below; the First Reading is Sirach 24:23–31; the Gospel is Luke 11:27–28; the Song at the Preparation of the Gifts is on page 343; for the rest of today's Mass turn to page 341.

Song of Meditation

Blessed and venerable are you, O Virgin Mary;
for without stain to your virginity
you became the Mother of the Savior.
O Virgin Mother of God,
he whom the whole world cannot contain,
being made man, shut himself up within your womb.

251

August 15 : The Assumption

Entrance Song

A great sign appeared in heaven:
a woman clothed with the sun,
and the moon was under her feet,
and upon her head a crown of twelve stars. REVELATION 12:1

> Sing to the Lord a new song,
> for he has done wondrous deeds. TURN TO PSALM 97
> Glory be to the Father.

Lord Have Mercy   Glory to God   Prayer

THE LITURGY OF THE WORD

First Reading
JUDITH 13:22, 23–25; 15:10

Songs of Meditation and Response

Hear, O daughter, and see;
turn your ear; for the king shall desire your beauty.
All glorious is the king's daughter as she enters;
her raiment is threaded with spun gold. PSALM 44

Alleluia, alleluia.
Mary has been taken up into heaven;
the choirs of the angels rejoice. Alleluia.

Gospel
LUKE 1:41–50

Homily   Creed   Prayer of the Faithful

THE LITURGY OF THE EUCHARIST

Song at the Preparation of the Gifts

I will put enmity between you and the woman,
between your seed and her seed.

GENESIS 3:15 TURN TO PSALM 44

Prayer over the Gifts

EUCHARISTIC PRAYER

TURN TO PAGE 401

Communion Song

All generations shall call me blessed;
because he who is mighty has done great things for me.

LUKE 1:48–49 TURN TO PSALM 117

Prayer after Communion

August 16 : Joachim : Grandfather of the Lord

Entrance Song

Lavishly he gives to the poor;
his generosity shall endure forever;
his horn shall be exalted in glory.

Happy the man who fears the Lord,
who greatly delights in his commands.

Glory be to the Father. TURN TO PSALM 111

First Reading

SIRACH 31:8–11

Songs of Meditation and Response

Lavishly he gives to the poor;
his generosity shall endure forever.
His posterity shall be mighty upon the earth;
the upright generation shall be blessed. PSALM 111

Alleluia, alleluia.
O Joachim, husband of Saint Anne,
father of the kind Virgin,
help your servants to save their souls. Alleluia.

Gospel

MATTHEW 1:1–16

Song at the Preparation of the Gifts

You crowned him with glory and honor.
You have given him rule over the works of your hand, O Lord.

TURN TO PSALM 8

Communion Song

The faithful and prudent servant
whom the master will set over his household
to give them their ration of grain in due time.

LUKE 12:42   TURN TO PSALM 43

August 17 : Hyacinth : Confessor

For today's Mass turn to page 325.

August 18 : Agapitus : Martyr

The Mass is of the preceding Sunday, with a commemoration of Agapitus.

August 19 : John Eudes : Confessor

For today's Mass turn to page 325.

August 20 : Bernard
Abbot and Doctor of the Church

The First Reading is Sirach 39:6–14; for the rest of today's Mass turn to page 323.

August 21 : Jane Frances de Chantal
Holy Woman

For today's Mass turn to page 336.

August 22 : The Immaculate Heart of Mary

Entrance Song

Let us draw near with confidence to the throne of grace,
that we may obtain mercy
and find grace to help in time of need.   HEBREWS 4:16

My heart overflows with a goodly theme;
as I sing my ode to the king.   TURN TO PSALM 44

Glory be to the Father.

First Reading

SIRACH 24:23–31

Songs of Meditation and Response

Let my heart rejoice in your salvation;
let me sing to the Lord, "He has been good to me."
Yes, I will sing to the name of the Lord, Most High. PSALM 12

They shall remember your name throughout all generations;
therefore shall nations praise you forever and ever. PSALM 44

Alleluia, alleluia.
My soul magnifies the Lord,
and my spirit rejoices in God my Savior. Alleluia.

LUKE 1:46–47

Gospel
JOHN 19:25–27

Song at the Preparation of the Gifts

My spirit rejoices in God my Savior;
because he who is mighty has done great things for me,
and holy is his name.   LUKE 1:47, 49   TURN TO PSALM 32

EUCHARISTIC PRAYER
TURN TO PAGE 401

Communion Song

Jesus said to his mother,
"Woman, behold your son."
Then he said to the disciple,
"Behold your mother."
And from that hour the disciple took her into his home.

JOHN 19:26–27   TURN TO PSALM 83

August 23 : Philip Benizi : Confessor
For today's Mass turn to page 326.

August 24 : Bartholomew : Apostle

Entrance Song

To me, your friends, O God,
are made exceedingly honorable;
their principality is exceedingly strengthened.

O Lord, you have probed me and you know me;
you know when I sit and when I stand.
Glory be to the Father. TURN TO PSALM 138

First Reading
I CORINTHIANS 12:27–31

Songs of Meditation and Response

You shall make them princes through all the land;
they shall remember your name, O Lord.
The place of your fathers your sons shall have;
therefore shall nations praise you. PSALM 44

Alleluia, alleluia.
The glorious choir of apostles
praises you, O Lord, Alleluia.

Gospel
LUKE 6:12–19

Song at the Preparation of the Gifts

To me, your friends, O God,
are made exceedingly honorable,
their principality is exceedingly strengthened.
TURN TO PSALM 138

EUCHARISTIC PRAYER
TURN TO PAGE 403

Communion Song
"You who have followed me shall sit on thrones
judging the twelve tribes of Israel," says the Lord.
MATTHEW 19:28 TURN TO PSALM 18

August 25 : Louis : Confessor

*The First Reading is Sirach 10:10–14; the Gospel is Luke 19:12–26; for the
rest of today's Mass turn to page 325.*

August 26 : Zephyrinus : Pope and Martyr

The Mass is of the preceding Sunday, with a commemoration of Zephyrinus.

August 27 : Joseph Calasanctius : Confessor

Entrance Song

Come, children, hear me;
I will teach you the fear of the Lord.

> I will bless the Lord at all times;
> his praise shall be ever in my mouth.   TURN TO PSALM 33

Glory be to the Father.

First Reading
WISDOM OF SOLOMON 10:10–14

Songs of Meditation and Response

The mouth of the just man tells of wisdom
and his tongue utters what is right.
The law of his God is in his heart,
and his steps do not falter.   PSALM 36

Alleluia, alleluia.
Blessed is the man who endures temptation;
for when he has been tried,
he will receive the crown of life. Alleluia.   JAMES 1:12

Gospel
MATTHEW 18:1–5

Song at the Preparation of the Gifts

The desire of the afflicted the Lord hears.
You pay heed to the strengthening of their hearts.

TURN TO PSALM 9

Communion Song

Let the little children come to me,
and do not hinder them,
for of such is the kingdom of God.

MARK 10:14   TURN TO PSALM 33

August 28 : Augustine : Bishop and Doctor of the Church

The second part of the Songs of Meditation and Response is printed below; for the rest of today's Mass turn to page 323.

Song of Meditation and Response

Alleluia, alleluia.
I have found David, my servant;
with my holy oil I have anointed him. Alleluia.

PSALM 88

August 29 : Beheading of John the Baptist

Entrance Song

I will speak of your decrees before kings
without being ashamed.
And I will delight in your commands,
which I love exceedingly.   PSALM 118

> It is good to give thanks to the Lord,
> to sing to your name, Most High.   TURN TO PSALM 91
>
> Glory be to the Father.

First Reading

JEREMIAH 1:17–19

Songs of Meditation and Response

The just man shall flourish like the palm tree,
like a cedar of Lebanon shall he grow
in the house of the Lord.
To proclaim your kindness at dawn
and your faithfulness throughout the night.   PSALM 91

Alleluia, alleluia.
The just shall blossom like the lily,
and flourish forever before the Lord. Alleluia.

HOSEA 14:6

Gospel

MARK 6:17–29

Song at the Preparation of the Gifts

O Lord, in your strength the just man is glad;
in your victory how greatly he rejoices!
You have granted him his heart's desire.

TURN TO PSALM 20

Communion Song

You placed on his head, O Lord,
a crown of precious stones. TURN TO PSALM 20

August 30 : Rose of Lima : Virgin

For today's Mass turn to page 332.

August 31 : Raymond Nonnatus : Confessor

For today's Mass turn to page 325.

September 1 : Giles : Abbot

The Mass is of the preceding Sunday, with a commemoration of Giles.

September 2 : Stephen : Confessor

The Gospel is Luke 19:12–26; for the rest of today's Mass turn to page 325.

September 3 : Pius X : Pope

Entrance Song

I have raised up the chosen one from the people;
with my holy oil I have anointed him,
that my hand may be always with him,
and that my arm may make him strong.

The favors of the Lord I will sing forever;
through all generations
my mouth shall proclaim your faithfulness. TURN TO PSALM 88

Glory be to the Father.

First Reading

I THESSALONIANS 2:2–8

Songs of Meditation and Response

I announced your justice in the vast assembly;
I did not restrain my lips as you, O Lord, know.
Your justice I kept not hid within my heart;
your faithfulness and your salvation I have spoken of.

PSALM 39

Alleluia, alleluia.
You spread the table before me;
you anoint my head with oil;
my cup overflows. Alleluia. PSALM 22

Gospel
JOHN 21:15-17

Song at the Preparation of the Gifts

Come, children, hear me;
I will teach you the fear of the Lord. TURN TO PSALM 33

Communion Song

My flesh is food indeed, and my blood is drink indeed.
He who eats my flesh and drinks my blood,
abides in me and I in him.

JOHN 6:56-57 TURN TO PSALM 22

September 5 : Lawrence Justinian : Bishop

For today's Mass turn to page 320.

September 8 : Birthday of Our Lady

Entrance Song

Hail, holy Mother, who gave birth to the King
who rules heaven and earth forever and ever.

My heart overflows with a goodly theme;
as I sing my ode to the king. TURN TO PSALM 44

Glory be to the Father.

First Reading
PROVERBS 8:22-35

Songs of Meditation and Response

Blessed and venerable are you, O Virgin Mary;
for without stain to your virginity
you became the Mother of the Savior.
O Virgin Mother of God,
he whom the whole world cannot contain, being made man
shut himself up within your womb.

Alleluia, alleluia.
You are happy, O Holy Virgin Mary,
and most worthy of all high praise;
for from you has risen the sun of justice,
Christ our God. Alleluia.

Gospel

MATTHEW 1:1–16

Song at the Preparation of the Gifts

Blessed are you, O Virgin Mary,
you who bore the Creator of all things;
you brought forth him who made you,
and you remain a Virgin forever. TURN TO PSALM 86

EUCHARISTIC PRAYER
TURN TO PAGE 401

Communion Song

Blessed is the womb of the Virgin Mary,
which bore the Son of the eternal Father.

TURN TO PSALM 88

September 9 : Peter Claver : Confessor

Entrance Song

The Lord has satisfied the longing soul:
those who sit in darkness and in the shadow of death,
bondsmen in want and in chains.

Let them give thanks to the Lord for his kindness
and his wondrous deeds to the children of men.

Glory be to the Father. TURN TO PSALM 106

First Reading
ISAIAH 58:6–10

Songs of Meditation and Response

He shall rescue the poor man from the powerful,
and the poor man when he has no one to help him.
He shall have pity for the poor and the needy,
and the lives of the poor he shall save.
From fraud and wickedness he shall redeem their lives,

and honorable shall be their name in his sight. PSALM 71
Alleluia, alleluia.
Rise, O Lord! O God, lift up your hand!
Forget not the afflicted.
On you the poor man depends,
of the fatherless you are the helper. Alleluia. PSALM 9

Gospel
LUKE 10:29–37

Song at the Preparation of the Gifts

I rescued the poor who cried out for help,
the orphans, and the unassisted;
the blessing of those in extremity came upon me,
and the heart of the widow I made joyful.
I was eyes to the blind, and feet to the lame;
I was a father to the needy.

JOB 29:12–13: 15–16 TURN TO PSALM 71

Communion Song

I myself will pasture my sheep;
I myself will give them rest, says the Lord God.
The lost I will seek out.
The strayed I will bring back,
the injured I will bind up, and the sick I will heal.

EZEKIEL 34:15–16 TURN TO PSALM 22

September 10 : Nicholas of Tolentine : Confessor
For today's Mass turn to page 326.

September 11 : Protus and Hyacinth : Martyrs
The Mass is of the preceding Sunday, with a commemoration of the Martyrs.

September 12 : Holy Name of Mary

*The Entrance Song is printed below; the First Reading is Sirach 24:23–31;
the Gospel is Luke 1:26–38; for the rest of today's Mass turn to page 339.*

Entrance Song

All the rich among the people seek your favor.
Behind her the virgins of her train are brought to the king.

Her neighbors are brought to you with gladness and joy.

My heart overflows with a goodly theme;
as I sing my ode to the king. TURN TO PSALM 44
Glory be to the Father.

September 14 : The Holy Cross

Entrance Song

But it behooves us to glory in the cross
of our Lord Jesus Christ;
in whom is our salvation, life, and resurrection;
by whom we are saved and delivered. GALATIANS 6:14

May God have pity on us and bless us;
may he let his face shine upon us;
and may he have pity on us. TURN TO PSALM 66
Glory be to the Father.

Lord Have Mercy   Glory to God   Prayer

THE LITURGY OF THE WORD

First Reading
PHILIPPIANS 2:5-11

Songs of Meditation and Response

Christ became obedient for us to death,
even to death on a cross.
Therefore God also has exalted him,
and has bestowed upon him the name that is above every name.
Alleluia, alleluia. PHILIPPIANS 2:8, 9
Sweet the wood, sweet the nails,
sweet the load that hangs on you!
You alone were worthy
to bear up the King and Lord of heaven. Alleluia.

Gospel
JOHN 12:31-36

263

Homily   Creed   Prayer of the Faithful

THE LITURGY OF THE EUCHARIST

Song at the Preparation of the Gifts

Protect your people, O Lord,
through the sign of the Holy Cross,
from the snares of their enemies,
that we may pay you a pleasing service,
and our sacrifice may be acceptable to you. Alleluia.

TURN TO PSALM 21

Prayer over the Gifts

EUCHARISTIC PRAYER
TURN TO PAGE 394

Communion Song

O our God, through the sign of the Cross,
deliver us from our enemies.   TURN TO PSALM 21

Prayer after Communion

September 15 : Seven Sorrows of Our Lady

Entrance Song

There were standing by the cross of Jesus his mother,
and his mother's sister, Mary of Cleophas,
and Salome, and Mary Magdalene.

"Woman, behold your son," said Jesus;
and to the disciple, "Behold your mother."

Glory be to the Father.   JOHN 19:25-27   TURN TO PSALM 21

First Reading

JUDITH 13:22-25

Songs of Meditation and Response

You are sorrowful and tearful, O Virgin Mary,
standing by the cross of the Lord Jesus,
your Son and Redeemer.
O Virgin Mother of God,

he whom the whole earth does not contain,
the author of life made man,
bears this torture of the cross.

Alleluia, alleluia.
Holy Mary, the Queen of heaven and Mistress of the world,
filled with sorrow, stood by the cross of Our Lord Jesus Christ.

> At the cross her station keeping,
>   Stood the mournful Mother weeping,
>   Close to Jesus to the last.
> Through her heart, his sorrow sharing,
>   All his bitter anguish bearing,
>   Now at length the sword had passed.
> Oh, how sad and sore distressed
>   Was that Mother highly blessed
>   Of the sole begotten One!
> Christ above in torment hangs,
>   She beneath beholds the pangs
>   Of her dying, glorious Son.
> Is there one who would not weep
>   'Whelmed in miseries so deep
>   Christ's dear Mother to behold?
> Can the human heart refrain
>   From partaking in her pain,
>   In that mother's pain untold?
> Bruised, derided, cursed, defiled,
>   She beheld her tender Child,
>   All with bloody scourges rent.
> For the sins of his own nation
>   Saw him hang in desolation
>   Till his spirit forth he sent.
> O sweet Mother! fount of love,
>   Touch my spirit from above,
>   Make my heart with yours accord.
> Make me feel as you have felt;
>   Make my soul to glow and melt
>   With the love of Christ, my Lord.
> Holy Mother, pierce me through,
>   In my heart each wound renew
>   Of my Savior crucified.

Let me share with you his pain,
　　Who for all our sins was slain,
　　Who for me in torments died.
Let me mingle tears with thee,
　　Mourning him who mourned for me,
　　All the days that I may live.
By the cross with you to stay,
　　There with you to weep and pray,
　　Is all I ask of you to give.
Virgin of all virgins blest!
　　Listen to my fond request:
　　Let me share your grief divine.
Let me, to my latest breath
　　In my body bear the death
　　Of that dying Son of yours.
Wounded with his every wound,
　　Steep my soul till it has swooned
　　In his very blood away.
Be to me, O Virgin, nigh,
　　Lest in flames I burn and die,
　　In his awful judgment day.
Christ, when you shall call me hence,
　　Be your Mother my defense,
　　Be your cross my victory.
While my body here decays,
　　May my soul your goodness praise,
　　Safe in heaven eternally.
　　Amen. Alleluia.

Gospel
JOHN 19:25–27

Song at the Preparation of the Gifts

Be mindful, O Virgin Mother of God,
when you stand in the sight of the Lord,
to speak good things for us,
and to turn away his wrath from us.

JEREMIAH 18:20　TURN TO PSALM 21

EUCHARISTIC PRAYER
TURN TO PAGE 401

Happy the heart of the Blessed Virgin Mary,
which, without dying, earned the palm of martyrdom
beneath the cross of our Lord. TURN TO PSALM 89

September 16 : Cornelius and Cyprian : Martyrs

For today's Mass turn to page 315.

September 17 : Stigmata of Francis

The Mass is of the preceding Sunday, with a commemoration of Francis.

September 18 : Joseph of Cupertino : Confessor

Entrance Song

The love of God is honorable wisdom
and they to whom she shall show herself, love her
by the sight and by the knowledge of her great works.

SIRACH 1:14–15

How lovely is your dwelling place, O Lord of hosts!
My soul yearns and pines for the courts of the Lord.

Glory be to the Father. TURN TO PSALM 83

First Reading

I CORINTHIANS 13:1–8

Songs of Meditation and Response

O Lord, you welcomed him with goodly blessings,
you placed on his head a crown of precious stones.
He asked life of you
and you gave him length of days forever and ever. PSALM 20

Alleluia, alleluia.
The eye of God looks favorably upon him;
he raises him free of the vile dust and lifts up his head. Alleluia

SIRACH 11:13

Gospel

MATTHEW 22:1–14

Song at the Preparation of the Gifts

But I, when they were ill, put on sackcloth.
I afflicted myself with fasting
and poured forth my prayers within my bosom.

TURN TO PSALM 34

Communion Song

I am afflicted and in pain;
let your saving help, O God, protect me.
I will praise the name of God in song,
and I will glorify him with thanksgiving. TURN TO PSALM 68

September 19 : Januarius and Companions
Martyrs

The Gospel is Matthew 24:3–13; for the rest of today's Mass turn to page 318.

September 20 : Eustace and Companions
Martyrs

The Mass is of the preceding Sunday, with a commemoration of the Martyrs.

September 21 : Matthew : Apostle

Entrance Song

The mouth of the just man tells of wisdom
and his tongue utters what is right.
The law of his God is in his heart.

Be not vexed over evildoers,
nor jealous of those who do wrong. TURN TO PSALM 36
Glory be to the Father.

First Reading

EZEKIEL 1:10–14

Songs of Meditation and Response

Happy the man who fears the Lord,
who greatly delights in his commands.
His posterity shall be mighty upon the earth;
the upright generation shall be blessed. PSALM 111

Alleluia, alleluia.
The glorious choir of Apostles
praises you, O Lord. Alleluia.

Gospel

MATTHEW 9:9–13

Song at the Preparation of the Gifts

O Lord, you placed on his head a crown of precious stones;
he asked life of you, and you gave it to him, alleluia.

TURN TO PSALM 20

EUCHARISTIC PRAYER

TURN TO PAGE 403

Communion Song

Great is his glory in your victory;
majesty and splendor you conferred upon him, O Lord.

TURN TO PSALM 20

September 22 : Thomas of Villanova : Bishop

For today's Mass turn to page 320.

September 23 : Linus : Pope and Martyr

For today's Mass turn to page 310.

September 24 : Our Lady of Ransom

The Mass is of the preceding Sunday, with a commemoration of Our Lady.

September 26 : North American Martyrs

Entrance Song

These are they who have come out of the great tribulation,
and have washed their robes
and made them white in the blood of the Lamb.   REVELATION 7:14

Praise the Lord, all you nations;
glorify him, all you peoples.   TURN TO PSALM 116
Glory be to the Father.

First Reading

2 CORINTHIANS 12:11–15

Songs of Meditation and Response

Our life was rescued like a bird from the fowlers' snare.
Broken was the snare, and we were freed.
Our help is in the name of the Lord,
who made heaven and earth. PSALM 123
Alleluia, alleluia.
As the sufferings of Christ abound in us,
so also through Christ does our comfort abound. Alleluia.

2 CORINTHIANS 1:5

Gospel

LUKE 6:17–23

Song at the Preparation of the Gifts

As gold in the furnace, the Lord proved them,
and as sacrificial offerings he took them to himself.

WISDOM OF SOLOMON 3:6 TURN TO PSALM 99

Communion Song

Christ will be glorified in my body,
whether through life or through death:
for to me to live is Christ and to die is gain.

PHILIPPIANS 1:20–21 TURN TO PSALM 18

September 27 : Cosmas and Damian : Martyrs

Entrance Song

At gatherings the wisdom of the saints is retold,
and the assembly sings their praises;
their name lives on and on. SIRACH 44:15, 14

Exult, you just, in the Lord;
praise from the upright is fitting. TURN TO PSALM 32
Glory be to the Father.

First Reading

WISDOM OF SOLOMON 5:16–20

Songs of Meditation and Response

When the just cry out, the Lord hears them,
and from all their distress he rescues them.
The Lord is close to the brokenhearted,
and those who are crushed in spirit he saves. PSALM 33

Alleluia, alleluia.
This is the true brotherhood
which overcame the wickedness of the world;
it followed Christ,
holding fast to the glorious heavenly kingdom. Alleluia.

Gospel
LUKE 6:17–23

Song at the Preparation of the Gifts

All who love your name shall glory in you,
for you, O Lord, bless the just man.
O Lord, you surround us with the shield of your good will.

TURN TO PSALM 5

Communion Song

They have given the corpses of your servants, O Lord,
as food to the birds of heaven,
the flesh of your faithful ones to the beasts of the earth.
With your great power free those doomed to death.

TURN TO PSALM 78

September 28 : Wenceslaus : Martyr

For today's Mass turn to page 313.

September 29
Holy Michael the Archangel

Entrance Song

Bless the Lord, all you his angels,
you mighty in strength, who do his bidding,
obeying his spoken word.

Bless the Lord, O my soul;
and, all my being, bless his holy name. TURN TO PSALM 102
Glory be to the Father.

Lord Have Mercy   Glory to God   Prayer

THE LITURGY OF THE WORD

First Reading
REVELATION 1:1–5

Songs of Meditation and Response

Bless the Lord, all you his angels,
you mighty in strength, who do his bidding.
Bless the Lord, O my soul;
and, all my being, bless his holy name.   PSALM 102
Alleluia, alleluia.
Saint Michael the Archangel, defend us in battle,
that we may not perish in the dreadful judgment. Alleluia.

Gospel
MATTHEW 18:1–10

Homily   Creed   Prayer of the Faithful

THE LITURGY OF THE EUCHARIST

Song at the Preparation of the Gifts

An Angel stood before the altar of the temple,
having a golden censer in his hand,
and there was given to him much incense;
and the smoke of the spices ascended before God. Alleluia.

REVELATION 8:3, 4 TURN TO PSALM 137

Prayer over the Gifts .

EUCHARISTIC PRAYER
TURN TO PAGE 405

Communion Song

All you angels of the Lord, bless the Lord,
sing a hymn, and exalt him above all forever.

DANIEL 3:58   TURN TO PSALM 102

Prayer after Communion

September 30 : Jerome : Doctor of the Church

For today's Mass turn to page 323.

October 1 : Remegius : Bishop

The Mass is of the preceding Sunday, with a commemoration of Remegius.

October 2 : Guardian Angels

Entrance Song

Bless the Lord, all you his angels,
you mighty in strength, who do his bidding,
obeying his spoken word.

Bless the Lord, O my soul;
and, all my being, bless his holy name.

Glory be to the Father.   TURN TO PSALM 102

First Reading

EXODUS 23:20–23

Songs of Meditation and Response

To his angels God has given command about you,
they guard you in all your ways.
Upon their hands they shall bear you up,
lest you dash your foot against a stone.   PSALM 90

Alleluia, alleluia.
Bless the Lord, all you his hosts,
his ministers, who do his will. Alleluia.   PSALM 102

Gospel

MATTHEW 18:1–10

Bless the Lord, all you his angels,
his ministers, who do his will,
obeying his spoken word.   TURN TO PSALM 102

Communion Song

All you angels of the Lord, bless the Lord,
sing a hymn, and exalt him above all forever.
DANIEL 3:58 TURN TO PSALM 148

October 3 : Theresa of the Child Jesus : Virgin

Entrance Song

Come from Lebanon, my bride,
come from Lebanon, come!
You have ravished my heart, my sister, my bride;
you have ravished my heart.   SONG OF SOLOMON 4:8–9

Praise the Lord, you children,
praise the name of the Lord.   TURN TO PSALM 112

Glory be to the Father.

First Reading
ISAIAH 66:12–14

Songs of Meditation and Response

I praise you, Father, Lord of heaven and earth,
that you did hide these things from the wise and prudent,
and did reveal them to little ones.   MATTHEW 11:25

You are my trust, O Lord, from my youth.   PSALM 70

Alleluia, alleluia.
Open up your petals, like roses planted near running waters;
send up a sweet odor like Lebanon.
Break forth in blossoms like the lily, and yield a smell.
And bring forth leaves in grace.
And praise with canticles
and bless the Lord in his works. Alleluia.   SIRACH 39:17–19

Gospel
MATTHEW 18:1–4

Song at the Preparation of the Gifts

My soul magnifies the Lord,
and my spirit rejoices in God my savior;
because he has regarded the lowliness of his handmaid.
He who is mighty has done great things for me.

LUKE 1:46–49   TURN TO PSALM 130

Communion Song

He led her about and taught her,
and he guarded her as the apple of his eye.
As an eagle he spread his wings to receive her
and bore her up on his pinions.
The Lord alone was her leader.

DEUTERONOMY 32:10–12   TURN TO PSALM 90

October 4 : Francis of Assisi : Confessor

Entrance Song

But as for me,
God forbid that I should glory,
save in the cross of our Lord Jesus Christ,
through whom the world is crucified to me,
and I to the world.

GALATIANS 6:14

With a loud voice I cry out to the Lord;
with a loud voice I beseech the Lord. TURN TO PSALM 141

Glory be to the Father.

First Reading
GALATIANS 6:14–18

Songs of Meditation and Response

The mouth of the just man tells of wisdom,
and his tongue utters what is right.
The law of his God is in his heart,
and his steps do not falter.

PSALM 36

Alleluia, alleluia.
Francis, poor and humble, enters heaven a rich man,
and he is welcomed with celestial hymns. Alleluia.

Gospel

MATTHEW 11:25-30

Song at the Preparation of the Gifts

My faithfulness and my kindness shall be with him,
and through my name shall his horn be exalted.

TURN TO PSALM 88

Communion Song

The faithful and prudent servant
whom the master will set over his household
to give them their ration of grain in due time.

LUKE 12:42   TURN TO PSALM 30

October 5 : Placid and Companions : Martyrs

The Mass is of the preceding Sunday, with a commemoration of the Martyrs.

October 6 : Bruno : Confessor

For today's Mass turn to page 325.

October 7 : Our Lady of the Rosary

Entrance Song

Let us all rejoice with the Lord,
keeping a feast-day in honor of the Blessed Virgin Mary,
on whose solemnity the angels rejoice
and unite in praising the Son of God.

My heart overflows with a goodly theme;
as I sing my ode to the king. TURN TO PSALM 44

Glory be to the Father.

First Reading

PROVERBS 8:22–24, 32–35

Songs of Meditation and Response

Because of truth and meekness and justice;
and may your right hand show you wondrous deeds.
Hear, O daughter, and see; turn your ear;
for the king shall desire your beauty. PSALM 44

Alleluia, alleluia.

The solemnity of the glorious Virgin Mary,
of the seed of Abraham,
sprung from the tribe of Juda,
of the royal line of David. Alleluia.

Gospel
LUKE 1:26–38

Song at the Preparation of the Gifts

In me is all grace of the way and of the truth,
in me is all hope of life and of virtue.
Like a rose planted near running waters I have budded forth.

SIRACH 24:25; 39:17 TURN TO PSALM 135

EUCHARISTIC PRAYER
TURN TO PAGE 401

Communion Song

Break forth in blossoms like the lily, and yield a smell.
And bring forth leaves in grace.
And praise with canticles and bless the Lord in his works.

SIRACH 39:19 TURN TO PSALM 135

October 8 : Bridget : Holy Woman

The First Reading is 1 Timothy 5:3–10; for the rest of today's Mass turn to page 336.

October 9 : John Leonard : Confessor

Entrance Song

At the Lord's word were his works brought into being.
As the rising sun is clear to all,
so the glory of the Lord shines upon all his works.

Sing to the Lord a new song; SIRACH 42:15–16
sing to the Lord, all you lands. TURN TO PSALM 95
Glory be to the Father.

First Reading
2 CORINTHIANS 4:1–6, 15–18

My heart was embittered and my soul was pierced.
Zeal for your house consumed me.   PSALMS 72 AND 68

He made my mouth a sharp-edged sword
and concealed me in the shadow of his arm.
He made me a polished arrow.   ISAIAH 49:2

Alleluia, alleluia.
A portent am I to many,
but you are my strong refuge! Alleluia.   PSALM 70

Gospel
LUKE 10:1–9

Song at the Preparation of the Gifts

I have become a minister of Christ
in virtue of the office that God has given me,
for I am to fulfill the word of God.

COLOSSIANS 1:25   TURN TO PSALM 132

Communion Song

The things that were gain to me,
these, for the sake of Christ, I have counted loss.

PHILIPPIANS 3:7   TURN TO PSALM 18

October 10 : Francis Borgia : Confessor
For today's Mass turn to page 327.

October 11 : Motherhood of Our Lady

Entrance Song

Behold, the virgin shall be with child and bear a son,
and shall name him Emmanuel.   ISAIAH 7:14

Sing to the Lord a new song,
for he has done wondrous deeds.   TURN TO PSALM 97

Glory be to the Father.

First Reading
SIRACH 24:23–31

Songs of Meditation and Response

A shoot shall sprout from the stump of Jesse,
and from his roots a bud shall blossom.
And the Spirit of the Lord shall rest upon him.   ISAIAH 11:1-2

Alleluia, alleluia.
O Virgin, Mother of God,
he whom the whole world cannot contain,
being made man, shut himself up within your womb. Alleluia.

Gospel

LUKE 2:43-51

Song at the Preparation of the Gifts

When Mary his mother had been betrothed to Joseph,
she was found to be with child by the Holy Spirit.

MATTHEW 1:18   TURN TO PSALM 2

EUCHARISTIC PRAYER

TURN TO PAGE 401

Communion Song

Blessed is the womb of the Virgin Mary,
which bore the Son of the eternal Father.

TURN TO PSALM 97

October 13 : Edward : Confessor

For today's Mass turn to page 325.

October 14 : Callistus : Pope and Martyr

For today's Mass turn to page 310.

October 15 : Theresa of Avila : Virgin

For today's Mass turn to page 332.

October 16 : Hedwig : Holy Woman

For today's Mass turn to page 336.

October 17 : Margaret Mary Alacoque : Virgin

Entrance Song

I delight to rest in his shadow,
and his fruit is sweet to my mouth.   SONG OF SOLOMON 2:3

How lovely is your dwelling place,
O Lord of hosts!
My soul yearns and pines
for the courts of the Lord. TURN TO PSALM 83
Glory be to the Father.

First Reading
EPHESIANS 3:8–9, 14–19

Songs of Meditation and Response

Deep waters cannot quench love,
nor floods sweep it away. SONG OF SOLOMON 8:7
My flesh and my heart waste away;
God is the God of my heart and my portion forever.
Alleluia, alleluia. PSALM 72
I belong to my lover
and for me he yearns. Alleluia. SONG OF SOLOMON 7:10

Gospel
MATTHEW 11:25–30

Song at the Preparation of the Gifts

What wealth is his, and what beauty!
grain that makes the chosen ones flourish,
and new wine, the maidens!
ZECHARIAH 9:17 TURN TO PSALM 32

Communion Song

I belong to my lover and my lover to me;
he browses among the lilies.
SONG OF SOLOMON 6:2 TURN TO PSALM 30

October 18 : Luke : Evangelist

Entrance Song

To me, your friends, O God,
are made exceedingly honorable;
their principality is exceedingly strengthened.

O Lord, you have probed me and you know me;
you know when I sit and when I stand.

Glory be to the Father. TURN TO PSALM 138

First Reading

2 CORINTHIANS 8:16–24

Songs of Meditation and Response

Through all the earth their voice resounds,
and to the ends of the world, their message.
The heavens declare the glory of God,
and the firmament proclaims his handiwork.   PSALM 18
Alleluia, alleluia.
I have chosen you out of the world,
that you should go and bear fruit,
and that your fruit should remain. Alleluia.   JOHN 15:16

Gospel

LUKE 10:1–9

Song at the Preparation of the Gifts

To me, your friends, O God,
are made exceedingly honorable;
their principality is exceedingly strengthened.

TURN TO PSALM 138

EUCHARISTIC PRAYER
TURN TO PAGE 403

Communion Song

You who have followed me shall sit upon thrones,
judging the twelve tribes of Israel.

MATTHEW 19:28   TURN TO PSALM 18

October 19 : Peter of Alcantara : Confessor

The First Reading is Philippians 3:7–12; for the rest of today's Mass turn to page 326.

October 20 : John Cantius : Confessor

Entrance Song

Man may be merciful to his fellow man,
but God's mercy reaches all flesh.
He has mercy, teaches and guides,
as a shepherd does his flock.   SIRACH 18:12–13

Happy the man who follows not the counsel of the wicked
nor sits in the company of the insolent. TURN TO PSALM I
Glory be to the Father.

First Reading
JAMES 2:12–17

Songs of Meditation and Response

Let them give thanks to the Lord for his kindness
and his wondrous deeds to the children of men.
Because he satisfied the longing soul
and filled the hungry soul with good things.   PSALM 106

Alleluia, alleluia.
He extends his arms to the needy,
and reaches out his hands to the poor. Alleluia.

PROVERBS 31:20

Gospel
LUKE 12:35–40

Song at the Preparation of the Gifts

I wore my honesty like a garment;
justice was my robe and my turban.
I was eyes to the blind, and feet to the lame was I;
I was a father to the needy.

JOB 29:14–16 TURN TO PSALM 118

Communion Song

Give, and it shall be given to you;
good measure, pressed down, shaken together, running over,
shall they pour into your lap.   LUKE 6:38 TURN TO PSALM 33

October 21 : Hilarion : Abbot
The Mass is of the preceding Sunday, with a commemoration of Hilarion.

October 23 : Anthony Mary Claret : Bishop
For today's Mass turn to page 322.

October 24 : Raphael : Archangel

*The Songs of Meditation and Response are printed below; the First Reading is
Tobias 12:7–15; the Gospel is John 5:1–4; for the rest of today's Mass turn
to page 271.*

Songs of Meditation and Response

The angel of the Lord, Raphael,
took and bound the devil. TOBIAS 8:3
Great is our Lord and mighty in power. PSALM 146
Alleluia, alleluia.
In the presence of the angels I will sing your praise;
I will worship at your holy temple
and give thanks to your name, O Lord. Alleluia. PSALM 137

October 25 : Isidore the Farmer : Confessor

*The First Reading is James 5:7–9, 11, 16–18; the Gospel is John 15:1–7;
for the rest of today's Mass turn to page 326.*

October 26 : Evaristus : Pope and Martyr

The Mass is of the preceding Sunday, with a commemoration of Evaristus.

October 28 : Simon and Jude : Apostles

*The second part of the Songs of Meditation and Response is printed below;
the First Reading is Ephesians 4:7–13; the Gospel is John 15:17–25; for the
rest of today's Mass turn to page 242.*

Song of Response

Alleluia, alleluia.
Your friends, O God, are made exceedingly honorable;
their principality is exceedingly strengthened. Alleluia.

PSALM 138

Last Sunday in October

Christ the King

Entrance Song

Worthy is the Lamb who was slain to receive power,
and divinity, and wisdom, and strength, and honor.
To him belong glory and dominion forever and ever.

REVELATION 5:12; 1:6

O God, with your judgment endow the king,
and with your justice, the king's son. TURN TO PSALM 71
Glory be to the Father.

Lord Have Mercy   Glory to God   Prayer

THE LITURGY OF THE WORD

First Reading
COLOSSIANS 1:12–20

Songs of Meditation and Response

He shall rule from sea to sea,
and from the River to the ends of the earth.
All kings shall pay him homage,
all nations shall serve him. PSALM 71

Alleluia, alleluia.
His dominion is an everlasting dominion
that shall not be taken away,
and his kingdom shall not be destroyed. Alleluia. DANIEL 7:14

Gospel
JOHN 18:33–37

Homily   Creed   Prayer of the Faithful

THE LITURGY OF THE EUCHARIST

Song at the Preparation of the Gifts

Ask of me and I will give you the nations for an inheritance
and the ends of the earth for your possession. TURN TO PSALM 2

Prayer over the Gifts

EUCHARISTIC PRAYER
TURN TO PAGE 400

Communion Song

The Lord is enthroned as king forever;
may the Lord bless his people with peace! TURN TO PSALM 28

Prayer after Communion

November 1 : All Saints Day

Entrance Song

Let us all rejoice in the Lord,
celebrating a feast-day in honor of all the saints,
on whose solemnity the angels rejoice,
and join in praising the Son of God.

Exult, you just, in the Lord;
praise from the upright is fitting. TURN TO PSALM 32
Glory be to the Father.

Lord Have Mercy   Glory to God   Prayer

THE LITURGY OF THE WORD

First Reading
REVELATION 7:2–12

Songs of Meditation and Response

Fear the Lord, all you his holy ones,
for nought is lacking to those who fear him.
But those who seek the Lord
want for no good thing.   PSALM 33
Alleluia, alleluia.
Come to me, all you who labor and are burdened,
and I will give you rest. Alleluia.   MATTHEW 11:28

Gospel
MATTHEW 5:1–12

Homily   Creed   Prayer of the Faithful

THE LITURGY OF THE EUCHARIST

Song at the Preparation of the Gifts

The souls of the just are in the hand of God,
and no torment shall touch them.

They seemed, in view of the foolish, to be dead;
but they are in peace. Alleluia.

WISDOM OF SOLOMON 3:1–3 TURN TO PSALM 112

Prayer over the Gifts

EUCHARISTIC PRAYER

TURN TO PAGE 405

Communion Song

Blessed are the pure of heart,
for they shall see God.
Blessed are the peacemakers,
for they shall be called children of God.
Blessed are they who suffer persecution for justice' sake,
for theirs is the kingdom of heaven.

MATTHEW 5:8–10 TURN TO PSALM 111

Prayer after Communion

November 2 : All Souls

*The different Masses which may be celebrated on this day all have the same
Songs, but different First Readings and Gospels.*

Entrance Song

Eternal rest grant unto them, O Lord:
and let perpetual light shine upon them.   4 ESDRAS 2:34–35

> To you we owe our hymn of praise, O God, in Sion;
> to you must vows be fulfilled in Jerusalem.
> Hear my prayer;
> to you all flesh must come.   TURN TO PSALM 64

First Reading

I CORINTHIANS 15:51–57

2 MACCABEES 12:43–46

REVELATION 14:13

Songs of Meditation and Response

Eternal rest grant unto them, O Lord;
and let perpetual light shine upon them.   4 ESDRAS 2:34–35

The just man shall be in everlasting remembrance;
an evil report he shall not fear.   PSALM III

Absolve, O Lord, the souls of all the faithful departed
from every bond of sin.
And by the help of your grace
may they deserve to escape the judgment of vengeance.
And to enjoy the blessedness of light eternal.

Day of wrath! O day of mourning!
    See fulfilled the prophets' warning,
    Heav'n and earth in ashes burning!

O what fear man's bosom rendeth
    When from heav'n the judge descendeth,
    On whose sentence all dependeth!

Wondrous sound the trumpet flingeth;
    Through earth's sepulchers it ringeth;
    All before the throne it bringeth.

Death is struck, and nature quaking,
    All creation is awaking,
    To its judge an answer making.

Lo! the book, exactly worded,
    Wherein all hath been recorded:
    Thence shall judgment be awarded.

When the judge his seat attaineth
    And each hidden deed arraigneth,
    Nothing unavenged remaineth.

What shall I, frail man, be pleading?
    Who for me be interceding,
    When the just are mercy needing?

King of majesty tremendous,
    Who dost free salvation send us,
    Fount of pity, then befriend us!

Think, good Jesus, my salvation
    Cost thy wondrous incarnation;
    Leave me not to reprobation!

Faint and weary, thou hast sought me,
    On the cross of suff'ring bought me.
    Shall such grace be vainly brought me?

Righteous judge! for sin's pollution
   Grant thy gift of absolution,
   Ere the day of retribution.

Guilty, now I pour my moaning,
   All my shame with anguish owning;
   Spare, O God, thy suppliant groaning!

Thou the sinful woman savedst;
   Thou the dying thief forgavest;
   And to me a hope vouchsafest.

Worthless are my prayers and sighing,
   Yet, good Lord, in grace complying,
   Rescue me from fires undying!

With thy favored sheep O place me,
   Nor among the goats abase me,
   But to thy right hand upraise me.

While the wicked are confounded,
   Doomed to flames of woe unbounded,
   Call me with thy saints surrounded.

Low I kneel, with heart submission:
   See, like ashes, my contrition;
   Help me in my last condition.

Ah! that day of tears and mourning!
   From the dust of earth returning,
   Man for judgment must prepare him;
   Spare, O God, in mercy spare him!

Lord, all pitying, Jesus blest,
   Grant them thine eternal rest. Amen.

Gospel

JOHN 5:25–29
JOHN 6:37–40
JOHN 6:51–55

Song at the Preparation of the Gifts

Lord Jesus Christ, King of glory,
deliver the souls of all the faithful departed
from the pains of hell and the deep pit,
deliver them from the lion's mouth,
may hell not swallow them up,

nor may they fall into darkness,
but may Michael, the holy standardbearer,
bring them into the holy light:
Which you once promised to Abraham and to his seed.
We offer you, O Lord, sacrifices and prayers of praise;
receive them for the souls whom we remember this day.
Grant, O Lord, that they may pass from death to life.
Which you once promised to Abraham and to his seed.

EUCHARISTIC PRAYER

TURN TO PAGE 404

Communion Song

May light eternal shine upon them, O Lord,
With your saints forever, for you are merciful.
Eternal rest grant unto them, O Lord,
and let perpetual light shine upon them.
With your saints forever, for you are merciful.

4 ESDRAS 2:34–35 TURN TO PSALM 129

November 4 : Charles : Bishop

For today's Mass turn to page 320.

November 5 : Martin de Porres : Confessor

For today's Mass turn to page 326.

November 8 : Four Crowned Martyrs

The Mass is of the preceding Sunday, with a commemoration of the Martyrs.

November 9

The Anniversary of the Dedication of St. John Lateran, The Cathedral Church of Rome

Entrance Song

How awesome is this place!
This is none other than the house of God;
this is the gate of heaven;
and it shall be called the court of God.   GENESIS 28:17

How lovely is your dwelling place, O Lord of hosts!
My soul yearns and pines for the courts of the Lord.
Glory be to the Father.   TURN TO PSALM 83

Lord Have Mercy   Glory to God   Prayer

THE LITURGY OF THE WORD

First Reading
REVELATION 21:2–5

Songs of Meditation and Response

This place was made by God, a priceless mystery;
it is without reproof.
O God, before whom stands the choir of angels,
hear the prayers of your servants.

Alleluia, alleluia.
I will worship at your holy temple
and give thanks to your name. Alleluia.   PSALM 137

Gospel
LUKE 19:1–10

Homily   Creed   Prayer of the Faithful

THE LITURGY OF THE EUCHARIST

Song at the Preparation of the Gifts

O Lord God, in the simplicity of my heart
I have joyfully offered all these things;
and I have seen with great joy your people
which is here present:
O God of Israel, keep this will. Alleluia.

I CHRONICLES 29:17, 18   TURN TO PSALM 137

Prayer over the Gifts

EUCHARISTIC PRAYER
TURN TO PAGE 405

Communion Song

"My house shall be called a house of prayer," says the Lord;
"in it everyone who asks receives:
  and he who seeks finds,
  and to him who knocks, it shall be opened."

MATTHEW 21:13   TURN TO PSALM 83

Prayer after Communion

November 10 : Andrew Avellino : Confessor

For today's Mass turn to page 325.

November 11 : Martin : Bishop

Entrance Song

The Lord made a covenant of friendship with him,
and made him a prince,
that he should possess the dignity of the priesthood forever.

Remember, O Lord, David   WISDOM OF SOLOMON 45:30
and all his meekness.   TURN TO PSALM 131
Glory be to the Father.

First Reading
SIRACH 44:16–27, 45:3–20

Songs of Meditation and Response

Behold, a great priest, who in his days pleased God.
There was not found the like to him,
who kept the law of the Most High.   SIRACH 44:16, 20
Alleluia, alleluia.
The blessed man, Saint Martin, Bishop of Tours,
has gone to rest;
angels and archangels, thrones, dominations, and powers
have received him. Alleluia.

Gospel
LUKE 11:33–36

Song at the Preparation of the Gifts

My faithfulness and my kindness shall be with him,
and through my name shall his horn be exalted.

TURN TO PSALM 88

Communion Song

Blessed is that servant
whom his master, when he comes, shall find watching.
Amen I say to you,
he will set him over all his goods.

MATTHEW 24:46–47   TURN TO PSALM 33

November 12 : Martin I : Pope

For today's Mass turn to page 310.

November 13 : Frances Cabrini : Virgin

Entrance Song

You have hold of my right hand;
with your counsel you guide me,
and in the end you will receive me in glory.

How good God is to Israel,
to those who are clean of heart.   TURN TO PSALM 72
Glory be to the Father.

First Reading

I CORINTHIANS 1:26–31

Songs of Meditation and Response

The God who guided me with strength
and kept my way unerring.
Who made my feet swift as those of hinds
and set me on the heights.   PSALM 17
Alleluia, alleluia.
I became all things to all men,
that I might save all. Alleluia.   I CORINTHIANS 9:22

Gospel

MATTHEW 11:25–30

Song at the Preparation of the Gifts

But for me, to be near God is my good;
to make the Lord God my refuge.
I shall declare all your works
in the gates of the daughter of Sion.   TURN TO PSALM 72

Communion Song

Come to me, all you who labor and are burdened,
and I will give you rest.

MATTHEW 11:28   TURN TO PSALM 33

November 14 : Josaphat : Bishop and Martyr

Entrance Song

Let us all rejoice in the Lord,
celebrating a feast-day
in honor of the blessed martyr Josaphat,
at whose martyrdom the angels rejoice
and give praise to the Son of God.

> Exult, you just, in the Lord;
> praise from the upright is fitting.   TURN TO PSALM 32

Glory be to the Father.

First Reading

HEBREWS 5:1–6

Songs of Meditation and Response

I have found David, my servant,
with my holy oil I have anointed him,
that my hand may be always with him,
and that my arm may make him strong.
No enemy shall have an advantage over him,
nor shall the son of iniquity have power to hurt him.

Alleluia, alleluia.   PSALM 88
This is the priest whom the Lord has crowned. Alleluia.

Gospel

JOHN 10:11–16

Song at the Preparation of the Gifts

Greater love than this no one has,
that one lay down his life for his friends.

JOHN 15:13   TURN TO PSALM 91

Communion Song

I am the good shepherd,
and I know my sheep, and mine know me.

JOHN 10:14 TURN TO PSALM 22

November 15 : Albert the Great
Bishop and Doctor of the Church

For today's Mass turn to page 323.

November 16 : Gertrude : Virgin

For today's Mass turn to page 332.

November 17
Gregory the Wonderworker : Bishop

The Gospel is Mark 11:22–24; for the rest of today's Mass turn to page 320.

November 18
Dedication of the Basilicas of Peter and Paul

For today's Mass turn to page 289.

November 19 : Elizabeth : Holy Woman

For today's Mass turn to page 336.

November 20 : Felix of Valois : Confessor

For today's Mass turn to page 326.

November 21 : Presentation of Our Lady

For today's Mass turn to page 339.

November 22 : Cecilia : Virgin and Martyr

*The Songs of Meditation and Response are printed below; the First Reading is
Sirach 51:13–17; for the rest of today's Mass turn to page 329.*

Hear, O daughter, and see; turn your ear;
for the king shall desire your beauty.

In your splendor and your beauty
ride on triumphant, and reign.   PSALM 44

Alleluia, alleluia.
The five virgins took oil in their vessels with the lamps:
and at midnight a cry arose,
"Behold the bridegroom is coming,
    go forth to meet Christ the Lord." Alleulia.

                              MATTHEW 25:4, 6

November 23 : Clement : Pope and Martyr

Entrance Song

The Lord says,
"My words that I have put into your mouth,
shall never leave your mouth;
and your gifts shall be accepted upon my altar."

    Happy the man who fears the Lord,   ISAIAH 59:21: 56:7
    who greatly delights in his commands.

    Glory be to the Father.   TURN TO PSALM III

First Reading
PHILIPPIANS 3:17–21; 4:1–3

Songs of Meditation and Response

Let them extol him in the assembly of the people;
and praise him in the council of the elders.
Let them give thanks to the Lord for his kindness
and his wondrous deeds to the children of men.

Alleluia, alleluia.   PSALM 106
You are Peter,
and upon this rock I will build my Church. Alleluia.

                              MATTHEW 16:18

Gospel
MATTHEW 16:13–19

Song at the Preparation of the Gifts

See, I place my words in your mouth:
behold, I set you over nations and over kingdoms,
to root up and to tear down,
and to build and to plant.

JEREMIAH 1:9–10   TURN TO PSALM 103

Communion Song

You are Peter,
and upon this rock I will build my Church.

MATTHEW 16:18   TURN TO PSALM 18

November 24
John of the Cross : Doctor of the Church

For today's Mass turn to page 323.

November 25 : Catherine : Virgin and Martyr

For today's Mass turn to page 329.

November 26 : Sylvester : Abbot

For today's Mass turn to page 327.

November 29 : Saturninus : Martyr

For today's Mass turn to page 314.

November 30 : Andrew : Apostle

Entrance Song

To me, your friends, O God, are made exceedingly honorable;
their principality is exceedingly strengthened.

O Lord, you have probed me and you know me;
you know when I sit and when I stand.   TURN TO PSALM 138

Glory be to the Father.

First Reading

ROMANS 10:10–18

Songs of Meditation and Response

You shall make them princes through all the land;
they shall remember your name, O Lord.
The place of your fathers your sons shall have;
therefore shall nations praise you.   PSALM 44

Alleluia, alleluia.
The Lord loved Andrew in an odor of sweetness. Alleluia.

Gospel
MATTHEW 4:18–22

Song at the Preparation of the Gifts

To me, your friends, O God, are made exceedingly honorable;
their principality is exceedingly strengthened.

TURN TO PSALM 138

EUCHARISTIC PRAYER
TURN TO PAGE 403

Communion Song

"Come, follow me, and I will make you fishers of men."
And at once they left the nets, and followed the Lord.

MATTHEW 4:19–20   TURN TO PSALM 18

December 2 : Bibliana : Virgin and Martyr

For today's Mass turn to page 330.

December 3 : Francis Xavier : Confessor

Entrance Song

I will speak of your decrees before kings,
without being ashamed.
And I will delight in your commands,
which I love exceedingly.   PSALM 118

Praise the Lord, all you nations;
glorify him, all you people!
For steadfast is his kindness toward us,
and the fidelity of the Lord endures forever.   PSALM 116

Glory be to the Father.

First Reading

ROMANS 10:10–18

Songs of Meditation and Response

The just man shall flourish like the palm tree,
like a cedar of Lebanon shall he grow
in the house of the Lord.
To proclaim your kindness at dawn,
and your faithfulness throughout the night.   PSALM 91

Alleluia, alleluia.
Blessed is the man who endures temptation;
for when he has been tried,
he will receive the crown of life. Alleluia.   JAMES 1:12

Gospel

MARK 16:15–18

Song at the Preparation of the Gifts

My faithfulness and my kindness shall be with him,
and through my name shall his horn be exalted.

TURN TO PSALM 88

Communion Song

Blessed is that servant,
whom his master, when he comes, shall find watching.
Amen I say to you,
he will set him over all his goods.

MATTHEW 24:46–47   TURN TO PSALM 137

December 4 : Peter Chrysologus : Bishop and Doctor of the Church

The Songs of Meditation and Response and the Communion Song are printed below; for the rest of today's Mass turn to page 323.

Songs of Meditation and Response

Behold a great priest, who in his days pleased God.
There was not found the like to him,
who kept the law of the Most High.   SIRACH 44:16

Alleluia, alleluia.
You are a priest forever,
according to the order of Melchisedec. Alleluia.

PSALM 109

Communion Song

"Master, you delivered to me five talents:
behold I have gained other five over and above."
"Well done, good and faithful servant,
because you have been faithful over a few things,
I will set you over many;
enter into the joy of your master."

MATTHEW 25:20–21   TURN TO PSALM 118

December 5 : Sabbas : Abbot

The Mass is of the preceding Sunday, with a commemoration of Sabbas.

December 6 : Nicholas : Bishop

Entrance Song

The Lord made a covenant of friendship with him,
and made him a prince,
that he should possess the dignity of priesthood forever.

Remember, O Lord, David SIRACH 45:30
and all his meekness. TURN TO PSALM 131

Glory be to the Father.

First Reading
HEBREWS 13:7–17

Songs of Meditation and Response

I have found David, my servant;
with my holy oil I have anointed him,
that my hand may be always with him,
and that my arm may make him strong.
No enemy shall have an advantage over him,
nor shall the son of iniquity have power to hurt him.

Alleluia, alleluia. PSALM 88
The just man shall flourish like the palm tree,
like a cedar of Lebanon shall he grow. Alleluia. PSALM 91

Gospel

MATTHEW 25:14–23

Song at the Preparation of the Gifts

My faithfulness and my kindness shall be with him,
and through my name shall his horn be exalted.

TURN TO PSALM 88

Communion Song

Once, by my holiness, have I sworn;
his posterity shall continue forever,
and his throne shall be like the sun before me;
like the moon, which remains forever—
a faithful witness in the sky.

TURN TO PSALM 88

December 7 : Ambrose
Bishop and Doctor of the Church

Entrance Song

In the midst of the assembly he opened his mouth;
and the Lord filled him
with the spirit of wisdom and understanding;
he clothed him with a robe of glory.   SIRACH 15:5

It is good to give thanks to the Lord,
to sing praise to your name, Most High.

Glory be to the Father.   TURN TO PSALM 91

First Reading

2 TIMOTHY 4:1–8

Songs of Meditation and Response

Behold a great priest, who in his days pleased God.
There was not found the like to him,
who kept the law of the Most High.   SIRACH 44:16, 20

Alleluia, alleluia.
The Lord has sworn, and he will not repent:
"You are a priest forever,
according to the order of Melchisedec." Alleluia.

PSALM 109

300

Song at the Preparation of the Gifts

My faithfulness and my kindness shall be with him,
and through my name shall his horn be exalted.

TURN TO PSALM 88

Communion Song

Once, by my holiness, have I sworn;
his posterity shall continue forever,
and his throne shall be like the sun before me;
like the moon, which remains forever—
a faithful witness in the sky.

TURN TO PSALM 88

December 8
The Immaculate Conception

Entrance Song

I will heartily rejoice in the Lord,
in my God is the joy of my soul;
for he has clothed me with a robe of salvation,
and wrapped me in a mantle of justice,
like a bride bedecked with her jewels.   ISAIAH 61:10

> I will extol you, O Lord, for you drew me clear
> and did not let my enemies rejoice over me.
> Glory be to the Father.   TURN TO PSALM 29

Lord Have Mercy   Glory to God   Prayer

THE LITURGY OF THE WORD

First Reading

PROVERBS 8:22–35

Songs of Meditation and Response

Blessed are you, O Virgin Mary,
by the Lord the most high God,

above all women upon the earth.
You are the glory of Jerusalem,
you are the joy of Israel,
you are the honor of our people. JUDITH 13:23; 15:10
Alleluia, alleluia.
You are all-beautiful, O Mary,
and there is in you no stain of original sin. Alleluia.

SONG OF SOLOMON 4:7

Gospel

LUKE 1:26–28

Homily   Creed   Prayer of the Faithful

THE LITURGY OF THE EUCHARIST

Song at the Preparation of the Gifts

Hail, Mary, full of grace, the Lord is with you;
blessed are you among women, alleluia.

LUKE 1:28   TURN TO PSALM 44

Prayer over the Gifts

EUCHARISTIC PRAYER
TURN TO PAGE 401

Communion Song

Glorious things are said of you, O Mary,
because he who is mighty has done great things for you.

TURN TO PSALM 84

Prayer after Communion

December 10 : Melchiades : Pope and Martyr
The Mass is of the preceding Sunday, with a commemoration of Melchiades.

December 11 : Damasus : Pope
For today's Mass turn to page 310.

Entrance Song

Hail, holy Mother, who gave birth to the King
who rules heaven and earth forever and ever.

My heart overflows with a goodly theme;
as I sing my ode to the king.   TURN TO PSALM 44

Glory be to the Father.

First Reading
SIRACH 24:23–31

Songs of Meditation and Response

Who is this that comes forth like the dawn,
as beautiful as the moon, as resplendent as the sun?
          SONG OF SOLOMON 6:9

Like the rainbow appearing in the cloudy sky;
like the blossoms on the branches in springtime.   SIRACH 50:8

Alleluia, alleluia.
The flowers appear on the earth,
the time of pruning the vines has come. Alleluia.
          SONG OF SOLOMON 2:12

Gospel
LUKE 1:39–47

Song at the Preparation of the Gifts

I have chosen and have sanctified this place,
that my name may be there
and my eyes and my heart may remain there forever.
          2 CHRONICLES 7:16 TURN TO PSALM 84

EUCHARISTIC PRAYER
TURN TO PAGE 401

Communion Song

He has not done this for any other nation;
his ordinances he has not made known to them.
          TURN TO PSALM 147

December 13 : Lucy : Virgin and Martyr

Entrance Song

You love justice and hate wickedness;
therefore God, your God, has anointed you
with the oil of gladness above your fellows.

My heart overflows with a goodly theme;
as I sing my ode to the king. TURN TO PSALM 44
Glory be to the Father.

First Reading

2 CORINTHIANS 10:17-18; 11:1-2

Songs of Meditation and Response

You love justice and hate wickedness.
Therefore, God, your God, has anointed you
with the oil of gladness.

Alleluia, alleluia.
Grace is poured out upon your lips;
thus God has blessed you forever. Alleluia. PSALM 44

Gospel

MATTHEW 13:44-52

Song at the Preparation of the Gifts

Behind her the virgins of her train are brought to the king.
Her neighbors are brought to you with gladness and joy;
they enter the palace of the Lord, the king. TURN TO PSALM 44

Communion Song

Princes persecute me without cause,
but my heart stands in awe of your word.
I rejoice at your promise, as one who has found rich spoil.

TURN TO PSALM 118

December 16 : Eusebius : Bishop and Martyr

For today's Mass turn to page 312.

December 21 : Thomas : Apostle

Entrance Song

To me, your friends, O God, are made exceedingly honorable;
their principality is exceedingly strengthened.

O Lord, you have probed me and you know me;
you know when I sit and when I stand. TURN TO PSALM 138

Glory be to the Father.

First Reading

EPHESIANS 2:19–22

Songs of Meditation and Response

Your friends, O God, are made exceedingly honorable:
their principality is exceedingly strengthened.
I will number them and they will outnumber the sands.

Alleluia, alleluia. PSALM 138

Exult, you just, in the Lord;
praise from the upright is fitting. Alleluia. PSALM 32

Gospel

JOHN 20:24–29

Song at the Preparation of the Gifts

Through all the earth their voice resounds,
and to the ends of the world, their message.

TURN TO PSALM 18

EUCHARISTIC PRAYER

TURN TO PAGE 403

Communion Song

Put in your hand and know the place of the nails,
and be not unbelieving but believing.

JOHN 20:27   TURN TO PSALM 115

305

Index of Feasts

Common and Votive Masses

Of a Pope

The alleluias in parentheses are recited during Eastertime.

Entrance Song

If you love me, Simon Peter,
feed my lambs, feed my sheep.
(Alleluia, alleluia.) JOHN 21:15-17

> I will extol you, O Lord, for you drew me clear
> and did not let my enemies rejoice over me.
>
> Glory be to the Father. TURN TO PSALM 29

First Reading

1 PETER 5:1-4, 10-11

Songs of Meditation and Response

During Eastertime:

Alleluia, alleluia.
You are Peter
and upon this rock I will build my Church. Alleluia.

MATTHEW 16:18

> You shall make them princes through all the land;
> they shall remember your name, O Lord,
> through all generations. Alleluia. PSALM 44

During the Rest of the Year:

Let them extol him in the assembly of the people;
and praise him in the council of the elders.
Let them give thanks to the Lord for his kindness
and his wondrous deeds to the children of men.

PSALM 106

And from Septuagesima to Easter add:

I announced your justice in the vast assembly;
I did not restrain my lips as you, O Lord, know.
Your justice I kept not hid within my heart,
your faithfulness and your salvation I have spoken of.
I have made no secret of your kindness
and your truth in the vast assembly. PSALM 39

From Pentecost to Septuagesima add:

Alleluia, alleluia.
You are Peter,
and upon this rock I will build my Church. Alleluia.

MATTHEW 16:18

Gospel

MATTHEW 16:13–19

Song at the Preparation of the Gifts

See, I place my words in your mouth!
Behold, I set you over nations and over kingdoms,
to root up and to tear down,
and to build and to plant. (Alleluia.)

JEREMIAH 1:9–10 TURN TO PSALM 106

Communion Song

You are Peter,
and upon this rock I will build my Church. (Alleluia.)

MATTHEW 16:18 TURN TO PSALM 39

Of a Bishop Martyr I

Entrance Song

The Lord made a covenant of friendship with him,
and made him a prince;
that he should possess the dignity of priesthood forever.

Remember, O Lord, David   SIRACH 45:30
and all his meekness.   TURN TO PSALM 131

Glory be to the Father.

First Reading

JAMES 1:12–18

Songs of Meditation and Response

I have found David, my servant;
with my holy oil I have anointed him,
that my hand may be always with him,
that my arm may make him strong.
No enemy shall have an advantage over him,
nor shall the son of iniquity have power to hurt him.

PSALM 88

From Pentecost to Septuagesima add:
Alleluia, alleluia.
You are a priest forever,
according to the order of Melchisedec. Alleluia.   PSALM 109

From Septuagesima to Easter add:
You have granted him his heart's desire;
you refused not the wish of his lips.
For you welcomed him with goodly blessings.
You placed on his head a crown of precious stones.   PSALM 20

Gospel
LUKE 14:26–33

Song at the Preparation of the Gifts
My faithfulness and my kindness shall be with him,
and through my name shall his horn be exalted.

TURN TO PSALM 88

Communion Song
Once by my holiness have I sworn:
his posterity shall continue forever,
and his throne shall be like the sun before me,
like the moon, perfect forever—
a faithful witness in the sky.   TURN TO PSALM 88

Of a Bishop Martyr   2

Entrance Song
Priests of the Lord, bless the Lord,
holy men of humble heart, praise God.

Bless the Lord, all you works of the Lord,
praise and exalt him above all forever.

DANIEL 3:84, 87, 57   TURN TO PSALM 148

Glory be to the Father.

First Reading
2 CORINTHIANS 1:3–7

Songs of Meditation and Response
You crowned him with glory and honor.
You have given him rule
over the works of your hands, O Lord.   PSALM 8

From Pentecost to Septuagesima add:

Alleluia, alleluia.

This is the priest whom the Lord has crowned. Alleluia.

From Septuagesima to Easter add:

Happy the man who fears the Lord,
who greatly delights in his commands.
His posterity shall be mighty upon the earth;
the upright generation shall be blessed.
Wealth and riches shall be in his house;
his generosity endures forever. PSALM III

Gospel
MATTHEW 16:24–27

Song at the Preparation of the Gifts

I have found David, my servant;
with my holy oil I have anointed him,
that my hand may be always with him,
and that my arm may make him strong.

TURN TO PSALM 88

Communion Song

You placed on his head, O Lord,
a crown of precious stones. TURN TO PSALM 20

Of a Martyr I

Entrance Song

O Lord, in your strength the just man is glad;
in your salvation how greatly he rejoices!
You have granted him his heart's desire.

For you welcomed him with goodly blessings,
you placed on his head a crown of precious stones.

Glory be to the Father. TURN TO PSALM 20

First Reading
WISDOM OF SOLOMON 10:10–14

Songs of Meditation and Response

Happy the man who fears the Lord,
who greatly delights in his commands.

His posterity shall be mighty upon the earth;
the upright generation shall be blessed. PSALM 111

From Pentecost to Septuagesima add:
Alleluia, alleluia.
You placed on his head, O Lord,
a crown of precious stones. Alleluia.

From Septuagesima to Easter add:
You have granted him his heart's desire:
you refused not the wish of his lips.
For you welcomed him with goodly blessings.
You placed upon his head a crown of precious stones.

PSALM 20

Gospel
MATTHEW 10:34–42

Song at the Preparation of the Gifts
You crowned him with glory and honor;
you have given him rule over the works of your hands, O Lord.

TURN TO PSALM 8

Communion Song
Whoever wishes to come after me,
let him deny himself,
and take up his cross, and follow me.

MATTHEW 16:24 TURN TO PSALM 111

Of a Martyr   2

Entrance Song
The just man is glad in the Lord and takes refuge in him;
all the upright of heart shall be praised.

Hear, O God, my voice in my lament;
from the dread enemy preserve my life.

Glory be to the Father. TURN TO PSALM 63

First Reading
2 TIMOTHY 2:8–10, 3:10–12

Songs of Meditation and Response
Though the just man fall, he does not lie prostrate,
for the hand of the Lord sustains him.

All the day he is kindly and lends,
and his descendants shall be blessed.   PSALM 36

From Pentecost to Septuagesima add:
Alleluia, alleluia.
He who follows me does not walk in darkness,
but will have the light of life eternal. Alleluia. JOHN 8:12

From Septuagesima to Easter add:
Happy the man who fears the Lord,
who greatly delights in his commands.
His posterity shall be mighty upon the earth;
the upright generation shall be blessed.
Wealth and riches shall be in his house;
his generosity shall endure forever.   PSALM 111

Gospel
MATTHEW 10:26–32

Song at the Preparation of the Gifts

O Lord, you placed on his head a crown of precious stones.
He asked life of you, and you gave it to him, alleluia.

TURN TO PSALM 20

Communion Song
Whoever serves me, let him follow me;
and where I am there also shall my servant be.

JOHN 12:26   TURN TO PSALM 123

Of Martyrs   I

Entrance Song

Let the prisoners' sighing come before you, O Lord;
repay our neighbors sevenfold into their bosoms;
avenge the blood of your saints which has been shed.

O God, the nations have come into your inheritance;
they have defiled your holy temple,
they have made Jerusalem as a place to keep fruit.

Glory be to the Father.   TURN TO PSALM 78

First Reading
WISDOM OF SOLOMON 3:1–8

Songs of Meditation and Response

God is glorious in his saints,
wonderful in majesty, a worker of wonders.
Your right hand, O Lord, is magnificent in power;
your right hand has shattered the enemy.

EXODUS 15:11, 6

From Pentecost to Septuagesima add:

Alleluia, alleluia.
The bodies of the saints are buried in peace,
but their name lives on and on. Alleluia.   SIRACH 44:14

From Septuagesima to Easter add:

Those that sow in tears
shall reap rejoicing.
Going, they went and wept,
casting their seeds.
But coming, they shall come with joyfulness,
carrying their sheaves.

PSALM 125

Gospel

LUKE 21:9–19

Song at the Preparation of the Gifts

God is wonderful in his saints;
the God of Israel is he
who gives power and strength to his people.
Blessed be God! Alleluia.   TURN TO PSALM 67

Communion Song

For if before men they were punished, God tried them;
as gold in the furnace he proved them,
and as sacrificial offerings he took them to himself.

WISDOM OF SOLOMON 3:4–6   TURN TO PSALM 125

Of Martyrs   2

Entrance Song

At gatherings the wisdom of the saints is retold,
and the assembly sings their praises;
their name lives on and on.   SIRACH 44:15, 14

Exult, you just, in the Lord;
praise from the upright is fitting. TURN TO PSALM 32
Glory be to the Father.

First Reading
WISDOM OF SOLOMON 5:16–20

Songs of Meditation and Response

We were rescued like a bird
from the fowlers' snare.
Broken was the snare,
and we were freed;
our help is in the name of the Lord,
who made heaven and earth. PSALM 123

From Pentecost to Septuagesima add:
Alleluia, alleluia.
The just feast and exult before God;
and they are glad and rejoice. Alleluia. PSALM 67

From Septuagesima to Easter add:
Those that sow in tears
shall reap rejoicing.
Going, they went and wept,
casting their seeds.
But coming, they shall come with joyfulness,
carrying their sheaves. PSALM 125

Gospel
LUKE 6:17–23

Song at the Preparation of the Gifts

Let the faithful exult in glory;
let them sing for joy upon their couches;
let the high praises of God be in their throats. Alleluia.

TURN TO PSALM 149

Communion Song

But I say to you, my friends:
do not be afraid of those who persecute you.

LUKE 12:4 TURN TO PSALM 123

Entrance Song

The salvation of the just is from the Lord;
he is their refuge in time of distress.

Be not vexed over evildoers,
nor jealous of those who do wrong.   TURN TO PSALM 36
Glory be to the Father.

First Reading
HEBREWS 10:32–38

Songs of Meditation and Response

The just cry out and the Lord hears them,
and from all their distress he rescues them.
The Lord is close to those who are brokenhearted;
and those who are crushed in spirit he saves.   PSALM 33

From Pentecost to Septuagesima add:

Alleluia, alleluia.
The white-robed army of Martyrs
praises you, O Lord. Alleluia.

From Septuagesima to Easter add:

Those that sow in tears
shall reap rejoicing.
Going, they went and wept,
casting their seeds.
But coming, they shall come with joyfulness,
carrying their sheaves.   PSALM 125

Gospel
LUKE 12:1–8

Song at the Preparation of the Gifts

The souls of the just are in the hand of God,
and no torment of death shall touch them.
They seemed, in view of the foolish, to be dead;
but they are in peace. Alleluia.

WISDOM OF SOLOMON 3:1–3   TURN TO PSALM 41

Communion Song
"What I tell you in darkness,
   speak it in the light," says the Lord,
"and what you hear whispered,
   preach it on the house tops."

MATTHEW 10:27   TURN TO PSALM 128

Of a Martyr During Eastertime

Entrance Song
You have sheltered me, O God,
against the council of malefactors, alleluia,
against the multitude of the workers of iniquity,
alleluia, alleluia.

   Hear, O God, my voice in lament;
   from the dread enemy preserve my life.

   Glory be to the Father.   TURN TO PSALM 63

First Reading
WISDOM OF SOLOMON 5:1–5

Songs of Meditation and Response
Alleluia, alleluia.
The heavens proclaim your wonders, O Lord,
and your faithfulness in the assembly of the holy ones. Alleluia.

PSALM 88

You placed on his head, O Lord,
a crown of precious stones. Alleluia.   PSALM 20

Gospel
JOHN 15:1–7

Song at the Preparation of the Gifts

The heavens proclaim your wonders, O Lord,
and your faithfulness in the assembly of the holy ones,
alleluia, alleluia.   TURN TO PSALM 88

Communion Song
The just man is glad in the Lord and takes refuge in him;
all the upright of heart shall be praised,
alleluia, alleluia.   TURN TO PSALM 63

Of Martyrs During Eastertime

Entrance Song

Let your faithful ones bless you, O Lord;
let them discourse of the glory of your kingdom,
alleluia, alleluia.

I will extol you, O my God and King,
and I will bless your name forever and ever.

Glory be to the Father.   TURN TO PSALM 144

First Reading
I PETER 1:3-7

Songs of Meditation and Response

Alleluia, alleluia.
Your faithful shall flourish like the lily, O Lord,
and be as the odor of balsam before you. Alleluia.

Precious in the eyes of the Lord
is the death of his faithful ones. Alleluia.   PSALM 115

Gospel
JOHN 15:5-11

Song at the Preparation of the Gifts

Be glad in the Lord, and rejoice, you just;
and exult, all you upright of heart,
alleluia, alleluia.   TURN TO PSALM 31

Communion Song

Exult, you just, in the Lord, alleluia;
praise from the upright is fitting, alleluia.

TURN TO PSALM 32

Of a Bishop I

The alleluias in parentheses are recited during Eastertime.

Entrance Song

The Lord made a covenant of friendship with him,
and made him a prince,
that he should possess the dignity of priesthood forever.
(Alleluia, alleluia.)   SIRACH 45:30

Remember, O Lord, David
and all his meekness.   TURN TO PSALM 131
Glory be to the Father.

First Reading
SIRACH 44:16-27, 45:3-20

Songs of Meditation and Response
During Eastertime:

Alleluia, alleluia.
You are a priest forever,
according to the order of Melchisedec. Alleluia. PSALM 109
This is the priest whom the Lord has crowned. Alleluia.

During the rest of the year:

Behold, a great priest,
who in his days pleased God.
There was not found the like to him,
who kept the law of the Most High.   SIRACH 44:16, 20

And from Septuagesima to Easter add:

Happy the man who fears the Lord,
who greatly delights in his commands.
His posterity shall be mighty upon the earth;
the upright generation shall be blessed.
Wealth and riches shall be in his house:
his generosity shall endure forever.   PSALM 111

From Pentecost to Septuagesima add:

Alleluia, alleluia.
You are a priest forever,
according to the order of Melchisedec. Alleluia.

PSALM 109

Gospel
MATTHEW 25:14-23

Song at the Preparation of the Gifts

I have found David, my servant;
with my holy oil I have anointed him,
that my hand may be always with him,
and that my arm may make him strong. (Alleluia.)

TURN TO PSALM 88

321

Communion Song

The faithful and prudent servant
whom the master will set over his household
to give them their ration of grain in due time. (Alleluia.)

LUKE 12:42 TURN TO PSALM 111

Of a Bishop 2

The alleluias in parentheses are recited during Eastertime.

Entrance Song

May your priests, O Lord, be clothed with justice;
let your faithful ones shout merrily for joy.
For the sake of David your servant,
reject not the plea of your anointed.
(Alleluia, alleluia.)

Remember, O Lord, David
and all his meekness.   TURN TO PSALM 131
Glory be to the Father.

First Reading
HEBREWS 7:23–27

Songs of Meditation and Response
During Eastertime:

Alleluia, alleluia.
The Lord has sworn, and he will not repent:
"You are a priest forever,
according to the order of Melchisedec." Alleluia.   PSALM 109

The Lord loved him and adorned him;
he clothed him with a robe of glory. Alleluia.   SIRACH 45:9

During the rest of the year:

Her priests I will clothe with salvation,
and her faithful ones shall shout merrily for joy.
In her will I make a horn to sprout forth for David;
I will place a lamp for my anointed.   PSALM 131

And from Septuagesima to Easter add:

Happy the man who fears the Lord,
who greatly delights in his commands.

His posterity shall be mighty upon the earth;
the upright generation shall be blessed.
Wealth and riches shall be in his house;
his generosity shall endure forever. PSALM 111

From Pentecost to Septuagesima add:
Alleluia, alleluia.
The Lord has sworn, and he will not repent:
"You are a priest forever,
according to the order of Melchisedec." Alleluia.
PSALM 109

Gospel
MATTHEW 24:42–47

Song at the Preparation of the Gifts
My faithfulness and my kindness shall be with him,
and through my name shall his horn be exalted. (Alleluia.)
TURN TO PSALM 88

Communion Song
Blessed is that servant
whom his master, when he comes, shall find watching.
Amen I say to you,
he will set him over all his goods. (Alleluia.)
MATTHEW 24:46–47 TURN TO PSALM 111

Of a Doctor of the Church

The alleluias in parentheses are recited during Eastertime.

Entrance Song
In the midst of the assembly he opened his mouth;
and the Lord filled him
with the spirit of wisdom and understanding;
he clothed him with a robe of glory. SIRACH 15:5
(Alleluia, alleluia.)

It is good to give thanks to the Lord,
to sing praise to your name, Most High.

Glory be to the Father. TURN TO PSALM 91

First Reading
2 TIMOTHY 4:1–8

Songs of Meditation and Response

During Eastertime:

Alleluia, alleluia.
The Lord loved him and adorned him;
he clothed him with a robe of glory. Alleluia. SIRACH 45:9
The just man shall blossom like the lily;
and shall flourish forever before the Lord. Alleluia. HOSEA 14:6

During the rest of the year:

The mouth of the just man tells of wisdom,
and his tongue utters what is right.
The law of his God is in his heart,
and his steps do not falter. PSALM 36

And from Septuagesima to Easter add:

Happy the man who fears the Lord,
who greatly delights in his commands.
His posterity shall be mighty upon the earth;
the upright generation shall be blessed.
Wealth and riches shall be in his house;
his generosity shall endure forever. PSALM 111

From Pentecost to Septuagesima add:

Alleluia, alleluia.
The Lord loved him and adorned him;
he clothed him with a robe of glory. Alleluia. SIRACH 45:9

Gospel
MATTHEW 5:13–19

Song at the Preparation of the Gifts
The just man shall flourish like the palm tree,
like a cedar of Lebanon shall he grow. (Alleluia.)
TURN TO PSALM 91

Communion Song
The faithful and prudent servant
whom the master will set over his household
to give them their ration of grain in due time. (Alleluia.)
LUKE 12:42 TURN TO PSALM 118

The alleluias in parentheses are recited during Eastertime.

Entrance Song

The mouth of the just man tells of wisdom,
and his tongue utters what is right.
The law of his God is in his heart.
(Alleluia, alleluia.)

Be not vexed over evildoers,
nor jealous of those who do wrong.　　TURN TO PSALM 36
Glory be to the Father.

First Reading

SIRACH 31:8–11

Songs of Meditation and Response

During Eastertime:

Alleluia, alleluia.
Blessed is the man who endures temptation;
for when he has been tried,
he shall receive the crown of life. Alleluia.　　JAMES 1:12
The Lord loved him and adorned him;
he clothed him with a robe of glory. Alleluia.　　SIRACH 45:9

During the rest of the year:

The just man shall flourish like the palm tree,
like a cedar of Lebanon shall he grow
in the house of the Lord.
To proclaim your kindness at dawn
and your faithfulness throughout the night.　　PSALM 91

And from Septuagesima to Easter add:

Happy the man who fears the Lord,
who greatly delights in his commands.
His posterity shall be mighty upon the earth;
the upright generation shall be blessed.
Wealth and riches shall be in his house;
his generosity shall endure forever.　　PSALM 111

From Pentecost to Septuagesima add:

Alleluia, alleluia.
Blessed is the man who endures temptation;

for when he has been tried,
he will receive the crown of life. Alleluia. JAMES 1:12

Gospel

LUKE 12:35-40

Song at the Preparation of the Gifts

My faithfulness and my kindness shall be with him,
and through my name shall his horn be exalted. (Alleluia.)

TURN TO PSALM 88

Communion Song

Blessed is that servant
whom his master, when he comes, shall find watching.
Amen I say to you,
he will set him over all his goods. (Alleluia.)

MATTHEW 24:46-47 TURN TO PSALM 65

Of a Confessor 2

The alleluias in parentheses are recited during Eastertime.

Entrance Song

The just man shall flourish like the palm tree,
like a cedar of Lebanon shall he grow,
planted in the house of our God.
(Alleluia, alleluia.)

It is good to give thanks to the Lord,
to sing praise to your name, Most High.

Glory be to the Father. TURN TO PSALM 91

First Reading

I CORINTHIANS 4:9-14

Songs of Meditation and Response

During Eastertime:

Alleluia, alleluia.
Happy the man who fears the Lord,
who greatly delights in his commands. Alleluia.

PSALM 111

The just man shall blossom like the lily,
and flourish forever before the Lord. Alleluia.

HOSEA 14:6

During the rest of the year:

The mouth of the just man tells of wisdom,
and his tongue utters what is right.
The law of his God is in his heart,
and his steps do not falter. PSALM 36

And from Septuagesima to Easter add:

Happy the man who fears the Lord,
who greatly delights in his commands.
His posterity shall be mighty upon the earth;
the upright generation shall be blessed.
Wealth and riches shall be in his house;
his generosity shall endure forever. PSALM 111

From Pentecost to Septuagesima add:

Alleluia, alleluia.
Happy the man who fears the Lord,
who greatly delights in his commands. Alleluia.
PSALM 111

Gospel
LUKE 12:32–34

Song at the Preparation of the Gifts

O Lord, in your strength the just man is glad;
in your victory how greatly he rejoices!
You have granted him his heart's desire. (Alleluia.)
TURN TO PSALM 20

Communion Song

Amen I say to you
that you, who have left all things and followed me,
shall receive a hundredfold,
and shall possess life everlasting. (Alleluia.)
MATTHEW 19:28–29   TURN TO PSALM 61

Of an Abbot

The alleluias in parentheses are recited during Eastertime.

Entrance Song

The mouth of the just man tells of wisdom,
and his tongue utters what is right.

The law of his God is in his heart.
(Alleluia, alleluia.)

> Be not vexed over evildoers,
> nor jealous of those who do wrong.

TURN TO PSALM 36

> Glory be to the Father.

First Reading
SIRACH 45:1–6

Songs of Meditation and Response
During Eastertime:
Alleluia, alleluia.
The just man shall flourish like the palm tree,
like a cedar of Lebanon shall he grow. Alleluia.   PSALM 91

The just man shall blossom like the lily,
and flourish forever before the Lord. Alleluia.   HOSEA 14:6

During the rest of the year:
O Lord, you welcomed him with goodly blessings,
you placed on his head a crown of precious stones.
He asked life of you
and you gave him length of days forever and ever.

PSALM 20

And from Septuagesima to Easter add:
Happy the man who fears the Lord,
who greatly delights in his commands.
His posterity shall be mighty upon the earth;
the upright generation shall be blessed.
Wealth and riches shall be in his house;
his generosity shall endure forever.   PSALM 111

From Pentecost to Septuagesima add:
Alleluia, alleluia.
The just man shall flourish like the palm tree,
like a cedar of Lebanon shall he grow. Alleluia.   PSALM 91

Gospel
MATTHEW 19:27–29

You have granted him his heart's desire, O Lord;
you refused not the wish of his lips;
you placed on his head a crown of precious stones. (Alleluia.)

TURN TO PSALM 20

Communion Song

The faithful and prudent servant
whom the master will set over his household
to give them their ration of grain in due time. (Alleluia.)

LUKE 12:42 TURN TO PSALM 33

Of a Virgin Martyr   I

The alleluias in parentheses are recited during Eastertime.

Entrance Song

I will speak of your decrees before kings
without being ashamed.
And I will delight in your commands,
which I love exceedingly.
(Alleluia, alleluia.)

> Happy are they whose way is blameless,
> who walk in the law of the Lord.   TURN TO PSALM 118
>
> Glory be to the Father.

First Reading

SIRACH 51:1–8, 12

Songs of Meditation and Response

During Eastertime:

Alleluia, alleluia.
Behind her the virgins of her train are brought to the king.
Her neighbors are brought to you with gladness. Alleluia.

In your splendor and your beauty
ride on triumphant, and reign. Alleluia.   PSALM 44

During the rest of the year:

You love justice and hate wickedness.
Therefore God, your God, has anointed you
with the oil of gladness.   PSALM 44

And from Septuagesima to Easter add:

Come, O spouse of Christ, receive the crown
which the Lord has prepared for you forever,
for the love of whom you shed your blood.

You love justice and hate wickedness;
therefore God, your God, has anointed you
with the oil of gladness above your fellows.
In your splendor and your beauty
ride on triumphant, and reign.   PSALM 44

From Pentecost to Septuagesima add:
Alleluia, alleluia.
Behind her the virgins of her train are brought to the king.
Her neighbors are brought to you with gladness. Alleluia.

PSALM 44

Gospel
MATTHEW 25:1–13

Song at the Preparation of the Gifts

Behind her the virgins of her train are brought to the king.
Her neighbors are brought to you with gladness and joy;
they enter the palace of the Lord, the King. (Alleluia.)

TURN TO PSALM 44

Communion Song

Let the proud be put to shame for oppressing me unjustly;
I will meditate on your precepts,
on your statutes, that I be not put to shame. (Alleluia.)

TURN TO PSALM 118

Of a Virgin Martyr   2

The alleluias in parentheses are recited during Eastertime.

Entrance Song

Sinners wait to destroy me,
but I pay heed to your decrees, O Lord.
I see that all fulfillment has its limits;
broad indeed is your command.
(Alleluia, alleluia.)

Happy are they whose way is blameless,
who walk in the law of the Lord. TURN TO PSALM 118
Glory be to the Father.

First Reading
SIRACH 51:13–17

Songs of Meditation and Response
During Eastertime:
Alleluia, alleluia.
This is a wise virgin,
and one of the number of the prudent. Alleluia.
Oh, how beautiful is the chaste generation with glory! Alleluia.

WISDOM OF SOLOMON 4:1

During the rest of the year:
God will help her with his countenance;
God is in her midst, she shall not be disturbed.
There is a stream whose runlets gladden the city of God;
the Most High has sanctified his dwelling. PSALM 45

And from Septuagesima to Easter add:
Come, spouse of Christ, receive the crown
which the Lord has prepared for you forever,
for the love of whom you shed your blood.

You love justice and hate wickedness;
therefore God, your God, has anointed you
with the oil of gladness above your fellows.
In your splendor and your beauty
ride on triumphant, and reign. PSALM 44

From Pentecost to Septuagesima add:
Alleluia, alleluia.
This is a wise virgin,
and one of the number of the prudent. Alleluia.

Gospel
MATTHEW 13:44–52

331

Song at the Preparation of the Gifts

Grace is poured out upon your lips;
thus God has blessed you forever and ever. (Alleluia.)

TURN TO PSALM 44

Communion Song

I have done judgment and justice, O Lord,
let not the proud slander me.
I was directed toward all your commandments;
I have hated all wicked ways. (Alleluia.)

TURN TO PSALM 118

Of a Virgin I

The alleluias in parentheses are recited during Eastertime.

Entrance Song

You love justice and hate wickedness;
therefore God, your God, has anointed you
with the oil of gladness above your fellows.
(Alleluia, alleluia.)

My heart overflows with a goodly theme,
as I sing my ode to the king. TURN TO PSALM 44
Glory be to the Father.

First Reading
2 CORINTHIANS 10:17–18, 11:1–2

Songs of Meditation and Response
During Eastertime:

Alleluia, alleluia.
Behind her the virgins of her train are brought to the king.
Her neighbors are brought to you with gladness. Alleluia.

In your splendor and beauty
ride on triumphant, and reign. Alleluia. PSALM 44

During the rest of the year:

In your splendor and your beauty
ride on triumphant, and reign.

Because of truth, and meekness, and justice;
and may your right hand show you wondrous deeds.

PSALM 44

And from Septuagesima to Easter add:
Hear, O daughter, and see,
and turn your ear; for the king shall desire your beauty.
All the rich among the people seek your favor;
the daughters of kings come in your honor.
Behind her the virgins of her train are brought to the king.
Her neighbors are brought to you.
They are brought with gladness and joy;
they enter the palace of the king.

PSALM 44

From Pentecost to Septuagesima add:
Alleluia, alleluia.
Behind her the virgins of her train are brought to the king.
Her neighbors are brought to you with gladness. Alleluia.

PSALM 44

Gospel
MATTHEW 25:1–13

Song at the Preparation of the Gifts

The daughters of kings come in your honor;
the queen takes her place at your right hand
in gold and colored clothing. (Alleluia.)

TURN TO PSALM 44

Communion Song
The five wise virgins took oil in their vessels with the lamps;
and at midnight a cry arose,
"Behold, the bridgeroom is coming,
go forth to meet Christ the Lord." (Alleluia.)

MATTHEW 25:4, 6   TURN TO PSALM 94

Of a Virgin   2

The alleluias in parentheses are recited during Eastertime.

Entrance Song
All the rich among the people seek your favor.
Behind her the virgins of her train are brought to the king.

333

Her neighbors are brought to you with gladness and joy.
(Alleluia, alleluia.)

My heart overflows with a goodly theme,
as I sing my ode to the king.   TURN TO PSALM 44

Glory be to the Father.

First Reading
I CORINTHIANS 7:25–34

Songs of Meditation and Response
During Eastertime:

Alleluia, alleluia.
This is a wise virgin,
and one of the number of the prudent. Alleluia.
O how beautiful is the chaste generation with glory! Alleluia
WISDOM OF SOLOMON 4:1

During the rest of the year:
The king shall desire your beauty,
for he is the Lord your God.
Hear, O daughter, and see;
and turn your ear.   PSALM 44

And from Septuagesima to Easter add:
For the king shall desire your beauty.
All the rich among the people seek your favor;
the daughters of kings come in your honor.
Behind her the virgins of her train are brought to the king;
her neighbors are brought with gladness and joy;
they enter the palace of the king.   PSALM 44

From Pentecost to Septuagesima add:
Alleluia, alleluia.
This is a wise virgin,
and one of the number of the prudent. Alleluia.

Gospel
MATTHEW 13:44–52

334

Song at the Preparation of the Gifts

Behind her the virgins of her train are brought to the king;
her neighbors are brought to you with gladness and joy;
they enter the palace of the Lord, the king. (Alleluia.)

TURN TO PSALM 44

Communion Song

The kingdom of heaven is like a merchant
in search of fine pearls.
When he finds a single pearl of great price,
he sells all that he has and buys it. (Alleluia.)

MATTHEW 13:45–46   TURN TO PSALM 83

Of a Martyred Woman

The alleluias in parentheses are recited during Eastertime.

Entrance Song

Sinners wait to destroy me,
but I pay heed to your decrees, O Lord.
I see that all fulfillment has its limits;
broad indeed is your command.
(Alleluia, alleluia.)

Happy are they whose way is blameless,
who walk in the law of the Lord.   TURN TO PSALM 118

Glory be to the Father.

First Reading
SIRACH 51:1–8, 12

Songs of Meditation and Response

During Eastertime:

Alleluia, alleluia.
In your splendor and your beauty
ride on triumphant, and reign. Alleluia.

Because of truth, and meekness, and justice;
may your right hand show you wondrous deeds. Alleluia.

PSALM 44

During the rest of the year:

You love justice and hate wickedness.
Therefore, God, your God, has anointed you
with the oil of gladness. PSALM 44

And from Septuagesima to Easter add:

Come, O spouse of Christ, receive forever the crown
which the Lord has prepared for you,
for whose love you shed your blood.

You love justice and hate wickedness;
therefore God, your God, has anointed you
with the oil of gladness above your fellows.
In your splendor and your beauty
ride on triumphant, and reign. PSALM 44

From Pentecost to Septuagesima add:

Alleluia, alleluia.
In your splendor and your beauty
ride on triumphant, and reign. Alleluia. PSALM 44

Gospel

MATTHEW 13:44–52

Song at the Preparation of the Gifts

Grace is poured out upon your lips;
thus God has blessed you forever, and ever. (Alleluia.)

TURN TO PSALM 44

Communion Song

Princes persecute me without cause,
but my heart stands in awe of your words.
I rejoice at your promise,
as one who has found rich spoil. (Alleluia.)

TURN TO PSALM 118

Of a Holy Woman

The alleluias in parentheses are recited during Eastertime.

Entrance Song

I know, O Lord, that your ordinances are just,
and in your faithfulness you have afflicted me.

Pierce my flesh with your fear;
I fear your ordinances.
(Alleluia, alleluia.)

> Happy are they whose way is blameless,
> who walk in the law of the Lord. TURN TO PSALM 118
>
> Glory be to the Father.

First Reading

PROVERBS 31:10–31

Songs of Meditation and Response

During Eastertime:

Alleluia, alleluia.
In your splendor and your beauty
ride on triumphant, and reign. Alleluia.

Because of truth, and meekness, and justice;
may your right hand show wondrous deeds. Alleluia.

PSALM 44

During the rest of the year:

Grace is poured out upon your lips;
thus God has blessed you forever.
Because of truth, and meekness, and justice;
and may your right hand show you wondrous deeds.

PSALM 44

And from Septuagesima to Easter add:

Come, O spouse of Christ,
receive the crown which the Lord has prepared for you forever.

You love justice and hate wickedness;
therefore God, your God, has anointed you
with the oil of gladness above your fellows.
In your splendor and your beauty,
ride on triumphant, and reign.

PSALM 44

From Pentecost to Septuagesima add:

Alleluia, alleluia.
In your splendor and your beauty
ride on triumphant, and reign. Alleluia.

PSALM 44

Gospel

MATTHEW 13:44–52

337

Song at the Preparation of the Gifts

Grace is poured out upon your lips;
thus God has blessed you forever, and ever. (Alleluia.)

TURN TO PSALM 44

Communion Song

You love justice and hate wickedness;
therefore God, your God, has anointed you
with the oil of gladness above your fellows. (Alleluia.)

TURN TO PSALM 44

Dedication of a Church

The Songs of Meditation and Response are printed below.
For the rest of this Mass turn to page 289.

Songs of Meditation and Response
During Eastertime:

Alleluia, alleluia.
I will worship at your holy temple
and give thanks to your name, Alleluia.   PSALM 137

The house of the Lord is well founded
upon a firm rock. Alleluia.

During the rest of the year:

This place was made by God, a priceless mystery;
it is without reproof.
O God, before whom stands the choir of angels,
hear the prayers of your servants.

And from Septuagesima to Easter add:

They who trust in the Lord are like Mount Sion,
which is immovable;
which forever stands.
Mountains are round about Jerusalem;
so the Lord is round about his people,
both now and forever.   PSALM 124

From Pentecost to Septuagesima add:

Alleluia, alleluia.
I will worship at your holy temple
and give thanks to your name. Alleluia.   PSALM 137

Of Our Lady

The alleluias in parentheses are recited during Eastertime.

Entrance Song

Hail, holy Mother, who gave birth to the King
who rules heaven and earth forever and ever.
(Alleluia, alleluia.)

> My heart overflows with a goodly theme;
> as I sing my ode to the king.   TURN TO PSALM 44
>
> Glory be to the Father.

First Reading

SIRACH 24:14–16

Songs of Meditation and Response

During Eastertime:

Alleluia, alleluia.
The rod of Jesse has blossomed:
a Virgin has brought forth God and man:
God has given peace,
reconciling in himself the lowest with the highest. Alleluia

NUMBERS 17:18

Hail, Mary, full of grace, the Lord is with you;
blessed are you among women. Alleluia.   LUKE 1:28

During the rest of the year:

Blessed and venerable are you, O Virgin Mary;
for without stain to your virginity
you became the Mother of the Savior.
O Virgin Mother of God,
he whom the whole world cannot contain, being made man,
shut himself up within your womb.

And from Septuagesima to Easter add:

Rejoice, O Virgin Mary,
for alone you have destroyed all heresies.
You believed the words of the Archangel Gabriel.
As a virgin, you brought forth God and man;
and after childbirth you remained an inviolate virgin.
O Mother of God, intercede for us.

During Advent add:

Alleluia, alleluia.
Hail, Mary, full of grace, the Lord is with you;
blessed are you among women. Alleluia.   LUKE 1:28

At other times add:

Alleluia, alleluia.
After childbirth you still remained an inviolate virgin:
O Mother of God, intercede for us. Alleluia.

Gospel
LUKE 11:27–28

Song at the Preparation of the Gifts

Hail, Mary, full of grace, the Lord is with you;
blessed are you among women
and blessed is the fruit of your womb. (Alleluia.)

LUKE 1:28, 42   TURN TO PSALM 23

EUCHARISTIC PRAYER
TURN TO PAGE 401

Communion Song

Blessed is the womb of the Virgin Mary,
which bore the Son of the eternal Father. (Alleluia.)

TURN TO PSALM 117

Our Lady on Saturday   1
DURING ADVENT

Entrance Song

Drop down dew, you heavens, from above,
and let the clouds rain the Just;
let the earth be opened and bud forth a Savior.   ISAIAH 45:8

You have favored, O Lord, your land;
you have restored the well-being of Jacob.

Glory be to the Father.   TURN TO PSALM 84

First Reading
ISAIAH 7:10–15

Songs of Meditation and Response

Lift up, O gates, your lintels;
reach up, you ancient portals,
that the King of glory may come in!
Who can ascend the mountain of the Lord?
or who may stand in his holy place?
He whose hands are sinless, whose heart is clean.

PSALM 23

Alleluia, alleluia.
Hail, Mary, full of grace, the Lord is with you;
blessed are you among women. Alleluia.　LUKE 1:28

Gospel

LUKE 1:26–38

Song at the Preparation of the Gifts

Hail, Mary, full of grace, the Lord is with you;
blessed are you among women,
and blessed is the fruit of your womb.

LUKE 1:28, 42　TURN TO PSALM 126

EUCHARISTIC PRAYER

TURN TO PAGE 401

Communion Song

Behold, a virgin shall be with child and bear a son,
and shall name him Emmanuel.

ISAIAH 7:14　TURN TO PSALM 24

Our Lady on Saturday　2
FROM CHRISTMAS TO THE PURIFICATION

Entrance Song

All the rich among the people seek your favor.
Behind her the virgins of her train are brought to the king.
Her neighbors are brought to you with gladness and joy.

My heart overflows with a goodly theme,
as I sing my ode to the king.　TURN TO PSALM 44

Glory be to the Father.

First Reading

TITUS 3:4–7

Songs of Meditation and Response

Fairer in beauty are you than the sons of men;
grace is poured out upon your lips.
My heart overflows with a goodly theme,
as I sing my ode to the king,
my tongue is nimble as the pen of a skillful scribe.

PSALM 44

Before Septuagesima add:

Alleluia, alleluia.
After childbirth, you still remained an inviolate virgin:
O Mother of God, intercede for us. Alleluia.

After Septuagesima add:

Rejoice, O Virgin Mary;
for alone you have destroyed all heresies.
You believed the words of the Archangel Gabriel.
As a virgin, you brought forth God and man;
and after childbirth, you remained an inviolate virgin.
O Mother of God, intercede for us.

Gospel

LUKE 2:15–20

Song at the Preparation of the Gifts

For you are happy, O holy Virgin Mary,
and most worthy of all praise;
for from you has risen the sun of justice, Christ our God.

TURN TO PSALM 2

EUCHARISTIC PRAYER
TURN TO PAGE 401

Communion Song

Blessed is the womb of the Virgin Mary,
which bore the Son of the eternal Father.

TURN TO PSALM 97

Our Lady on Saturday 3

*The second part of the Songs of Meditation and Response for the time before
Septuagesima, and the Song at the Preparation of the Gifts are printed below.
For the rest of this Mass, turn to page 339.*

Song of Response

Alleluia, alleluia.
The rod of Jesse has blossomed:
a Virgin has brought forth God and man:
God has given peace,
reconciling in himself the lowest with the highest. Alleluia.

NUMBERS 17:8

Song at the Preparation of the Gifts

You are happy, O holy Virgin Mary,
and most worthy of all praise,
since from you has risen the sun of justice, Christ our God.

TURN TO PSALM 122

Our Lady on Saturday 4

*The Song at the Preparation of the Gifts is printed below; the Gospel is
John 19:25–27. For the rest of this Mass, turn to page 339.*

Song at the Preparation of the Gifts

Blessed are you, O Virgin Mary,
who bore the Creator of all things;
you brought forth him who made you,
and you remain forever a virgin, alleluia.

TURN TO PSALM 117

Our Lady on Saturday 5

For this Mass, turn to page 339.

The Holy Trinity

The Songs of Meditation and Response are printed below. The First Reading is 2 Corinthians 13:11, 13, and the Gospel is John 15:16–17, 16:1–4. For the rest of this Mass, turn to page 137.

Songs of Meditation and Response

During Eastertime:

Alleluia, alleluia.
Blessed are you, O Lord, the God of our fathers,
and praiseworthy forever. Alleluia. DANIEL 3:52

Let us bless the Father and the Son
with the Holy Spirit. Alleluia.

During the rest of the year:

Blessed are you, O Lord,
who look into the depths from your throne upon the cherubim.
Blessed are you, O Lord, in the firmament of heaven,
and praiseworthy forever. DANIEL 3:55–56

And from Septuagesima to Easter add:

With all our hearts we confess you,
we praise you, we bless you,
God the Father unbegotten,
the only-begotten Son,
the Holy Spirit, the Consoler,
holy and undivided Trinity.
For you are great and do wonderful things;
you alone are God.
To you be praise, to you glory,
to you thanksgiving for eternal ages, O blessed Trinity.

From Pentecost to Septuagesima add:

Alleluia, alleluia.
Blessed are you, O Lord, the God of our fathers,
and praiseworthy forever. Alleluia. DANIEL 3:52

Of the Holy Spirit

The alleluias in parentheses are recited during Eastertime.

Entrance Song

The spirit of the Lord fills the world,
is all-embracing, and knows man's utterance.
(Alleluia, alleluia.) WISDOM OF SOLOMON 1:7

God arises; his enemies are scattered,
and those who hate him flee before him.
Glory be to the Father. TURN TO PSALM 67

TURN TO PSALM 67

First Reading
ACTS OF THE APOSTLES 8:14–17

Songs of Meditation and Response
During Eastertime:

Alleluia, alleluia.
Send forth your spirit, and they shall be created;
and you shall renew the face of the earth. Alleluia. PSALM 103

Come, O Holy Spirit, fill the hearts of your faithful;
and kindle in them the fire of your love. Alleluia.

During the rest of the year:

Happy the nation whose God is the Lord,
the people he has chosen for his own inheritance.
By the word of the Lord the heavens were made;
by the breath of his mouth all their hosts. PSALM 32

And from Septuagesima to Easter add:

Send forth your spirit, and they shall be created;
and you shall renew the face of the earth.
O Lord, how good and sweet is your spirit within us!

PSALM 103

Come, O Holy Spirit, fill the hearts of your faithful;
and kindle in them the fire of your love.

From Pentecost to Septuagesima add:

Alleluia, alleluia.
Come, O Holy Spirit, fill the hearts of your faithful;
and kindle in them the fire of your love. Alleluia.

345

Gospel

JOHN 14:23-31

Song at the Preparation of the Gifts

Confirm, O God, what you have wrought in us;
from your temple, which is in Jerusalem,
kings shall offer gifts to you, alleluia. TURN TO PSALM 67

EUCHARISTIC PRAYER
TURN TO PAGE 398

Communion Song

Suddenly there came a sound from heaven,
as of a violent wind blowing,
where they were sitting,
and they were all filled with the Holy Spirit,
speaking of the wonderful works of God, alleluia.

ACTS OF THE APOSTLES 2:2, 4 TURN TO PSALM 103

Of Christ, the Great High Priest

The alleluias in parentheses are recited during Eastertime.

Entrance Song

The Lord has sworn and he will not repent:
"You are a priest forever,
according to the order of Melchisedec."
(Alleluia, alleluia.)

> The Lord said to my Lord:
> "Sit at my right hand." TURN TO PSALM 109
> Glory be to the Father.

First Reading
HEBREWS 5:1-11

Songs of Meditation and Response

During Eastertime:

Alleluia, alleluia.
But Jesus, because he continues forever,
has an everlasting priesthood. Alleluia. HEBREWS 7:24

The Spirit of the Lord is upon me
because he has anointed me;
to bring good news to the poor he has sent me,
to heal the contrite of heart. Alleluia.   LUKE 4:18

During the rest of the year:
The Spirit of the Lord is upon me
because he has anointed me.
To bring good news to the poor he has sent me,
to heal the contrite of heart.   LUKE 4:18

And from Septuagesima to Easter add:
Rise, O Lord! O God, lift up your hand!
Forget not the afflicted!
You do see, for you behold misery and sorrow.
On you the unfortunate man depends;
of the fatherless you are the helper.   PSALM 9

From Pentecost to Septuagesima add:
Alleluia, alleluia.
But Jesus, because he continues forever,
has an everlasting priesthood. Alleluia.   HEBREWS 7:24

Gospel
LUKE 22:14–20

Song at the Preparation of the Gifts
Christ having offered one sacrifice for sins,
has taken his seat forever at the right hand of God;
for by one offering he has perfected forever
those who are sanctified. (Alleluia.)

HEBREWS 10:12–14   TURN TO PSALM 2

Communion Song
"This is the body which shall be given up for you.
  This cup is the new covenant in my blood," says the Lord.
"Do this as often as you drink it,
  in remembrance of me." (Alleluia.)

I CORINTHIANS 11:24–25   TURN TO PSALM 98

Of Our Lord's Passion

The alleluias in parentheses are recited during Eastertime.

Entrance Song

The Lord Jesus Christ humbled himself unto death,
even to death on a cross;
therefore God also exalted him
and has bestowed upon him the name
that is above every name. PHILIPPIANS 2:8–9

(Alleluia, alleluia.)

The favors of the Lord I will sing forever;
through all generations. TURN TO PSALM 88
Glory be to the Father.

First Reading
ZECHARIAH 12:10–11, 13:6–7

During Eastertime:

Alleluia, alleluia.
Hail, our king:
you alone pitied our errors;
obedient to the Father, you were led to be crucified
like a meek lamb to the slaughter. Alleluia.

Glory to you, to you hosanna;
to you triumph and victory;
to you the crown of highest praise and honor! Alleluia.

During the rest of the year:

Insult has broken my heart, and I am weak;
I looked for sympathy, but there was none;
for comforters, and I found none.
Rather they put gall in my food,
and in my thirst they gave me vinegar to drink. PSALM 68

And from Septuagesima to Easter add:

Yet it was our infirmities that he bore,
our sufferings that he endured.
While we thought of him as stricken,
as one smitten by God and afflicted.
But he was pierced for our offenses,
crushed for our sins.

348

Upon him was the chastisement that makes us whole,
by his stripes we were healed. ISAIAH 53:4–5

From Pentecost to Septuagesima add:
Alleluia, alleluia.
Hail, our king;
you alone pitied our errors;
obedient to the Father, you were led to be crucified
like a meek lamb to the slaughter. Alleluia.

Gospel
JOHN 19:28–35

Song at the Preparation of the Gifts
Wicked men rose up against me;
pitilessly they sought to slay me without mercy;
and they did not spare to spit in my face;
with lances they wounded me, and all my bones are shaken. (Alleluia.)

TURN TO PSALM 21

EUCHARISTIC PRAYER
TURN TO PAGE 394

Communion Song
They have pierced my hands and my feet:
they have numbered all my bones. (Alleluia.) TURN TO PSALM 21

The Holy Eucharist
The Songs of Meditation and Response are given below.
For the rest of this Mass turn to page 139.

Songs of Meditation and Response
During Eastertime:
Alleluia, alleluia.
The disciples recognized the Lord Jesus
in the breaking of the bread. Alleluia. LUKE 24:35

My flesh is food indeed, and my blood is drink indeed.
He who eats my flesh, and drinks my blood,
abides in me and I in him. Alleluia. JOHN 6:56–57

During the rest of the year:
The eyes of all look hopefully to you, O Lord;
and you give them their food in due season.

You open your hand;
and satisfy the desire of every living thing.   PSALM 144

And from Septuagesima to Easter add:

From the rising of the sun, even to its setting,
my name is great among the nations.
And everywhere they bring sacrifice to my name,
and a pure offering;
for great is my name among the nations.   MALACHI 1:11

Come, eat of my bread,
and drink of the wine I have mixed for you.

PROVERBS 9:5

From Pentecost to Septuagesima add:

Alleluia, alleluia.
My flesh is food indeed, and my blood is drink indeed.
He who eats my flesh, and drinks my blood,
abides in me and I in him. Alleluia.   JOHN 6:56–57

The Sacred Heart

DURING EASTERTIME

*The Songs of Meditation and Response, the Song at the Preparation of the Gifts
and the Communion Song are given below. For the rest of this Mass, turn to
page 144.*

Songs of Meditation and Response

Alleluia, alleluia.
Take my yoke upon you and learn from me,
for I am meek and humble of heart;
and you will find rest for your souls. Alleluia.

Come to me, all you who labor and are burdened,
and I will give you rest. Alleluia.   MATTHEW 11:28–29

Song at the Preparation of the Gifts

Holocausts or sin-offerings you sought not;
then said I, "Behold I come;
in the written scroll it is prescribed for me,
to do your will, O my God, is my delight,
and your law is within my heart!" Alleluia.

TURN TO PSALM 39

Communion Song

If anyone thirst,
let him come to me and drink.
Alleluia, alleluia.   JOHN 7:37   TURN TO PSALM 32

The Sacred Heart

FROM SEPTUAGESIMA TO EASTER

The Songs of Meditation and Response are given below.
For the rest of this Mass, *turn to page 144.*

Songs of Meditation and Response

Good and upright is the Lord;
thus he shows sinners the way.
He guides the humble to justice;
he teaches the humble his way.   PSALM 24

Merciful and gracious is the Lord,
slow to anger and abounding in kindness.
He will not always chide,
nor does he keep his wrath forever.
Not according to our sins does he deal with us,
nor does he requite us according to our crimes.

PSALM 102

AT ALL OTHER TIMES
For this Mass, turn to page 144.

Of the Angels

The alleluias in parentheses are recited during Eastertime.

Entrance Song

Bless the Lord, all you his angels,
you mighty in strength, who do his bidding,
obeying his spoken word.
(Alleluia, alleluia.)

Bless the Lord, O my soul;
and, all my being, bless his holy name.

Glory be to the Father.   TURN TO PSALM 102

First Reading

REVELATION 5:11–14

Songs of Meditation and Response

During Eastertime:

Alleluia, alleluia.
In the presence of the angels I will sing your praise;
I will worship at your holy temple
and give thanks to your name. Alleluia.   PSALM 137

An angel of the Lord came down from heaven,
and drawing near rolled back the stone,
and sat upon it. Alleluia.   MATTHEW 28:2

During the rest of the year:

Praise the Lord from the heavens,
praise him in the heights.
Praise him, all you his angels,
praise him, all you his hosts.   PSALM 148

And from Septuagesima to Easter add:

Bless the Lord, all you his angels,
you mighty in strength, who do his bidding.
Bless the Lord, all you his hosts,
his ministers, who do his will.
Bless the Lord, all his works, everywhere in his domain.
Bless the Lord, O my soul!   PSALM 102

From Pentecost to Septuagesima add:

Alleluia, alleluia.
In the presence of the angels I will sing your priase;
I will worship at your holy temple
and give thanks to your name. Alleluia.   PSALM 137

Gospel

JOHN 1:47–51

Song at the Preparation of the Gifts

An angel stood near the altar of the temple,
having a golden censer in his hand,

and there was given to him much incense:
and the smoke of the perfumes ascended before God. (Alleluia.)

REVELATION 8:3, 4 TURN TO PSALM 137

Communion Song

Angels, archangels, thrones and dominations,
principalities, and powers, the virtues of the heavens,
cherubim and seraphim, bless the Lord forever. (Alleluia.)

TURN TO PSALM 148

Joseph, Husband of Our Lady

The alleluias in parentheses are recited during Eastertime.

Entrance Song

The Lord is our help and our shield:
in him our hearts rejoice;
in his holy name we trust.
(Alleluia, alleluia.)   PSALM 32

    O shepherd of Israel, hearken,
    O guide of the flock of Joseph!   TURN TO PSALM 79
    Glory be to the Father.

First Reading
GENESIS 49:22–26

Songs of Meditation and Response
During Eastertime:

Alleluia, alleluia.
In whatever tribulation they shall cry to me,
I will hear them,
and be their protector always. Alleluia.

Make us lead, O Joseph, an innocent life;
and may it ever be safe under your patronage. Alleluia.

During the rest of the year:

O Lord, you welcomed him with goodly blessings,
you placed on his head a crown of pure gold.
He asked life of you:
you gave him length of days forever and ever.   PSALM 20

And from Septuagesima to Easter add:

Happy the man who fears the Lord,
who greatly delights in his commands.
His posterity shall be mighty upon the earth;
the upright generation shall be blessed.
Wealth and riches shall be in his house;
his generosity shall endure forever. PSALM III

From Pentecost to Septuagesima add:

Alleluia, alleluia.
Make us lead, O Joseph, an innocent life;
and may it ever be safe under your patronage. Alleluia.

Gospel

LUKE 3:21–23

Song at the Preparation of the Gifts

Glorify the Lord, O Jerusalem,
for he has strengthened the bars of your gates,
he has blessed your children within you. (Alleluia.)

TURN TO PSALM 147

EUCHARISTIC PRAYER

TURN TO PAGE 402

Communion Song

And Jacob begot Joseph, the husband of Mary,
and of her was born Jesus who is called Christ. (Alleluia.)

MATTHEW 1:16 TURN TO PSALM 126

The Apostles Peter and Paul

DURING EASTERTIME

Entrance Song

You have protected me, O God,
from the assembly of the malignant, alleluia:
from the multitude of the workers of iniquity,
alleluia, alleluia.

Hear, O God, my prayer when I make supplication to you:
deliver my soul from the fear of the enemy.

Glory be to the Father. TURN TO PSALM 63

First Reading

ACTS OF THE APOSTLES 5:12–16

Songs of Meditation and Response

Alleluia, alleluia.
The heavens shall confess your wonders, O Lord;
and your truth in the church of the saints. Alleluia.

O Lord, you placed on his head   PSALM 88
a crown of precious stones. Alleluia.   PSALM 20

Gospel

MATTHEW 19:27–29

Song at the Preparation of the Gifts

The heavens proclaim your wonders, O Lord,
and your faithfulness in the assembly of the holy ones,
alleluia, alleluia.   TURN TO PSALM 88

EUCHARISTIC PRAYER

TURN TO PAGE 403

Communion Song

The just man is glad in the Lord and takes refuge in him;
in him glory all the upright of heart,
alleluia, alleluia.   TURN TO PSALM 63

The Apostles Peter and Paul

FROM PENTECOST TO EASTER

*The second part of the Songs of Meditation and Response for the time between
Septuagesima and Easter is printed below. The First Reading is Acts of the
Apostles 5:12–16 and the Gospel is Matthew 19:27–29. For the rest of this
Mass, turn to page 228.*

Songs of Meditation and Response

Those that sow in tears shall reap rejoicing.
Although they go forth weeping,
carrying the seed to be sown.
They shall come back rejoicing,
carrying their sheaves.   PSALM 125

Peter : Apostle

The alleluias in parentheses are recited during Eastertime.

Entrance Song

During Eastertime:

You have sheltered me, O God,
against the council of malefactors, alleluia,
against the multitude of the workers of iniquity,
alleluia, alleluia.

> Hear O God, my voice in lament;
> from the dread enemy preserve my life.

> Glory be to the Father. TURN TO PSALM 63

During the rest of the year:

To me, your friends, O God,
are made exceedingly honorable;
their principality is exceedingly strengthened.

> O Lord, you have probed me and you know me;
> you know when I sit and when I stand.

> Glory be to the Father. TURN TO PSALM 138

First Reading

ACTS OF THE APOSTLES 12:1–11

Songs of Meditation and Response

During Eastertime:

Alleluia, alleluia.
Let them give thanks to the Lord for his kindness
and his wondrous deeds to the children of men. Alleluia.

You are Peter, PSALM 106
and upon this rock I will build my Church. Alleluia.

MATTHEW 16:18

During the rest of the year:

> You shall make them princes through all the land;
> they shall remember your name, O Lord.
> The place of your fathers your sons shall have;
> therefore shall nations praise you. PSALM 44

And from Septuagesima to Easter add:

You are Peter,
and upon this rock I will build my Church.
And the gates of hell shall not prevail against it.
And I will give you the keys of the kingdom of heaven.
And whatever you shall bind on earth
shall be bound in heaven. And whatever you shall loose on earth
shall be loosed in heaven. MATTHEW 16:18–19

From Pentecost to Septuagesima add:

Alleluia, alleluia.
You are Peter,
and upon this rock I will build my Church. Alleluia.

MATTHEW 16:18

Gospel
MATTHEW 16:13–19

Song at the Preparation of the Gifts

You shall make them princes through all the land;
they shall remember your name, O Lord,
through all generations. (Alleluia.) TURN TO PSALM 44

EUCHARISTIC PRAYER
TURN TO PAGE 403

Communion Song

You are Peter,
and upon this rock I will build my Church. (Alleluia.)

MATTHEW 16:18 TURN TO PSALM 18

Of All the Apostles

DURING EASTERTIME

Entrance Song

You have protected me, O God,
from the assembly of the malignant, alleluia:
from the multitude of the workers of iniquity,
alleluia, alleluia.

Hear, O God, my prayer when I make supplication to you:
deliver my soul from the fear of the enemy.

Glory be to the Father. TURN TO PSALM 63

First Reading
EPHESIANS 4:7–13

Songs of Meditation and Response

Alleluia, alleluia.
The heavens proclaim your wonders, O Lord,
and your faithfulness in the assembly of the holy ones. Alleluia.

PSALM 88

I have chosen you from the world and have appointed you
that you should go and bear fruit,
and that your fruit should remain. Alleluia. JOHN 15:16

Gospel
MATTHEW 19:27–29

Song at the Preparation of the Gifts

You shall make them princes through all the land.
I will make your name memorable through all generations;
therefore shall all generations praise you forever and ever,
alleluia, alleluia. TURN TO PSALM 44

EUCHARISTIC PRAYER
TURN TO PAGE 403

Communion Song

Through all the earth their voice resounds,
and to the end of the world, their message,
alleluia, alleluia. TURN TO PSALM 18

Of All the Apostles

FROM PENTECOST TO EASTER

*The second part of the Songs of Meditation and Response for the time from
Septuagesima to Easter is printed below. The First Reading is Ephesians 4:7–13
and the Gospel is Matthew 19:27–29. For the rest of this Mass, turn to page 283,
the Feast of Simon and Jude.*

Song of Response

Those that sow in tears shall reap rejoicing.
Although they go forth weeping,
carrying the seed to be sown.
They shall come back rejoicing,
carrying their sheaves. PSALM 125

Of All the Saints

DURING EASTERTIME

Entrance Song

Let your faithful ones bless you, O Lord.
Let them discourse of the glory of your kingdom,
alleluia, alleluia.

I will extol you, O my God and King,
and I will bless your name forever and ever.

Glory be to the Father. TURN TO PSALM 144

First Reading

REVELATION 7:2–12

Song of Response

Alleluia, alleluia.
Your faithful shall flourish like the lily, O Lord,
and be as the odor of balsam before you. Alleluia.

Precious in the eyes of the Lord
is the death of his faithful ones. Alleluia. PSALM 115

Gospel

MATTHEW 5:1–12

Song at the Preparation of the Gifts

Be glad in the Lord and rejoice, you just;
exult, all you upright of heart,
alleluia, alleluia. TURN TO PSALM 31

Communion Song

Exult, you just, in the Lord, alleluia;
praise from the upright is fitting, alleluia.

TURN TO PSALM 32

Of All the Saints

FROM PENTECOST TO EASTER

*The Entrance Song, and the second part of the Songs of Meditation and Response
for the time from Septuagesima to Easter are printed below. For the rest of this
Mass, turn to page 285.*

Entrance Song

They shall judge nations and rule over peoples,
and the Lord shall be their King forever.

Exult, you just, in the Lord;   WISDOM OF SOLOMON 3:8
praise from the upright is fitting.   TURN TO PSALM 32
Glory be to the Father.

Song of Response

Those that sow in tears shall reap rejoicing.
Going, they went and wept,
casting their seeds.
But coming, they shall come with joyfulness,
carrying their sheaves.   PSALM 125

Of the Holy Cross

The alleluias in parentheses are recited during Eastertime.

Entrance Song

But it behooves us to glory in the cross
of our Lord Jesus Christ:
in whom is our salvation, life and resurrection:
by whom we are saved and delivered.
(Alleluia, alleluia.)   GALATIANS 6:14

May God have pity on us and bless us;
may he let his face shine upon us;
and may he have pity on us.   TURN TO PSALM 66
Glory be to the Father.

First Reading
PHILIPPIANS 2:8–11

Songs of Meditation and Response

During Eastertime:

Alleluia, alleluia.
Say among the nations:
The Lord has reigned from the wood. Alleluia. PSALM 95

Sweet the wood, sweet the nails,
sweet the load that hangs on you:
you alone were worthy
to bear up the king and Lord of heaven. Alleluia.

During the rest of the year:

Christ became obedient for us to death,
even to death on a cross.
Therefore, God also has exalted him,
and has bestowed upon him the name that is above every name.

PHILIPPIANS 2:8–9

And from Septuagesima to Easter add:

We adore you, O Christ, and we bless you:
because by your cross you redeemed the world.
We adore your cross, O Lord,
we commemorate your glorious passion;
have mercy on us, you who suffered for us.
O blessed cross, you alone were worthy
to bear the Lord and king of the heavens.

From Pentecost to Septuagesima add:

Alleluia, alleluia.
Sweet the wood, sweet the nails,
sweet the load that hangs on you:
you alone were worthy
to bear up the king and Lord of heaven. Alleluia.

Gospel
MATTHEW 20:17–19

Song at the Preparation of the Gifts

Through the sign of the holy cross,
protect your people, O Lord,
from the snares of all enemies,

361

that we may pay you a pleasing service,
and our sacrifice may be acceptable. (Alleluia.)

TURN TO PSALM 21

EUCHARISTIC PRAYER

TURN TO PAGE 394

Communion Song

By the sign of the cross, our God,
deliver us from our enemies. (Alleluia.)

TURN TO PSALM 68

For Peace

The alleluias in parentheses are recited during Eastertime.

Entrance Song

Give peace, O Lord, to those who have hoped in you,
and let your prophets be proved true.
Hear the prayers of your servant,
and of your people Israel.
(Alleluia, alleluia.)   SIRACH 36:18

I rejoiced because they said to me,
"We will go up to the house of the Lord."

Glory be to the Father.   TURN TO PSALM 121

First Reading

2 MACCABEES 1:1–5

Songs of Meditation and Response

During Eastertime:

Alleluia, alleluia.
Glorify the Lord, O Jerusalem;
praise your God, O Sion. Alleluia.

He has granted peace in your borders;
with the best of wheat he fills you. Alleluia. PSALM 147

During the rest of the year:

Pray for the peace of Jerusalem!
May those who love you prosper!
May peace be within your walls,
prosperity in your buildings.   PSALM 121

And from Septuagesima to Easter add:

God is renowned in Juda;
in Israel great is his name.
In the city of peace is his abode;
his dwelling is in Sion.
There he shattered the flashing shafts of the bow,
shield and sword, and weapons of war.   PSALM 75

From Pentecost to Septuagesima add:

Alleluia, alleluia.
Glorify the Lord, O Jerusalem;
praise your God, O Sion. Alleluia.   PSALM 147

Gospel
JOHN 20:19–23

Song at the Preparation of the Gifts

Praise the Lord, for he is good;
sing to his name, for it is sweet.
All that he wills he does
in heaven and on earth. (Alleluia.)   TURN TO PSALM 134

Communion Song

"Peace I leave with you,
my peace I give to you," says the Lord. (Alleluia.)
JOHN 14:27   TURN TO PSALM 75

For Christian Unity
The alleluias in parentheses are recited during Eastertime.

Entrance Song

Save us, O Lord, our God,
and gather us from among the nations,
that we may give thanks to your holy name
and glory in praising you.
(Alleluia, alleluia.)

Give thanks to the Lord, for he is good,
for his kindness endures forever!   TURN TO PSALM 105

Glory be to the Father.

First Reading

EPHESIANS 4:1–7, 13–21

Songs of Meditation and Response

During Eastertime:

Alleluia, alleluia.
Glorify the Lord, O Jerusalem;
praise your God, O Sion. Alleluia.

He has granted peace in your borders;
with the best of wheat he fills you. Alleluia.   PSALM 147

During the rest of the year:

Pray for the peace of Jerusalem!
May those who love you prosper!
May peace be within your walls,
prosperity in your buildings.   PSALM 121

And from Septuagesima to Easter add:

God is renowned in Juda;
in Israel great is his name.
In the city of peace is his abode;
his dwelling is in Sion.
There he shattered the flashing shafts of the bow,
shield and sword, and weapons of war.   PSALM 75

From Pentecost to Septuagesima add:

Alleluia, alleluia.
Glorify the Lord, O Jerusalem;
praise your God, O Sion. Alleluia.   PSALM 147

Gospel

JOHN 17:1, 11–23

Song at the Preparation of the Gifts

May God grant you to be of one mind toward one another;
that, one in spirit,
you may with one mouth glorify our God. (Alleluia.)

ROMANS 15:5–6   TURN TO PSALM 121

Communion Song

The bread is one,
and we though many, are one body,

all of us who partake of the one bread,
and of the one chalice. (Alleluia.)

I CORINTHIANS 10:17   TURN TO PSALM 22

For the Increase of the Faith

The alleluias in parentheses are recited during Eastertime.

Entrance Song

May God have pity on us and bless us;
may he let his face shine upon us;
and may he have pity on us.
So may your ways be known upon earth;
among all nations, your salvation.
(Alleluia, alleluia.)

> May the peoples praise you, O God;
> may all the peoples praise you! TURN TO PSALM 66
> Glory be to the Father.

First Reading
SIRACH 36:1–10, 17–19

Songs of Meditation and Response
During Eastertime:

Alleluia, alleluia.
Sing joyfully to God, all you lands;
serve the Lord with gladness;
come before him with joyful song. Alleluia.

Know that the Lord is God;
he made us, his we are. Alleluia.   PSALM 99

During the rest of the year:

May the peoples praise you, O God;
may all the peoples praise you!
The earth has yielded its fruits.
God, our God, has blessed us.
May God bless us,
and may all the ends of the earth fear him! PSALM 66

And from Septuagesima to Easter add:

Tell the glory of the Lord among the nations;
among all peoples, his wondrous deeds.
For great is the Lord and highly to be praised;
awesome is he, beyond all gods.
For all the gods of the nations are devils,
but the Lord made the heavens. PSALM 95

From Pentecost to Septuagesima add:

Alleluia, alleluia.
Sing joyfully to God, all you lands;
serve the Lord with gladness;
come before him with joyful song. Alleluia. PSALM 99

Gospel
MATTHEW 9:35–38

Song at the Preparation of the Gifts

Give to the Lord, you families of nations,
give to the Lord glory and praise;
give to the Lord the glory due his name!
Bring gifts, and enter his courts;
worship the Lord in his holy court. (Alleluia.)

TURN TO PSALM 95

Communion Song

Praise the Lord, all you nations;
glorify him, all you peoples!
For steadfast is his kindness toward us,
and the fidelity of the Lord endures forever. (Alleluia.)

PSALM 116 TURN TO PSALM 148

For the Sick

The alleluias in parentheses are recited during Eastertime.

Entrance Song

Hearken, O God, to my prayer;
turn not away from my pleading;
give heed to me, and answer me.
(Alleluia, alleluia.)

I rock with grief, and am troubled
at the voice of the enemy and the clamor of the wicked.

Glory be to the Father. TURN TO PSALM 54

First Reading

JAMES 5:13–16

Songs of Meditation and Response

During Eastertime:

Alleluia, alleluia.
Hear, O Lord, my prayer,
and let my cry come to you. Alleluia. PSALM 101
In God my heart trusts, and I find help;
then my flesh flourishes again
and with my song I give him thanks. Alleluia. PSALM 27

During the rest of the year:

Have pity on me, O Lord, for I am languishing;
heal me, O Lord.
For my body is in terror;
my soul, too, is utterly terrified. PSALM 6

And from Septuagesima to Easter add:

Have pity on me, O Lord, for I am in distress;
with sorrow my eye is consumed;
my soul also, and my body.
For my life is spent with grief and my years with sighing.
My strength has failed through affliction,
and my bones are consumed. PSALM 30

From Pentecost to Septuagesima add:

Alleluia, alleluia.
O Lord, hear my prayer,
and let my cry come to you. Alleluia. PSALM 101

Gospel

MATTHEW 8:5–13

Song at the Preparation of the Gifts

Hearken, O God, to my prayer;
turn not away from my pleading;
give heed to me and answer me. (Alleluia.)

TURN TO PSALM 54

Communion Song

Let your face shine upon your servant;
save me in your kindness.
O Lord, let me not be put to shame,
for I call upon you. (Alleluia.) TURN TO PSALM 30

For Forgiveness of Sins

The alleluias in parentheses are recited during Eastertime.

Entrance Song

You have mercy on all, O Lord,
and hate none of the things which you have made,
overlooking the sins of men for the sake of repentance,
and sparing them: because you are the Lord our God.
(Alleluia, alleluia.) WISDOM OF SOLOMON 11:24, 25, 27

Have pity on me, O God; have pity on me,
for in you I take refuge. TURN TO PSALM 56

Glory be to the Father.

First Reading
ROMANS 7:22–25

Songs of Meditation and Response

During Eastertime:

Alleluia, alleluia.
A just judge is God, strong and patient;
is he angry every day? Alleluia. PSALM 7

Let me hear the sounds of joy and gladness;
the bones you have crushed shall rejoice. Alleluia.

PSALM 50

During the rest of the year:

Pardon our sins, O Lord;
why should the nations say, "Where is their God?"
Help us, O God our savior;
because of the glory of your name, O Lord, deliver us.

PSALM 78

And from Septuagesima to Easter add:

Out of the depths I cry to you, O Lord;
Lord, hear my voice!

Let your ears be attentive
to the prayer of your servant.
If you, O Lord, mark iniquities,
Lord, who can stand it?
But with you is forgiveness,
and by reason of your law I have waited for you, O Lord.

PSALM 129

From Pentecost to Septuagesima add:
Alleluia, alleluia.
A just judge is God, strong and patient;
is he angry every day? Alleluia.

PSALM 7

Gospel

LUKE 11:9–13

Song at the Preparation of the Gifts

O Lord, hear my prayer,
and let my cry come to you. (Alleluia.)

TURN TO PSALM 101

Communion Song

Ask and you shall receive;
seek, and you shall find;
knock and it shall be opened to you.
For everyone who asks receives;
and he who seeks finds;
and to him who knocks it shall be opened. (Alleluia.)

LUKE 11:9–10 TURN TO PSALM 50

For the Favor of Dying Well

The alleluias in parentheses are recited during Eastertime.

Entrance Song

Give light to my eyes that I may not sleep in death
lest my enemy say, "I have overcome him."
(Alleluia, alleluia.)

How long, O Lord? Will you utterly forget me?
How long will you hide your face from me?

Glory be to the Father.

TURN TO PSALM 12

First Reading

ROMANS 14:7–12

Songs of Meditation and Response

During Eastertime:

Alleluia, alleluia.
When Israel came forth from Egypt,
the house of Jacob from a people of alien tongue. Alleluia.

My heart is steadfast; PSALM 113
I will sing and chant praise to you, my glory. Alleluia. PSALM 107

During the rest of the year:

Even though I walk in the midst of the shadow of death
I fear no evil; for you are at my side, O Lord.
With your rod and your staff that give me courage. PSALM 22

And from Septuagesima to Easter add:

Bring me out of distress, O Lord;
put an end to my affliction and my suffering,
and take away all my sins.
To you I lift up my soul, O Lord.
In you, O my God, I trust;
let me not be put to shame,
let not my enemies exult over me.
No one who waits for you shall be put to shame;
those shall be put to shame who heedlessly break faith. PSALM 24

From Pentecost to Septuagesima add:

Alleluia, alleluia.
In you, O Lord, I take refuge;
let me never be put to shame.
In your justice rescue me and save me,
incline your ear to me, make haste to deliver me! Alleluia. PSALM 30

Gospel

LUKE 21:34–36

Song at the Preparation of the Gifts

My trust is in you, O Lord;
I say, "You are my God."
In your hands is my destiny. (Alleluia.) TURN TO PSALM 30

Communion Song

O Lord, I will tell of your singular justice.
O God, you have taught me from my youth;
and now that I am old and gray,
O God, forsake me not. (Alleluia.)   TURN TO PSALM 70

For Vocations

The alleluias in parentheses are recited during Eastertime.

Entrance Song

By the sea of Galilee the Lord saw two brothers,
Peter and Andrew,
and he called to them,
"Come, follow me,
and I will make you fishers of men."
(Alleluia, alleluia.)   MATTHEW 4:18–19

>   The heavens declare the glory of God,
>   and the firmament proclaims his handiwork.

>   Glory be to the Father.   TURN TO PSALM 18

First Reading
I SAMUEL 3:1–10

Songs of Meditation and Response
During Eastertime:

Alleluia, alleluia.
Happy they who dwell in your house, O Lord!
Continually they praise you. Alleluia.   PSALM 83

Break forth in blossoms and yield a smell.
And bring forth leaves in grace.
And praise with Canticles
and bless the Lord in his works. Alleluia.   SIRACH 39:19

During the rest of the year:

One thing I ask of the Lord; this I seek:
to dwell in the house of the Lord all the days of my life.
That I may gaze on the loveliness of the Lord
and contemplate his temple.   PSALM 26

And from Septuagesima to Easter add:

How lovely is your dwelling place, O Lord of hosts!
My soul yearns and pines for the courts of the Lord.
My heart and my flesh cry out for the living God.
Even the sparrow finds a home,
and the swallow a nest in which she puts her young:
your altars, O Lord of hosts, my king and my God.   PSALM 83

From Pentecost to Septuagesima add:

Alleluia, alleluia.
Happy they who dwell in your house, O Lord!
Continually they praise you. Alleluia.   PSALM 83

Gospel
JOHN 1:35–51

Song at the Preparation of the Gifts

O Lord, my allotted portion and my cup,
you it is who hold fast my lot. (Alleluia.)

TURN TO PSALM 15

Communion Song

Hear now, all you who fear God,
while I declare what he has done for me. (Alleluia.)

TURN TO PSALM 65

For the Preservation of Vocations
The alleluias in parentheses are recited during Eastertime.

Entrance Song

Rejoice, O hearts that seek the Lord!
Look to the Lord, and be strengthened;
seek his face evermore.
(Alleluia, alleluia.)

> Give thanks to the Lord, and invoke his name;
> make known among the nations his deeds.

> Glory be to the Father.   TURN TO PSALM 104

First Reading
I JOHN 2:14–17

Songs of Meditation and Response

During Eastertime:

Alleluia, alleluia.
But I, like a green olive tree in the house of God,
trust in the kindness of God forever and ever. Alleluia.

Hear now, all you who fear God,
while I declare what he has done for me. Alleluia.

PSALM 51

PSALM 65

During the rest of the year:

You have hold of my right hand;
with your counsel you guide me,
and in the end you will receive me in glory.
How good God is to Israel,
to those who are clean of heart!

PSALM 72

And from Septuagesima to Easter add:

Who can ascend the mountain of the Lord?
Or who may stand in his holy place?
He whose hands are sinless, whose heart is clean,
who desires not what is vain,
nor swears deceitfully to his neighbor.
He shall receive a blessing from the Lord,
and a reward from God his savior.

PSALM 23

From Pentecost to Septuagesima add:

Alleluia, alleluia.
But I, like a green olive tree in the house of God,
trust in the kindness of God forever and ever. Alleluia.

PSALM 51

Gospel

JOHN 15:1–9

Song at the Preparation of the Gifts

It is good to give thanks to the Lord,
and to sing praise to your name, Most High. (Alleluia.)

TURN TO PSALM 91

Communion Song

Holy Father, keep in your name
those whom you have given me,

that they may be one even as we are;
sanctify them in the truth. (Alleluia.)

JOHN 17:11, 17   TURN TO PSALM 14

For Vocations to the Religious Life
The alleluias in parentheses are recited during Eastertime.

Entrance Song

Look down from heaven, and see,
take care of this vine,
and protect what your right hand has planted.
(Alleluia, alleluia.)

O shepherd of Israel, hearken,
O guide of the flock of Joseph. TURN TO PSALM 79

Glory be to the Father.

First Reading
EPHESIANS 4:1–6, 23–24

Songs of Meditation and Response
During Eastertime:

Alleluia, alleluia.
May you be blessed by the Lord,
who made heaven and earth. Alleluia. PSALM 113

Happy the nation whose God is the Lord,
the people he has chosen for his own inheritance. Alleluia.

PSALM 32

During the rest of the year:

Serve the Lord with gladness;
come before him with joyful song.
Know that the Lord is God;
he made us, his we are. PSALM 99

And from Septuagesima to Easter add:

Pray for the peace of Jerusalem!
May those who love you prosper!
Because of my relatives and friends

I will say, "Peace be within you!"
Because of the house of the Lord, our God,
I will pray for your good.　　　　　PSALM 121

From Pentecost to Septuagesima add:
Alleluia, alleluia.
May you be blessed by the Lord,
who made heaven and earth. Alleluia.　　　PSALM 113

Gospel
LUKE 9:57-62

Song at the Preparation of the Gifts
I will go in to the altar of God,
the God of my gladness and joy. (Alleluia.)
TURN TO PSALM 42

Communion Song
Behold how good it is, and how pleasant,
where brethren dwell at one!
For there the Lord has pronounced his blessing. (Alleluia.)
TURN TO PSALM 132

For Any Need
The alleluias in parentheses are recited during Eastertime.

Entrance Song
"I am the salvation of the people," says the Lord.
"From whatever tribulation they shall cry to me,
I will hear them;
and I will be their Lord forever."
(Alleluia, alleluia.)

　　Hearken, my people, to my teaching;
　　incline your ears to the words of my mouth.
　　Glory be to the Father.　　TURN TO PSALM 77

First Reading
JEREMIAH 14:7-9

375

Songs of Meditation and Response

During Eastertime:

Alleluia, alleluia.
Pardon our sins, O Lord;
why should the nations say, "Where is their God?" Alleluia.

I will rejoice and be glad of your kindness,   PSALM 78
when you have seen my affliction
and watched over me in my distress. Alleluia.   PSALM 30

During the rest of the year:

You saved us, O Lord, from our foes,
and those who hated us you put to shame.
In God we gloried day by day;
your name we praised always.   PSALM 43

And from Septuagesima to Easter add:

Bring me out of distress, O Lord;
put an end to my affliction and my suffering,
and take away all my sins.
To you I lift up my soul, O Lord.
In you, O my God, I trust;
let me not be put to shame,
let not my enemies exult over me.
No one who waits for you shall be put to shame;
those shall be put to shame who heedlessly break faith.

PSALM 24

From Pentecost to Septuagesima add:

Alleluia, alleluia.
Pardon our sins, O Lord;
why should the nations say, "Where is their God?" Alleluia.

PSALM 78

Gospel
MARK 11:22–26

Song at the Preparation of the Gifts

Though I walk amid distress, you preserve me;
against the anger of my enemies you raise your hand;
your right hand saves me. (Alleluia.)   TURN TO PSALM 137

Communion Song

Remember your word to your servant, O Lord,
This is my comfort in my affliction. (Alleluia.)

TURN TO PSALM 118

The Day and Anniversary of the Pope's Coronation

The alleluias in parentheses are recited during Eastertime.

Entrance Song

The Lord made a covenant of friendship with him,
and made him a prince;
that he should possess the dignity of priesthood forever.
(Alleluia.) SIRACH 45:30

Remember, O Lord, David
and all his meekness. TURN TO PSALM 131

Glory be to the Father.

First Reading

I PETER 1:1–7

During Eastertime:

Alleluia, alleluia.
Let them give thanks to the Lord for his kindness
and his wondrous deeds to the children of men. Alleluia.

You are Peter, PSALM 106
and upon this rock I will build my Church. Alleluia.

MATTHEW 16:18

During the rest of the year:

Let them extol him in the assembly of the people
and praise him in the council of the elders.
Let them give thanks to the Lord for his kindness
and his wondrous deeds to the children of men. PSALM 106

And from Septuagesima to Easter add:

You are Peter,
and upon this rock I will build my Church.
And the gates of hell shall not prevail against it;

and I will give you the keys of the kingdom of heaven.
Whatever you shall bind on earth
shall be bound in heaven.
And whatever you shall loose on earth
shall be loosed in heaven.　　　　　MATTHEW 16:18–19

From Pentecost to Septuagesima add:
Alleluia, alleluia.
You are Peter,
and upon this rock I will build my Church. Alleluia.
　　　　　　　　　　　　　　　　　MATTHEW 16:18

Gospel
MATTHEW 16:13–19

Song at the Preparation of the Gifts

You are Peter,
and upon this rock I will build my Church,
and the gates of hell shall not prevail against it;
and I will give you the keys of the kingdom of heaven.
(Alleluia.)　　　　MATTHEW 16:18–19　TURN TO PSALM 88

Communion Song

You are Peter
and upon this rock I will build my Church. (Alleluia.)
　　　　　　MATTHEW 16:18　TURN TO PSALM 39

The Profession Day of Men
The alleluias in parentheses are recited during Eastertime.

Entrance Song

In the written scroll it is prescribed for me:
to do your will, O my God, is my delight,
and your law is within my heart.
(Alleluia, alleluia.)

　　　I have waited, waited for the Lord,
　　　and he stooped toward me.　　TURN TO PSALM 39
　　　Glory be to the Father.

First Reading
PHILIPPIANS 3:7–14

Songs of Meditation and Response

During Eastertime:

Alleluia, alleluia.
But as for me, God forbid that I should glory,
save in the cross of our Lord Jesus Christ,
through whom the world is crucified to me,
and I to the world. Alleluia.   GALATIANS 6:14

Behold, how good it is, and how pleasant,
where brethren dwell at one! Alleluia.   PSALM 132

During the rest of the year:

I will bring holocausts to your house;
to you I will fulfill the vows which my lips uttered.
Hear now, all you who fear God,
while I declare what he has done for me.   PSALM 65

And from Septuagesima to Easter add:

O God, my God, to you do I watch at break of day.
For you my flesh pines and my soul thirsts.   PSALM 62

A clean heart create for me, O God,
and a steadfast spirit renew within me.   PSALM 50

From Pentecost to Septuagesima add:

Alleluia, alleluia.
But as for me, God forbid that I should glory,
save in the cross of our Lord Jesus Christ,
through whom the world is crucified to me,
and I to the world. Alleluia.   GALATIANS 6:14

Gospel

MARK 10:17–21

Song at the Preparation of the Gifts

O Lord God, in the simplicity of my heart
I have joyfully offered all these things:
O God of Israel, keep forever this will. (Alleluia.)

I CHRONICLES 29:17–18   TURN TO PSALM 132

Communion Song

Taste and see how good the Lord is:
happy the man who takes refuge in him. (Alleluia.)

TURN TO PSALM 33

The Profession Day of Women

The alleluias in parentheses are recited during Eastertime.

Entrance Song

Hear, O daughter, and see: turn your ear,
forget your people and your father's house;
and the king shall desire your beauty.
(Alleluia, alleluia.)

> My heart overflows with a goodly theme;
> as I sing my ode to the king. TURN TO PSALM 44
> Glory be to the Father.

First Reading

I CORINTHIANS 7:6–8, 25:29–32, 34

Songs of Meditation and Response

During Eastertime:

Alleluia, alleluia.
My lover belongs to me and I to him;
he browses among the lilies, Alleluia.

SONG OF SOLOMON 2:16

Happy they who dwell in your house, O Lord;
continually they praise you. Alleluia. PSALM 83

During the rest of the year:

I hold the kingdom of this world
and all its allurements in contempt
for the love of my Lord Jesus Christ,
whom I have seen, whom I have loved,
and in whom is my belief and my delight.

My heart overflows with a goodly theme;
as I sing my ode to the king. PSALM 44

And from Septuagesima to Easter add:

Hear, O Lord, the sound of my call;
have pity on me, and answer me.
Of you my heart speaks, you my glance seeks;
your presence, O Lord, I seek.

You are my helper: cast me not off,
forsake me not, O God my savior. PSALM 26

From Pentecost to Septuagesima add:
Alleluia, alleluia.
My lover belongs to me and I to him;
he browses among the lilies. Alleluia.

SONG OF SOLOMON 2:16

Gospel
MATTHEW 25:1–13

Song at the Preparation of the Gifts

You have loosed, O Lord, my bonds;
to you will I offer sacrifice of thanksgiving
and I will call upon the name of the Lord. (Alleluia.)

TURN TO PSALM 115

Communion Song

But for me, to be near God is my good;
to make the Lord God my refuge. (Alleluia.)

TURN TO PSALM 72

Anniversary of a Bishop's Election
or Consecration

The First Reading is Hebrews 5:1–4, and the Gospel is Mark 13:33–37.
For the rest of this Mass turn to page 322.

Index of Common and Votive Masses

COMMON MASSES

VOTIVE MASSES

The Order of Worship

THE MOST IMPORTANT EVENT in the life of the Church is the celebration of Mass. Everything else takes its place according to its relationship to the Eucharist. It is to reveal more fully the profound meaning and power of the Mass that the Second Vatican Council began a program of liturgical reform. That reform is aimed not only at the forms and rites of worship, but also at our very understanding of the sacred liturgy.

Of all the names for the holy sacrifice of the Mass, the Council chose "The Most Sacred Mystery of the Eucharist." The Mass is called a mystery because it is the outward sign of an inner reality. It commemorates the death and the resurrection of Jesus—the "paschal mystery" of Christ's passage from death to life, which the Church proclaims until the Lord comes again. The Mass is called the Eucharist because it is a thanksgiving. Its central prayer of blessing and consecration begins with the great invitation to the people of God: Let us give thanks to the Lord our God. . . . Let us offer the Eucharist to the Father.

No words can exhaust the meaning of the Eucharist which we celebrate. It is a deed, a sacrifice of praise and love. It is a sacrifice of the Body and Blood of Jesus, in the form of a sacred meal, the paschal banquet which God shares with his people. It is the sign and the cause of the unity of Christians, the promise of future glory. The Eucharist, which we commonly call the Mass, is the great act of the Christian assembly. God and man meet in Christ. Man is made holy, God is given honor through Christ. The roles of priest and congregation differ at Mass, but there is a part for each. The people's part is faith and devotion, sorrow for sin, joined to glad praise and thanks—and all this is expressed outwardly, publicly, socially, by words, responses, acclamations, common prayer and song.

What is given here is intended as an outline of the Mass structure, the plan for the order of worship. Included are those parts which may at times pertain to the people, and which are not found elsewhere in the book, as well as the common responses of the people. Those who are not familiar with the Mass, or who wish to refresh their understanding of it, will find the following outline and commentary a helpful guide to the sequence of prayers, readings and songs, and to the relation of one part to another. In order that the faithful may become familiar with the Latin text also, in accordance with Article 36 of the Constitution on the Sacred Liturgy, the Latin text of the dialogue and of the Ordinary chants is to be found on page 796.

Our celebration begins with the entrance of the priest and his assistants. They proceed first to the altar, which the priest salutes, and then to the presidential chair, where he will preside during the first part of the Mass. This procession is usually accompanied by the singing of a hymn, or by the common recitation or singing of the verses of the Entrance Song, or Introit, given for the day.

Preparation Prayers

Usually during the singing of the Entrance Song the priest and his assistants will pause for the following prayers. In some places, the congregation takes part in these prayers if there is no singing.

Priest: In the name of the Father, and of the Son, and of the Holy Spirit. Amen. I will go to the altar of God.

Assistants: To God who gives joy to my youth.

Priest: Our help is in the name of the Lord.

Assistants: Who made heaven and earth.

The priest then confesses his sins.

Assistants: May almighty God have mercy on you, forgive you your sins, and bring you to life everlasting.

Priest: Amen.

Assistants: I confess to almighty God, to blessed Mary ever Virgin, to blessed Michael the Archangel, to blessed John the Baptist, to the holy apostles Peter and Paul, to all the saints, and to you, father, that I have sinned exceedingly in thought, word, and deed; through my fault, through my fault, through my most grievous fault.

Therefore I beseech blessed Mary ever Virgin, blessed Michael the Archangel, blessed John the Baptist, the holy apostles Peter and Paul, all the saints, and you, father, to pray to the Lord our God for me.

Priest: May almighty God have mercy on you, forgive you your sins, and bring you to life everlasting.

Assistants: Amen.

Priest: May the almighty and merciful Lord grant us pardon, absolution, and remission of our sins.

Assistants: Amen.

Priest: O God, you will give us life again.

Assistants: And your people will rejoice in you.

Priest: Show us, O Lord, your kindness.

Assistants: And grant us your salvation.

Priest: O Lord, hear my prayer.
Assistants: And let my cry come to you.
Priest: The Lord be with you.
Assistants: And with your spirit.
Priest: Let us pray. . . .

go to Pron of Book

Lord Have Mercy

The acclamation, Lord Have Mercy, is a brief litany of supplication to Christ as Lord. By acknowledging our need for it, we open ourselves to the saving action of God which the Mass is. It may be sung or recited. The text for this and the following prayer may be found on the inside front cover.

Glory to God

This hymn of praise is introduced by the priest and then sung or recited by all. It is said or sung on most Sundays, on the feasts of saints, and on all other days when the theme of the celebration is festive.

Prayer

The Entrance Rite concludes with a prayer which collects our various intentions into the principal petition of the Church for this day.

Priest: The Lord be with you.
People: AND WITH YOUR SPIRIT.
Priest: Let us pray. . . .

After all have prayed silently for a few moments, we listen as the priest recites a prayer in the name of the entire congregation. Then we express our affirmation of this prayer which ends:

Priest: . . . forever and ever.
People: AMEN.

THE LITURGY OF THE WORD

We have assembled in Christ's name. He is present among us now, speaking to us. During this part of the Mass we listen, think about what is said, respond with common song to express the unity the Word brings us, and finally we make our requests, our prayer to the Father.

First Reading

We listen to one or more readings before the Gospel, sincerely accepting them as chapters in our history as God's holy people, as warnings from outspoken men about our need to be faithful to the law of love, or as explanations of the Christian's way of life.

Songs of Meditation and Response

After each of the readings before the Gospel a response, which may be sung, is made by the people and/or the choir. This is a time for reflection upon what has been said, a time for seeing its relevance here and now.

Gospel

The proclamation of the Gospel is the high point in the Liturgy of the Word. We stand as a sign of our respect and great attention. Before the Gospel the priest greets the people and announces the reading.

> *Priest*: The Lord be with you.
> *People*: AND WITH YOUR SPIRIT.
> *Priest*: A reading from the holy Gospel according to ———.
> *People*: GLORY TO YOU, O LORD.

Homily

The homily is a short talk by the priest in which the message of Scripture is made more alive, more real, more meaningful for modern man. We listen to it as to the readings; for it, too, is God's Word for us.

Creed

Since Sundays are special days of celebration, renewals of Easter Sunday, the reminder of Christ's rising and our own, we make a special profession of our faith by reciting or singing the Creed, which is introduced by the priest. Apart from Sundays, it is said or sung only on great feasts. The text may be found on the inside back cover.

Prayer of the Faithful

> *Priest*: The Lord be with you.
> *People*: AND WITH YOUR SPIRIT.
> *Priest*: Let us pray.

The Liturgy of the Word ends with prayers of petition for all of our needs and those of our brothers, to each of which the people make a response such as "LORD, HAVE MERCY," or "LORD, HEAR OUR PRAYER." These petitions are made because in the readings we have become aware that God is our Father, that he loves us, that we have been given the freedom of those he has called to be his children. They are summed up in a concluding prayer by the priest, to which the people say "AMEN."

Having listened to God's Word in faith, expressed in our responses of praise and petition, we begin the Liturgy of the Eucharist. First the gifts are brought forward and prepared at the altar. During this time of preparation a hymn may be sung, or the Song at the Preparation of the Gifts, given for the day, may be sung or recited by the people.

When the priest has completed his preparation of the bread and wine at the altar, he asks the servers and other ministers gathered around him to pray that our work of sacrificial worship will be acceptable to God. In some cases, if there is no singing by the people at this time, they may join the priest's assistants in their response:

Priest: Brethren, pray that my sacrifice and yours may be acceptable to God the Father almighty.

Assistants: May the Lord receive the sacrifice from your hands to the praise and glory of his name, for our welfare and that of all his holy Church.

After a few moments of silent prayer, the priest concludes the preparations with the Prayer over the Gifts which ends:

Priest: . . . forever and ever.
People: AMEN.

EUCHARISTIC PRAYER

The Eucharistic Prayer (pages 389–410) begins with a short dialogue between the priest and the people. The people join in the song, Holy, Holy, Holy, and approve and ratify the entire prayer, or Canon, by answering AMEN at the end. The Eucharistic Prayer itself is recited by the priest in the name of all. It is a prayer of thanksgiving to the Father for all of our sacred history, for all he does for us now. And through this thanksgiving we recall Jesus, his saving death, resurrection and ascension, and especially we recall the Last Supper. This remembering and giving thanks and the offering and sharing of the Body and Blood of Jesus constitute our celebration of our salvation from sin and death. Following the great AMEN we prepare to share the holy meal by reciting or singing the Our Father and the Lamb of God. During the communion meal itself a song will usually be sung after the verses provided for are recited.

Prayer after Communion

The communion, like the other parts of the Mass, concludes with a prayer. This is usually a petition that what we have just done in this holy meal may have a real effect upon us.

Priest: The Lord be with you.
People: AND WITH YOUR SPIRIT.
Priest: Let us pray. . . .

After all pray silently, the priest recites the Prayer after Communion which ends:

Priest: . . . forever and ever.
People: AMEN.

The Dismissal

The celebration of the Eucharist concludes with a reminder to the people of the peace that is now theirs in Christ and which, in his name, they are to accomplish among all men.

Priest: The Lord be with you.
People: AND WITH YOUR SPIRIT.
Priest: The Mass is ended. Go in peace.
People: THANKS BE TO GOD.

When some other liturgical celebration is to follow the Mass immediately, instead of "The Mass is ended. Go in peace," the priest says: "Let us bless the Lord." The people answer: "THANKS BE TO GOD." When the Mass of the Dead is celebrated, the priest says: "May they rest in peace." The people answer: "AMEN."

Priest: May almighty God bless you, the Father, and the Son, + and the Holy Spirit.

People: AMEN.

While the priest leaves the altar, the people often sing a hymn.

THE
EUCHARISTIC
PRAYER

The Eucharistic Prayer

CHRISTMAS

Priest: The Lord be with you.
People: AND WITH YOUR SPIRIT.
Priest: Lift up your hearts.
People: WE HAVE LIFTED THEM UP TO THE LORD.
Priest: Let us give thanks to the Lord our God.
People: IT IS RIGHT AND JUST.

IT IS TRULY right and just,
proper and helpful toward salvation,
that we always and everywhere give thanks to you, O Lord,
holy Father, almighty and eternal God;
for the brightness of your glory
has made itself manifest to the eyes of our mind
by the mystery of the Word made flesh,
and we are drawn to the love of things unseen
through him whom we acknowledge as God,
now seen by men.
Therefore with the Angels and Archangels,
the Thrones and Dominations, and all the militant hosts of heaven,
we continuously praise your glory in song, and say:

HOLY, HOLY, HOLY LORD GOD OF HOSTS.
HEAVEN AND EARTH ARE FILLED WITH YOUR GLORY.
HOSANNA IN THE HIGHEST.
BLESSED IS HE WHO COMES IN THE NAME OF THE LORD.
HOSANNA IN THE HIGHEST.

TURN TO PAGE 407

The Eucharistic Prayer

EPIPHANY

Priest: The Lord be with you.
People: AND WITH YOUR SPIRIT.
Priest: Lift up your hearts.
People: WE HAVE LIFTED THEM UP TO THE LORD.
Priest: Let us give thanks to the Lord our God.
People: IT IS RIGHT AND JUST.

IT IS TRULY right and just,
proper and helpful toward salvation,
that we always and everywhere give thanks to you, O Lord,
holy Father, almighty and eternal God;
for your only-begotten Son restored our human nature
by the new light of his immortality
when he appeared in the substance of man's mortal nature.
Therefore with the Angels and Archangels,
the Thrones and Dominations, and all the militant hosts of heaven,
we continuously praise your glory in song, and say:

> HOLY, HOLY, HOLY LORD GOD OF HOSTS.
> HEAVEN AND EARTH ARE FILLED WITH YOUR GLORY.
> HOSANNA IN THE HIGHEST.
> BLESSED IS HE WHO COMES IN THE NAME OF THE LORD.
> HOSANNA IN THE HIGHEST.

TURN TO PAGE 407

The Eucharistic Prayer

LENT

Priest: The Lord be with you.
People: AND WITH YOUR SPIRIT.
Priest: Lift up your hearts.
People: WE HAVE LIFTED THEM UP TO THE LORD.
Priest: Let us give thanks to the Lord our God.
People: IT IS RIGHT AND JUST.

IT IS TRULY right and just,
proper and helpful toward salvation,
that we always and everywhere give thanks to you, O Lord,
holy Father, almighty and eternal God,
for using our bodily fasting to curb our vices,
to elevate our minds,
and to bestow upon us virtue and its reward,
through Christ our Lord.
Through the same Christ the Angels acclaim your majesty,
the Dominations adore you,
and the Powers worship in awe.
Through him also the heavens and the Virtues of heaven
join the blessed Seraphim in one grand chorus of joyous praise.
We beg you, let our voices blend with theirs,
as in humble praise we say:

HOLY, HOLY, HOLY LORD GOD OF HOSTS.
HEAVEN AND EARTH ARE FILLED WITH YOUR GLORY.
HOSANNA IN THE HIGHEST.
BLESSED IS HE WHO COMES IN THE NAME OF THE LORD.
HOSANNA IN THE HIGHEST.

TURN TO PAGE 407

The Eucharistic Prayer

THE HOLY CROSS

Priest: The Lord be with you.
People: AND WITH YOUR SPIRIT.
Priest: Lift up your hearts.
People: WE HAVE LIFTED THEM UP TO THE LORD.
Priest: Let us give thanks to the Lord our God.
People: IT IS RIGHT AND JUST.

IT IS TRULY right and just,
proper and helpful toward salvation,
that we always and everywhere give thanks to you, O Lord,
holy Father, almighty and eternal God;
for you ordained that the salvation of mankind
should be accomplished upon the tree of the cross,
in order that life might be restored
through the very instrument which brought death,
and that Satan, who conquered us through the tree,
might also be overcome by it;
through Christ our Lord.
Through the same Christ the Angels acclaim your majesty,
the Dominations adore you, and the Powers worship in awe.
Through him also the heavens and the Virtues of heaven
join the blessed Seraphim in one grand chorus of joyous praise.
We beg you, let our voices blend with theirs,
as in humble praise we say:

HOLY, HOLY, HOLY LORD GOD OF HOSTS.
HEAVEN AND EARTH ARE FILLED WITH YOUR GLORY.
HOSANNA IN THE HIGHEST.
BLESSED IS HE WHO COMES IN THE NAME OF THE LORD.
HOSANNA IN THE HIGHEST.

TURN TO PAGE 407

The Eucharistic Prayer

HOLY CHRISM

Priest: The Lord be with you.
People: AND WITH YOUR SPIRIT.
Priest: Lift up your hearts.
People: WE HAVE LIFTED THEM UP TO THE LORD.
Priest: Let us give thanks to the Lord our God.
People: IT IS RIGHT AND JUST.

It is TRULY right and just,
proper and helpful toward salvation,
that we humbly implore your mercy to strengthen this chrism
and so make it a sacrament of life and perfect salvation
for those who are to be remade in the spiritual bath of baptism.
After the corruption of their first birth has been submerged,
may each one of them, when this sacred oil is poured on him,
be a holy temple redolent with the sweet fragrance
of innocent life pleasing to you.
By this mystery which you have instituted
richly bestow upon them royal, priestly and prophetical honor
and clothe them with the robe of immortality,
through Christ our Lord.
Through the same Christ the Angels acclaim your majesty,
the Dominations adore you, and the Powers worship in awe.
Through him also the heavens and the Virtues of heaven
join the blessed Seraphim in one grand chorus of joyous praise.
We beg you, let our voices blend with theirs,
as in humble praise we say:

HOLY, HOLY, HOLY LORD GOD OF HOSTS.
HEAVEN AND EARTH ARE FILLED WITH YOUR GLORY.
HOSANNA IN THE HIGHEST.
BLESSED IS HE WHO COMES IN THE NAME OF THE LORD.
HOSANNA IN THE HIGHEST.

TURN TO PAGE 407

The Eucharistic Prayer

EASTER

Priest: The Lord be with you.
People: AND WITH YOUR SPIRIT.
Priest: Lift up your hearts.
People: WE HAVE LIFTED THEM UP TO THE LORD.
Priest: Let us give thanks to the Lord our God.
People: IT IS RIGHT AND JUST.

It is truly right and just,
proper and helpful toward salvation,
that we always praise you, O Lord,
but more especially so on this day
(on this night *or* at this season)
when Christ our Pasch was sacrificed.
For he is the true Lamb
who has taken away the sins of the world,
who overcame death for us by dying himself
and who restored us to life by his own resurrection.
Therefore with the Angels and Archangels,
the Thrones and Dominations, and all the militant hosts of heaven,
we continually praise your glory in song, and say:

> HOLY, HOLY, HOLY LORD GOD OF HOSTS.
> HEAVEN AND EARTH ARE FILLED WITH YOUR GLORY.
> HOSANNA IN THE HIGHEST.
> BLESSED IS HE WHO COMES IN THE NAME OF THE LORD.
> HOSANNA IN THE HIGHEST.

TURN TO PAGE 407

The Eucharistic Prayer

ASCENSION

Priest: The Lord be with you.
People: AND WITH YOUR SPIRIT.
Priest: Lift up your hearts.
People: WE HAVE LIFTED THEM UP TO THE LORD.
Priest: Let us give thanks to the Lord our God.
People: IT IS RIGHT AND JUST.

IT IS TRULY right and just,
proper and helpful toward salvation,
that we always and everywhere give thanks to you, O Lord,
holy Father, almighty and eternal God,
through Christ our Lord;
who appeared openly to all his disciples after his resurrection,
and was taken up to heaven before their eyes,
so that he might make us sharers in his own divinity.
Therefore with the Angels and Archangels,
the Thrones and Dominations, and all the militant hosts of heaven,
we continuously praise your glory in song, and say:

HOLY, HOLY, HOLY LORD GOD OF HOSTS.
HEAVEN AND EARTH ARE FILLED WITH YOUR GLORY.
HOSANNA IN THE HIGHEST.
BLESSED IS HE WHO COMES IN THE NAME OF THE LORD.
HOSANNA IN THE HIGHEST.

TURN TO PAGE 407

The Eucharistic Prayer

THE HOLY SPIRIT

Priest: The Lord be with you.
People: AND WITH YOUR SPIRIT.
Priest: Lift up your hearts.
People: WE HAVE LIFTED THEM UP TO THE LORD.
Priest: Let us give thanks to the Lord our God.
People: IT IS RIGHT AND JUST.

IT IS TRULY right and just,
proper and helpful toward salvation,
that we always and everywhere give thanks to you, O Lord,
holy Father, almighty and eternal God,
through Christ our Lord;
who ascended above the heavens to sit at your right hand,
and (on this day) he sent forth the Holy Spirit upon the children
 of adoption,
as he had promised.
Therefore the whole world is jubilant with unrestrained joy,
and the Virtues on high, with the Powers of the angelic choir,
continuously praise your glory in song, and say:

HOLY, HOLY, HOLY LORD GOD OF HOSTS.
HEAVEN AND EARTH ARE FILLED WITH YOUR GLORY.
HOSANNA IN THE HIGHEST.
BLESSED IS HE WHO COMES IN THE NAME OF THE LORD.
HOSANNA IN THE HIGHEST.

TURN TO PAGE 407

The Eucharistic Prayer

THE SACRED HEART

Priest: The Lord be with you.
People: AND WITH YOUR SPIRIT.
Priest: Lift up your hearts.
People: WE HAVE LIFTED THEM UP TO THE LORD.
Priest: Let us give thanks to the Lord our God.
People: IT IS RIGHT AND JUST.

IT IS TRULY right and just,
proper and helpful toward salvation,
that we always and everywhere give thanks to you, O Lord,
holy Father, almighty and eternal God,
who decreed that your only-begotten Son
should be pierced by a soldier's lance
as he hung upon the cross,
so that from his open heart,
as from a treasury of divine bounty,
streams of mercy and grace might pour forth upon us,
and, ever burning with love for us,
it might be a haven of peace for the devout
and a safe refuge for the penitent.
Therefore with the Angels and Archangels,
the Thrones and Dominations, and all the militant hosts of heaven,
we continuously praise your glory in song, and say:

HOLY, HOLY, HOLY LORD GOD OF HOSTS.
HEAVEN AND EARTH ARE FILLED WITH YOUR GLORY.
HOSANNA IN THE HIGHEST.
BLESSED IS HE WHO COMES IN THE NAME OF THE LORD.
HOSANNA IN THE HIGHEST.

TURN TO PAGE 407

The Eucharistic Prayer

CHRIST THE KING

Priest: The Lord be with you.
People: AND WITH YOUR SPIRIT.
Priest: Lift up your hearts.
People: WE HAVE LIFTED THEM UP TO THE LORD.
Priest: Let us give thanks to the Lord our God.
People: IT IS RIGHT AND JUST.

IT IS TRULY right and just,
proper and helpful toward salvation,
that we always and everywhere give thanks to you, O Lord,
holy Father, almighty and eternal God,
who anointed your only-begotten Son,
Jesus Christ our Lord, with the oil of gladness
to be a priest forever and king of the whole world,
so that by offering himself on the altar of the cross
as a pure victim and a peace offering,
he might perform the sacrificial rite of mankind's redemption.
All creation thereby has been made subject to his dominion
that he might present to your infinite majesty
a universal and everlasting Kingdom—
a Kingdom of truth and life, of holiness and grace,
a Kingdom of justice, of love, and of peace.
Therefore with the Angels and Archangels,
the Thrones and Dominations, and all the militant hosts of heaven,
we continuously praise your glory in song, and say:

> HOLY, HOLY, HOLY LORD GOD OF HOSTS.
> HEAVEN AND EARTH ARE FILLED WITH YOUR GLORY.
> HOSANNA IN THE HIGHEST.
> BLESSED IS HE WHO COMES IN THE NAME OF THE LORD.
> HOSANNA IN THE HIGHEST.

TURN TO PAGE 407

The Eucharistic Prayer

THE BLESSED VIRGIN MARY

Priest: The Lord be with you.
People: AND WITH YOUR SPIRIT.
Priest: Lift up your hearts.
People: WE HAVE LIFTED THEM UP TO THE LORD.
Priest: Let us give thanks to the Lord our God.
People: IT IS RIGHT AND JUST.

IT IS TRULY right and just,
proper and helpful toward salvation,
that we always and everywhere give thanks to you, O Lord,
holy Father, almighty and eternal God,
and praise, honor, and extol you
on this feast of the blessed ever-virgin Mary.
For without losing the glory of her virginity
she conceived your only-begotten Son
by the overshadowing of the Holy Spirit,
and she brought forth to the world
Jesus Christ our Lord, the eternal light.
Through the same Christ the Angels acclaim your majesty,
the Dominations adore you, and the Powers worship in awe.
Through him also the heavens and the Virtues of heaven
join the blessed Seraphim in one grand chorus of joyous praise.
We beg you, let our voices blend with theirs,
as in humble praise we say:

HOLY, HOLY, HOLY LORD GOD OF HOSTS.
HEAVEN AND EARTH ARE FILLED WITH YOUR GLORY.
HOSANNA IN THE HIGHEST.
BLESSED IS HE WHO COMES IN THE NAME OF THE LORD.
HOSANNA IN THE HIGHEST.

TURN TO PAGE 407

The Eucharistic Prayer

SAINT JOSEPH

Priest: The Lord be with you.
People: AND WITH YOUR SPIRIT.
Priest: Lift up your hearts.
People: WE HAVE LIFTED THEM UP TO THE LORD.
Priest: Let us give thanks to the Lord our God.
People: IT IS RIGHT AND JUST.

IT IS TRULY right and just,
proper and helpful toward salvation,
that we always and everywhere give thanks to you, O Lord,
holy Father, almighty and eternal God;
and glorify, honor, and extol you with fitting praise
on this feast of blessed Joseph.
For he is the just man whom you gave as husband to the virgin
    Mother of God;
the faithful and prudent servant whom you set over your family
as foster-father to protect your only-begotten Son,
conceived by the overshadowing of the Holy Spirit,
Jesus Christ our Lord.
Through the same Jesus Christ the Angels acclaim your majesty,
the Dominations adore you, and the Powers worship in awe.
Through him also the heavens and the Virtues of heaven
join the blessed Seraphim in one grand chorus of joyous praise.
We beg you, let our voices blend with theirs,
as in humble praise we say:

    HOLY, HOLY, HOLY LORD GOD OF HOSTS.
    HEAVEN AND EARTH ARE FILLED WITH YOUR GLORY.
    HOSANNA IN THE HIGHEST.
    BLESSED IS HE WHO COMES IN THE NAME OF THE LORD.
    HOSANNA IN THE HIGHEST.

TURN TO PAGE 407

The Eucharistic Prayer

THE APOSTLES

Priest: The Lord be with you.
People: AND WITH YOUR SPIRIT.
Priest: Lift up your hearts.
People: WE HAVE LIFTED THEM UP TO THE LORD.
Priest: Let us give thanks to the Lord our God.
People: IT IS RIGHT AND JUST.

IT IS TRULY right and just,
proper and helpful toward salvation,
that we humbly implore you, O Lord, our eternal shepherd,
never to desert your flock,
but to guard and protect it always through your blessed Apostles,
so that it may be governed by the same rulers
whom you have set over it to carry on your work as its shepherds.
Therefore with the Angels and Archangels,
the Thrones and Dominations, and all the militant hosts of heaven,
we continuously praise your glory in song, and say:

HOLY, HOLY, HOLY LORD GOD OF HOSTS.
HEAVEN AND EARTH ARE FILLED WITH YOUR GLORY.
HOSANNA IN THE HIGHEST.
BLESSED IS HE WHO COMES IN THE NAME OF THE LORD.
HOSANNA IN THE HIGHEST.

TURN TO PAGE 407

The Eucharistic Prayer

THE DEAD

Priest: The Lord be with you.
People: AND WITH YOUR SPIRIT.
Priest: Lift up your hearts.
People: WE HAVE LIFTED THEM UP TO THE LORD.
Priest: Let us give thanks to the Lord our God.
People: IT IS RIGHT AND JUST.

It is truly right and just,
proper and helpful toward salvation,
that we always and everywhere give thanks to you, O Lord,
holy Father, almighty and eternal God,
through Christ our Lord.
In the same Christ the hope of a blessed resurrection has dawned
for us,
bringing all who are under the certain, sad sentence of death
the consoling promise of future immortality.
For those who have been faithful, O Lord,
life is not ended but merely changed;
and when this earthly abode dissolves,
an eternal dwelling place awaits them in heaven.
Therefore with the Angels and Archangels,
the Thrones and Dominations, and all the militant hosts of heaven,
we continuously praise your glory in song, and say:

HOLY, HOLY, HOLY LORD GOD OF HOSTS.
HEAVEN AND EARTH ARE FILLED WITH YOUR GLORY.
HOSANNA IN THE HIGHEST.
BLESSED IS HE WHO COMES IN THE NAME OF THE LORD.
HOSANNA IN THE HIGHEST.

TURN TO PAGE 407

The Eucharistic Prayer

WEEKDAYS

Priest: The Lord be with you.
People: AND WITH YOUR SPIRIT.
Priest: Lift up your hearts.
People: WE HAVE LIFTED THEM UP TO THE LORD.
Priest: Let us give thanks to the Lord our God.
People: IT IS RIGHT AND JUST.

IT IS TRULY right and just,
proper and helpful toward salvation,
that we always and everywhere give thanks to you, O Lord,
holy Father, almighty and eternal God,
through Christ our Lord.
Through the same Christ the Angels acclaim your majesty,
the Dominations adore you,
and the Powers worship in awe.
Through him also the heavens and the Virtues of heaven
join the blessed Seraphim
in one grand chorus of joyous praise.
We beg you, let our voices blend with theirs,
as in humble praise we say:

HOLY, HOLY, HOLY LORD GOD OF HOSTS.
HEAVEN AND EARTH ARE FILLED WITH YOUR GLORY.
HOSANNA IN THE HIGHEST.
BLESSED IS HE WHO COMES IN THE NAME OF THE LORD.
HOSANNA IN THE HIGHEST.

TURN TO PAGE 407

The Eucharistic Prayer

THE HOLY TRINITY

Priest: The Lord be with you.
People: AND WITH YOUR SPIRIT.
Priest: Lift up your hearts.
People: WE HAVE LIFTED THEM UP TO THE LORD.
Priest: Let us give thanks to the Lord our God.
People: IT IS RIGHT AND JUST.

IT IS TRULY right and just,
proper and helpful toward salvation,
that we always and everywhere give thanks to you, O Lord,
holy Father, almighty and eternal God;
for with your only-begotten Son and the Holy Spirit
you are one God, one Lord,
not in the unity of a single person,
but in the Trinity of one substance.
For what we believe of your glory, through your revelation,
that we also believe of your Son, and of the Holy Spirit
without difference or distinction.
So that in confessing the true and eternal Godhead,
we adore the distinction of persons, oneness in being,
    and equality in majesty.
This the Angels and Archangels,
the Cherubim and Seraphim praise,
and unceasingly chant each day, saying with one voice:

    HOLY, HOLY, HOLY LORD GOD OF HOSTS.
    HEAVEN AND EARTH ARE FILLED WITH YOUR GLORY.
    HOSANNA IN THE HIGHEST.
    BLESSED IS HE WHO COMES IN THE NAME OF THE LORD.
    HOSANNA IN THE HIGHEST.

TURN TO PAGE 407

M ost merciful father, we humbly pray and entreat you through Jesus Christ, your Son, our Lord, to accept and bless these gifts, these holy things we owe to you, these sacred unblemished offerings.

W e offer them to you in the first place on behalf of your holy Catholic Church: be pleased to keep her in peace throughout the world, to watch over her, to guide her and to gather all men into unity with her; together with your servant our pope, our bishop, and all those right-believing teachers who have the guardianship of the catholic and apostolic faith.

R emember, Lord, your servants, and all here present: you know their faith and have seen their devotedness. On their behalf we offer you, or they themselves offer, this sacrifice of praise for themselves and all who are theirs, for the redeeming of their souls, for the safety and salvation they hope for; they direct their prayers to you, the eternal, the living and the true God.

U nited in one fellowship, we reverently call to mind, first, the glorious ever-virgin Mary, mother of our God and Lord Jesus Christ, and also blessed Joseph her husband, and then your blessed apostles and martyrs Peter and Paul, Andrew, James, John, Thomas, James, Philip, Bartholomew, Matthew, Simon and Thaddeus, Linus, Cletus, Clement, Sixtus, Cornelius, Cyprian, Lawrence, Chrysogonus, John and Paul, Cosmas and Damian, and all your saints. Grant through their merits and prayers that we may at all times be helped by your power and protection. Through the same Christ our Lord. Amen.

T his, then, is the offering
that we, the servants of your altar,
together with your whole family,
make to you:

Lord, be pleased to accept it.
Order our days in your peace,
save us from everlasting doom,
number us in the flock of your chosen ones.
Through Christ our Lord. Amen.

Be pleased, O God, to bless this offering,
wholly to accept and approve it,
to perfect it and make it worthy of your acceptance;
that thus it may become for us
the Body and the Blood of your dearly beloved Son,
our Lord Jesus Christ.

He, on the day before he suffered,
took bread in his holy and worshipful hands
and, with eyes lifted heavenwards
to you, God, his almighty Father,
giving thanks to you, he blessed the bread,
broke it,
and gave it to his disciples, saying:
Take it, all of you, and eat of it,
for this is my body.

In the same way, after supper,
he took this noble cup in his holy and worshipful hands
and, again giving thanks to you, he blessed it
and gave it to his disciples, saying:
Take it, all of you, and drink of it,
for this is the cup of my blood,
of the new and everlasting covenant,
the mystery of faith
which shall be shed for you
and for many others

for forgiveness of sins.
As often as you do these things,
you shall do them in memory of me.

Accordingly, Lord, remembering the blessed passion
of the same Christ your Son, our Lord,
his resurrection from the shades of death
and his ascension to glory in heaven,
we your servants and your holy people
offer to your resplendent majesty—
from your own gifts bestowed on us—
the sacrifice that is perfect,
the sacrifice that is holy,
the sacrifice that is without blemish:
the holy Bread of eternal life
and the Cup of everlasting salvation.

Be pleased to look on these offerings with favor and contentment;
accept them as you were pleased to accept
the offerings of your holy servant Abel,
the sacrifice of our father Abraham,
and that of your high priest Melchisedech—
a holy sacrifice, an unblemished victim.

We humbly entreat you, almighty God,
to command that these offerings be carried by your holy angel
to your altar on high,
in the sight of your divine majesty;
so that we,
receiving your Son's most sacred Body and Blood
by partaking at the altar here,
may be filled with every blessing and grace from heaven.
Through the same Christ our Lord. Amen.

Rемемвеr too, Lord, your servants, who have gone before us from this world, signed with the seal of faith, and are sleeping the sleep of peace. We pray you, Lord, to lead these, and all who rest in Christ, into the place of happiness, light, and peace. Through the same Christ our Lord. Amen.

All of us too, sinners, but your servants, put our trust in your countless mercies. Be pleased, then, to give us a place in the fellowship of your holy apostles and martyrs, with John, Stephen, Matthias, Barnabas, Ignatius, Alexander, Marcellinus, Peter, Felicity, Perpetua, Agatha, Lucy, Agnes, Cecilia, Anastasia, and with all your saints. Admit us to their company, not weighing our merits, but freely granting us forgiveness. Through Christ our Lord.

It is through him, Lord, that you unceasingly create all these good things, and hallow them, give them life, bless them, and bestow them on us.

> Through him and with him and in him
> are given to you, God the almighty Father,
> in the unity of the Holy Spirit
> all honor and glory
> for ever and ever.

> Per ipsum, et cum ipso, et in ipso,
> est tibi Deo Patri omnipotenti,
> in unitate Spiritus Sancti,
> omnis honor et gloria,
> per omnia saecula saeculorum.

AMEN

The Eucharistic Banquet

Priest: Let us pray: Taught by our Savior's command and formed by the word of God, we dare to say:

All: OUR FATHER, WHO ART IN HEAVEN,
HALLOWED BE THY NAME;
THY KINGDOM COME;
THY WILL BE DONE ON EARTH AS IT IS IN HEAVEN.
GIVE US THIS DAY OUR DAILY BREAD;
AND FORGIVE US OUR TRESPASSES
AS WE FORGIVE THOSE WHO TRESPASS AGAINST US;
AND LEAD US NOT INTO TEMPTATION,
BUT DELIVER US FROM EVIL.

Priest: Deliver us, we beg you, O Lord, from every evil, past, present, and to come; and by the intercession of the blessed and glorious ever-virgin Mary, mother of God, of the blessed apostles Peter and Paul, of Andrew, and all the saints, in your mercy grant peace in our days, that by your compassionate aid we may be ever free from sin and sheltered from all turmoil. Through Jesus Christ, your Son, our Lord, who lives and reigns with you in the unity of the Holy Spirit, God, forever and ever.

People: AMEN.
Priest: May the peace of the Lord be always with you.
People: AND WITH YOUR SPIRIT.

The priest prays that the mingling of the Body and Blood of Christ may be a source of everlasting life for us.

411

People: LAMB OF GOD, WHO TAKE AWAY THE SINS OF THE WORLD, HAVE MERCY ON US.

LAMB OF GOD, WHO TAKE AWAY THE SINS OF THE WORLD, HAVE MERCY ON US.

LAMB OF GOD, WHO TAKE AWAY THE SINS OF THE WORLD, GRANT US PEACE.

In Masses of the Dead: GRANT THEM REST *is said twice,*
then GRANT THEM ETERNAL REST.

The priest prays for peace and for the unity of the Church, which is sometimes expressed by a gesture of fraternal love called the Kiss of Peace. The priest then prepares for his own communion by saying a few prayers quietly.

Priest: Behold the lamb of God, behold him who takes away the sins of the world.

People (three times): LORD, I AM NOT WORTHY THAT YOU SHOULD COME UNDER MY ROOF. SPEAK BUT THE WORD AND MY SOUL WILL BE HEALED.

During the distribution of communion the following dialogue takes place:

Priest: The Body of Christ.

Communicant: AMEN.

Turn to the Mass of the day for the Communion Song.

THE
HYMNAL

THE HYMNAL

MUSIC AND SONG have an important place in liturgy. Through them men may express more fully their beliefs, hopes, joys and sorrows, and in this way both manifest and build a unity among themselves. This Hymnal is intended to provide a variety in kinds and styles of song for use at worship in all its forms. For the best use of the Hymnal, a cross reference index for the various seasons and feasts and one for different occasions and themes may be found on page 803.

The first section of the Hymnal, Numbers 1 through 101, contains the hymns themselves. A complete index of the hymns and the other materials in the Hymnal will be found on page 553.

Numbers 102 through 130 are antiphons, most of which may be used with the psalms if the latter are sung in the simple manner described on page 549. The third section of the Hymnal, Numbers 131 through 135, provides music for some of the Holy Week antiphons in the order in which they occur during Holy Week.

The fourth section, Numbers 136 through 163, provides music for the ordinary parts of the English sung Mass. These are taken from J. Gerald Phillips' "Mass in the Vernacular," C. Alexander Peloquin's "Mass for Parishes," Joseph Roff's "People's Mass in Honor of Pope John," and Marcel Rooney's "Mass in Honor of the Immaculate Conception," with a musical setting for the Creed by Joseph Roff and a setting for the "Lamb of God" at Masses for the Dead by Cyril Reilly. Finally, the following approved musical settings are included: three settings of the Our Father, two settings of the Preface, two settings of the Holy, Holy, Holy, and one setting each of the Orations, Kiss of Peace, Dismissal and Pontifical Blessing.

The Hymnal concludes with ten musical patterns for singing the psalms, Numbers 164 through 173. These are explained in the instruction to the choir director on page 550.

A Child is Born in Bethlehem

MODE I

1 A Child is born in Beth - le - hem, Al - le - lu - ia;
2 Our Broth - er in the flesh is he, Al - le - lu - ia;
3 The Ma - gi Kings come from a - far, Al - le - lu - ia;
4 Gold, in - cense, myrrh they of - fer him, Al - le - lu - ia;

Re - joice, re - joice Je - ru - sa - lem, Al - le - lu - ia, Al - le - lu - ia.
Our King for all e - ter - ni - ty, Al - le - lu - ia, Al - le - lu - ia.
Led on by faith in heav - en's star, Al - le - lu - ia, Al - le - lu - ia.
And bend - ing low they wor - ship him, Al - le - lu - ia, Al - le - lu - ia.

Let grate - ful hearts now sing A song of joy and

ho - ly praise to Christ the new - born King!

Traditional, *Tr.* IRVIN UDULUTSCH

2

A Great and Mighty Wonder

ROSA MYSTICA   76.76.676   Traditional, har. by MICHAEL PRAETORIUS, 1609, a[

1 A great and migh-ty won-der To-day on earth is done
Be-hold, a vir-gin moth-er Brings forth God's on-ly Son.

Re-peat the hymn a-gain! "To God on high be

glo-ry, And peace on earth to men!"

2 The Word made Flesh has come now
   To live with us on earth,
   And angel choirs sing praises,
      Proclaim to all his birth. *Refrain*

3 While thus they praise your maker
   Those bright angelic bands,
   Rejoice you fields and mountains,
      You oceans clap your hands. *Ref*

4 Since all he comes to comfort
   By all he be adored,
   The infant born in Bethl'hem,
      The Saviour and the Lord. *Refrain*

ST. GERMANUS, 634–734; *after* J. M. NEALE,

416

Behold, a Rose of Judah

The tune is the same as No. 2.

1 Behold, a Rose of Judah from tender branch has sprung!
A Rose from Root of Jesse, as prophets long had sung.
It bore a flower bright,
That blossomed in the winter, when half spent was the night.

2 This Rose of royal beauty of which Isaiah sings,
Is Mary, maiden Mother, and Christ the flow'r she brings.
By God's unique design,
Remaining still a Virgin, she bore her child divine.

3 We pray thee, Virgin Mother, the Queen of heav'n and earth:
Obtain for us from Jesus the blessings of his birth.
By his humility,
May we live as God's children in peace and unity.

Es ist ein' Ros' entsprungen, 15th c. Tr. IRVIN UDULUTSCH, O.F.M. *Cap.*

Hark! A Thrilling Voice is Sounding

MERTON   87.87   WILLIAM HENRY MONK, 1850

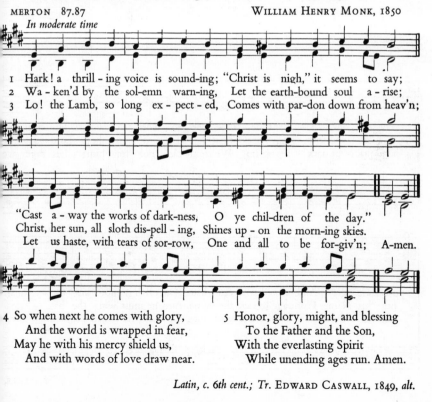

In moderate time

1 Hark! a thrill-ing voice is sound-ing; "Christ is nigh," it seems to say;
2 Wa-ken'd by the sol-emn warn-ing, Let the earth-bound soul a-rise;
3 Lo! the Lamb, so long ex-pect-ed, Comes with par-don down from heav'n;

"Cast a-way the works of dark-ness, O ye chil-dren of the day."
Christ, her sun, all sloth dis-pell-ing, Shines up-on the morn-ing skies.
Let us haste, with tears of sor-row, One and all to be for-giv'n; A-men.

4 So when next he comes with glory,
And the world is wrapped in fear,
May he with his mercy shield us,
And with words of love draw near.

5 Honor, glory, might, and blessing
To the Father and the Son,
With the everlasting Spirit
While unending ages run. Amen.

Latin, c. 6th cent.; Tr. EDWARD CASWALL, 1849, *alt.*

417

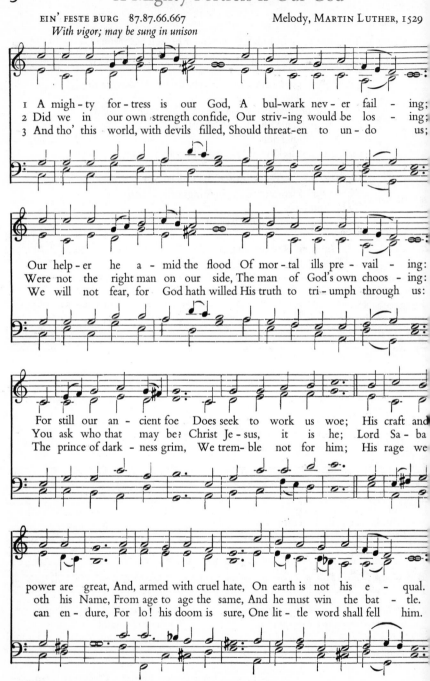

5   A Mighty Fortress is Our God

EIN' FESTE BURG   87.87.66.667   Melody, MARTIN LUTHER, 1529

With vigor; may be sung in unison

1 A migh-ty for-tress is our God, A bul-wark nev-er fail - ing;
2 Did we in our own strength confide, Our striv-ing would be los - ing;
3 And tho' this world, with devils filled, Should threat-en to un-do us;

Our help-er he a-mid the flood Of mor-tal ills pre-vail - ing:
Were not the right man on our side, The man of God's own choos - ing:
We will not fear, for God hath willed His truth to tri-umph through us:

For still our an-cient foe Does seek to work us woe; His craft and
You ask who that may be? Christ Je-sus, it is he; Lord Sa-ba
The prince of dark-ness grim, We trem-ble not for him; His rage we

power are great, And, armed with cruel hate, On earth is not his e - qual.
oth his Name, From age to age the same, And he must win the bat - tle.
can en-dure, For lo! his doom is sure, One lit-tle word shall fell him.

418

4 That word above all earthly powers,
   No thanks to them, abideth;
The Spirit and the gifts are ours
   Through him who with us sideth:
Let goods and kindred go,
This mortal life also;
The body they may kill:
God's truth abideth still,
   His kingdom is for ever.

MARTIN LUTHER, 1529; *Tr.* FREDERICK HENRY HEDGE, 1852, *alt.*

All Hail the Power of Jesus' Name

CORONATION   86.86.86   OLIVER HOLDEN, 1793
Majestically, in strict time throughout

1 All hail the power of Je - sus 'Name! Let an - gels pros-trate fall;
2 Crown him, ye mar - tyrs of our God, Who from his al - tar call:
3 Hail him, the Heir of Da - vid's line, Whom Da - vid Lord did call,

Bring forth the roy - al di - a - dem, And crown him Lord of all!
Praise him whose way of pain ye trod, And crown him Lord of all!
The God in - car - nate, Man di - vine, And crown him Lord of all!

Bring forth the roy - al di - a - dem, And crown him Lord of all!
Praise him whose way of pain ye trod, And crown him Lord of all!
The God in - car - nate, Man di - vine, And crown him Lord of all!

EDWARD PERRONET, 1779, *alt.*

ST. THEODULPH 76.76.D   MELCHIOR TESCHNER, pub. 1615

Majestically; may be sung in unison

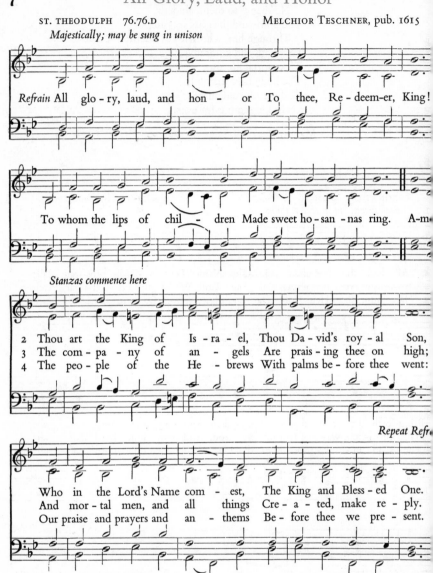

Refrain All glo-ry, laud, and hon-or To thee, Re-deem-er, King!

To whom the lips of chil-dren Made sweet ho-san-nas ring. A-m

Stanzas commence here

2 Thou art the King of Is-ra-el, Thou Da-vid's roy-al Son,
3 The com-pa-ny of an-gels Are prais-ing thee on high;
4 The peo-ple of the He-brews With palms be-fore thee went:

Repeat Refr

Who in the Lord's Name com-est, The King and Bless-ed One.
And mor-tal men, and all things Cre-a-ted, make re-ply.
Our praise and prayers and an-thems Be-fore thee we pre-sent.

5 To thee before thy passion
 They sang hymns of praise:
 To thee, now high exalted,
 Our melody we raise
 Refrain

6 Thou didst accept their praises;
 Accept the prayers we bring,
 Who in all good delightest,
 Thou good and gracious King.
 Refrain

ST. THEODULPH, c. 820; *Tr.* JOHN MASON NEALE, I

The Strife is O'er, The Battle Done

VICTORY   8 8 8, with Alleluias

With dignity

PALESTRINA, 1588;
adapted with Alleluias by WILLIAM H. MONK, 1861

Al – le – lu – ia! Al – le – lu – ia! Al – le – lu – ia!

Org. *p*

1 The strife is o'er, the bat – tle done, The vic – to –
2 The powers of death have done their worst, But Christ their
3 The three sad days are quick – ly sped, He ri – ses

ry of life is won; The song of tri – umph
le – gions has dis – persed: Let shout of ho – ly
glo – rious from the dead: All glo – ry to our

has be – gun. Al – le – lu – ia!
joy out – burst. Al – le – lu – ia!
ris – en Head! Al – le – lu – ia!   A – men.

He closed the yawning gates of hell,
The bars from heav'n's high portals fell;
Let hymns of praise his triumphs tell!
　　　　　　　　Alleluia!

5 Lord! by the stripes which wounded thee,
From death's dread sting thy servants free,
That we may live and sing to thee.
　　　　　　　　Alleluia! Amen.

Latin, pub. Cologne, 1695; Tr. FRANCIS POTT, *1861, alt.*

421

9 Alleluia! Sing to Jesus

HYFRYDOL 87.87.D ROWLAND HUGH PRICHARD, c. 1830

With dignity

1 Al - le - lu - ia! sing to Je - sus! His the scep - ter, his the throne
2 Al - le - lu - ia! not as or - phans Are we left in sor - row now;
3 Al - le - lu - ia! Bread of Hea - ven, You on earth our food, our stay!

Al - le - lu - ia! his the tri - umph, His the vic - to - ry a - lone
Al - le - lu - ia! he is near us, Faith be - lieves, nor ques - tions how
Al - le - lu - ia! here the sin - ful Flee to you from day to day

Hark! the songs of peace - ful Si - on Thun - der like a migh - ty flood
Though the cloud from sight re - ceived him, When the for - ty days were o'er,
In - ter - ces - sor, friend of sin - ners, Earth's Re - deem - er, plead for me,

Je - sus out of ev - 'ry na - tion Has re - deemed us by his blood
Shall our hearts for - get his prom - ise, "I am with you ev - er - more"
Where the songs of all the sin - less Sweep a - cross the crys - tal sea.

4 Alleluia! King eternal,
  Thee the Lord of lords we own:
  Alleluia! born of Mary,
  Earth thy footstool, heav'n thy throne;
  Thou within the veil hast entered,
  Robed in flesh, our great High Priest:
  Thou on earth both Priest and Victim
  In the eucharistic feast.

5 Alleluia! sing to Jesus!
  All his scepter, his the throne;
  Alleluia! his the triumph,
  His the victory alone;
  Hark! the songs of holy Sion
  Thunder like a mighty flood;
  Jesus out of every nation
  Hath redeemed us by his blood.

A - men.

WILLIAM CHATTERTON DIX, 1866, *alt.*

Praise the Lord, Ye Heavens

The tune is the same as No. 9   *Based on Psalm 148*

1 Praise the Lord, ye heav'ns, adore him;
  Praise him, angels in the height;
  Sun and moon, rejoice before him;
  Praise him, all ye stars of light.
  Praise the Lord, for he has spoken;
  Worlds his mighty voice obeyed;
  Laws which never shall be broken
  For their guidance he has made.

2 Praise the Lord, for he is glorious,
  Never shall his promise fail;
  God has made his saints victorious,
  Sin and death shall not prevail.
  Praise the God of our salvation;
  Hosts on high, his power proclaim;
  Heaven and earth and all creation
  Praise and magnify his name.

3 Worship, honor, glory, blessing,
  Lord, we offer unto you
  Young and old, your praises expressing,
  All glad homage that is due.
  All the saints in heav'n adore you,
  We would bow before your throne;
  As the angels serve before you.
  So on earth your will be done.

Verses 1, 2: Foundling Hospital Collection, c. 1801. Verse 3: EDWARD OSLER, 1836

11 As With Gladness Men of Old

DIX 77.77.77
Joyfully

CONRAD KOCHER, 1838, *alt.*

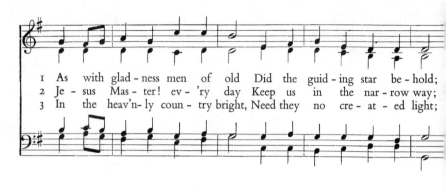

1 As with glad-ness men of old Did the guid-ing star be-hold;
2 Je - sus Mas - ter! ev - 'ry day Keep us in the nar - row way;
3 In the heav'n-ly coun - try bright, Need they no cre - at - ed light;

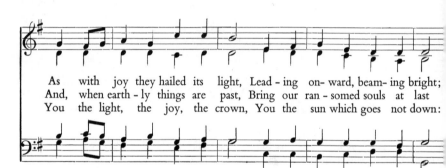

As with joy they hailed its light, Lead-ing on-ward, beam-ing bright;
And, when earth - ly things are past, Bring our ran - somed souls at last
You the light, the joy, the crown, You the sun which goes not down:

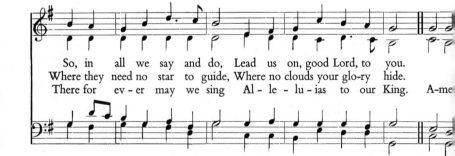

So, in all we say and do, Lead us on, good Lord, to you.
Where they need no star to guide, Where no clouds your glo-ry hide.
There for ev - er may we sing Al - le - lu - ias to our King. A-me

WILLIAM CHATTERTON DIX, 1860,

Break Forth, O Beauteous Heavenly Light

SCHOP 87.87.88.77
Joyously; may be sung in unison

JOHANN SCHOP, 1641
har. J. S. BACH, 1734

Break forth, O beau-teous heav'n-ly light, And ush-er in the morn-ing; You shep-herds do not fear this sight, But hear the an-gel's warn-ing. This child, this lit-tle help-less boy Shall be our con-fi-dence and joy, The powers of hell o'er-throw-ing, At last our peace be-stow-ing.

JOHANN RIST, 1641; *Hymnal Version*, 1940, alt.

425

87.87.87

EDMUND KESTEL, O.S.B., 1946

Triumphantly

1 Burst - ing forth from Phar-aoh's pris - on, Al - le - lu - ia let us sin
2 World-wide ta - ble, Hea - ven's vi - sion, Let the Al - le - lu - ia rin
3 To the Fa - ther, Son, and Spir - it, Al - le - lu - ia on the wir

REFRAIN

Al - le - lu - ia, Christ is ris - en, Al - le - lu ia to our King

rit.

Al - le - lu - ia, Christ is ris - en, Al - le - lu - ia to our King.

PATRICK CUMMINS, O.S.B., 1

Come, Holy Ghost

HOLY SPIRIT 88.88.8

L. LAMBILLOTTE (ABRIDGED)

1 Come Ho - ly Ghost, Cre - a - tor blest, And in our hearts take up your rest; Come with your grace and heav'n - ly aid To fill the hearts which you have made.

2 O, Com - fort - er, to you we cry, The heav'n - ly gift of God Most High; The Fount of Life, And sweet a - noint - ing from a - bove, And sweet a - noint - ing from a - bove.

3 O Ho - ly Ghost, Through you a - lone, Know we the Fa - ther and the Son; Be this our firm un - chang - ing creed, That you do from them both pro - ceed, That you do from them both pro - ceed.

4 Praise we the Lord, Fa - ther and Son, And Ho - ly Spir - it with them one; And may the Son on us be - stow All gifts that from the Spir - it flow, All gifts that from the Spir - it flow.

Tr. REV. E. CASWALL, *alt.*

15

Christ, the Lord, is Risen Again

CHRIST IST ERSTANDEN 77. 77, with Alleluia   GERMAN CAROL, XII CENT.

Joyfully. In unison

1 Christ, the Lord, is ris'n a- gain, Christ has bro- ken ev- 'ry cha
2 He who gave for us his life, Who for us en- dured the str

Hark, an- gel- ic voic- es cry, Sing- ing ev- er- more on
Is our Pas- chal Lamb to- day; We too sing for joy, and

3 He who bore all pain and loss
  Comfortless upon the Cross,
  Lives in glory now on high,
  Pleads for us, and hears our cry:
              Alleluia!

4 He who slumbered in the grave,
  Is exalted now to save;
  Through creation now it rings
  That the Lamb is King of kings,
              Alleluia!

5 Now he bids us tell abroad
  How the lost may be restored,
  How the penitent forgiven,
  How we too may enter heaven,
              Alleluia!

6 You, our Paschal Lamb indeed,
  Christ, your ransomed people feed;
  Take our sins and guilt away,
  Let your people sing today.
              Alleluia!

From The Lutheran Service Book and Hymnal, by permission of the Commission on The Liturg
Hy

Al – le – lu – ia! Al – le – lu – ia, Al – le – lu – ia,

Al – le – lu – ia. Hark, an – gel – ic voic – es cry,

Sing – ing ev – er – more on high, Al – le – lu – ia.

MICHAEL WEISSE, *cir.* 1480–1534; *Tr.* CATHERINE WINKWORTH, 1829–78, *alt.*

16

Come, Thou Holy Spirit, Come

R. F. Twynham

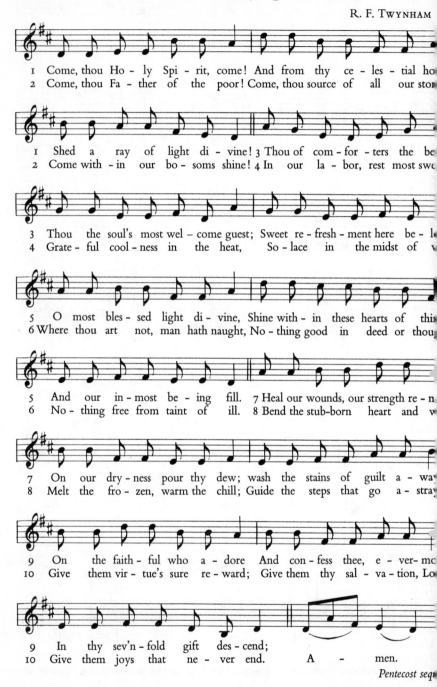

1 Come, thou Holy Spi - rit, come! And from thy ce - les - tial ho
2 Come, thou Fa - ther of the poor! Come, thou source of all our stor

1 Shed a ray of light di - vine! 3 Thou of com - for - ters the be
2 Come with - in our bo - soms shine! 4 In our la - bor, rest most swe

3 Thou the soul's most wel - come guest; Sweet re - fresh - ment here be - l
4 Grate - ful cool - ness in the heat, So - lace in the midst of v

5 O most bles - sed light di - vine, Shine with - in these hearts of thi
6 Where thou art not, man hath naught, No - thing good in deed or thou

5 And our in - most be - ing fill. 7 Heal our wounds, our strength re - n
6 No - thing free from taint of ill. 8 Bend the stub - born heart and v

7 On our dry - ness pour thy dew; wash the stains of guilt a - wa
8 Melt the fro - zen, warm the chill; Guide the steps that go a - stra

9 On the faith - ful who a - dore And con - fess thee, e - ver - mo
10 Give them vir - tue's sure re - ward; Give them thy sal - va - tion, Lo

9 In thy sev'n - fold gift des - cend;
10 Give them joys that ne - ver end. A - men.

Pentecost seq

430

Come to the Banquet

CHANT

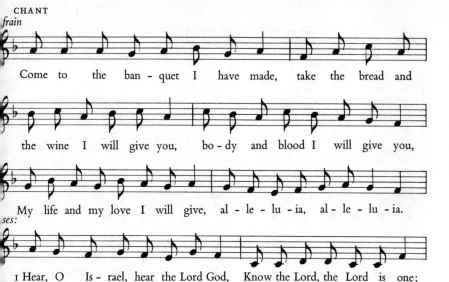

Come to the ban-quet I have made, take the bread and
the wine I will give you, bo-dy and blood I will give you,
My life and my love I will give, al-le-lu-ia, al-le-lu-ia.

1 Hear, O Is-rael, hear the Lord God, Know the Lord, the Lord is one;
2 We were once a cap-tive peo-ple, Till that day of jub-i-lee,

I your God and you my peo-ple, Till this cov-e-nant is done.
Brought us Christ the Eas-ter vic-tim, Slain to set his peo-ple free.

Victim worthy of the Father,
Paschal Lamb made Lamb of God;
Death brings life to captive people,
Breaking hell with royal rod.

5 God's own people called to banquet,
Gathered at the cov'nant meal,
Flesh and blood feed hungry children;
Here Christ's body is made real.

Christ is risen, Alleluia!
Come the Victor from the tomb!
Come and feast now at the marriage
Of the Lamb made mankind's groom.

6 Sent forth from this holy banquet,
Witnesses for all the earth,
Till the Lord returns in glory
Bringing all the world new birth.

Verses for Advent, Christmas, or Epiphany

Hear the cry of John the Baptist,
"Turn to God, prepare his ways!"
Hear Isaiah's songs of servant,
Hear the mother's hymn of praise!

4 Christ is come now, Alleluia!
Glory seen in God's own son,
Full of grace and full of favor,
Sing to him while ages run.

Word made flesh to help his brothers,
Savior comes to enter strife.
Great exchange beyond all hoping,
Mankind shares in God's own life.

5 In the star that led the sages,
In the water John has poured,
In the wine at Cana banquet,
All the earth now sees its Lord!

Chorus: JOSEPH NOLAN *Verses:* GABRIEL HUCK, 1965

18 Crown Him with Many Crowns

DIADEMATA 66.86.D

GEORGE J. ELVEY, 1868

With vigor

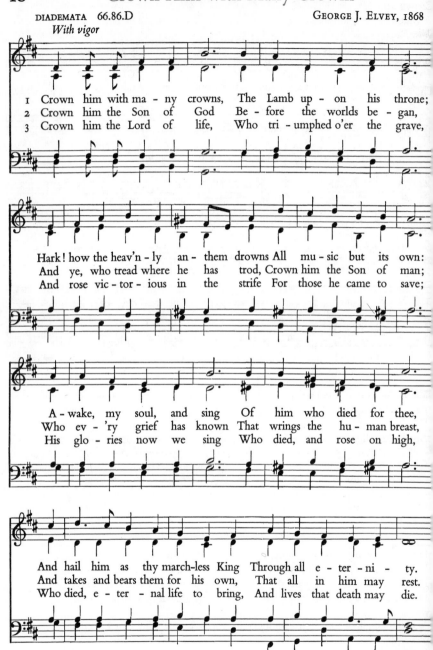

1 Crown him with ma - ny crowns, The Lamb up - on his throne;
2 Crown him the Son of God Be - fore the worlds be - gan,
3 Crown him the Lord of life, Who tri - umphed o'er the grave,

Hark! how the heav'n - ly an - them drowns All mu - sic but its own:
And ye, who tread where he has trod, Crown him the Son of man;
And rose vic - tor - ious in the strife For those he came to save;

A - wake, my soul, and sing Of him who died for thee,
Who ev - 'ry grief has known That wrings the hu - man breast,
His glo - ries now we sing Who died, and rose on high,

And hail him as thy march-less King Through all e - ter - ni - ty.
And takes and bears them for his own, That all in him may rest.
Who died, e - ter - nal life to bring, And lives that death may die.

Crown him of lords the Lord,
  Who over all shall reign,
Who once on earth, the incarnate Word,
  For ransomed sinners slain,
Now lives in realms of light,
  Where saints with angels sing
Their songs before him day and night,
  Their God, Redeemer, King.

5 Crown him the Lord of heav'n,
    Enthroned in worlds above;
  Crown him the King, to whom is giv'n
    The wondrous name of Love.
  Crown him with many crowns,
    As thrones before him fall,
  Crown him, ye kings, with many crowns,
    For he is King of all.

MATTHEW BRIDGES, 1851

In Christ There Is No East or West

MCKEE C.M.
With dignity

Negro Melody adapted by
HARRY T. BURLEIGH, 1939

In Christ there is no East or West, In him no South or North,
In him shall true hearts ev-'ry-where Their high com-mun-ion find;

But one great fel-low-ship of love Thro' out the whole wide earth.
His ser-vice is the gold-en cord Close-bind-ing all man-kind.

Join hands, then, brothers of the faith,
  What'er your race may be!
Who serves my Father as a son
  Is surely kin to me.

4 In Christ now meet both East and West,
    In him meet South and North,
  All Christly souls are one in him,
    Throughout the whole wide earth.

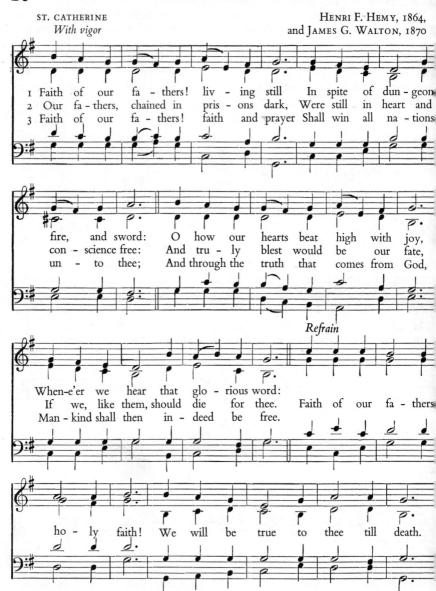

ST. CATHERINE
With vigor

HENRI F. HEMY, 1864,
and JAMES G. WALTON, 1870

1 Faith of our fa - thers! liv - ing still In spite of dun - geon
2 Our fa - thers, chained in pris - ons dark, Were still in heart and
3 Faith of our fa - thers! faith and prayer Shall win all na - tions

fire, and sword: O how our hearts beat high with joy,
con - science free: And tru - ly blest would be our fate,
un - to thee; And through the truth that comes from God,

Refrain

When-e'er we hear that glo - rious word:
If we, like them, should die for thee. Faith of our fa - thers
Man - kind shall then in - deed be free.

ho - ly faith! We will be true to thee till death.

4 Faith of our fathers! we will love
  Both friend and foe in all our strife;
  And preach thee, too, as love knows how,
  By kindly deeds and virtuous life. *Refrain*

FREDERICK WILLIAM FABER, 1849,

1

Faithful Cross

MODE I

1 Faith - ful Cross, O tree all beau - teous, Tree all peer - less
2 Sing, my tongue, the Sa - vior's glo - ry; Tell his tri - umph

and di - vine: Not a grove on earth can show us
far and wide; Tell a - loud the fa - mous sto - ry

Such a leaf and flower as thine; Sweet the nails and
Of his bo - dy cru - ci - fied; How up - on the

sweet the wood La - den with so sweet a load.
cross a vic - tim Van - quish - ing in death he died.

For additional verses turn to page 519. VENATUS FORTUNATUS, *c.* 609

Almighty Father Strong to Save

MELITA 88.88.88

JOHN B. DYKES, 1861

In moderate time

1 Al-migh-ty Fa-ther, strong to save, Whose arm has bound the
2 O Christ, the Lord of hill and plain O'er which our traf-fic
3 O Spir-it whom the Fa-ther sent To spread a-broad the

rest-less wave, Who bids the migh-ty o-cean deep Its
runs a-main By moun-tain pass or val-ley low; Where-
fir-ma-ment; O Wind of hea-ven, by thy might Save

own ap-point-ed lim-its keep: O hear us when we
ev-er, Lord, thy breth-ren go, Pro-tect them by thy
all who dare the ea-gle's flight, And keep them by thy

cry to thee For those in per-il on the sea.
guard-ing hand From ev-'ry per-il on the land.
watch-ful care From ev-'ry per-il in the air. A-men.

4 O Trinity of love and power,
　Our brethren shield in danger's hour;
　From rock and tempest, fire and foe,
　Protect them wheresoe'er they go;
　　Thus evermore shall rise to thee
　　Glad praise from air and land and sea.
　　　　　　　Amen.

From A Missionary Service Book, 1937
Stanzas 1 *and* 4, WILLIAM WHITING, 1860, *alt.*

3　Ye Holy Angels Bright

DARWELL　66.66.44.44　　　　　　　JOHN DARWELL, 1770
With dignity

1 Ye ho-ly an-gels bright, Who wait at God's right hand, Or
2 Ye bless-ed souls at rest, Who ran this earth-ly race And
3 Ye saints, who toil be-low, A-dore your heav'n-ly King, And

through the realms of light Fly at your Lord's com-mand, As-sist our
now, from sin re-leased, Be-hold the Sa-viour's face, God's prais-es
on-ward as ye go Some joy-ful an-them sing; Take what he

song, For else the theme Too high doth seem For mor-tal tongue.
sound, As in his sight With sweet de-light Ye do a-bound.
gives And praise him still, Through good or ill, Who ev-er lives!

RICHARD BAXTER, 1672, *and* JOHN HAMPDEN GURNEY, 1838

437

Father, We Gather Here to Praise You

98.98.D

Joseph Roff

1 Fa - ther we gath - er here to praise you, You are th
2 Je - sus, the Mas - ter, went to Ca - na; For bride an

love that makes us one. Be here a - mong us at this
groom he worked new sign: Teach - er of love made ban-que

wed - ing, Make strong this wonder now be - gun.
joy - ous, Love came in gift of new-made wine.

Fa - ther you made us to be like you, To have this
See now the mar - riage of your peo - ple, Your Church u -

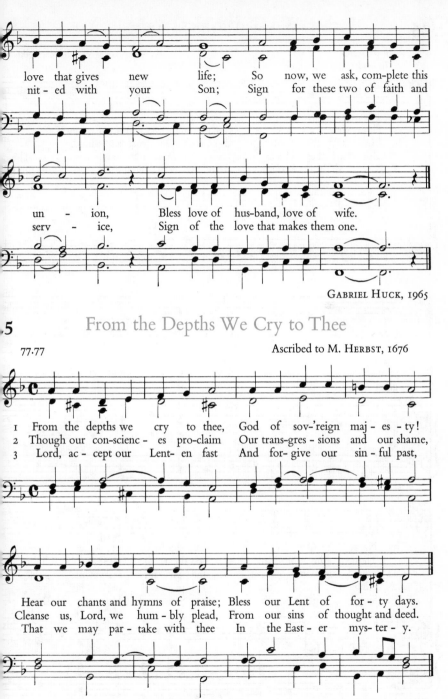

love that gives new life; So now, we ask, com-plete this
nit - ed with your Son; Sign for these two of faith and

un - ion, Bless love of hus-band, love of wife.
serv - ice, Sign of the love that makes them one.

GABRIEL HUCK, 1965

5 From the Depths We Cry to Thee

77·77   Ascribed to M. HERBST, 1676

1 From the depths we cry to thee, God of sov'reign maj - es - ty!
2 Though our con-scienc - es pro-claim Our trans-gres - sions and our shame,
3 Lord, ac - cept our Lent- en fast And for-give our sin - ful past,

Hear our chants and hymns of praise; Bless our Lent of for - ty days.
Cleanse us, Lord, we hum - bly plead, From our sins of thought and deed.
That we may par - take with thee In the East - er mys- ter - y.

SISTER M. TERESINE, O.S.F. *Stanza 2,* A. G. MCDOUGALL, *alt.*

439

SINE NOMINE   R. VAUGHAN WILLIAMS, 1906
In moderate time, unison

1 For   all   the   saints,   who from their la - bors rest,   Who
2 Thou wast their rock,   their for - tress, and their might:
3 O   may thy   sol -   diers, faith - ful, true, and bold,
7 But   lo! there breaks   a   yet more glo-rious day;   The
8 From earth's wide bounds,   from   o - cean's far - thest coast,   Through

thee . . . . . by   faith   be - fore the world con - fessed,
Thou, Lord, their Cap -   tain   in   the well - fought fight;
Fight   as   the   saints   who   no - bly fought of   old,
saints . . . . . . tri - umph - ant   rise in bright ar - ray;
gates . . . . . . of   pearl   streams in the count - less host,

Thy Name   O   Je -   sus, be   for   ev - er   blest.
Thou   in the dark - ness drear, the one true   light.
And win,   with them,   the vic - tor's crown of gold.
The King   of   glo -   ry pass - es   on   his way.
Sing - ing to Fa -   ther, Son, and Ho - ly   Ghost,

Al - le-lu - ia, al - le-lu - ia!

In harmony

A-men.

In harmony

4 O blest com-mun - ion, fel-low-ship di - vine! We fee-bly strug-gle,
5 And when the strife is fierce, the war-fare long, Steals on the ear the
6 The gold-en eve-ning bright-ens in the west; Soon, soon to faith - ful

they in glo-ry shine; Yet all are one in thee, for all are
dis-tant tri-umph song, And hearts are brave a-gain, and arms are
war-riors com-eth rest; . . . Sweet is the calm of pa-ra-dise the

thine.
strong. Al - le-lu - ia, al - le-lu - ia!
blest.

WILLIAM WALSHAM HOW, 1864
Reprinted from The English Hymnal *by permission of Oxford University Press*

Father, We Thank You

RENDEZ A DIEU   98.98.D

LOUIS BOURGEOIS, 1543

With dignity

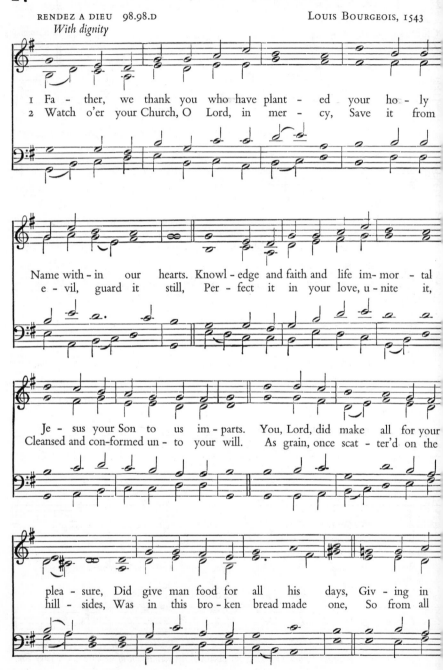

1 Fa - ther, we thank you who have plant - ed your ho - ly
2 Watch o'er your Church, O Lord, in mer - cy, Save it from

Name with - in our hearts. Knowl - edge and faith and life im - mor - tal
e - vil, guard it still, Per - fect it in your love, u - nite it,

Je - sus your Son to us im - parts. You, Lord, did make all for your
Cleansed and con-formed un - to your will. As grain, once scat - ter'd on the

plea - sure, Did give man food for all his days, Giv - ing in
hill - sides, Was in this bro - ken bread made one, So from all

Christ the Bread e - ter - nal; yours is the power, be yours the praise.
lands your Church be gath - er'd In - to your king-dom by your Son. A - men.

Greek, from the Didache, c. 110; *Tr.* F. BLAND TUCKER, 1941, *alt.*

God, My King, Your Might Confessing

STUTTGART 87.87
Majestically

Adapted from a Melody by
C. F. WITT, Gotha, 1715

1 God, my King, your might con-fess - ing, Ev - er will I bless your Name;
2 Hon - or great our God be - fits now; Who his ma - jes - ty can reach?
3 They shall talk of all your glo - ry, On your might and great-ness dwell,

Day by day your throne ad-dress-ing, Still will I your praise pro-claim.
Age to age his works transmits now, Age to age his power shall teach.
Speak of your dread acts the sto - ry, And your deeds of won - der tell. A-men.

4 Nor shall fail from memory's treasure
   Works by love and mercy wrought,
   Works of love surpassing measure,
    Works of mercy passing thought.

5 Full of kindness and compassion,
   Slow to anger, vast in love,
   God is good to all creation;
    All his works his goodness prove.

6 All your works, O Lord, shall bless you;
   You shall all your saints adore:
   King supreme shall they confess you,
   And proclaim your sov'reign power. Amen.

RICHARD MANT, 1824; *based on Psalm* 145

Glory to God

C. Rivers

Refrain

Glo - ry to God, glo - ry, O praise Him, al - le - lu - ia!

Glo - ry to God, glo - ry, O praise the name of the Lord.

Verses
Ref

1 Bless the Lord, all you works of the Lord; Praise and glo-ri-fy Him for-ev-e

Ref

2 Sun and moon, bless the Lord; Bless the Lord, you stars of heav -

Ref

3 Fire and heat, bless the Lord; Bless the Lord, you frost and cold

Ref

4 Dew and rain, bless the Lord; Bless the Lord, you ice and snow

Ref

5 Light and dark-ness, bless the Lord; Bless the Lord, you nights and days.

Ref

6 Light-nings and clouds, bless the Lord; Bless the Lord, you winds of heav -

DANIEL 3: 5

7 Now let the earth bless the Lord; Praise and glo-ri-fy Him for-ev-er.

Refrain

8 Moun-tains and hills, bless the Lord; Bless the Lord, you grow-ing trees.

Refrain

9 Springs of the earth, bless the Lord; Bless the Lord, you seas and riv-ers.

Refrain

0 Crea-tures of the sea, bless the Lord; Bless the Lord, you birds of the air.

Refrain

1 Crea-tures wild and tame, bless the Lord; Praise and glo-ri-fy Him for-ev-er.

Refrain

2 Now let the Church bless the Lord; Let His peo-ple praise His name.

Refrain

3 Priests of the Lord, bless the Lord; Praise His name both night and day.

Refrain

4 Souls of the just, bless the Lord; Bless the Lord, you hum-ble of heart.

Refrain

5 Bless the Lord, you saints of the Lord; Peo-ples near and far, praise His name.

Refrain

6 Praise to the Fa-ther and to the Son, To the Ho-ly Spir-it, Three in One.

445

76, 76, with Refrain   MAINZ MELODY

1 God Fa-ther, praise and glo-ry your chil-dren come to sing.
2 And you, Lord Co-e-ter-nal, God's sole be-got-ten Son;
3 O Ho-ly Ghost, Cre-a-tor, the Gift of God most high;

Good will and peace to man-kind, the gifts your king-dom brings.
O Je-sus, King a-noint-ed, You have re-demp-tion won.
Life, love and ho-ly wis-dom, Our weakness now sup-ply.

Refrain

O most Ho-ly Trin-i-ty, Un-di-vid-ed U-ni-ty

Ho-ly God, Might-y God, God Im-mor-tal, be a-dored.

Anon. Tr. JOHN ROTHENSTEINER, 1936,

God of Our Fathers

NATIONAL HYMN

GEORGE WILLIAM WARREN, 1892

With vigor

1 God of our fa - thers, whose al-migh -ty hand Leads forth in beau - ty
2 Your love a - lone can teach us to be free, to make a world that

all the star - ry band Of shin - ing worlds in splen-dor through the
lives in u - ni - ty; Be then our rul - er, guar-dian, guide, and

skies, Our grate - ful songs be- fore your throne a - rise.
stay, your word our law, your paths our cho- sen way. A-men.

3 Refresh your people on their toilsome way,
   Lead us from night to never-ending day;
   Fill all our lives with love and grace and peace;
   Our song of grateful praise shall never cease.
                Amen.

DANIEL CRANE ROBERTS, 1876, *alt.*

447

God is Love

32

C. RIVERS

Refrain

God is love, And he who a-bides in love a-bides in God And God in him.

VERSES

I JOHN 4

1 The love of Christ has gath-ered us to geth-er. Let us re-joice in him And be glad.

JOHN 13

2 By this shall all know that we are his dis-ci-ples, If we have love One for an-oth-er.

ROM. 13

3 Owe no man an-y-thing ex-cept to love one an-oth-er. For he who loves his neigh-bor will ful-fill The whole Law

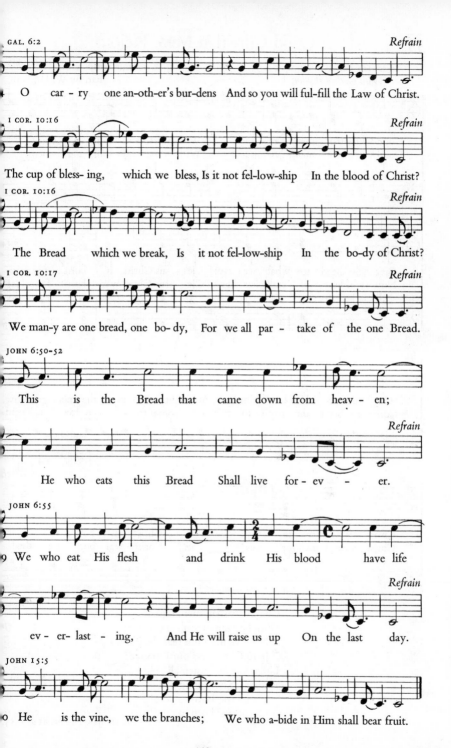

GAL. 6:2   *Refrain*

O car - ry one an-oth-er's bur-dens And so you will ful-fill the Law of Christ.

I COR. 10:16   *Refrain*

The cup of bless- ing, which we bless, Is it not fel-low-ship In the blood of Christ?

I COR. 10:16   *Refrain*

The Bread which we break, Is it not fel-low-ship In the bo-dy of Christ?

I COR. 10:17   *Refrain*

We man-y are one bread, one bo- dy, For we all par - take of the one Bread.

JOHN 6:50-52

This is the Bread that came down from heav - en;

                                         Refrain

He who eats this Bread Shall live for - ev - er.

JOHN 6:55

9 We who eat His flesh and drink His blood have life

                                         Refrain

ev - er-last - ing, And He will raise us up On the last day.

JOHN 15:5

o He is the vine, we the branches; We who a-bide in Him shall bear fruit.

449

IN DULCI JUBILO 66. 77. 78. 55
With marked rhythm

Fourteenth century Melody
har. by W. D., 1918

1 Good Chris-tian men, re - joice, With heart, and soul, and voice;
2 Good Chris-tian men, re - joice, With heart, and soul, and voice;

Give you heed to what we say: Je - sus Christ is born to- day;
Now you hear of end - less bliss: Je - sus Christ was born for this!

Ox and ass be - fore him bow, And he is in the man - ger now.
Come to bring the truth to men. He comes to set us free a - gain

Christ is born to - day! Christ is born to - day!
Christ was born for this! Christ was born for this!

3 Good Christian men, rejoice,
 With heart, and soul, and voice;
   Now ye need not fear the grave:
   Jesus Christ was born to save!
 Listen one and listen all
 Answer to his loving call.
   Christ was born to save!
   Christ was born to save!

JOHN MASON NEALE, 1853,

Great King of Peace

VILMA G. LITTLE, 1952   JOSEPH ROFF, 1959

Moderato

1. Great King of Peace, hear now Thy people's cry, In this dark hour of peril be Thou nigh: Bid sinful strife through-out the world to cease, And grant us Peace.
2. Re-mem-ber, Lord, we have no hope but Thee, None oth-er cham-pion on our side we see: Stretch forth Thine arm to bring us prompt re-lease, And grant us Peace.
3. So here we bow be-neath Thy chast-'ning rod, And cry for mer-cy in Thy sight, O God: Spurn not our firm re-solve from sin to cease, And grant us Peace.

451

TRADITIONAL MELODY

1 Hail! ho-ly Queen en-throned a-bove, O Ma - ri - a! Hai
2 Our life, our sweet-ness here be-low, O Ma - ri - a! Ou
3 To thee we cry poor sons of Eve, O Ma - ri - a! To
4 Turn then most gra-cious Ad - vo-cate, O Ma - ri - a! Tow
5 When this our ex - ile is com-plete, O Ma - ri - a! Sho

Moth-er of mer - cy and of love,
hope in sor-row and in woe,
thee we sigh, we mourn, we grieve, O Ma - ri - a! Tri-umph all ye
us thine eyes com- pas- sion-ate,
us thy Son, our Je - sus sweet,

Cher - u - bim, Sing with us ye Ser - a - phim, Heav'n and earth re

sound the hymn: Sal - ve, Sal - ve, Sal - ve Re - gi - na!

Hail the Day That Sees Him Rise

LLANFAIR 77.77, with Alleluias
Triumphantly

Melody, ROBERT WILLIAMS, 1817,
har. by JOHN ROBERTS, 1837

Hail the day that sees him rise,
There the glo - rious tri - umph waits; Al — — le - lu - ia!
See! he lifts his hands a - bove;

Glo - rious to his na - tive skies;
Lift your heads, e - ter - nal gates! Al — — le - lu - ia!
See! he shows the prints of love:

Christ, a - while to mor - tals giv'n,
Wide un - fold the ra - diant scene; Al — — le - lu - ia!
Hark! his gra - cious lips be - stow,

In unison

En - ters now the high - est heav'n!
Take the King of glo - ry in! Al — — le - lu - ia! A-men.
Bless- ings on his Church be - low.

4 Lord beyond our mortal sight, Alleluia!
Raise our hearts to reach thy height, Alleluia!
There your face unclouded see, Alleluia!
All creation shall be free. Alleluia!

Amen.

CHARLES WESLEY, 1739, *alt.*

SALVE FESTA DIES   Irregular, with Refrain   R. VAUGHAN WILLIAMS, 1906

For Ascension and Pentecost, verses 2 and 5 may be omitted.

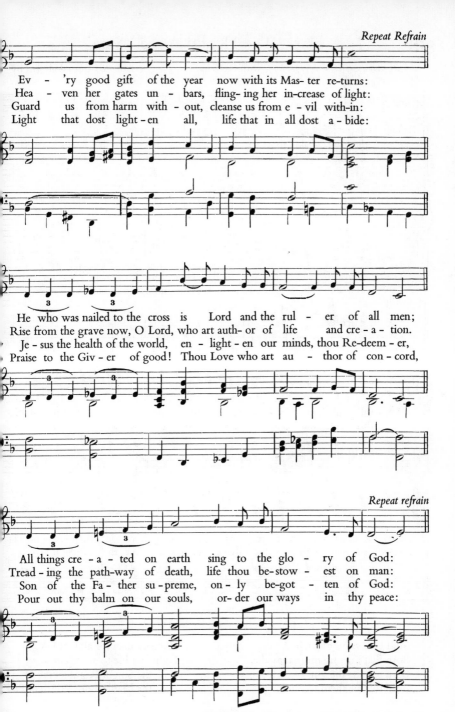

Ev - 'ry good gift of the year now with its Mas- ter re-turns:
Hea - ven her gates un - bars, fling- ing her in-crease of light:
Guard us from harm with - out, cleanse us from e - vil with-in:
Light that dost light - en all, life that in all dost a - bide:

He who was nailed to the cross is Lord and the rul - er of all men;
Rise from the grave now, O Lord, who art auth- or of life and cre - a - tion.
Je - sus the health of the world, en - light - en our minds, thou Re-deem - er,
Praise to the Giv - er of good! Thou Love who art au - thor of con - cord,

Repeat refrain

All things cre - a - ted on earth sing to the glo - ry of God:
Tread - ing the path-way of death, life thou be-stow - est on man:
Son of the Fa - ther su - preme, on - ly be-got - ten of God:
Pour out thy balm on our souls, or- der our ways in thy peace:

VENANTIUS HONORIUS FORTUNATUS, 530–609

455

Hark, The Herald Angels Sing

MENDELSSOHN 77.77.77.77, with Refrain

Vigorously

Adapted from a chorus by
FELIX MENDELSSOHN, 1840

1 Hark! the her - ald an - gels sing Glo - ry to the new - born King!
2 Christ, by high - est heav'n a - dored; Christ, the ev - er - last - ing Lord;

Peace on earth and mer - cy mild, God and sin - ners rec - on - ciled!
Late in time be - hold him come, Off - spring of the Vir - gin's womb

Joy - ful, all ye na - tions, rise, Join the tri - umph of the skies;
In this man, our God we see; Praise to him shall ev - er be,

With the an - gel - ic host pro - claim Christ is born in Beth - le - hem!
Pleased as man with man to dwell; Je - sus, our Em - man - u - el!

3 Mild he lays his glory by,
Born that man no more may die,
Born to raise the sons of earth,
Born to give them second birth.

Comes a man for all that lives,
Light and life to all he gives,
Hail, the Sun of Righteousness!
Hail, the heav'n-born Prince of Peac

CHARLES WESLEY, 1739, ·

Holy God, We Praise Thy Name

TE DEUM 78.78.77   VIENNA, c. 1774

1 Ho - ly God, we praise thy Name! Lord of all we
2 Hark! the loud ce - les - tial hymn An - gel choirs a -

bow be - fore thee; All on earth thy scep - ter claim,
bove are rais - ing; Cher - u - bim and Ser - a - phim

All in heav'n a - bove a - dore thee: In - fi - nite thy
In un - ceas - ing cho - rus prais - ing; Fill the heav'ns with

vast do - main, Ev - er - last - ing is thy reign.
sweet ac - cord; Ho - ly, ho - ly, ho - ly Lord!

Ascribed to ST. NICETAS, 415. *Tr.* C. WALWORTH, 1900

NICAEA   11 12.12 10   JOHN B. DYKES, 1861
With dignity

1 Ho - ly, Ho - ly, Ho - ly! Lord God Al - migh - ty!
2 Ho - ly, Ho - ly, Ho - ly! all the saints a - dore thee,
3 Ho - ly, Ho - ly, Ho - ly! though the dark - ness hide thee,

Ear - ly in the morn - ing our song shall rise to thee:
Cast - ing down their gold-en crowns a - round the glass - y sea;
Though the eye of sin - ful man thy glo - ry may not see,

Ho - ly, Ho - ly, Ho - ly! mer - ci - ful and migh - ty,
Cher - u - bim and ser - a - phim fall - ing down be - fore thee,
On - ly thou art ho - ly; there is none be - side thee,

God in three Per - sons, bless - ed Tri - ni - ty.
Who were, and are, and ev - er - more shall be.
Per - fect in power, in love, and pu - ri - ty. A - men.

4 Holy, Holy, Holy! Lord God Almighty!
    All thy works shall praise thy Name, in earth, and sky, and sea;
   Holy, Holy, Holy! merciful and mighty,
    God in three Persons, blessed Trinity. Amen.

REGINALD HEBER, 18

How Blessed Are We

FROM HEAVEN HIGH

Melody Pub. Leipzig, 1539

In moderate time

1 How bless'd are we who share this Bread, The Flesh and Blood of
2 Oh, Lord, we eat this Bread of life, The Bread you give to
3 Our fa-thers fed on heav'n-ly food, The Man-na gath-ered

Christ our Lord. May love u — nite us grate-ful - ly
faith - ful sons. The peace of Christ, your Son, is ours
in the wild. Your God - sent Bread we now re - ceive,

As sons of God who live in peace.
U - nit - ing us who do your will.
Our dai - ly food of last - ing strength. A-men.

This banquet brings eternal life,
A life of love and unity.
For we now live in Jesus Christ
And share with Him His risen might.
Give thanks to Jesus, saving Lord,
Our paschal victim, newly slain.
He shares His Father's love with us,
He makes us worthy sons of God.

6 Lord, Jesus Christ, we beg your grace,
We turn to you, our hope and guide.
This Bread unites us, faithful sons,
Awaiting perfect unity.

7 Give praise to God for He is good,
To Him who made us like Himself.
To Christ, His Son, who set us free,
To God's great gift, our Source of life.

JAMES McMULLEN, S. J.

42

It Is Good to Give Thanks to the Lord

R. F. TWYNHAM

With joyful movement

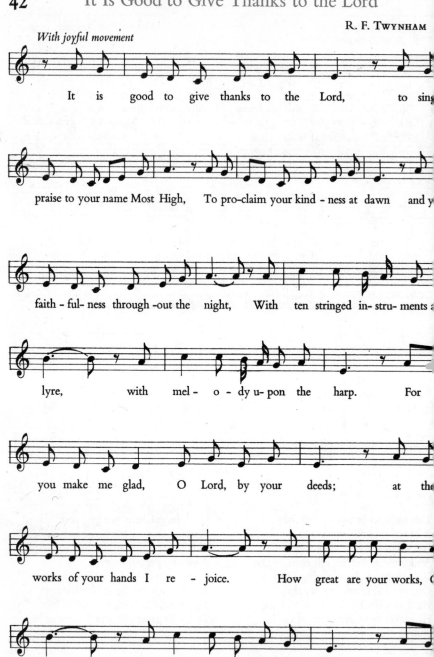

It is good to give thanks to the Lord, to sing

praise to your name Most High, To pro-claim your kind - ness at dawn and y

faith - ful- ness through -out the night, With ten stringed in- stru- ments

lyre, with mel - o - dy u- pon the harp. For

you make me glad, O Lord, by your deeds; at the

works of your hands I re - joice. How great are your works, (

Lord! How ve - ry deep are your thoughts! The

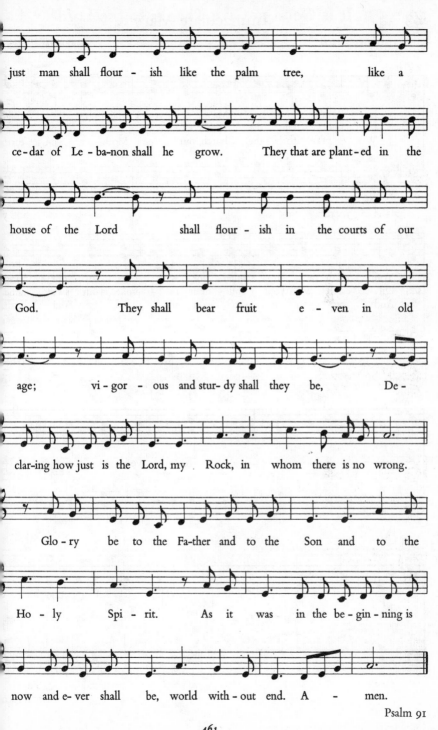

just man shall flour - ish like the palm tree, like a
ce - dar of Le - ba - non shall he grow. They that are plant - ed in the
house of the Lord shall flour - ish in the courts of our
God. They shall bear fruit e - ven in old
age; vi - gor - ous and stur - dy shall they be, De -
clar - ing how just is the Lord, my Rock, in whom there is no wrong.
Glo - ry be to the Fa - ther and to the Son and to the
Ho - ly Spi - rit. As it was in the be - gin - ning is
now and e - ver shall be, world with - out end. A - men.

Psalm 91

461

43

Immaculate Mary

1 Im - mac - u - late Ma - ry, your prais - es we sing.
2 In heav - en the bless - ed your glo - ry pro - claim
3 We pray for the Church, our true Moth - er on earth

You reign now in splen - dor with Je - sus our King.
On earth we your chil - dren in - voke your sweet name.
And beg you to watch o'er the land of our birth.

A - ve, A - ve, A - ve Ma - ri - a!

A - ve, A - ve, A - ve Ma - ri - a!

ANONYMO

462

Jerusalem, My Happy Home

LAND OF REST

With unhurried simplicity

Traditional American Melody,
coll. and har. by ANNABEL MORRIS BUCHANAN

Je - ru - sa - lem, my hap - py home, When shall I come to thee?
Thy saints are crowned with glo-ry great; They see God face to face;
There Da - vid stands with harp in hand As mas - ter of the choir:

When shall my sor - rows have an end? Thy joys when shall I see?
They tri - umph still, they still re - joice: Most hap - py is their case.
Ten thou - sand times that man were blest That might this mu - sic hear.

4 Our Lady sings Magnificat
    With tune surpassing sweet;
  And all the virgins bear their part,
    Sitting about her feet.

5 There Magdalen hath left her moan,
    And cheerfully doth sing
  With blessed saints, whose harmony
    In every street doth ring.

6 Jerusalem, Jerusalem,
    God grant that I may see
  Thine endless joy, and of the same
    Partaker ever be!

F. B. P., *c. 16th cent.*

Jesus Christ Is Risen Today

EASTER HYMN   77.77, with Alleluias   *Lyra Davidica*, 1708, alt.

Stately

1 Je - sus Christ is ris'n to day,
2 Hymns of praise then let us sing, Al - le - lu - ia!
3 But the pains which he en - dured,

Our tri - umph-ant ho - ly day,
Un - to Christ, our heav'n-ly King, Al - le - lu - ia!
Our sal - va - tion have pro - cured;

Who did once up - on the cross,
Who en-dured the cross and grave, Al - le - lu - ia!
Now a - bove the sky he's King,

Suf - fer to re - deem our loss.
Sin - ners to re - deem and save. Al - le - lu - ia! A-men
Where the an - gels ev - er sing.

4 Sing we to our God above, Alleluia!
  Praise eternal as his love; Alleluia!
  Praise him, all ye heav'nly host, Alleluia!
  Father, Son, and Holy Ghost. Alleluia! Amen

Latin, 14th cent.; *Tr.* TATE *and* BRADY, 1698; *St.* 4, CHARLES WES

Let All Mortal Flesh Keep Silence

PICARDY 87.87.87   Traditional French Melody, 17th cent.

Unison, in strict rhythm, slowly

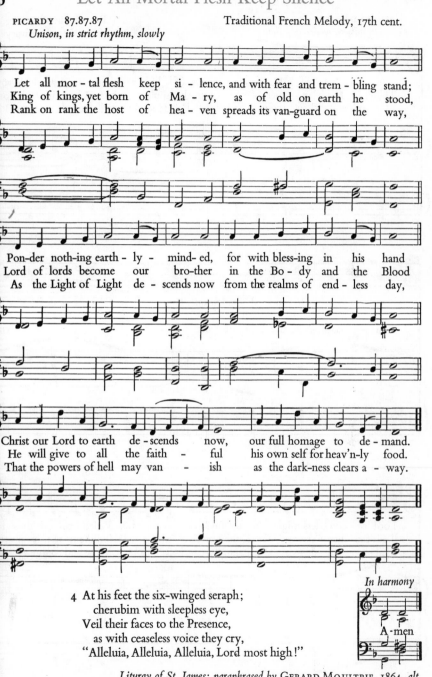

Let all mor - tal flesh keep si - lence, and with fear and trem - bling stand;
King of kings, yet born of Ma - ry, as of old on earth he stood,
Rank on rank the host of hea - ven spreads its van-guard on the way,

Pon-der noth-ing earth - ly - mind- ed, for with bless-ing in his hand
Lord of lords become our bro-ther in the Bo - dy and the Blood
As the Light of Light de - scends now from the realms of end - less day,

Christ our Lord to earth de -scends now, our full homage to de - mand.
He will give to all the faith - ful his own self for heav'n-ly food.
That the powers of hell may van - ish as the dark-ness clears a - way.

4 At his feet the six-winged seraph;
 cherubim with sleepless eye,
Veil their faces to the Presence,
 as with ceaseless voice they cry,
 "Alleluia, Alleluia, Alleluia, Lord most high!"

In harmony

A -men

Liturgy of St. James; paraphrased by GERARD MOULTRIE, 1864, *alt.*

Jesus, Son of Mary

ADORO DEVOTE 11 11. 11 11
In unison, moderately slow

Benedictine Plainsong
Mode V, 13th century

1 Je - sus, Son of Ma - ry, Fount of life a - lone, Here we hail you
2 Think, O Lord, in mer - cy On the souls of those Who, in faith gon
3 Of - ten were they wound - ed In the dead - ly strife; Heal them, Good Ph

pres - ent On your al - tar throne. Humbly we a - dore you
from us, Now in death re - pose. Here 'mid stress and con - flic
si - cian, With the balm of life. Ev -'ry taint of e - vil,

Lord of end - less might, In the mys - tic sym - bols Veiled from earthly sigh
Toils can nev - er cease; There, the war-fare end - ed, Bid them rest in peace.
Frail - ty and de - cay, Good and gra-cious Sa - viour, Cleanse and purge a-way.

4 Rest eternal grant them,
    After weary fight;
    Shed on them the radiance
    Of your Heav'nly light.
    Lead them onward, upward,
    To the holy place,
    Where your saints made perfect
    Gaze upon your face. Amen.

A - men.

Written in Swahili; Tr. EDMUND S. PALMER, 1906
By permission of the Oxford University Press

8 Lord, Who Throughout These Forty Days

ST. FLAVIAN   JOHN DAY'S *Psalter*, 1562
Moderately slow

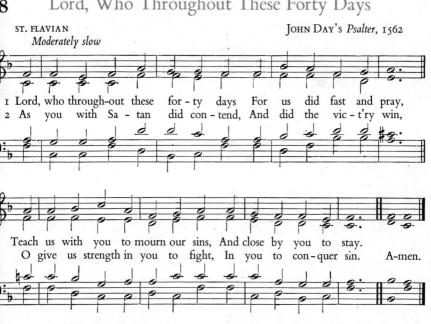

1 Lord, who through-out these for - ty days For us did fast and pray,
2 As you with Sa - tan did con - tend, And did the vic - t'ry win,

Teach us with you to mourn our sins, And close by you to stay.
O give us strength in you to fight, In you to con - quer sin. A-men.

3 As you did hunger bear and thirst,
    So teach us, gracious Lord,
    To die to self, and chiefly live
    By your most holy word.

4 And through these days of penitence,
    And through your Passiontide,
    Yea, evermore, in life and death,
    Jesus! with us abide.

5 Abide with us, that so, this life
    Of suff'ring overpast,
    An Easter of unending joy
    We may attain at last! Amen.

CLAUDIA F. HERNAMAN, 1873, *alt.*

Like the Deer that Yearns

R. F. TWYNHAM, 1965

Move!

Like the deer that yearns for run-ning streams, so my soul is yearn-ing

yearn-ing for you my God. My soul is thirst-ing for God, the God of r

life; when can I en-ter and see; see the face of God? M

tears have become my bread, by night by day, as I hear it said all the d

long: "Where, where is your God?" These things will I re-member as

pour out my soul: how I would lead the re-joic - ing crowd in-to the

house of God, a-mid cries of gladness and thanks-giv-ing, the throng wild wi

joy. Why are you cast down my soul, why groan within me? Hope in Go

hope in God; I will praise him still, My Sa-vior and my God. M

soul is cast down with - in me as I think of you, from the

coun-try of Jor-dan and Mount Her-mon, from the Hill of Mi - zar. Deep

is call - ing on deep in the roar of wa - ters: Your

tor-rents and all your waves swept, swept, swept o - ver me. By

day the Lord will send his lov-ing kind-ness; by night I will sing to him,

praise the God of my life. I will say to God, my rock:"Why have you for-

got-ten me? Why do I go mourn-ing op - pressed, op - pressed by the

foe?" With cries that pierce me to the heart, pierce me to the heart, my

en - e - mies re - vile me, say-ing to me all the day long:

"Where, where, where is your God?" Why are you cast down, my soul why

groan within me? Hope in God; hope in God; I will praise him still, my

Sa-vior and my God; my Sa-vior and my God.

Psalm 41, *the Grail translation*

469

UNDE ET MEMORES   10 10. 10 10. 10 10   WILLIAM H. MONK, 1875, *alt.*

Do not drag

1 Lord, who at thy first Eu - cha - rist did pray   That all thy Church mig
2 For all   thy Church, O Lord, we in - ter - cede;   Make all   our sad di
3 We pray thee too for wan - d'rers from thy fold;   O bring them back, goo

be for ev - er   one, Grant us   at ev - 'ry   Eu - cha-rist to   say
vi - sions soon to   cease; Draw us   the near - er   each to each, we plead,
Shep-herd of the   sheep, Back to   the faith which saints be-lieved of old,

With long - ing heart and soul, "Thy will be done."   O   may we all one
By draw - ing all   to thee, O Prince of Peace;   Thus   may we all one
Back to the Church which still that faith doth keep;   Soon may we all one

bread, one bo - dy be, Through this blest sac - ra - ment of u - ni - ty.
bread, one bo - dy be, Through this blest sac - ra - ment of u - ni - ty.
bread, one bo - dy be, Through this blest sac - ra - ment of u - ni - ty.

WILLIAM HARRY TURTON, 188

1

Master of Eager Youth

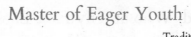

MONKS GATE
Brightly

Traditional Sussex Melody,
arr. by R. VAUGHAN WILLIAMS, 1904

1 Mas - ter of ea - ger youth, Con - trol - ling, guid - ing,
2 You are our migh - ty Lord, Our strength in sad - ness,
3 Good Shep - herd of your sheep, Your own de - fend - ing,

Lift - ing our hearts to truth, New power pro - vid - ing;
The Fa - ther's con-quering Word, True source of glad - ness;
In love your chil - dren keep To life un - end - ing.

Shep - herd of in - no - cence, You are our Con - fi -
Your Name we glo - ri - fy, O Je - sus, throned on
You are your - self the Way: Lead us then day by

dence; To you our sure De - fence, We bring our prais - es.
high, Who gave your - self to die For man's sal - va - tion.
day In your own steps, we pray, O Lord most ho - ly. A-men.

ST. CLEMENT OF ALEXANDRIA, *c.* 200; *paraphrased by* F. BLAND TUCKER, 1939, *alt.*

Now Thank We All Our God

JOHANN CRUEGER, 1647
adapted by FELIX MENDELSSOHN, 1840

NUN DANKET   67.67.66.66
In unison, majestically

1 Now thank we all our God, With heart, and hands, and voic - es,
2 O may this boun- teous God Thro' all our life be near us!
3 All praise and thanks to God The Fa - ther now be giv - en,

Who won-drous things has done, In whom his world re - joic - es;
With ev - er- joy - ful hearts And bless - ed peace to cheer us;
The Son, and him who reigns With them in high - est hea - ven,

Who from our moth - er's arms Has blessed us on our way
And keep us in his grace, And guide us when per - plext,
E - ter - nal, Tri - une God, Whom earth and heav'n a - dore;

With count - less gifts of love, And still is ours to - day.
And free us from all ills In this world and the next.
For thus it was, is now, And shall be, ev - er - more. A - men

MARTIN RINKART, *c.* 1630; *Tr.* CATHERINE WINKWORTH, 1858, *a*

3

Now Yield We Thanks and Praise

DARMSTADT 67.67.66.66
Slow

AHASUERUS FRITSCH, 1679
arr. and har. by J. S. BACH

1 Now yield we thanks and praise To Christ en-throned in glo-ry,
2 What trib-ute shall we pay To him who came in weak-ness,

And on this day of days Tell out re-demp-tion's sto-ry,
And in a man-ger lay To teach his peo-ple meek-ness?

We tru-ly have be-lieved That on this bless-ed morn,
Let ev-'ry house be bright; Let prais-es nev-er cease:

In ho-li-ness con-ceived, The Son of God was born.
With mer-cies in-fi-nite Our Christ hath brought us peace.

HOWARD CHANDLER ROBBINS, 1929, *alt.*

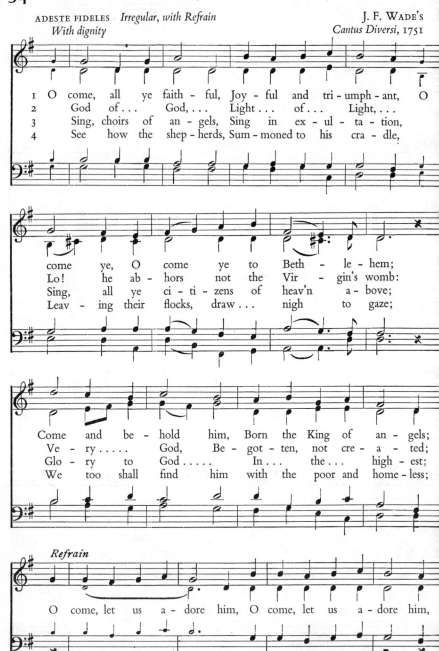

ADESTE FIDELES *Irregular, with Refrain*   J. F. WADE'S
With dignity   *Cantus Diversi,* 1751

1 O come, all   ye faith - ful, Joy - ful and tri - umph - ant,   O
2   God of ... God, ... Light ... of ... Light, ...
3   Sing, choirs of an - gels, Sing in ex - ul - ta - tion,
4   See how the shep - herds, Sum - moned to his cra - dle,

come   ye,   O   come   ye   to   Beth - le - hem;
Lo!   he   ab - hors   not   the   Vir - gin's womb:
Sing,   all   ye   ci - ti - zens   of   heav'n   a - bove;
Leav - ing their flocks, draw ... nigh to gaze;

Come   and   be - hold   him,   Born   the   King   of   an - gels;
Ve - ry .....   God,   Be - got - ten,   not   cre - a - ted;
Glo - ry   to   God .....   In ...   the ...   high - est;
We   too   shall   find   him   with   the   poor   and   home - less;

Refrain

O   come,   let   us   a - dore   him,   O   come,   let   us   a - dore   him,

474

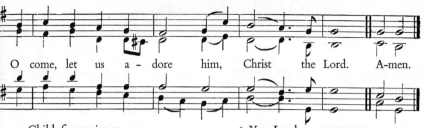

O come, let us a-dore him, Christ the Lord. A-men.

5 Child, for us sinners	6 Yea, Lord, we greet you,
Poor and in the manger,	Born this happy morning;
We would embrace you with love and awe;	Jesus, to you be glory giv'n;
Who would not love you,	Word of the Father,
Loving us so dearly? *Refrain*	Now in flesh appearing; *Refrain*

Latin, 18th cent.; Tr. FREDERICK OAKELEY *and others*

O God, Our Help in Ages Past

ST. ANNE
Majestically

WILLIAM CROFT, 1708

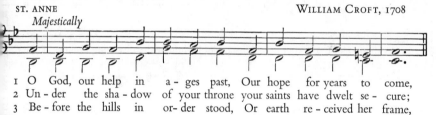

1 O God, our help in a-ges past, Our hope for years to come,
2 Un-der the sha-dow of your throne your saints have dwelt se-cure;
3 Be-fore the hills in or-der stood, Or earth re-ceived her frame,

Our shel-ter from the storm-y blast, And our e-ter-nal home:
Suf-fi-cient is your arm a-lone, And our de-fence is sure.
From ev-er-last-ing you are God, To end-less years the same.

A thousand ages in your sight	5 Time, like an ever-rolling stream,
Are like an evening gone;	Bears all its sons away;
Short as the watch that ends the night	They fly, forgotten, as a dream
Before the rising sun.	Dies at the opening day.

6 O God, our help in ages past,
Our hope for years to come,
Be then our guide while life shall last,
And our eternal home.

A-men.

ISAAC WATTS, 1719; *based on Psalm 90*

56 O Come, Good Spirit

10 10. 10 10. 10 10

R. F. TWYNHAM, 1965

1 O come, good Spi-rit, come fill all the ea-rth, And in these wa-t
2 Once wa-ters part-ed, saved God's cho-sen flock, And faith brought wa-t

give this child new birth. So when the sav-ing heal-ing wa-ter's poured
flow-ing from a rock. All signs of Spir-it's liv-ing water here,

She
He shall be born our sister
brother in the Lord. Be glad! sing out! Go
That saves, re-fresh-es all who would come near

show to all the earth The life in Christ that comes in this new birth!

476

3 To Nicodemus Jesus spoke of breath,
   Of birth in Spirit through a water's death.
   For men in living waters are to die,
   And rise again to live and testify.

Refrain:

   Be glad! Sing out! Go show to all the earth
   The life in Christ that comes in this new birth.

4 This water brings the death that Jesus died,
   This water is the death he crucified.
   This tomb keeps all we men refuse to give
   To Christ our risen Lord in whom we live. *Refrain.*

5 O creature water, source of life restored,
   The Church's womb made fruitful by her Lord.
   The mother of all things on earth that live,
   The spring that now has Christ's own life to give. *Refrain.*

6 In signs that we can hear and feel and see,
   The Spirit comes to set his people free.
   No longer turned to self in pride and fear,
   As God's own children live in love sincere. *Refrain.*

GABRIEL HUCK, 1965

Rise up, O Men of God

FESTAL SONG S.M.   WILLIAM H. WALTER, 1894

With vigor

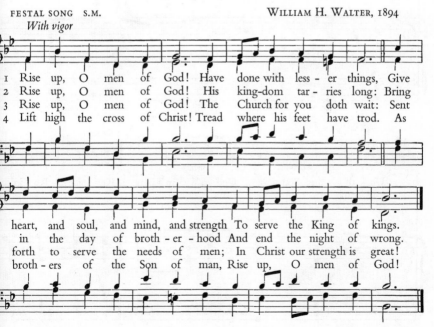

1 Rise up, O men of God! Have done with less-er things, Give
2 Rise up, O men of God! His king-dom tar-ries long: Bring
3 Rise up, O men of God! The Church for you doth wait: Sent
4 Lift high the cross of Christ! Tread where his feet have trod. As

heart, and soul, and mind, and strength To serve the King of kings.
in the day of broth-er-hood And end the night of wrong.
forth to serve the needs of men; In Christ our strength is great!
broth-ers of the Son of man, Rise up, O men of God!

By permission of the author WILLIAM PIERSON MERRILL, 1911

VENI EMMANUEL

In unison, boldly

Melody adapted from plainsong, Mode I;
by THOMAS HELMORE, 1854

1 O come, O come, Em - man - u - el, And ran - som cap - tive
2 O come, now Wis - dom from on high, Who or - ders all thing
3 O come, O come, now Lord of might, Who to your tribes on

Is - ra - el, That mourns in lone - ly ex - ile here
migh - ti - ly; To us the path of knowl - edge show,
Si - nai's height In an - cient times you gave the law,

Refrain

Un - til the Son of God ap - pear. Re - joice! Re - joice
And teach us in her ways to go.
In cloud, and ma - jes - ty, and awe.

Em - man - u - el Shall come to you, O Is - ra - el!

4 O come, now Rod of Jesse's stem,
From every foe deliver them
That trust your mighty power to save,
And give them vict'ry o'er the grave.
    Rejoice! Rejoice! Emmanuel
    Shall come to you, O Israel!

5 O come, now Key of David, come,
And open wide our heav'nly home;
Make safe the way that leads on high,
And close the path to misery.
    Rejoice! Rejoice! Emmanuel
    Shall come to you, O Israel!

6 O come, now Day-spring from on high,
And cheer us by your drawing nigh;
Disperse the gloomy clouds of night,
And death's dark shadow put to flight.
    Rejoice! Rejoice! Emmanuel
    Shall come to you, O Israel!

7 O come, Desire of nations, bind
In one the hearts of all mankind;
Bid now our sad divisions cease,
And be yourself our King of Peace.
    Rejoice! Rejoice! Emmanuel
    Shall come to you, O Israel!

A-men.

Hymnal Version, based on Latin, c. 9th cent.; St. 1, 3, 4, 5, 6, pub. Cologne, 1710

ST. ALPHONSUS

1 O God of love - li - ness, O Lord of Heav'n a - bo
2 Thou art blest Three in One, Yet un - di - vid - ed st
3 To think Thou art my God! O thought for - ev - er bl

How wor - thy to pos - sess my heart's de - vot - ed love!
Thou art that One a - lone whose love my heart can fill.
My heart has ov - er-flow'd with joy with - in my breast;

So sweet Thy coun - te-nance, so gra - cious to be-hol
The heav'ns, the earth be - low were fash - ioned by Thy wor
My soul so full of bliss is plunged as in a sea

That one, one on - ly glance To me were bliss un - told!
How a - mia - ble art Thou, My ev - er dear-est Lord
Deep in the sweet a - byss Of ho - ly char - i - ty.

Silesian Melody pub. 1842; arr. JOSEPH R

Christ is the World's True Light

ST. JOAN 67.67.66.66 MISSIONS   PERCY E. B. COLLER, 1941

Sturdily

Christ is the world's true Light, It's Cap - tain of sal - va - tion,
In Christ all ra - ces meet, Their an - cient feuds for - get - ting,

The Day - star clear and bright Of ev - 'ry man and na - tion;
The whole round world com - plete, From sun - rise to its set - ting:

New life, new hope a - wakes, Wher - e'er men own his sway:
When Christ is throned as Lord, Men shall for - sake their fear,

Free - dom her bond - age breaks, And night is turned to day.
To plough-share beat the sword, To prun-ing - hook the spear. A - men.

3 One Lord, in one great Name   The world has waited long,
   Unite us all who own thee;   Has travailed long in pain;
Cast out our pride and shame   To heal its ancient wrong,
   That hinder to enthrone thee;   Come, Prince of Peace, and reign. Amen

GEORGE WALLACE BRIGGS, 1933

O Holy Lord, by All Adored

BOHEMIAN BRETHREN 87.87.887 Melody of the Unitas Fratrum, pub. 156

Unison, in moderate time

1 O ho - ly Lord, by all a - dored, Our weak-ness - es con

2 To God on high, be thanks and praise, Who brings us all to -

fess - ing, To you this day your chil-dren pray, Our ho - ly fait

geth - er; His care shall guide us all our days, And harm shall reac

pro - fess - ing! Ac - cept, O King, the gifts we bring, Our

us nev - er. In him we trust with faith as - sured; Of

words of praise, the songs we raise; And grant us, Lord, your bless - ing

all that live he is the Lord, For - ev - er and for - ev - er.

Tradit

O Sacred Head, Sore Wounded

PASSION CHORALE 76.76 D
Solemnly, but not too slow

HANS LEO HASSLER, 1601
adapted and har. by J. S. BACH

O sa - cred head, sore wound - ed, De - filed and put to scorn;
Your beau - ty, long de - sir - ed, Has van - ished from our sight;

O king - ly head, sur - round - ed With mock - ing crown of thorn:
Your power is all ex - pir - ed, And quenched the light of light.

What sor - row mars your grand - eur? Can death your bloom de - flower?
From us for whom you died then, Hide not so far your grace:

O coun - te - nance whose splen - dor The hosts of heav'n a - dore!
Show us, O Love most longed for, The bright - ness of your face. A - men.

3 My days are few, O fail not,
   With your immortal power,
To hold me that I fear not
   In death's most frightful hour:

That I may fight befriended,
   And see in my last strife
To me your arms extended
   Upon the cross of life. Amen

PAULUS GERHARDT, 1656; *Tr.* ROBERT BRIDGES, 1899, *alt.*

O Saving Victim

O SALUTARIS L.M.   ABBÉ DUGUET, C.D., 1767

1 O Sav - ing Vic - tim, o - pening wide The
2 To your great name be end - less praise, Im

gate of heav'n to man be - low! Our foes press on from
mor - tal God - head, One in Three; Oh, grant us end - less

ev - 'ry side: Your aid sup - ply, your strength be - stow.
length of days When our true na - tive land we see. A - men.

3 The word of God from heaven sent—
  Yet biding at the Father's side,
  Upon his destined work intent,
  Came to his life's dark eventide.

4 To foes upon his death agreed—
  Christ, ere surrendered by his friend,
  Surrendered first himself to feed
  His friends with life that knows no e

ST. THOMAS AQUINAS, 1227-74; *Tr.* E. CASWELL, 1814-78,

Of That Branch in Ancient Garden

87.87.87

EDMUND KESTEL, O.S.B., 1946

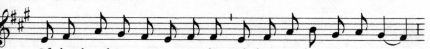

1 Of that branch in an-cient gar - den, Did thy Fa- ther make thy tree,
2 By thy words on road to pas - sion, Words that set thy chil- dren free,
3 To thy Fa - ther be all glo - ry, E - qual glo- ry, Lord, to thee,

On that tree with thee up - lift - ed, Let us tri - umph, Lord, with thee.
Thou the Vine and we the branch-es, Let us tri - umph, Lord, with thee.
By the Spir - it's e - qual glo - ry, Let us tri - umph, Lord, with thee.

On that tree with thee up - lift - ed, Let us tri - umph, Lord, with thee.
Thou the Vine and we the branch-es, Let us tri - umph, Lord, with thee.
By the Spir - it's e - qual glo - ry, Let us tri - umph, Lord, with thee.

PATRICK CUMMINS, O.S.B., 1946

O FILII ET FILIAE 8 8 8, with Alleluia   French, 15th cent.; Solesmes Version,
Before the first stanza   Mode II

Al - le - lu - ia!   Al - le - lu - ia!   Al - le - lu - ia!

In unison

1 O sons and daugh - ters, let us sing! The King of heav'n, the
2 That Eas - ter morn, at break of day, The faith - ful wo - men
3 An an - gel clad in white they see, Who sat, and spoke un

glo - rious King, O'er death to - day rose tri - umph-ing. Al-le - lu - ia!
went their way To seek the tomb where Je - sus lay. Al-le - lu - ia!
to the three, "Your Lord goes now to Gal - i - lee." Al-le - lu - ia!

After the last stanza

Al – le – lu – ia! Al – le – lu – ia! Al – le – lu – ia!

4 That night the apostles met in fear;
  Among them came their Lord most dear,
  And said, "My peace be on all here."
                    Alleluia!

5 When Thomas first the tidings heard,
  How they had seen the risen Lord,
  He doubted the disciples' word.
                    Alleluia!

6 "My pierced side, O Thomas, see;
  My hands, my feet, I show to thee;
  Not faithless, but believing be."
                    Alleluia!

7 No longer Thomas then denied,
  He saw the feet, the hands, the side;
  "You are my Lord and God," he cried.
                    Alleluia!

8 How happy all who do not see
  Yet place all faith and trust in me
  True witnesses now may they be!
                    Alleluia!

9 On this most holy day of days,
  To God your hearts and voices raise,
  In laud, and jubilee, and praise.
                    Alleluia!

JEAN TISSERAND, *15th cent.; Tr.* JOHN MASON NEALE, *1852, alt.*

Of the Father's Love Begotten

DIVINUM MYSTERIUM 87.87.877   13th century Plainsong, Mode V

Flowing, not slow

1 Of the Fa-ther's love be-got-ten, Ere the worlds be-gan to be,
2 O ye heights of heav'n a-dore him; An-gel hosts, his prais-es sing;

He is Al-pha and O-me-ga, He the source, the end-ing he
Powers, do-min-ions, bow be-fore him, And ex-tol our God and King

Of the things that are, that have . . . . . been, And that
Let no tongue on earth be si - - - lent, Ev - ry

fu - ture years shall see, Ev - er - more and ev - er - more!
voice in con - cert ring, Ev - er - more and ev - er - more!

3 Christ, to thee with God the Father,
  And, O Holy Ghost, to thee,
  Hymn and chant and high thanksgiving,
  And unwearied praises be:
  Honor, glory, and dominion,
  And eternal victory,
  Evermore and evermore!

A - men.

AURELIUS CLEMENS PRUDENTIUS, 348-413; *Tr.* J. M. NEALE, 1859

On This Day, the First of Days

7

LUEBECK 77.77

With spirit

JOHANN A. FREYLINGHAUSEN, 1704

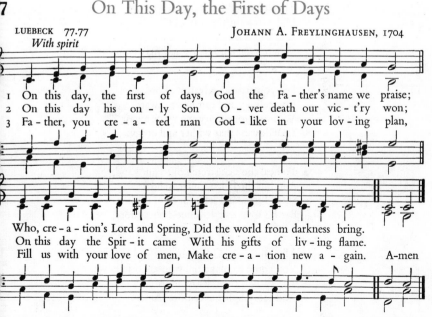

1 On this day, the first of days, God the Fa - ther's name we praise;
2 On this day his on - ly Son O - ver death our vic - t'ry won;
3 Fa - ther, you cre - a - ted man God - like in your lov - ing plan,

Who, cre - a - tion's Lord and Spring, Did the world from darkness bring.
On this day the Spir - it came With his gifts of liv - ing flame.
Fill us with your love of men, Make cre - a - tion new a - gain. A-men

LE MANS BREVIARY, 1748; *Tr.* H. W. BAKER, 1821-77, *alt.*

WINCHESTER NEW
With solemnity

Adapted from
Musikalisches Handbuch, HAMBURG, 1690

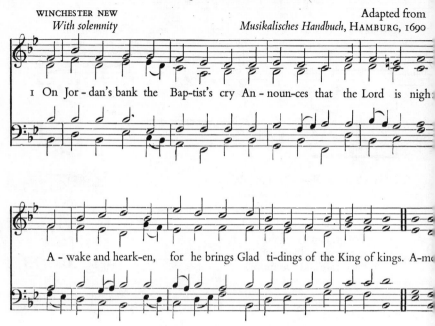

1 On Jor-dan's bank the Bap-tist's cry An-noun-ces that the Lord is nigh:

A-wake and heark-en, for he brings Glad ti-dings of the King of kings. A-men

2 Then cleansed be every breast from sin;
Make straight the way of God within,
And let each heart prepare a home
Where such a mighty guest may come.

3 For you are our salvation, Lord,
Our refuge, and our great reward;
Without your grace we waste away
Like flowers that wither and decay.

4 To heal the sick stretch out your hand,
And bid the fallen sinner stand;
Shine forth, and let your light restore
Earth's own true loveliness once more.

5 All praise, eternal Son, to you
You come to make the whole world new;
The Father, then, let us adore
And Holy Spirit evermore. Amen.

CHARLES COFFIN, 1736; *Tr.* JOHN CHANDLER, 1837,

Once in Royal David's City

IRBY 87.87.77   HENRY J. GAUNTLETT, 1858

Cheerfully

1 Once in roy - al Da - vid's ci - ty Stood a low - ly cat - tle shed,
2 He came down to earth from hea - ven, Who is God and Lord of all,
3 And, thro' all his won - drous childhood, He would hon - or and o - bey,

Where a moth - er laid her ba - by In a man - ger for his bed:
And his shel - ter was a sta - ble, And his cra - dle was a stall;
Love, and watch the low - ly maid - en In whose gen - tle arms he lay;

Ma - ry was that moth - er mild, Je - sus Christ her lit - tle child.
With the poor, and mean, and low - ly, Lived on earth our Sa - viour ho - ly.
Chris - tian chil - dren all must be Mild, o - be - dient, good as he.

4 For he is our childhood's pattern;
     Day by day like us he grew;
He was little, weak, and helpless,
     Tears and smiles like us he knew;
And he feeleth for our sadness,
And he shareth in our gladness.

5 And our eyes at last shall see him,
     Through his own redeeming love;
For that child so dear and gentle
     Is our Lord in heav'n above;
And he leads his children on
To the place where he is gone.

OLD HUNDREDTH L.M.
With great dignity

LOUIS BOURGEOIS, 1551

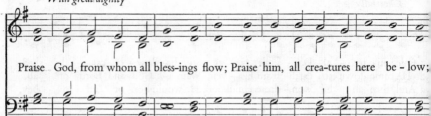

Praise God, from whom all bless-ings flow; Praise him, all crea-tures here be-low;

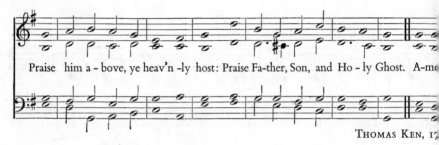

Praise him a-bove, ye heav'n-ly host: Praise Fa-ther, Son, and Ho-ly Ghost. A-me

THOMAS KEN, 17

71 All People That on Earth Do Dwell

The tune is the same as No. 70.

1 All people that on earth do dwell,
    Sing to the Lord with cheerful voice;
Him serve with fear, his praise forth tell,
    Come ye before him and rejoice.

2 Know that the Lord is God indeed;
    Without our aid he did us make:
We are his folk, he doth us feed,
    And for his sheep he doth us take.

3 O enter then his gates with praise,
    Approach with joy his courts unto;
Praise, laud, and bless his Name always,
    For it is seemly so to do.

4 For why? the Lord our God is good,
    His mercy is for ever sure;
His truth at all times firmly stood,
    And shall from age to age endure. Amen.

WILLIAM KETHE, 1561; *based on Psalm 1*

Praise, My Soul, the King of Heaven

LAUDA ANIMA 87.87.87

JOHN GOSS, 1869

With movement

1. Praise, my soul, the King of hea - ven; To his feet your
2. Praise him for his grace and fa - vor To our fa - thers
3. Fa - ther - like he tends and spares us; Well our fee - ble

trib - ute bring; Ran - somed, healed, re - stored, for - giv - en,
in dis - tress; Praise him still the same as ev - er,
frame he knows; In his hand he gen - tly bears us,

Ev - er - more his prais - es sing: Al - le - lu - ia!
Slow to chide, and swift to bless: Al - le - lu - ia!
Res - cues us from all our foes. Al - le - lu - ia!

Al - le - lu - ia! Praise the ev - er - last - ing King.
Al - le - lu - ia! Glo - rious in his faith - ful - ness.
Al - le - lu - ia! Wide - ly yet his mer - cy flows.

4 Angels, help us to adore him; Dwellers all in time and space.
  You behold him face to face; Alleluia! Alleluia!
  Sun and moon, bow down before him, Praise with us the God of grace.

HENRY FRANCIS LYTE, 1834, *alt; based on Psalm 103*

493

NEWMAN C.M.
In unison, fervently

RICHARD RUNCIMAN TERRY, 1912

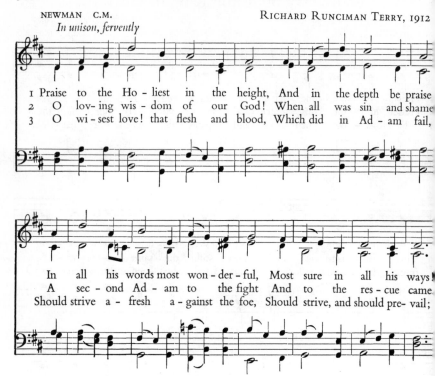

1 Praise to the Ho - liest in the height, And in the depth be praise
2 O lov- ing wis - dom of our God! When all was sin and shame
3 O wi - sest love! that flesh and blood, Which did in Ad - am fail,

In all his words most won - der - ful, Most sure in all his ways!
A sec - ond Ad - am to the fight And to the res - cue came.
Should strive a - fresh a - gainst the foe, Should strive, and should pre- vail;

4 And that a higher gift than grace
  Should flesh and blood refine:
  God's presence and his very self,
  And essence all-divine.

5 O generous love! that he who smote
  In Man for man the foe,
  The double agony in Man
  For man should undergo;

6 And in the garden secretly,
  And on the cross on high,
  Should teach his brethren, and inspire
  To suffer and to die.

7 Praise to the Holiest in the height,
  And in the depth be praise;
  In all his words most wonderful,
  Most sure in all his ways!

A - m

JOHN HENRY NEWMAN,

Praise to the Lord, the Almighty

PRAISE TO THE LORD   14.14.478
Joyfully, with dignity

Stralsund Gesangbuch, 1665
The Chorale Book for England, 1863

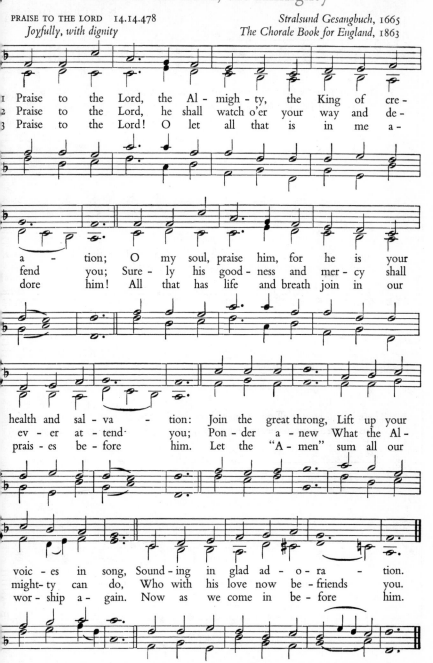

1. Praise to the Lord, the Al - migh - ty, the King of cre - a - tion; O my soul, praise him, for he is your health and sal - va - tion: Join the great throng, Lift up your voic - es in song, Sound - ing in glad ad - o - ra - tion.

2. Praise to the Lord, he shall watch o'er your way and de - fend you; Sure - ly his good - ness and mer - cy shall ev - er at - tend you; Pon - der a - new What the Al - might - y can do, Who with his love now be - friends you.

3. Praise to the Lord! O let all that is in me a - dore him! All that has life and breath join in our prais - es be - fore him. Let the "A - men" sum all our wor - ship a - gain. Now as we come in be - fore him.

JOACHIM NEANDER, 1680, *alt.*

495

See Your People

Unison

R. F. TWYNHAM, 1965

1 See your peo-ple here be-fore you Hear our prayers and give us peace.
2 See ex-am-ple Je-sus gave us, Wash-ing his dis-ci-ples' feet.

Help these cho-sen men to serve us, May their pa-tient love in-crease.
Though he was their Lord and Mas-ter, Gave him-self in love com-plete.

These shall be for all our mem-bers, Hel-pers al-ways in the Lord.
Thus to rule means being ser-vant, Min-is-ter and guard-ian too:

May their ser-vice be most faith-ful; Make their minds of one ac-cord.
Spokes-man for a ho-ly peo-ple, Sent to nour-ish and re-new.

GABRIEL HUCK, 1

Sing of Mary

PLEADING SAVIOUR 87.87.D
Somewhat slowly

Plymouth Collection,
New York, 1855

1 Sing of Ma - ry, pure and low - ly, Vir - gin moth - er un - de - filed,
2 Sing of Je - sus, son of Ma - ry, In the home at Na - za - reth.

Sing of God's own Son most ho - ly, Who be - came her lit - tle child.
Toil and la - bor can not wea - ry Love en - dur - ing un - to death.

Fair - est child of fair - est moth - er, God the Lord who came to earth,
Con - stant was the love he gave her, Though he went forth from her side,

Word made flesh, our ve - ry broth - er, Takes our na - ture by his birth.
Forth to preach, and heal, and suf - fer, Till on Cal - va - ry he died. A-men.

3 Glory be to God the Father;
   Glory be to God the Son;
  Glory be to God the Spirit;
   Glory while the ages run.

From the heart of blessed Mary,
  From all saints the song ascends,
And the church the strain re-echoes
  Unto earth's remotest ends. Amen.

Anonymous, c. 1914

ST. GERTRUDE 65.65.D., with Refrain   ARTHUR S. SULLIVAN, 1871

In march time

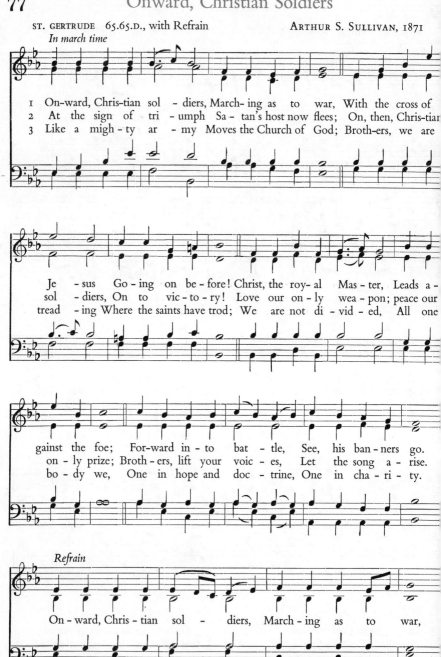

1 On-ward, Chris-tian sol - diers, March- ing as to war, With the cross of
2 At the sign of tri - umph Sa - tan's host now flees; On, then, Chris-tian
3 Like a migh - ty ar - my Moves the Church of God; Broth-ers, we are

Je - sus Go - ing on be - fore! Christ, the roy- al Mas - ter, Leads a -
sol - diers, On to vic - to - ry! Love our on - ly wea - pon; peace our
tread - ing Where the saints have trod; We are not di - vid - ed, All one

gainst the foe; For-ward in - to bat - tle, See, his ban - ners go.
on - ly prize; Broth - ers, lift your voic - es, Let the song a - rise.
bo - dy we, One in hope and doc - trine, One in cha - ri - ty.

Refrain

On - ward, Chris - tian sol - diers, March - ing as to war,

With the cross of Je - sus Go - ing on be - fore! A-men.

4 Onward, then, ye people,
Join our happy throng;
Blend with ours your voices
In our thankful song:

Glory, laud, and honor,
Unto Christ the King;
This through countless ages
Men and angels sing. *Refrain* Amen.

SABINE BARING-GOULD, 1864 *alt.*

Silent Night

HOLY NIGHT Irregular
Steadily, in moderate time

FRANZ GRUEBER, 1818
harmonized by CARL REINECKE

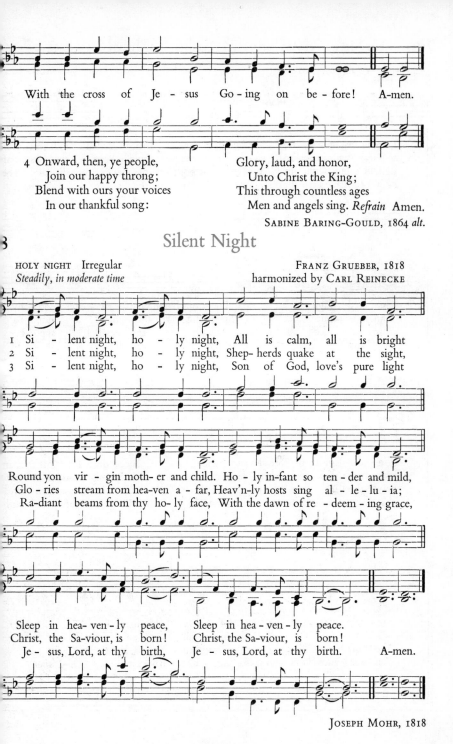

1 Si - lent night, ho - ly night, All is calm, all is bright
2 Si - lent night, ho - ly night, Shep- herds quake at the sight,
3 Si - lent night, ho - ly night, Son of God, love's pure light

Round yon vir - gin moth- er and child. Ho - ly in-fant so ten - der and mild,
Glo - ries stream from hea-ven a - far, Heav'n-ly hosts sing al - le - lu - ia;
Ra-diant beams from thy ho- ly face, With the dawn of re - deem - ing grace,

Sleep in hea - ven - ly peace, Sleep in hea - ven - ly peace.
Christ, the Sa-viour, is born! Christ, the Sa-viour, is born!
Je - sus, Lord, at thy birth, Je - sus, Lord, at thy birth. A-men.

JOSEPH MOHR, 1818

499

Sing: My Tongue, Acclaim Christ Present

FIRST TUNE   87.87.87   MODE III

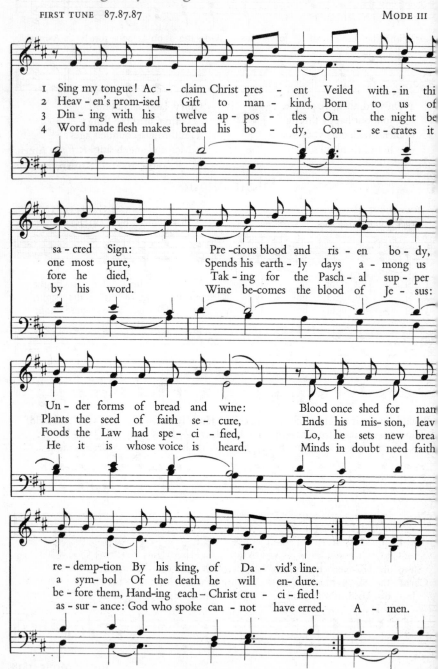

1 Sing my tongue! Ac - claim Christ pres - ent   Veiled with - in thi[s]
2 Heav - en's prom-ised   Gift   to   man - kind,   Born   to   us   of
3 Din - ing with his   twelve ap - pos - tles   On   the night be -
4 Word made flesh makes bread his bo - dy,   Con - se - crates it

sa - cred   Sign: Pre -cious blood and   ris - en   bo - dy,
one most   pure,   Spends his earth - ly   days   a - mong us
fore he   died,   Tak - ing for the   Pasch - al   sup - per
by   his   word.   Wine be-comes the blood of   Je - sus:

Un - der forms of bread and   wine: Blood once shed for   man[kind's]
Plants the seed   of faith se - cure,   Ends his mis - sion, leav[es]
Foods the Law had spe - ci - fied,   Lo, he sets new brea[d]
He   it   is   whose voice is   heard.   Minds in doubt need faith[']

re - demp-tion By his king, of   Da - vid's line.
a   sym-bol Of the death he   will   en - dure.
be - fore them, Hand-ing each – Christ cru - ci - fied!
as - sur - ance: God who spoke can - not   have erred.   A - men.

5 Bowing low, then, offer homage
  To a Sacrament so great!
  Here is new and perfect worship;
  All the old must terminate.
  Senses cannot grasp this marvel:
  Faith must serve to compensate.

6 Praise and glorify the Father,
  Bless his Son's life-giving Name,
  Singing their eternal God-head,
  Power, majesty and fame,
  Offering their Holy Spirit
  Equal worship and acclaim. Amen.

ST. THOMAS AQUINAS, 1274. Tr. MELVIN FARRELL, S.S.

Sing, My Tongue, Acclaim Christ Present

SECOND TUNE 87.87.87

Trier, 17th cent.
Cantus Diversi, 1751

1 Sing, my tongue! Ac-claim Christ pres-ent Veiled with-in this sa-cred sign:
2 Hea-ven's promised Gift to man-kind, Born to us of one most pure,
3 Din-ing with his twelve a-pos-tles On the night be-fore he died,
4 Word made flesh makes bread his bo-dy, Con-se-crates it by his word.

Pre-cious blood and ris-en bo-dy, Un-der forms of bread and wine:
Spends his earth-ly days a-mong us, Plants the seed of faith se-cure,
Tak-ing for the Pasch-al sup-per Foods the Law had spe-ci-fied,
Wine be-comes the blood of Je-sus: He it is whose voice is heard.

Blood once shed for man's re-demption By his King, of Da-vid's line.
Ends his mis-sion, leaves a sym-bol Of the death he will en-dure.
Lo, he sets new bread be-fore them, Handing each Christ cru-ci-fied!
Minds in doubt need faith's as-sur-ance: God who spoke can-not have erred. A-men.

ST. THOMAS AQUINAS, 1274. Tr. MELVIN FARRELL, S.S.

SALZBURG   77.77.D
With great dignity

Melody by Jakob Hintze, 1678, *alt.*
harmonized by J. S. Bach, 1685–1750

1 Songs of thank-ful-ness and praise, Je-sus, Lord, to you we raise,
2 Man-i-fest at Jor-dan's stream, Pro-phet, Priest, and King su-preme;

Man-i-fest-ed by the star To the sa-ges from a-far;
And at Ca-na, wed-ding guest, In your God-head man-i-fest;

Branch of roy-al Da-vid's stem In your birth at Beth-le-hem;
Man-i-fest in power di-vine, Changing wa-ter in-to wine;

An-thems be to you ad-dressed, God in man made man-i-fest.
An-thems be to you ad-dressed, God in man made man-i-fest. A-men

3 Manifest in making whole
   Palsied limbs and fainting soul;
   Manifest in valiant fight,
   Quelling all the devil's might;
   Manifest in gracious will,
   Ever bringing good from ill;
   Anthems be to you addressed,
   God in man made manifest.

4 Grant us grace to see you, Lord,
   Mirrored in your holy word;
   May we imitate you here,
   Live as men who know no fear;
   That we like to you may be
   At your great epiphany;
   And may praise you, ever blest,
   God in man made manifest. Amen.

Christopher Wordsworth, 1862, *alt*

At the Lamb's High Feast We Sing

The tune is the same as No. 79

1 At the Lamb's high feast we sing
Praise to our victorious King,
He has washed us in the tide
Flowing from his pierced side;
Praise we him, whose love divine
Gives his sacred Blood for wine,
Gives his Body for the feast,
Christ the victim, Christ the priest.

2 Where the Paschal blood is poured,
Death's dark angel sheathes his sword;
Israel's hosts triumphant go
Through the wave that drowns the foe.
Praise we Christ, whose blood was shed,
Paschal victim, Paschal bread;
With sincerity and love
Eat we manna from above. Amen.

3 Mighty victim from the sky,
Hell's fierce powers beneath you lie;
You have conquered in the fight,
You have brought us life and light:
Now no more can death appall,
Now no more the grave enthrall;
You have opened paradise,
And in you your saints shall rise.

4 Easter triumph, Easter joy,
Sin alone can this destroy;
From sin's power now set us free
Souls new-born, O Lord we'll be.
Hymns of glory songs of praise,
Father, unto you we raise:
Lord, all praise to you;
Praise the Spirit ever new. Amen

Latin; Tr. ROBERT CAMPBELL, 1849, *alt.*

The Great Creator of the Worlds

TALLIS' ORDINAL

THOMAS TALLIS, c. 1567

Moderately slow

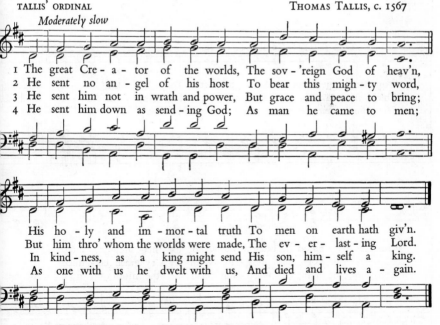

1 The great Cre-a-tor of the worlds, The sov-'reign God of heav'n,
2 He sent no an-gel of his host To bear this migh-ty word,
3 He sent him not in wrath and power, But grace and peace to bring;
4 He sent him down as send-ing God; As man he came to men;

His ho-ly and im-mor-tal truth To men on earth hath giv'n.
But him thro' whom the worlds were made, The ev-er-last-ing Lord.
In kind-ness, as a king might send His son, him-self a king.
As one with us he dwelt with us, And died and lives a-gain.

From Epistle to Diognetus, c. 150; Tr. F. BLAND TUCKER, 1939

AURELIA   76.76.D.   SAMUEL SEBASTIAN WESLEY, 1864
In moderate time

1 The Church's one foun-da-tion Is Je-sus Christ her Lord;
2 E-lect from ev-'ry na-tion, Yet one o'er all the earth,
3 Though with a scorn-ful won-der Men see her sore op-prest,

She is his new cre-a-tion By wa-ter and the word:
Her char-ter of sal-va-tion, One Lord, one faith, one birth;
By schisms rent a-sun-der, By her-e-sies dis-trest;

From heav'n he came and sought her To be his ho-ly bride;
One ho-ly Name she bless-es, Par-takes one ho-ly food,
Yet saints their watch are keep-ing, Their cry goes up, "How long?"

With his own blood he bought her, And for her life he died.
And to one hope she press-es, With ev-'ry grace en-dued.
And soon the night of weep-ing Shall be the morn of song. A-men.

4 'Mid toil and tribulation,
　　and tumult of her war,
She waits the consummation
　　Of peace for evermore;
Till with the vision glorious
　　Her longing eyes are blest,
And the great Church victorious
　　Shall be the Church at rest.

5 Yet she on earth hath union
　　With God, the Three in One,
And mystic sweet communion
　　With those whose rest is won.
O happy ones and holy!
　　Lord, give us grace that we
Like them, the meek and lowly,
　　On high may dwell with thee. Amen.

SAMUEL JOHN STONE, 1866

4　The God Whom Earth and Sea and Sky

L. M.

J. S. BACH, 1685–1750

1 The God whom earth and sea and sky
　A - dore and laud and mag - ni - fy,
　Whose might they own, whose praise they tell,
　In Ma - ry's bo - dy deigned to dwell.

2 O Moth - er blest! the chos - en shrine
　Where - in the Ar - chi - tect di - vine,
　Whose hand con - tains the earth and sky,
　Vouch - safed in hid - den guise to lie:

3 Blest in the mes - sage Gab - riel brought;
　Blest in the work the Spi - rit wrought;
　Most blest, to bring to hu - man birth
　The long de - sired of all the earth.

4 O Lord, the Vir - gin - born, to thee
　E - ter - nal praise and glo - ry be,
　Whom with the Fa - ther we a - dore
　And Ho - ly Ghost for ev - er - more.

VENANTIUS FORTUNATUS, c. 530–609; Tr. J. M. NEALE, 1818–1866

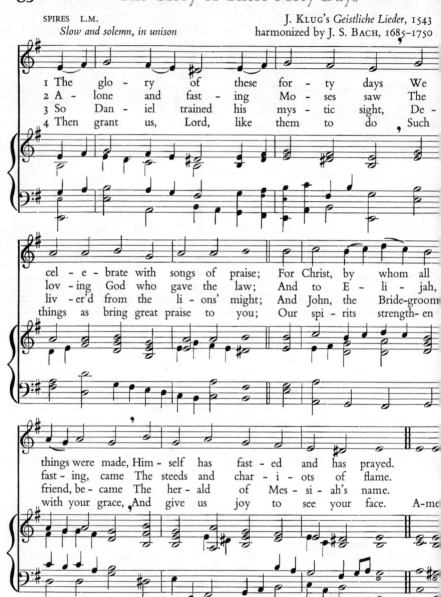

SPIRES   L.M.

Slow and solemn, in unison

J. KLUG's *Geistliche Lieder*, 1543
harmonized by J. S. BACH, 1685–1750

1 The glo - ry of these for - ty days We
2 A - lone and fast - ing Mo - ses saw The
3 So Dan - iel trained his mys - tic sight, De -
4 Then grant us, Lord, like them to do, Such

cel - e - brate with songs of praise; For Christ, by whom all
lov - ing God who gave the law; And to E - li - jah,
liv - er'd from the li - ons' might; And John, the Bride-groom
things as bring great praise to you; Our spi - rits strength- en

things were made, Him - self has fast - ed and has prayed.
fast - ing, came The steeds and char - i - ots of flame.
friend, be - came The her - ald of Mes - si - ah's name.
with your grace, And give us joy to see your face. A-me

5 O Father, Son, and Spirit blest,
   To you be every prayer addressed
   And by all mankind be adored,
   From age to age, the only Lord. Amen.

Latin, 6th cent.; Tr. MAURICE F. BELL, 1906,

6

The Lord Is My True Shepherd

BASED ON PSALM 22   76.76.D.

JOSEPH MOHR
Acc. by REV. EUGENE LINDUSKY, O.S.C.

1 The Lord is my true Shep-herd, no want or fear I know;
2 He sets for me a ban-quet be-fore my watching foes,

Through pas-tures green he leads me, where liv-ing wa-ters flow;
A-noints my head with glad-ness, my cup, it o-ver-flows;

Though I should walk in dark ness, no dan-ger will I fear
His mer-cy shall pur-sue me, His good-ness calm my fears;

His rod and staff, my com-fort, when Christ my Lord is near.
His house shall be my dwell-ing through ev-er-last-ing years.

REV. EUGENE LINDUSKY, O.S.C.

MAINZ, 1900
Harmonization, R. F. TWYNHAM

87.87 Refrain

1 To Je - sus Christ, our sov - 'reign King, Who is the world's Sal -
2 Thy reign ex - tend, O King be - nign, To ev - 'ry land an
3 To Thee and to Thy Church, great King, We pledge our hearts' ob

va - tion, All praise and hom - age do we bring And
na - tion; For in Thy king - dom, Lord di - vine, A -
la - tion; Un - til be - fore Thy throne we sing In

thanks and ad - o - ra - tion.
lone we find sal - va - tion. Christ Je - sus, Vic - tor! Christ Je - su
end - less ju - bi - la - tion.

Rul - er! Christ Je - sus, Lord and Re - deem - er!

MSGR. MARTIN B. HELLRIEC

The Master Came

The tune is the same as No. 87

The Master came to bring good news,
The news of love and freedom,
To heal the sick and seek the poor,
To build the peace-ful kingdom.

Refrain:
Father, forgive us! Through Jesus, hear us!
As we forgive one another.

To seek the sinners Jesus came,
To live among the friendless,
To show them love that they might share
The kingdom that is endless. *Refrain.*

2 Through Jesus Christ the Law's fulfilled,
The man who lived for others.
The law of Christ is love alone,
To serve now all our brothers. *Refrain.*

4 Forgive us, Lord, as we forgive
And seek to help each other.
Forgive us, Lord, and we shall live
To pray and work together. *Refrain.*

GABRIEL HUCK, 1965

Shepherd of Souls

ST. AGNES   C.M.   JOHN B. DYKES, 1866
Quietly

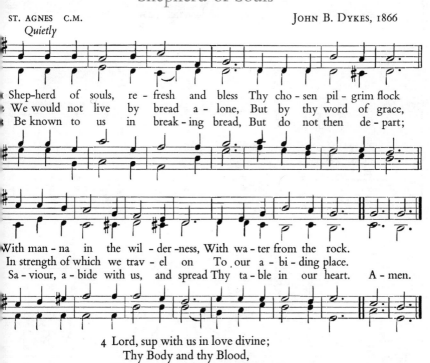

Shep-herd of souls, re-fresh and bless Thy cho-sen pil-grim flock
We would not live by bread a-lone, But by thy word of grace,
Be known to us in break-ing bread, But do not then de-part;

With man-na in the wil-der-ness, With wa-ter from the rock.
In strength of which we trav-el on To our a-bi-ding place.
Sa-viour, a-bide with us, and spread Thy ta-ble in our heart.   A-men.

4 Lord, sup with us in love divine;
Thy Body and thy Blood,
That living bread, that heav'nly wine,
Be our immortal food. Amen

JAMES MONTGOMERY, 1825, *alt.*

509

90

Bless the Lord, O My Soul

IPPOLITOV-IVANOV (M. G. H. G.)

Bless the Lord O my soul: Bless-ed are you, O Lord

Bless the Lord, O my soul: And all that is with-in

me, bless his ho-ly name. Bless the Lord, O my soul: And

get not all his prais - es. Who for - gives all your

i - qui - ties, Who heals all your dis - eas - es, Who re -

deems your life from de - struc - tion, Who crowns you with lov-ing

kind - ness and ten - der mer - cies. Bless the Lord,

O my soul: And all that is with - in me, bless his ho - ly

name. Bless - ed are you, O Lord.

91

Wake, Awake, for Night is Flying

SLEEPERS, WAKE   898.898.664.448
Broad and solemn; may be sung in unison

Melody, PHILIP NICOLAI, 1599
arr. and har. by J. S. BACH, 1731

1 Wake, a-wake, for night is fly-ing, The watch-men on th
2 Si-on hears the watch-men sing-ing, And all her heart w

heights are cry-ing, A-wake, Je-ru-sa-lem, at last
joy is spring-ing, She wakes, she ris-es from her gloo

Mid-night hears the wel-come voic-es And at the thrill-in
For her Lord comes down all glo-rious, The strong in grace, i

cry re-joic-es: Come forth, ye vir-gins, night is past
truth vic-to-rious, Her Star is ris'n, her Light is come

The Bride - groom comes, a - wake, Your lamps with glad - ness take;
Ah come, thou bless - ed One, God's own be - lov - ed Son,

Al - le - lu - ia! And for his mar - riage feast pre - pare,
Al - le - lu - ia! We fol - low till the halls we see

For ye must go to meet him there.
Where thou hast bid us sup with thee. A - men.

3 Now let all the heavens adore thee,
   And men and angels sing before thee,
      With harp and cymbal's clearest tone;
   Of one pearl each shining portal,
   Where we are with the choir immortal
      Of angels round thy dazzling throne;
         Nor eye hath seen, nor ear
         Hath yet attained to hear
            What there is ours;
   But we rejoice, and sing to thee
   Our hymn of joy eternally. Amen.

PHILIP NICOLAI, 1556-1608. *Tr.* CATHERINE WINKWORTH, 1829-78

513

92

We Long for You, O Lord

C. Reilly

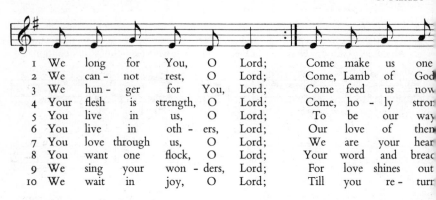

1 We long for You, O Lord; Come make us one
2 We can - not rest, O Lord; Come, Lamb of God
3 We hun - ger for You, Lord; Come feed us now
4 Your flesh is strength, O Lord; Come, ho - ly stron
5 You live in us, O Lord; To be our way
6 You live in oth - ers, Lord; Our love of then
7 You love through us, O Lord; We are your hear
8 You want one flock, O Lord; Your word and bread
9 We sing your won - ders, Lord; For love shines out
10 We wait in joy, O Lord; Till you re - turn

with You in love; We long for You, O Lord.
and give us peace; We can - not rest, O Lord.
with liv - ing bread; We hun - ger for You, Lord.
One, make us strong; Your flesh is strength, O Lord.
and Truth and Life; You live in us, O Lord.
is love of You; You live in oth - ers, Lord.
and hands and voice; You love through us, O Lord.
can make us one; You want one flock, O Lord.
in all You do; We sing your won - ders, Lord.
to take us home, We wait in joy, O Lord.

REFRAIN AND DOXOLOGY (Dox. after last stanza only)

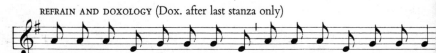

Ris - en Sav - ior, King of glo - ry, Come to- day in mys - ter - y:
(Dox.) Fa - ther, Son, and Ho - ly Spir - it, Let us share your fam - i - ly,

Let us share your death and ris - ing Till You come in maj - es - ty
Lov- ing You and one an - oth - er, Prais- ing You e - ter - nal - ly

C. Reilly, 19

Were You There

Irregular
With deep reverence

Were you there when they cru - ci - fied my Lord? Were you
Were you there when they nailed him to the tree? Were you
Were you there when they laid him in the tomb? Were you
Were you there when they rolled the stone a - way? Were you

there when they cru - ci - fied my Lord?
there when they nailed him to the tree? Oh! . . . .
there when they laid him in the tomb?
there when they rolled the stone a - way?

Some-times it caus - es me to trem - ble, trem - ble, trem- ble.

Were you there when they cru - ci - fied my Lord?
Were you there when they nailed him to the tree?
Were you there when they laid him in the tomb?
Were you there when they rolled the stone a - way?

Negro Spiritual

FRANKFORT   887.887.48.48   PHILIP NICOLAI, 1599,
With breadth; may be sung in unison   arr. J. S. BACH, c. 1730

1 With hearts re-newed by   liv-ing faith, We lift   our thoughts in
2 So   rich God's grace   in   Je-sus Christ, That we   are called as

grate-ful   prayer   To   God   our   grac-ious   Fa-   ther,
sons   of   light   To   bear   the   pledge of   glo-   ry.

Whose plan   it   was   to   make us   sons Through his   own   Son's re-
Through him   in   whom all   full-ness dwells, We   of-fer   God   our

demp-tive   death,   That   res-cued   us   from   dark-   ness.
gift   of   self   In   un-ion   with   the   Spi-   rit.

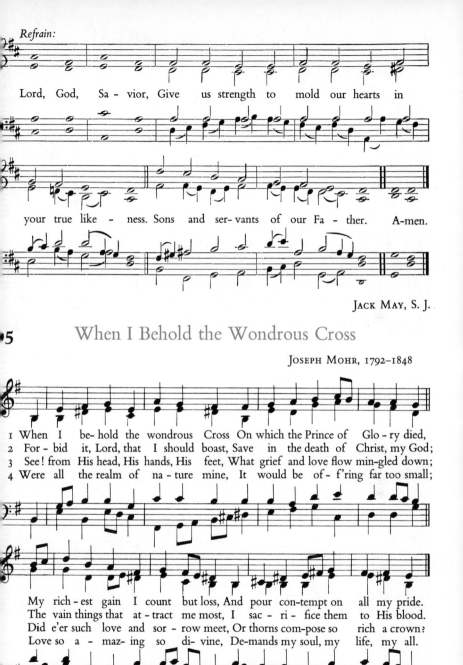

Refrain:

Lord, God, Sa - vior, Give us strength to mold our hearts in your true like - ness. Sons and ser - vants of our Fa - ther. A - men.

JACK MAY, S. J.

When I Behold the Wondrous Cross

JOSEPH MOHR, 1792–1848

1 When I be- hold the wondrous Cross On which the Prince of Glo - ry died,
2 For - bid it, Lord, that I should boast, Save in the death of Christ, my God;
3 See! from His head, His hands, His feet, What grief and love flow min-gled down;
4 Were all the realm of na - ture mine, It would be of- f'ring far too small;

My rich - est gain I count but loss, And pour con-tempt on all my pride.
The vain things that at - tract me most, I sac - ri - fice them to His blood.
Did e'er such love and sor - row meet, Or thorns com-pose so rich a crown?
Love so a - maz - ing so di - vine, De-mands my soul, my life, my all.

ISAAC WATTS, 1674–1748, *alt.*

517

What Child Is This?

GREENSLEEVES 87.87, with Refrain — English, before 1642

In moderate time

1 What child is this, who, laid to rest, On Mary's lap is sleep-ing?
2 Why lies he in such low-li-ness Where ox and ass are feed-ing?

Whom an-gels greet with an-thems sweet, While shepherds watch are keep-ing?
Good Christian, fear: for sin-ners here The si-lent Word is plead-ing.

Refrain

This, this is Christ the King, Whom shep-herds guard and an-gels sing:

Haste, haste to bring him praise, The babe, the son of Ma-ry.

3 So bring him incense, gold, and myrrh,
Come, peasant, king, to own him,
The King of kings salvation brings,
Let loving hearts enthrone him.
Refrain

WILLIAM CHATTERTON DIX, c. 1865, *a*

7

Where Charity and Love Are

JOSEPH ROFF

Refrain

Where char-i-ty and love are, there is God.

Verses

1 The love of Christ has gathered us to-geth — er. Let us rejoice in him and
2 When, therefore, we are assembled to-geth — er, Let us take heed, that we be
   not divided
3 Let us also with the bless-ed see Your face in glory, O Christ

be glad. Let us fear and love the liv-ing God.
in mind. Let malicious quarrels and con - ten-tions cease;
our God; There to possess immeasurable and hap-py joy

And let us love one another with a sin-cere heart. *Refrain.*
And let Christ our God dwell a — mong us. *Refrain.*
For infinite ages of a - ges. A — men. *Refrain.*

Ye Watchers and Ye Holy Ones

VIGILES ET SANCTI 88.44.88.44.444

Melody, Cologne *Gesangbuch*, 1623

Boldly, in unison

1 Ye watch-ers and ye ho - ly ones, Bright ser - aphs, cher- u- bim, a
2 O high - er than the cher - u - bim, More glo - rious than the ser - a

thrones, Raise the glad strain, Al - le - lu - ia! Cry
phim, Lead their prais - es, Al - le - lu - ia! Thou

out, do - min - ions, princedoms, powers, Vir - tues, arch-an - gels, an - gel
bear - er of the e - ter - nal Word, Most gra - cious, mag -ni - fy th

choirs,
Lord,
Al - le - lu - ia, Al - le - lu - ia, Al - le -

lu - ia, Al - le - lu - ia, Al - le - lu - ia!

Respond, ye souls in endless rest,
Ye patriarchs and prophets blest,
  Alleluia, Alleluia!
Ye holy twelve, ye martyrs strong,
All saints triumphant, raise the song
Alleluia, Alleluia, Alleluia, Alleluia, Alleluia!

4 O friends, in gladness let us sing,
Supernal anthems echoing,
  Alleluia, Alleluia!
To God the Father, God the Son,
And God the Spirit, Ever one,
Alleluia, Alleluia, Alleluia, Alleluia, Alleluia!

ATHELSTAN RILEY, 1909

All Creatures of Our God and King

The tune is the same as No. 98

1 All creatures of our God and King,
  Lift up your voice and with us sing
    Alleluia, alleluia!
  Thou burning sun with golden beam,
  Thou silver moon with softer gleam:

2 Thou rushing winds that are so strong,
  Ye clouds that sail in heaven along,
    O praise him, alleluia!
  Thou rising morn, in praise rejoice,
  Ye lights of evening, find a voice:
                                    Refrain

Refrain O praise him, O praise him, Alleluia, alleluia, alleluia!

3 Thou flowing water, pure and clear,
　Make music for thy Lord to hear,
　　Alleluia, alleluia!
　Thou fire so masterful and bright,
　That gives to man both warmth and light:

Refrain O praise him, O praise him,
　　Alleluia, alleluia, alleluia!

4 Dear mother earth, who day by day
　Unfolds new blessings on our way,
　　O praise him, alleluia!
　The flowers and fruits that in thee grow,
　Let them his glory also show:
　　　　　　　　　　　Refrain

5 And all ye men of tender heart,
　Forgiving others, take your part,
　　O sing ye, alleluia!
　Ye who long pain and sorrow bear,
　Praise God and on him cast your care:
　　　　　　　　　　　Refrain

6 And thou, most kind and gentle death,
　Waiting to hush our latest breath,
　　O praise him, alleluia!
　Lead then to home the child of God,
　And Christ our Lord the way once tro☐
　　　　　　　　　　　Refrain

7 Let all things their Creator bless,
　And worship him in humbleness;
　　O praise him, alleluia!
　Praise, praise the Father, praise the Son
　And praise the Spirit, ever One:
　　　　　　　　　　　Refrain

ST. FRANCIS OF ASSISI, 1182–12☐
TR. WILLIAM H. DRAPER, 1855–1933, ☐

100　　　　While Shepherds Watched

WINCHESTER OLD
In moderate time

Melody from T. EST'S
Whole Book of Psalmes, 1592

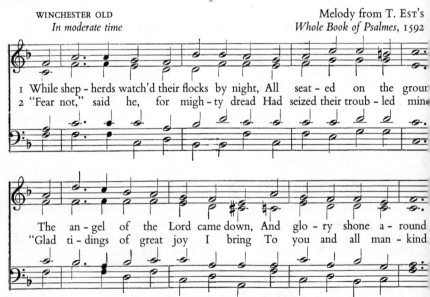

1 While shep-herds watch'd their flocks by night, All seat-ed on the grour☐
2 "Fear not," said he, for migh-ty dread Had seized their troub-led min☐

The an-gel of the Lord came down, And glo-ry shone a-round
"Glad ti-dings of great joy I bring To you and all man-kind

'To you, in David's town, this day
  Is born of David's line
The Saviour, who is Christ the Lord;
  And this shall be the sign:

'The heav'nly Babe you there shall find
  To human view displayed,
All meanly wrapped in swathing bands,
  And in a manger laid."

5 So spoke the angel, then with him
   Appeared a glorious throng;
  To sing the praise of God to men
   In bright and joyful song.

6 "All glory be to God on high
   And on the earth be peace;
  Good will to men from heav'n shall now
   Begin and never cease."

NAHUM TATE, 1700, *alt.*

Angels from the Realms of Glory

REGENT SQUARE 87.87.87   HENRY SMART, 1867
In moderate time

An-gels, from the realms of glo-ry, Wing your flight o'er all the earth;
Shep-herds in the field a-bid-ing, Watch-ing o'er your flocks by night,

Ye, who sang cre-a-tion's sto-ry, Now pro-claim Mes-si-ah's birth:
God with man is now re-sid-ing; Yon-der shines the in-fant Light:

Refrain

Come and wor-ship, come and wor-ship, Wor-ship Christ, the new-born King.

ages, leave your contemplations;
  Brighter visions beam afar:
eek the great Desire of nations;
  Ye have seen his natal star: *Refrain*

4 Saints before the altar bending,
   Watching long in hope and fear,
  Suddenly the Lord, descending,
   In his temple shall appear: *Refrain*

JAMES MONTGOMERY, 1810

523

102   R. F. TWYNHAM, 1965

All you peoples clap your hands; shout to God with cries of glad- ne

103   R. F. TWYNHAM, 1965

Al - le - lu - ia, al - le - lu - ia, al - le - lu - ia.

104   R. F. TWYNHAM, 1965

Al - le - lu - ia, al - le - lu - ia, al - le - lu - ia.

105   R. F. TWYNHAM, 1965

At - tend to my sigh - ing; heed my call for help, m

king   and   my   God.   To   you   I   pray, O   Lord.

R. F. TWYNHAM, 1965

De - li - ver us, O   God of Is - ra - el from all   our   tri - bu - la-tions.

R. F. TWYNHAM, 1965

Drop down dew, you   hea-vens, from a-bove   and   let the clouds rain the   just.

R. F. TWYNHAM, 1965

Hap-py they who dwell in your house. Con-tin-u- al- ly   they   praise you.

109

R. F. TWYNHAM, 1965

He gave them the bread of hea- ven; man ate the bread of an - gels.

110

R. F. TWYNHAM, 1965

He rained man-na u - pon them for food and gave them hea-ven-ly bread.

111

R. F. TWYNHAM, 1965

He shall call u - pon me, and I will an - swer him;

I will de - li - ver him and glo - ri - fy him.

112

GREGORY MURRAY, O.S.B.

His good-ness shall fol - low me al - ways, to the end of my day

JOSEPH GELINEAU, S.J.

I place all my trust in you, my God: all my hope is in your mer - cy.

R. F. TWYNHAM, 1965

In my dis - stress I called u - pon the
Lord; from his ho - ly tem - ple he has heard my voice.

R. F. TWYNHAM, 1965

Let all the earth wor - ship you, O God, and sing
praise to you, sing praise to your name, Most High High.

116 R. F. Twynham, 1965

Let us glo-ry in the cross of our Lord, Je-su

Christ; in whom is our sal-va-tion life and re-sur-rec-tion.

117 R. F. Twynham, 1965

May God grant you to be of one mind with one a-no-ther.

118 Joseph Gelineau, s.j.

My shep-herd is the Lord, no-thing in-deed shall I want.

119 R. F. Twynham, 1965

O Lord be not far from me; O my help, has-ten to aid me. aid me.

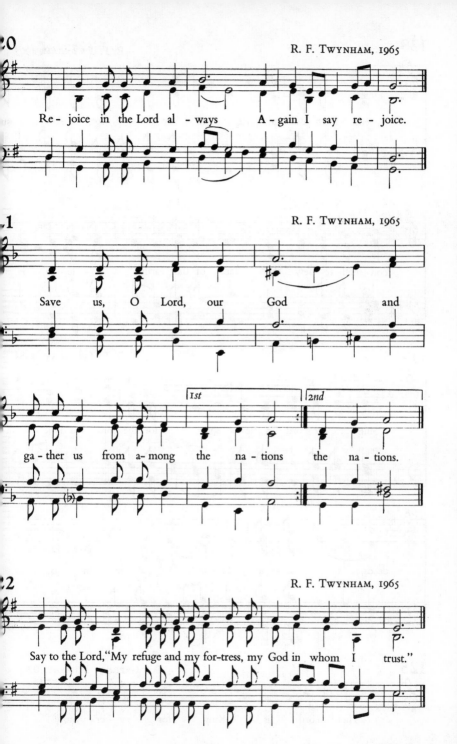

R. F. TWYNHAM, 1965

Re - joice in the Lord al - ways A - gain I say re - joice.

R. F. TWYNHAM, 1965

Save us, O Lord, our God and

1st   2nd

ga - ther us from a - mong the na - tions the na - tions.

R. F. TWYNHAM, 1965

Say to the Lord, "My refuge and my for-tress, my God in whom I trust."

123 R. F. Twynham, 1965

Send forth your spi - rit, and they shall be cre - a - ted, an

You shall re - new the face of the earth, al - le - lu - ia.

124 R. F. Twynham, 1965

Sing to the Lord a new song, for the Lord has done won-dr

deeds, al - le - lu - ia, al - le - lu - ia.

125 Gregory Murray, O.S.B.

The Lord is King for ev - er - more.

26

R. F. TWYNHAM, 1965

The Lord said to me, "You are my son; this day I have be-got-ten you."

27

R. F. TWYNHAM, 1965

The Spi-rit of the Lord has filled the earth, al-le-lu-ia, al-le-lu-ia.

28

R. F. TWYNHAM, 1965

This is the day the Lord has made; let us be glad and re-joice in it.

29

R. F. TWYNHAM, 1965

1st 2nd

To you I lift up my soul; in you, O my God, I trust I trust.

30

GREGORY MURRAY, O.S.B.

We shall go up with joy to the house of our God.

131 R. F. TWYNHAM, 1965

Ho - san - na   to   the   Son   of   Da -   vid!

Bles - sed   is   he   who   comes   in   the   name   of   the   Lord.   O

King   of   Is - ra - el: Ho - san - na   in   the   high - est.

132 R. F. TWYNHAM, 1965

The   child - ren   of   the   He - brews,   bear - ing   o - live

bran - ches, went to meet the Lord cry - ing a -

loud and say - ing, Ho - san - na in the high - est.

33

"A new command-ment I give you, that you love one a -

no - ther, as I have loved you," says the Lord, says the Lord.

134 R. F. Twynham, 1965

My peo - ple what have I done un - to you? or in what have I of- fend - ed you? An - swer me. Ho - ly God. Ho - ly God. Ho - ly migh-ty one. Ho-ly migh - ty one. Ho - ly im-mor-tal one, have mer - cy on us. Ho - ly im - mor - tal one, have mer - cy on us.

135 R. F. Twynham, 1965

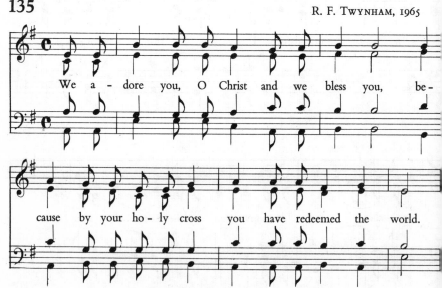

We a - dore you, O Christ and we bless you, be- cause by your ho - ly cross you have redeemed the world.

Priest: The Lord be with you. *People:* And with your spir - it.

Priest: Let us pray. O God... and ev - er *People:* A - men.

37 Lord Have Mercy

J. GERALD PHILLIPS

Lord, have mer - cy.

Lord, have mer-cy. Lord, have mer - cy.

Christ, have mer - cy.

Christ, have mer - cy. Christ, have mer - cy.

Lord, have mer - cy.

Lord, have mer - cy. Lord, have mer - cy.

Mass in the Vernacular

138 Lord Have Mercy

C. ALEXANDER PELOQUIN

Lord, have mer - cy. Lord, have mer - cy.

Lord, have mer - cy. Christ, have mer - cy.

Christ, have mer - cy. Christ, have mer - cy.

Lord, have mer - cy. Lord, have mer -

cy. Lord, have mer - cy. *Mass for Parishe*

139 Lord Have Mercy

JOSEPH ROFF

Lord, have mer - cy. Lord, have mer-cy. Lord, have mer - cy.

Christ, have mer - cy. Christ, have mer-cy. Christ, have mer - cy.

Lord, have mer-cy. Lord, have mer - cy. Lord, have mer - cy.

People's Mass in Honor of Pope John

140 Lord Have Mercy

MARCEL ROONEY, O.S.B.

Lord, have mer - cy. Lord, have mer - cy. Lord, have mer-cy.

536

Christ, have mer - cy. Christ, have mer- cy. Christ, have mer- cy.

Lord, have me-rcy. Lord, have mer-cy. Lord have mer - cy.

Mass in Honor of the Immaculate Conception

141 Glory to God

J. GERALD PHILLIPS

Glo - ry to God in the high - est.

And on earth peace, peace to men of good will.

We praise You. We bless You. We wor-ship You.

We glo - ri - fy You. We give You thanks for Your great glo - ry.

Lord God, heav - en- ly King, God the Fa - ther al - might - y.

Lord Je - sus Christ, the on - ly be - got - ten Son.

Lord God, Lamb of God, Son of the Fa - ther.

You, who take a - way the sins of the world, have mer - cy on us.

537

You, who take a-way the sins of the world, re-ceive our prayer

You, who sit at the right hand of the Fa - ther, have mer-cy on

us. For You a-lone are ho - ly. You a-lone are Lord.

You a - lone, O Je - sus Christ, are most high, With the Ho - ly

Spir - it, in the glo-ry of God the Fa - ther. A - men.

Mass in the Vernacular

142 Glory to God

C. ALEXANDER PELOQUIN

Glo-ry to God in the high - est. And on earth peace to

men of good will. We praise you. We bless you.

We wor-ship you. We glo-ri-fy you. We

give you thanks for your great glo - ry. Lord God,

heav-en-ly King, God the Fa-ther al-might - y.

538

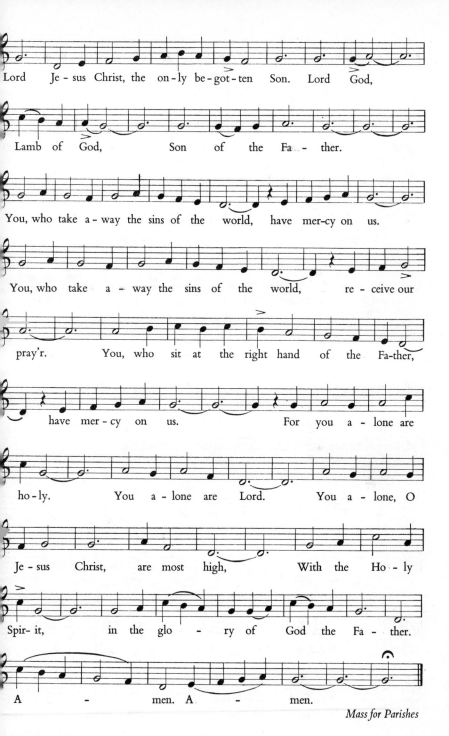

Lord Je - sus Christ, the on - ly be - got - ten Son. Lord God, Lamb of God, Son of the Fa - ther. You, who take a - way the sins of the world, have mer - cy on us. You, who take a - way the sins of the world, re - ceive our pray'r. You, who sit at the right hand of the Fa - ther, have mer - cy on us. For you a - lone are ho - ly. You a - lone are Lord. You a - lone, O Je - sus Christ, are most high, With the Ho - ly Spir - it, in the glo - ry of God the Fa - ther. A - men. A - men.

Mass for Parishes

JOSEPH ROFF

Glo - ry to God in the high - est. And on earth peace to

men of good will. We praise you. We bless you. We wor - ship you.

We glo - ri - fy you. We give you thanks for your great glo - ry

Lord God, heavenly King, God the Fa - ther al - might- y. Lord Je-sus Chri

the on - ly- be - got - ten Son. Lord God, Lamb of Go

Son of the Fa - ther. You, who take a- way the sins of the worl

have mer- cy on us. You, who take a-way the sins of the worl

re - ceive our prayer. You, who sit at the right hand of the

Fa-ther, have mer - cy on us. For you a - lone are ho - ly.

You a - lone are Lord. With the Ho - ly Spir - it,

in the glo - ry of God the Fa - ther. A - men

540

People's Mass in Honor of Pope J

JOSEPH ROFF

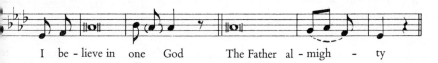

I be - lieve in one God The Father al - migh - ty

Maker of heaven | and earth,
> and of all things visible and in | visible.

And I believe in one Lord, | Jesus Christ,
> the only begotten | Son of God.

Born of his Father before all | ages.
> God of God, Light of Light, true God of | true God.

Begotten, not made, of one substance with the | Father.
> By whom all | things were made.

Who for us men and for our sal | vation
> came down from | heaven.

And he became flesh by the Holy Spirit of the Virgin | Mary:
> and was | made man.

He was also cruci | fied for us,
> suffered under Pontius Pilate, and was | buried.

And on the third day he | rose again,
> according to the | Scriptures.

He ascended into | heaven
> and sits at the right hand of the | Father.

He will come again in glory to judge the living | and the dead.
> And of his kingdom there will | be no end.

And I believe in the Holy Spirit, the Lord and Giver | of life,
> who proceeds from the Father | and the Son.

Who together with the Father and the Son is adored and | glorified,
> and who spoke through the | prophets.

And one holy, Catholic, and Apos | tolic Church.
> I confess one baptism for the forgiveness | of sins.

And I await the resurrection | of the dead.
> And the life of the world to | come. Amen.

People's Mass in Honor of Pope John

145 Preface

Priest: The Lord be with you. *People:* And with your spir - it.

Priest: Lift up your heart. *People:* We have lift - ed them up to the Lord

Priest: Let us give thanks to the Lord our God. *People:* It is right and just

146 Preface

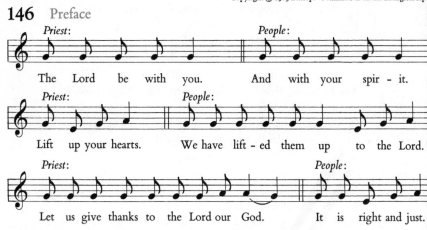

Priest: The Lord be with you. *People:* And with your spir - it.

Priest: Lift up your hearts. *People:* We have lift - ed them up to the Lord.

Priest: Let us give thanks to the Lord our God. *People:* It is right and just.

147 Holy, Holy, Holy

J. GERALD PHILLIPS

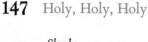

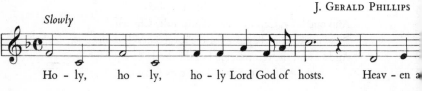

Slowly

Ho - ly, ho - ly, ho - ly Lord God of hosts. Heav - en a

earth are filled with Your glo - ry. Ho - san - na, ho - san - na,

san-na in the high-est. Bless-ed is He who comes in the name of the

Lord. Ho - san - na, ho - san - na, ho-san-na in the high - est.

Mass in the Vernacular

8 Holy, Holy, Holy

Strong

C. Alexander Peloquin

Ho - ly, ho - ly, ho - ly Lord God of hosts.

Heaven and earth are filled with your glo - ry. Ho - san - na

in the high - est. Bless - ed is he who comes in the name of the

Lord. Ho - san - na in the high - est.

Mass for Parishes

9 Holy, Holy, Holy

Joseph Roff

Ho - ly, ho - ly, ho - ly Lord God of hosts.

Heaven and earth are filled with your glo - ry. Ho - san - na in the

high - est. Bless - ed is he who comes in the name of the Lord.

Ho - san - na in the high - est.

People's Mass in Honor of Pope John

543

150 Holy, Holy, Holy   MARCEL ROONEY, O.S.B.

Ho - ly, ho - ly, ho - ly, Lord God of hosts! Hea-ven and earth filled with your glo - ry. Ho-san - na in the high-est. Bless- ed he who comes in the name of the Lord. Ho-san - na in the high-est.

Mass in Honor of the Immaculate Concep

151 Holy, Holy, Holy

Ho - ly, ho - ly, ho - ly Lord God of Hosts. Heav-en and earth filled with your glo - ry. Ho-san-na in the high-est. Bless-ed is who comes in the name of the Lord. Ho-san - na in the high - est.

152 Holy, Holy, Holy

Ho - ly, ho - ly, ho - ly Lord God of hosts. Heaven and earth are filled with your glo - ry. Hosanna in the high - Blessed is he who comes in the name of the Lord. Hosanna in the high-est

Let us pray: Taught by our Sa - vior's com - mand and formed

by the word of God, we dare to say: Our Fa - ther,

who art in heav - en, hal - lowed be thy name; thy king-dom come;

thy will be done on earth as it is in heav - en. Give us this

day our dai - ly bread; and for - give us our tres - pass - es

as we for - give those who tres-pass a - gainst us; and lead us not

in - to temp -ta - tion, but de - liv - er us from e - vil.

4 Our Father

Let us pray: Taught by our Sa - vior's command and formed by the word of God,

we dare to say: Our Fa - ther who art in heav - en, hallowed be thy name;

thy king-dom come; thy will be done on earth as it is in heav - en.

Give us this day our dai - ly bread; and for-give us our tres - pass - es

as we forgive those who tres - pass a - gainst us;

and lead us not in - to temp-ta - tion, but de - liv - er us from e -

155 Our Father

Let us pray: Taught by our Sa-vior's com - mand and formed by th

word of God, we dare to say: Our Fa - ther, who art in heav

hal - lowed be thy name; thy kingdom come; thy will be done on

as it is in heav-en. Give us this day our dai - ly bread; and

give us our tres-pass - es as we for-give those who tres-pass a - gainst u

and lead us not in-to temp - ta - tion, but de-liv-er us from e - vi

Priest: *People:*

May the peace of the Lord be al-ways with you.   And with your spir - it.

Copyright © 1965 Bishops' Commission on the Liturgical Apostolate.

57 Lamb of God

J. Gerald Phillips

Devoutly

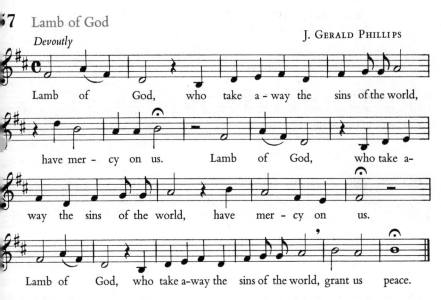

Lamb of God, who take a-way the sins of the world, have mer - cy on us. Lamb of God, who take a-way the sins of the world, have mer - cy on us. Lamb of God, who take a-way the sins of the world, grant us peace.

58 Lamb of God

C. Alexander Peloquin

With sorrow

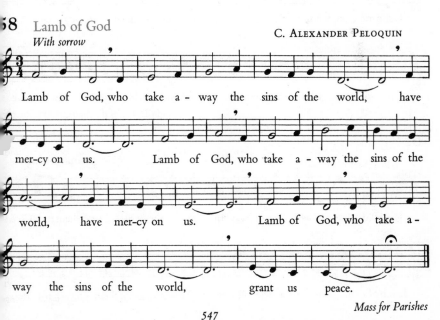

Lamb of God, who take a - way the sins of the world, have mer-cy on us. Lamb of God, who take a - way the sins of the world, have mer-cy on us. Lamb of God, who take a - way the sins of the world, grant us peace.

Mass for Parishes

159 Lamb of God

JOSEPH ROFF

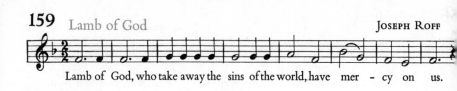

Lamb of God, who take away the sins of the world, have mer - cy on us.

Lamb of God, who take away the sins of the world, have mer - cy on us.

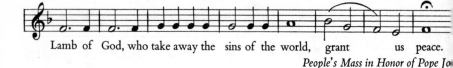

Lamb of God, who take away the sins of the world, grant us peace.

People's Mass in Honor of Pope Jo

160 Lamb of God

MARCEL ROONEY, O.S.B.

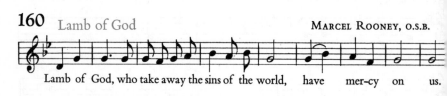

Lamb of God, who take away the sins of the world, have mer-cy on us.

Lamb of God, who take away the sins of the world, have mer-cy on us.

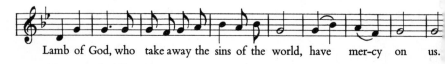

Lamb of God who take a-way the sins of the world, grant us peace.

Mass in Honor of the Immaculate Concepti

161 Lamb of God

(At Masses of the dead)

CYRIL A. REILLY

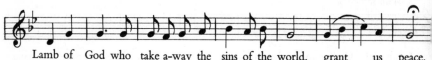

Lamb of God, who take a- way the sins of the world, grant them rest. *(Repea*

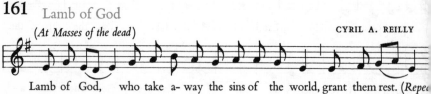

Lamb of God, who take a- way the sins of the world, grant them e-ter - nal rest.

548

Priest:

The Mass is end - ed. Go in peace.

People:

Thanks be to God.

en the Glory to God is omitted:

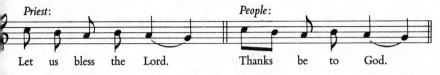

Priest:

Let us bless the Lord.

People:

Thanks be to God.

Requiem Masses:

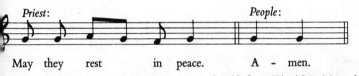

Priest:

May they rest in peace.

People:

A - men.

Copyright © 1965 Bishops' Commission on the Liturgical Apostolate.

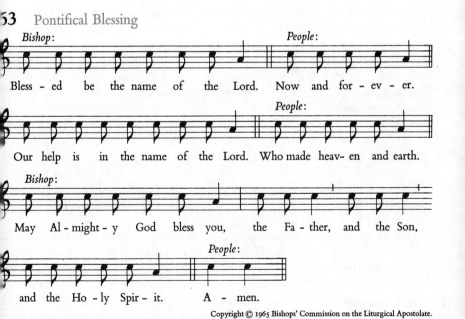

Bishop:

Bless - ed be the name of the Lord.

People:

Now and for - ev - er.

Our help is in the name of the Lord.

People:

Who made heav- en and earth.

Bishop:

May Al - might - y God bless you, the Fa - ther, and the Son,

and the Ho - ly Spir - it.

People:

A - men.

Copyright © 1965 Bishops' Commission on the Liturgical Apostolate.

Singing the Psalms: To the Choir Directo

SONG has always had a special place in the celebration of the Eucharist. Althoug
singing is particularly suited to some parts of the Mass (the chants between t
readings and the Holy, Holy, Holy, for example), song will also accompany certa
actions, especially the various processions (Entrance Song, Song at the Preparation
the Gifts, Communion Song). Today the whole congregation is encouraged to join
song with the trained choir. An ideal form for such participation may be seen in t
arrangement of the Introit or Entrance Song. First there is a theme line, called t
antiphon, then a psalm is begun. If the psalm is continued, the antiphon may be r
peated. The people will usually sing this antiphon, while the choir sings the psalm.

Although it is often the custom today to sing hymns during those parts of the Ma
where the Missal provides antiphons and/or psalms, we are encouraged to restore t
ancient tradition of alternating between choir and congregation and using, as much
possible, the psalms and other scriptural texts of the Mass being celebrated. This w
allow the people to become familiar with sung psalms, and to understand better t
significance of the season or feast which is usually given in the theme line or antipho

In the hymnal section are many antiphons suited to various feasts and seasor
Ordinarily such antiphons will be used at the direction of the choir master in conne
tion with a psalm. The ten simple musical patterns below are meant to be used for t
psalms when the latter are sung with the antiphons in the hymnal (except those an
phons by Gelineau and Murray which have their own psalm tones). When an appr
priate antiphon has been selected, the musical pattern in the same key must be foun
First, the congregation will sing the antiphon; then the choir will begin the verses
the psalm or other text given in the proper parts of the Mass being celebrated. Aft
singing these verses, they may continue with the psalm recommended, which will
found in the psalter. The choir and the congregation will then alternate in singin
when directed, the people will repeat the antiphon between verses of the psalm.

Each verse of a psalm has two parts when sung by the choir. Ordinarily a psal
verse will be printed this way, but sometimes it appears that a verse has three or mo
parts, or lines. Whenever this occurs, the choir director usually indicates beforeha
which lines will be joined together. For example, in the second verse of Psalm Tw
(page 557), the first line would be considered half of the verse, and the following tw
lines would be joined to form the second half.

The first half of a verse will be sung with the notes on the first half of any one of t
following ten musical patterns. The second half of the verse will be sung with the not
on the second line. It is important to notice that in both lines the last three syllables w
be sung with the last three notes, though at times the natural accent of the words ma
suggest a change at the fourth or the second syllable from the end. This is precisely wl
a trained choir under the direction of the choir master can best sing the psalm vers
Since the antiphons are simple and easy to learn, they belong to the whole congregatio

54 KEY OF C   PSALM 17

For who is God   ex - cept the Lord? Who is a rock,   Save our God?

55 KEY OF D   PSALM 66

May God have pity on us   and bless us; may he let his face shine up-on us.

56 KEY OF E♭   PSALM 106

"Give thanks to the Lord, for   he is good, for his kindness endures   for-ev-er.

57 KEY OF E   PSALM 33

I will bless the Lord   at all times; his praise shall be ever   in my mouth.

58 KEY OF F   PSALM 137

I will give thanks to you,   for you have heard the words
    O Lord, with all my heart,   . . . of the angels I will sing your praise;

169 KEY OF G   PSALM 75

God is renowned   in Ju-da;   in Israel great   is his name

170 KEY OF D MINOR   PSALM 39

I have waited, waited   for the Lord, and he stooped toward   me and heard my cry

171 KEY OF E MINOR   PSALM 115

I believed even   when I said, "I am greatly   af-flict-ed.

172 KEY OF F MINOR   PSALM 2

Why do the   na-tions rage   and the peoples   ut-ter fol-ly

173 KEY OF B MINOR   PSALM 119

In my distress I called   to the Lord and he   ans-wered me
Woe is me that I sojourn   in Mo-soch, that I dwell amid the tents of Ce-dar

Index of First Lines of Hymns, Antiphons and Sung Masses

The numbers below are hymn numbers, *not* page numbers

553

ANTIPHONS

ANTIPHONS FOR HOLY WEEK

MUSIC FOR SUNG MASSES

THE
PSALTER

Introduction

THE PSALMS are prayers for Christians of today. They are part of holy Scripture, the product of the varied attitudes and styles of generations of poets who sang about the majesty of God, the sinfulness of man and the beauty of nature.

The psalms are prayers, but prayers of many kinds. Some are well thought out and carefully written expressions of a man's devotion to God's law or his love of sacred history. Others are like painful cries from men in trouble and in danger, or the spontaneous shouts of joyful warriors after a great victory.

The psalter is a book of many moods. On one occasion the beauty and goodness of a psalm will come with the readiness of our own feelings; on other occasions, especially when we pray the psalms in the liturgy, we adopt for ourselves the attitudes expressed, thus entering into these traditional prayers which for centuries have been a medium for God's communication with his beloved people and his revelation to them.

The psalms in all their variety were used in the Jewish liturgy, and so have from the earliest times been a most important part of Christian worship. Thus the Book of Psalms became the prayerbook and the song book of God's people.

But for Jews and Christians alike the psalter was more than a book to be used in the liturgy. It was the source of inspiration and reflection: about oneself, about the love of God for men, about sin and forgiveness, about hardship and how the poor become God's special people—about almost every aspect of life. The psalmists saw God as present and acting in all. Praying the psalms will make this attitude our own.

Psalm 1

1 HAPPY the man who follows not
    the counsel of the wicked
Nor walks in the way of sinners,
    nor sits in the company of the insolent,

2 But delights in the law of the Lord
    and meditates on his law day and night.

3 He is like a tree
    planted near running water,
That yields its fruit in due season,
    and whose leaves never fade.
    Whatever he does, prospers.

4 Not so the wicked, not so;
    they are like chaff which the wind drives away.

5 Therefore in judgment the wicked shall not stand,
    nor shall sinners, in the assembly of the just.

6 For the Lord watches over the way of the just,
    but the way of the wicked vanishes.

Psalm 2

1 WHY DO the nations rage
    and the peoples utter folly?

2 The kings of the earth rise up,
    and the princes conspire together
    against the Lord and against his anointed:

3 "Let us break their fetters
    and cast their bonds from us!"

4 He who is throned in heaven laughs;
    the Lord derides them.

5 Then in anger he speaks to them;
    he terrifies them in his wrath:

6 "I myself have set up my king
    on Sion, my holy mountain."

7 I will proclaim the decree of the Lord:
    The Lord said to me, "You are my son;
    this day I have begotten you.

8 Ask of me and I will give you
    the nations for an inheritance
    and the ends of the earth for your possession.

9   You shall rule them with an iron rod;
        you shall shatter them like an earthen dish."

10   And now, O kings, give heed;
        take warning, you rulers of the earth.
11   Serve the Lord with fear, and rejoice before him;
12   with trembling pay homage to him,
        Lest he be angry and you perish from the way,
        when his anger blazes suddenly.
        Happy are all who take refuge in him!

Psalm 3

2   O LORD, how many are my adversaries!
        Many rise up against me!
3   Many are saying of me,
        "There is no salvation for him in God."
4   But you, O Lord, are my shield;
        my glory, you lift up my head!

5   When I call out to the Lord,
        he answers me from his holy mountain.
6   When I lie down in sleep,
        I wake again, for the Lord sustains me.
7   I fear not the myriads of people
        arrayed against me on every side.

8   Rise up, O Lord!
        Save me, my God!
     For you strike all my enemies on the cheek;
        the teeth of the wicked you break.
9   Salvation is the Lord's!
        Upon your people be your blessing!

Psalm 4

2   WHEN I call, answer me, O my just God,
        you who relieve me when I am in distress;
        Have pity on me, and hear my prayer!

3   Men of rank, how long will you be dull of heart?
        Why do you love what is vain and seek after falsehood?
4   Know that the Lord does wonders for his faithful one;
        the Lord will hear me when I call upon him.

5   Tremble, and sin not;
      reflect, upon your beds, in silence.
6   Offer just sacrifices,
      and trust in the Lord.

7   Many say, "Oh, that we might see better times!"
      O Lord, let the light of your countenance shine upon us!
8   You put gladness into my heart,
      more than when grain and wine abound.
9   As soon as I lie down, I fall peacefully asleep,
      for you alone, O Lord,
      bring security to my dwelling.

Psalm 5

2   HEARKEN to my words, O Lord,
      attend to my sighing.
3   Heed my call for help,
      my king and my God!
4   To you I pray, O Lord;
      at dawn you hear my voice;
      at dawn I bring my plea expectantly before you.

5   For you, O God, delight not in wickedness;
      no evil man remains with you;
6   the arrogant may not stand in your sight.
    You hate all evildoers;
7   you destroy all who speak falsehood;
    The bloodthirsty and the deceitful
      the Lord abhors.

8   But I, because of your abundant kindness,
      will enter your house;
    I will worship at your holy temple
9   in fear of you, O Lord;
    Because of my enemies, guide me in your justice;
      make straight your way before me.

10   For in their mouth there is no sincerity;
      their heart teems with treacheries.
    Their throat is an open grave;
      they flatter with their tongue.
11   Punish them, O God;
      let them fall by their own devices;

For their many sins, cast them out
    because they have rebelled against you.

12 But let all who take refuge in you
    be glad and exult forever.
Protect them, that you may be the joy
    of those who love your name.
13 For you, O Lord, bless the just man;
    you surround him with the shield of your good will.

Psalm 6

2 O Lord, reprove me not in your anger,
    nor chastise me in your wrath.
3 Have pity on me, O Lord, for I am languishing;
    heal me, O Lord, for my body is in terror;
4 My soul, too, is utterly terrified;
    but you, O Lord, how long . . .?

5 Return, O Lord, save my life;
    rescue me because of your kindness,
6 For among the dead no one remembers you;
    in the nether world who gives you thanks?

7 I am wearied with sighing;
    every night I flood my bed with weeping;
    I drench my couch with my tears.
8 My eyes are dimmed with sorrow;
    they have aged because of all my foes.

9 Depart from me, all evildoers,
    for the Lord has heard the sound of my weeping;
10 The Lord has heard my plea;
    the Lord has accepted my prayer.
11 All my enemies shall be put to shame in utter terror;
    they shall fall back in sudden shame.

Psalm 7

2 O Lord, my God, in you I take refuge;
    save me from all my pursuers and rescue me,
3 Lest I become like the lion's prey,
    to be torn to pieces, with no one to rescue me.

4   O Lord, my God, if I am at fault in this,
        if there is guilt on my hands,
5   If I have repaid my friend with evil,
        I who spared those who without cause were my foes—
6   Let the enemy pursue and overtake me;
        let him trample my life to the ground,
        and lay my glory in the dust.

7   Rise up, O Lord, in your anger;
        rise against the fury of my foes;
        wake to the judgment you have decreed.
8   Let the assembly of the peoples surround you;
        above them on high be enthroned.
9   The Lord judges the nations.
      Do me justice, O Lord, because I am just,
        and because of the innocence that is mine.
10   Let the malice of the wicked come to an end,
        but sustain the just,
        O searcher of heart and soul, O just God.

11   A shield before me is God,
        who saves the upright of heart;
12   A just judge is God,
        a God who punishes day by day.
13   Unless they be converted, God will sharpen his sword;
        he will bend and aim his bow,
14   Prepare his deadly weapons against them,
        and use fiery darts for arrows.

15   He who conceived iniquity and was pregnant with mischief,
        brings forth failure.
16   He has opened a hole, he has dug it deep,
        but he falls into the pit which he has made.
17   His mischief shall recoil upon his own head;
        upon the crown of his head his violence shall rebound.
18   I will give thanks to the Lord for his justice,
        and sing praise to the name of the Lord Most High.

Psalm 8

2   O Lord, our Lord,
        how glorious is your name over all the earth!
        You have exalted your majesty above the heavens.
3   Out of the mouths of babes and sucklings

you have fashioned praise because of your foes,
to silence the hostile and the vengeful.

4 When I behold your heavens, the work of your fingers,
the moon and the stars which you set in place—
5 What is man that you should be mindful of him,
or the son of man that you should care for him?

6 You have made him little less than the angels,
and crowned him with glory and honor.
7 You have given him rule over the works of your hands,
putting all things under his feet:
8 All sheep and oxen,
yes, and the beasts of the field,
9 The birds of the air, the fishes of the sea,
and whatever swims the paths of the seas.
10 O Lord, our Lord,
how glorious is your name over all the earth!

Psalm 9a

2 I WILL give thanks to you, O Lord, with all my heart;
I will declare all your wondrous deeds.
3 I will be glad and exult in you;
I will sing praise to your name, Most High,
4 Because my enemies are turned back,
overthrown and destroyed before you.

5 For you upheld my right and my cause,
seated on your throne, judging justly.
6 You rebuked the nations and destroyed the wicked;
their name you blotted out forever and ever.
7 The enemies are ruined completely forever;
the remembrance of the cities you uprooted has perished.

8 But the Lord sits enthroned forever;
he has set up his throne for judgment.
9 He judges the world with justice;
he governs the peoples with equity.
10 The Lord is a stronghold for the oppressed,
a stronghold in times of distress.
11 They trust in you who cherish your name,
for you forsake not those who seek you, O Lord.

12 Sing praise to the Lord enthroned in Sion;

proclaim among the nations his deeds;

13 For the avenger of blood has remembered;
  he has not forgotten the cry of the afflicted.

14 Have pity on me, O Lord; see how I am afflicted by my foes,
  you who have raised me up from the gates of death,
15 That I may declare all your praises
  and, in the gates of the daughter of Sion, rejoice in your salvation.

16 The nations are sunk in the pit they have made;
  in the snare they set, their foot is caught;
17 In passing sentence, the Lord is manifest;
  the wicked are trapped by the work of their own hands.

18 To the nether world the wicked shall turn back,
  all the nations that forget God.
19 For the needy shall not always be forgotten,
  nor shall the hope of the afflicted forever perish.
20 Rise, O Lord, let not man prevail;
  let the nations be judged in your presence.
21 Strike them with terror, O Lord;
  let the nations know that they are but men.

Psalm 9b

1 WHY, O Lord, do you stand aloof?
  Why hide in times of distress?
2 Proudly the wicked harass the afflicted,
  who are caught in the devices the wicked have contrived.

3 For the wicked man glories in his greed,
  and the covetous blasphemes, sets the Lord at nought.
4 The wicked man boasts, "He will not avenge it";
  "There is no God," sums up his thoughts.
5 His ways are secure at all times;
  your judgments are far from his mind;
  all his foes he scorns.
6 He says in his heart, "I shall not be disturbed;
  from age to age I shall be without misfortune."

7 His mouth is full of cursing, guile and deceit;
  under his tongue are mischief and iniquity.
8 He lurks in ambush near the villages;

in hiding he murders the innocent;
  his eyes spy upon the unfortunate.
9 He waits in secret like a lion in his lair;
  he lies in wait to catch the afflicted;
  he catches the afflicted and drags them off in his net.
10 He stoops and lies prone
  till by his violence fall the unfortunate.
11 He says in his heart, "God has forgotten;
  he hides his face, he never sees."

12 Rise, O Lord! O God, lift up your hand!
  Forget not the afflicted!
13 Why should the wicked man despise God,
  saying in his heart, "He will not avenge it"?
14 You do see, for you behold misery and sorrow,
  taking them in your hands.
  On you the unfortunate man depends;
  of the fatherless you are the helper.
15 Break the strength of the wicked and of the evildoer;
  punish their wickedness; let them not survive.

16 The Lord is king forever and ever;
  the nations have perished out of his land.
17 The desire of the afflicted you hear, O Lord;
  strengthening their hearts, you pay heed
18 To the defense of the fatherless and the oppressed,
  that man, who is of earth, may terrify no more.

Psalm 10

1 IN THE Lord I take refuge; how can you say to me,
  "Flee to the mountain like a bird!
2 For, see, the wicked bend the bow;
  they place the arrow on the string
  to shoot in the dark at the upright of heart.
3 When the pillars are overthrown,
  what can the just man do?"

4 The Lord is in his holy temple;
  the Lord's throne is in heaven.
  His eyes behold,
  his searching glance is on mankind.
5 The Lord searches the just and the wicked;
  the lover of violence he hates.

6 He rains upon the wicked fiery coals and brimstone;
a burning blast is their allotted cup.
7 For the Lord is just, he loves just deeds;
the upright shall see his face.

Psalm 11

2 HELP, O Lord! for no one now is dutiful;
faithfulness has vanished from among men.
3 Everyone speaks falsehood to his neighbor;
with smooth lips they speak, and double heart.

4 May the Lord destroy all smooth lips,
every boastful tongue,
5 Those who say, "We are heroes with our tongues;
our lips are our own; who is lord over us?"

6 "Because they rob the afflicted, and the needy sigh,
now will I arise," says the Lord;
"I will grant safety to him who longs for it."

7 The promises of the Lord are sure,
like tried silver, freed from dross, sevenfold refined.
8 You, O Lord, will keep us
and preserve us always from this generation,
9 While about us the wicked strut
and in high place are the basest of men.

Psalm 12

2 HOW LONG, O Lord? Will you utterly forget me?
How long will you hide your face from me?
3 How long shall I harbor sorrow in my soul,
grief in my heart day after day?
How long will my enemy triumph over me?
4 Look, answer me, O Lord, my God!

Give light to my eyes that I may not sleep in death
5 lest my enemy say, "I have overcome him";
Lest my foes rejoice at my downfall
6 though I trusted in your kindness.
Let my heart rejoice in your salvation;
let me sing of the Lord, "He has been good to me."

Psalm 13

1 THE FOOL says in his heart,
   "There is no God."
   Such are corrupt; they do abominable deeds;
     there is not one who does good.
2 The Lord looks down from heaven upon the children of men,
     to see if there be one who is wise and seeks God.
3 All alike have gone astray; they have become perverse;
     there is not one who does good, not even one.

4 Will all these evildoers never learn,
     they who eat up my people just as they eat bread?
   They have not called upon the Lord;
5   then they shall be in great fear,
       for God is with the just generation.
6 You would confound the plans of the afflicted,
     but the Lord is his refuge.

7 Oh, that out of Sion would come the salvation of Israel!
     When the Lord restores the well-being of his people,
     then shall Jacob exult and Israel be glad.

Psalm 14

1 O LORD, who shall sojourn in your tent?
     Who shall dwell on your holy mountain?

2 He who walks blamelessly and does justice;
     who thinks the truth in his heart
3   and slanders not with his tongue;
   Who harms not his fellow man,
     nor takes up a reproach against his neighbor;
4 By whom the reprobate is despised,
     while he honors those who fear the Lord;
   Who, though it be to his loss, changes not his pledged word;
5   who lends not his money at usury
       and accepts no bribe against the innocent.

   He who does these things
     shall never be disturbed.

566

Psalm 15

1 KEEP ME, O God, for in you I take refuge;
2   I say to the Lord, "My Lord are you.
   Apart from you I have no good."
3 How wonderfully has he made me cherish
   the holy ones who are in his land!
4 They multiply their sorrows
   who court other gods.
   Blood libations to them I will not pour out,
   nor will I take their names upon my lips.
5 O Lord, my allotted portion and my cup,
   you it is who hold fast my lot.
6 For me the measuring lines have fallen on pleasant sites;
   fair to me indeed is my inheritance.

7 I bless the Lord who counsels me;
   even in the night my heart exhorts me.
8 I set the Lord ever before me;
   with him at my right hand I shall not be disturbed.
9 Therefore my heart is glad and my soul rejoices,
   my body, too, abides in confidence;
10 Because you will not abandon my soul to the nether world,
   nor will you suffer your faithful one to undergo corruption.
11 You will show me the path to life,
   fullness of joys in your presence,
   the delights at your right hand forever.

Psalm 16

1 HEAR, O Lord, a just suit;
   attend to my outcry;
   hearken to my prayer from lips without deceit.
2 From you let my judgment come;
   your eyes behold what is right.
3 Though you test my heart, searching it in the night,
   though you try me with fire, you shall find no malice in me.
4 My mouth has not transgressed after the manner of man;
   according to the words of your lips I have kept the ways of
5 My steps have been steadfast in your paths,   [the law.
   my feet have not faltered.

6 I call upon you, for you will answer me, O God;
   incline your ear to me; hear my word.

7 Show your wondrous kindness,
    O savior of those who flee
    from their foes to refuge at your right hand.
8 Keep me as the apple of your eye;
    hide me in the shadow of your wings
9   from the wicked who use violence against me.

My ravenous enemies beset me;
10   they shut up their cruel hearts,
    their mouths speak proudly.
11 Their steps even now surround me;
    crouching to the ground, they fix their gaze,
12 Like lions hungry for prey,
    like young lions lurking in hiding.

13 Rise, O Lord, confront them and cast them down;
    rescue me by your sword from the wicked,
14   by your hand, O Lord, from mortal men:
From mortal men whose portion in life is in this world,
    where with your treasures you fill their bellies.
Their sons are enriched
    and bequeath their abundance to their little ones.
15 But I in justice shall behold your face;
    on waking, I shall be content in your presence.

Psalm 17

2   I LOVE YOU, O Lord, my strength,
3   O Lord, my rock, my fortress, my deliverer.
    My God, my rock of refuge,
        my shield, the horn of my salvation, my stronghold!
4   Praised be the Lord, I exclaim,
        and I am safe from my enemies.

5   The breakers of death surged round about me,
        the destroying floods overwhelmed me;
6   The cords of the nether world enmeshed me,
        the snares of death overtook me.
7   In my distress I called upon the Lord
        and cried out to my God;
    From his temple he heard my voice,
        and my cry to him reached his ears.

8   The earth swayed and quaked;

the foundations of the mountains trembled
and shook when his wrath flared up.

9 Smoke rose from his nostrils,
and a devouring fire from his mouth
that kindled coals into flame.

10 And he inclined the heavens and came down,
with dark clouds under his feet.

11 He mounted a cherub and flew,
borne on the wings of the wind.

12 And he made darkness the cloak about him;
dark, misty rain-clouds his wrap.

13 From the brightness of his presence
coals were kindled to flame.

14 And the Lord thundered from heaven,
the Most High gave forth his voice;

15 He sent forth his arrows to put them to flight,
with frequent lightnings he routed them.

16 Then the bed of the sea appeared,
and the foundations of the world were laid bare,
At the rebuke of the Lord,
at the blast of the wind of his wrath.

17 He reached out from on high and grasped me;
he drew me out of the deep waters.

18 He rescued me from my mighty enemy
and from my foes, who were too powerful for me.

19 They attacked me in the day of my calamity,
but the Lord came to my support.

20 He set me free in the open,
and rescued me, because he loves me.

21 The Lord rewarded me according to my justice;
according to the cleanness of my hands he requited me;

22 For I kept the ways of the Lord
and was not disloyal to my God;

23 For his ordinances were all present to me,
and his statutes I put not from me,

24 But I was wholehearted toward him,
and I was on my guard against guilt.

25 And the Lord requited me according to my justice,
according to the cleanness of my hands in his sight.

26 Toward the faithful you are faithful,
toward the wholehearted you are wholehearted,

27 Toward the sincere you are sincere,
but toward the crooked you are astute;

28   For lowly people you save
       but haughty eyes you bring low;
29   You indeed, O Lord, give light to my lamp;
       O my God, you brighten the darkness about me;
30   For with your aid I run against an armed band,
       and by the help of my God I leap over a wall.
31   God's way is unerring,
       the promise of the Lord is fire-tried;
       he is a shield to all who take refuge in him.

32   For who is God except the Lord?
       Who is a rock, save our God?
33   The God who girded me with strength
       and kept my way unerring;
34   Who made my feet swift as those of hinds
       and set me on the heights;
35   Who trained my hands for war
       and my arms to bend a bow of brass.

36   You have given me your saving shield;
       your right hand has upheld me,
       and you have stooped to make me great.
37   You made room for my steps;
       unwavering was my stride.
38   I pursued my enemies and overtook them,
       nor did I turn again till I made an end of them.
39   I smote them and they could not rise;
       they fell beneath my feet.

40   And you girded me with strength for war;
       you subdued my adversaries beneath me.
41   My enemies you put to flight before me,
       and those who hated me you destroyed.
42   They cried for help—but no one saved them;
       to the Lord—but he answered them not.
43   I ground them fine as the dust before the wind;
       like the mud in the streets I trampled them down.

44   You rescued me from the strife of the people;
       you made me head over nations;
       A people I had not known became my slaves;
45   as soon as they heard me they obeyed.
       The foreigners fawned and cringed before me;
46   they staggered forth from their fortresses.

47 The Lord live! And blessed be my Rock!
  Extolled be God my savior.
48 O God, who granted me vengeance,
  who made peoples subject to me
49 and preserved me from my enemies,
  Truly above my adversaries you exalt me
  and from the violent man you have rescued me.
50 Therefore will I proclaim you, O Lord, among the nations,
  and I will sing praise to your name,
51 You who gave great victories to your king
  and showed kindness to your anointed,
  to David and his posterity forever.

Psalm 18

2 THE HEAVENS declare the glory of God,
  and the firmament proclaims his handiwork.
3 Day pours out the word to day,
  and night to night imparts knowledge;
4 Not a word nor a discourse
  whose voice is not heard;
5 Through all the earth their voice resounds,
  and to the ends of the world, their message.

  He has pitched a tent there for the sun,
6 which comes forth like the groom from his bridal chamber
  and, like a giant, joyfully runs its course.
7 At one end of the heavens it comes forth,
  and its course is to their other end;
  nothing escapes its heat.

8 The law of the Lord is perfect,
  refreshing the soul;
  The decree of the Lord is trustworthy,
  giving wisdom to the simple.
9 The precepts of the Lord are right,
  rejoicing the heart;
  The command of the Lord is clear,
  enlightening the eye;
10 The fear of the Lord is pure,
  enduring forever;
  The ordinances of the Lord are true,
  all of them just;
11 They are more precious than gold,

than a heap of purest gold;
Sweeter also than syrup
  or honey from the comb.

12 Though your servant is careful of them,
  very diligent in keeping them,
13 Yet who can detect failings?
  Cleanse me from my unknown faults!
14 From wanton sin especially, restrain your servant;
  let it not rule over me.
Then shall I be blameless and innocent
  of serious sin.
15 Let the words of my mouth and the thought of my heart
  find favor before you,
    O Lord, my rock and my redeemer.

Psalm 19

2 THE LORD answer you in time of distress;
  the name of the God of Jacob defend you!
3 May he send you help from the sanctuary,
  from Sion may he sustain you.
4 May he remember all your offerings
  and graciously accept your holocaust.
5 May he grant you what is in your heart
  and fulfill your every plan.
6 May we shout for joy at your victory
  and raise the standards in the name of our God.
  The Lord grant all your requests!

7 Now I know that the Lord has given victory to his anointed,
  that he has answered him from his holy heaven
  with the strength of his victorious right hand.
8 Some are strong in chariots; some, in horses;
  but we are strong in the name of the Lord, our God.
9 Though they bow down and fall,
  yet we stand erect and firm.

10 O Lord, grant victory to the king,
  and answer us when we call upon you.

Psalm 20

2 O LORD, in your strength the king is glad;
  in your victory how greatly he rejoices!

3   You have granted him his heart's desire;
        you refused not the wish of his lips.
4   For you welcomed him with goodly blessings,
        you placed on his head a crown of pure gold.
5   He asked life of you: you gave him
        length of days forever and ever.
6   Great is his glory in your victory;
        majesty and splendor you conferred upon him.
7   For you made him a blessing forever;
        you gladdened him with the joy of your presence.
8   For the king trusts in the Lord,
        and through the kindness of the Most High he stands unshaken.

9   May your hand reach all your enemies,
        may your right hand reach your foes!
10 Make them burn as though in a fiery furnace,
        when you appear.
    May the Lord consume them in his anger;
        let fire devour them.
11 Destroy their fruit from the earth
        and their posterity from among men.
12 Though they intend evil against you,
        devising plots, they cannot succeed,
13 For you shall put them to flight;
        you shall aim your shafts against them.
14 Be extolled, O Lord, in your strength!
        We will sing, chant the praise of your might.

Psalm 21

2   MY GOD, my God, why have you forsaken me,
        far from my prayer, from the words of my cry?
3   O my God, I cry out by day, and you answer not;
        by night, and there is no relief for me.
4   Yet you are enthroned in the holy place,
        O glory of Israel!
5   In you our fathers trusted;
        they trusted, and you delivered them.
6   To you they cried, and they escaped;
        in you they trusted, and they were not put to shame.

7   But I am a worm, not a man;
        the scorn of men, despised by the people.
8   All who see me scoff at me;

they mock me with parted lips, they wag their heads:

9   "He relied on the Lord; let him deliver him,
           let him rescue him, if he loves him."
10   You have been my guide since I was first formed,
           my security at my mother's breast.
11   To you I was committed at birth,
           From my mother's womb you are my God.

12   Be not far from me, for I am in distress;
           be near, for I have no one to help me.
13   Many bullocks surround me;
           the strong bulls of Basan encircle me.
14   They open their mouths against me
           like ravening and roaring lions.

15   I am like water poured out;
           all my bones are racked.
       My heart has become like wax
           melting away within my bosom.
16   My throat is dried up like baked clay,
           my tongue cleaves to my jaws;
           to the dust of death you have brought me down.

17   Indeed, many dogs surround me,
           a pack of evildoers closes in upon me;
       They have pierced my hands and my feet;
18   I can count all my bones.
               They look on and gloat over me;
19   they divide my garments among them,
               and for my vesture they cast lots.

20   But you, O Lord, be not far from me;
           O my help, hasten to aid me.
21   Rescue my soul from the sword,
           my loneliness from the grip of the dog.
22   Save me from the lion's mouth;
           from the horns of the wild bulls, my wretched life.

23   I will proclaim your name to my brethren;
           in the midst of the assembly I will praise you:
24   "You who fear the Lord, praise him;
           all you descendants of Jacob, give glory to him;
           revere him, all you descendants of Israel!
25   For he has not spurned nor disdained

the wretched man in his misery,
Nor did he turn his face away from him,
　　but when he cried out to him, he heard him."
26　So by your gift will I utter praise in the vast assembly;
　　I will fulfill my vows before those who fear him.
27　The lowly shall eat their fill;
　　they who seek the Lord shall praise him:
　　"May your hearts be ever merry!"

28　All the ends of the earth
　　shall remember and turn to the Lord;
　　All the families of the nations
　　shall bow down before him.
29　For dominion is the Lord's,
　　and he rules the nations.
30　To him alone shall bow down
　　all who sleep in the earth;
　　Before him shall bend
　　all who go down into the dust.
　　And to him my soul shall live;
31　my descendants shall serve him.
　　Let the coming generation be told of the Lord
32　　that they may proclaim to a people yet to be born
　　the justice he has shown.

Psalm 22

1　THE LORD is my shepherd; I shall not want.
2　　In verdant pastures he gives me repose;
　　Beside restful waters he leads me;
3　　he refreshes my soul.
　　He guides me in right paths
　　for his name's sake.
4　Even though I walk in the dark valley
　　I fear no evil; for you are at my side
　　With your rod and your staff
　　. that give me courage.

5　You spread the table before me
　　in the sight of my foes;
　　You anoint my head with oil;
　　my cup overflows.
6　Only goodness and kindness follow me
　　all the days of my life;

And I shall dwell in the house of the Lord
　　for years to come.

Psalm 23

1　THE LORD'S are the earth and its fullness;
　　the world and those who dwell in it.
2　For he founded it upon the seas
　　and established it upon the rivers.

3　Who can ascend the mountain of the Lord?
　　or who may stand in his holy place?
4　He whose hands are sinless, whose heart is clean,
　　who desires not what is vain,
　　nor swears deceitfully to his neighbor.
5　He shall receive a blessing from the Lord,
　　a reward from God his savior.
6　Such is the race that seeks for him,
　　that seeks the face of the God of Jacob.

7　Lift up, O gates, your lintels;
　　reach up, you ancient portals,
　　that the king of glory may come in!
8　Who is this king of glory?
　　The Lord, strong and mighty,
　　the Lord, mighty in battle.
9　Lift up, O gates, your lintels;
　　reach up, you ancient portals,
　　that the king of glory may come in!
10　Who is this king of glory?
　　The Lord of hosts; he is the king of glory.

Psalm 24

1　To YOU I lift up my soul,
2　　O Lord, my God.
In you I trust; let me not be put to shame,
　　let not my enemies exult over me.
3　No one who waits for you shall be put to shame;
　　those shall be put to shame who heedlessly break faith.

4　Your ways, O Lord, make known to me;
　　teach me your paths,

5 Guide me in your truth and teach me,
    for you are God my savior,
    and for you I wait all the day.

6 Remember that your compassion, O Lord,
    and your kindness are from of old.

7 The sins of my youth and my frailties remember not;
    in your kindness remember me,
    because of your goodness, O Lord.

8 Good and upright is the Lord;
    thus he shows sinners the way.

9 He guides the humble to justice,
    he teaches the humble his way.

10 All the paths of the Lord are kindness and constancy
    toward those who keep his covenant and his decrees.

11 For your name's sake, O Lord,
    you will pardon my guilt, great as it is.

12 When a man fears the Lord,
    he shows him the way he should choose.

13 He abides in prosperity,
    and his descendants inherit the land.

14 The friendship of the Lord is with those who fear him,
    and his covenant, for their instruction.

15 My eyes are ever toward the Lord,
    for he will free my feet from the snare.

16 Look toward me, and have pity on me,
    for I am alone and afflicted.

17 Relieve the troubles of my heart,
    and bring me out of my distress.

18 Put an end to my affliction and my suffering,
    and take away all my sins.

19 Behold, my enemies are many,
    and they hate me violently.

20 Preserve my life, and rescue me;
    let me not be put to shame, for I take refuge in you.

21 Let integrity and uprightness preserve me,
    because I wait for you, O Lord.

22 Redeem Israel, O God,
    from all its distress!

Psalm 25

1 Do ME justice, O Lord! for I have walked in integrity,
    and in the Lord I trust without wavering.
2 Search me, O Lord, and try me;
    test my soul and my heart.

3 For your kindness is before my eyes,
    and I walk in your truth.
4 I stay not with worthless men,
    nor do I consort with hypocrites.
5 I hate the assembly of evildoers,
    and with the wicked I will not stay.
6 I wash my hands in innocence,
    and I go around your altar, O Lord,
7 Giving voice to my thanks,
    and recounting all your wondrous deeds.
8 O Lord, I love the house in which you dwell,
    the tenting-place of your glory.

9 Gather not my soul with those of sinners,
    nor with men of blood my life.
10 On their hands are crimes,
    and their right hands are full of bribes.
11 But I walk in integrity;
    redeem me, and have pity on me.
12 My foot stands on level ground;
    in the assemblies I will bless the Lord.

Psalm 26

1 The Lord is my light and my salvation;
    whom should I fear?
The Lord is my life's refuge;
    of whom should I be afraid?
2 When evildoers come at me
    to devour my flesh,
My foes and my enemies
    themselves stumble and fall.
3 Though an army encamp against me,
    my heart will not fear;
Though war be waged upon me,
    even then will I trust.

4   One thing I ask of the Lord;
        this I seek:
    To dwell in the house of the Lord
        all the days of my life,
    That I may gaze on the loveliness of the Lord
        and contemplate his temple.
5   For he will hide me in his abode
        in the day of trouble;
    He will conceal me in the shelter of his tent,
        he will set me high upon a rock.
6   Even now my head is held high
        above my enemies on every side.
    And I will offer in his tent
        sacrifices with shouts of gladness;
    I will sing and chant praise to the Lord.

7   Hear, O Lord, the sound of my call;
        have pity on me, and answer me.
8   Of you my heart speaks; you my glance seeks;
        your presence, O Lord, I seek.
9   Hide not your face from me;
        do not in anger repel your servant.
    You are my helper: cast me not off;
        forsake me not, O God my savior.
10 Though my father and mother forsake me,
        yet will the Lord receive me.

11 Show me, O Lord, your way,
        and lead me on a level path,
        because of my adversaries.
12 Give me not up to the wishes of my foes;
        for false witnesses have risen up against me,
        and such as breathe out violence.
13 I believe that I shall see the bounty of the Lord
        in the land of the living.
14 Wait for the Lord with courage;
        be stouthearted, and wait for the Lord.

Psalm 27

1   To you, O Lord, I call;
        O my Rock, be not deaf to me,
    Lest, if you heed me not,
        I become one of those going down into the pit.

2   Hear the sound of my pleading, when I cry to you,
        lifting up my hands toward your holy shrine.
3   Drag me not away with the wicked,
        with those who do wrong,
     Who speak civilly to their neighbors
        though evil is in their hearts.
4   Repay them for their deeds,
        for the evil of their doings.
     For the work of their hands repay them;
        give them their deserts.
5   Because they consider not
        the deeds of the Lord nor the work of his hands,
        may he tear them down and not build them up.

6   Blessed be the Lord,
        for he has heard the sound of my pleading;
7   the Lord is my strength and my shield.
     In him my heart trusts, and I find help;
        then my heart exults, and with my song I give him thanks.

8   The Lord is the strength of his people,
        the saving refuge of his anointed.
9   Save your people, and bless your inheritance;
        feed them, and carry them forever!

Psalm 28

1   GIVE TO the Lord, you sons of God,
        give to the Lord glory and praise,
2   Give to the Lord the glory due his name;
        adore the Lord in holy attire.

3   The voice of the Lord is over the waters,
        the God of glory thunders,
        the Lord, over vast waters.
4   The voice of the Lord is mighty;
        the voice of the Lord is majestic.
5   The voice of the Lord breaks the cedars,
        the Lord breaks the cedars of Lebanon.
6   He makes Lebanon leap like a calf
        and Sarion like a young wild bull.
7   The voice of the Lord strikes fiery flames;
8   the voice of the Lord shakes the desert,
        the Lord shakes the wilderness of Cades.

9   The voice of the Lord twists the oaks and strips the forests,
    and in his temple all say, "Glory!"

10 The Lord is enthroned above the flood;
    the Lord is enthroned as king forever.
11 May the Lord give strength to his people;
    may the Lord bless his people with peace!

Psalm 29

2   I WILL extol you, O Lord, for you drew me clear
    and did not let my enemies rejoice over me.

3   O Lord, my God,
    I cried out to you and you healed me.
4   O Lord, you brought me up from the nether world;
    you preserved me from among those going down into the pit.
5   Sing praise to the Lord, you his faithful ones,
    and give thanks to his holy name.
6   For his anger lasts but a moment;
    a lifetime, his good will.
    At nightfall, weeping enters in,
    but with the dawn, rejoicing.

7   Once, in my security, I said,
    "I shall never be disturbed."
8   O Lord, in your good will you had endowed me with majesty
                                                    [and strength;
    but when you hid your face I was terrified.

9   To you, O Lord, I cried out;
    with the Lord I pleaded:
10 "What gain would there be from my lifeblood,
    from my going down into the grave?
    Would dust give you thanks
    or proclaim your faithfulness?
11 Hear, O Lord, and have pity on me;
    O Lord, be my helper."

12 You changed my mourning into dancing;
    you took off my sackcloth and clothed me with gladness,
13 That my soul might sing praise to you without ceasing;
    O Lord, my God, forever will I give you thanks.

2   IN YOU, O Lord, I take refuge;
        let me never be put to shame.
    In your justice rescue me,
3   incline your ear to me, make haste to deliver me!
    Be my rock of refuge,
        a stronghold to give me safety.
4   You are my rock and my fortress;
        for your name's sake you will lead and guide me.
5   You will free me from the snare they set for me,
        for you are my refuge.
6   Into your hands I commend my spirit;
        you will redeem me, O Lord, O faithful God.
7   You hate those who worship vain idols,
        but my trust is in the Lord.
8   I will rejoice and be glad of your kindness,
        when you have seen my affliction
        and watched over me in my distress,
9   Not shutting me up in the grip of the enemy
        but enabling me to move about at large.

10   Have pity on me, O Lord, for I am in distress;
        with sorrow my eye is consumed; my soul also, and my body.
11   For my life is spent with grief
        and my years with sighing;
    My strength has failed through affliction,
        and my bones are consumed.
12   For all my foes I am an object of reproach,
        a laughingstock to my neighbors, and a dread to my friends;
        they who see me abroad flee from me.
13   I am forgotten like the unremembered dead;
        I am like a dish that is broken.
14   I hear the whispers of the crowd, that frighten me from every side,
        as they consult together against me, plotting to take my life.
15   But my trust is in you, O Lord;
        I say, "You are my God."
16   In your hands is my destiny; rescue me
        from the clutches of my enemies and my persecutors.
17   Let your face shine upon your servant;
        save me in your kindness.
18   O Lord, let me not be put to shame, for I call upon you;
        let the wicked be put to shame;
        let them be reduced to silence in the nether world.

19   Let dumbness strike their lying lips
      that speak insolence against the just in pride and scorn.

20   How great is the goodness, O Lord,
      which you have in store for those who fear you,
  And which, toward those who take refuge in you,
      you show in the sight of men.

21   You hide them in the shelter of your presence
      from the plottings of men;
  You screen them within your abode
      from the strife of tongues.

22   Blessed be the Lord whose wondrous kindness
      he has shown me in a fortified city.

23   Once I said in my anguish,
      "I am cut off from your sight";
  Yet you heard the sound of my pleading
      when I cried out to you.

24   Love the Lord, all you his faithful ones!
      The Lord keeps those who are constant,
      but more than requites those who act proudly.

25   Take courage and be stouthearted,
      all you who hope in the Lord.

Psalm 31

1   HAPPY is he whose fault is taken away,
      whose sin is covered.

2   Happy the man to whom the Lord imputes not guilt,
      in whose spirit there is no guile.

3   As long as I would not speak, my bones wasted away
      with my groaning all the day,

4   For day and night your hand was heavy upon me;
      my strength was dried up as by the heat of summer.

5   Then I acknowledged my sin to you,
      my guilt I covered not.
  I said, "I confess my faults to the Lord,"
      and you took away the guilt of my sin.

6   For this shall every faithful man pray to you
      in time of stress.
  Though deep waters overflow,
      they shall not reach him.

7   You are my shelter; from distress you will preserve me;
      with glad cries of freedom you will ring me round.

8   I will instruct you and show you the way you should walk;
      I will counsel you, keeping my eye on you.
9   Be not senseless like horses or mules:
      with bit and bridle their temper must be curbed,
      else they will not come near you.

10   Many are the sorrows of the wicked,
      but kindness surrounds him who trusts in the Lord.
11   Be glad in the Lord and rejoice, you just;
      exult, all you upright of heart.

Psalm 32

1   EXULT, you just, in the Lord;
      praise from the upright is fitting.
2   Give thanks to the Lord on the harp;
      with the ten-stringed lyre chant his praises.
3   Sing to him a new song;
      pluck the strings skillfully, with shouts of gladness.
4   For upright is the word of the Lord,
      and all his works are trustworthy.
5   He loves justice and right;
      of the kindness of the Lord the earth is full.

6   By the word of the Lord the heavens were made;
      by the breath of his mouth all their host.
7   He gathers the waters of the sea as in a flask;
      in cellars he confines the deep.

8   Let all the earth fear the Lord;
      let all who dwell in the world revere him.
9   For he spoke, and it was made;
      he commanded, and it stood forth.
10   The Lord brings to nought the plans of nations;
      he foils the designs of peoples.
11   But the plan of the Lord stands forever;
      the design of his heart, through all generations.
12   Happy the nation whose God is the Lord,
      the people he has chosen for his own inheritance.

13   From heaven the Lord looks down;
      he sees all mankind.
14   From his fixed throne he beholds
      all who dwell on the earth,

15 He who fashioned the heart of each,
    he who knows all their works.

16 A king is not saved by a mighty army,
    nor is a warrior delivered by great strength.
17 Useless is the horse for safety;
    great though its strength, it cannot provide escape.
18 But see, the eyes of the Lord are upon those who fear him,
    upon those who hope for his kindness,
19 To deliver them from death
    and preserve them in spite of famine.

20 Our soul waits for the Lord,
    who is our help and our shield,
21 For in him our hearts rejoice;
    in his holy name we trust.
22 May your kindness, O Lord, be upon us
    who have put our hope in you.

Psalm 33

2 I WILL bless the Lord at all times;
    his praise shall be ever in my mouth.
3 Let my soul glory in the Lord;
    the lowly will hear me and be glad.
4 Glorify the Lord with me,
    let us together extol his name.

5 I sought the Lord, and he answered me
    and delivered me from all my fears.
6 Look to him that you may be radiant with joy,
    and your faces may not blush with shame.
7 When the afflicted man called out, the Lord heard,
    and from all his distress he saved him.
8 The angel of the Lord encamps
    around those who fear him, and delivers them.
9 Taste and see how good the Lord is;
    happy the man who takes refuge in him.
10 Fear the Lord, you his holy ones,
    for nought is lacking to those who fear him.
11 The great grow poor and hungry;
    but those who seek the Lord want for no good thing.

12 Come, children, hear me;
    I will teach you the fear of the Lord.

13	Which of you desires life,
	and takes delight in prosperous days?
14	Keep your tongue from evil
	and your lips from speaking guile;
15	Turn from evil, and do good;
	seek peace, and follow after it.
16	The Lord has eyes for the just,
	and ears for their cry.
17	The Lord confronts the evildoers,
	to destroy remembrance of them from the earth.
18	When the just cry out, the Lord hears them,
	and from all their distress he rescues them.
19	The Lord is close to the brokenhearted;
	and those who are crushed in spirit he saves.
20	Many are the troubles of the just man,
	but out of them all the Lord delivers him;
21	He watches over all his bones;
	not one of them shall be broken.
22	Vice slays the wicked,
	and the enemies of the just pay for their guilt.
23	But the Lord redeems the lives of his servants;
	no one incurs guilt who takes refuge in him.

Psalm 34

1 FIGHT, O Lord, against those who fight me;
    war against those who make war upon me.
2 Take up the shield and buckler,
    and rise up in my defense.
3 Brandish the lance, and block the way
    in the face of my pursuers;
  Say to my soul,
    "I am your salvation."
4 Let those be put to shame and disgraced
    who seek my life;
  Let those be turned back and confounded
    who plot evil against me.
5 Let them be like chaff before the wind,
    with the angel of the Lord driving them on.
6 Let their way be dark and slippery,
    with the angel of the Lord pursuing them.

7 For without cause they set their snare for me,
    without cause they dug a pit against my life.

8　Let ruin come upon them unawares,
　　and let the snare they have set catch them;
　　into the pit they have dug let them fall.
9　But I will rejoice in the Lord,
　　I will be joyful because of his salvation.
10　All my being shall say,
　　"O Lord, who is like you,
　　The rescuer of the afflicted man from those too strong for him,
　　of the afflicted and the needy from their despoilers?"
11　Unjust witnesses have risen up;
　　things I knew not of, they lay to my charge.
12　They have repaid me evil for good,
　　bringing bereavement to my soul.

13　But I, when they were ill, put on sackcloth;
　　I afflicted myself with fasting
　　and poured forth prayers within my bosom.
14　As though it were a friend of mine, or a brother, I went about;
　　like one bewailing a mother, I was bowed down in mourning.
15　Yet when I stumbled they were glad and gathered together;
　　they gathered together striking me unawares.
　　They tore at me without ceasing;
16　they put me to the test; they mocked me,
　　gnashing their teeth at me.

17　O Lord, how long will you look on?
　　Save me from the roaring beasts; from the lions, my only life.
18　I will give you thanks in the vast assembly,
　　in the mighty throng I will praise you.
19　Let not my unprovoked enemies rejoice over me;
　　let not my undeserved foes wink knowingly.
20　For civil words they speak not,
　　but against the peaceful in the land
　　they fashion treacherous speech.
21　And they open wide their mouths against me,
　　saying, "Aha, aha! We saw him with our own eyes!"
22　You, O Lord, have seen; be not silent;
　　Lord, be not far from me!
23　Awake, and be vigilant in my defense;
　　in my cause, my God and my Lord.
24　Do me justice, because you are just, O Lord;
　　my God, let them not rejoice over me.
25　Let them not say in their hearts, "Aha! This is what we wanted!"
　　Let them not say, "We have swallowed him up!"

26   Let all be put to shame and confounded
      who are glad at my misfortune.
    Let those be clothed with shame and disgrace
      who glory over me.

27   But let those shout for joy and be glad
      who favor my just cause;
    And may they ever say, "The Lord be glorified;
      he wills the prosperity of his servant!"

28   Then my tongue shall recount your justice,
      your praise, all the day.

Psalm 35

2   SIN SPEAKS to the wicked man in his heart;
      there is no dread of God before his eyes,

3   For he beguiles himself with the thought
      that his guilt will not be found out or hated.

4   The words of his mouth are empty and false;
      he has ceased to understand how to do good.

5   He plans wickedness in his bed;
      he sets out on a way that is not good,
      with no repugnance for evil.

6   O Lord, your kindness reaches to heaven;
      your faithfulness, to the clouds.

7   Your justice is like the mountains of God;
      your judgments, like the mighty deep;
      man and beast you save, O Lord.

8   How precious is your kindness, O God!
      The children of men take refuge in the shadow of your wings.

9   They have their fill of the prime gifts of your house;
      from your delightful stream you give them to drink.

10   For with you is the fountain of life,
      and in your light we see light.

11   Keep up your kindness toward your friends,
      your just defense of the upright of heart.

12   Let not the foot of the proud overtake me
      nor the hand of the wicked disquiet me.

13   See how the evildoers have fallen;
      they are thrust down and cannot rise.

Psalm 36

1 BE NOT vexed over evildoers,
   nor jealous of those who do wrong;
2 For like grass they quickly wither,
   and like green herbs they wilt.

3 Trust in the Lord and do good,
   that you may dwell in the land and enjoy security.
4 Take delight in the Lord,
   and he will grant you your heart's requests.

5 Commit to the Lord your way;
   trust in him, and he will act.
6 He will make justice dawn for you like the light;
   bright as the noonday shall be your vindication.

7 Leave it to the Lord,
   and wait for him;
   Be not vexed at the successful path
   of the man who does malicious deeds.

8 Give up your anger, and forsake wrath;
   be not vexed, it will only harm you.
9 For evildoers shall be cut off,
   but those who wait for the Lord shall possess the land.

10 Yet a little while, and the wicked man shall be no more;
   though you mark his place he will not be there.
11 But the meek shall possess the land,
   they shall delight in abounding peace.

12 The wicked man plots against the just
   and gnashes his teeth at them;
13 But the Lord laughs at him,
   for he sees that his day is coming.

14 A sword the wicked draw; they bend their bow
   to bring down the afflicted and the poor,
   to slaughter those whose path is right.
15 But their swords shall pierce their own hearts,
   and their bows shall be broken.

16 Better is the scanty store of the just

than the great wealth of the wicked,
17   For the power of the wicked shall be broken,
but the Lord supports the just.

18   The Lord watches over the lives of the wholehearted;
their inheritance lasts forever.
19   They are not put to shame in an evil time;
in days of famine they have plenty.

20   But the wicked perish,
and the enemies of the Lord, like the beauty of the meadows,
vanish; like smoke they vanish.

21   The wicked man borrows and does not repay;
the just man is kindly and gives,
22   But those whom he blesses shall possess the land,
while those he curses shall be cut off.

23   By the Lord are the steps of a man made firm,
and he approves his way.
24   Though he fall, he does not lie prostrate,
for the hand of the Lord sustains him.

25   Neither in my youth, nor now that I am old,
have I seen a just man forsaken
nor his descendants begging bread.
26   All the day he is kindly and lends,
and his descendants shall be blessed.

27   Turn from evil and do good,
that you may abide forever;
28   For the Lord loves what is right,
and forsakes not his faithful ones.

Criminals are destroyed,
and the posterity of the wicked is cut off.
29   The just shall possess the land
and dwell in it forever.

30   The mouth of the just man tells of wisdom
and his tongue utters what is right.
31   The law of his God is in his heart,
and his steps do not falter.

32 The wicked man spies on the just,
   and seeks to slay him.
33 The Lord will not leave him in his power
   nor let him be condemned when he is on trial.

34 Wait for the Lord,
   and keep his way;
   He will promote you to ownership of the land;
   when the wicked are destroyed, you shall look on.

35 I saw a wicked man, fierce,
   and stalwart as a flourishing, age-old tree.
36 Yet as I passed by, lo! he was no more;
   I sought him, but he could not be found.

37 Watch the wholehearted man, and mark the upright;
   for there is a future for the man of peace.
38 Sinners shall all alike be destroyed;
   the future of the wicked shall be cut off.

39 The salvation of the just is from the Lord;
   he is their refuge in time of distress.
40 And the Lord helps them and delivers them;
   he delivers them from the wicked and saves them,
   because they take refuge in him.

Psalm 37

2 O Lord, in your anger punish me not,
   in your wrath chastise me not;
3 For your arrows have sunk deep in me,
   and your hand has come down upon me.
4 There is no health in my flesh because of your indignation;
   there is no wholeness in my bones because of my sin,
5 For my iniquities have overwhelmed me;
   they are like a heavy burden, beyond my strength.

6 Noisome and festering are my sores
   because of my folly,
7 I am stooped and bowed down profoundly;
   all the day I go in mourning,
8 For my loins are filled with burning pains;
   there is no health in my flesh.
9 I am numbed and severely crushed;
   I roar with anguish of heart.

591

10   O Lord, all my desire is before you;
      from you my groaning is not hid.

11   My heart throbs; my strength forsakes me;
      the very light of my eyes has failed me.

12   My friends and my companions stand back because of my affliction;
      my neighbors stand afar off.

13   Men lay snares for me seeking my life;
      they look to my misfortune, they speak of ruin,
      treachery they talk of all the day.

14   But I am like a deaf man, hearing not,
      like a dumb man who opens not his mouth.

15   I am become like a man who neither hears
      nor has in his mouth a retort.

16   Because for you, O Lord, I wait;
      you, O Lord my God, will answer

17   When I say, "Let them not be glad on my account
      who, when my foot slips, glory over me."

18   For I am very near to falling,
      and my grief is with me always.

19   Indeed, I acknowledge my guilt;
      I grieve over my sin.

20   But my undeserved enemies are strong;
      many are my foes without cause.

21   Those who repay evil for good
      harass me for pursuing good.

22   Forsake me not, O Lord;
      my God, be not far from me!

23   Make haste to help me,
      O Lord my salvation!

Psalm 38

2   I SAID, "I will watch my ways,
      so as not to sin with my tongue;
      I will set a curb on my mouth."
    While the wicked man was before me

3   I kept dumb and silent;
      I refrained from rash speech.
    But my grief was stirred up;

4   hot grew my heart within me;
      in my thoughts, a fire blazed forth.
    I spoke out with my tongue:

5   Let me know, O Lord, my end
       and what is the number of my days,
       that I may learn how frail I am.

6   A short span you have made my days,
       and my life is as nought before you;
       only a breath is any human existence.

7   A phantom only, man goes his ways;
       like vapor only are his restless pursuits;
       he heaps up stores, and knows not who will use them.

8   And now, for what do I wait, O Lord?
       In you is my hope.

9   From all my sins deliver me;
       a fool's taunt let me not suffer.

10   I was speechless and opened not my mouth,
       because it was your doing;

11   Take away your scourge from me;
       at the blow of your hand I wasted away.

12   With rebukes for guilt you chasten man;
       you dissolve like a cobweb all that is dear to him;
       only a breath is any man.

13   Hear my prayer, O Lord;
       to my cry give ear;
       to my weeping be not deaf!
     For I am but a wayfarer before you,
       a pilgrim like all my fathers.

14   Turn your gaze from me, that I may find respite
       ere I depart and be no more.

Psalm 39

2   I HAVE waited, waited for the Lord,
       and he stooped toward me and heard my cry.

3   He drew me out of the pit of destruction,
       out of the mud of the swamp;
     He set my feet upon a crag;
       he made firm my steps.

4   And he put a new song into my mouth,
       a hymn to our God.
     Many shall look on in awe
       and trust in the Lord.

5   Happy the man who makes the Lord his trust;

who turns not to idolatry
or to those who stray after falsehood.

6 How numerous have you made,
O Lord, my God, your wondrous deeds!
And in your plans for us
there is none to equal you;
Should I wish to declare or to tell them,
they would be too many to recount.

7 Sacrifice or oblation you wished not,
but ears open to obedience you gave me.
Holocausts or sin-offerings you sought not;
8 then said I, "Behold I come;
in the written scroll it is prescribed for me,
9 To do your will, O my God, is my delight,
and your law is within my heart!"
10 I announced your justice in the vast assembly;
I did not restrain my lips, as you, O Lord, know.
11 Your justice I kept not hid within my heart;
your faithfulness and your salvation I have spoken of;
I have made no secret of your kindness and your truth
in the vast assembly.

12 Withhold not, O Lord, your compassion from me;
may your kindness and your truth ever preserve me.
13 For all about me are evils beyond reckoning;
my sins so overcome me that I cannot see;
They are more numerous than the hairs of my head,
and my heart fails me.

14 Deign, O Lord, to rescue me;
O Lord, make haste to help me.
15 Let all be put to shame and confusion
who seek to snatch away my life.
Let them be turned back in disgrace
who desire my ruin.
16 Let them be dismayed in their shame
who say to me, "Aha, aha!"
17 But may all who seek you
exult and be glad in you,
And may those who love your salvation
say ever, "The Lord be glorified."
18 Though I am afflicted and poor,
yet the Lord thinks of me.

594

You are my help and my deliverer;
O my God, hold not back!

Psalm 40

2 HAPPY is he who has regard for the lowly and the poor;
in the day of misfortune the Lord will deliver him.
3 The Lord will keep and preserve him;
he will make him happy on the earth,
and not give him over to the will of his enemies.
4 The Lord will help him on his sickbed,
he will take away all his ailment when he is ill.

5 Once I said, "O Lord, have pity on me;
heal me, though I have sinned against you.
6 My enemies say the worst of me:
'When will he die and his name perish?'
7 When one comes to see me, he speaks without sincerity;
his heart stores up malice;
when he leaves he gives voice to it outside.
8 All my foes whisper together against me;
against me they imagine the worst:
9 'A malignant disease fills his frame';
and 'Now that he lies ill, he will not rise again.'
10 Even my friend who had my trust
and partook of my bread, has raised his heel against me.
11 But you, O Lord, have pity on me, and raise me up,
that I may repay them."
12 That you love me I know by this,
that my enemy does not triumph over me,
13 But because of my integrity you sustain me
and let me stand before you forever.

14 Blessed be the Lord, the God of Israel,
from all eternity and forever. Amen. Amen.

Psalm 41

2 As THE hind longs for the running waters,
so my soul longs for you, O God.
3 Athirst is my soul for God, the living God.
When shall I go and behold the face of God?
4 My tears are my food day and night,
as they say to me day after day, "Where is your God?"

5   Those times I recall,
     now that I pour out my soul within me,
When I went with the throng
     and led them in procession to the house of God,
Amid loud cries of joy and thanksgiving,
     with the multitude keeping festival.

6   Why are you so downcast, O my soul?
       Why do you sigh within me?
     Hope in God! For I shall again be thanking him,
      in the presence of my savior and my God.

7   Within me my soul is downcast;
     so will I remember you
From the land of the Jordan and of Hermon,
     from Mount Misar.

8   Deep calls unto deep
     in the roar of your cataracts;
All your breakers and your billows
     pass over me.

9   By day the Lord bestows his grace,
     and at night I have his song,
     a prayer to my living God.

10   I sing to God, my Rock:
     "Why do you forget me?
Why must I go about in mourning,
     with the enemy oppressing me?"

11   It crushes my bones that my foes mock me,
     as they say to me day after day, "Where is your God?"

12   Why are you so downcast, O my soul?
       Why do you sigh within me?
     Hope in God! For I shall again be thanking him,
      in the presence of my savior and my God.

Psalm 42

1   Do ME justice, O God, and fight my fight
     against a faithless people;
     from the deceitful and impious man rescue me.

2   For you, O God, are my strength.
     Why do you keep me so far away?
Why must I go about in mourning,
     with the enemy oppressing me?

3   Send forth your light and your fidelity;
     they shall lead me on

And bring me to your holy mountain,
    to your dwelling-place.
4   Then I will go in to the altar of God,
    the God of my gladness and joy;
Then will I give you thanks upon the harp,
    O God, my God!
5   Why are you so downcast, O my soul?
        Why do you sigh within me?
        Hope in God! For I shall again be thanking him,
    in the presence of my savior and my God.

Psalm 43

2   O GOD, our ears have heard,
    our fathers have declared to us,
The deeds you did in their days,
    in days of old:
3   How with your own hand
    you rooted out the nations and planted them;
    you smashed the peoples, but for them you made room.

4   For not with their own sword did they conquer the land,
    nor did their own arm make them victorious,
But it was your arm and your right hand
    and the light of your countenance, in your love for them.
5   You are my king and my God,
    who bestowed victories on Jacob.
6   Our foes through you we struck down;
    through your name we trampled down our adversaries.
7   For not in my bow did I trust,
    nor did my sword save me;
8   But you saved us from our foes,
    and those who hated us you put to shame.
9   In God we gloried day by day;
    your name we praised always.

10   Yet now you have cast us off and put us in disgrace,
    and you go not forth with our armies.
11   You have let us be driven back by our foes;
    those who hated us plundered us at will,
12   You marked us out as sheep to be slaughtered;
    among the nations you scattered us.
13   You sold your people for no great price;
    you made no profit from the sale of them.

14 You made us the reproach of our neighbors,
  the mockery and the scorn of those around us.
15 You made us a byword among the nations,
  a laughingstock among the peoples.
16 All the day my disgrace is before me,
  and shame covers my face
17 At the voice of him who mocks and blasphemes,
  and in the presence of the enemy and the avenger.

18 All this has come upon us, though we have not forgotten you,
  nor have we been disloyal to your covenant;
19 Our hearts have not shrunk back,
  nor our steps turned aside from your path,
20 Though you thrust us down into a place of misery
  and covered us over with darkness.
21 If we had forgotten the name of our God
  and stretched out our hands to a strange god,
22 Would not God have discovered this?
  For he knows the secrets of the heart.
23 Yet for your sake we are being slain all the day;
  we are looked upon as sheep to be slaughtered.

24 Awake! Why are you asleep, O Lord?
  Arise! Cast us not off forever!
25 Why do you hide your face,
  forgetting our woe and our oppression?
26 For our souls are bowed down to the dust,
  our bodies are pressed to the earth.
27 Arise, help us!
  Redeem us for your kindness' sake.

Psalm 44

2 MY HEART overflows with a goodly theme;
  as I sing my ode to the king,
  my tongue is nimble as the pen of a skillful scribe.

3 Fairer in beauty are you than the sons of men;
  grace is poured out upon your lips;
  thus God has blessed you forever.
4 Gird your sword upon your thigh, O mighty one!
  In your splendor and your majesty ride on triumphant
5 In the cause of truth and for the sake of justice;
  and may your right hand show you wondrous deeds.

6 Your arrows are sharp; peoples are subject to you;
    the king's enemies lose heart.
7 Your throne, O God, stands forever and ever;
    a tempered rod is your royal scepter.
8 You love justice and hate wickedness;
    therefore God, your God, has anointed you
    with the oil of gladness above your fellow kings.
9 With myrrh and aloes and cassia your robes are fragrant;
    from ivory palaces string music brings you joy.
10 The daughters of kings come to meet you;
    the queen takes her place at your right hand in gold of Ophir.

11 Hear, O daughter, and see; turn your ear,
    forget your people and your father's house.
12 So shall the king desire your beauty;
    for he is your lord, and you must worship him.
13 And the city of Tyre is here with gifts;
    the rich among the people seek your favor.
14 All glorious is the king's daughter as she enters;
    her raiment is threaded with spun gold.
15 In embroidered apparel she is borne in to the king;
    behind her the virgins of her train are brought to you.
16 They are borne in with gladness and joy;
    they enter the palace of the king.

17 The place of your fathers your sons shall have;
    you shall make them princes through all the land.
18 I will make your name memorable through all generations;
    therefore shall nations praise you forever and ever.

Psalm 45

2 GOD IS our refuge and our strength,
    an ever-present help in distress.
3 Therefore we fear not, though the earth be shaken
    and mountains plunge into the depths of the sea;
4 Though its waters rage and foam
    and the mountains quake at its surging.
    The Lord of hosts is with us;
    our stronghold is the God of Jacob.

5 There is a stream whose runlets gladden the city of God,
    the holy dwelling of the Most High.

6   God is in its midst; it shall not be disturbed;
       God will help it at the break of dawn.
7   Though nations are in turmoil, kingdoms totter,
       his voice resounds, the earth melts away,
8   The Lord of hosts is with us;
         our stronghold is the God of Jacob.

9   Come! behold the deeds of the Lord,
       the astounding things he has wrought on earth:
10   He has stopped wars to the end of the earth:
       the bow he breaks; he splinters the spears;
       he burns the shields with fire.
11   Desist! and confess that I am God,
       exalted among the nations, exalted upon the earth.
12   The Lord of hosts is with us;
         our stronghold is the God of Jacob.

Psalm 46

2   ALL YOU peoples, clap your hands,
       shout to God with cries of gladness,
3   For the Lord, the Most High, the awesome
       is the great king over all the earth.
4   He brings peoples under us;
       nations under our feet.
5   He chooses for us our inheritance,
       the glory of Jacob, whom he loves.

6   God mounts his throne amid shouts of joy;
       the Lord, amid trumpet blasts.
7   Sing praise to God, sing praise;
       sing praise to our king, sing praise.

8   For king of all the earth is God;
       sing hymns of praise.
9   God reigns over the nations,
       God sits upon his holy throne.
10   The princes of the peoples are gathered together
       with the people of the God of Abraham.
       For God's are the guardians of the earth;
       he is supreme.

Psalm 47

2   GREAT is the Lord and wholly to be praised
     in the city of our God.

3   His holy mountain, fairest of heights,
     is the joy of all the earth;
    Mount Sion, "the recesses of the North,"
     is the city of the great King.

4   God is with her castles;
     renowned is he as a stronghold.

5   For lo! the kings assemble,
     they come on together;

6   They also see, and at once are stunned,
     terrified, routed;

7   Quaking seizes them there;
     anguish, like a woman's in labor,

8   As though a wind from the east
     were shattering ships of Tharsis.

9   As we had heard, so have we seen
     in the city of the Lord of hosts,
    In the city of our God;
     God makes it firm forever.

10   O God, we ponder your kindness
     within your temple.

11   As your name, O God, so also your praise
     reaches to the ends of the earth.
    Of justice your right hand is full;
     let Mount Sion be glad,

12   Let the cities of Juda rejoice,
     because of your judgments.

13   Go about Sion, make the round;
     count her towers.

14   Consider her ramparts,
     examine her castles,
    That you may tell a future generation

15   that such is God,
    Our God forever and ever;
     he will guide us.

2   HEAR THIS, all you peoples;
     hearken, all who dwell in the world,
3   Of lowly birth or high degree,
     rich and poor alike.
4   My mouth shall speak wisdom;
     prudence shall be the utterance of my heart.
5   My ear is intent upon a proverb;
     I will set forth my riddle to the music of the harp.

6   Why should I fear in evil days
     when my wicked ensnarers ring me round?
7   They trust in their wealth;
     the abundance of their riches is their boast.
8   Yet in no way can a man redeem himself,
     or pay his own ransom to God;
9   Too high is the price to redeem one's life;
     he would never have enough
10   to remain alive always and not see destruction.

11   For he can see that wise men die,
     and likewise the senseless and the stupid pass away,
     leaving to others their wealth.
12   Tombs are their homes forever,
     their dwellings through all generations,
     though they have called lands by their names.
13   Thus man, for all his splendor, does not abide;
     he resembles the beasts that perish.

14   This is the way of those whose trust is folly,
     the end of those contented with their lot:
15   Like sheep they are herded into the nether world;
     death is their shepherd, and the upright rule over them.
     Quickly their form is consumed;
     the nether world is their palace.
16   But God will redeem me
     from the power of the nether world by receiving me.

17   Fear not when a man grows rich,
     when the wealth of his house becomes great,
18   For when he dies, he shall take none of it;
     his wealth shall not follow him down.

19 Though in his lifetime he counted himself blessed,
"They will praise you for doing well for yourself,"
20 He shall join the circle of his forebears
who shall never more see light.
21 Man, for all his splendor, if he have not prudence,
resembles the beasts that perish.

Psalm 49

GOD THE LORD has spoken and summoned the earth,
from the rising of the sun to its setting.
2 From Sion, perfect in beauty,
God shines forth.
3 May our God come and not be deaf to us!
Before him is a devouring fire;
around him is a raging storm.
4 He summons the heavens from above,
and the earth, to the trial of his people:
5 "Gather my faithful ones before me,
those who have made a covenant with me by sacrifice."
6 And the heavens proclaim his justice;
for God himself is the judge.

7 "Hear, my people, and I will speak;
Israel, I will testify against you;
God, your God, am I.
8 Not for your sacrifices do I rebuke you,
for your holocausts are before me always.
9 I take from your house no bullock,
no goats out of your fold.
10 For mine are all the animals of the forests,
beasts by the thousand on my mountains.
11 I know all the birds of the air,
and whatever stirs in the plains, belongs to me.
12 If I were hungry, I should not tell you,
for mine are the world and its fullness.
13 Do I eat the flesh of strong bulls,
or is the blood of goats my drink?
14 Offer to God praise as your sacrifice
and fulfill your vows to the Most High;
15 Then call upon me in time of distress;
I will rescue you, and you shall glorify me."

16 But to the wicked man God says:

"Why do you recite my statutes,
and profess my covenant with your mouth,
17 Though you hate discipline
and cast my words behind you?
18 When you see a thief, you keep pace with him,
and with adulterers you throw in your lot.
19 To your mouth you give free rein for evil,
you harness your tongue to deceit.
20 You sit speaking against your brother;
against your mother's son you spread rumors.
21 When you do these things, shall I be deaf to it?
Or think you that I am like yourself?
I will correct you by drawing them up before your eyes.

22 "Consider this, you who forget God,
lest I rend you and there be no one to rescue you.
23 He that offers praise as a sacrifice glorifies me;
and to him that goes the right way
I will show the salvation of God."

Psalm 50

3 HAVE mercy on me, O God, in your goodness;
in the greatness of your compassion wipe out my offense.
4 Thoroughly wash me from my guilt
and of my sin cleanse me.

5 For I acknowledge my offense,
and my sin is before me always:
6 "Against you only have I sinned,
and done what is evil in your sight"—
That you may be justified in your sentence,
vindicated when you condemn.
7 Indeed, in guilt was I born,
and in sin my mother conceived me;
8 Behold, you are pleased with sincerity of heart,
and in my inmost being you teach me wisdom.

9 Cleanse me of sin with hyssop, that I may be purified;
wash me, and I shall be whiter than snow.
10 Let me hear the sounds of joy and gladness;
the bones you have crushed shall rejoice.
11 Turn away your face from my sins,
and blot out all my guilt.

12   A clean heart create for me, O God,
        and a steadfast spirit renew within me.
13   Cast me not out from your presence,
        and your holy spirit take not from me.
14   Give me back the joy of your salvation,
        and a willing spirit sustain in me.

15   I will teach transgressors your ways,
        and sinners shall return to you.
16   Free me from blood guilt, O God, my saving God;
        then my tongue shall revel in your justice.
17   O Lord, open my lips,
        and my mouth shall proclaim your praise.
18   For you are not pleased with sacrifices;
        should I offer a holocaust, you would not accept it.
19   My sacrifice, O God, is a contrite spirit;
        a heart contrite and humbled, O God, you will not spurn.

20   Be bountiful, O Lord, to Sion in your kindness
        by rebuilding the walls of Jerusalem;
21   Then shall you be pleased with due sacrifices,
        burnt offerings and holocausts;
        then shall they offer up bullocks on your altar.

Psalm 51

3   WHY DO you glory in evil,
        you champion of infamy?
4   All the day you plot harm;
        your tongue is like a sharpened razor, you practiced deceiver!
5   You love evil rather than good,
        falsehood rather than honest speech.
6   You love all that means ruin,
        you of the deceitful tongue!

7   God himself shall demolish you;
        forever he shall break you;
    He shall pluck you from your tent,
        and uproot you from the land of the living.

8   The just shall look on with awe;
        then they shall laugh at him:
9   "This is the man who made not
        God the source of his strength,

But put his trust in his great wealth,
   and his strength in harmful plots."
10   But I, like a green olive tree
   in the house of God,
Trust in the kindness of God
   forever and ever.
11   I will thank you always for what you have done,
   and proclaim the goodness of your name
   before your faithful ones.

Psalm 52

2   THE FOOL says in his heart,
   "There is no God."
Such are corrupt; they do abominable deeds;
   there is not one who does good.
3   God looks down from heaven upon the children of men
   to see if there be one who is wise and seeks God.
4   All alike have gone astray; they have become perverse;
   there is not one who does good, not even one.

5   Will all these evildoers never learn,
   they who eat up my people just as they eat bread,
   who call not upon God?
6   There they were in great fear,
   where no fear was,
For God has scattered the bones of your besiegers;
   they are put to shame, because God has rejected them.

7   Oh, that out of Sion would come the salvation of Israel!
   When God restores the well-being of his people,
   then shall Jacob exult and Israel be glad.

Psalm 53

3   O GOD, by your name save me,
   and by your might defend my cause.
4   O God, hear my prayer;
   hearken to the words of my mouth.
5   For haughty men have risen up against me,
   and fierce men seek my life;
   they set not God before their eyes.

6 Behold, God is my helper;
the Lord sustains my life.
7 Turn back the evil upon my foes;
in your faithfulness destroy them.
8 Freely will I offer you sacrifice;
I will praise your name, O Lord, for its goodness,
9 Because from all distress you have rescued me,
and my eyes look down upon my enemies.

Psalm 54

2 HEARKEN, O God, to my prayer;
turn not away from my pleading;
3 give heed to me, and answer me.
I rock with grief, and am troubled
4 at the voice of the enemy and the clamor of the wicked.
For they bring down evil upon me,
and with fury they persecute me.
5 My heart quakes within me;
the terror of death has fallen upon me.
6 Fear and trembling come upon me.
and horror overwhelms me,
7 And I say, "Had I but wings like a dove,
I would fly away and be at rest.
8 Far away I would flee;
I would lodge in the wilderness.
9 I would hasten to find shelter
from the violent storm and the tempest."

10 Engulf them, O Lord; divide their counsels,
for in the city I see violence and strife;
11 day and night they prowl about upon its walls.
Evil and mischief are in its midst;
12 treachery is in its midst;
oppression and fraud never depart from its streets.
13 If an enemy had reviled me,
I could have borne it;
If he who hates me had vaunted himself against me,
I might have hidden from him.
14 But you, my other self,
my companion and my bosom friend!
15 You, whose comradeship I enjoyed;
at whose side I walked in procession in the house of God!

16	Let death surprise them;
	let them go down alive to the nether world,
	for evil is in their dwellings, in their very midst.
17	But I will call upon God,
	and the Lord will save me.
18	In the evening, and at dawn, and at noon,
	I will grieve and moan,
	and he will hear my voice.
19	He will give me freedom and peace
	from those who war against me,
	for many there are who oppose me.
20	God will hear me and will humble them
	from his eternal throne;
	For improvement is not in them,
	nor do they fear God.
21	Each one lays hands on his associates,
	and violates his pact.
22	Softer than butter is his speech,
	but war is in his heart;
	His words are smoother than oil,
	but they are drawn swords.
23	Cast your care upon the Lord,
	and he will support you;
	never will he permit the just man to be disturbed.
24	And you, O God, will bring them down
	into the pit of destruction;
	Men of blood and deceit shall not live out half their days.
	But I trust in you, O Lord.

Psalm 55

2	HAVE pity on me, O God, for men trample upon me;
	all the day they press their attack against me.
3	My adversaries trample upon me all the day;
	yes, many fight against me.
4	O Most High, when I begin to fear,
	in you will I trust.
5	In God, in whose promise I glory,
	in God I trust without fear;
	what can flesh do against me?
6	All the day they molest me in my efforts;
	their every thought is of evil against me.
7	They gather together in hiding,

they watch my steps.
As they have waited for my life,
8   because of their wickedness keep them in view:
in your wrath bring down the peoples, O God.
9 My wanderings you have counted;
    my tears are stored in your flask;
are they not recorded in your book?
10 Then do my enemies turn back,
    when I call upon you;
now I know that God is with me.
11   In God, in whose promise I glory,
12   in God I trust without fear;
what can flesh do against me?

13 I am bound, O God, by vows to you;
    your thank offerings I will fulfill.
14 For you have rescued me from death,
    my feet, too, from stumbling;
that I may walk before God in the light of the living.

Psalm 56

2 HAVE pity on me, O God; have pity on me,
    for in you I take refuge.
In the shadow of your wings I take refuge,
    till harm pass by.
3 I call to God the Most High,
    to God, my benefactor.
4 May he send from heaven and save me;
    may he make those a reproach who trample upon me;
may God send his kindness and his faithfulness.
5 I lie prostrate in the midst of lions
    which devour men;
Their teeth are spears and arrows,
    their tongue is a sharp sword.
6   Be exalted above the heavens, O God;
    above all the earth be your glory!

7 They have prepared a net for my feet;
    they have bowed me down;
They have dug a pit before me,
    but they fall into it.
8 My heart is steadfast, O God; my heart is steadfast;
    I will sing and chant praise.

9   Awake, O my soul; awake, lyre and harp!
         I will wake the dawn.

10   I will give thanks to you among the peoples, O Lord,
         I will chant your praise among the nations,

11   For your kindness towers to the heavens,
         and your faithfulness to the skies.

12   Be exalted above the heavens, O God;
         above all the earth be your glory!

Psalm 57

2   Do YOU indeed like gods pronounce justice
         and judge fairly, you men of rank?

3   Nay, you willingly commit crimes;
         on earth you look to the fruits of extortion.

4   From the womb the wicked are perverted;
         astray from birth have the liars gone.

5   Theirs is poison like a serpent's,
         like that of a stubborn snake that stops its ears,

6   That it may not hear the voice of enchanters
         casting cunning spells.

7   O God, smash their teeth in their mouths;
         the jaw-teeth of the lions, break, O Lord!

8   Let them vanish like water flowing off;
         when they draw the bow, let their arrows be headless shafts.

9   Let them dissolve like a melting snail,
         like an untimely birth that never sees the sun.

10   Unexpectedly, like a thorn-bush,
         or like thistles, let the whirlwind carry them away.

11   The just man shall be glad when he sees vengeance;
         he shall bathe his feet in the blood of the wicked.

12   And men shall say, "Truly there is a reward for the just;
         truly there is a God who is judge on earth!"

Psalm 58

2   RESCUE me from my enemies, O my God;
         from my adversaries defend me.

3   Rescue me from evildoers;
         from bloodthirsty men save me.

4   For behold, they lie in wait for my life;
         mighty men come together against me.
         Not for any offense or sin of mine, O Lord;

5 for no guilt of mine they hurry to take up arms.
Rouse yourself to see it, and aid me,
6 for you are the Lord of hosts, the God of Israel.
Arise; punish all the nations;
 have no pity on any worthless traitors.
7 Each evening they return, they snarl like dogs
  and prowl about the city.
8 Though they bay with their mouths,
 and blasphemies are on their lips—
"Who is there to listen?"—
9 You, O Lord, laugh at them;
 you deride all the nations.
10 O my strength! for you I watch;
  for you, O God, are my stronghold,
11 my gracious God!

May God come to my aid;
 may he show me the fall of my foes.
12 O God, slay them, lest they beguile my people;
 shake them by your power, and bring them down,
 O Lord our shield!
13 By the sin of their mouths and the word of their lips
 let them be caught in their arrogance,
 for the lies they have told under oath.
14 Consume them in wrath; consume, till they are no more;
 that men may know that God is the ruler of Jacob,
 yes, to the ends of the earth.

15 Each evening they return, they snarl like dogs
  and prowl about the city;
16 They wander about as scavengers;
 if they are not filled, they howl.
17 But I will sing of your strength
 and revel at dawn in your kindness;
You have been my stronghold,
 my refuge in the day of distress.
18 O my strength! your praise will I sing;
  for you, O God, are my stronghold,
  my gracious God!

Psalm 59

3 O God, you have rejected us and broken our defenses;
 you have been angry; rally us!

4   You have rocked the country and split it open;
     repair the cracks in it, for it is tottering.
5   You have made your people feel hardships;
     you have given us stupefying wine.
6   You have raised for those who fear you a banner
     to which they may flee out of bowshot
7   That your loved ones may escape;
     help us by your right hand, and answer us!

8   God promised in his sanctuary:
     "Exultantly I will apportion Sichem,
     and measure off the valley of Socchoth.
9   Mine is Galaad, and mine Manasse;
     Ephraim is the helmet for my head; Juda, my scepter;
10   Moab shall serve as my washbowl;
     upon Edom I will set my shoe;
     I will triumph over Philistia."

11   Who will bring me into the fortified city?
     Who will lead me into Edom?
12   Have not you, O God, rejected us,
     so that you go not forth, O God, with our armies?
13   Give us aid against the foe,
     for worthless is the help of men.
14   Under God we shall do valiantly;
     it is he who will tread down our foes.

Psalm 60

2   HEAR, O God, my cry;
     listen to my prayer!
3   From the earth's end I call to you
     as my heart grows faint.
   You will set me high upon a rock; you will give me rest,
4   for you are my refuge,
     a tower of strength against the enemy.
5   Oh, that I might lodge in your tent forever,
     take refuge in the shelter of your wings!

6   You indeed, O God, have accepted my vows;
     you granted me the heritage of those who fear your name.
7   Add to the days of the king's life;
     let his years be many generations;

8 Let him sit enthroned before God forever;
   bid kindness and faithfulness preserve him.
9 So will I sing the praises of your name forever,
   fulfilling my vows day by day.

Psalm 61

2 ONLY in God is my soul at rest;
   from him comes my salvation.
3 He only is my rock and my salvation,
   my stronghold; I shall not be disturbed at all.
4 How long will you set upon a man and all together beat him down
   as though he were a sagging fence, a battered wall?
5 Truly from my place on high they plan to dislodge me;
   they delight in lies;
They bless with their mouths,
   but inwardly they curse.

6 Only in God be at rest, my soul,
   for from him comes my hope.
7 He only is my rock and my salvation,
   my stronghold; I shall not be disturbed.
8 With God is my safety and my glory,
   he is the rock of my strength; my refuge is in God.
9 Trust in him at all times, O my people!
   Pour out your hearts before him;
   God is our refuge!

10 Only a breath are mortal men;
   an illusion are men of rank;
In a balance they prove lighter,
   all together, than a breath.
11 Trust not in extortion; in plunder take no empty pride;
   though wealth abound, set not your heart upon it.
12 One thing God said; these two things which I heard:
13 that power belongs to God, and yours, O Lord, is kindness;
   and that you render to everyone according to his deeds.

Psalm 62

2 O GOD, you are my God whom I seek;
   for you my flesh pines and my soul thirsts
   like the earth, parched, lifeless and without water.

3   Thus have I gazed toward you in the sanctuary
      to see your power and your glory,
4   For your kindness is a greater good than life;
      my lips shall glorify you.

5   Thus will I bless you while I live;
      lifting up my hands, I will call upon your name.
6   As with the riches of a banquet shall my soul be satisfied,
      and with exultant lips my mouth shall praise you.
7   I will remember you upon my couch,
      and through the night-watches I will meditate on you:
8   That you are my help,
      and in the shadow of your wings I shout for joy.
9   My soul clings fast to you;
      your right hand upholds me.

10   But they shall be destroyed who seek my life,
      they shall go into the depths of the earth;
11   They shall be delivered over to the sword,
      and shall be the prey of jackals.
12   The king, however, shall rejoice in God;
      everyone who swears by him shall glory,
      but the mouths of those who speak falsely shall be stopped.

Psalm 63

2   HEAR, O God, my voice in my lament;
      from the dread enemy preserve my life.
3   Shelter me against the council of malefactors,
      against the tumult of evildoers,
4   Who sharpen their tongues like swords,
      who aim like arrows their bitter words,
5   Shooting from ambush at the innocent man,
      suddenly shooting at him without fear.
6   They resolve on their wicked plan;
      they conspire to set snares,
      saying, "Who will see us?"
7   They devise a wicked scheme,
      and conceal the scheme they have devised;
      deep are the thoughts of each heart.

8   But God shoots his arrows at them;
      suddenly they are struck.

9   He brings them down by their own tongues;
       all who see them nod their heads.
10   And all men fear and proclaim the work of God,
       and ponder what he has done.
11   The just man is glad in the Lord and takes refuge in him;
       in him glory all the upright of heart.

Psalm 64

2   To YOU we owe our hymn of praise,
       O God, in Sion;
   To you must vows be fulfilled,
       you who hear prayers.
3   To you all flesh must come
4   because of wicked deeds.
   We are overcome by our sins;
       it is you who pardon them.
5   Happy the man you choose, and bring
       to dwell in your courts.
   May we be filled with the good things of your house,
       the holy things of your temple!

6   With awe-inspiring deeds of justice you answer us,
       O God our savior,
   The hope of all the ends of the earth
       and of the distant seas.
7   You set the mountains in place by your power,
       you who are girt with might;
8   You still the roaring of the seas,
       the roaring of their waves and the tumult of the peoples.
9   And the dwellers at the earth's ends are in fear at your marvels;
       the farthest east and west you make resound with joy.

10   You have visited the land and watered it;
       greatly have you enriched it.
   God's watercourses are filled;
       you have prepared the grain.
11   Thus have you prepared the land: drenching its furrows,
       breaking up its clods,
   Softening it with showers,
       blessing its yield.
12   You have crowned the year with your bounty,
       and your paths overflow with a rich harvest;

13	The untilled meadows overflow with it,
	and rejoicing clothes the hills.
14	The fields are garmented with flocks
	and the valleys blanketed with grain.
	They shout and sing for joy.

Psalm 65

1	SHOUT joyfully to God, all you on earth,
2	sing praise to the glory of his name;
	proclaim his glorious praise.
3	Say to God, "How tremendous are your deeds!
	for your great strength your enemies fawn upon you.
4	Let all on earth worship and sing praise to you,
	sing praise to your name!"

5	Come and see the works of God,
	his tremendous deeds among men.
6	He has changed the sea into dry land;
	through the river they passed on foot;
	therefore let us rejoice in him.
7	He rules by his might forever;
	his eyes watch the nations;
	rebels may not exalt themselves.
8	Bless our God, you peoples,
	loudly sound his praise;
9	He has given life to our souls,
	and has not let our feet slip.
10	For you have tested us, O God!
	You have tried us as silver is tried by fire;
11	You have brought us into a snare;
	you laid a heavy burden on our backs.
12	You let men ride over our heads;
	we went through fire and water,
	but you have led us out to refreshment.

13	I will bring holocausts to your house;
	to you I will fulfill the vows
14	Which my lips uttered
	and my words promised in my distress.
15	Holocausts of fatlings I will offer you,
	with burnt offerings of rams;
	I will sacrifice oxen and goats.

16 Hear now, all you who fear God, while I declare
    what he has done for me.
17 When I appealed to him in words,
    praise was on the tip of my tongue.
18 Were I to cherish wickednesss in my heart,
    the Lord would not hear;
19 But God has heard;
    he has hearkened to the sound of my prayer.
20 Blessed be God who refused me not
    my prayer or his kindness!

Psalm 66

2 MAY GOD have pity on us and bless us;
    may he let his face shine upon us.
3 So may your way be known upon earth;
    among all nations, your salvation.
4   May the peoples praise you, O God;
        may all the peoples praise you!

5 May the nations be glad and exult
    because you rule the peoples in equity;
    the nations on the earth you guide.
6   May the peoples praise you, O God;
        may all the peoples praise you!

7 The earth has yielded its fruits;
    God, our God, has blessed us.
8 May God bless us,
    and may all the ends of the earth fear him!

Psalm 67

2 GOD ARISES; his enemies are scattered,
    and those who hate him flee before him.
3 As smoke is driven away, so are they driven;
    as wax melts before the fire,
    so the wicked perish before God.
4 But the just rejoice and exult before God;
    they are glad and rejoice.

5 Sing to God, chant praise to his name,
    extol him who rides upon the clouds,

Whose name is the Lord;
   exult before him.
6 The father of orphans and the defender of widows
   is God in his holy dwelling.
7 God gives a home to the forsaken;
   he leads forth prisoners to prosperity;
   only rebels remain in the parched land.

8 O God, when you went forth at the head of your people,
   when you marched through the wilderness,
9 The earth quaked; it rained from heaven at the presence of God,
   at the presence of God, the God of Israel.
   This is Sinai.
10 A bountiful rain you showered down, O God,
   upon your inheritance;
   you restored the land when it languished;
11 Your flock settled in it;
   in your goodness, O God, you provided it for the needy.

12 The Lord gives the word;
   women bear the glad tidings, a vast army:
13 "Kings and their hosts are fleeing, fleeing,
   and the household shall divide the spoils.
14 Though you rested among the sheepfolds,
   the wings of the dove shone with silver,
   and her pinions with a golden hue.
15 While the Almighty dispersed the kings there,
   snow fell on Salmon."

16 High the mountains of Basan;
   rugged the mountains of Basan.
17 Why look you jealously, you rugged mountains,
   at the mountain God has chosen for his throne,
   where the Lord himself will dwell forever?
18 The chariots of God are myriad, thousands on thousands;
   the Lord advances from Sinai to the sanctuary.
19 You have ascended on high, taken captives,
   received men as gifts—
   even rebels; the Lord God enters his dwelling.

20 Blessed day by day be the Lord,
   who bears our burdens; God, who is our salvation.
21 God is a saving God for us;
   the Lord, my Lord, controls the passageways of death.

22 Surely God crushes the heads of his enemies,
   the hairy crowns of those who stalk about in their guilt.
23 The Lord said: "I will fetch them back from Basan;
   I will fetch them back from the depths of the sea,
24 So that you will bathe your feet in blood;
   the tongues of your dogs will have their share of your enemies."

25 They view your progress, O God,
   the progress of my God, my King, into the sanctuary;
26 The singers lead, the minstrels follow,
   in their midst the maidens play on timbrels.
27 In your choirs bless God;
   bless the Lord, you of Israel's wellspring!
28 There is Benjamin, the youngest, leading them;
   the princes of Juda in a body,
   the princes of Zabulon, the princes of Nephthali.

29 Show forth, O God, your power,
   the power, O God, with which you took our part;
30 For your temple in Jerusalem
   let the kings bring you gifts.
31 Rebuke the wild beast of the reeds,
   the herd of strong bulls and the bullocks, the nations.
   Let them prostrate themselves with bars of silver;
   scatter the peoples who delight in war.
32 Let nobles come from Egypt;
   let Ethiopia extend its hands to God.

33 You kingdoms of the earth, sing to God,
   chant praise to the Lord
34 who rides on the heights of the ancient heavens.
   Behold, his voice resounds, the voice of power:
35 "Confess the power of God!"
   Over Israel is his majesty;
   his power is in the skies.
36 Awesome in his sanctuary is God, the God of Israel;
   he gives power and strength to his people.
   Blessed be God!

Psalm 68

2 SAVE ME, O God,
   for the waters threaten my life;
3 I am sunk in the abysmal swamp

where there is no foothold;
I have reached the watery depths;
the flood overwhelms me.

4　I am wearied with calling,
my throat is parched;
My eyes have failed
with looking for my God.

5　Those outnumber the hairs of my head
who hate me without cause.
Too many for my strength
are they who wrongfully are my enemies.
Must I restore what I did not steal?

6　O God, you know my folly,
and my faults are not hid from you.

7　Let not those who wait for you be put to shame through me,
O Lord, God of Hosts.
Let not those who seek you blush for me,
O God of Israel,

8　Since for your sake I bear insult,
and shame covers my face.

9　I have become an outcast to my brothers,
a stranger to my mother's sons,

10　Because zeal for your house consumes me,
and the insults of those who blaspheme you fall upon me.

11　I humbled myself with fasting,
and this was made a reproach to me.

12　I made sackcloth my garment,
and I became a byword for them.

13　They who sit at the gate gossip about me,
and drunkards make me the butt of their songs.

14　But I pray to you, O Lord,
for the time of your favor, O God!
In your great kindness answer me
with your constant help.

15　Rescue me out of the mire; may I not sink!
may I be rescued from my foes,
and from the watery depths.

16　Let not the flood-waters overwhelm me,
nor the abyss swallow me up,
nor the pit close its mouth over me.

17　Answer me, O Lord, for bounteous is your kindness;
in your great mercy turn toward me.

18   Hide not your face from your servant;
      in my distress, make haste to answer me.
19   Come and ransom my life;
      as an answer for my enemies, redeem me.
20   You know my reproach, my shame and my ignominy;
      before you are all my foes.
21   Insult has broken my heart, and I am weak,
      I looked for sympathy, but there was none;
      for comforters, and I found none.
22   Rather they put gall in my food,
      and in my thirst they gave me vinegar to drink.

23   Let their own table be a snare before them,
      and a net for their friends.
24   Let their eyes grow dim so that they cannot see,
      and keep their backs always feeble.
25   Pour out your wrath upon them;
      let the fury of your anger overtake them.
26   Let their encampment become desolate;
      in their tents let there be no one to dwell.
27   For they kept after him whom you smote,
      and added to the pain of him you wounded.
28   Heap guilt upon their guilt,
      and let them not attain to your reward.
29   May they be erased from the book of the living,
      and not be recorded with the just!

30   But I am afflicted and in pain;
      let your saving help, O God, protect me.
31   I will praise the name of God in song,
      and I will glorify him with thanksgiving;
32   This will please the Lord more than oxen
      or bullocks with horns and divided hooves:
33   "See, you lowly ones, and be glad;
      you who seek God, may your hearts be merry!
34   For the Lord hears the poor,
      and his own who are in bonds he spurns not.
35   Let the heavens and the earth praise him,
      the seas and whatever moves in them!"

36   For God will save Sion
      and rebuild the cities of Juda.
      They shall dwell in the land and own it,

37 and the descendants of his servants shall inherit it,
and those who love his name shall inhabit it.

Psalm 69

2 DEIGN, O God, to rescue me;
O Lord, make haste to help me.
3 Let them be put to shame and confounded
who seek my life.
Let them be turned back in disgrace
who desire my ruin.
4 Let them retire in their shame
who say to me, "Aha, aha!"
5 But may all who seek you
exult and be glad in you,
And may those who love your salvation
say ever, "God be glorified!"
6 But I am afflicted and poor;
O God, hasten to me!
You are my help and my deliverer;
O Lord, hold not back!

Psalm 70

1 IN YOU, O Lord, I take refuge;
let me never be put to shame.
2 In your justice rescue me, and deliver me;
incline your ear to me, and save me.
3 Be my rock of refuge,
a stronghold to give me safety,
for you are my rock and my fortress.
4 O my God, rescue me from the hand of the wicked,
from the grasp of the criminal and the violent.
5 For you are my hope, O Lord;
my trust, O God, from my youth.
6 On you I depend from birth;
from my mother's womb you are my strength;
constant has been my hope in you.
7 A portent am I to many,
but you are my strong refuge!
8 My mouth shall be filled with your praise,
with your glory day by day.

Cast me not off in my old age;
    as my strength fails, forsake me not,
10   For my enemies speak against me,
    and they who keep watch against my life take counsel together.
11   They say, "God has forsaken him;
    pursue and seize him,
    for there is no one to rescue him."
12   O God, be not far from me;
    my God, make haste to help me.
13   Let them be put to shame and consumed who attack my life;
    let them be wrapped in ignominy and disgrace who seek to
                                      [harm me.
14   But I will always hope
    and praise you ever more and more.
15   My mouth shall declare your justice,
    day by day your salvation,
    though I know not their extent.
16   I will treat of the mighty works of the Lord;
    O God, I will tell of your singular justice.

17   O God, you have taught me from my youth,
    and till the present I proclaim your wondrous deeds;
18   And now that I am old and gray,
    O God, forsake me not
   Till I proclaim your strength
    to every generation that is to come.
19   Your power and your justice,
    O God, reach to heaven.
   You have done great things;
    O God, who is like you?
20   Though you have made me feel many bitter afflictions,
    you will again revive me;
    from the depths of the earth you will once more raise me.

21   Renew your benefits toward me,
    and comfort me over and over.
22   So will I give you thanks with music on the lyre,
    for your faithfulness, O my God!
   I will sing your praises with the harp,
    O Holy One of Israel!
23   My lips shall shout for joy
    as I sing your praises;
   My soul also, which you have redeemed,

    and my tongue day by day shall discourse on your justice:
        How shamed and how disgraced
            are those who sought to harm me!

Psalm 71

1   O GOD, with your judgment endow the king,
        and with your justice, the king's son;
2   He shall govern your people with justice
        and your afflicted ones with judgment.
3   The mountains shall yield peace for the people,
        and the hills justice.
4   He shall defend the afflicted among the people,
        save the children of the poor,
        and crush the oppressor.

5   May he endure as long as the sun,
        and like the moon through all generations.
6   He shall be like rain coming down on the meadow,
        like showers watering the earth.
7   Justice shall flower in his days,
        and profound peace, till the moon be no more.

8   May he rule from sea to sea,
        and from the River to the ends of the earth.
9   His foes shall bow before him,
        and his enemies shall lick the dust.
10   The kings of Tharsis and the Isles shall offer gifts;
        the kings of Arabia and Saba shall bring tribute.
11   All kings shall pay him homage,
        all nations shall serve him.

12   For he shall rescue the poor man when he cries out,
        and the afflicted when he has no one to help him.
13   He shall have pity for the lowly and the poor;
        the lives of the poor he shall save.
14   From fraud and violence he shall redeem them,
        and precious shall their blood be in his sight.

15   May he live to be given the gold of Arabia,
        and to be prayed for continually;
        day by day shall they bless him.
16   May there be an abundance of grain upon the earth;

on the tops of the mountains the crops shall rustle like Lebanon;
    the city dwellers shall flourish like the verdure of the fields.
17 May his name be blessed forever;
    as long as the sun his name shall remain.
In him shall all the tribes of the earth be blessed;
    all the nations shall proclaim his happiness.

18 Blessed be the Lord, the God of Israel,
    who alone does wondrous deeds.
19 And blessed forever be his glorious name;
    may the whole earth be filled with his glory.
    Amen. Amen.

20 The prayers of David the son of Jesse are ended.

Psalm 72

1 How GOOD God is to the upright;
    the Lord, to those who are clean of heart!
2 But, as for me, I almost lost my balance;
    my feet all but slipped,
3 Because I was envious of the arrogant
    when I saw them prosper though they were wicked.

4 For they are in no pain;
    their bodies are sound and sleek;
5 They are free from the burdens of mortals,
    and are not afflicted like the rest of men.
6 So pride adorns them as a necklace;
    as a robe violence enwraps them.
7 Out of their crassness comes iniquity;
    their fancies overflow their hearts.
8 They scoff and speak evil;
    outrage from on high they threaten.
9 They set their mouthings in place of heaven,
    and their pronouncements roam the earth:
10 "So he brings his people to such a pass
    that they have not even water!"
11 And they say, "How does God know?"
    And, "Is there any knowledge in the Most High?"
12 Such, then, are the wicked;
    always carefree, while they increase in wealth.

13 Is it but in vain I have kept my heart clean
        and washed my hands as an innocent man?
14 For I suffer affliction day after day
        and chastisement with each new dawn.
15 Had I thought, "I will speak as they do,"
        I had been false to the fellowship of your children.
16 Though I tried to understand this
        it seemed to me too difficult,
17 Till I entered the sanctuary of God
        and considered their final destiny.

18 You set them, indeed, on a slippery road;
        you hurl them down to ruin.
19 How suddenly they are made desolate!
        They are completely wasted away amid horrors.
20 As though they were the dream of one who had awakened, O Lord,
        so will you, when you arise, set at nought these phantoms.
21 Because my heart was embittered
        and my soul was pierced,
22 I was stupid and understood not;
        I was like a brute beast in your presence.

23 Yet with you I shall always be;
        you have hold of my right hand;
24 With your counsel you guide me,
        and in the end you will receive me in glory.
25 Whom else have I in heaven?
        And when I am with you, the earth delights me not.
26 Though my flesh and my heart waste away,
        God is the rock of my heart and my portion forever.
27 For indeed, they who withdraw from you perish;
        you destroy everyone who is unfaithful to you.
28 But for me, to be near God is my good;
        to make the Lord God my refuge.
    I shall declare all your works
        in the gates of the daughter of Sion.

Psalm 73

1 WHY, O GOD, have you cast us off forever?
        Why does your anger smolder against the sheep of your pasture?
2 Remember your flock which you built up of old,
        the tribe you redeemed as your inheritance,
        Mount Sion, where you took up your abode.

3   Turn your steps toward the utter ruins;
        toward all the damage the enemy has done in the sanctuary.

4   Your foes roar triumphantly in your shrine;
        they have set up their tokens of victory.
5   They are like men coming up with axes to a clump of trees;
6   and now with chisel and hammer they hack at all its paneling.
7   They set your sanctuary on fire;
        the place where your name abides they have razed and profaned.
8   They said in their hearts, "Let us destroy them;
        burn all the shrines of God in the land."

9   Deeds on our behalf we do not see; there is no prophet now,
        and no one of us knows how long. . . .
10   How long, O God, shall the foe blaspheme?
        Shall the enemy revile your name forever?
11   Why draw back your hand
        and keep your right hand idle beneath your cloak?

12   Yet, O God, my king from of old,
        you doer of saving deeds on earth,
13   You stirred up the sea by your might;
        you smashed the heads of the dragons in the waters.
14   You crushed the heads of Leviathan,
        and made food of him for the dolphins.
15   You released the springs and torrents;
        you brought dry land out of the primeval waters.
16   Yours is the day, and yours the night;
        you fashioned the moon and the sun.
17   You fixed all the limits of the land;
        summer and winter you made.

18   Remember how the enemy has blasphemed you, O Lord,
        and how a stupid people has reviled your name.
19   Give not to the vulture the life of your dove;
        be not forever unmindful of the lives of your afflicted ones.
20   Look to your covenant,
        for the hiding places in the land and the plains are full of violence.
21   May the humble not retire in confusion;
        may the afflicted and the poor praise your name.
22   Arise, O God; defend your cause;
        remember how the fool blasphemes you day after day.
23   Be not unmindful of the voice of your foes;
        the uproar of those who rebel against you is unceasing.

Psalm 74

2   WE GIVE you thanks, O God, we give thanks,
     and we invoke your name; we declare your wondrous deeds.

3   "When I seize the appointed time,
     I will judge with equity.
4   Though the earth and all who dwell in it quake,
     I have set firm its pillars.
5   I say to the boastful: Boast not;
     and to the wicked: Lift not up your horns."

6   Lift not up your horns against the Most High;
     speak not haughtily against the Rock.
7   For neither from the east nor from the west,
     neither from the desert nor from the mountains—
8   But God is the judge;
     one he brings low; another he lifts up.
9   For a cup is in the Lord's hand,
     full of spiced and foaming wine,
     And he pours out from it; even to the dregs they shall drain it;
     all the wicked of the earth shall drink.

10   But as for me, I will exult forever;
     I will sing praise to the God of Jacob.
11   And I will break off the horns of all the wicked;
     the horns of the just shall be lifted up.

Psalm 75

2   GOD IS renowned in Juda;
     in Israel great is his name.
3   In Salem is his abode;
     his dwelling is in Sion.
4   There he shattered the flashing shafts of the bow,
     shield and sword, and weapons of war.

5   Resplendent you came, O powerful One,
     from the everlasting mountains.
6   Despoiled are the stouthearted;
     they sleep their sleep;
     the hands of all the mighty ones have failed.
7   At your rebuke, O God of Jacob,
     chariots and steeds lay stilled.

8 You are terrible; and who can withstand you
       for the fury of your anger?
9 From heaven you made your intervention heard;
       the earth feared and was silent
10 When God arose for judgment,
       to save all the afflicted of the earth.

11 For wrathful Edom shall glorify you,
       and the survivors of Hamath shall keep your festivals.
12 Make vows to the Lord, your God, and fulfill them;
       let all round about him bring gifts to the terrible Lord
13 Who checks the pride of princes,
       who is terrible to the kings of the earth.

Psalm 76

2 ALOUD to God I cry;
       aloud to God, to hear me;
3   on the day of my distress I seek the Lord.
   By night my hands are stretched out without flagging;
       my soul refuses comfort.
4 When I remember God, I moan;
       when I ponder, my spirit grows faint.
5 You keep my eyes watchful;
       I am troubled and cannot speak.
6 I consider the days of old;
7   the years long past I remember.
   In the night I meditate in my heart;
       I ponder, and my spirit broods:
8 "Will the Lord reject forever
       and nevermore be favorable?
9 Will his kindness utterly cease,
       his promise fail for all generations?
10 Has God forgotten pity?
       Does he in anger withhold his compassion?"
11 And I say, "This is my sorrow,
       that the right hand of the Most High is changed."
12 I remember the deeds of the Lord;
       yes, I remember your wonders of old.
13 And I meditate on your works;
       your exploits I ponder.

14 O God, your way is holy;
       what great god is there like our God?

15	You are the God who works wonders;
	among the peoples you have made known your power.
16	With your strong arm you redeemed your people,
	the sons of Jacob and Joseph.
17	The waters saw you, O God;
	the waters saw you and shuddered;
	the very depths were troubled.
18	The clouds poured down water;
	the skies gave forth their voice;
	your arrows also sped abroad.
19	Your thunder resounded in the whirlwind;
	your lightning illumined the world;
	the earth quivered and quaked.
20	Through the sea was your way,
	and your path through the deep waters,
	though your footsteps were not seen.
21	You led your people like a flock
	under the care of Moses and Aaron.

Psalm 77

1	HEARKEN, my people, to my teaching;
	incline your ears to the words of my mouth.
2	I will open my mouth in a parable,
	I will utter mysteries from of old.
3	What we have heard and know,
	and what our fathers have declared to us,
4	We will not hide from their sons;
	we will declare to the generation to come
	The glorious deeds of the Lord and his strength
	and the wonders that he wrought.
5	He set it up as a decree in Jacob,
	and established it as a law in Israel,
	That what he commanded our fathers
	they should make known to their sons;
6	So that the generation to come might know,
	their sons yet to be born,
	That they too may rise and declare to their sons
7	that they should put their hope in God,
	And not forget the deeds of God
	but keep his commands,
8	And not be like their fathers,
	a generation wayward and rebellious,

A generation that kept not its heart steadfast
  nor its spirit faithful toward God.

9 The sons of Ephraim, ordered ranks of bowmen,
     retreated in the day of battle.
10 They kept not the covenant with God;
     according to his law they would not walk;
11 And they forgot his deeds,
     the wonders he had shown them.
12 Before their fathers he did wondrous things,
     in the land of Egypt, in the plain of Soan.
13 He cleft the sea and brought them through,
     and he made the waters stand as in a mound.
14 He led them with a cloud by day,
     and all night with a glow of fire.
15 He cleft the rocks in the desert
     and gave them water in copious floods.
16 He made streams flow from the crag
     and brought the waters forth in rivers.

17 But they sinned yet more against him,
     rebelling against the Most High in the wasteland,
18 And they tempted God in their hearts
     by demanding the food they carved.
19 Yes, they spoke against God, saying,
     "Can God spread a table in the desert?
20 For when he struck the rock, waters gushed forth,
     and the streams overflowed;
   Can he also give bread
     and provide meat for his people?"
21 Then the Lord heard and was enraged;
     and fire blazed up against Jacob,
     and anger rose against Israel,
22 Because they believed not God
     nor trusted in his help.
23 Yet he commanded the skies above
     and the doors of heaven he opened;
24 He rained manna upon them for food
     and gave them heavenly bread.
25 The bread of the mighty was eaten by men;
     even a surfeit of provisions he sent them.
26 He stirred up the east wind in the heavens,
     and by his power brought on the south wind.

27 And he rained meat upon them like dust,
    and, like the sand of the sea, winged fowl,
28 Which fell in the midst of their camp
    round about their tents.
29 So they ate and were wholly surfeited;
    he had brought them what they craved.
30 They had not given over their craving,
    and their food was still in their mouths,
31 When the anger of God rose against them
    and slew their best men,
    and laid low the young men of Israel.

32 Yet for all this they sinned still more
    and believed not in his wonders.
33 Therefore he quickly ended their days
    and their years with sudden destruction.
34 While he slew them they sought him
    and inquired after God again,
35 Remembering that God was their Rock
    and the Most High God, their redeemer.
36 But they flattered him with their mouths
    and lied to him with their tongues,
37 Though their hearts were not steadfast toward him,
    nor were they faithful to his covenant.
38 Yet he, being merciful, forgave their sin
    and destroyed them not;
    Often he turned back his anger
    and let none of his wrath be roused.
39 He remembered that they were flesh,
    a passing breath that returns not.

40 How often they rebelled against him in the desert
    and grieved him in the wilderness!
41 Again and again they tempted God
    and provoked the Holy One of Israel.
42 They remembered not his hand
    nor the day he delivered them from the foe,
43 When he wrought his signs in Egypt
    and his marvels in the plain of Soan,
44 And changed into blood their streams—
    their running water, so that they could not drink;
45 He sent among them flies that devoured them
    and frogs that destroyed them.

46	He gave their harvest to the caterpillar,
	the fruits of their toil to the locust.
47	He killed their vines with hail
	and their sycamores with frost.
48	He gave over to the hail their beasts
	and their flocks to the lightning.
49	He loosed against them his fierce anger,
	wrath and fury and strife,
	a detachment of messengers of doom.
50	When he measured the course of his anger
	he spared them not from death,
	and delivered their beasts to the plague.
51	He smote every first-born in Egypt,
	the first fruits of manhood in the tents of Ham;
52	But his people he led forth like sheep
	and guided them like a herd in the desert.
53	He led them on secure and unafraid,
	while he covered their enemies with the sea.
54	And he brought them to his holy land,
	to the mountains his right hand had won.
55	And he drove out nations before them;
	he distributed their inheritance by lot,
	and settled the tribes of Israel in their tents.

56	But they tempted and rebelled against God the Most High,
	and kept not his decrees.
57	They turned back and were faithless like their fathers;
	they recoiled like a treacherous bow.
58	They angered him with their high places
	and with their idols roused his jealousy.
59	God heard and was enraged
	and utterly rejected Israel.
60	And he forsook the tabernacle in Silo,
	the tent where he dwelt among men.
61	And he surrendered his strength into captivity,
	his glory into the hands of the foe.
62	He abandoned his people to the sword
	and was enraged against his inheritance.
63	Fire consumed their young men,
	and their maidens were not betrothed.
64	Their priests fell by the sword,
	and their widows sang no dirges.

65 Then the Lord awoke, as wakes from sleep
    a champion overcome with wine;
66 And he put his foes to flight
    and cast them into everlasting disgrace.
67 And he rejected the tent of Joseph,
    and the tribe of Ephraim he chose not;
68 But he chose the tribe of Juda,
    Mount Sion which he loved.
69 And he built his shrine like heaven,
    like the earth which he founded forever.
70 And he chose David, his servant,
    and took him from the sheepfolds;
71 From following the ewes he brought him
    to shepherd Jacob, his people,
    and Israel, his inheritance.
72 And he tended them with a sincere heart,
    and with skillful hands he guided them.

Psalm 78

1 O GOD, the nations have come into your inheritance;
    they have defiled your holy temple,
    they have laid Jerusalem in ruins.
2 They have given the corpses of your servants
    as food to the birds of heaven,
    the flesh of your faithful ones to the beasts of the earth.
3 They have poured out their blood like water
    round about Jerusalem,
    and there is no one to bury them.
4 We have become the reproach of our neighbors,
    the scorn and derision of those around us.

5 O Lord, how long? Will you be angry forever?
    Will your jealousy burn like fire?
6 Pour out your wrath upon the nations that acknowledge you not,
    upon the kingdoms that call not upon your name;
7 For they have devoured Jacob
    and laid waste his dwelling.
8 Remember not against us the iniquities of the past;
    may your compassion quickly come to us,
    for we are brought very low.

9 Help us, O God our savior,
    because of the glory of your name;

Deliver us and pardon our sins
    for your name's sake.
10 Why should the nations say,
    "Where is their God?"
Let it be known among the nations in our sight
    that you avenge the shedding of your servants' blood.

11 Let the prisoners' sighing come before you;
    with your great power free those doomed to death.
12 And repay our neighbors sevenfold into their bosoms
    the disgrace they have inflicted on you, O Lord.
13 Then we, your people and the sheep of your pasture,
    will give thanks to you forever;
    through all generations we will declare your praise.

Psalm 79

2 O SHEPHERD of Israel, hearken,
    O guide of the flock of Joseph!
From your throne upon the cherubim, shine forth
3   before Ephraim, Benjamin and Manasse.
Rouse your power,
    and come to save us.
4   O Lord of hosts, restore us;
      if your face shine upon us, then we shall be safe.

5 O Lord of hosts, how long will you burn with anger
    while your people pray?
6 You have fed them with the bread of tears
    and given them tears to drink in ample measure.
7 You have left us to be fought over by our neighbors,
    and our enemies mock us.
8   O Lord of hosts, restore us;
      if your face shine upon us, then we shall be safe.

9 A vine from Egypt you transplanted;
    you drove away the nations and planted it.
10 You cleared the ground for it,
    and it took root and filled the land.
11 The mountains were hidden in its shadow;
    by its branches, the cedars of God.
12 It put forth its foliage to the Sea,
    its shoots as far as the River.

13	Why have you broken down its walls, so that every passer-by plucks its fruit,
14	The boar from the forest lays it waste, and the beasts of the field feed upon it?
15	Once again, O Lord of hosts, look down from heaven, and see; Take care of this vine,
16	and protect what your right hand has planted the son of man whom you yourself made strong.

17	Let those who would burn it with fire or cut it down perish before you at your rebuke.
18	May your help be with the man of your right hand, with the son of man whom you yourself made strong.
19	Then we will no more withdraw from you; give us new life, and we will call upon your name.
20	O Lord of hosts, restore us; if your face shine upon us, then we shall be safe.

Psalm 80

2	SING joyfully to God our strength; acclaim the God of Jacob.
3	Take up a melody, and sound the timbrel, the pleasant harp and the lyre.
4	Blow the trumpet at the new moon, at the full moon, on our solemn feast;
5	For it is a statute in Israel, an ordinance of the God of Jacob,
6	Who made it a decree for Joseph when he came forth from the land of Egypt.

	An unfamiliar speech I hear:
7	"I relieved his shoulder of the burden; his hands were freed from the basket.

8	In distress you called, and I rescued you;
	   Unseen, I answered you in thunder;
	   I tested you at the waters of Meriba.

9	Hear, my people, and I will admonish you; O Israel, will you not hear me?
10	There shall be no strange god among you nor shall you worship any alien god.
11	I, the Lord, am your God

who led you forth from the land of Egypt;
    open wide your mouth, and I will fill it.

12 "But my people heard not my voice,
    and Israel obeyed me not;
13 So I gave them up to the hardness of their hearts;
    they walked according to their own counsels.
14 If only my people would hear me,
    and Israel walk in my ways,
15 Quickly would I humble their enemies;
    against their foes I would turn my hand.
16 Those who hated the Lord would seek to flatter me,
    but their fate would endure forever,
17 While Israel I would feed with the best of wheat,
    and with honey from the rock I would fill them."

Psalm 81

1 GOD ARISES in the divine assembly;
    he judges in the midst of the gods.

2 "How long will you judge unjustly
    and favor the cause of the wicked?
3 Defend the lowly and the fatherless;
    render justice to the afflicted and the destitute.
4 Rescue the lowly and the poor;
    from the hand of the wicked deliver them.

5 "They know not, neither do they understand;
    they go about in darkness;
    all the foundations of the earth are shaken.
6 I said: You are gods,
    all of you sons of the Most High;
7 Yet like men you shall die,
    and fall like any prince."
8 Rise, O God; judge the earth,
    for yours are all the nations.

Psalm 82

2 O GOD, do not remain unmoved;
    be not silent, O God, and be not still!
3 For behold, your enemies raise a tumult,
    and they who hate you lift up their heads.

4   Against your people they plot craftily;
      they conspire against those whom you protect.

5   They say, "Come, let us destroy their nation;
      let the name of Israel be remembered no more!"

6   Yes, they consult together with one mind,
      and against you they are allied:

7   The tents of Edom and the Ismaelites,
      Moab and the Agarenes,

8   Gebal and Ammon and Amalec,
      Philistia with the inhabitants of Tyre;

9   The Assyrians, too, are leagued with them;
      they are the forces of the sons of Lot.

10   Deal with them as with Madian;
      as with Sisara and Jabin at the torrent Cison,

11   Who perished at Endor;
      they became dung on the ground.

12   Make their nobles like Oreb and Zeb;
      all their chiefs like Zebee and Salmana,

13   Who said, "Let us take for ourselves
      the dwelling place of God."

14   O my God, make them like leaves in a whirlwind,
      like chaff before the wind.

15   As a fire raging in a forest,
      as a flame setting the mountains ablaze,

16   So pursue them with your tempest
      and rout them with your storm.

17   Darken their faces with disgrace,
      that men may seek your name, O Lord.

18   Let them be shamed and put to rout forever;
      let them be confounded and perish,

19   Knowing that you alone are the Lord,
      the Most High over all the earth.

Psalm 83

2   How LOVELY is your dwelling place,
      O Lord of hosts!

3   My soul yearns and pines
      for the courts of the Lord.
    My heart and my flesh
      cry out for the living God.

4   Even the sparrow finds a home,
        and the swallow a nest
        in which she puts her young—
    Your altars, O Lord of hosts,
        my king and my God!

5   Happy they who dwell in your house!
        continually they praise you.
6   Happy the men whose strength you are!
        their hearts are set upon the pilgrimage:
7   When they pass through the arid valley,
        they make a spring of it;
        the early rain clothes it with generous growth.
8   They go from strength to strength;
        they shall see the God of gods in Sion.

9   O Lord of hosts, hear my prayer;
        hearken, O God of Jacob!
10   O God, behold our shield,
        and look upon the face of your anointed.
11   I had rather one day in your courts
        than a thousand elsewhere;
    I had rather lie at the threshold of the house of my God
        than dwell in the tents of the wicked.
12   For a sun and a shield is the Lord God;
        grace and glory he bestows;
    The Lord withholds no good thing
        from those who walk in sincerity.
13   O Lord of hosts,
        happy the men who trust in you!

Psalm 84

2   YOU HAVE favored, O Lord, your land;
        you have restored the well-being of Jacob.
3   You have forgiven the guilt of your people;
        you have covered all their sins.
4   You have withdrawn all your wrath;
        you have revoked your burning anger.

5   Restore us, O God our savior,
        and abandon your displeasure against us.
6   Will you be ever angry with us,
        prolonging your anger to all generations?

7   Will you not instead give us life;
        and shall not your people rejoice in you?
8   Show us, O Lord, your kindness,
        and grant us your salvation.

9   I will hear what God proclaims:
        the Lord—for he proclaims peace
    To his people, and to his faithful ones,
        and to those who put in him their hope.
10 Near indeed is his salvation to those who fear him,
        glory dwelling in our land.
11 Kindness and truth shall meet;
        justice and peace shall kiss.
12 Truth shall spring out of the earth,
        and justice shall look down from heaven.
13 The Lord himself will give his benefits;
        our land shall yield its increase.
14 Justice shall walk before him,
        and salvation, along the way of his steps.

Psalm 85

1   INCLINE your ear, O Lord; answer me,
        for I am afflicted and poor.
2   Keep my life, for I am devoted to you;
        save your servant who trusts in you.
3   You are my God; have pity on me, O Lord,
        for to you I call all the day.
4   Gladden the soul of your servant,
        for to you, O Lord, I lift up my soul;
5   For you, O Lord, are good and forgiving,
        abounding in kindness to all who call upon you.
6   Hearken, O Lord, to my prayer
        and attend to the sound of my pleading.
7   In the day of my distress I call upon you,
        for you will answer me.

8   There is none like you among the gods, O Lord,
        and there are no works like yours.
9   All the nations you have made shall come
        and worship you, O Lord,
        and glorify your name.
10 For you are great, and you do wondrous deeds;
        you alone are God.

11 Teach me, O Lord, your way
    that I may walk in your truth;
    direct my heart that it may fear your name.
12 I will give thanks to you, O Lord my God,
    with all my heart,
    and I will glorify your name forever.
13 Great has been your kindness toward me;
    you have rescued me from the depths of the nether world.
14 O God, the haughty have risen up against me,
    and the company of fierce men seeks my life,
    nor do they set you before their eyes.
15 But you, O Lord, are a God merciful and gracious,
    slow to anger, abounding in kindness and fidelity.
16 Turn toward me, and have pity on me;
    give your strength to your servant,
    and save the son of your handmaid.
17 Grant me a proof of your favor,
    that my enemies may see, to their confusion,
    that you, O Lord, have helped and comforted me.

Psalm 86

His FOUNDATION upon the holy mountains
2   the Lord loves:
The gates of Sion,
    more than any dwelling of Jacob.
3 Glorious things are said of you,
    O city of God!
4 I tell of Egypt and Babylon
    among those that know the Lord;
Of Philistia, Tyre, Ethiopia:
    "This man was born there."
5 And of Sion they shall say:
    "One and all were born in her;
And he who has established her
    is the Most High Lord."
6 They shall note, when the peoples are enrolled:
    "This man was born there."
7 And all shall sing, in their festive dance:
    "My home is within you."

Psalm 87

2   O Lᴏʀᴅ, my God, by day I cry out;
      at night I clamor in your presence.

3   Let my prayer come before you;
      incline your ear to my call for help.

4   For my soul is surfeited with troubles
      and my life draws near to the nether world.

5   I am numbered with those who go down into the pit;
      I am a man without strength.

6   My couch is among the dead,
      like the slain who lie in the grave,
  Whom you remember no longer
      and who are cut off from your care.

7   You have plunged me into the bottom of the pit,
      into the dark abyss.

8   Upon me your wrath lies heavy,
      and with all your billows you overwhelm me.

9   You have taken my friends away from me;
      you have made me an abomination to them;
      I am imprisoned, and I cannot escape.

10   My eyes have grown dim through affliction;
      daily I call upon you, O Lord;
      to you I stretch out my hands.

11   Will you work wonders for the dead?
      Will the shades arise to give you thanks?

12   Do they declare your kindness in the grave,
      your faithfulness among those who have perished?

13   Are your wonders made known in the darkness,
      or your justice in the land of oblivion?

14   But I, O Lord, cry out to you;
      with my morning prayer I wait upon you.

15   Why, O Lord, do you reject me;
      why hide from me your face?

16   I am afflicted and in agony from my youth;
      I am dazed with the burden of your dread.

17   Your furies have swept over me;
      your terrors have cut me off.

18   They encompass me like water all the day;
      on all sides they close in upon me.

19   Companion and neighbor you have taken away from me;
      my only friend is darkness.

Psalm 88

2   THE FAVORS of the Lord I will sing forever;
      through all generations my mouth shall proclaim your
                                      [faithfulness.

3   For you have said, "My kindness is established forever";
      in heaven you have confirmed your faithfulness:

4   "I have made a covenant with my chosen one,
      I have sworn to David my servant:

5   Forever will I confirm your posterity
      and establish your throne for all generations."

6   The heavens proclaim your wonders, O Lord,
      and your faithfulness, in the assembly of the holy ones.

7   For who in the skies can rank with the Lord?
      Who is like the Lord among the sons of God?

8   God is terrible in the council of the holy ones;
      he is great and awesome beyond all round about him.

9   O Lord, God of hosts, who is like you?
      Mighty are you, O Lord, and your faithfulness surrounds you.

10   You rule over the surging of the sea;
      you still the swelling of its waves.

11   You have crushed Rahab with a mortal blow;
      with your strong arm you have scattered your enemies.

12   Yours are the heavens, and yours is the earth;
      the world and its fullness you have founded;

13   North and south you created;
      Thabor and Hermon rejoice at your name.

14   Yours is a mighty arm;
      strong is your hand, exalted your right hand.

15   Justice and judgment are the foundation of your throne;
      kindness and truth go before you.

16   Happy the people who know the joyful shout;
      in the light of your countenance, O Lord, they walk.

17   At your name they rejoice all the day,
      and through your justice they are exalted.

18   For you are the splendor of their strength,
      and by your favor our horn is exalted.

19   For to the Lord belongs our shield,
      and to the Holy One of Israel, our king.

20   Once you spoke in a vision,

and to your faithful ones you said:
"Of a stripling I have made a champion;
over the people I have set a youth.
21 I have found David, my servant;
with my holy oil I have anointed him,
22 That my hand may be always with him,
and that my arm may make him strong.

23 "No enemy shall deceive him,
nor shall the wicked afflict him.
24 But I will crush his foes before him
and those who hate him I will smite.
25 My faithfulness and my kindness shall be with him,
and through my name shall his horn be exalted.
26 I will set his hand upon the sea,
his right hand upon the rivers.

27 "He shall say of me, 'You are my father,
my God, the Rock, my savior.'
28 And I will make him the first-born,
highest of the kings of the earth.
29 Forever I will maintain my kindness toward him,
and my covenant with him stands firm.
30 I will make his posterity endure forever
and his throne as the days of heaven.

31 "If his sons forsake my law
and walk not according to my ordinances,
32 If they violate my statutes
and keep not my commands,
33 I will punish their crime with a rod
and their guilt with stripes.
34 Yet my kindness I will not take from him,
nor will I belie my faithfulness.

35 "I will not violate my covenant;
the promise of my lips I will not alter.
36 Once, by my holiness, have I sworn;
I will not be false to David.
37 His posterity shall continue forever,
and his throne shall be like the sun before me;
38 Like the moon, which remains forever—
a faithful witness in the sky."

39 Yet you have rejected and spurned
   and been enraged at your anointed.
40 You have renounced the covenant with your servant,
   and defiled his crown in the dust.
41 You have broken down all his walls;
   you have laid his strongholds in ruins.
42 All who pass by the way have plundered him;
   he is made the reproach of his neighbors.

43 You have exalted the right hands of his foes,
   you have gladdened all his enemies.
44 You have turned back his sharp sword
   and have not sustained him in battle.
45 You have deprived him of his luster
   and hurled his throne to the ground.
46 You have shortened the days of his youth;
   you have covered him with shame.

47 How long, O Lord? Will you hide yourself forever?
   Will your wrath burn like fire?
48 Remember how short my life is;
   how frail you created all the children of men!
49 What man shall live, and not see death,
   but deliver himself from the power of the nether world?
50 Where are your ancient favors, O Lord,
   which you pledged to David by your faithfulness?
51 Remember, O Lord, the insults to your servants:
   I bear in my bosom all the accusations of the nations
52 With which your enemies have reviled, O Lord,
   with which they have reviled your anointed on his way!

53 Blessed be the Lord forever.
   Amen, and amen!

Psalm 89

1 O Lord, you have been our refuge
   through all generations.
2 Before the mountains were begotten
   and the earth and the world were brought forth,
   from everlasting to everlasting you are God.
3 You turn man back to dust,
   saying, "Return, O children of men."
4 For a thousand years in your sight

are as yesterday, now that it is past,
    or as a watch of the night.
5   You make an end of them in their sleep;
    the next morning they are like the changing grass,
6   Which at dawn springs up anew,
    but by evening wilts and fades.

7   Truly we are consumed by your anger,
    and by your wrath we are put to rout.
8   You have kept our iniquities before you,
    our hidden sins in the light of your scrutiny.
9   All our days have passed away in your indignation;
    we have spent our years like a sigh.
10   Seventy is the sum of our years,
    or eighty, if we are strong,
    And most of them are fruitless toil,
    for they pass quickly and we drift away.
11   Who knows the fury of your anger
    or your indignation toward those who should fear you?

12   Teach us to number our days aright,
    that we may gain wisdom of heart.
13   Return, O Lord! How long?
    Have pity on your servants!
14   Fill us at daybreak with your kindness,
    that we may shout for joy and gladness all our days.
15   Make us glad, for the days when you afflicted us,
    for the years when we saw evil.
16   Let your work be seen by your servants
    and your glory by their children;
17   And may the gracious care of the Lord our God be ours;
    prosper the work of our hands for us!
    Prosper the work of our hands!

Psalm 90

1   You who dwell in the shelter of the Most High,
    who abide in the shadow of the Almighty,
2   Say to the Lord, "My refuge and my fortress,
    my God, in whom I trust."
3   For he will rescue you from the snare of the fowler,
    from the destroying pestilence.
4   With his pinions he will cover you,

and under his wings you shall take refuge;
his faithfulness is a buckler and a shield.
5 You shall not fear the terror of the night
nor the arrow that flies by day;
6 Not the pestilence that roams in darkness
nor the devastating plague at noon.
7 Though a thousand fall at your side,
ten thousand at your right side,
near you it shall not come.
8 Rather with your eyes shall you behold
and see the requital of the wicked,
9 Because you have the Lord for your refuge;
you have made the Most High your stronghold.
10 No evil shall befall you,
nor shall affliction come near your tent,
11 For to his angels he has given command about you,
that they guard you in all your ways.
12 Upon their hands they shall bear you up,
lest you dash your foot against a stone.
13 You shall tread upon the asp and the viper;
you shall trample down the lion and the dragon.

14 Because he clings to me, I will deliver him;
I will set him on high because he acknowledges my name.
15 He shall call upon me, and I will answer him;
I will be with him in distress;
I will deliver him and glorify him;
16 with length of days I will gratify him
and will show him my salvation.

Psalm 91

2 It is good to give thanks to the Lord,
to sing praise to your name, Most High,
3 To proclaim your kindness at dawn
and your faithfulness throughout the night,
4 With ten-stringed instrument and lyre,
with melody upon the harp.
5 For you make me glad, O Lord, by your deeds;
at the works of your hands I rejoice.

6 How great are your works, O Lord!
How very deep are your thoughts!

7	A senseless man knows not,
	nor does a fool understand this.
8	Though the wicked flourish like grass
	and all evildoers thrive,
9	They are destined for eternal destruction;
	while you, O Lord, are the Most High forever.

10	For behold, your enemies, O Lord,
	for behold, your enemies shall perish;
	all evildoers shall be scattered.
11	You have exalted my horn like the wild bull's;
	you have anointed me with rich oil.
12	And my eye has looked down upon my foes,
	and my ears have heard of the fall of my wicked adversaries.

13	The just man shall flourish like the palm tree,
	like a cedar of Lebanon shall he grow.
14	They that are planted in the house of the Lord
	shall flourish in the courts of our God.
15	They shall bear fruit even in old age;
	vigorous and sturdy shall they be,
16	Declaring how just is the Lord,
	my Rock, in whom there is no wrong.

Psalm 92

1	THE LORD is king, in splendor robed;
	robed is the Lord and girt about with strength;
	And he has made the world firm,
	not to be moved.
2	Your throne stands firm from of old;
	from everlasting you are, O Lord.

3	The floods lift up, O Lord,
	the floods lift up their voice;
	the floods lift up their tumult.
4	More powerful than the roar of many waters,
	more powerful than the breakers of the sea—
	powerful on high is the Lord.

5	Your decrees are worthy of trust indeed;
	holiness befits your house,
	O Lord, for length of days.

Psalm 93

1 GOD OF vengeance, Lord,
    God of vengeance, show yourself.
2 Rise up, judge of the earth;
    render their deserts to the proud.
3 How long, O Lord, shall the wicked,
    how long shall the wicked glory,
4 Mouthing insolent speeches,
    boasting, all the evildoers?

5 Your people, O Lord, they trample down,
    your inheritance they afflict.
6 Widow and stranger they slay,
    the fatherless they murder,
7 And they say, "The Lord sees not;
    the God of Jacob perceives not."

8 Understand, you senseless ones among the people;
    and, you fools, when will you be wise?
9 Shall he who shaped the ear not hear?
    or he who formed the eye not see?
10 Shall he who instructs nations not chastise,
    he who teaches men knowledge?
11 The Lord knows the thoughts of men,
    and that they are vain.

12 Happy the man whom you instruct, O Lord,
    whom by your law you teach,
13 Giving him rest from evil days,
    till the pit be dug for the wicked.
14 For the Lord will not cast off his people,
    nor abandon his inheritance;
15 But judgment shall again be with justice,
    and all the upright of heart shall follow it.

16 Who will rise up for me against the wicked?
    Who will stand by me against the evildoers?
17 Were not the Lord my help,
    I would soon dwell in the silent grave.
18 When I say, "My foot is slipping,"
    your kindness, O Lord, sustains me;
19 When cares abound within me,
    your comfort gladdens my soul.

20 How could the tribunal of wickedness be leagued with you,
    which creates burdens in the guise of law?
21 Though they attack the life of the just
    and condemn innocent blood,
22 Yet the Lord is my stronghold,
    and my God the Rock of my refuge.
23 And he will requite them for their evildoing,
    and for their wickedness he will destroy them;
    the Lord, our God, will destroy them.

Psalm 94

1 COME, let us sing joyfully to the Lord;
    let us acclaim the Rock of our salvation.
2 Let us greet him with thanksgiving;
    let us joyfully sing psalms to him
3 For the Lord is a great God,
    and a great king above all gods;
4 In his hands are the depths of the earth,
    and the tops of the mountains are his.
5 His is the sea, for he has made it,
    and the dry land, which his hands have formed.

6 Come, let us bow down in worship;
    let us kneel before the Lord who made us.
7 For he is our God,
    and we are the people he shepherds, the flock he guides.

Oh, that today you would hear his voice:
8   "Harden not your hearts as at Meriba,
    as in the day of Massa in the desert,
9 Where your fathers tempted me;
    they tested me though they had seen my works.
10 Forty years I loathed that generation,
    and I said: They are a people of erring heart,
    and they know not my ways.
11 Therefore I swore in my anger:
    They shall not enter into my rest."

Psalm 95

1 Sing to the Lord a new song;
    sing to the Lord, all you lands.

2   Sing to the Lord; bless his name;
      announce his salvation, day after day.
3   Tell his glory among the nations;
      among all peoples, his wondrous deeds.

4   For great is the Lord and highly to be praised;
      awesome is he, beyond all gods.
5   For all the gods of the nations are things of nought,
      but the Lord made the heavens.
6   Splendor and majesty go before him;
      praise and grandeur are in his sanctuary.

7   Give to the Lord, you families of nations,
      give to the Lord glory and praise;
8   give to the Lord the glory due his name!
   Bring gifts, and enter his courts;
9   worship the Lord in holy attire.
   Tremble before him, all the earth;
10   say among the nations: The Lord is king.
   He has made the world firm, not to be moved;
      he governs the peoples with equity.

11   Let the heavens be glad and the earth rejoice;
      let the sea and what fills it resound;
12   let the plains be joyful and all that is in them!
   Then shall all the trees of the forest exult
13   before the Lord, for he comes;
      for he comes to rule the earth.
   He shall rule the world with justice
      and the peoples with his constancy.

Psalm 96

1   THE LORD is king; let the earth rejoice;
      let the many isles be glad.
2   Clouds and darkness are round about him,
      justice and judgment are the foundation of his throne.
3   Fire goes before him
      and consumes his foes round about.
4   His lightnings illumine the world;
      the earth sees and trembles.
5   The mountains melt like wax before the Lord,
      before the Lord of all the earth.

6   The heavens proclaim his justice,
       and all peoples see his glory.

7   All who worship graven things are put to shame,
       who glory in the things of nought;
       all gods are prostrate before him.

8   Sion hears and is glad,
       and the cities of Juda rejoice
       because of your judgments, O Lord.

9   Because you, O Lord, are the Most High over all the earth,
       exalted far above all gods.

10   The Lord loves those that hate evil;
       he guards the lives of his faithful ones;
       from the hand of the wicked he delivers them.

11   Light dawns for the just;
       and gladness, for the upright of heart.

12   Be glad in the Lord, you just,
       and give thanks to his holy name.

Psalm 97

1   SING to the Lord a new song,
       for he has done wondrous deeds;
    His right hand has won victory for him,
       his holy arm.

2   The Lord has made his salvation known:
       in the sight of the nations he has revealed his justice.

3   He has remembered his kindness and his faithfulness
       toward the house of Israel.
    All the ends of the earth have seen
       the salvation by our God.

4   Sing joyfully to the Lord, all you lands;
       break into song; sing praise.

5   Sing praise to the Lord with the harp,
       with the harp and melodious song.

6   With tumpets and the sound of the horn
       sing joyfully before the King, the Lord.

7   Let the sea and what fills it resound,
       the world and those who dwell in it;

8   Let the rivers clap their hands,
       the mountains shout with them for joy

9 Before the Lord, for he comes,
    for he comes to rule the earth;
    He will rule the world with justice
    and the peoples with equity.

Psalm 98

1 THE LORD is king; the peoples tremble;
    he is throned upon the cherubim; the earth quakes.
2 The Lord in Sion is great,
    he is high above all the peoples.
3 Let them praise your great and awesome name;
    holy is he!

4 The King in his might loves justice;
    you have established equity;
    justice and judgment in Jacob you have wrought.
5   Extol the Lord, our God,
      and worship at his footstool;
      holy is he!

6 Moses and Aaron were among his priests,
    and Samuel, among those who called upon his name;
    they called upon the Lord, and he answered them.
7 From the pillar of cloud he spoke to them;
    they heard his decrees and the law he gave them.
8 O Lord, our God, you answered them;
    a forgiving God you were to them,
    though requiting their misdeeds.
9   Extol the Lord, our God,
      and worship at his holy mountain;
      for holy is the Lord, our God.

Psalm 99

1 SING joyfully to the Lord, all you lands;
2   serve the Lord with gladness;
    come before him with joyful song.
3 Know that the Lord is God;
    he made us, his we are;
    his people, the flock he tends.
4 Enter his gates with thanksgiving,
    his courts with praise;
5 Give thanks to him; bless his name, for he is good:

the Lord, whose kindness endures forever,
and his faithfulness, to all generations.

Psalm 100

1 Of KINDNESS and judgment I will sing;
to you, O Lord, I will sing praise.
2 I will persevere in the way of integrity;
when will you come to me?

I will walk in the integrity of my heart,
within my house;
3 I will not set before my eyes
any base thing.
I hate him who does perversely;
he shall not remain with me.
4 A crooked heart shall be far from me;
evil I will not know.
5 Whoever slanders his neighbor in secret,
him will I destroy.
The man of haughty eyes and puffed-up heart
I will not endure.
6 My eyes are upon the faithful of the land,
that they may dwell with me.
He who walks in the way of integrity
shall be in my service.
7 He shall not dwell within my house
who practices deceit.
He who speaks falsehood shall not stand
before my eyes.
8 Each morning I will destroy
all the wicked of the land,
And uproot from the city of the Lord
all evildoers.

Psalm 101

2 O Lord, hear my prayer,
and let my cry come to you.
3 Hide not your face from me
in the day of my distress.
Incline your ear to me;
in the day when I call, answer me speedily.

4 For my days vanish like smoke,
  and my bones burn like fire.
5 Withered and dried up like grass is my heart;
  I forget to eat my bread.
6 Because of my insistent sighing
  I am reduced to skin and bone.
7 I am like a desert owl;
  I have become like an owl among the ruins.
8 I am sleepless, and I moan;
  I am like a sparrow alone on the housetop.
9 All the day my enemies revile me;
  in their rage against me they make a curse of me.
10 For I eat ashes like bread
  and mingle my drink with tears,
11 Because of your fury and your wrath;
  for you lifted me up only to cast me down.
12 My days are like a lengthening shadow,
  and I wither like grass.

13 But you, O Lord, abide forever,
  and your name through all generations.
14 You will arise and have mercy on Sion,
    for it is time to pity her,
    for the appointed time has come.
15 For her stones are dear to your servants,
  and her dust moves them to pity.
16 And the nations shall revere your name, O Lord,
  and all the kings of the earth your glory,
17 When the Lord has rebuilt Sion
  and appeared in his glory;
18 When he has regarded the prayer of the destitute,
  and not despised their prayer.

19 Let this be written for the generation to come,
  and let his future creatures praise the Lord:
20 "The Lord looked down from his holy height,
  from heaven he beheld the earth,
21 To hear the groaning of the prisoners,
  to release those doomed to die"—
22 That the name of the Lord may be declared in Sion;
  and his praise, in Jerusalem,
23 When the peoples gather together,
  and the kingdoms, to serve the Lord.

24   He has broken down my strength in the way;
  he has cut short my days.
25   I say: O my God,
Take me not hence in the midst of my days;
  through all generations your years endure.
26   Of old you established the earth,
  and the heavens are the work of your hands.
27   They shall perish, but you remain
  though all of them grow old like a garment.
Like clothing you change them, and they are changed,
28   but you are the same, and your years have no end.
29   The children of your servants shall abide,
  and their posterity shall continue in your presence.

Psalm 102

1   Bless the Lord, O my soul;
  and all my being, bless his holy name.
2   Bless the Lord, O my soul,
  and forget not all his benefits;
3   He pardons all your iniquities,
  he heals all your ills.
4   He redeems your life from destruction,
  he crowns you with kindness and compassion,
5   He fills your lifetime with good;
  your youth is renewed like the eagle's.

6   The Lord secures justice
  and the rights of all the oppressed.
7   He has made known his ways to Moses,
  and his deeds to the children of Israel.
8   Merciful and gracious is the Lord,
  slow to anger and abounding in kindness.
9   He will not always chide,
  nor does he keep his wrath forever.
10   Not according to our sins does he deal with us,
  nor does he requite us according to our crimes.

11   For as the heavens are high above the earth,
  so surpassing is his kindness toward those who fear him.
12   As far as the east is from the west,
  so far has he put our transgressions from us.
13   As a father has compassion on his children,
  so the Lord has compassion on those who fear him,

14 For he knows how we are formed;
   he remembers that we are dust.

15 Man's days are like those of grass;
   like a flower of the field he blooms;
16 The wind sweeps over him and he is gone,
   and his place knows him no more.
17 But the kindness of the Lord is from eternity
   to eternity toward those who fear him,
   And his justice toward children's children
18 among those who keep his covenant
   and remember to fulfill his precepts.

19 The Lord has established his throne in heaven,
   and his kingdom rules over all.
20 Bless the Lord, all you his angels,
   you mighty in strength, who do his bidding,
   obeying his spoken word.
21 Bless the Lord, all you his hosts,
   his ministers, who do his will.
22 Bless the Lord, all his works,
   everywhere in his domain.
   Bless the Lord, O my soul!

Psalm 103

1 Bless the Lord, O my soul!
   O Lord, my God, you are great indeed!
   You are clothed with majesty and glory,
2 robed in light as with a cloak.
   You have spread out the heavens like a tent-cloth;
3 you have constructed your palace upon the waters.
   You make the clouds your chariot;
   you travel on the wings of the wind.
4 You make the winds your messengers,
   and flaming fire your ministers.

5 You fixed the earth upon its foundation,
   not to be moved forever;
6 With the ocean, as with a garment, you covered it;
   above the mountains the waters stood.
7 At your rebuke they fled,
   at the sound of your thunder they took to flight;

8 As the mountains rose, they went down the valleys
  to the place you had fixed for them.
9 You set a limit they may not pass,
  nor shall they cover the earth again.

10 You send forth springs into the watercourses
  that wind among the mountains,
11 And give drink to every beast of the field,
  till the wild asses quench their thirst.
12 Beside them the birds of heaven dwell;
  from among the branches they send forth their song.
13 You water the mountains from your palace;
  the earth is replete with the fruit of your works.
14 You raise grass for the cattle,
  and vegetation for men's use,
 Producing bread from the earth,
15 and wine to gladden men's hearts,
 So that their faces gleam with oil,
  and bread fortifies the hearts of men.
16 Well watered are the trees of the Lord,
  the cedars of Lebanon, which he planted;
17 In them the birds build their nests;
  fir trees are the home of the stork.
18 The high mountains are for wild goats;
  the cliffs are a refuge for rock-badgers.

19 You made the moon to mark the seasons;
  the sun knows the hour of its setting.
20 You bring darkness, and it is night;
  then all the beasts of the forest roam about;
21 Young lions roar for the prey
  and seek their food from God.
22 When the sun rises, they withdraw
  and couch in their dens.
23 Man goes forth to his work
  and to his tillage till the evening.

24 How manifold are your works, O Lord!
  In wisdom you have wrought them all—
  the earth is full of your creatures;
25 The sea also, great and wide,
  in which are schools without number
  of living things both small and great,

26   And where ships move about
        with Leviathan, which you formed to make sport of it.

27   They all look to you
        to give them food in due time.
28   When you give it to them, they gather it;
        when you open your hand,
        they are filled with good things.
29   If you hide your face, they are dismayed;
        if you take away their breath, they perish
        and return to their dust.
30   When you send forth your spirit, they are created,
        and you renew the face of the earth.

31   May the glory of the Lord endure forever;
        may the Lord be glad in his works!
32   He who looks upon the earth, and it trembles;
        who touches the mountains, and they smoke!
33   I will sing to the Lord all my life;
        I will sing praise to my God while I live.
34   Pleasing to him be my theme;
        I will be glad in the Lord.
35   May sinners cease from the earth,
        and may the wicked be no more.
        Bless the Lord, O my soul!   Alleluia.

Psalm 104

1   GIVE thanks to the Lord, invoke his name;
        make known among the nations his deeds.
2   Sing to him, sing his praise,
        proclaim all his wondrous deeds.
3   Glory in his holy name;
        rejoice, O hearts that seek the Lord!
4   Look to the Lord in his strength;
        seek to serve him constantly.
5   Recall the wondrous deeds that he has wrought,
        his portents, and the judgments he has uttered,
6   You descendants of Abraham, his servants,
        sons of Jacob, his chosen ones!

7   He, the Lord, is our God;
        throughout the earth his judgments prevail.

8	He remembers forever his covenant
	which he made binding for a thousand generations—
9	Which he entered into with Abraham
	and by his oath to Isaac;
10	Which he established for Jacob by statute,
	for Israel as an everlasting covenant,
11	Saying, "To you will I give the land of Chanaan
	as your allotted inheritance."
12	When they were few in number,
	a handful, and strangers there,
13	Wandering from nation to nation
	and from one kingdom to another people,
14	He let no man oppress them,
	and for their sake he rebuked kings:
15	"Touch not my anointed,
	and to my prophets do no harm."
16	When he called down a famine on the land
	and ruined the crop that sustained them,
17	He sent a man before them,
	Joseph, sold as a slave;
18	They had weighed him down with fetters,
	and he was bound with chains,
19	Till his prediction came to pass
	and the word of the Lord proved him true.
20	The king sent and released him,
	the ruler of the peoples set him free.
21	He made him lord of his house
	and ruler of all his possessions,
22	That he might train his princes to be like him
	and teach his elders wisdom.
23	Then Israel came to Egypt,
	and Jacob sojourned in the land of Ham.
24	He greatly increased his people
	and made them stronger than their foes,
25	Whose hearts he changed, so that they hated his people,
	and dealt deceitfully with his servants.
26	He sent Moses his servant;
	Aaron, whom he had chosen.
27	They wrought his signs among them,
	and wonders in the land of Ham.

28 He sent the darkness; it grew dark,
  but they rebelled against his words.
29 He turned their waters into blood
  and killed their fish.
30 Their land swarmed with frogs,
  even in the chambers of their kings.
31 He spoke, and there came swarms of flies;
  gnats, throughout all their borders.
32 For rain he gave them hail,
  with flashing fires throughout their land.
33 He struck down their vines and their fig trees
  and shattered the trees throughout their borders.
34 He spoke, and there came locusts
  and grasshoppers without number;
35 And they devoured every plant throughout the land;
  they devoured the fruit of their soil.
36 Then he struck every first-born throughout their land,
  the first fruits of all their manhood.
37 And he led them forth laden with silver and gold,
  with not a weakling among their tribes.
38 Egypt rejoiced at their going,
  for the dread of them had fallen upon it.

39 He spread a cloud to cover them
  and fire to give them light by night.
40 They asked, and he brought them quail,
  and with bread from heaven he satisfied them.
41 He cleft the rock, and the water gushed forth;
  it flowed through the dry lands like a stream,
42 For he remembered his holy word
  to his servant Abraham.
43 And he led forth his people with joy;
  with shouts of joy, his chosen ones.

44 And he gave them the lands of the nations,
  and they took what the peoples had toiled for,
45 That they might keep his statutes
  and observe his laws. Alleluia.

Psalm 105

1 GIVE thanks to the Lord, for he is good,
  for his kindness endures forever.

2 Who can tell the mighty deeds of the Lord,
     or proclaim all his praises?
3 Happy are they who observe what is right,
     who do always what is just.
4 Remember me, O Lord, as you favor your people;
     visit me with your saving help,
5 That I may see the prosperity of your chosen ones,
     rejoice in the joy of your people,
     and glory with your inheritance.

6 We have sinned, we and our fathers;
     we have committed crimes; we have done wrong.
7 Our fathers in Egypt
     considered not your wonders;
   They remembered not your abundant kindness,
     but rebelled against the Most High at the Red Sea.
8 Yet he saved them for his name's sake,
     to make known his power.
9 He rebuked the Red Sea, and it was dried up,
     and he led them through the deep as through a desert.
10 He saved them from hostile hands
     and freed them from the hands of the enemy.
11 The waters covered their foes;
     not one of them was left.
12 Then they believed his words
     and sang his praises.

13 But soon they forgot his works;
     they waited not for his counsel.
14 They gave way to craving in the desert
     and tempted God in the wilderness.
15 He gave them what they asked
     but sent a wasting disease against them.

16 They envied Moses in the camp,
     and Aaron, the holy one of the Lord.
17 The earth opened and swallowed up Dathan,
     and covered the faction of Abiram.
18 Fire broke out against their faction;
     a flame consumed the wicked.

19 They made a calf in Horeb
     and adored a molten image;

20	They exchanged their glory for the image of a grass-eating bullock.
21	They forgot the God who had saved them, who had done great deeds in Egypt,
22	Wondrous deeds in the land of Ham, terrible things at the Red Sea.

23	Then he spoke of exterminating them,
	    but Moses, his chosen one,
	Withstood him in the breach
	    to turn back his destructive wrath.

24	Yet they despised the desirable land; they believed not his word.
25	They murmured in their tents, and obeyed not the voice of the Lord.
26	Then with raised hand he swore against them to let them perish in the desert,
27	To scatter their descendants among the nations, and to disperse them over the lands.
28	And they submitted to the rites of Beelphegor and ate the sacrifices of dead gods.
29	They provoked him by their deeds, and a plague attacked them.
30	Then Phinees stood forth in judgment and the plague was checked;
31	And it was imputed to him for merit through all generations forever.
32	They angered him at the waters of Meriba, and Moses fared ill on their account,
33	For they embittered his spirit, and the rash utterance passed his lips.
34	They did not exterminate the peoples, as the Lord had commanded them,
35	But mingled with the nations and learned their works.
36	They served their idols, which became a snare for them.
37	They sacrificed their sons and their daughters to demons,
38	And they shed innocent blood, the blood of their sons and their daughters,

Whom they sacrificed to the idols of Chanaan,
    desecrating the land with bloodshed;
39   They became defiled by their works,
    and wanton in their crimes.

40   And the Lord grew angry with his people,
    and abhorred his inheritance;
41   He gave them over into the hands of the nations,
    and their foes ruled over them.
42   Their enemies oppressed them,
    and they were humbled under their power.
43   Many times did he rescue them,
    but they embittered him with their counsels
    and were brought low by their guilt.
44   Yet he had regard for their affliction
    when he heard their cry;
45   And for their sake he was mindful of his covenant
    and relented, in his abundant kindness,
46   And he won for them compassion
    from all who held them captive.

47   Save us, O Lord, our God,
    and gather us from among the nations,
    That we may give thanks to your holy name
    and glory in praising you.

48   Blessed be the Lord, the God of Israel,
    through all eternity!
    Let all the people say, Amen!   Alleluia.

Psalm 106

1   "Give thanks to the Lord, for he is good,
    for his kindness endures forever!"
2   Thus let the redeemed of the Lord say,
    those whom he has redeemed from the hand of the foe
3   And gathered from the lands,
    from the east and the west, from the north and the south.

4   They went astray in the desert wilderness;
    the way to an inhabited city they did not find.
5   Hungry and thirsty,
    their life was wasting away within them.

6   They cried to the Lord in their distress;
        from their straits he rescued them.

7   And he led them by a direct way
      to reach an inhabited city.

8   Let them give thanks to the Lord for his kindness
        and his wondrous deeds to the children of men,

9   Because he satisfied the longing soul
      and filled the hungry soul with good things.

10   They dwelt in darkness and gloom,
      bondsmen in want and in chains,

11   Because they had rebelled against the words of God
      and scorned the counsel of the Most High.

12   And he humbled their hearts with trouble;
      when they stumbled, there was no one to help them.

13   They cried to the Lord in their distress;
        from their straits he rescued them.

14   And he led them forth from darkness and gloom
      and broke their bonds asunder.

15   Let them give thanks to the Lord for his kindness
        and his wondrous deeds to the children of men,

16   Because he shattered the gates of brass
      and burst the bars of iron.

17   Stricken because of their wicked ways
      and afflicted because of their sins,

18   They loathed all manner of food,
      so that they were near the gates of death.

19   They cried to the Lord in their distress;
        from their straits he rescued them.

20   He sent forth his word to heal them
      and to snatch them from destruction.

21   Let them give thanks to the Lord for his kindness
        and his wondrous deeds to the children of men.

22   Let them make thank offerings
      and declare his works with shouts of joy.

23   They who sailed the sea in ships,
      trading on the deep waters,

24   These saw the works of the Lord
      and his wonders in the abyss.

25   His command raised up a storm wind
      which tossed its waves on high.

26 They mounted up to heaven; they sank to the depths;
   their hearts melted away in their plight.

27 They reeled and staggered like drunken men,
   and all their skill was swallowed up.

28   They cried to the Lord in their distress;
           from their straits he rescued them.

29 He hushed the storm to a gentle breeze,
   and the billows of the sea were stilled;

30 They rejoiced that they were calmed,
   and he brought them to their desired haven.

31   Let them give thanks to the Lord for his kindness
           and his wondrous deeds to the children of men.

32 Let them extol him in the assembly of the people
   and praise him in the council of the elders.

33 He changed rivers into desert,
   water springs into thirsty ground,

34 Fruitful land into salt marsh,
   because of the wickedness of its inhabitants.

35 He changed the desert into pools of water,
   waterless land into water springs.

36 And there he settled the hungry,
   and they built a city to dwell in.

37 They sowed fields and planted vineyards,
   And they obtained a fruitful yield.

38 He blessed them, and they became very many;
   nor did he suffer their cattle to decrease.

39 And they dwindled and were brought low
   through oppression, affliction and sorrow.

40 But he who pours out contempt upon princes,
   and sends them astray through a trackless waste,

41 Lifted up the needy out of misery
   and made the families numerous like flocks.

42 The upright see this and rejoice,
   and all wickedness closes its mouth.

43 Who is wise enough to observe these things
   and to understand the favors of the Lord?

Psalm 107

2   MY HEART is steadfast, O God; my heart is steadfast;
         I will sing and chant praise.

3 Awake, O my soul; awake, lyre and harp;
  I will wake the dawn.
4 I will give thanks to you among the peoples, O Lord;
  I will chant your praise among the nations,
5 For your kindness towers to the heavens,
  and your faithfulness to the skies.
6 Be exalted above the heavens, O God;
  over all the earth be your glory!
7 That your loved ones may escape,
  help us by your right hand, and answer us.

8 God promised in his sanctuary:
  "Exultantly I will apportion Sichem,
  and measure off the valley of Succhoth;
9 Mine is Galaad, and mine Manasse,
  Ephraim is the helmet for my head; Juda, my scepter;
10 Moab shall serve as my washbowl;
  upon Edom I will set my shoe;
  I will triumph over Philistia."

11 Who will bring me into the fortified city?
  Who will lead me into Edom?
12 Have not you, O God, rejected us,
  So that you go not forth, O God, with our armies?
13 Give us aid against the foe,
  for worthless is the help of men.
14 Under God we shall do valiantly;
  it is he who will tread down our foes.

Psalm 108

1 O GOD, whom I praise, be not silent,
2 for they have opened wicked and treacherous mouths
  against me.
They have spoken to me with lying tongues,
3 and with words of hatred they have encompassed me
  and attacked me without cause.
4 In return for my love they slandered me,
  but I prayed.
5 They repaid me evil for good
  and hatred for my love.

6 Raise up a wicked man against him,
  and let the accuser stand at his right hand.

7	When he is judged, let him go forth condemned,
	and may his plea be in vain.
8	May his days be few;
	may another take his office.
9	May his children be fatherless,
	and his wife a widow.
10	May his children be roaming vagrants and beggars;
	may they be cast out of the ruins of their homes.
11	May the usurer ensnare all his belongings,
	and strangers plunder the fruit of his labors.
12	May there be no one to do him a kindness,
	nor anyone to pity his orphans.
13	May his posterity meet with destruction;
	in the next generation may their name be blotted out.
14	May the guilt of his fathers be remembered by the Lord;
	let not his mother's sin be blotted out;
15	May they be continually before the Lord,
	till he banish the memory of these parents from the earth,
16	Because he remembered not to show kindness,
	but persecuted the wretched and poor
	and the brokenhearted, to do them to death.
17	He loved cursing; may it come upon him;
	he took no delight in blessing; may it be far from him.
18	And may he be clothed with cursing as with a robe;
	may it penetrate into his entrails like water
	and like oil into his bones;
19	May it be for him like a garment which covers him,
	like a girdle which is always about him.
20	May this be the recompense from the Lord upon my accusers
	and upon those who speak evil against me.
21	But do you, O God, my Lord,
	deal kindly with me for your name's sake;
	in your generous kindness rescue me;
22	For I am wretched and poor,
	and my heart is pierced within me.
23	Like a lengthening shadow I pass away;
	I am swept away like the locust.
24	My knees totter from my fasting,
	and my flesh is wasted of its substance.
25	And I am become a mockery to them;
	when they see me, they shake their heads.
26	Help me, O Lord, my God;
	save me, in your kindness,

27	And let them know that this is your hand;

27 And let them know that this is your hand;
   that you, O Lord, have done this.
28 Let them curse, but do you bless;
   may my adversaries be put to shame,
   but let your servant rejoice.
29 Let my accusers be clothed with disgrace
   and let them wear their shame like a mantle.
30 I will speak my thanks earnestly to the Lord,
   and in the midst of the throng I will praise him,
31 For he stood at the right hand of the poor man,
   to save him from those who would condemn him.

Psalm 109

1 THE LORD said to my Lord: "Sit at my right hand
   till I make your enemies your footstool."
2 The scepter of your power the Lord will stretch forth from Sion:
   "Rule in the midst of your enemies.
3 Yours is princely power
   in the day of your birth, in holy splendor;
   before the daystar, like the dew, I have begotten you."

4 The Lord has sworn, and he will not repent:
   "You are a priest forever,
   according to the order of Melchisedec."

5 The Lord is at your right hand;
   he will crush kings on the day of his wrath.
6 He will do judgment on the nations, heaping up corpses;
   he will crush heads over the wide earth.
7 From the brook by the wayside he will drink;
   therefore will he lift up his head.

Psalm 110

1 I WILL give thanks to the Lord with all my heart
   in the company and assembly of the just.
2 Great are the works of the Lord,
   exquisite in all their delights.
3 Majesty and glory are his work,
   and his justice endures forever.
4 He has won renown for his wondrous deeds;
   gracious and merciful is the Lord.

5   He has given food to those who fear him;
        he will forever be mindful of his covenant.
6   He has made known to his people the power of his works,
        giving them the inheritance of the nations.
7   The works of his hands are faithful and just;
        sure are all his precepts,
8   Reliable forever and ever,
        wrought in truth and equity.
9   He has sent deliverance to his people;
        he has ratified his covenant forever;
        holy and awesome is his name.
10 The fear of the Lord is the beginning of wisdom;
        prudent are all who live by it.
        His praise endures forever.

Psalm 111

1   HAPPY the man who fears the Lord,
        who greatly delights in his commands.
2   His posterity shall be mighty upon the earth;
        the upright generation shall be blessed.
3   Wealth and riches shall be in his house;
        his generosity shall endure forever.
4   He dawns through the darkness, a light for the upright;
        he is gracious and merciful and just.
5   Well for the man who is gracious and lends,
        who conducts his affairs with justice;
6   He shall never be moved;
        the just man shall be in everlasting remembrance.
7   An evil report he shall not fear;
        his heart is firm, trusting in the Lord.
8   His heart is steadfast; he shall not fear
        till he looks down upon his foes.
9   Lavishly he gives to the poor;
        his generosity shall endure forever;
        his horn shall be exalted in glory.
10 The wicked man shall see it and be vexed;
        he shall gnash his teeth and pine away;
        the desire of the wicked shall perish.

Psalm 112

1   PRAISE, you servants of the Lord,
        praise the name of the Lord.

2   Blessed be the name of the Lord
        both now and forever.
3   From the rising to the setting of the sun
        is the name of the Lord to be praised.

4   High above all nations is the Lord;
        above the heavens is his glory.
5   Who is like the Lord, our God, who is enthroned on high
6   and looks upon the heavens and the earth below?

7   He raises up the lowly from the dust;
        from the dunghill he lifts up the poor
8   To seat them with princes,
        with the princes of his own people.
9   He establishes in her home the barren wife
        as the joyful mother of children.

Psalm 113a

1   WHEN Israel came forth from Egypt,
        the house of Jacob from a people of alien tongue,
2   Juda became his sanctuary,
        Israel his domain.

3   The sea beheld and fled;
        Jordan turned back.
4   The mountains skipped like rams,
        the hills like the lambs of the flock.

5   Why is it, O sea, that you flee?
        O Jordan, that you turn back?
6   You mountains, that you skip like rams?
        You hills, like the lambs of the flock?

7   Before the face of the Lord, tremble, O earth,
        before the face of the God of Jacob,
8   Who turned the rock into pools of water,
        the flint into flowing springs.

Psalm 113b

1   NOT TO us, O Lord, not to us
        but to your name give glory
        because of your kindness, because of your truth.

2 Why should the pagans say,
  "Where is their God?"
3 Our God is in heaven;
  whatever he wills, he does.

4 Their idols are silver and gold,
  the handiwork of men.
5 They have mouths but speak not;
  they have eyes but see not;
6 They have ears but hear not;
  they have noses but smell not;
7 They have hands but feel not;
  they have feet but walk not;
  they utter no sound from their throat.
8 Their makers shall be like them,
  everyone that trusts in them.

9 The house of Israel trusts in the Lord;
  he is their help and their shield.
10 The house of Aaron trusts in the Lord;
  he is their help and their shield.
11 Those who fear the Lord trust in the Lord;
  he is their help and their shield.
12 The Lord remembers us and will bless us:
  he will bless the house of Israel;
  he will bless the house of Aaron;
13 He will bless those who fear the Lord,
  both the small and the great.
14 May the Lord bless you more and more,
  both you and your children.
15 May you be blessed by the Lord,
  who made heaven and earth.
16 Heaven is the heaven of the Lord,
  but the earth he has given to the children of men.
17 It is not the dead who praise the Lord,
  nor those who go down into silence;
18 But we bless the Lord,
  both now and forever.

Psalm 114

1 I LOVE the Lord because he has heard
  my voice in supplication,

2   Because he has inclined his ear to me
        the day I called.
3   The cords of death encompassed me;
        the snares of the nether world seized upon me;
        I fell into distress and sorrow,
4   And I called upon the name of the Lord,
    "O Lord, save my life!"

5   Gracious is the Lord and just;
        yes, our God is merciful.
6   The Lord keeps the little ones;
        I was brought low, and he saved me.
7   Return, O my soul, to your tranquillity,
        for the Lord has been good to you.
8   For he has freed my soul from death,
        my eyes from tears, my feet from stumbling.
9   I shall walk before the Lord
        in the lands of the living.

Psalm 115

1   I BELIEVED, even when I said,
    "I am greatly afflicted";
2   I said in my alarm,
    "No man is dependable."

3   How shall I make a return to the Lord
        for all the good he has done for me?
4   The cup of salvation I will take up,
        and I will call upon the name of the Lord;
5   My vows to the Lord I will pay
        in the presence of all his people.
6   Precious in the eyes of the Lord
        is the death of his faithful ones.

7   O Lord, I am your servant;
        I am your servant, the son of your handmaid;
        you have loosed my bonds.
8   To you will I offer sacrifice of thanksgiving,
        and I will call upon the name of the Lord.
9   My vows to the Lord I will pay
        in the presence of all his people,
10 In the courts of the house of the Lord,
        in your midst, O Jerusalem.

Psalm 116

1   PRAISE the Lord, all you nations;
                glorify him, all you peoples!

2   For steadfast is his kindness toward us,
                and the fidelity of the Lord endures forever.

Psalm 117

1   GIVE thanks to the Lord, for he is good,
                for his mercy endures forever.

2   Let the house of Israel say,
                "His mercy endures forever."

3   Let the house of Aaron say,
                "His mercy endures forever."

4   Let those who fear the Lord say,
                "His mercy endures forever."

5   In my straits I called upon the Lord;
                the Lord answered me and set me free.

6   The Lord is with me; I fear not;
                what can man do against me?

7   The Lord is with me to help me,
                and I shall look down upon my foes.

8   It is better to take refuge in the Lord
                than to trust in man.

9   It is better to take refuge in the Lord
                than to trust in princes.

10   All the nations encompassed me;
                in the name of the Lord I crushed them.

11   They encompassed me on every side;
                in the name of the Lord I crushed them.

12   They encompassed me like bees,
                they flared up like fire among thorns;
                in the name of the Lord I crushed them.

13   I was hard pressed and was falling,
                but the Lord helped me.

14   My strength and my courage is the Lord,
                and he has been my savior.

15   The joyful shout of victory
                in the tents of the just:
        "The right hand of the Lord has struck with power:

16   the right hand of the Lord is exalted;
         the right hand of the Lord has struck with power."
17   I shall not die, but live,
         and declare the works of the Lord.
18   Though the Lord has indeed chastised me,
         yet he has not delivered me to death.

19   Open to me the gates of justice;
         I will enter them and give thanks to the Lord.

20   This gate is the Lord's;
         the just shall enter it.

21   I will give thanks to you, for you have answered me
         and have been my savior.

22   The stone which the builders rejected
         has become the cornerstone.
23   By the Lord has this been done;
         it is wonderful in our eyes.

24   This is the day the Lord has made;
         let us be glad and rejoice in it.
25   O Lord, grant salvation!
         O Lord, grant prosperity!

26   Blessed is he who comes in the name of the Lord;
         we bless you from the house of the Lord.
27   The Lord is God, and he has given us light.
      Join in procession with leafy boughs
         up to the horns of the altar.

28   You are my God, and I give thanks to you;
         O my God, I extol you.
29   Give thanks to the Lord, for he is good;
         for his kindness endures forever.

Psalm 118

1   HAPPY are they whose way is blameless,
         who walk in the law of the Lord.
2   Happy are they who observe his decrees,
         who seek him with all their heart,
3   And do no wrong,
         but walk in his ways.

4 You have commanded that your precepts
      be diligently kept.
5 Oh, that I might be firm in the ways
      of keeping your statutes!
6 Then should I not be put to shame
      when I beheld all your commands.
7 I will give you thanks with an upright heart,
      when I have learned your just ordinances.
8 I will keep your statutes;
      do not utterly forsake me.

9 How shall a young man be faultless in his way?
      By keeping to your words.
10 With all my heart I seek you;
      let me not stray from your commands.
11 Within my heart I treasure your promise,
      that I may not sin against you.
12 Blessed are you, O Lord;
      teach me your statutes.
13 With my lips I declare
      all the ordinances of your mouth.
14 In the way of your decrees I rejoice,
      as much as in all riches.
15 I will meditate on your precepts
      and consider your ways.
16 In your statutes I will delight;
      I will not forget your words.

17 Be good to your servant, that I may live
      and keep your words.
18 Open my eyes, that I may consider
      the wonders of your law.
19 I am a wayfarer of earth;
      hide not your commands from me.
20 My soul is consumed with longing
      for your ordinances at all times.
21 You rebuke the accursed proud,
      who turn away from your commands.
22 Take away from me reproach and contempt,
      for I observe your decrees.
23 Though princes meet and talk against me,
      your servant meditates on your statutes.
24 Yes, your decrees are my delight;
      they are my counselors.

25 I lie prostrate in the dust;
    give me life according to your word.
26 I declared my ways, and you answered me;
    teach me your statutes.
27 Make me understand the way of your precepts,
    and I will meditate on your wondrous deeds.
28 My soul weeps for sorrow;
    strengthen me according to your words.
29 Remove from me the way of falsehood,
    and favor me with your law.
30 The way of truth I have chosen;
    I have set your ordinances before me.
31 I cling to your decrees;
    O Lord, let me not be put to shame.
32 I will run the way of your commands
    when you give me a docile heart.

33 Instruct me, O Lord, in the way of your statutes,
    that I may exactly observe them.
34 Give me discernment, that I may observe your law
    and keep it with all my heart.
35 Lead me in the path of your commands,
    for in it I delight.
36 Incline my heart to your decrees
    and not to gain.
37 Turn away my eyes from seeing what is vain;
    by your way give me life.
38 Fulfill for your servant
    your promise to those who fear you.
39 Turn away from me the reproach which I dread,
    for your ordinances are good.
40 Behold, I long for your precepts;
    in your justice give me life.

41 Let your kindness come to me, O Lord,
    your salvation according to your promise.
42 So shall I have an answer for those who reproach me,
    for I trust in your words.
43 Take not the word of truth from my mouth,
    for in your ordinances is my hope;
44 And I will keep your law continually,
    forever and ever.
45 And I will walk at liberty,
    because I seek your precepts.

46 I will speak of your decrees before kings
  without being ashamed.
47 And I will delight in your commands,
  which I love.
48 And I will lift up my hands to your commands
  and meditate on your statutes.

49 Remember your word to your servant
  since you have given me hope.
50 My comfort in my affliction is
  that your promise gives me life.
51 Though the proud scoff bitterly at me,
  I turn not away from your law.
52 I remember your ordinances of old, O Lord,
  and I am comforted.
53 Indignation seizes me because of the wicked
  who forsake your law.
54 Your statutes are the theme of my song
  in the place of my exile.
55 By night I remember your name, O Lord,
  and I will keep your law.
56 This has been mine,
  that I have observed your precepts.

57 I have said, O Lord, that my part
  is to keep your words.
58 I entreat you with all my heart,
  have pity on me according to your promise.
59 I considered my ways
  and turned my feet to your decrees.
60 I was prompt and did not hesitate
  in keeping your commands.
61 Though the snares of the wicked are twined about me,
  your law I have not forgotten.
62 At midnight I rise to give you thanks
  because of your just ordinances.
63 I am the companion of all who fear you
  and keep your precepts.
64 Of your kindness, O Lord, the earth is full;
  teach me your statutes.

65 You have done good to your servant,
  O Lord, according to your word.

66   Teach me wisdom and knowledge,
        for in your commands I trust.
67   Before I was afflicted I went astray,
        but now I hold to your promise.
68   You are good and bountiful;
        teach me your statutes.
69   Though the proud forge lies against me,
        with all my heart I will observe your precepts.
70   Their heart has become gross and fat;
        as for me, your law is my delight.
71   It is good for me that I have been afflicted,
        that I may learn your statutes.
72   The law of your mouth is to me more precious
        than thousands of gold and silver pieces.

73   Your hands have made me and fashioned me;
        give me discernment that I may learn your commands.
74   Those who fear you shall see me and be glad,
        because I hope in your word.
75   I know, O Lord, that your ordinances are just,
        and in your faithfulness you have afflicted me.
76   Let your kindness comfort me
        according to your promise to your servants.
77   Let your compassion come to me that I may live,
        for your law is my delight.
78   Let the proud be put to shame for oppressing me unjustly;
        I will meditate on your precepts.
79   Let those turn to me who fear you
        and acknowledge your decrees.
80   Let my heart be perfect in your statutes,
        that I be not put to shame.

81   My soul pines for your salvation;
        I hope in your word.
82   My eyes strain after your promise;
        when will you comfort me?
83   Though I am shriveled like a leathern flask in the smoke,
        I have not forgotten your statutes.
84   How many are the days of your servant?
        When will you do judgment on my persecutors?
85   The proud have dug pits for me;
        this is against your law.
86   All your commands are steadfast;
        they persecute me wrongfully; help me!

87	They have all but put an end to me on the earth,
	but I have not forsaken your precepts.
88	In your kindness give me life,
	that I may keep the decrees of your mouth.

89	Your word, O Lord, endures forever;
	it is firm as the heavens.
90	Through all generations your truth endures;
	you have established the earth, and it stands firm.
91	According to your ordinances they still stand firm:
	all things serve you.
92	Had not your law been my delight,
	I should have perished in my affliction.
93	Never will I forget your precepts,
	for through them you give me life.
94	I am yours; save me,
	for I have sought your precepts.
95	Sinners wait to destroy me,
	but I pay heed to your decrees.
96	I see that all fulfillment has its limits;
	broad indeed is your command.

97	How I love your law, O Lord!
	It is my meditation all the day.
98	Your command has made me wiser than my enemies,
	for it is ever with me.
99	I have more understanding than all my teachers
	when your decrees are my meditation.
100	I have more discernment than the elders,
	because I observe your precepts.
101	From every evil way I withhold my feet,
	that I may keep your words.
102	From your ordinances I turn not away,
	for you have instructed me.
103	How sweet to my palate are your promises,
	sweeter than honey to my mouth!
104	Through your precepts I gain discernment;
	therefore I hate every false way.

105	A lamp to my feet is your word,
	a light to my path.
106	I resolve and swear
	to keep your just ordinances.

107	I am very much afflicted; O Lord, give me life according to your word.
108	Accept, O Lord, the free homage of my mouth, and teach me your decrees.
109	Though constantly I take my life in my hands, yet I forget not your law.
110	The wicked have laid a snare for me, but from your precepts I have not strayed.
111	Your decrees are my inheritance forever; the joy of my heart they are.
112	I intend in my heart to fulfill your statutes always, to the letter.

113	I hate men of divided heart, but I love your law.
114	You are my refuge and my shield; in your word I hope.
115	Depart from me, you wrongdoers, and I will observe the commands of my God.
116	Sustain me as you have promised, that I may live; disappoint me not in my hope.
117	Help me, that I may be safe and ever delight in your statutes.
118	You despise all who stray from your statutes, for their deceitfulness is in vain.
119	You account all the wicked of the earth as dross; therefore I love your decrees.
120	My flesh shudders with dread of you, and I fear your ordinances.

121	I have fulfilled just ordinances; leave me not to my oppressors.
122	Be surety for the welfare of your servant; let not the proud oppress me.
123	My eyes strain after your salvation and your just promise.
124	Deal with your servant according to your kindness, and teach me your statutes.
125	I am your servant; give me discernment that I may know your decrees.
126	It is time for the Lord to act: they have broken your law.
127	For I love your command more than gold, however fine.

128   For in all your precepts I go forward;
       every false way I hate.

129   Wonderful are your decrees;
       therefore I observe them.

130   The revelation of your words sheds light,
       giving understanding to the simple.

131   I gasp with open mouth
       in my yearning for your commands.

132   Turn to me in pity
       as you turn to those who love your name.

133   Steady my footsteps according to your promise,
       and let no iniquity rule over me.

134   Redeem me from the oppression of men,
       that I may keep your precepts.

135   Let your countenance shine upon your servant,
       and teach me your statutes.

136   My eyes shed streams of tears
       because your law has not been kept.

137   You are just, O Lord,
       and your ordinance is right.

138   You have pronounced your decrees in justice
       and in perfect faithfulness.

139   My zeal consumes me,
       because my foes forget your words.

140   Your promise is very sure,
       and your servant loves it.

141   I am mean and contemptible,
       but your precepts I have not forgotten.

142   Your justice is everlasting justice,
       and your law is permanent.

143   Though distress and anguish have come upon me,
       your commands are my delight.

144   Your decrees are forever just;
       give me discernment that I may live.

145   I call out with all my heart; answer me, O Lord;
       I will observe your statutes.

146   I call upon you; save me,
       and I will keep your decrees.

147   Before dawn I come and cry out;
       I hope in your words.

148 My eyes greet the night watches
      in meditation on your promise.
149 Hear my voice according to your kindness, O Lord;
      according to your ordinance give me life.
150 I am attacked by malicious persecutors
      who are far from your law.
151 You, O Lord, are near,
      and all your commands are permanent.
152 Of old I know from your decrees,
      that you have established them forever.

153 Behold my affliction, and rescue me,
      for I have not forgotten your law.
154 Plead my cause, and redeem me;
      for the sake of your promise give me life.
155 Far from sinners is salvation,
      because they seek not your statutes.
156 Your compassion is great, O Lord;
      according to your ordinances give me life.
157 Though my persecutors and my foes are many,
      I turn not away from your decrees.
158 I beheld the apostates with loathing,
      because they kept not to your promise.
159 See how I love your precepts, O Lord;
      in your kindness give me life.
160 Permanence is your word's chief trait;
      each of your just ordinances is everlasting.

161 Princes persecute me without cause
      but my heart stands in awe of your word.
162 I rejoice at your promise,
      as one who has found rich spoil.
163 Falsehood I hate and abhor;
      your law I love.
164 Seven times a day I praise you
      for your just ordinances.
165 Those who love your law have great peace,
      and for them there is no stumbling block.
166 I wait for your salvation, O Lord,
      and your commands I fulfill.
167 I keep your decrees
      and love them deeply.
168 I keep your precepts and your decrees,
      for all my ways are before you.

169 Let my cry come before you, O Lord;
    in keeping with your word, give me discernment.
170 Let my supplication reach you;
    rescue me according to your promise.
171 My lips pour forth your praise,
    because you teach me your statutes.
172 May my tongue sing of your promise,
    for all your commands are just.
173 Let your hand be ready to help me,
    for I have chosen your precepts.
174 I long for your salvation, O Lord,
    and your law is my delight.
175 Let my soul live to praise you,
    and may your ordinances help me.
176 I have gone astray like a lost sheep; seek your servant,
    because your commands I do not forget.

Psalm 119

1 IN MY distress I called to the Lord,
    and he answered me.
2 O Lord, deliver me from lying lip,
    from treacherous tongue.

3 What will he inflict on you, with more besides,
    O treacherous tongue?
4 Sharp arrows of a warrior
    with fiery coals of brushwood.

5 Woe is me that I sojourn in Mosoch,
    that I dwell amid the tents of Cedar!
6 All too long have I dwelt
    with those who hate peace.
7 When I speak of peace,
    they are ready for war.

Psalm 120

1 I LIFT UP my eyes toward the mountains;
    whence shall help come to me?
2 My help is from the Lord,
    who made heaven and earth.

3 May he not suffer your foot to slip;
 may he slumber not who guards you:
4 Indeed he neither slumbers nor sleeps,
 the guardian of Israel.

5 The Lord is your guardian; the Lord is your shade;
 he is beside you at your right hand.
6 The sun shall not harm you by day,
 nor the moon by night.

7 The Lord will guard you from all evil;
 he will guard your life.
8 The Lord will guard your coming and your going,
 both now and forever.

Psalm 121

1 I REJOICED because they said to me,
 "We will go up to the house of the Lord."
2 And now we have set foot
 within your gates, O Jerusalem—
3 Jerusalem, built as a city
 with compact unity.

4 To it the tribes go up,
 the tribes of the Lord,
 According to the decree for Israel,
 to give thanks to the name of the Lord.
5 In it are set up judgment seats,
 seats for the house of David.

6 Pray for the peace of Jerusalem!
 May those who love you prosper!
7 May peace be within your walls,
 prosperity in your buildings.
8 Because of my relatives and friends
 I will say, "Peace be within you!"
9 Because of the house of the Lord, our God,
 I will pray for your good.

Psalm 122

1 To YOU I lift up my eyes
 who are enthroned in heaven.

2   Behold, as the eyes of servants
                are on the hands of their masters,
        As the eyes of a maid
                are on the hands of her mistress,
        So are our eyes on the Lord, our God,
                till he have pity on us.

3   Have pity on us, O Lord, have pity on us,
                for we are more than sated with contempt;
4   Our souls are more than sated
                with the mockery of the arrogant,
                with the contempt of the proud.

Psalm 123

1   HAD NOT the Lord been with us,
                let Israel say,
2   had not the Lord been with us—
    When men rose up against us,
3   then would they have swallowed us alive.
    When their fury was inflamed against us,
4   then would the waters have overwhelmed us;
    The torrent would have swept over us;
5   over us then would have swept
                the raging waters.

6   Blessed be the Lord, who did not leave us
                a prey to their teeth.
7   We were rescued like a bird
                from the fowlers' snare;
    Broken was the snare,
                and we were freed.
8   Our help is in the name of the Lord,
                who made heaven and earth.

Psalm 124

1   THEY who trust in the Lord are like Mount Sion,
                which is immovable; which forever stands.
2   Mountains are round about Jerusalem;
                so the Lord is round about his people,
                both now and forever.

3   For the scepter of the wicked shall not remain

upon the territory of the just,
    Lest the just put forth
        to wickedness their hands.

4   Do good, O Lord, to the good
        and to the upright of heart.
5   But such as turn aside to crooked ways
        may the Lord lead away with the evildoers!
        Peace be upon Israel!

Psalm 125

1   WHEN the Lord brought back the captives of Sion,
        we were like men dreaming.
2   Then our mouth was filled with laughter,
        and our tongue with rejoicing.
    Then they said among the nations,
        "The Lord has done great things for them."
3   The Lord has done great things for us;
        we are glad indeed.

4   Restore our fortunes, O Lord,
        like the torrents in the southern desert.
5   Those that sow in tears
        shall reap rejoicing.
6   Although they go forth weeping,
        carrying the seed to be sown,
    They shall come back rejoicing,
        carrying their sheaves.

Psalm 126

1   UNLESS the Lord build the house,
        they labor in vain who build it.
    Unless the Lord guard the city,
        in vain does the guard keep vigil.
2   It is vain for you to rise early
        or put off your rest,
    You that eat hard-earned bread,
        for he gives to his beloved in sleep.

3   Behold, sons are a gift from the Lord;
        the fruit of the womb is a reward.

4   Like arrows in the hand of a warrior
      are the sons of one's youth.
5   Happy the man whose quiver is filled with them;
      they shall not be put to shame when they contend
      with enemies at the gate.

Psalm 127

1   HAPPY are you who fear the Lord,
      who walk in his ways!
2   For you shall eat the fruit of your handiwork;
      happy shall you be, and favored.
3   Your wife shall be like a fruitful vine
      in the recesses of your home;
      Your children like olive plants
      around your table.
4   Behold, thus is the man blessed
      who fears the Lord.

5   The Lord bless you from Sion:
      may you see the prosperity of Jerusalem
      all the days of your life;
6   May you see your children's children.
      Peace be upon Israel!

Psalm 128

1   MUCH have they oppressed me from my youth,
      let Israel say,
2   Much have they oppressed me from my youth;
      yet they have not prevailed against me.
3   Upon my back the plowers plowed;
      long did they make their furrows.
4   But the just Lord has severed
      the cords of the wicked.

5   May all be put to shame and fall back
      that hate Sion.
6   May they be like grass on the housetops,
      which withers before it is plucked;
7   With which the reaper fills not his hand,
      nor the gatherer of sheaves his arms;
8   And those that pass by say not,

"The blessing of the Lord be upon you!
We bless you in the name of the Lord!"

Psalm 129

1 OUT OF the depths I cry to you, O Lord;
    Lord, hear my voice!
2 Let your ears be attentive
    to my voice in supplication:

3 If you, O Lord, mark iniquities,
    Lord, who can stand?
4 But with you is forgiveness,
    that you may be revered.

5 I trust in the Lord;
    my soul trusts in his word.
6 My soul waits for the Lord
    more than sentinels wait for the dawn.

More than sentinels wait for the dawn,
    let Israel wait for the Lord,
7 For with the Lord is kindness
    and with him is plenteous redemption;
8 And he will redeem Israel
    from all their iniquities.

Psalm 130

1 O LORD, my heart is not proud,
    nor are my eyes haughty;
I busy not myself with great things,
    nor with things too sublime for me.
2 Nay rather, I have stilled and quieted
    my soul like a weaned child.
Like a weaned child on its mother's lap,
    so is my soul within me.
3 O Israel, hope in the Lord,
    both now and forever.

Psalm 131

1 REMEMBER, O Lord, for David
    all his anxious care:

2   How he swore to the Lord,
        vowed to the Mighty One of Jacob:

3   "I will not enter the house I live in,
        nor lie on the couch where I sleep;

4   I will give my eyes no sleep
        my eyelids no rest,

5   Till I find a place for the Lord,
        a dwelling for the Mighty One of Jacob."

6   Behold, we heard of it in Ephratha;
        we found it in the fields of Jaar.

7   Let us enter into his dwelling,
        let us worship at his footstool.

8   Advance, O Lord, to your resting place,
        you and the ark of your majesty.

9   May your priests be clothed with justice;
        let your faithful ones shout merrily for joy.

10   For the sake of David your servant,
        reject not the plea of your anointed.

11   The Lord swore to David
        a firm promise from which he will not withdraw:
    "Your own offspring
        I will set upon your throne;

12   If your sons keep my covenant
        and the decrees which I shall teach them,
    Their sons, too, forever
        shall sit upon your throne."

13   For the Lord has chosen Sion;
        he prefers her for his dwelling.

14   "Sion is my resting place forever;
        in her will I dwell, for I prefer her.

15   I will bless her with abundant provision,
        her poor I will fill with bread.

16   Her priests I will clothe with salvation,
        and her faithful ones shall shout merrily for joy.

17   In her will I make a horn to sprout forth for David;
        I will place a lamp for my anointed.

18   His enemies I will clothe with shame,
        but upon him my crown shall shine."

Psalm 132

1 BEHOLD, how good it is, and how pleasant,
where brethren dwell at one!
2 It is as when the precious ointment upon the head
runs down over the beard, the beard of Aaron,
till it runs down upon the collar of his robe.
3 It is a dew like that of Hermon,
which comes down upon the mountains of Sion;
For there the Lord has pronounced his blessing,
life forever.

Psalm 133

1 COME, bless the Lord,
all you servants of the Lord
Who stand in the house of the Lord
during the hours of night.
2 Lift up your hands toward the sanctuary,
and bless the Lord.

3 May the Lord bless you from Sion,
the maker of heaven and earth.

Psalm 134

1 PRAISE the name of the Lord;
Praise, you servants of the Lord
2 Who stand in the house of the Lord,
in the courts of the house of our God.
3 Praise the Lord, for the Lord is good;
sing praise to his name, which we love;
4 For the Lord has chosen Jacob for himself,
Israel for his own possession.

5 For I know that the Lord is great;
our Lord is greater than all gods.
6 All that the Lord wills he does
in heaven and on earth,
in the seas and in all the deeps.
7 He raises storm clouds from the end of the earth;
with the lightning he makes the rain;
he brings forth the winds from his storehouse.

8	He smote the first-born in Egypt,
	both of man and of beast.
9	He sent signs and wonders
	into your midst, O Egypt,
	against Pharao and against all his servants.
10	He smote many nations
	and slew mighty kings:
11	Sehon, king of the Amorrites,
	and Og, king of Basan,
	and all the kings of Chanaan;
12	And he made their land a heritage,
	the heritage of Israel his people.
13	Your name, O Lord, endures forever;
	Lord is your title through all generations,
14	For the Lord defends his people,
	and is merciful to his servants.

15 The idols of the nations are silver and gold,
      the handiwork of men.
16 They have mouths but speak not;
      they have eyes but see not;
17 They have ears but hear not,
      nor is there breath in their mouths.
18 Their makers shall be like them,
      everyone that trusts in them.

19 House of Israel, bless the Lord,
      house of Aaron, bless the Lord,
20 House of Levi, bless the Lord;
      you who fear the Lord, bless the Lord.
21 Blessed from Sion be the Lord,
      who dwells in Jerusalem.

Psalm 135

1 GIVE thanks to the Lord, for he is good,
      for his mercy endures forever;
2 Give thanks to the God of gods,
      for his mercy endures forever;
3 Give thanks to the Lord of lords,
      for his mercy endures forever;

4 Who alone does great wonders,
      for his mercy endures forever;

5	Who made the heavens in wisdom,
	for his mercy endures forever;
6	Who spread out the earth upon the waters,
	for his mercy endures forever;
7	Who made the great lights,
	for his mercy endures forever;
8	The sun to rule over the day,
	for his mercy endures forever;
9	The moon and the stars to rule over the night,
	for his mercy endures forever;
10	Who smote the Egyptians in their first-born,
	for his mercy endures forever;
11	And brought out Israel from their midst,
	for his mercy endures forever;
12	With a mighty hand and an outstretched arm,
	for his mercy endures forever;
13	Who split the Red Sea in twain,
	for his mercy endures forever;
14	And led Israel through its midst,
	for his mercy endures forever;
15	But swept Pharao and his army into the Red Sea,
	for his mercy endures forever;
16	Who led his people through the wilderness,
	for his mercy endures forever;
17	Who smote great kings,
	for his mercy endures forever;
18	And slew powerful kings,
	for his mercy endures forever;
19	Sehon, king of the Amorrites,
	for his mercy endures forever;
20	And Og, king of Basan,
	for his mercy endures forever;
21	And made their land a heritage,
	for his mercy endures forever;
22	The heritage of Israel his servant,
	for his mercy endures forever;
23	Who remembered us in our abjection,
	for his mercy endures forever;
24	And freed us from our foes,
	for his mercy endures forever;
25	Who gives food to all flesh,
	for his mercy endures forever.

Give thanks to the God of heaven,
    for his mercy endures forever.

Psalm 136

1 BY THE streams of Babylon
       we sat and wept
       when we remembered Sion.
2 On the aspens of that land
       we hung up our harps,
3 Though there our captors asked of us
       the lyrics of our songs,
   And our despoilers urged us to be joyous:
   "Sing for us the songs of Sion!"

4 How could we sing a song of the Lord
       in a foreign land?
5 If I forget you, Jerusalem,
       may my right hand be forgotten!
6 May my tongue cleave to my palate
       if I remember you not,
   If I place not Jerusalem
       ahead of my joy.

7 Remember, O Lord, against the children of Edom,
       the day of Jerusalem,
   When they said, "Raze it, raze it
       down to its foundations!"
8 O daughter of Babylon, you destroyer,
       happy the man who shall repay you
       the evil you have done us!
9 Happy the man who shall seize and smash
       your little ones against the rock!

Psalm 137

1 I WILL give thanks to you, O Lord, with all my heart,
       for you have heard the words of my mouth;
       in the presence of the angels I will sing your praise;
2 I will worship at your holy temple
       and give thanks to your name,
   Because of your kindness and your truth;
       for you have made great above all things
       your name and your promise.

3   When I called, you answered me;
        you built up strength within me.

4   All the kings of the earth shall give thanks to you, O Lord,
        when they hear the words of your mouth;
5   And they shall sing of the ways of the Lord:
        "Great is the glory of the Lord."
6   The Lord is exalted, yet the lowly he sees,
        and the proud he knows from afar.

7   Though I walk amid distress, you preserve me;
        against the anger of my enemies you raise your hand;
        your right hand saves me.
8   The Lord will complete what he has done for me;
        your kindness, O Lord, endures forever;
        forsake not the work of your hands.

Psalm 138

1   O Lord, you have probed me and you know me;
2   you know when I sit and when I stand;
        you understand my thoughts from afar.
3   My journeys and my rest you scrutinize,
        with all my ways you are familiar.
4   Even before a word is on my tongue,
        behold, O Lord, you know the whole of it.
5   Behind me and before, you hem me in
        and rest your hand upon me.
6   Such knowledge is too wonderful for me;
        too lofty for me to attain.

7   Where can I go from your spirit?
        from your presence where can I flee?
8   If I go up to the heavens, you are there;
        if I sink to the nether world, you are present there.
9   If I take the wings of the dawn,
        if I settle at the farthest limits of the sea,
10 Even there your hand shall guide me,
        and your right hand hold me fast.
11 If I say, "Surely the darkness shall hide me,
        and night shall be my light"—
12 For you darkness itself is not dark,
        and night shines as the day.
        Darkness and light are the same.

13	Truly you have formed my inmost being;

13   Truly you have formed my inmost being;
      you knit me in my mother's womb.

14   I give you thanks that I am fearfully, wonderfully made;
      wonderful are your works.
  My soul also you knew full well;

15   nor was my frame unknown to you
  When I was made in secret,
      when I was fashioned in the depths of the earth.

16   Your eyes have seen my actions;
      in your book they are all written;
      my days were limited before one of them existed.

17   How weighty are your designs, O God;
      how vast the sum of them!

18   Were I to recount them, they would outnumber the sands;
      did I reach the end of them, I should still be with you.

19   If only you would destroy the wicked, O God,
      and the men of blood were to depart from me!

20   Wickedly they invoke your name;
      your foes swear faithless oaths.

21   Do I not hate, O Lord, those who hate you?
      Those who rise up against you do I not loathe?

22   With a deadly hatred I hate them;
      they are my enemies.

23   Probe me, O God, and know my heart;
      try me, and know my thoughts;

24   See if my way is crooked,
      and lead me in the way of old.

Psalm 139

2   DELIVER me, O Lord, from evil men;
      preserve me from violent men,

3   From those who devise evil in their hearts,
      and stir up wars every day.

4   They make their tongues sharp as those of serpents;
      the venom of asps is under their lips.

5   Save me, O Lord, from the hands of the wicked;
      preserve me from violent men
  Who plan to trip up my feet—

6   the proud who have hidden a trap for me;
  They have spread cords for a net;
      by the wayside they have laid snares for me.

7   I say to the Lord, you are my God;
         hearken, O Lord, to my voice in supplication.
8   O God, my Lord, my strength and my salvation;
         you are my helmet in the day of battle!

9   Grant not, O Lord, the desires of the wicked;
         further not their plans.
10   Those who surround me lift up their heads;
         may the mischief which they threaten overwhelm them.
11   May he rain burning coals upon them;
         may he cast them into the depths, never to rise.

12   A man of wicked tongue shall not abide in the land;
         evil shall abruptly entrap the violent man.
13   I know that the Lord renders
         justice to the afflicted, judgment to the poor.
14   Surely the just shall give thanks to your name;
         the upright shall dwell in your presence.

Psalm 140

1   O Lord, to you I call; hasten to me;
         hearken to my voice when I call upon you.
2   Let my prayer come like incense before you;
         the lifting up of my hands, like the evening sacrifice.

3   O Lord, set a watch before my mouth,
         a guard at the door of my lips.
4   Let not my heart incline to the evil
         of engaging in deeds of wickedness
     With men who are evildoers;
         and let me not partake of their dainties.
5   Let the just man strike me; that is kindness;
         let him reprove me; it is oil for the head,
     Which my head shall not refuse,
         but I will still pray under these afflictions.
6   Their judges were cast down over the crag,
         and they heard how pleasant were my words
7   As when a plowman breaks furrows in the field,
         so their bones are strewn by the edge of the nether world.

8   For toward you, O God, my Lord, my eyes are turned;
         in you I take refuge; strip me not of life.

9   Keep me from the trap they have set for me,
        and from the snares of evildoers.
10   Let all the wicked fall, each into his own net,
        while I escape.

Psalm 141

2   WITH a loud voice I cry out to the Lord;
        with a loud voice I beseech the Lord.
3   My complaint I pour out before him;
        before him I lay bare my distress.
4   When my spirit is faint within me,
        you know my path.

       In the way along which I walk
        they have hid a trap for me.
5   I look to the right to see,
        but there is no one who pays me heed.
       I have lost all means of escape;
        there is no one who cares for my life.

6   I cry out to you, O Lord;
        I say, "You are my refuge,
         my portion in the land of the living."
7   Attend to my cry,
        for I am brought low indeed.
       Rescue me from my persecutors,
        for they are too strong for me.
8   Lead me forth from prison,
        that I may give thanks to your name.
       The just shall gather around me
        when you have been good to me.

Psalm 142

1   O LORD, hear my prayer;
        hearken to my pleading in your faithfulness;
        in your justice answer me.
2   And enter not into judgment with your servant,
        for before you no living man is just.

3   For the enemy pursues me;
        he has crushed my life to the ground;
        he has left me dwelling in the dark, like those long dead.

4   And my spirit is faint within me,
        my heart within me is appalled.
5   I remember the days of old;
        I meditate on all your doings,
        the works of your hands I ponder.
6   I stretch out my hands to you;
        my soul thirsts for you like parched land.

7   Hasten to answer me, O Lord,
        for my spirit fails me.
    Hide not your face from me
        lest I become like those who go down into the pit.
8   At dawn let me hear of your kindness,
        for in you I trust.
    Show me the way in which I should walk,
        for to you I lift up my soul.
9   Rescue me from my enemies, O Lord,
        for in you I hope.

10 Teach me to do your will,
        for you are my God.
    May your good spirit guide me
        on level ground.
11 For your name's sake, O Lord, preserve me;
        in your justice free me from distress,
12 And in your kindness destroy my enemies;
        bring to nought all my foes,
        for I am your servant.

Psalm 143

1   BLESSED be the Lord, my rock,
        who trains my hands for battle, my fingers for war;
2   My refuge and my fortress,
        my stronghold, my deliverer,
    My shield, in whom I trust,
        who subdues peoples under me.

3   Lord, what is man, that you notice him;
        the son of man, that you take thought of him?
4   Man is like a breath;
        his days, like a passing shadow.
5   Incline your heavens, O Lord, and come down;
        touch the mountains, and they shall smoke;

6   Flash forth lightning, and put them to flight,
       shoot your arrows, and rout them;
7   Reach out your hand from on high—
          Deliver me and rescue me from many waters,
          from the hands of aliens,
8   Whose mouths swear false promises
          while their right hands are raised in perjury.

9   O God, I will sing a new song to you;
       with a ten-stringed lyre I will chant your praise,
10   You who give victory to kings,
       and deliver David, your servant.
11   From the evil sword deliver me;
         and rescue me from the hands of aliens,
        Whose mouths swear false promises
         while their right hands are raised in perjury.

12   May our sons be like plants
       well-nurtured in their youth,
    Our daughters like wrought columns
       such as stand at the corners of the temple.
13   May our garners be full,
       affording every kind of store;
    May our sheep be in the thousands,
       and increase to myriads in our meadows;
14   may our oxen be well laden.
    May there be no breach in the walls, no exile,
       no outcry in our streets.
15   Happy the people for whom things are thus;
       happy the people whose God is the Lord.

Psalm 144

1   I WILL extol you, O my God and King,
       and I will bless your name forever and ever.
2   Every day will I bless you,
       and I will praise your name forever and ever.
3   Great is the Lord and highly to be praised;
       his greatness is unsearchable.
4   Generation after generation praises your works
       and proclaims your might.

5   They speak of the splendor of your glorious majesty
       and tell of your wondrous works.

6	They discourse of the power of your terrible deeds
	and declare your greatness.
7	They publish the fame of your abundant goodness
	and joyfully sing of your justice.
8	The Lord is gracious and merciful,
	slow to anger and of great kindness.
9	The Lord is good to all
	and compassionate toward all his works.

10 Let all your works give you thanks, O Lord,
and let your faithful ones bless you.
11 Let them discourse of the glory of your kingdom
and speak of your might,
12 Making known to men your might
and the glorious splendor of your kingdom.
13 Your kingdom is a kingdom for all ages,
and your dominion endures through all generations.

The Lord is faithful in all his words
and holy in all his works.
14 The Lord lifts up all who are falling
and raises up all who are bowed down.
15 The eyes of all look hopefully to you,
and you give them their food in due season;
16 You open your hand
and satisfy the desire of every living thing.

17 The Lord is just in all his ways
and holy in all his works.
18 The Lord is near to all who call upon him,
to all who call upon him in truth.
19 He fulfills the desire of those who fear him,
he hears their cry and saves them.
20 The Lord keeps all who love him,
but all the wicked he will destroy.

21 May my mouth speak the praise of the Lord,
and may all flesh bless his holy name
forever and ever.

Psalm 145

1 PRAISE the Lord, O my soul;
2 I will praise the Lord all my life;
I will sing praise to my God while I live.

3   Put not your trust in princes,
        in man, in whom there is no salvation.

4   When his spirit departs he returns to his earth;
        on that day his plans perish.

5   Happy he whose help is the God of Jacob,
        whose hope is in the Lord, his God,

6   Who made heaven and earth,
        the sea and all that is in them;
     Who keeps faith forever,

7   secures justice for the oppressed,
        gives food to the hungry.
     The Lord sets captives free;

8   the Lord gives sight to the blind.
     The Lord raises up those that were bowed down;
        the Lord loves the just.

9   The Lord protects strangers;
        the fatherless and the widow he sustains,
        but the way of the wicked he thwarts.

10   The Lord shall reign forever;
        your God, O Sion, through all generations. Alleluia

Psalm 146

1   PRAISE the Lord, for he is good;
        sing praise to our God, for he is gracious;
        it is fitting to praise him.

2   The Lord rebuilds Jerusalem;
        the dispersed of Israel he gathers.

3   He heals the brokenhearted
        and binds up their wounds.

4   He tells the number of the stars;
        he calls each by name.

5   Great is our Lord and mighty in power;
        to his wisdom there is no limit.

6   The Lord sustains the lowly;
        the wicked he casts to the ground.

7   Sing to the Lord with thanksgiving;
        sing praise with the harp to our God,

8   Who covers the heavens with clouds,
        who provides rain for the earth;
     Who makes grass sprout on the mountains
        and herbs for the service of men;

9	Who gives food to the cattle, and to the young ravens when they cry to him.
10	In the strength of the steed he delights not, nor is he pleased with the fleetness of men.
11	The Lord is pleased with those who fear him, with those who hope for his kindness.

Psalm 147

12	GLORIFY the Lord, O Jerusalem; praise you God, O Sion.
13	For he has strengthened the bars of your gates; he has blessed your children within you.
14	He has granted peace in your borders; with the best of wheat he fills you.
15	He sends forth his command to the earth; swiftly runs his word!
16	He spreads snow like wool; frost he strews like ashes.
17	He scatters his hail like crumbs; before his cold the waters freeze.
18	He sends his word and melts them; he lets his breeze blow and the waters run.
19	He has proclaimed his word to Jacob, his statutes and his ordinances to Israel.

20	He has not done thus for any other nation;
	      his ordinances he has not made known to them.
	      Alleluia.

Psalm 148

1	PRAISE the Lord from the heavens, praise him in the heights;
2	Praise him, all you his angels, praise him, all you his hosts.
3	Praise him, sun and moon; praise him, all you shining stars.
4	Praise him, you highest heavens, and you waters above the heavens.
5	Let them praise the name of the Lord, for he commanded and they were created;
6	He established them forever and ever; he gave them a duty which shall not pass away.

7	Praise the Lord from the earth,
	you sea monsters and all depths;
8	Fire and hail, snow and mist,
	storm winds that fulfill his word;
9	You mountains and all you hills,
	you fruit trees and all you cedars;
10	You wild beasts and all tame animals,
	you creeping things and you winged fowl.

11	Let the kings of the earth and all peoples,
	the princes and all the judges of the earth,
12	Young men too, and maidens,
	old men and boys,
13	Praise the name of the Lord,
	for his name alone is exalted;
	His majesty is above earth and heaven,
14	and he has lifted up the horn of his people.
	Be this his praise from all his faithful ones,
	from the children of Israel, the people close to him.
	Alleluia.

Psalm 149

1	SING to the Lord a new song
	of praise in the assembly of the faithful.
2	Let Israel be glad in their maker,
	let the children of Sion rejoice in their king.
3	Let them praise his name in the festive dance,
	let them sing praise to him with timbrel and harp.
4	For the Lord loves his people,
	and he adorns the lowly with victory.
5	Let the faithful exult in glory;
	let them sing for joy upon their couches;
6	let the high praises of God be in their throats.

7	And let two-edged swords be in their hands:
	to execute vengeance on the nations,
	punishments on the peoples;
8	To bind their kings with chains,
	their nobles with fetters of iron;
9	To execute on them the written sentence.
	This is the glory of all his faithful. Alleluia.

Psalm 150

1 PRAISE the Lord in his sanctuary,
   praise him in the firmament of his strength.
2 Praise him for his mighty deeds,
   praise him for his sovereign majesty.
3 Praise him with the blast of the trumpet,
   praise him with lyre and harp,
4 Praise him with timbrel and dance,
   praise him with strings and pipe.
5 Praise him with sounding cymbals,
   praise him with clanging cymbals.
6 Let everything that has breath
   praise the Lord!   Alleluia.

Song of Sirach

1   COME to our aid, O God of the universe,
      and put all the nations in dread of you!
2   Raise your hand against the heathen,
      that they may realize your power.
3   As you have used us to show them your holiness,
      so now use them to show us your glory.
4   Thus they will know, as we know,
      that there is no God but you.

5   Give new signs and work new wonders;
      show forth the splendor of your right hand and arm.
6   Rouse your anger, pour out wrath,
      humble the enemy, scatter the foe.
7   Hasten the day, bring on the time;
      crush the heads of the hostile rulers.
8   Let raging fire consume the fugitive,
      and your people's oppressors meet destruction.

9   Gather all the tribes of Jacob,
      that they may inherit the land as of old.
10   Show mercy to the people called by your name;
      Israel, whom you named your first-born.
11   Take pity on your holy city,
      Jerusalem, your dwelling place.
12   Fill Sion with your majesty,
      your temple with your glory.

13   Give evidence of your deeds of old;
      fulfill the prophecies spoken in your name.
14   Reward those who have hoped in you,
      and let your prophets be proved true.
15   Hear the prayer of your servants,
      for you are ever gracious to your people.
16   Thus it will be known to the very ends of the earth
      that you are the eternal God.

SIRACH 36

57	BLESS the Lord, all you works of the Lord,
	praise and exalt him above all forever.
58	Angels of the Lord, bless the Lord.
59	You heavens, bless the Lord.
60	All you waters above the heavens, bless the Lord.
61	All you hosts of the Lord, bless the Lord.
62	Sun and moon, bless the Lord.
63	Stars of heaven, bless the Lord.
64	Every shower and dew bless the Lord.
65	All you winds, bless the Lord.
66	Fire and heat bless the Lord.
67	Cold and chill bless the Lord.
68	Dew and rain, bless the Lord.
69	Frost and chill, bless the Lord.
70	Ice and snow bless the Lord.
71	Nights and days bless the Lord.
72	Light and darkness, bless the Lord.
73	Lightnings and clouds bless the Lord.
74	Let the earth bless the Lord;
	praise and exalt him above all forever.
75	Mountains and hills, bless the Lord.
76	Everything growing from the earth, bless the Lord.
77	You springs, bless the Lord.
78	Seas and rivers, bless the Lord.
79	You dolphins and all water creatures, bless the Lord.
80	All you birds of the air bless the Lord.
81	All you beasts, wild and tame, bless the Lord.
82	You sons of men, bless the Lord.
83	O Israel, bless the Lord.
	Praise and exalt him above all forever.
84	Priests of the Lord, bless the Lord.
85	Servants of the Lord, bless the Lord.
86	Spirits and souls of the just, bless the Lord.
87	Holy men of humble heart, bless the Lord.
88	Anania, Azaria, Misael, bless the Lord;
	praise and exalt him above all forever.
52	Blessed are you, O Lord, the God of our fathers,
	praiseworthy and exalted above all forever.

DANIEL 3

46   MY SOUL magnifies the Lord,
47   and my spirit rejoices in God my Savior,
48   because he has regarded the lowliness of his handmaid;
      for, behold, henceforth all generations shall call me blessed;
49   because he who is mighty has done great things for me,
      and holy is his name;
50   and his mercy is from generation to generation
      on those who fear him.
51   He has shown might with his arm;
      he has scattered the proud in the conceit of their heart.
52   He has put down the mighty from their thrones,
      and has exalted the lowly.
53   He has filled the hungry with good things,
      and the rich he has sent away empty.
54   He has given help to Israel, his servant,
      mindful of his mercy—
55   Even as he spoke to our fathers—
      to Abraham and to his posterity forever.

LUKE I

68 BLESSED be the Lord, the God of Israel,
    because he has visited and wrought redemption for his people,
69 and has raised up a horn of salvation for us,
    in the house of David his servant,
70 as he promised through the mouth of his holy ones,
    the prophets from of old;
71 salvation from our enemies,
    and from the hand of all who hate us,
72 to show mercy to our forefathers
    and to be mindful of his holy covenant,
73 of the oath that he swore to Abraham our father,
    that he would grant us,
74 that, delivered from the hand of our enemies,
    we should serve him without fear,
75 in holiness and justice before him
    all our days.

76 And you, child, shall be called the prophet of the Most High,
    for you shall go before the face of the Lord to prepare his ways,
77 to give to his people knowledge of salvation
    through forgiveness of their sins,
78 because of the loving-kindness of our God,
    wherewith the Orient from on high has visited us,
79 to shine on those who sit in darkness and in the shadow of death,
    to guide our feet into the way of peace.

LUKE 1:68-79

Songs from the Book of Revelation

HOLY, holy, holy, the Lord God almighty,
  who was, and who is, and who is coming.

REVELATION 4:8

THEREFORE they are before the throne of God,
  and serve him day and night in his temple,
  and he who sits upon the throne will dwell with them.
They shall neither hunger nor thirst any more,
  neither shall the sun strike them nor any heat.
For the Lamb who is in the midst of the throne will shepherd them,
  and will guide them to the fountains of the waters of life,
  and God will wipe away every tear from their eyes.

REVELATION 7:15-17

GREAT and marvelous are thy works,
  O Lord God almighty;
just and true are thy ways,
  O King of the ages.
Who will not fear thee, O Lord, and magnify thy name?
  for thou alone art holy.
For all nations will come and worship before thee;
  because thy judgments are manifest.

REVELATION 15:3-4

ALLELUIA! for the Lord, our God almighty, now reigns!
  Let us be glad and rejoice, and give glory to him;
for the marriage of the Lamb has come,
  and his spouse has prepared herself.

REVELATION 19:6-7

The Sacraments

Baptism

BAPTISM is the sacrament of the new life that comes through death.
We die with Christ so as to be born again in his life.

Water signifies death. It reminds us of drowning, and recalls the
story of the Flood. When the water is poured over our heads we die to
selfishness and sin.

Water also signifies life. It causes things to grow; it reminds us of
the story of creation: God's Spirit moving over the waters and bringing
all things into existence. When the water is poured over our heads, we
come to life in Christ.

Baptism is a sacrament of resurrection, of passage through water
from death to life. It is a sign of the resurrection of the Lord, who con-
quers death in us; and a promise of our own resurrection in Christ after
death.

In baptism we become sons of God by becoming members of his
people, the Church. The baptismal font is often called the womb of the
Church, for from its waters come the new sons and daughters of the
parish family. A baptism is always a parish celebration, because the
newly baptized is born into the faith and life of the parish family, and
all rejoice at the birth.

Baptism is really the first of three sacraments. Born again in Christ,
we will be sealed by the Holy Spirit in confirmation so that we may share
in the central sacrament of love, the holy Eucharist.

The Baptism of Infants

*Priest and people gather at the entrance of the church to meet the parents and
sponsors who are bringing the infants to be baptized. An appropriate hymn may
be sung, such as No. 58 or No. 86; or a few verses from Psalm 8, Psalm 28,
or Psalm 41 may be recited.*

Interrogations

Priest: Peace be with you.

The priest then asks the name of each child individually, and the sponsors reply.

Priest (naming each child): What do you ask of the Church of God?
Sponsors: FAITH.

Priest: What does faith offer you?

Sponsors: ETERNAL LIFE.

Priest: If, then, you wish to enter into life, keep the commandments: you shall love the Lord your God with your whole heart, and with your whole soul, and with your whole mind, and your neighbor as yourself.

Breathings

The priest then breathes three times on the face of each infant. His action recalls the Book of Genesis: "Then the Lord God formed man out of the dust of the ground and breathed into his nostrils the breath of life, and man became a living being."

Priest: Depart from him, unclean spirit, and give place to the Holy Spirit, the Consoler.

Sign of the Cross

Priest: Receive the mark of the cross on your forehead and within your heart. Embrace the faith with its divine teachings. So live that you will indeed be a temple of God.

The priest prays that God will guard the children he has called to his Church through the never-failing power of the cross.

Laying on of Hands

The priest places his hand on the head of each infant. Then he prays that God, who has called these children to walk in the faith, may perfect them in his service.

Giving of Salt

Salt is a sign of hospitality. It is also a pledge that the infant to be baptized will have a taste for heavenly wisdom and be preserved from the corruption of sin. The priest blesses the salt, asking that it may become a health-giving sacrament, and a perfect medicine. Then he places a bit of salt into the mouth of each infant.

Priest: Receive the salt which is the symbol of wisdom. May it bring you God's favor for life everlasting.

People: AMEN.

Priest: Peace be with you.

People: AND WITH YOUR SPIRIT.

The priest then prays that the infants may grow up to be fervent in spirit, joyful in hope, and zealous in the Lord's service.

Preparatory Purifications

At this point the name of each child may be written in the official book of the parish, a sign that each of them is to become a member of the parish family. While this is being done a hymn may be sung, such as No. 119 or No. 106, or a few verses of Psalm 41 or Psalm 50 may be recited.

The priest solemnly exorcizes the children in the name of the Father, and of the Son, and of the Holy Spirit. Next he makes the sign of the cross on the head of each child.

Priest: Accursed devil, never dare to desecrate this sign of the holy cross which we are tracing upon his forehead. Through the same Christ our Lord.

All: AMEN.

The priest places his hand on the head of each child, and then prays that all of them may receive true knowledge so that they may live up to the grace of their baptism.

Entrance into the Church

The priest places his stole upon the first infant and invites all of them to enter the church.

Priest: Enter into the temple of God, so that you may have part with Christ in everlasting life.

All: AMEN.

Then all together enter the church and proceed to the baptistry. An appropriate hymn may be sung, such as No. 91 or No. 130, or a few verses of Psalm 83 or Psalm 121 may be recited.

Apostles' Creed and Lord's Prayer

When the singing is concluded, the priest invites the sponsors to say the Apostles' Creed and the Lord's Prayer together with him.

I BELIEVE IN GOD, THE FATHER ALMIGHTY, CREATOR OF HEAVEN AND EARTH; AND IN JESUS CHRIST, HIS ONLY SON, OUR LORD, WHO WAS CONCEIVED BY THE HOLY SPIRIT, BORN OF THE VIRGIN MARY, SUFFERED UNDER PONTIUS PILATE, WAS CRUCIFIED, DIED, AND WAS BURIED. HE DESCENDED INTO HELL; THE THIRD DAY HE AROSE AGAIN FROM THE DEAD; HE ASCENDED INTO HEAVEN, SITTETH AT THE RIGHT HAND OF GOD, THE FATHER ALMIGHTY; FROM THENCE HE SHALL COME TO JUDGE THE LIVING AND THE DEAD. I

BELIEVE IN THE HOLY SPIRIT, THE HOLY CATHOLIC CHURCH, THE COM-
MUNION OF SAINTS, THE FORGIVENESS OF SINS, THE RESURRECTION OF THE
BODY, AND LIFE EVERLASTING. AMEN.

OUR FATHER, WHO ART IN HEAVEN, HALLOWED BE THY NAME; THY KING-
DOM COME; THY WILL BE DONE ON EARTH AS IT IS IN HEAVEN. GIVE US
THIS DAY OUR DAILY BREAD; AND FORGIVE US OUR TRESPASSES AS WE
FORGIVE THOSE WHO TRESPASS AGAINST US; AND LEAD US NOT INTO
TEMPTATION, BUT DELIVER US FROM EVIL. AMEN.

Solemn Exorcism

*The priest then exorcises the children, praying that they may become temples of
the living God and that the Holy Spirit may dwell in them. Then he touches
the ears and nostrils of each child.*

Priest: Ephpheta, which means "Be opened," so that you may perceive the fragrance of God's sweetness. But you, O devil, depart; for the
judgment of God has come.

Renunciation of Satan

The priest then speaks to the sponsors of each of the children separately.

Priest: Do you renounce Satan?
Sponsors: I DO RENOUNCE HIM.
Priest: And all his works?
Sponsors: I DO RENOUNCE THEM.
Priest: And all his allurements?
Sponsors: I DO RENOUNCE THEM.

Anointing

*The priest then anoints each child with oil, making the sign of the cross on the
breast and between the shoulders.*

Priest: I anoint you with the oil of salvation in Christ Jesus our Lord,
so that you may have everlasting life.
All: AMEN.

Profession of Faith

The sponsors and the parents then bring each child to the baptismal font itself.

Priest: Do you believe in God, the Father almighty, creator of heaven
and earth?
Sponsors: I DO BELIEVE.

Priest: Do you believe in Jesus Christ, his only Son, our Lord, who was born into this world and who suffered?

Sponsors: I DO BELIEVE.

Priest: Do you believe also in the Holy Spirit, the holy Catholic Church, the communion of saints, the forgiveness of sins, the resurrection of the body and life everlasting?

Sponsors: I DO BELIEVE.

Priest: Do you wish to be baptized?

Sponsors: I DO.

Pouring of the Water

The priest then pours water on the head of the infant three times, in the form of a cross.

Priest: I baptize you in the name of the Father, and of the Son, and of the Holy Spirit.

When all have been baptized, an appropriate hymn may be sung, such as No. 56 or No. 126, or a few verses of Psalm 41 or Psalm 95 may be recited.

Anointing with Chrism

The priest anoints the head of each child in the form of a cross as a sign of his priesthood.

Priest: May almighty God, the Father of our Lord Jesus Christ, who has given you a new birth by means of water and the Holy Spirit and forgiven all your sins, anoint you with the Chrism of salvation in the same Christ Jesus our Lord, so that you may have everlasting life.

All: AMEN.

Priest: Peace be with you.

All: AND WITH YOUR SPIRIT.

Reception of Baptismal Robes

The priest places a white garment on each of the newly baptized.

Priest: Receive this white garment. Never let it become stained, so that when you stand before the judgment seat of our Lord Jesus Christ, you may have life everlasting.

All: AMEN.

Reception of Baptismal Candles

The priest gives a lighted candle to the sponsors of each child.

Priest: Receive this burning light, and keep the grace of your baptism throughout a blameless life. Observe the commandments of God. Then, when the Lord comes to the heavenly wedding feast, you will be able to meet him with all the saints in the halls of heaven, and live forever and ever.

All: AMEN.

Conclusion

Priest: Go in peace, and the Lord be with you.
All: AMEN.

An appropriate closing hymn may be sung, such as No. 98 or No. 124, or a few verses of Psalm 117 or Psalm 135 may be recited.

Thanksgiving after Childbirth

In many places it is customary to express in a special service the joy and gratitude of the parish, parents, relatives and friends, at the birth of a child. This rite, which includes a blessing of the mother and her child, either follows the baptism, as a conclusion to the sacramental celebration, or takes place at another time.

Entrance

Parents and friends stand in the baptistry or at the entrance of the church. The mother holds her child and a lighted candle. The priest sprinkles all with holy water.

Priest: Peace be with you.

Then the priest turns to the mother: Come into the temple of God; adore the Son of the Blessed Virgin Mary, adore him who granted that you should bear a child.

The priest then leads everyone into the church and to the altar. At this time an appropriate hymn, such as No. 14 or No. 130, may be sung.

Magnificat

When all are assembled at the altar, all together sing or say the Magnificat, page 708.

Prayers

When the Magnificat is concluded, all kneel.

Priest: Lord, have mercy.
People: CHRIST, HAVE MERCY. LORD, HAVE MERCY.

Priest: Our Father . . . And lead us not into temptation.
People: BUT DELIVER US FROM EVIL.
Priest: O Lord, hear my prayer.
People: AND LET MY CRY COME TO YOU.
Priest: The Lord be with you.
People: AND WITH YOUR SPIRIT.

The priest prays that mother and child may attain the joys of everlasting life. Then the priest prays that the child may grow so as to be pleasing to God.

Conclusion

The priest then sprinkles mother and child with holy water.

Priest: May the peace and blessing of almighty God, the Father, and the Son, and the Holy Spirit, descend upon you and remain forever.
People: AMEN.

The Baptism of Adults

The practice of preparing for the baptism of adults in several distinct steps goes back to the early Church, in which much of the Lenten liturgy was devoted to the instruction and preparation of the catechumens who were to be baptized on Easter Sunday. For an adult, baptism involves a very profound change in attitude and way of life, a conscious and deliberate turning to Christ in his Church. The candidate is helped and encouraged in this process by the parish family he seeks to enter. He is officially recognized as a catechumen, one who seeks baptism, and every member of the parish takes on a responsibility of assisting him in his new birth in Christ. Each step is a celebration of the entire parish, for new members are to be born into God's family.

THE FIRST STEP

Entrance

An appropriate hymn, such as No. 91 or No. 121, may be sung, as the priest and his ministers enter and kneel before the altar. When the singing is completed, the priest rises.

Priest: O God, come to my assistance.
All: O LORD, MAKE HASTE TO HELP ME.
Priest: Glory be to the Father, and to the Son, and to the Holy Spirit.

All: AS IT WAS IN THE BEGINNING, IS NOW, AND EVER SHALL BE, WORLD WITHOUT END. AMEN.

Priest and people may sing or recite all or part of the psalms listed below:

> Thus speaks the Lord:
> I will pour out upon you cleansing waters,
> and you shall be washed of all your stains.
>
> TURN TO PSALM 8, PSALM 28, PSALM 41

Reception of the Catechumens

Priest: Lord, have mercy.
All: CHRIST, HAVE MERCY. LORD, HAVE MERCY.
Priest: Our Father . . . And lead us not into temptation.
All: BUT DELIVER US FROM EVIL.
Priest: O Lord, hear my prayer.
All: AND LET MY CRY COME TO YOU.
Priest: The Lord be with you.
All: AND WITH YOUR SPIRIT.

Prayer

The priest prays that the faith of the parish, into which the candidates are to be baptized, might be preserved; he prays also for himself and for the candidates.

The priest calls each candidate by name, and the candidate answers: PRESENT. *Now the candidates are officially recognized by the parish as catechumens.*

Priest: What do you ask of the Church of God?
Catechumens: FAITH.
Priest: What does faith offer you?
Catechumens: ETERNAL LIFE.

The priest tells the catechumens about the life they must lead and the faith they must have.

Renunciation of Satan

Priest: Do you renounce Satan?
Catechumens: I DO RENOUNCE HIM.
Priest: And all his works?
Catechumens: I DO RENOUNCE THEM.
Priest: And all his allurements?
Catechumens: I DO RENOUNCE THEM.

First Profession of Faith

Priest: Do you believe in God, the Father almighty, creator of heaven and earth?

Catechumens: I DO BELIEVE.

Priest: Do you believe in Jesus Christ, his only Son, our Lord, who was born into this world and who suffered?

Catechumens: I DO BELIEVE.

Priest: Do you believe also in the Holy Spirit, the holy Catholic Church, the communion of saints, the forgiveness of sins, the resurrection of the body and life everlasting?

Catechumens: I DO BELIEVE.

After this profession of faith a hymn may be sung, such as No. 30 or No. 124, or Psalm 61 or Psalm 90 may be recited. If a number of catechumens are to be signed individually, additional verses may be sung or recited when convenient during the following ceremony.

Solemn Signing with the Cross

Priest (breathing on the catechumens): Depart from them, unclean spirit, and give place to the Holy Spirit, the Consoler. *(Again breathing on the catechumens)*: Through this rite of breathing upon you, receive the good Spirit and the blessing of God.

Priest: Peace be to you.

Catechumens: AND WITH YOUR SPIRIT.

Priest (making the sign of the cross on the forehead and on the breast of each catechumen): (Name), receive the mark of the cross on your forehead and within your heart. Embrace the faith with its divine teachings. So live that you will indeed be a temple of God. Having entered into the Church of God, be happy in knowing that you have escaped the snares of death.

Then to all the catechumens: Worship only God, the Father almighty, and Jesus Christ, his only Son, our Lord, who will come to judge the living and the dead and the world by fire.

Catechumens: AMEN.

Prayer

The priest asks God to show the catechumens the way of faith, leading them out of darkness so that they may profess the faith.

Once again each catechumen comes before the priest, who makes the sign of the cross on his forehead, ears, eyes, nose, mouth, breast and shoulders.

Priest: I sign you on the forehead that you may take up the Lord's cross.

I sign you on the ears that you may listen attentively to God's commands.

I sign you on the eyes that you may see God's glory.

I sign you on the nostrils that you may perceive the sweet fragrance of Christ.

I sign you on the mouth that you may speak words of life.

I sign you on the breast that you may believe in God.

I sign you on the shoulders that you may take upon yourself the yoke of his service.

Then to all the catechumens: I sign you all in the name of the Father, and of the Son, and of the Holy Spirit that you may have eternal life and live forever.

Catechumens: AMEN.

Prayers

The priest says three prayers in the name of the entire parish, asking God to protect the catechumens by the power of Christ's cross, to bring them to the new birth of baptism, and to make them children of the promise and new members of his Church.

Priest: Go in peace, and the Lord be with you.

All: AMEN.

An appropriate closing hymn is sung, such as No. 10 or No. 72, or Psalm 3 or Psalm 24 may be recited.

THE SECOND STEP

Entrance

An appropriate hymn, such as No. 74 or No. 39, may be sung, or Psalm 50 or Psalm 141 recited, as the priest and his ministers enter and kneel before the altar. When this is completed, the priest rises and says:

Priest: O God, come to my assistance.

All: O LORD, MAKE HASTE TO HELP ME.

Priest: Glory be to the Father, and to the Son, and to the Holy Spirit.

All: AS IT WAS IN THE BEGINNING, IS NOW, AND EVER SHALL BE, WORLD WITHOUT END. AMEN.

Blessing of the Salt

The priest blesses the salt, asking God that it may become a perfect medicine for the catechumens.

Prayer

The priest asks God to hear the prayers of the catechumens he has called to his Church.

Tasting of the Salt

Each of the catechumens approaches the priest to receive a taste of salt. If there are several catechumens, this is an appropriate time for a hymn, such as No. 73 or No. 105. When giving the catechumen a taste of the salt, the priest says:

Priest: (Name), receive the salt, which is a symbol of wisdom. May it bring you God's favor for life everlasting.

Catechumen: AMEN.

Priest: Peace be to you.

Catechumen: AND WITH YOUR SPIRIT.

Prayer

In the name of the entire parish the priest asks God, who has given the catechumens a taste of blessed salt, to feed them with the bread of heaven and lead them to baptism.

Priest: Go in peace, and the Lord be with you.

All: AMEN.

An appropriate closing hymn is sung, such as No. 79 or No. 52, or Psalm 27 or Psalm 113 may be recited.

THE THIRD STEP

The third, fourth and fifth steps are sometimes combined into a single exorcism. An appropriate hymn, such as No. 30 or No. 21, may be sung, or Psalm 50 or Psalm 130 recited, as the priest and his ministers enter and kneel before the altar. When this is completed, the priest rises and says:

Priest: O God, come to my assistance.

All: O LORD, MAKE HASTE TO HELP ME.

Priest: Glory be to the Father, and to the Son, and to the Holy Spirit.

All: AS IT WAS IN THE BEGINNING, IS NOW, AND EVER SHALL BE, WORLD WITHOUT END. AMEN.

Priest (to the catechumens): Kneel down, chosen ones of God, and say the Our Father.

The catechumens kneel and recite the Our Father.

Priest: Stand up; end your prayer by saying: Amen.

Catechumens: AMEN.

Priest (to the sponsors): Make the sign of the cross on them with me. In the name of the Father, and of the Son, and of the Holy Spirit.

Prayer

The priest asks God to lead the catechumens to the grace of baptism.

Exorcism

The priest solemnly expels the powers of evil with the sign of the cross.

Priest: Go in peace, and the Lord be with you.
All: AMEN.

An appropriate closing hymn is sung, such as No. 86 or No. 116, or Psalm 35 or Psalm 143 may be recited.

THE FOURTH STEP

An appropriate hymn, such as No. 16 or No. 73, may be sung, or Psalm 50 or Psalm 22 recited, as the priest and his ministers enter and kneel before the altar. When this is completed, the priest rises.

Priest: O God, come to my assistance.
All: O LORD, MAKE HASTE TO HELP ME.
Priest: Glory be to the Father, and to the Son, and to the Holy Spirit.
All: AS IT WAS IN THE BEGINNING, IS NOW, AND EVER SHALL BE, WORLD WITHOUT END. AMEN.

Priest (to the catechumens): Kneel down, chosen ones of God, and say the Our Father.

The catechumens kneel and recite the Our Father.

Priest: Stand up; end your prayer by saying: Amen.
Catechumens: AMEN.

Priest (to the sponsors): Make the sign of the cross on them with me. In the name of the Father, and of the Son, and of the Holy Spirit.

Prayer

The priest asks God to accept the catechumens and to guard them as they prepare for baptism.

Exorcism

The priest solemnly expels the powers of evil in the name of the Holy Trinity.

Priest: Go in peace, and the Lord be with you.
All: AMEN.

An appropriate closing hymn is sung, such as No. 99 or No. 90, or Psalm 5 or Psalm 32 may be recited.

THE FIFTH STEP

An appropriate hymn, such as No. 10 or No. 72, may be sung, or Psalm 50 or Psalm 12 recited, as the priest and his ministers enter and kneel before the altar. When this is completed, the priest rises and says:

Priest: O God, come to my assistance.
All: O LORD, MAKE HASTE TO HELP ME.
Priest: Glory be to the Father, and to the Son, and to the Holy Spirit.
All: AS IT WAS IN THE BEGINNING, IS NOW, AND EVER SHALL BE, WORLD WITHOUT END. AMEN.
Priest (to the catechumens): Kneel down, chosen ones of God, and say the Our Father.

The catechumens kneel and recite the Our Father.

Priest: Stand up; end your prayer by saying: Amen.
Catechumens: AMEN.
Priest (to the sponsors): Make the sign of the cross on them with me. In the name of the Father, and of the Son, and of the Holy Spirit.

Exorcism

The priest solemnly expels the powers of evil with the sign of the cross.

Prayer

The priest asks God to give the catechumens the light of his wisdom and to prepare them for baptism.

Priest: Go in peace, and the Lord be with you.
All: AMEN.

An appropriate closing hymn may be sung, such as No. 42 or No. 5, or Psalm 76 or Psalm 102 may be recited.

THE SIXTH STEP

The priest and his ministers meet the catechumens at the entrance of the church. An appropriate hymn may be sung, such as No. 29 or No. 130, or Psalm 50 or Psalm 121 recited. Then the priest says:

Priest: O God, come to my assistance.

All: O LORD, MAKE HASTE TO HELP ME.

Priest: Glory be to the Father, and to the Son, and to the Holy Spirit.

All: AS IT WAS IN THE BEGINNING, IS NOW, AND EVER SHALL BE, WORLD WITHOUT END. AMEN.

Entrance into the Church

The priest leads the catechumens into the church.

Priest: Enter into the holy Church of God that you may receive the blessing of our Lord Jesus Christ and may have part with him and his saints.

All: AMEN.

Once the catechumens have reached their position inside the church, they prostrate themselves in silent adoration. A brief hymn may be sung at this point, such as No. 72 or No. 118, or Psalm 42 or Psalm 83 may be recited.

Apostles' Creed and Lord's Prayer

The catechumens rise, and with the priest they recite the Apostles' Creed and the Lord's Prayer:

I BELIEVE IN GOD, THE FATHER ALMIGHTY, CREATOR OF HEAVEN AND EARTH; AND IN JESUS CHRIST, HIS ONLY SON, OUR LORD, WHO WAS CONCEIVED BY THE HOLY SPIRIT, BORN OF THE VIRGIN MARY, SUFFERED UNDER PONTIUS PILATE, WAS CRUCIFIED, DIED, AND WAS BURIED. HE DESCENDED INTO HELL; THE THIRD DAY HE AROSE AGAIN FROM THE DEAD; HE ASCENDED INTO HEAVEN, SITTETH AT THE RIGHT HAND OF GOD, THE FATHER ALMIGHTY; FROM THENCE HE SHALL COME TO JUDGE THE LIVING AND THE DEAD. I BELIEVE IN THE HOLY SPIRIT, THE HOLY CATHOLIC CHURCH, THE COMMUNION OF SAINTS, THE FORGIVENESS OF SINS, THE RESURRECTION OF THE BODY, AND LIFE EVERLASTING. AMEN.

OUR FATHER, WHO ART IN HEAVEN, HALLOWED BE THY NAME; THY KINGDOM COME; THY WILL BE DONE ON EARTH AS IT IS IN HEAVEN. GIVE US THIS DAY OUR DAILY BREAD; AND FORGIVE US OUR TRESPASSES AS WE FORGIVE THOSE WHO TRESPASS AGAINST US; AND LEAD US NOT INTO TEMPTATION, BUT DELIVER US FROM EVIL. AMEN.

Exorcism

The priest solemnly expels the powers of evil in the name of Jesus Christ.

Priest (touching the ears of each catechumen): Ephpheta, which means

"Be opened," *(then he touches the nostrils)* so that you may receive the fragrance of God's sweetness. But you, O devil, depart; for the judgment of God has come.

An appropriate hymn may now be sung, such as No. 119 or No. 5, or Psalm 31 or Psalm 38 may be recited. Then the priest calls each catechumen by name, and the catechumen answers: PRESENT.

Renunciation of Satan

Priest: Do you renounce Satan?
Catechumens: I DO RENOUNCE HIM.
Priest: And all his works?
Catechumens: I DO RENOUNCE THEM.
Priest: And all his allurements?
Catechumens: I DO RENOUNCE THEM.

Then the priest anoints each of the catechumens with the oil of catechumens.

Priest: I anoint you with the oil of salvation in Christ Jesus our Lord, so that you may have everlasting life.
Catechumen: AMEN.
Priest: Peace be to you.
Catechumen: AND WITH YOUR SPIRIT.

When the anointings are completed, the priest prays over all the catechumens.

Priest: Go forth, unclean spirit, and pay homage to the living and true God. Depart, unclean spirit, and give place to Jesus Christ, his Son. Depart, unclean spirit, and give place to the Holy Spirit, the Consoler.
Priest: Go in peace, and the Lord be with you.
All: AMEN.

An appropriate closing hymn may be sung, such as No. 99 or No. 39, or Psalm 77 or Psalm 104 may be recited.

THE SEVENTH STEP

An appropriate hymn, such as No. 14 or No. 49, may be sung, or Psalm 50 or Psalm 35 recited, as the priest and his ministers enter and assemble with the catechumens and sponsors near the baptismal font. All kneel for a time in prayer. When the singing is completed, the priest rises.

Priest: O God, come to my assistance.
All: O LORD, MAKE HASTE TO HELP ME.

Priest: Glory be to the Father, and to the Son, and to the Holy Spirit.
All: AS IT WAS IN THE BEGINNING, IS NOW, AND EVER SHALL BE, WORLD WITHOUT END. AMEN.

The priest calls each catechumen by name, and the catechumen answers:
PRESENT.

Profession of Faith

Priest: Do you believe in God, the Father almighty, creator of heaven and earth?
Catechumens: I DO BELIEVE.
Priest: Do you believe in Jesus Christ, his only Son, our Lord, who was born into this world and who suffered?
Catechumens: I DO BELIEVE.
Priest: Do you believe also in the Holy Spirit, the holy Catholic Church, the communion of saints, the forgiveness of sins, the resurrection of the body and life everlasting?
Catechumens: I DO BELIEVE.
Priest: What is it that you are seeking?
Catechumens: BAPTISM.
Priest: Do you wish to be baptized?
Catechumens: I DO.

Pouring of the Water

Then the priest baptizes each of the catechumens.

Priest: I baptize you in the name of the Father, and of the Son, and of the Holy Spirit.

An appropriate hymn may now be sung, such as No. 126 or No. 56, or Psalm 41 or Psalm 95 may be recited.

Anointing

Then the priest anoints each of the catechumens.

Priest: May almighty God, the Father of our Lord Jesus Christ, who has given you a new birth by means of water and the Holy Spirit and forgiven all your sins, anoint you with the Chrism of salvation in the same Christ Jesus our Lord, so that you may have life everlasting.
Newly Baptized: AMEN.
Priest: Peace be to you.
Newly Baptized: AND WITH YOUR SPIRIT.

Reception of Baptismal Robes

Then the sponsors give white garments to the newly baptized, while the priest says:

Priest: Receive this white garment. Never let it become stained, so that, when you stand before the judgment seat of our Lord Jesus Christ, you may have life everlasting.

Newly Baptized: AMEN.

Reception of Baptismal Candles

Then the sponsors give lighted candles to the newly baptized.

Priest: Receive this burning light, and keep the grace of your baptism throughout a blameless life. Observe the commandments of God. Then when the Lord comes to the heavenly wedding feast, you will be able to meet him with all the saints in the halls of heaven, and live forever and ever.

Newly Baptized: AMEN.

Priest: Go in peace, and the Lord be with you.

All: AMEN.

An appropriate closing hymn may be sung, such as No. 99 or No. 13, or Psalm 117 or Psalm 135 may be recited.

A Renewal of Baptismal Promises

The commitment to live Christ's life which every Christian takes on at baptism is intensified at confirmation and renewed at every Mass. But sometimes a more special and solemn renewal should be made. This is regularly done each year in the Easter vigil of the Lord's resurrection, when the whole Christian community celebrates its share in Christ's rising to new life. It may also be done before other important events in the life of the individual or the community: before weddings, confirmations and ordinations, for example, or before a graduation or after a retreat.

The following rite is merely suggested for such occasions; it will be altered to suit particular needs.

Entrance

An opening hymn, such as No. 81 or No. 79, is sung as the priest and his ministers enter and kneel before the altar; or all may recite together Psalm 22, 41, 62, 71 or 89.

Scripture Reading

Suggested Readings: John 3:1–21; John 4:5–14; John 20:19–29; Romans 6:3–11; Romans 8:5–17; 1 Peter 3:18–22.

Homily

The priest may preach a brief homily.

Blessing of the Water

The priest blesses the water, which God has made a sign of baptism.

The Renewal

Some explanation of the promises is necessary. The comments given here are intented as suggestions; ordinarily the priest or leader will give his own commentary.

Priest: Your baptism began as love and faith in action. You came to your Father and he gave you the gift of his own life, made you his child. We shall now renew the promises of our baptism, which for most of us were made by others. Now we will make them for ourselves, in gratitude and with a spirit of dedication. What is it, then, that you asked of the Church of God at baptism and that you still desire today?

People: FAITH.

Priest: What does faith offer you?

People: ETERNAL LIFE.

Priest: If, then, it is life that you wish, keep the commandments. Love the Lord your God with your whole being, and love your neighbor as yourself.

Do not ask, Who is my neighbor? Remember that our Lord has taught us that every man is our neighbor, and that what you do to others you do to Jesus.

Renunciation of Satan

In your baptism you renounced the devil. This means that with God's help you would free yourselves from evil and live as God's children. It is a choice you make: between Christ and the works of darkness. How do you renounce the devil? By refusing to place your good above that of another, and by devoting yourself to works of love and goodness. Decide now that you will serve the Lord alone.

Since you realize what it is to make these promises, I ask you: Do you renounce Satan?

People: WE DO RENOUNCE HIM.
Priest: And all his works?
People: WE DO RENOUNCE THEM.
Priest: And all his allurements?
People: WE DO RENOUNCE THEM.

Profession of Faith

Priest: In baptism you profess your faith. To say, I believe, means, I accept God's Word; I accept Jesus Christ. It means: I take my stand; I build my house upon this rock which is Christ. The rains and floods and winds may come, but I shall not be moved.

What does it mean to say, I believe? It means: I guide my life by these truths; I am willing to live for them or to die for them. I shall teach them by words, but even more by action. So now we reaffirm our faith.

Do you believe in God, the Father almighty, creator of heaven and earth?

People: WE DO BELIEVE.

Priest: Do you believe in Jesus Christ, his only Son, our Lord, who was born into this world and who suffered?

People: WE DO BELIEVE.

Priest: Do you believe also in the Holy Spirit, the holy Catholic Church, the communion of saints, the forgiveness of sins, the resurrection of the body and life everlasting?

People: WE DO BELIEVE.

Lord's Prayer

Priest: Now we say the prayer that was said at our baptism and that we repeat at every renewal of our covenant with the Father. It reminds us that we are called every day to live our commitment and that our lives must be lives of building and doing: thy kingdom come, thy will be done. Above all, say this prayer knowing that each of us can speak to God as Father. Let us pray to him together, as our Lord Jesus Christ has taught us to pray:

All: OUR FATHER . . .

Priest: Then the waters flowed, the Holy Trinity was invoked, and you were Christ-ened, made over to be like Christ. Then the Father could say: This is my beloved son. Now you can live his life, branches joined to Christ, the true vine. Your life can be fruitful now. Children of God, live up to your commitment.

As the priest sprinkles everyone with water, an appropriate hymn, such as No. 45 or No. 56, may be sung; or Psalm 117 or Psalm 50 may be recited.

Response

Priest: Strip away everything vicious, everything deceitful: pretenses, jealousies and disparaging remarks of all kinds.

People: LIKE NEWBORN BABES, WE CRAVE PURE MILK FOR OUR MINDS, THAT BY IT WE MAY GROW UP INTO SALVATION, SINCE NOW WE HAVE TASTED THE SWEETNESS OF THE LORD.

Priest: Come to him, the living stone, rejected indeed by men, but choice and precious before God.

People: WE TOO ARE LIVING STONES, BUILT INTO A SPIRITUAL TEMPLE.

Priest: Your vocation is to a holy priesthood, to offer pleasing spiritual sacrifices to God through Jesus Christ.

People: FOR SCRIPTURE SAYS: SEE, I AM LAYING A STONE IN SION, A CHOICE AND PRECIOUS CORNERSTONE, AND HE WHO PUTS HIS BELIEF IN IT WILL NOT BE DISAPPOINTED.

Priest: Yours, then, is the honor because you believe.

People: WE ARE A CHOSEN RACE, A ROYAL HOUSE, A PRIESTHOOD, A HOLY NATION, A PEOPLE GOD TAKES AS HIS OWN, THAT WE MAY DECLARE THE PRAISES OF HIM WHO CALLED US OUT OF DARKNESS INTO HIS WONDERFUL LIGHT.

Priest: Once you were not a people.

People: NOW WE ARE GOD'S PEOPLE.

Priest: Once there was no mercy for you.

People: NOW WE HAVE FOUND MERCY.

A closing hymn, such as No. 52 or No. 65, may be sung; or Psalm 64, 135, or 148 may be recited.

Confirmation

CONFIRMATION furthers our initiation into the Christian community. It is our anointing in the Spirit of God's love, our consecration into the priestly work begun by Christ.

In baptism we enter the Church and its life, which is Christ. Confirmation strengthens and perfects this new life in the Holy Spirit, the Spirit of that peace and love which are the foundation of the Church's unity.

The bishop lays his hands on our heads and asks God the Father that we may receive the fullness of the Spirit as the Apostles did after Jesus rose from the dead. The Spirit that filled Jesus, that is the life of the Risen Lord, is the Spirit he promised to send us, building up the life we began to live in baptism. Spirit means breath and thus life itself. A man's spirit may be strong, or it may be broken; unafraid or cowardly. In confirmation we have the Spirit of Jesus, the Spirit of love, of peace, of wisdom.

We are anointed with oil, a sign of our Christian calling to be a royal priesthood and a nation of prophets. As priests we must offer God praise and thanksgiving for ourselves and for all men. As prophets, we must speak the truth to all, guided by the Spirit, unafraid of any consequences. We are signed with the cross, a reminder that we are Christ's to the extent that we embrace his cross and share his risen life.

Confirmation prepares for the great sacrament, the Eucharist. The Spirit comes that we may more fully understand what we do in the sign of our unity with one another in God's love. The Spirit provides us with the resources to live the life of our new faith.

As confirmed and consecrated Christians we are made more conscious of our need to give witness to the Spirit of God in the world. Confirmation helps us demonstrate in our lives the peace and the love of Christ and his community. As Christians we are brothers of Christ, and our lives are to be filled with his Spirit.

The Rite of Confirmation

Whenever possible, confirmation will occur within the celebration of the Eucharist. After the Gospel the bishop will ordinarily preach a homily. Then the candidates will advance to kneel before the bishop. At this point an appropriate hymn may be sung, such as No. 29 or No. 127, or Psalm 67 or 103 may be recited.

Outside Mass there would be an opening hymn or psalm, followed by the reading of Acts of the Apostles 8:14–17 and John 14:23–31 or other appropriate selections. Between the two readings appropriate psalm verses may be recited or another hymn sung. After the Gospel reading the bishop preaches a homily, then the candidates take their places before him. Before or after they approach the bishop the promises of baptism may be renewed; see page 729.

Invocation of the Spirit

When the candidates are kneeling before him and the song or psalm is finished, the bishop says:

Bishop: May the Holy Spirit descend upon you and the power of the Most High preserve you from sin.
People: AMEN.
Bishop: Our help is in the name of the Lord.
People: WHO MADE HEAVEN AND EARTH.
Bishop: O Lord, hear my prayer.
People: AND LET MY CRY COME TO YOU.
Bishop: The Lord be with you.
People: AND WITH YOUR SPIRIT.
Bishop: Let us pray. Almighty and eternal God, who in your kindness gave to these your servants a new birth through water and the Holy Spirit, and granted to them remission of all their sins; send forth from heaven upon them your sevenfold Spirit, the Holy Consoler.
People: AMEN.
Bishop: The Spirit of wisdom and understanding.
People: AMEN.
Bishop: The Spirit of counsel and fortitude.
People: AMEN.
Bishop: The Spirit of knowledge and piety.
People: AMEN.

The bishop concludes the prayer by asking that those to be confirmed may be filled with the Spirit and sealed with the sign of the cross.

The Confirming

The bishop then anoints each candidate with chrism in the sign of the cross. While this is being done an appropriate hymn, such as No. 16 or No. 123, may be sung, or all together may recite Psalm 88 or 131.

Bishop: I sign you with the sign of the cross and I confirm you with the Chrism of salvation. In the name of the Father, and of the Son, and of the Holy Spirit.

The Newly Confirmed: AMEN.

The bishop strikes the newly confirmed lightly on the cheek, a form of the kiss of peace.

Bishop: Peace be with you.

When the anointing is finished, the following is sung or recited:

Strengthen, O God, what you have wrought in us,
from your holy temple, which is in Jerusalem.
Glory be to the Father, and to the Son,
and to the Holy Spirit.
As it was in the beginning, is now, and ever shall be,
world without end. Amen.
Strengthen, O God, what you have wrought in us,
from your holy temple, which is in Jerusalem.

Bishop: Show us, O Lord, your mercy.
People: AND GRANT US YOUR SALVATION.
Bishop: O Lord, hear my prayer.
People: AND LET MY CRY COME TO YOU.
Bishop: The Lord be with you.
People: AND WITH YOUR SPIRIT.

The bishop prays that the Holy Spirit may live in the newly confirmed and make them temples of his glory.

Conclusion

Bishop: Behold, so will the man be blessed who fears the Lord. May the Lord bless you from Sion, so that you may see the prosperity of Jerusalem all the days of your life and may have life everlasting.

People: AMEN.

An appropriate hymn may be sung, such as No. 5 or No. 71. In the Mass, with the bishop's permission, the newly confirmed may receive both bread and wine, as a fuller sign of their participation in the eucharistic meal.

735

Penance

PENANCE is the sacrament of reconciliation. Through our selfishness we have deliberately separated ourselves from God and our fellow Christians. In penance we return to God by returning to the unity of his people, the Church.

The best introduction to the sacrament of penance is found in the story of the prodigal son. Like the young man who left his father's house to squander his inheritance in selfish pleasure, we have deliberately turned away from the family of Christians to indulge our selfishness and pride. In baptism we were born into God's family as sons and daughters, to share the life of Christ in the unity of the Church. But we have rejected our Father, decided to live our own lives, shattered the unity of God's people.

Like the prodigal son we find ourselves alone in the misery of our sin. We raise our eyes to the Church, the house of our Father, and long for the unity, the goodness and the peace we once knew within it. We no longer have any place in the family we deserted, yet there is no hope for us outside it.

Penance is a sign of our Father's great love for us, a love which accepts our sorrow and renews our life in Christ. It is a sign of our reconciliation with the Church: the fellow Christians we deserted have continued to pray for us. They have kept Christ's love alive in the world. Had they not done so, we could not return.

Penance is never merely an individual affair. We return to Christ through our fellow Christians, and the perfect sign of our reconciliation with him comes when we share with them in the Eucharist, the great sacrament of unity in the love of Christ.

Examination of Conscience

St. Paul tells us that we have been set free from the law. As Christians we are called not to keep a set of rules but to live the love of Christ. St. Augustine advises us: "Love, then do what you want."

Sin is never simply a matter of breaking a rule, even a commandment of God. Sin is always personal, a refusal to love, a turning away from God and neighbor. Sin is our failure to live the Christian life into which we were baptized.

In our thoughts and actions we discover our failures as Christians.

By reviewing what we have thought and what we have done, we find that we have—or have not—love for God and our neighbor.

Most of us have a favorite method of examining our consciences. Some review the Ten Commandments and the precepts of the Church; others concentrate on their responsibilities as parents, students, workers, and members of society; others prefer some other method. The questions which follow are not intended to replace such examinations. They may be read from time to time as an addition to what we usually do to prepare ourselves for the sacrament of penance.

FOR ADULTS

What kind of an employee am I? Do I put in a fair day's work? Do I usually do my work well? Take an interest in the performance and good name of my employer? Take care of my employer's property? Do I try to understand the problems of ownership and management? If I belong to a union, do I take an active and responsible part and support it with time and money?

Do I take personal responsibility for all my actions or excuse myself from their consequences because I act under another's orders?

Am I friendly and fair with the people with whom I deal at work? Am I honest with those above me—telling them what I think, but willing to work hard even when decisions go against me? Do I try to avoid office intrigue and gossip? Do I refuse to blame others for everything that goes wrong? Do I cooperate honestly with those who work with me, sometimes going out of my way to give an encouraging or friendly word? Do I admit mistakes? Forgive the mistakes of others?

Do I recognize my subordinates as human beings? Do I take a personal interest in them? Am I willing to give time and energy to train them, and at the same time, am I willing to learn from them? Do I often ask them to work too hard? Not hard enough? Do I make an effort to be clear and precise when giving directions? Do I leave room for individual initiative?

If I deal with the public, do I usually make an effort to be helpful and friendly? Am I honest, and do I avoid taking advantage of people? Do I damage my employer by the way I treat customers?

What kind of employer am I? Do I pay a just wage? Am I fair in hiring and advancing my employees? Do I take a personal interest in them? Show a proper concern for their health and well-being? Am I harsh, arbitrary or unreasonable? Do I habitually disregard the feelings of those who work for me? Do I recognize their right to organize and bargain collectively?

Do I recognize my obligation to train my employees? To help them fully utilize their talents? Am I willing to give young people a chance? Do I make provision for the needs of my older employees?

Are my business practices ethical? Do I recognize my suppliers and competitors as human beings, and refuse to take unfair advantage of them? Do I try to give my customers a fair product or service for a fair price?

Is my advertising honest? Do I deliberately take advantage of people's ignorance, insecurity or greed?

Do I accept the responsibility my company has in community affairs? Does my company contribute its share, particularly in time and talent, to the needs of the community?

As a professional person, do I make an honest effort to live up to the ideals of my profession? Do I take the time necessary to keep up with developments in my field? Do I respect my colleagues? Am I constantly re-evaluating my professional practice?

Do I look on my life as one of service? Am I willing to help those in need? Are my fees reasonable? Do I make an effort always to treat those I serve as human beings? Am I arrogant?

Do I have a proper concern for the welfare of my client, student or patient? Do I do the best I can for him, even when he does not appreciate it, and even when I could have done less?

Do I take part in professional and civic organizations? Do I concern myself with community problems?

Do I allow myself to become too busy, taking on so many things that I cannot do a decent job at any one of them? Do I waste a good deal of time because I am not organized? Do I waste the time of others?

What kind of husband am I? Do I spend enough time with my family? Do I allow my work to consume so much of my time, energy and interest that I cannot give my wife and children the attention they require? Do I spend too much time or money on my personal amusement?

Do I love my wife? Do I share things with her, and put her interests above all others? Am I concerned for her happiness, careful never to take her for granted? Do I help and encourage her? Ask her advice, but avoid leaving all the painful and difficult decisions to her? Am I often

738

unreasonable? Do I use her love for me to take advantage of her? Do I respect my wife? Never belittle her before other people? Do I willingly do the things she asks me? Do I allow her great freedom in expressing her needs and talents?

Do I love my children? Do I know them as individuals? Do I talk to them? Play with them? Help them with their work and listen to their problems? Do I discipline my children according to their own needs and not according to my convenience? Do I give them example they can imitate? Do I give my children the affection they need, without playing favorites? Do I know and respect their friends? Am I concerned with their education, not only with getting them through school? Do I exercise enough control over my children's activities? Do I allow them to start making decisions on their own? Do I encourage freedom and independent thought, especially in teenagers? Do I allow my children's mistakes to prejudice me in the future? Do I guide and encourage them to choose good books, magazines, music, television and movies? Do I respect their likes and dislikes in all fields, trying to understand those that differ from my own?

Do I provide for my family? Am I too much concerned with luxuries or with status symbols? Do I live beyond my means? Do I take proper care of myself? Do I plan for the future without losing the present?

Do I make sure that my family does not become closed within its own small concerns? Do I encourage an interest in the affairs of our neighborhood, city, state and nation?

What kind of wife am I? Do I take proper care of my family, providing an atmosphere of love and security in which all can grow and mature? Do I run my home efficiently, without becoming obsessed by my routine? Do I waste a great deal of time? Do I make sure that I take some time for leisure?

Do I love my husband? Am I concerned about his needs? Do I place his interests above all others? Do I help and encourage him, and make an effort to understand his problems? Do I often nag or belittle him? Do I take him for granted? Do I use his love for me to take advantage of him? Do I respect him? Am I overanxious, not relying enough on the responsibility of each family member? Do I do willingly the things my husband asks me?

Do I love my children? Do I care for them as individuals? Am I patient with them? Do I take time out to talk to them, play with them, help them with their work, and listen to their problems? Am I careful to help them grow, and not to smother them in my affection? Am I often unreasonable with them? Do I discipline my children? Do I comfort them and show them the affection they need? Do I take the time to teach my children? Do I take enough interest in their education, in their ideals and ambitions? Do I allow them to learn by helping me about the house? Do I give them the kind of example they can follow? Do I make a conscious effort to provide them with good things to read, to discuss things with them, to supervise the television they watch, the movies they see, the music they listen to?

Do I make an effort to broaden my own interests? Do I avoid gossip and neighborhood feuds? Do I plan family activities which will be interesting and beneficial to all? Do I realize the importance of leisure activities and give them the attention they deserve?

Do I take a reasonable share in the financial concerns of my family? Am I responsible in the way I spend money? Am I overly concerned? Do I distinguish between essentials and luxuries?

If I work, do I let my job take the interest and devotion the family should have? If I do not work, am I sufficiently involved in activities outside the house?

As a single person, am I careful to avoid selfishness? Am I concerned about other members of my family? Do I contribute, not only financially, but of my time and abilities, to the rest of my family? Do I make an effort to broaden my own knowledge, concern and activities?

If I live alone, do I organize my activities so as not to waste too much time? Do I waste time and money on trifles? If I live with others, am I considerate of their wishes? Do I share things with them, while respecting their need for privacy?

If I am a student, do I take my work seriously? Do I want to learn? Do I do outside reading? How many books not assigned in class do I read in a year? How many journals in my field do I read? Do I try to think through what my professors are saying? Do I ask questions? Are my criticisms constructive? Do I realize that self-education is the most important kind? Do I contribute to those campus activities whose goal is a better school or society? Am I interested only in income and status after graduation or do I realize my responsibility to serve the community?

Do I take a responsible part in the political affairs of my city, state and nation? Do I make an effort to follow these affairs closely enough to vote intelligently? Do I vote for the man I consider best qualified? Do I decide on bond issues and the like on the basis of the facts as I have been able to discover them, and not merely on the basis of avoiding higher taxes or of securing some special privilege?

Do I substitute slogans for thinking in political matters? Do I listen to those who disagree with me? Do I ever contribute to those organizations and candidates who seem best qualified for political responsibility? Do I combat ignorance, indifference, hatred and violence? Am I too hasty to judge and categorize others?

Do I make an effort to discover the implications of my religious belief to local, state and national politics? Do I make any effort to see that every citizen in my community is treated fairly and decently? Have I ever considered the morality of nuclear warfare, and have I ever communicated my judgment to those charged with making national policy?

Do I respect just political authority? Are my criticisms constructive? Do I make any effort to think out alternatives to policies with which I disagree? Have I done anything to join with others in order to effect these alternatives?

Do I support local, state and national officials when I think they are right? Do I ever try to interest others in their support? Do I avoid seeking special interests which will not serve the common good?

Am I aware of the social implications of my Christian life? Do I avoid and condemn any form of racial prejudice, wherever and however it might be practiced? Do I try to eliminate any form of prejudice in myself, and do I speak out against it whenever I encounter it? What have I done to remove this evil from the community in which I live? How have I supported those who are working to remove it from the state and national level?

What have I done for people who are poorer than I am? Do I encourage and support efforts to allow every member of society to live a decent life? Have I helped to make happier the lives of the sick, the old or those in prison?

Do I realize what human rights are and do I work to make them realities in every life? Through gossip or by other means do I destroy the good name of another? Do I uphold by word and deed the right of every person to live where he wishes? Do I ridicule those who exercise their right to protest?

Do I work for peace? Am I willing to involve myself in efforts to find peaceful solutions to neighborhood, community and state problems? Do I do what I can to promote international peace? Do I encourage my representatives to seek every possibility for achieving genuine peace in the world? Do I recognize that no nation, religion or social system claims a monopoly on all truth?

Do I allow a proper love of country to turn into a narrow nationalism, or do I actively recognize the brotherhood of all men? Do I support and encourage efforts to assist underdeveloped nations, to give men all over the world a chance to help themselves? Am I willing to make sacrifices to see that this is done?

Do I live as a member of my parish family? Do I contribute time, ability and money to the parish in which I am a member? Do I take an interest in parish affairs? Am I willing to take on the responsibility of organizing and working on these affairs so that they genuinely contribute to the common life of my parish? Do I avoid getting involved in parochial activities for their own sake, ignoring the obligations which my parish has to the larger community in which it exists? Do I realize that my parish is not a self-contained unit? That we cannot use all or often even most of our resources for our own needs, when the needs of our fellow Christians and others in our city, state and world are more pressing? What have I done to see that a proper portion of the parish resources are spent outside the parish?

Do I deal honestly with my pastor and his assistants? Do I respect them and listen to them? Do I tell them what I think? Do I simply criticize, or do I take the responsibility of offering constructive suggestions about the running of my parish? Do I think of my parish chiefly in terms of the services it provides me and my family?

Do I work for unity with all other Christians? Do I try to learn about other beliefs? Do I respect other religions, and do I try to see in their traditions authentic elements which I may have forgotten in my own? Do I ever discuss religion with other Christians? Pray with them? Cooperate with them in common activities? Do I work well with those of no religious faith, without being condescending, and try to appreciate the values in their lives which I may have forgotten in my own?

FOR CHILDREN

What kind of a student am I? Do I study hard, even subjects I don't like? Do I try to get my work done every day? Do I ask questions, and try to be interested in my subjects? Do I read things in newspapers, magazines and books about the things I am studying in school, even when I don't have to? Do I do my own work? Do I cheat?

Do I ask my teacher or my parents when I don't understand something? Do I try not to get discouraged when the work seems difficult? Do I do extra work if I find a subject easy?

Do I help my schoolmates? Do I dislike those who get better marks than I do, or look down on those who don't do as well? Do I spend time worrying about marks? Do I ever ask myself whether I am learning anything, and try to figure out why I am not learning more? Do I show off?

Do I pay attention to my teacher? Do I try to do the things he or she asks me to do? Do I ever say, "Thank you," when he or she helps me with something? Do I make fun of him or her? Do I always tell the truth, and do I try to be polite?

Do I obey the rules of my school? Do I take care of the furniture and books, and try to make it a pleasant place to work? Do I take part in school activities, and help out in school projects? Am I careful of others?

Do I love my mother and father? Do I talk to them and tell them about my day? Do I tell them the truth? Do I try to do what they ask me to? Do I try to help them about the house? Do I try to be cheerful and pleasant? Am I polite to them? Do I take care of my own things? Do I ever tell them that I love them?

Do I love my brothers and sisters? Am I kind to them? Do I share things with them? Do I play with them, and help them with their work? Do I take care of my younger brothers and sisters? Do I leave my older brothers and sisters alone when they want to be by themselves? Do I help with and enjoy the things my family does all together? Do I often get angry? Do I often sulk? Do I become jealous when my parents or relatives praise or pay special attention to one of my brothers or sisters?

Do I take care of furniture and all the things my family owns? Do I try to think up ways to make our home more pleasant? Do I volunteer for jobs around the house? Do I ever sweep the walks, cut the grass, do the dishes, or clean a room?

Do I think of others? Am I noisy when someone is trying to work or to rest? Do I interfere when my parents or brothers and sisters are doing something by themselves? Do I make my parents speak to me three or four times before I do what they ask?

743

How am I in my neighborhood? Am I polite to people? Do I respect their feelings and their property? Do I make fun of people? Do I ever share my toys with other boys and girls? Am I a bully?

Do I help other people? Do I try to like them? Do I speak to them, and answer if they speak to me?

Do I know anything about my neighborhood and about my city? Do I read the newspaper to see what is going on? Do I ever watch the news on television, or a program that teaches me something?

The Rite of Penance

Before going to confession, the penitent should spend some time examining his conscience for sins he has committed since his last confession (see page 736). He should spend more time asking God to make him truly sorry for the hurt he has done to others, and begging his help to live a more truly human and Christian life in the future.

Before entering the confessional, the penitent should say an act of contrition.

Entering the Confessional

When he enters the confessional and the priest turns to him and blesses him, the penitent begins: THANK YOU FOR THE BLESSING, FATHER.

Confession

He then tells the priest how long it has been since his last confession, and tells his sins, simply and directly. When he has finished he may say something like this:

FOR THESE AND ALL THE SINS OF MY PAST LIFE I AM SORRY AND I ASK THE PARDON OF THE LORD FROM YOU, FATHER, TOGETHER WITH WHATEVER PENANCE YOU THINK BEST.

Absolution

Then the penitent listens to the priest and the penance he imposes. He also listens to the words of forgiveness. (Sometimes the priest may omit all but the third of these prayers.)

Priest: May almighty God have mercy on you, forgive you your sins, and bring you to life everlasting.
Penitent: AMEN.
Priest: May the almighty and merciful Lord grant you pardon, absolution, and remission of your sins.
Penitent: AMEN.

Priest: May our Lord Jesus Christ absolve you, and by his authority I absolve you from every bond of excommunication and interdict, to the extent of my power and your need. Finally I absolve you from your sins, in the name of the Father, and of the Son, and of the Holy Spirit.

Penitent: AMEN.

Priest: May the passion of our Lord Jesus Christ, the merits of the Blessed Virgin Mary and of all the saints, and also whatever good you do and evil you endure be cause for the remission of your sins, the increase of grace, and the reward of everlasting life.

Penitent: AMEN.

Penance

After leaving the confessional, the penitent performs the penance the priest assigned him, either immediately or on another occasion.

Marriage

MARRIAGE is the sacrament of love between man and woman. In its celebration, a couple become one in their love for each other, and a sign of the love Christ has for his Church.

A man and a woman wish to give themselves entirely to each other. They wish to unite their individual lives into a new life together. They invite God and man to witness and to bless their pledge of faithfulness and love.

Out of their love a new family is to be born within the parish family. So the parish gathers, in the persons of parents, relatives and friends, to witness and to approve the decision the couple has made.

The Christian lives in Christ, and so the new life which is begun in Christian marriage is Christ's life. The love which unites Christian husband and wife is Christ's love.

The union of a Christian man and woman is a sign of the union between Christ and his Church; their love is a sign of his love for his Church. Out of their love for each other, husband and wife are to show forth Christ's love in the world. Their love is to be fruitful in producing new life, and in spreading Christ's peace and his love in the world.

In the marriage rite, it is the couple themselves who are ministers of the sacrament to each other. They take each other for better or worse. They exchange rings as a sign of their fidelity. It is their words of choice which are the sign of God's power acting in them.

The celebration of marriage ordinarily takes place within the celebration of the Eucharist. The love and unity of marriage are perfected in the Eucharist, the sacrament of love and unity. For a man and woman united in Christ, the Eucharist will always be a special sign of the love which binds them together.

Blessing of an Engagement

Since the months before marriage are an important preparation in many ways, a couple intending marriage may seek the blessing of the Church and the support of the parish family during this time. The couple promises to grow in love for each other so as to be better prepared for the day on which they will give themselves to each other entirely.

This rite may also be used for groups, perhaps during a series of pre-Cana conferences. It may be celebrated in the church, in the home, or in any suitable place. The pastor or another may act as leader.

Entrance

An appropriate hymn, such as No. 29 or No. 118, may be sung.

Priest: Hear the word of the Lord, O nations,
    proclaim it on distant coasts, and say:
People: HE WHO SCATTERED ISRAEL, NOW GATHERS THEM TOGETHER,
    HE GUARDS THEM AS A SHEPHERD HIS FLOCK.
    THE LORD SHALL RANSOM JACOB,
    HE SHALL REDEEM HIM FROM THE HAND OF HIS CONQUEROR.
Priest: Shouting they shall mount the heights of Sion,
    they shall come streaming to the Lord's blessings:
People: THE GRAIN, THE WINE, AND THE OIL,
    THE SHEEP AND THE OXEN.
    THEY THEMSELVES SHALL BE LIKE WATERED GARDENS,
    NEVER AGAIN SHALL THEY LANGUISH.
Priest: Then the young girls shall make merry and dance,
    and young men and old as well.
People: THE LORD SHALL TURN THEIR MOURNING TO JOY,
    HE WILL CONSOLE AND GLADDEN THEM AFTER THEIR SORROWS.

JEREMIAH 31:10–13

Reading

SIRACH 51:23–30

Response

Priest: Stern as death is love,
People: RELENTLESS AS A BLAZING FIRE IS DEVOTION.
    DEEP WATERS CANNOT QUENCH LOVE,
    NOR FLOODS SWEEP IT AWAY.   SONG OF SOLOMON 8:6–7

Homily

The leader may give a short homily.

Exchange of Promises

If a ring is to be given, the man places it on the finger of his fiancée while making his promise.

Man: BEFORE GOD AND THESE PEOPLE, I LOVE YOU AND I PROMISE TO GROW IN THAT LOVE IN PREPARATION FOR OUR MARRIAGE.

Woman: BEFORE GOD AND THESE PEOPLE, I LOVE YOU AND I PROMISE TO GROW IN THAT LOVE IN PREPARATION FOR OUR MARRIAGE.

Prayer

Priest: Let us pray.

Father, you know that it is not good for a person to be alone, and that only through sharing all in love can we become your true sons and daughters. May you give this couple wisdom, and bless them, and may the time ahead be one of right decisions and honest preparations. We ask this through Jesus Christ our Lord.

People: AMEN.

Conclusion

An appropriate hymn, such as No. 52 or No. 72, may be sung; or all recite together Psalm 148.

Bible Service Before Marriage

The following service may be used the night before a wedding, perhaps in connection with the wedding rehearsal, with the wedding party and close relatives and friends of the couple taking part, to provide a few moments of meditation on the meaning and importance of the sacrament which is to be celebrated. The pastor or someone else may serve as leader, in the church or elsewhere.

Entrance

An appropriate hymn, such as No. 14 or No. 118, may be sung.

Priest: The house of Israel trusts in the Lord.
He is their help and their shield.
People: THOSE WHO FEAR THE LORD TRUST IN THE LORD.
HE IS THEIR HELP AND THEIR SHIELD.
THE LORD REMEMBERS US AND WILL BLESS US;
HE WILL BLESS THE HOUSE OF ISRAEL.
Priest: He will bless those who fear the Lord,
both the small and the great.
People: MAY THE LORD BLESS YOU MORE AND MORE,
BOTH YOU AND YOUR CHILDREN.

MAY YOU BE BLESSED BY THE LORD,
WHO MADE HEAVEN AND EARTH.

Priest: Heaven is the home of the Lord,
but the earth he has given to the children of men.

People: WE GIVE THANKS TO THE LORD,
NOW AND FOREVER. PSALM 113

Reading

GENESIS 2:18–24 OR I CORINTHIANS 13:1–10

Response

If there are two readings, the following may be recited between them:

Priest: Set a seal on your heart,
as a seal on your arm.

People: FOR STERN AS DEATH IS LOVE,
RELENTLESS AS A BLAZING FIRE IS DEVOTION;
DEEP WATERS CANNOT QUENCH LOVE,
NOR FLOODS SWEEP IT AWAY. SONG OF SOLOMON 8:6–7

Homily

The priest may give a short homily.

Prayer

Priest: Let us pray.

Father, this couple is soon to become one in marriage. Favor them
so that they may live by your holy word. Make them strong in constant
fidelity and real affection for one another, and let their love be a sign
to the world of your love for men. Help them to grow in loving service,
Lord, and support them in times of hardship and suffering. We ask this
through Jesus Christ our Lord.

People: AMEN.

Priest: May the Lord bless you and keep you. May the Lord make
his face shine upon you and be gracious to you. May the Lord give
you peace.

People: AMEN.

Conclusion

*An appropriate hymn, such as No. 83 or No. 124, may be sung; or all together
recite Psalm 127.*

Mass on the Day of Marriage

An appropriate hymn, such as No. 24 or No. 128, may be sung as the ministers of the Mass, together with the bridal party, enter the church and come in procession toward the sanctuary. The alleluias in parentheses are recited during Eastertime.

Entrance Song

May the God of Israel join you together;
and may he be with you,
who was merciful to two only children;
and now, O Lord, make them bless you more fully.
(Alleluia, alleluia.)   TOBIT 7:15, 8:19

> Blessed are all who fear the Lord,
> who walk in his ways.   TURN TO PSALM 127
>
> Glory be to the Father.

Lord Have Mercy   Glory to God   Prayer

THE LITURGY OF THE WORD

First Reading
EPHESIANS 5:22–33

Songs of Meditation and Response

During Eastertime:

Alleluia, alleluia.
May the Lord send you help from the sanctuary,
from Sion may he sustain you. Alleluia.   PSALM 19

May the Lord bless you from Sion,
the maker of heaven and earth. Alleluia.   PSALM 133

At other times:

Your wife shall be like a fruitful vine
in the recesses of your home.
Your children like olive plants
around your table.   PSALM 127

And from Septuagesima to Easter add:

Behold, thus is the man blessed
who fears the Lord.

The Lord bless you from Sion:
may you see the prosperity of Jerusalem
all the days of your life.
May you see your children's children.
Peace be upon Israel! PSALM 127

From Pentecost to Septuagesima add:

Alleluia, alleluia.
May the Lord send you help from the sanctuary,
from Sion may he sustain you. Alleluia. PSALM 19

Gospel
MATTHEW 19:3–6

Homily

Marriage Promise

When the homily is concluded, all stand.

Priest (to bridegroom): (Name), do you take (Name), here present, for your lawful wife according to the rite of our holy mother, the Church?

Bridegroom: I DO.

Priest (to bride): (Name), do you take (Name), here present, for your lawful husband according to the rite of our holy mother, the Church?

Bride: I DO.

The priest asks the couple to join hands, and to repeat after him in turn:

I, (NAME), TAKE YOU, (NAME), FOR MY LAWFUL WIFE (HUSBAND), TO HAVE AND TO HOLD, FROM THIS DAY FORWARD, FOR BETTER, FOR WORSE, FOR RICHER, FOR POORER, IN SICKNESS AND IN HEALTH, UNTIL DEATH DO US PART.

Confirmation of the Marriage Bond

Priest: By the authority of the Church I ratify and bless the bond of marriage you have contracted. In the name of the Father, and of the Son, and of the Holy Spirit.

People: AMEN.

Priest: I call upon all of you here present to be witnesses of this holy union which I have now blessed. "Man must not separate what God has joined together."

751

Blessing of the Rings

Priest: Our help is in the name of the Lord.
People: WHO MADE HEAVEN AND EARTH.
Priest: O Lord, hear my prayer.
People: AND LET MY CRY COME TO YOU.
Priest: The Lord be with you.
People: AND WITH YOUR SPIRIT.

The priest prays that the couple who are to wear the rings may keep faith with each other in peace.

Giving the Rings

Priest: Now that you have sealed a truly Christian marriage, give these wedding rings to each other, saying after me:

When exchanging rings, the groom, then the bride, say in turn:

IN THE NAME OF THE FATHER, AND OF THE SON, AND OF THE HOLY SPIRIT. TAKE AND WEAR THIS RING AS A SIGN OF OUR MARRIAGE VOWS.

Priest: In the name of the Father, and of the Son, and of the Holy Spirit. Amen. Strengthen, O God, what you have wrought in us.
People: FROM YOUR HOLY TEMPLE, WHICH IS IN JERSUALEM.

The Lord's Prayer

Priest: Lord, have mercy.
People: CHRIST, HAVE MERCY.
Priest: Lord, have mercy.
　　　　　Our Father . . . And lead us not into temptation.
People: BUT DELIVER US FROM EVIL.
Priest: Save your servants.
People: WHO TRUST IN YOU, MY GOD.
Priest: Send them help, O Lord, from your sanctuary.
People: AND SUSTAIN THEM FROM SION.
Priest: Be a tower of strength for them, O Lord.
People: AGAINST THE ATTACK OF THE ENEMY.
Priest: O Lord, hear my prayer.
People: AND LET MY CRY COME TO YOU.
Priest: The Lord be with you.
People: AND WITH YOUR SPIRIT.

The priest asks God to keep faithful the couple he has united by his authority.

Blessing

Priest: May almighty God bless you by the Word of his mouth, and unite your hearts in the enduring bond of pure love.

People: AMEN.

Priest: May you be blessed in your children, and may the love that you lavish on them be returned a hundredfold.

People: AMEN.

Priest: May the peace of Christ dwell always in your hearts and in your home; may you have true friends to stand by you, both in joy and in sorrow. May you be ready with help and consolation for all those who come to you in need; and may the blessings promised to the compassionate descend in abundance on your house.

People: AMEN.

Priest: May you be blessed in your word and enjoy its fruits. May cares never cause you distress, nor the desire for earthly possessions lead you astray; but may your hearts' concern be always for the treasures laid up for you in the life of heaven.

People: AMEN.

Priest: May the Lord grant you fullness of years, so that you may reap the harvest of a good life, and, after you have served him with loyalty in his kingdom on earth, may he take you up into his eternal dominions in heaven. Through our Lord Jesus Christ, his Son, who lives and reigns with him in the unity of the Holy Spirit, God, forever and ever.

People: AMEN.

Prayer of the Faithful

THE LITURGY OF THE EUCHARIST

Song at the Preparation of the Gifts

My trust is in you, O Lord;
I say, "You are my God."
In your hands is my destiny. (Alleluia.)

TURN TO PSALM 30

Prayer over the Gifts

EUCHARISTIC PRAYER

TURN TO PAGE 405

Nuptial Blessing

After the Lord's Prayer the priest offers a long prayer for the health, prosperity and peace of the newly married couple.
With the bishop's permission, the couple may receive both bread and wine.

Communion Song

Behold, thus is the man blessed
who fears the Lord;
may you see your children's children.
Peace be upon Israel! (Alleluia.) TURN TO PSALM 127

Prayer after Communion

Final Blessing

After he says, "The Mass is ended. Go in peace," the priest offers a final prayer for the married couple and sprinkles them with water before giving the final blessing.

Marriage Outside of Mass

If for any reason it is necessary to celebrate marriage outside the celebration of the Eucharist, the rite is the same as given above, except that it begins with a prayer by the priest, and the First Reading and the Gospel from the Marriage Mass are read. Also, all together recite Psalm 127 before the nuptial blessing.

BLESSING FOR WEDDING ANNIVERSARIES

This is a service of blessing, renewal and thanksgiving, which may be celebrated on any anniversary of a couple's marriage. It is most appropriate in connection with a Mass. With the bishop's permission, the couple celebrating their anniversary may receive both bread and wine.

Entrance

Depending upon circumstances, an appropriate hymn may be sung, such as No. 42 or No. 76; or all together may recite Psalm 91.

Priest: Our help is in the name of the Lord.
People: WHO MADE HEAVEN AND EARTH.
Priest: O Lord, hear my prayer.
People: AND LET MY CRY COME TO YOU.

Priest: The Lord be with you.
People: AND WITH YOUR SPIRIT.

Prayer

The priest prays that God will be the source and goal of all we do. (If Mass is not to be celebrated, the First Reading from the Marriage Mass, Ephesians 5: 22-33, may be read here, and the priest may preach a brief homily.)

Renewal of Marriage Vows

Priest (to husband): (Name), do you renew and confirm your taking of (Name), here present, for your wedded wife?
Husband: I DO.
Priest (to wife): (Name), do you renew and confirm your taking of (Name), here present, for your wedded husband?
Wife: I DO.

The priest asks the married couple to join hands and then says:

Priest: May the blessing of almighty God, the Father, and the Son, and the Holy Spirit, descend upon you and remain forever.
People: AMEN.

Blessing

Priest: Behold, thus is the man blessed who fears the Lord.

All turn to Psalm 127 (or 116) and recite it together.

Priest: Behold, thus is the man blessed who fears the Lord.
Priest: Lord, have mercy.
People: CHRIST, HAVE MERCY. LORD, HAVE MERCY.
Priest: Our Father . . . And lead us not into temptation.
People: BUT DELIVER US FROM EVIL.
Priest: O Lord, hear my prayer.
People: AND LET MY CRY COME TO YOU.
Priest: The Lord be with you.
People: AND WITH YOUR SPIRIT.

Final Prayer

The priest prays that God will be good to those who have come to give thanks to him. He then sprinkles the couple with water.

If Mass is not to be celebrated, the service may be concluded with a hymn, such as No. 39 or No. 52; or all together may recite Psalm 144.

Sometime during the weeks immediately before a woman is to give birth, the parish community into which the child will be born, represented by the priest and members of the family, may ask God's blessing on what is to take place. In the church or home, they may first recite together a psalm, such as Psalm 144, and then the priest (or someone else) leads the group in prayer.

Priest: Our help is in the name of the Lord.
People: WHO MADE HEAVEN AND EARTH.
Priest: Save your servant.
People: WHO TRUSTS IN YOU, MY GOD.
Priest: Be a tower of strength for her, O Lord.
People: AGAINST THE ATTACK OF THE ENEMY.
Priest: Let the enemy have no power against her.
People: AND LET NOT THE SON OF EVIL DRAW NEAR TO HARM HER.
Priest: Send her aid, O Lord, from your holy place.
People: AND WATCH OVER HER FROM SION.
Priest: O Lord, hear my prayer.
People: AND LET MY CRY COME TO YOU.
Priest: The Lord be with you.
People: AND WITH YOUR SPIRIT.

Prayers

The priest prays that God, who has protected his people in the past, may guard the welfare of mother and child. He then sprinkles the expectant mother with water.

Reading

John 15:1–17 may be read. The priest may give a short homily.

Psalm

All turn to Psalm 66 and recite it together. The psalm concludes with GLORY BE TO THE FATHER, *and the rite continues:*

Priest: Let us bless the Father, and the Son, and the Holy Spirit.
People: LET US PRAISE AND GLORIFY HIM FOREVER.
Priest: God has given his angels charge over you.
People: TO KEEP YOU IN ALL YOUR WAYS.
Priest: O Lord, hear my prayer.

People: AND LET MY CRY COME TO YOU.
Priest: The Lord be with you.
People: AND WITH YOUR SPIRIT.

Prayer

The priest asks God's peace and his light for the family.
He concludes the service:

Priest: May the blessing of almighty God, the Father, and the Son, and the Holy Spirit, descend upon you and your child and remain forever.

People: AMEN.

Anointing of the Sick

THE ANOINTING OF THE SICK is the sacrament of healing. Overcome by illness, we ask that we may be restored to health. At the same time, we recognize our spiritual weakness and ask to be restored to the fullness of Christian life.

We should not hesitate to ask God for relief from sickness and suffering. He has invited us to come to him for our needs; he has told us to call him Father. It is a sign of faith in him when we ask him to cure a disease or heal an injury.

The victory of Christ's resurrection did not remove sickness and suffering from our lives, but it did transform them. For a Christian, illness is not something to be borne with stoic endurance. It is a participation in Christ's suffering and death which will lead us to a participation in his rising and lasting triumph.

But our physical illness is also a sign of our spiritual illness, and the weakness of our bodies is a reminder of the weakness of our souls. For this weakness also we draw strength from the power of Christ in this sacrament.

Anointing with oil can be the sign of many things, of kingship, for instance, or of special power. In this sacrament, the anointings signify healing. As oils of one kind or another have always been used in treating diseases and injuries, so the blessed oil of the sick is the sign of the healing that Christ brings to body and soul.

Occasionally it will happen that the sick person to be anointed is quite close to death, and there is little hope of recovery. In such cases, the anointing is for the world to come, an anointing to the glory of life after death. Such an anointing will be followed by Viaticum, the final Eucharist of Christian passage through death to unending life.

Of course, the whole parish family is concerned about the illness of any one of its members. The unity established in the Eucharist should be especially evident as members of the parish gather to pray with and for their brother or sister who is sick. Together we ask God that he restore the sick person in body and soul, so that he or she may return to a full share in the eucharistic life of our parish.

THE RITE OF ANOINTING

Although this rite is ordinarily celebrated in the home or hospital room of the sick person, on occasion it may be done publicly, even in church.

Entrance

If the priest comes to the room of the sick person, he first greets those who are gathered there and asks God's blessing on them.

Priest: Peace to this house.
People: AND TO ALL WHO DWELL THEREIN.
Priest (sprinkling with water the sick person, the room and all those present): Sprinkle me, O Lord, with hyssop, and I shall be purified; wash me, and I shall be whiter than snow.

Our help is in the name of the Lord.
People: WHO MADE HEAVEN AND EARTH.
Priest: The Lord be with you.
People: AND WITH YOUR SPIRIT.

The priest prays that his visit may, through the power of God, bring health and happiness to all present.

Confession

If the sick person desires to receive the sacrament of penance, he does so at this time. When this is concluded and all have returned to the room, all present say together:

All: I CONFESS TO ALMIGHTY GOD,
　　　TO BLESSED MARY EVER VIRGIN,
　　　TO BLESSED MICHAEL THE ARCHANGEL,
　　　TO BLESSED JOHN THE BAPTIST,
　　　TO THE HOLY APOSTLES PETER AND PAUL,
　　　TO ALL THE SAINTS,
　　　AND TO YOU, FATHER,
　　　THAT I HAVE SINNED EXCEEDINGLY
　　　IN THOUGHT, WORD, AND DEED;
　　　THROUGH MY FAULT,
　　　THROUGH MY FAULT,
　　　THROUGH MY MOST GRIEVOUS FAULT.
　　　THEREFORE I BESEECH BLESSED MARY EVER VIRGIN,
　　　BLESSED MICHAEL THE ARCHANGEL,
　　　BLESSED JOHN THE BAPTIST,
　　　THE HOLY APOSTLES PETER AND PAUL,
　　　ALL THE SAINTS,

759

AND YOU, FATHER,
TO PRAY TO THE LORD OUR GOD FOR ME.

Priest: May almighty God have mercy on you, forgive you your sins, and bring you to life everlasting.

People: AMEN.

Priest: May the almighty and merciful Lord grant you pardon, absolution, and remission of your sins.

People: AMEN.

Reading and Homily

The priest may then read a passage from Scripture, such as James 5:14–18, and perhaps say a few words to the sick person and all present.

Prayer

Priest: Let us kneel down and pray. Lord, have mercy.

People: CHRIST, HAVE MERCY. LORD, HAVE MERCY.

Priest: Lord, that you would visit and strengthen this sick man (woman).

People: WE BESEECH YOU, HEAR US.

Priest: That you would give him (her) life and health.

People: WE BESEECH YOU, HEAR US.

Priest: That you would grant him (her) the grace of the Holy Spirit.

People: WE BESEECH YOU, HEAR US.

Priest: Lamb of God, who take away the sins of the world.

People: SPARE US, O LORD.

Priest: Lamb of God, who take away the sins of the world.

People: GRACIOUSLY HEAR US, O LORD.

Priest: Lamb of God, who take away the sins of the world.

People: HAVE MERCY ON US.

Prayer

The priest then prays that the power of sickness and of sin might be destroyed.

The Anointings

The priest then anoints the sick person with oil, making a sign of the cross on his eyes, ears, nose, mouth, hands and feet, saying:

May the Lord forgive you by this holy anointing and his most loving mercy whatever sins you have committed by the use of your sight.

Sick Person: AMEN.

May the Lord forgive you by this holy anointing and his most loving mercy whatever sins you have committed by the use of your hearing.

Sick Person: AMEN.

May the Lord forgive you by this holy anointing and his most loving mercy whatever sins you have committed by the use of your sense of smell.

Sick Person: AMEN.

May the Lord forgive you by this holy anointing and his most loving mercy whatever sins you have committed by the use of your sense of taste and the power of speech.

Sick Person: AMEN.

May the Lord forgive you by this holy anointing and his most loving mercy whatever sins you have committed by the use of your sense of touch.

Sick Person: AMEN.

May the Lord forgive you by this holy anointing and his most loving mercy whatever sins you have committed by the use of your power to walk.

Sick Person: AMEN.

Concluding Prayers

Priest: Lord, have mercy.
People: CHRIST, HAVE MERCY. LORD, HAVE MERCY.
Priest: Our Father . . . And lead us not into temptation.
People: BUT DELIVER US FROM EVIL.
Priest: Save your servant.
People: WHO TRUSTS IN YOU, MY GOD.
Priest: Send him (her) help, O Lord, from your sanctuary.
People: AND SUSTAIN HIM (HER) FROM SION.
Priest: Be a tower of strength for him (her), O Lord.
People: AGAINST THE ATTACK OF THE ENEMY.
Priest: Let the enemy have no power over him (her).
People: AND LET NOT THE SON OF EVIL DARE TO HARM HIM (HER).

Priest: O Lord, hear my prayer.
People: AND LET MY CRY COME TO YOU.
Priest: The Lord be with you.
People: AND WITH YOUR SPIRIT.

The priest then says three prayers for the physical and spiritual health of the sick person.

If time permits, all together may then recite Psalm 30 or Psalm 101. When he is ready to leave, the priest blesses the sick person:

Priest: May the blessing of almighty God, the Father, and the Son, and the Holy Spirit, descend upon you and remain forever.
People: AMEN.

Liturgy of the Dead

THE LITURGY OF DEATH is an Easter liturgy. It is the celebration of the completion of a Christian's passover, which he began at baptism when he underwent a real death. Dying, Christ destroyed our death, and rising, he restored our life. In baptism we entered into this mystery: we passed over in the Lord. It is the completion of baptism and of the Eucharist, the memorial of Christ's dying and rising, which have planted in us a trust that God's free gift of love, which gave us life, will not let us pass completely from existence.

The liturgy of the dead is an Easter liturgy because it finds all its meaning in the resurrection of Jesus. His rising is the basis of our hope that we too will rise. This is the mystery of the grain of seed that falls into the ground and dies so that it can come to life. This is Paul's vision of the resurrection which is going to happen because Christ was raised from the dead. The liturgy of burial, then, is a joyful shout: "I am sure that neither death, nor life, nor things present, nor things to come, nor anything else in all creation, will be able to separate us from the love of God in Christ Jesus our Lord" (Romans 8:38–39). We do not, as Christians, have some special knowledge that the world lacks; we have only a belief that God is love and that in this love we shall rise to new life.

This joy does not make grief something unchristian or mourning a thing for unbelievers. Christianity does not destroy humanity, and the very love which it gives us for one another brings a deep sorrow at separation. The Church can rejoice in her child who has embraced his passover, but she has also consolation for those who must grieve at being left alone.

SERVICE FOR A CHRISTIAN WAKE

A Memorial Service

This service may take place in the parish church, the funeral home, or the home of the deceased. It is most fitting in the parish church, perhaps with the faithful gathered around the baptistry to show the close connection between baptism and death. As a sign of the power of Christ's resurrection, which gives victory over death, the Easter candle may be lighted. The songs, readings and prayers may vary as needed. When it is a child who has died, perhaps the psalms and readings about the Good

Shepherd are most appropriate. The readings, prayers and songs suggested may also be used as a memorial service appropriate during the month of November, or to commemorate the death of national and world leaders.

Entrance

An appropriate hymn, such as No. 44 or No. 129, may be sung; or the service may begin immediately with the recitation of the following psalms:

Priest: If you, O Lord, mark iniquities,
O Lord, who can stand?

Turn to Psalm 129. (Instead of the usual ending, "Glory be to the Father," the following is said at the end of all psalms during the liturgy of the dead: ETERNAL REST GRANT UNTO HIM, O LORD, AND LET PERPETUAL LIGHT SHINE UPON HIM.) *Afterwards the priest prays that God's love may bring the Christian to unending happiness.*

Priest: They shall rejoice in the Lord,
the bones that are brought low in the dust.

Turn to Psalm 50. Afterwards the following is prayed:

Priest: Come to his aid, O saints of God;
People: HASTEN TO MEET HIM, ANGELS OF THE LORD;
TAKING UP HIS SOUL,
PRESENTING IT IN THE SIGHT OF THE MOST HIGH.
Priest: May you be received by Christ, who has called you;
and may the angels bring you into the bosom of Abraham.
People: TAKING UP HIS SOUL,
PRESENTING IT IN THE SIGHT OF THE MOST HIGH.
Priest: Eternal rest grant unto him, O Lord;
and let perpetual light shine upon him.
People: PRESENTING HIS SOUL IN THE SIGHT OF THE MOST HIGH.

If the funeral Mass is to begin at this point, turn to page 767.

Priest: Let us pray.
Father in heaven, your son wept at the grave of his friend Lazarus. Please feel sorrow with those who mourn and comfort them with your love. Give them confidence in your care and let them realize that all things work together for good in those who love God. We ask this through Christ our Lord.
People: AMEN.

Reading

The reading or readings may be selected from the following: Genesis 3:16–19; Job 7:16–21; 10:1–12; 14:1–12; 17:1–3, 11–15; 19:20–27; 33:14–28; Ecclesiastes 3:1–8; 3:14–22; Ezekiel 37:1–14; Jonah 1:1–16; 2:1–10; John 6:35–70; 11:1–27; Romans 8:1–25; 1 Corinthians 15:51–57.

When the dead person is a child, the following may be most appropriate: Ezekiel 34:11–16; 1 Peter 2:1–10 and John 10:1–15.

Response

If there are to be two readings, the following may be recited between them:

Priest: And I saw a new heaven and a new earth.
For the first heaven and the first earth passed away,
and the sea is no more.

People: AND I SAW THE HOLY CITY, NEW JERUSALEM,
COMING DOWN OUT OF HEAVEN FROM GOD,
MADE READY AS A BRIDE ADORNED FOR HER HUSBAND.

Priest: And I heard a loud voice from the throne saying,
"Behold the dwelling of God with men,
and he will dwell with them,

People: AND THEY WILL BE HIS PEOPLE,
AND GOD HIMSELF WILL BE WITH THEM AS THEIR GOD.
AND GOD WILL WIPE AWAY EVERY TEAR FROM THEIR EYES.

Priest: And death shall be no more;
Neither shall there be mourning,
nor crying, nor pain any more,
for the former things have passed away."

People: AND HE WHO WAS SITTING ON THE THRONE SAID,
"BEHOLD, I MAKE ALL THINGS NEW!"

REVELATION 21:1–5

Homily and Prayer

After the last reading there may be a short homily and a period of silent prayer. This may be followed by the Prayer of the Faithful as during Mass, including prayers for the deceased and the mourners, and for all who have fallen asleep in the Lord. At the end, this prayer may be recited:

Priest: Let us pray. We seem to give them back to you, O Lord, who first gave them to us. Yet as you did not lose them in giving, so we do not lose them by their return. Not as the world gives do you give, O lover of souls. What you give you do not take away, for what is yours is ours also if we belong to you. And life is eternal and love is immortal, and death is only a horizon, and a horizon is nothing save the limit of our sight. Lift us up, strong son of God, that we may see further; cleanse our eyes, that we may see more clearly; draw us closer to yourself that we may know ourselves to be nearer our loved ones who are with you. And while you prepare a place for us, prepare us also for that happy place, that where you are we may be also forevermore.   BEDE JARRETT

People: AMEN.

Conclusion

To conclude the service a hymn may be sung, such as No. 86 or No. 90; or all together may recite Psalm 24, 117 or 145, or the Song of the Three Young Men, page 707.

If the wake is to include the recitation of the rosary, the following scripture passages may be used for the five decades:

1. And to Adam God said, "Cursed be the ground because of you; in toil shall you eat of it all the days of your life; thorns and thistles shall it bring forth to you, and you shall eat the plants of the field. In the sweat of your brow you shall eat bread, till you return to the ground, since out of it you were taken; for dust you are and unto dust you shall return."
    GENESIS 3:17-19

2. Man, born of woman, is short-lived and full of trouble. Like a flower that springs up and fades, swift as a shadow that does not abide. You know the number of his months; you have fixed the limit which he cannot pass. When a man dies, all vigor leaves him; when man expires, where then is he?   JOB 14:1, 2, 5, 10

3. There is an appointed time for everything, and a time for every affair under the heavens. A time to be born, and a time to die; a time to plant, and a time to uproot the plant. A time to kill, and a time to heal; a time to tear down, and a time to build. A time to weep, and a time to laugh; a time to mourn, and a time to dance. A time to scatter stones, and a time to gather them; a time to embrace, and a time to be far from embraces.   ECCLESIASTES 3:1-5

4. But as it is, Christ has risen from the dead, the first-fruits of those who have fallen asleep. For since by a man came death, by a man also comes resurrection of the dead. For as in Adam all die, so in Christ all will be made to live.   I CORINTHIANS 15:20-22

5. And God will dwell with them. And they will be his people, and

God himself will be with them as their God. And God will wipe away every tear from their eyes. And death shall be no more; neither shall there be mourning, nor crying, nor pain any more, for the former things have passed away. REVELATION 21:3–4

Mass on the Day of Burial

The funeral Mass is a memorial of Christ's dying and rising; every time we eat the Bread, we proclaim the Lord's death until he comes. In the presence of the body of one who sleeps in the Lord, this new celebration of Christ's own passover, in which we all share, should take on new meaning. By sharing in the Bread, receiving communion at this Mass, the faithful are united with their departed brother or sister in the risen Lord.

If hymns are to be sung at the Mass, the following may be used: No. 44, No. 47 or No. 98. At sung Masses, any of the musical settings provided for the ordinary chants may be used, as found in the Hymnal, beginning page 533.

The songs of the funeral Masses are the same as those on the Mass of All Souls Day, page 286. The first reading is 1 Thessalonians 4:13–18, and the Gospel is John 11:21–27.

If the psalms and prayers beginning on page 764 have not been recited previously, they are said at the door of the church before the Mass begins.

PRAYER AFTER MASS

The priest prays that God will hear the prayers of the Christian people and in his great mercy give life to the departed Christian.

The following may be sung or recited:

DELIVER ME, O LORD, FROM EVERLASTING DEATH ON THAT DAY OF TERROR;
WHEN THE HEAVENS AND THE EARTH WILL BE SHAKEN.
AS YOU COME TO JUDGE THE WORLD BY FIRE.
   I AM IN FEAR AND TREMBLING
      AT THE JUDGMENT AND THE WRATH THAT IS TO COME.
WHEN THE HEAVENS AND THE EARTH WILL BE SHAKEN.
   THAT DAY WILL BE A DAY OF WRATH, OF MISERY, AND OF RUIN:
   A DAY OF GRANDEUR AND GREAT HORROR.
AS YOU COME TO JUDGE THE WORLD BY FIRE.
   ETERNAL REST GRANT UNTO THEM, O LORD,

AND LET PERPETUAL LIGHT SHINE UPON THEM.
DELIVER ME, O LORD, FROM EVERLASTING DEATH ON THAT DAY OF TERROR:
WHEN THE HEAVENS AND THE EARTH WILL BE SHAKEN.
AS YOU COME TO JUDGE THE WORLD BY FIRE.

Priest: Lord, have mercy.
People: CHRIST, HAVE MERCY. LORD, HAVE MERCY.
Priest: Our Father . . . And lead us not into temptation.
People: BUT DELIVER US FROM EVIL.
Priest: From the gate of hell.
People: RESCUE HIS SOUL, O LORD.
Priest: May he rest in peace.
People: AMEN.
Priest: O Lord, hear my prayer.
People: AND LET MY CRY COME TO YOU.
Priest: The Lord be with you.
People: AND WITH YOUR SPIRIT.

Prayer

The priest prays that the faith of the departed Christian may bring him to the joys he hoped for.

Conclusion

A hymn, such as No. 18 or No. 45, may be sung as the body is taken from the church.

AT THE GRAVE

The following prayers take place at the graveside or nearby:

Priest: I am the resurrection and the life;
People: HE WHO BELIEVES IN ME, EVEN IF HE DIES, SHALL LIVE;
AND WHOEVER LIVES AND BELIEVES IN ME, SHALL NEVER DIE.

Turn to the Song of Zachary, page 709. At the end of this canticle, before repeating the above verses, say: ETERNAL REST GRANT UNTO HIM, O LORD.
AND LET PERPETUAL LIGHT SHINE UPON HIM.

Prayer

The priest may then bless the grave and ask all to remember those whom God has taken to himself from this world.

Priest: Lord, have mercy.

People: CHRIST, HAVE MERCY. LORD, HAVE MERCY.

Priest: Our Father . . . And lead us not into temptation.

People: BUT DELIVER US FROM EVIL.

Priest: From the gate of hell.

People: RESCUE HIS SOUL, O LORD.

Priest: May he rest in peace.

People: AMEN.

Priest: O Lord, hear my prayer.

People: AND LET MY CRY COME TO YOU.

Priest: The Lord be with you.

People: AND WITH YOUR SPIRIT.

Prayer

The priest prays that as the faith of the departed Christian made him one with the Church on earth, it may now unite him to the Church in heaven.

Conclusion

Priest: May he rest in peace.

People: AMEN.

Priest: May his soul and the souls of all the faithful departed through the mercy of God rest in peace.

People: AMEN.

THE BURIAL OF A YOUNG CHILD

When a young child has died, the following rites are used instead of the above. At the home or the mortuary the following prayers are recited.

Psalm

Priest: Blessed be the name of the Lord.

People: NOW AND FOREVER.

Turn to Psalm 112 and recite it together. The Glory Be to the Father is said at the end; then the above verse is repeated.

Mass

If Mass is celebrated, it is the Mass of the day or a Votive Mass.

After the Mass

Priest: This child shall receive a blessing from the Lord,

People: AND MERCY FROM GOD, HIS SALVATION,
FOR THIS IS THE RACE OF THOSE WHO SEEK THE LORD.

Turn to Psalm 23 and recite it together. Afterwards the above verse is repeated.

Priest: Lord, have mercy.
People: CHRIST, HAVE MERCY. LORD, HAVE MERCY.
Priest: Our Father . . . And lead us not into temptation.
People: BUT DELIVER US FROM EVIL.
Priest: Because of my innocence you have received me.
People: AND GIVEN ME A PLACE IN YOUR SIGHT FOREVER.
Priest: The Lord be with you.
People: AND WITH YOUR SPIRIT.

The priest prays that we may all someday share in the happiness that now belongs to this child.

Conclusion

The following hymns may be appropriate at the conclusion of the service, at various times during the preceding Mass, or at the cemetery. Nos. 9, 44, or 90.

At the Grave

At the graveside or nearby the following prayers are recited:

Priest: Young men and maidens, old men and boys,
People: LET THEM PRAISE THE NAME OF THE LORD.

Turn to Psalm 148 and recite it together. Afterwards the above verse is repeated.

Priest: Lord, have mercy.
People: CHRIST, HAVE MERCY. LORD, HAVE MERCY.
Priest: Our Father . . . And lead us not into temptation.
People: BUT DELIVER US FROM EVIL.
Priest: Let little children come to me.
People: FOR OF SUCH IS THE KINGDOM OF HEAVEN.
Priest: The Lord be with you.
People: AND WITH YOUR SPIRIT.

Prayer

The priest prays as above that the child's joy may some day be ours.

* * *

The special Mass which may be offered on the anniversary of a death is the same as the Mass on All Souls Day, page 286, with the second readings listed.

The Mass for the dead which may be offered on certain days which have no other liturgical celebration is the same as the Mass of All Souls Day, page 286, with the third readings listed.

PARISH
SERVICES
AND
PRAYERS

Service of Christian Unity

THE FOLLOWING service is both a prayer for Christian unity and an expression of the unity all Christians already have in the body of Christ. It follows the structure of the service prepared each year for the Church Unity Octave by the Graymoor Friars and the National Council of Churches.

Entrance

Priest: Save us, O Lord our God.
People: AND GATHER US FROM AMONG THE NATIONS.
Priest: That we may give thanks to thy holy name.
People: AND GLORY IN THY PRAISE.   PSALM 105:47

An appropriate hymn, such as No. 19 or No. 83, may be sung; or all together may recite Psalm 100.

Prayer

Priest: Let us pray. Sovereign Lord, Ruler of the universe, look down from heaven upon your Church, upon all your people, and upon your little flock, and save all of us, your unworthy servants, the creatures of your flock, and give us your peace, your love, and your assistance. Send down upon us the free gift of your Holy Spirit so that with a clean heart and a good conscience we may kiss one another with holy love, not deceitfully nor hypocritically, nor to control each other's freedom, but blamelessly and purely in the bonds of peace and of love. For there is only one Body, and one Spirit and one Faith as we have been called in one hope of our calling so that we might all come to you and to your infinite love in Jesus Christ our Lord, with whom you are blessed with your all-holy, good, and life-giving Spirit, now and through endless ages.

People: AMEN.

LITURGY OF ST. MARK; PRAYER BEFORE THE KISS OF PEACE

Readings

For a first reading: Genesis 12:1–5; Exodus 19:3–8; Ezekiel 36:24–28; Isaiah 53:1–12; Joel 3:1–15; Psalm 95; Deuteronomy 7:14–24; Hosea 2:16–23.

For a second reading: Romans 15:7–13; 1 Peter 2:9–12; Luke 1:68–79; Hebrews 2:10–18; Acts 10:34–48; 1 Corinthians 10:1–13; Ephesians 6:10–20; Revelation 21:1–7.

Confession of Faith

All together say the Apostles' Creed, page 726.

Homily

The priest may preach a brief homily.

Litany

Priest: Let us give thanks to God our Father for the gift of unity.
Blessed be thou, O God our Father,
by the precious blood of thy Son, and by His resurrection
from the dead.
thou hast reconciled all things to thyself;
thou gatherest into unity thy children who are scattered
abroad.

People: GLORY BE TO THEE FOR EVER AND EVER.

Priest: By thy Holy Spirit, so freely given to us,
by the new birth of our baptism,
thou dost make of all believers a single body,
to feed them with one bread.

People: GLORY BE TO THEE FOR EVER AND EVER.

Priest: We give thanks to thee, O God our Father,
for the ecumenical movement
and for those who suffer, pray and work in the cause of unity.

People: GLORY BE TO THEE FOR EVER AND EVER.

Priest: We give thee thanks for this day and for this hour
in which thou gatherest us, to praise thee, to repent,
and to await in hope the visible unity of all Christian people.

People: GLORY BE TO THEE FOR EVER AND EVER.

Priest: In the presence of our Lord Jesus Christ, let us in penitence
confess our sins against unity:
Before thee, O Lord, we are ashamed:
We have brought division into thy great work of unity.

People: LORD, HAVE MERCY UPON US.

Priest: In our confession of the truth
we have often been hard and exclusive.

People: LORD, HAVE MERCY UPON US.

Priest: We have forgotten the beam in our own eye
seeing only the mote in our brother's eye.

People: LORD, HAVE MERCY UPON US.

Priest: We have been ignorant and scornful of our brethren; we have often sought to triumph over them.

People: LORD, HAVE MERCY UPON US.

Priest: We have drawn boundaries between thy children whether of race or nation or culture or class.

People: LORD, HAVE MERCY UPON US.

Priest: By our divisions we have hindered the witness of love, and the spread of the Gospel throughout the world.

People: LORD, HAVE MERCY UPON US.

Priest: May the Holy Spirit carry to the Father our prayer for unity: O Lord, forbid us to acquire the habit of our divisions. Save us from considering as normal that which is a scandal to the world and an offense against thy love.

People: UNITE US IN LOVE AND IN TRUTH.

Priest: Deliver us, O Lord, from a spirit of narrowness, of bitterness, or of prejudice. Teach us to recognize the gifts of thy grace in all those who call upon thee with an honest heart.

People: UNITE US IN LOVE AND IN TRUTH.

Priest: Deepen our faithfulness to thy Word. Do not allow us to be led astray by our own delusions or to walk rashly on paths which are not of thy choosing.

People: UNITE US IN LOVE AND IN TRUTH.

Priest: By thy power, O Lord, gather thy scattered flock. Unite it under the authority of thy Son, so that the purpose of thy love may be fulfilled and that the world may know thee, the one true God, and him whom thou has sent, Jesus Christ.

People: AMEN.

Intercession

The priest or another may mention particular intentions, such as the success of an approaching dialogue, the end of a local misunderstanding, the growth of an ecumenical project.

The Lord's Prayer

All together pray the Our Father.

Blessing and Dismissal

The clergymen present give their blessings, and then the service may conclude with an appropriate hymn, such as No. 29 or No. 86; or all together may recite Psalm 22, 24, or 66.

Commissioning Service

THE LIFE of a parish is its growth toward maturity in Christ. The sign of this growth is an ever deeper involvement in the mission of Jesus and of the Church: to serve and to save all men.

From time to time, perhaps as the climax of a parish retreat or during a celebration on the feastday of the patron of the parish, the entire community may wish to recall the dedication to mature Christian responsibility and service which should mark the life of each member. On such occasions the following rite may serve to emphasize the vocation of every Christian to be an intelligent and responsible witness to Christ in the world.

This rite may also be used when individuals are called to particular types of service within the parish community. The installation of a pastor or of an assistant priest, for instance, is an appropriate time to stress the ideal of Christian service, as are occasions on which new lectors, commentators, organists, choir members, or leaders of parish organizations are commissioned.

The following commissioning rite may also be used when members of the parish are embarking for service outside the parish: at the departure of lay missionaries, for instance, or of Peace Corps volunteers, or of teachers who are going to devote some of their time to the underprivileged in another part of this country or abroad.

The pastor or other leader will adapt the service to suit the occasion.

Entrance

An opening hymn, such as No. 89 or No. 123, may be sung; or all together may recite Psalm 18, 84, 94 or 145.

Readings

Suggested readings: Matthew 20:17–28; 25:31–40; Luke 6:12–23; John 13:1–17; 17:1–19; 1 Corinthians 9:17–27; 13:1–13; James 2:14–26; 1 John 3:14–24; 4:7–21.

Response

If there are two readings, the following may be recited between them:

THE SPIRIT OF THE LORD GOD IS UPON ME.
BECAUSE THE LORD HAS ANOINTED ME;
HE HAS SENT ME TO BRING GLAD TIDINGS TO THE LOWLY

TO HEAL THE BROKEN HEARTED,
TO PROCLAIM LIBERTY TO THE CAPTIVES AND RELEASE TO THE PRISONERS,
TO COMFORT ALL WHO MOURN,
TO GIVE THEM OIL OF GLADNESS IN PLACE OF MOURNING
A GLORIOUS MANTLE INSTEAD OF A LISTLESS SPIRIT.

ISAIAH 61:1-3

Homily

The priest may preach a brief homily.

Action

Some fitting action may take place here, perhaps the solemn signing with the cross. When this service is used for installing various parish officials to their offices, something appropriate to that office may be used. A new pastor, for instance, might be led to the chair from which he will preside over the church; new lectors may be given copies of the Scripture; leaders of parish organizations may be given something symbolizing their work. On any occasion, the exchange of the kiss of peace or shaking hands to signify peace and unity would be fitting.

Prayer

Priest: Father, you have given us a great variety of ways through which we may serve one another. But in all of them, we come to know the one Lord, for you work all things in all of us. What your Spirit does in any of us, he does for the good of all. Some are wise; they are wise for all. Some have great learning; they share it with all. Others have great faith; and all may believe. Others may be able to teach, to administer, to speak well, to heal, to clean, to sing, to pray. Whatever a man can do, he should do for all, to serve his brothers, for we form but one body in your Son, Jesus. We ask, Father, that the service you have given us to do, as individuals and as a community, may be done in the Spirit, that we may never appear to have all perfections, while lacking the love without which they are nothing. Bring us to perfect maturity in your Son, Jesus. We ask this in his name. Amen.

Conclusion

Priest: The Lord bless you and keep you. The Lord make his face shine upon you and be gracious to you. The Lord give you peace.

People: AMEN.

A closing hymn, such as No. 5 or No. 94, may be sung; or all together may recite Psalm 135 or 148.

Service for the Visit of the Bishop

THE BISHOP is the sign of the unity of the Church in his diocese. He is sent by the Father to serve his family, to teach them, to give witness to the Gospel and to be their high priest. Between each Christian and his bishop there is a close bond, which the sheer size of today's dioceses often obscures. Thus the visit of a bishop is a particularly important event in the life of a parish, and the service should make clear this close tie between the bishop and the faithful.

Entrance

The service may begin with an appropriate hymn, such as No. 83 or No. 86; or all together may recite Psalm 22, 110, 112 or 137.

Prayer

Afterwards, the priest, who has accompanied the bishop into the church, may recite the following prayer:

Priest: Let us pray. Father, you visit your children and comfort them with your love. Give our community your favor. May we experience your own coming in the visit of him in whom you live. We ask this through Christ our Lord.

People: AMEN.

First Reading

Many passages from the Constitution on the Church by the Vatican Council may be appropriate, especially from Chapter Three. The following Scripture passages may also be used: 1 Timothy 6:11–16; 2 Timothy 1:6–14; 4:1–8; Titus 2:11, 3:8; 1 Peter 5:1–11.

Response

Between the readings the following may be recited:

Priest: The favors of the Lord I will sing forever;
through all generations my mouth shall proclaim your faithfulness.
For you have said, "My kindness is established forever";
in heaven you have confirmed your faithfulness.

People: "I HAVE MADE A COVENANT WITH MY CHOSEN ONE,
I HAVE SWORN TO DAVID MY SERVANT:
FOREVER WILL I CONFIRM YOUR POSTERITY
AND ESTABLISH YOUR THRONE FOR ALL GENERATIONS."

Priest: The heavens proclaim your wonders, O Lord,
and your faithfulness, in the assembly of the holy ones.
Yours are the heavens and yours is the earth;
the world and its fullness you have founded.

People: JUSTICE AND JUDGMENT ARE THE FOUNDATION OF YOUR
THRONE;
KINDNESS AND TRUTH GO BEFORE YOU.

Priest: Once you spoke in a vision,
and to your faithful ones you said:
"I have found David, my servant:
with my holy oil I have anointed him,
that my hand may be always with him,
and that my arm may make him strong.

People: "FOREVER I WILL MAINTAIN MY KINDNESS TOWARD HIM,
AND MY COVENANT WITH HIM STANDS FOREVER."

PSALM 88

Second Reading

Matthew 10:1–14; 20:20–28; 28:16–20; John 10:1–16; 13:1–16.

Homily

The bishop may give a brief homily.

Action

*Following this the bishop may be formally greeted by representatives of the
parish with the kiss of peace or by shaking hands, or he may lead the parish in
the Lord's Prayer, or he may wish to perform some act of service as a sign
of his office.*

Prayer

Afterwards, the bishop may recite the following prayer:

Let us pray. Holy Father, almighty and everlasting God, in the fullness
of time through your eternal Son you reconciled mankind to yourself,
and after his glorious resurrection and ascension he manifested through
his holy Church your love and righteous will towards all men. Let your
Holy Spirit descend with sevenfold power upon the bishop, clergy and
people of this diocese. Enable us to worship that men may know and
adore the beauty of your holiness; to live and labor that we may declare
the greatness of your love; to learn and teach that we may be faithful
stewards of your truth. We ask this through Christ our Lord. Amen.

FROM A DIOCESAN SERVICE BOOK

To conclude the service, a hymn, such as No. 39 or No. 52, may be sung; or all together may recite Psalm 32, 95, 97, 144, or 148.

Litany of the Saints

Lord, have mercy. CHRIST, HAVE MERCY.
Lord, have mercy. Christ hear us. CHRIST, GRACIOUSLY HEAR US.
God, the Father in heaven, HAVE MERCY ON US.
God, the Son, Redeemer of the world, HAVE MERCY ON US.
God, the Holy Spirit, HAVE MERCY ON US.
Holy Trinity, one God, HAVE MERCY ON US.

Holy Mary, PRAY FOR US.
Holy Mother of God, PRAY FOR US.
Holy Virgin of Virgins, PRAY FOR US.
St. Michael, PRAY FOR US.
St. Gabriel, PRAY FOR US.
St. Raphael, PRAY FOR US.
All holy angels and archangels, PRAY FOR US.
All holy orders of blessed spirits, PRAY FOR US.
St. John the Baptist, PRAY FOR US.
St. Joseph, PRAY FOR US.
All holy patriarchs and prophets, PRAY FOR US.
St. Peter, PRAY FOR US.
St. Paul, PRAY FOR US.
St. Andrew, PRAY FOR US.
St. James, PRAY FOR US.
St. John, PRAY FOR US.
St. Thomas, PRAY FOR US.
St. James, PRAY FOR US.
St. Philip, PRAY FOR US.
St. Bartholomew, PRAY FOR US.
St. Matthew, PRAY FOR US.
St. Simon, PRAY FOR US.
St. Thaddeus, PRAY FOR US.
St. Matthias, PRAY FOR US.
St. Barnabas, PRAY FOR US.
St. Luke, PRAY FOR US.

St. Mark, PRAY FOR US.

All holy apostles and evangelists, PRAY FOR US.

All holy disciples of the Lord, PRAY FOR US.

All holy Innocents, PRAY FOR US.

St. Stephen, PRAY FOR US.

St. Lawrence, PRAY FOR US.

St. Vincent, PRAY FOR US.

SS. Fabian and Sebastian, PRAY FOR US.

SS. John and Paul, PRAY FOR US.

SS. Cosmas and Damian, PRAY FOR US.

SS. Gervase and Protase, PRAY FOR US.

All holy Martyrs, PRAY FOR US.

St. Sylvester, PRAY FOR US.

St. Gregory, PRAY FOR US.

St. Ambrose, PRAY FOR US.

St. Augustine, PRAY FOR US.

St. Jerome, PRAY FOR US.

St. Martin, PRAY FOR US.

St. Nicholas, PRAY FOR US.

All holy bishops and confessors, PRAY FOR US.

All holy doctors, PRAY FOR US.

St. Anthony, PRAY FOR US.

St. Benedict, PRAY FOR US.

St. Bernard, PRAY FOR US.

St. Dominic, PRAY FOR US.

St. Francis, PRAY FOR US.

All holy priests and levites, PRAY FOR US.

All holy monks and hermits, PRAY FOR US.

St. Mary Magdalen, PRAY FOR US.

St. Agatha, PRAY FOR US.

St. Lucy, PRAY FOR US.

St. Agnes, PRAY FOR US.

St. Cecilia, PRAY FOR US.

St. Catherine, PRAY FOR US.

St. Anastasia, PRAY FOR US.

All holy virgins and widows, PRAY FOR US.

All holy saints of God, INTERCEDE FOR US.

Be merciful, SPARE US, O LORD.

Be merciful, GRACIOUSLY HEAR US, O LORD.

From all evil, DELIVER US, O LORD.

From all sin, DELIVER US, O LORD.

From your wrath, DELIVER US, O LORD.

From sudden and unprovided death, DELIVER US, O LORD.

From the snares of the devil, DELIVER US, O LORD.

From anger, hatred, and all ill will, DELIVER US, O LORD.

From all lewdness, DELIVER US, O LORD.

From lightning and tempest, DELIVER US, O LORD.

From the scourge of earthquakes, DELIVER US, O LORD.

From plague, famine, and war, DELIVER US, O LORD.

From everlasting death, DELIVER US, O LORD.

By the mystery of your holy incarnation, DELIVER US, O LORD.

By your coming, DELIVER US, O LORD.

By your birth, DELIVER US, O LORD.

By your baptism and holy fasting, DELIVER US, O LORD.

By your cross and passion, DELIVER US, O LORD.

By your death and burial, DELIVER US, O LORD.

By your holy resurrection, DELIVER US, O LORD.

By your wondrous ascension, DELIVER US, O LORD.

By the coming of the Holy Spirit, the Advocate, DELIVER US, O LORD.

On the day of judgment, DELIVER US, O LORD.

We sinners, WE BEG YOU TO HEAR US.

That you spare us, THIS WE ASK YOU, HEAR OUR PRAYER.

That you pardon us, THIS WE ASK YOU, HEAR OUR PRAYER.

That you bring us to true penance, THIS WE ASK YOU, HEAR OUR PRAYER.

That you govern and preserve your holy Church,
  THIS WE ASK YOU, HEAR OUR PRAYER.

That you preserve our Holy Father and all ranks in the Church in holy
  religion, THIS WE ASK YOU, HEAR OUR PRAYER.

That you humble the enemies of holy Church,
  THIS WE ASK YOU, HEAR OUR PRAYER.

That you give peace and true concord to all Christian rulers,
  THIS WE ASK YOU, HEAR OUR PRAYER.

That you give peace and unity to the whole Christian world,
  THIS WE ASK YOU, HEAR OUR PRAYER.

That you restore to the unity of the Church all who have strayed from
  the truth, and lead all unbelievers to the light of the Gospel,
  THIS WE ASK YOU, HEAR OUR PRAYER.

That you confirm and preserve us in your holy service,
THIS WE ASK YOU, HEAR OUR PRAYER.
That you lift up our minds to heavenly desires,
THIS WE ASK YOU, HEAR OUR PRAYER.
That you grant everlasting blessings to all our benefactors,
THIS WE ASK YOU, HEAR OUR PRAYER.
That you deliver our souls and the souls of our brethren, relatives, and
benefactors from everlasting damnation,
THIS WE ASK YOU, HEAR OUR PRAYER.
That you give and preserve the fruits of the earth,
THIS WE ASK YOU, HEAR OUR PRAYER.
That you grant eternal rest to all the faithful departed,
THIS WE ASK YOU, HEAR OUR PRAYER.
That you graciously hear us, THIS WE ASK YOU, HEAR OUR PRAYER.
Son of God, THIS WE ASK YOU, HEAR OUR PRAYER.

Lamb of God, who take away the sins of the world, SPARE US, O LORD.
Lamb of God, who take away the sins of the world,
GRACIOUSLY HEAR US, O LORD.
Lamb of God, who take away the sins of the world, HAVE MERCY ON US.

Christ, hear us. CHRIST, GRACIOUSLY HEAR US.
Lord, have mercy. CHRIST, HAVE MERCY.
Lord, have mercy.

> *Priest*: Our Father . . . And lead us not into temptation.
> *People*: BUT DELIVER US FROM EVIL.

*After the Our Father, turn to Psalm 69. The psalm concludes with the Glory
Be to the Father.*

> *Priest*: Save your servants.
> *People*: WHO TRUST IN YOU, MY GOD.
> *Priest*: Let us find in you, Lord, a fortified tower.
> *People*: IN THE FACE OF THE ENEMY.
> *Priest*: Let the enemy have no power over us.
> *People*: AND THE SON OF INIQUITY BE POWERLESS TO HARM US.
> *Priest*: Lord, deal not with us as our sins deserve.
> *People*: NOR TAKE RETRIBUTION ON US ON ACCOUNT OF OUR SINS.
> *Priest*: Let us pray for our sovereign Pontiff.
> *People*: THE LORD PRESERVE HIM AND RENEW HIS LIFE, MAKE HIM
HAPPY ON EARTH, AND DELIVER HIM FROM THE ILL WILL OF HIS ENEMIES.

Priest: Let us pray for our benefactors.

People: LORD, FOR THE GLORY OF YOUR NAME, REWARD WITH EVER-LASTING LIFE ALL THOSE WHO DO GOOD TO US.

Priest: Let us pray for the faithful departed.

People: LORD, GRANT THEM ETERNAL REST, AND LET PERPETUAL LIGHT SHINE UPON THEM.

Priest: May they rest in peace.

People: AMEN.

Priest: For our absent brethren.

People: SAVE YOUR SERVANTS WHO TRUST IN YOU, MY GOD.

Priest: Lord, send them aid from your holy place.

People: AND WATCH OVER THEM FROM SION.

Priest: O Lord, hear my prayer.

People: AND LET MY CRY COME TO YOU.

Priest: The Lord be with you.

People: AND WITH YOUR SPIRIT.

Depending on the occasion, various prayers are recited by the priest. When these are finished, the litany concludes:

Priest: The Lord be with you.

People: AND WITH YOUR SPIRIT.

Priest: May the almighty and merciful Lord graciously hear us.

People: AMEN.

Priest: May the souls of the faithful departed through the mercy of God rest in peace.

People: AMEN.

The Way of the Cross

GOD FORBID that I should glory save in the cross of our Lord Jesus Christ." The cross sums up the love story of God and man. So it can never be something over and done with. Rather, it is the meaning of each Christian's life in the world. By thinking about the cross we can begin to see how Paul could say that it is the power of God for us, and how he could tell us to proclaim Christ nailed to the cross, realizing that on the cross we are crucified to the world and the world to us. We know that the cross and the empty tomb cannot be separated: death itself was slain by Christ's dying—and life came back in his resurrection.

Devotion to the way of the cross can prepare us to celebrate the

Eucharist, since these are simply fourteen meditations on that love of Jesus which brought him to die and rise, and it is this dying and rising which every Eucharist recalls, proclaims and prepares us to share: "With Christ I am nailed to the cross. It is now no longer I that live, but Christ lives in me." The stations of the cross, then, like the Eucharist, are a Passover celebration, a renewal of our life in Christ Jesus.

The service given below may be a private or a public meditation. In private, the various passages can be read and thought over. In public, the service might begin with an entrance song, such as Hymn No. 93 or No. 95, or all together may recite Psalm 21. After this there may be a reading from Scripture (for example: Isaiah 49:1–7; Jeremiah 20:7–13; John 13:31–35; 15:1–15; 16:2–33). Each station will then consist of a silent meditation on the scriptural passage, followed by a short verse and response and, if desired after some of the stations, a verse of an appropriate hymn.

It was the Lord who sent me to prophesy against this house and city all that you have heard. Now, therefore, reform your ways and your deeds; listen to the voice of the Lord your God, so that the Lord will repent of the evil with which he threatens you. As for me, I am in your hands; do with me what you think good and right. But mark well: if you put me to death, it is innocent blood you bring on yourselves, on this city and on its citizens. For in truth it was the Lord who sent me to you, to speak all these things for you to hear.

JEREMIAH 26:12–15

Priest: The Lord sent him to speak the truth to us.
People: LET US LISTEN TO THE VOICE OF THE LORD.

Though he was harshly treated, he submitted and opened not his mouth; like a lamb led to the slaughter or a sheep before the shearers, he was silent and opened not his mouth. Oppressed and condemned he was taken away, and who would have thought any more of his destiny? When he was cut off from the land of the living, and smitten for the sin of his people, a grave was assigned him among the wicked and a burial place with evildoers, though he had done no wrong nor spoken any falsehood. For the Lord was pleased to crush him in infirmity.

ISAIAH 53:7–10

Priest: Come to me, all you who labor and are burdened.
People: TAKE MY YOKE UPON YOU, AND LEARN FROM ME.

3 O Lord, my God, by day I cry out; at night I clamor in your presence. Let my prayer come before you; incline your ear to my call for help, for my soul is surfeited with troubles and my life draws near to the nether world. I am numbered with those who go down into the pit; I am a man without strength. My couch is among the dead, like the slain who lie in the grave, whom you remember no longer and who are cut off from your care. You have plunged me into the bottom of the pit, into the dark abyss. Upon me your wrath lies heavy, and with all your billows you overwhelm me. You have taken my friends away from me; you have made me an abomination to them; I am imprisoned, and I cannot escape. PSALM 87

Priest: If anyone wishes to come after me.
People: LET HIM TAKE UP HIS CROSS AND FOLLOW ME.

4 I sought him whom my heart loves—I sought him but I did not find him. I will arise and go about the city; in the streets and crossings I will seek him whom my heart loves. I sought him but I did not find him. The watchmen came upon me as they made their rounds of the city: Have you seen him whom my heart loves? I had hardly left them when I found him. I took hold of him and would not let him go. SONG OF SOLOMON 3:1–4

Priest: He shall be great and shall be called the Son of the Most High.
People: AND HE SHALL SAVE HIS PEOPLE FROM THEIR SINS.

5 I am a man who knows affliction from the rod of his anger, one whom he has led and forced to walk in darkness not in the light; against me alone he brings back his hand again and again all the day. He has worn away my flesh and my skin, he has broken all my bones; he has beset me round with poverty and weariness; he has left me to dwell in the dark like those long dead. He has hemmed me in with no escape and weighed me down with chains; even when I cry out for help, he stops my prayer; he has blocked my ways with fitted stones, and turned my paths aside. He has broken my teeth with gravel, pressed my face in the dust. My soul is deprived of peace, I have forgotten what happiness is. I tell myself that my future is lost; all that I hoped for from the Lord. LAMENTATIONS 3:1–9; 16–18

Priest: Bear one another's burdens.
People: AND SO YOU WILL FULFILL THE LAW OF CHRIST.

6 Who would believe what we have heard? To whom has the arm of the Lord been revealed? He grew up like a sapling before him, like a shoot from the parched earth. There was in him no stately bearing to make us look at him, nor appearance that would attract us to him. He was spurned and avoided by men, a man of suffering, accustomed to infirmity, one of those from whom men hide their faces; spurned, and we held him in no esteem. Yet it was our infirmities that he bore, our sufferings that he endured, while we thought of him as stricken, as one smitten by God and afflicted. But he was pierced for our offenses, crushed for our sins; upon him was the chastisement that makes us whole. By his stripes we were healed. We had all gone astray like sheep, each following his own way; but the Lord laid upon him the guilt of us all. ISAIAH 53:1-6

Priest: His appearance was marred beyond that of man.
People: WE SAW NO BEAUTY IN HIM TO WIN OUR HEARTS.

7 Come, all you who pass by the way, look and see whether there is any suffering like my suffering, which has been dealt me when the Lord afflicted me on the day of his blazing wrath. From on high he sent fire down into my very frame; he spread a net for my feet and overthrew me. He left me desolate, in pain all the day. He has kept watch over my sins; by his hand they have been plaited. They have settled about my neck; he brought my strength to its knees. The Lord has delivered me into their grip; I am unable to rise. At this I weep; my eyes run with tears. Far from me are all who could console me, any who might revive me. My sons were reduced to silence when the enemy prevailed. LAMENTATIONS 1:12-16

Priest: To the weak he became weak.
People: TO SAVE THOSE WHO SUFFER.

8 O God, you know my folly, and my faults are not hid from you. Let not those who wait for you be put to shame through me. Since for your sake I bear insult, and shame covers my face. I have become an outcast to my brothers, a stranger to my mother's sons, because zeal for your house consumes me, and the insults of those who blaspheme you fall upon me. I humbled myself with fasting, and this was made a reproach to me; I made sackcloth my garment, and I became a byword to them. They who sit at the gate gossip about me, and drunkards make me the butt of their songs. But I pray to you, O Lord, for the time

of your favor. In your great kindness, answer me with your constant help. PSALM 68:6-14

Priest: I am the vine and you are the branches.

People: IF YOU ABIDE IN ME, AND I IN YOU, YOU SHALL BEAR MUCH FRUIT.

9   I have waited, waited for the Lord, and he stooped toward me and heard my cry. He drew me out of the pit of destruction, out of the mud of the swamp. He set my feet upon a crag; he made firm my steps. Sacrifice and oblation you wished not, O God, but ears open to obedience you gave me. Holocausts or sin-offerings you sought not; then said I, "Behold I come. In the written scroll it is prescribed for me, to do your will, O my God, is my delight, and your law is within my heart." Deign, O Lord, to rescue me; O Lord, make haste to help me. Let all be put to shame and confusion who seek to snatch away my life. Let them be turned back in disgrace who desire my ruin. Though I am afflicted and poor, yet the Lord thinks of me. You are my help and my deliverer. PSALM 39

Priest: My task is to do the will of him who sent me.

People: AND TO ACCOMPLISH HIS WORK.

10   Naked I came forth from my mother's womb, and naked I shall go back again. The Lord gave and the Lord has taken away; blessed be the name of the Lord. The arrows of the Almighty pierce me, and my spirit drinks in their poison. The terrors of God are arrayed against me. Oh, that I might have my request, and that God would decide to crush me, that he would put forth his hand and cut me off. Then I should still have consolation and could exult through unremitting pain, because I have not transgressed the commands of the Holy One. What strength have I that I should endure? And what is my limit that I should be patient? Have I the strength of stones, or is my flesh of bronze? Have I no helper, and has advice deserted me? JOB 1:21, 6:4, 8-13

Priest: They divided my garments among them.

People: AND THEY CAST LOTS FOR MY CLOTHING.

11   My spirit is broken, my lamp of life extinguished; my burial is at hand. I am indeed mocked, and my eyes grow dim. My lot is described as evil, and I am become a byword to the people. My eye has grown blind with anguish, and all my frame is shrunken to a shadow. Upright men are astonished at this, and the innocent aroused against the

wicked. If I cry out "Injustice!" I am not heard. I cry for help, but there is no redress. He has barred my way and I cannot pass; he has veiled my path in darkness. He breaks me down on every side, and I am gone; my hope he has uprooted like a tree.   JOB 17:1-8; 19:7-10

Priest: With Christ I am nailed to the cross.
People: IT IS NOW NO LONGER I WHO LIVE, BUT CHRIST LIVES IN ME.

I2 Have this mind in you which was also in Christ Jesus, who, though he was by nature God, did not consider being equal to God a thing to be clung to, but emptied himself, taking the nature of a slave and being made like unto men. And appearing in the form of man, he humbled himself, becoming obedient to death, even to death on a cross.   PHILIPPIANS 2:5-8

Priest: And I, if I be lifted up from the earth.
People: I WILL DRAW ALL THINGS TO ME.

I3 In this we have come to know his love, that he laid down his life for us; and we likewise ought to lay down our life for the brethren. He who has the goods of this world and sees his brother in need and closes his heart to him, how does the love of God abide in him? My dear children, let us not love in word, neither with the tongue, but in deed and in truth.   I JOHN 3:16-18

Priest: Stronger than death is love; its flames are a blazing fire.
People: DEEP WATERS CANNOT QUENCH LOVE, NOR FLOODS SWEEP IT AWAY.

I4 Hear the word of the Lord. Thus says the Lord God to these bones: I will bring spirit into you, that you may come to life. I will put sinews upon you, make flesh grow over you, cover you with skin, and put spirit in you so that you may come to life. From the four winds come, O Spirit, and breathe into these slain that they may come to life. O my people, I will open your graves and have you rise from them, and bring you back to the land of Israel. I will put my spirit in you that you may live; thus you shall know that I am the Lord.

EZEKIEL 37:5-14

Priest: If we have died with Christ, we shall live together with him.
People: FOR CHRIST, HAVING RISEN FROM THE DEAD, DIES NOW NO MORE.

When the stations are made in public, a hymn, such as No. 18 or No. 64, may follow the last station, or all together may recite Psalm 117.

The Rosary

W E PRAY the rosary to make meaningful in our lives what Jesus said and did. There can be no best way to do this. The quotations from Scripture given here may be an aid in grasping the mystery of Jesus.

Joyful

1   You have found favor with God. And, now, you shall conceive and bear a son, and you shall call his name Jesus. He shall be great, and shall be called the Son of the Most High; and the Lord God will give him the throne of David his father; and of his kingdom there shall be no end.   LUKE 1:30-33

2   And his mercy is from generation to generation on those who fear him. He has put down the mighty from their thrones, and has exalted the lowly. He has filled the hungry with good things, and the rich he has sent away empty.   LUKE 1:50-53

3   I bring you good news of great joy which shall be to all the people; for today in the town of David a Savior has been born to you, who is Christ the Lord.   LUKE 2:10-11

4   Behold, this child is destined for the fall and for the rise of many in Israel, and for a sign that shall be contradicted.   LUKE 2:34

5   And he went down with them and came to Nazareth, and was subject to them; and his mother kept all these things carefully in her heart. And Jesus advanced in wisdom and age and grace before God and men.   LUKE 2:51-52

Sorrowful

6   "My soul is sad, even unto death. Wait here and watch with me." And going forward a little, he fell prostrate and prayed, saying, "Father, if it is possible, let this cup pass away from me; yet not as I will, but as you will."   MATTHEW 26:38-39

7   It was our infirmities that he bore, our sufferings that he suffered. He was pierced for our offenses, crushed for our sins; upon him was the chastisement that makes us whole; by his stripes we were healed.   ISAIAH 53:4-5

8   And the soldiers, plaiting a crown of thorns, put it upon his head, and arrayed him in a purple cloak. And they kept coming

to him and saying, "Hail, King of the Jews!" and striking him. Pilate therefore again went outside and said to them, "Behold, I bring him out to you." Jesus therefore came forth wearing the crown of thorns and the purple cloak. And Pilate said to them, "Behold, the man!"

JOHN 19:2-5

9 Fear not, you shall not be put to shame; you need not blush, for you shall not be disgraced. For he who has become your husband is your Maker; his name is the Lord of hosts; your redeemer is the Holy One of Israel, called God of all the earth. Though the mountains leave their place and the hills be shaken, my love shall never leave you nor my covenant of peace be shaken.

ISAIAH 54:4, 5, 10

10 Has not God turned to foolishness the wisdom of this world? For the Jews ask for signs, and the Greeks look for wisdom; but we, for our part, preach a crucified Christ—to the Jews indeed a stumbling-block and to the Gentiles foolishness, but to those who are called, both Jews and Greeks, Christ, the power of God and the wisdom of God.

I CORINTHIANS 1:20-24

Glorious

11 This Jesus, delivered up by the settled purpose and foreknowledge of God, you have crucified and slain by the hands of wicked men. But God has raised him up, having loosed the sorrows of hell, because it was not possible that he should be held fast by it. This Jesus God has raised up, and we are all witnesses of it.

ACTS OF THE APOSTLES 2:23, 24, 32

12 Jesus said to her, "Do not touch me, for I have not yet ascended to my Father, but go to my brethren and say to them, 'I ascend to my Father and your Father, to my God and your God.'"

JOHN 20:17

13 And it shall happen in the last days, God says, that I will pour out a portion of my spirit upon all mankind; your sons and daughters shall prophesy, your young men shall see visions, and your old men shall dream dreams. Yes, even upon my servants and my handmaids will I pour out a portion of my spirit in those days.

JOEL 3:1-2

14 I delight to rest in his shadow, and his fruit is sweet to my mouth. He brings me into the banquet hall and his emblem

over me is love. Strengthen me. For I am faint with love. His left hand is under my head and his right arm embraces me.

SONG OF SOLOMON 2:3–6

15 He has shown might with his arm. He has exalted the lowly; he has given help to Israel, his servant, mindful of his mercy.

LUKE 1:51, 52, 54

Benediction

Entrance

The rite begins with the singing of a hymn appropriate to the occasion or the season, such as No. 32 or No. 63 or No. 109; or all together may recite a psalm, such as Psalm 22 or 33. While this is being done, the priest puts the Blessed Sacrament out on the altar.

Reading

There may be a reading from Scripture, such as: John 6:1–14, 27–40, or 47–58; 21:1–13; Luke 24:13–35; 1 Corinthians 11:23–32; 12:12–27; 1 John 4:7–21.

Homily

The priest may preach a brief homily.

Hymn

The last two verses of hymn No. 79 are always sung, and then:

Priest: You have given them the bread of heaven.
People: WHICH HAS ALL DELIGHT WITHIN IT.

Prayer

The priest then prays that our love for Christ's body and blood will bring us to true salvation.

Blessing

The priest then gives the blessing.

Divine Praises

Blessed be God.
Blessed be his holy name.
Blessed be Jesus Christ, true God and true man.

Blessed be the name of Jesus.
Blessed be his most sacred heart.
Blessed be his most precious blood.
Blessed be Jesus in the most holy sacrament of the altar.
Blessed be the Holy Spirit, the Paraclete.
Blessed be the great mother of God, Mary most holy.
Blessed be her holy and immaculate conception.
Blessed be her glorious assumption.
Blessed be the name of Mary, virgin and mother.
Blessed be Saint Joseph, her most chaste spouse.
Blessed be God in his angels and in his saints.

Conclusion

The rite concludes with the singing of a hymn, such as No. 39 or No. 50.

Forty Hours

T HE FORTY HOURS devotion usually begins with the celebration of Mass and a procession in honor of the Blessed Sacrament. During this procession, Hymn No. 79 is sung. Afterwards, the Litany of the Saints is sung or recited as found on page 782.

The Mass of the Holy Eucharist (page 349) may be celebrated during these three days. If Mass is not celebrated on the first two evenings, a bible service may be held, closing with Benediction (as above).

At the closing of the Forty Hours, the Litany of the Saints is repeated after Mass. Hymn No. 79 is sung again, and the celebration concludes with Benediction (as above).

Latin Text

In order that the faithful may become familiar with the Latin text also, in accordance with Article 36 of the Constitution on the Sacred Liturgy the following dialogue and Ordinary chants are given:

Preparation Prayers

Priest: + In nomine Patris, et Filii, et Spiritus Sancti. Amen.
Assistants: Ad Deum qui laetificat juventutem meam.
Priest: + Adjutorium nostrum in nomine Domini.
Assistants: Qui fecit caelum et terram.

The priest then confesses his sins.

Assistants: Misereatur tui omnipotens Deus, et, dimissis peccatis tuis, perducat te ad vitam aeternam.
Priest: Amen.
Assistants: Confiteor Deo omnipotenti, beatae Mariae semper Virgini, beato Michaeli Archangelo, beato Joanni Baptistae, sanctis Apostolis Petro et Paulo, omnibus sanctis, et tibi, pater, quia peccavi nimis cogitatione, verbo et opere: mea culpa, mea culpa, mea maxima culpa. Ideo precor beatam Mariam semper Virginem, beatum Michaelem Archangelum, beatum Joannem Baptistam, sanctos Apostolos Petrum et Paulum, omnes sanctos, et te, pater, orare pro me ad Dominum Deum nostrum.
Priest: Misereatur vestri omnipotens Deus, et, dimissis peccatis vestris, perducat vos ad vitam aeternam.
Assistants: Amen.
Priest: + Indulgentiam, absolutionem et remissionem peccatorum nostrorum tribuat nobis omnipotens et misericors Dominus.
Assistants: Amen.

Lord, Have Mercy

Kyrie, eleison. Kyrie, eleison. Kyrie, eleison.
Christe, eleison. Christe, eleison. Christe, eleison.
Kyrie, eleison. Kyrie, eleison. Kyrie, eleison.

Glory to God

Gloria in excelsis Deo,
Et in terra pax

hominibus bonae voluntatis.
Laudamus te.
Benedicimus te.
Adoramus te.
Glorificamus te.
Gratias agimus tibi propter magnam gloriam tuam.
Domine Deus, Rex caelestis, Deus Pater omnipotens.
Domine Fili unigenite, Jesu Christe.
Domine Deus, Agnus Dei, Filius Patris.
Qui tollis peccata mundi, miserere nobis.
Qui tollis peccata mundi, suscipe deprecationem nostram.
Qui sedes ad dexteram Patris, miserere nobis.
Quoniam tu solus Sanctus, tu solus Dominus,
    tu solus Altissimus, Jesu Christe.
Cum Sancto Spiritu + in gloria Dei Patris. Amen.

Prayer

Priest: Dominus vobiscum.
People: Et cum spiritu tuo.
Priest: Oremus . . .
People: Amen.

Gospel

Priest: Dominus vobiscum.
People: Et cum spiritu tuo.
Priest: + Sequentia sancti Evangelii secundum . . .
People: Gloria tibi, Domine.

Creed

Credo in unum Deum, Patrem omnipotentem, factorem caeli et terrae,
    visibilium omnium et invisibilium.
Et in unum Dominum Jesum Christum, Filium Dei unigenitum, et ex
    Patre natum ante omnia saecula,
Deum et Deo, Lumen et Lumine, Deum verum de Deo vero.
Genitum non factum, consubstantialem Patri, per quem omnia facta sunt.
Qui propter nos homines, et propter nostram salutem, descendit de
    caelis,
Et incarnatus est de Spiritu Sancto, ex Maria Virgine et homo factus est.

797

Crucifixus etiam pro nobis, sub Pontio Pilato passus et sepultus est.

Et resurrexit tertia die, secundum Scripturas.

Et ascendit caelum, sedit ad dexteram Patris.

Et iterum venturus est cum gloria, judicare vivos et mortuos, cojus regni non erit finis.

Et in Spiritus Sanctum, Dominum, et vivificantum: qui ex Patre Filioque procedit.

Qui cum Patre et Filio simul adoratur, et conglorificatur: qui locutus est per prophetas.

Et unam, sanctam, catholicam et apostolicam Ecclesiam.

Confiteor unum baptisma in remissionem peccatorum.

Et exspecto resurrectionem mortuorum,

Et vitam + venturi saeculi. Amen.

Priest: Dominus vobiscum.
People: Et cum spiritu tuo.
Priest: Oremus . . .

Pray Brethren

Priest: Orate, fratres, ut meum ac vestrum sacrificium acceptabile fiat apud Deum Patrem omnipotentem.

People: Suscipiat Dominus sacrificium de manibus tuis, ad laudem et gloriam nominis sui, ad utilitatem quoque nostram, totiusque Ecclesiae suae sanctae.

Priest: Amen.

Prayer Over the Offerings

Priest: . . . per omnia saecula saeculorum.
People: Amen.

Preface Dialogue

Priest: Dominus vobiscum.
People: Et cum spiritu tuo.
Priest: Sursum corda.
People: Habemus ad Dominum.
Priest: Gratias agamus Domino Deo nostro.
People: Dignum et justum est.

Holy, Holy, Holy

Sanctus, sanctus, sanctus,
Dominus Deus Sabaoth.

Pleni sunt caeli et terra gloria tua:
Hosanna in excelsis.
Benedictus + qui venit in nomine Domini:
Hosanna in excelsis.

Our Father

Priest: Praeceptis salutaribus moniti, et divina institutione formati, audemus dicere:

People: Pater noster, qui es in caelis, sanctificetur nomen tuum, adveniat regnum tuum, fiat voluntas tua, sicut in caelo et in terra. Panem nostrum quotidianum da nobis hodie, et dimitte nobis debita nostra sicut et nos dimittimus debitoribus nostris, et ne nos inducas in tentationem, sed libera nos a malo. Amen.

Deliver Us, O Lord

Priest: Libera nos, quaesumus, Domine, ab omnibus malis praeteritis, praesentibus, et futuris, et intercedente beata et gloriosa semper Virgione Dei Genitrice Maria, cum beatis Apostolis tuis Petro et Paulo, atque Andrea, et omnibus Sanctis, da + propitius pacem in diebus nostris: ut ope misericordiae tuae adjuti, et a peccato simus semper liberi, et ab omni perturbatione securi. Per eundem Dominum nostrum Jesum Christum Filium tuum, qui tecum vivit et regnat in unitate Spiritus Sancti, Deus, per omnia saecula saeculorum.

People: Amen.

Priest: Pax Domini sit semper vobiscum.

People: Et cum spiritu tuo.

Lamb of God

Agnus Dei, qui tollis peccata mundi, miserere nobis.
Agnus Dei, qui tollis peccata mundi, miserere nobis.
Agnus Dei, qui tollis peccata mundi, dona nobis pacem.

Lord, I Am Not Worthy

The following words, repeated three times, may be said by the people aloud in Latin with the celebrant:

Domine, non sum dignus ut intres sub tectum meum:
sed tantum dic verbo, et sanabitur anima mea.

During Communion

Priest: Corpus Christi.
People: Amen.

Prayer After Communion

Priest: Dominus vobiscum.
People: Et cum spiritu tuo.
Priest: Oremus . . .

Dismissal

Priest: Dominus vobiscum.
People: Et cum spiritu tuo.
Priest: Ite, missa est.
People: Deo gratias.

Blessing

Priest: Benedicat vos omnipotens Deus, Pater, + et Filius,
et Spiritus Sanctus.
People: Amen.

INDICES

Index of Hymns and Antiphons

Index of Psalms and Canticles

FOR SEASONS AND FEASTS

Advent: 13, 24, 79, 84
Christmas: 2, 18, 86, 97
Epiphany: 23, 71

Septuagesima—Lent—Passiontime: 6, 16, 21, 23, 30, 34, 37, 40, 76, 70

Easter: 29, 117

Ascension: 20, 28, 46, 96, 98
Pentecost: 47, 103

Apostles: 18, 88
Martyrs: 12, 55, 78, 123, 125
Holy Men and Women: 1, 14, 20, 23, 25, 36, 44, 91, 111, 127, Song of Mary

OCCASIONS

Baptism: 35, 41, 50, 92, 94, 113, 117
Eucharist: 22, 23, 41, 62, 64, 77, 127
Weddings, anniversaries, the family: 19, 44, 126, 127
Penance: 6, 31, 37, 40, 50, 129, 138
Sickness: 15, 17, 30, 40, 129
Death and burial: 15, 29, 64, 89, 102

Morning prayer: 3, 5, 18, 89, 94, 107, 142, Song of Zachary
Evening prayer: 4, 62, 90, 102, 133, Song of Mary
Church dedication or anniversary: 25, 26, 47, 83, 86, 92, 126

THEMES

Assembly of the Faithful, the Church: 49, 77, 79, 99, 104
Beauty of Nature: 8, 64, 92, 103, 146, 147, Song of the Three Young Men
Faith and confidence: 1, 3, 10, 15, 26, 45, 61, 70, 90, 130, Song of Mary
Fidelity: 17, 24, 27, 36, 88, Song of Zachary, Song of Sirach
Forgiveness: 24, 31, 50, 85, 129
Good Shepherd: 22, 67, 76, 79
Hope: 12, 21, 41, 61, 79, 130, 140
Joy: 4, 22, 103, 148
Justice: 7, 39, 81
Loving kindness of God: 5, 8, 17, 76, 80, 102, 135, 138, 144, Song of Mary

Peace: 28, 71, 84, 121, 127
Petition: 16, 42, 65, 106, 127, 141, 143, Song of Sirach
Praise: 8, 28, 32, 45, 46, 65, 67, 80, 92, 95, 97, 99, 112, 116, 134, 143, 148, 149, 150, Song of the Three Young Men, Songs from the Book of Revelation
Salvation history: 32, 43, 77, 88, 103, 104, 105, 106, 113, 131, 134, 135
Sorrow: 6, 31, 38, 54, 67, 89, 136
Suffering: 17, 21, 30, 101, 122
Thanksgiving: 4, 8, 90, 29, 53, 57, 66, 91, 114, 115, 123, 135, 137
Unity: 105, 132

General Index

Designed by George Lilly and Don Joyce.
Composed in Monotype Bembo with Bembo Titling display
by Clarke & Way, Inc., New York.
Offset by The Press of The World Publishing Company,
Cleveland, on Missal Encyclopedia Text
supplied by Mead Papers, Inc.
Bound by The World Publishing Company
in Columbia Bayside Vellum.
Special thanks are due Mrs. Beatrice Warde and Stanley Morison
of The Monotype Corporation Ltd., London,
for their generous typographical advice.

Creed

I believe in one God.

The Father almighty, maker of heaven and earth,
  and of all things visible and invisible.
And I believe in one Lord, Jesus Christ,
  the only-begotten Son of God.
Born of the Father before all ages.
God of God, Light of Light, true God of true God.
Begotten, not made,
  of one substance with the Father.
By whom all things were made.
Who for us men and for our salvation came down from heaven.